TELECOMMUNICATIONS IN BUSINESS

BUSINESS

Strategy and Application

TELECOMMUNICATIONS IN BUSINESS

Strategy and Application

John Vargo
Ray Hunt
Both of the University of Canterbury

Irwin
McGraw-Hill

Boston, Massachusetts   Burr Ridge, Illinois   Dubuque, Iowa
Madison, Wisconsin   New York, New York   San Francisco, California   St. Louis, Missouri

Irwin/McGraw-Hill

A Division of The **McGraw·Hill** *Companies*

©Richard D. Irwin, a Times Mirror Higher Education Group, Inc. company, 1996

Irwin Book Team

Publisher: *Tom Casson*
Senior sponsoring editor: *Rick Williamson*
Developmental editor: *Christine Wright*
Marketing manager: *Michelle Hudson*
Production supervisor: *Dina L. Treadaway*
Assistant manager, desktop services: *Jon Christopher*
Project editor: *Beth Cigler*
Designer: *Larry J. Cope*
Cover illustration: *Carlos Alejandro*
Compositor: *Douglas & Gayle Limited*
Typeface: *11/13 Times Roman*
Printer: *R. R. Donnelley & Sons Company*

Library of Congress Cataloging-In-Publication Data

Vargo, John.
    Telecommunications in business: strategy and application / John
Vargo, Ray Hunt.
        p.   cm.
    Includes index.
    ISBN 0-256-19787-3
    1. Business enterprises—Communication systems.   2. Local area
networks (Computer networks)   3. Wide area networks (Computer
networks)   4. Internet (Computer network)   I. Hunt, Ray.
II. Title.
HD30.335.V37   1996
650′.0285′46—dc20   95–40750

Printed in the United States of America
    4 5 6 7 8 9 0 DO 2 1 0 9

PREFACE

Introduction

In the world of flexible markets, rapid-response management, stringent quality requirements, and increasingly global competition, there is a strong need for management education in the arena of telecommunications-based information technology (TBIT). This enabling technology, based on local and wide area computer networks, acts as a lever to gain efficiency and effectiveness while targeting new competitive advantage through cooperative efforts. Given the tremendous spread of global networks and rapid rise of the Internet, there is a need for concise and practical management education in this dynamic field. It is the purpose of this textbook to address these issues with contemporary teaching materials. Our observations of the current availability of textbooks in this field now follow.

- There are many computer science and engineering textbooks that address technical topics in the area of local and wide area networking technologies. These books are concerned with the bits and bytes as well as the details of protocol standards and other technical aspects. However, they are often mathematical in their orientation, which

makes them less appropriate for the needs of many business or commerce students.
- There are many MIS textbooks that address various management, marketing, and other business issues in the area of computing, but which (at the most) only include a single chapter on networking. Such coverage is frequently superficial and inadequate.
- There are few books that address the crucial, timely issue of how computer networks can be used to make business more competitive.

Audience

This textbook is suitable for students taking upper-level undergraduate business courses in information systems, or for MBAs needing a strong managerial grasp of this critical field of technology. The text assumes that the student has taken an introductory computing course and has a basic knowledge of computing and simple jargon and terminology, but it makes no assumption on students' knowledge of computer networks. The book also is suitable for managers who require more information on how they can use networks to make their businesses more efficient and competitive. This book often uses techniques of strategic analysis and decision making, and the various exercises address a wide range of examples in which networks have the potential to make business more competitive.

Objectives of the Book

Upon completion of the study of this book, the reader should be able to

1. Describe and evaluate the computer network as part of an organization's strategic plan.
2. Identify and describe the wide range of network applications in business.
3. Explain what the Internet is and how it can be used for business applications in a competitive environment.
4. Describe the key principles and components required to support wide area networking applications in business.
5. Describe the key principles and components required to support local area networking applications in business.
6. Apply tools and techniques for analyzing and assessing computer network opportunities.
7. Analyze opportunities and formulate strategies for sustaining organizational success.
8. Analyze network opportunities and formulate strategies for achieving personal goals in a business setting.
9. Evaluate the computer network requirements for a business.
10. Properly evaluate alternative network solutions and select the most appropriate.
11. Explain the functions and requirements of network management and security.
12. Discuss emerging and future network applications, and their implications for business opportunities.

Outline of the Book

The book is divided into 12 chapters, the titles of which will now be given together with a brief outline.

The chapters are:

Chapter 1	Strategic planning and network technology
Chapter 2	Networked business applications
Chapter 3	The Internet—a global communications resource
Chapter 4	Wide area networks (WANs): principles and components
Chapter 5	Local area networks (LANs): principles and components
Chapter 6	Techniques for analyzing and assessing network opportunities
Chapter 7	Networking opportunities for improving organizational performance
Chapter 8	Networking opportunities for improving personal performance
Chapter 9	Determining business networking requirements
Chapter 10	Evaluation and selection of alternatives
Chapter 11	Network management and security
Chapter 12	Future developments in business networking

Chapter 1 introduces the concepts of strategic planning and computer networking and discusses how they are an important part of an organization's strategic plan. This chapter shows how competitive advantage can be gained through business networking, and how an organization's strategic direction can benefit through networking.

Chapter 1 also demonstrates how information technology can be used to increase an organization's responsiveness to internal strengths and weaknesses as well as to external opportunities and threats.

Chapter 2 looks at the business applications that can benefit from both wide and local area networks. Examples of many familiar wide area network applications are discussed, including telemarketing, teleshopping, travel reservation systems, order entry systems, point-of-sale and stock management systems, and financial services (including electronic funds transfer, foreign exchange, and investment services). A variety of other topics, such as manufacturing systems, electronic messaging systems, and teleconferencing, are also included. Chapter 2 covers how local area networks also play an important part in many of the ways in which we do business; a number of the examples in this chapter illustrate the use of local area networks to access and process information in the wider area.

Chapter 3 is concerned with the Internet, its technology, supporting applications, and its business use. Commercial access to the Internet as well as to its related services and facilities available are covered in this chapter along with a discussion of the user tools available for gaining access to Internet resources (FTP, Telnet, Archie, Gopher, WAIS, World Wide Web, and its browsers). Issues of Internet security and performance are also covered, as well as the emerging range of business uses for this "network of networks."

Chapters 4 and 5 are primarily concerned with the principles and components of local and wide area networks, such as the various building blocks comprising these networks, as well as the purchased or leased equipment needed to set up and use such networks. These chapters discuss a number of technical terms such as cables, switches, modems, multiplexers, software, servers, workstations, hubs, repeaters, bridges, routers, and gateways in only as much detail as is necessary to understand how they work and what they are used for. Chapters 4 and 5 will also look at the

variety of network services available from service providers, such as the local telecom suppliers and other international operators, as well as a variety of the well-known local area network systems (including NetBIOS, Novell/NetWare, UNIX, Windows NT, Banyan/VINES, and Appleshare).

Chapter 6 covers the analyses and assessment of network opportunities within organizations using a range of models and techniques, such as a strategic planning model, critical success factors, data and process modeling, association matrices, and models of business operation.

Chapter 7 examines network opportunities for sustaining organizational success, including analyzing and measuring organizational performance, opportunities for business process reengineering, and support for organizational groups with groupware and workflow applications. Also covered are topics such as taking advantage of short-term opportunities, niche marketing via computer networks, and turning risk and uncertainty into organizational advantage.

Chapter 8 looks at network opportunities for achieving personal goals in a business setting with improved communications, assistance in better utilization of time and support for research activities and other business tasks, including personal productivity improvements.

Chapters 9 and 10 are concerned with the determination of business computer network requirements and the evaluation and selection of alternatives, and it describes how factors such as user requirements and performance parameters, including response time, up-time, data quality, and storage, all have an important effect in the determination of these requirements. Chapters 9 and 10 also discuss techniques such as cost-benefit analysis, and they evaluate factors such as reliability, maintenance, flexibility, risk conditions, as well as acquisition factors.

Chapter 11 discusses the management and security of networks and also the fundamentals of network management in light of the open, mixed vendor, distributed, and integrated systems currently in operation by many businesses. Security is discussed in terms of risk analysis, disaster recovery, computer security models, and encryption standards.

Finally, Chapter 12 looks at the emerging as well as the potential future developments in computer networking that will affect business in the early 21st century. Topics include the paperless office, integrated electronic commerce, and enterprise integration. Chapter discussion includes developments in high-speed networking systems with a focus on ATM. The chapter concludes with seven key trends thought to shape the future of this dynamic field.

Support material

An instructor's manual is available to those instructors adopting the text. This manual includes solutions to end-of-chapter questions and cases, teaching suggestions, lecture outlines, and suggestions for use of the Power Point presentation slides. The manual also includes two longer cases and their solutions, which are suitable for use as projects in the course. Strategic planning, organizational analysis, network design, system selection and security, and management are all addressed. The manual will also be available on disk and will contain a Power Point presentation disk. A Test Bank containing over 1200 true-false, multiple choice, fill-in-the-blank, and other test questions will be available to adopters. It is available as a test manual and in computerized form (Computest IV).

About the Authors

John Vargo and **Ray Hunt** bring complementary backgrounds and skills to the arena of telecommunications for business—Ray from the computer science perspective, and John from the business or commercial view.

John is a member of the Faculty of Commerce at the University of Canterbury, Christchurch, New Zealand, and is a senior lecturer in information

systems. Originally trained in accounting and business consulting, he has worked as a consultant for industry and government in both New Zealand and the United States, especially in the areas of strategic planning and the effective use of information technology. John's specialty areas include business information systems and strategic advantage of information technologies, and he has addressed conferences in Europe, the United States, Australia, and New Zealand. John's broad background in commerce, accounting, and information systems development has given him exceptional insight into the integration of new technologies into competitive organizations.

Ray is a senior lecturer in the department of computer science at the University of Canterbury, New Zealand. He has worked as a telecommunications consultant in both the private and public sectors and has been responsible for the design of a number of major networks. He has given numerous courses on data communications and network architecture for industry in New Zealand, Singapore, and Hong Kong, and has addressed conferences in Australia, Singapore, Hong Kong, the United States, and the United Kingdom. Currently he works in conjunction with various telecommunications companies on aspects of network design, performance, security, and management, and he is the supervisor for a number of industry-sponsored research projects in these areas.

Acknowledgments

Any book worth its weight in blood, sweat, and tears must be a real team effort. We would like to express our appreciation to those who were part of this team. First of all, our thanks to the staff at the Open Learning Institute (OLI) in Hong Kong who encouraged and helped us in the germination of this project. Our thanks, too, for their permission to take this work to the world. Without their help at the beginning we would not have seen this final product. Our special thanks to Steve Elliot, who is now at the University of New South Wales, Australia. Also, our heartfelt thanks to Graham Mead of Graham Mead Associates, Hong Kong, who brought us in touch with the OLI.

We must also express our gratitude to our many colleagues at the University of Canterbury who encouraged us and shared their insights during the writing of this text. Their help was invaluable, as was the support from our departments, and the university community.

Naturally, our families often bore the brunt of our absence, and so we must thank them for their understanding and willingness to release us to do the work necessary to see this project to completion. We truly appreciate their encouragement and support.

Although the final decisions and responsibilities regarding material included in this text lie with us, we are deeply indebted to the fine reviewers who gave us such invaluable input on content. This book is richer for their candor and insight. We believe the students who use this book will be, too, because of the reviewers' willingness to help. Reviewers of this text were

Lyne Bouchard, Laval University
Abhijit Chaudhury, UMass—Boston

Kevin Crowston, University of Michigan—Ann Arbor
Abhijit Gopal, University of Calgary
Linda Johnson, Western Kentucky University
Yvonne Lederer-Antonucci, Widener University
Roger McGrath, University of South Florida
Janet Urlaub, Sinclair Community College
Anthony Verstraete, Pennsylvania State University

Our final thanks go to the wonderful team at Richard D. Irwin. Rick Williamson and Christine Wright gave encouragement and prodding in the right direction, and this was always done in a happy spirit and with a desire to see excellence as the final product. Beth Cigler coordinated all efforts that transformed our "rough carpentry" into a beautifully crafted book. Many thanks to all members of the team who helped us complete this textbook with typical Irwin quality.

CONTENTS IN BRIEF

1   Strategic Planning and Network Technology   1

2   Networked Business Applications   33

3   The Internet: A Global Communications Resource   91

4   Wide Area Networks (WANs): Principles and Components   121

5   Local Area Networks (LANs): Principles and Components   167

6   Techniques for Analyzing and Assessing Networking Opportunities   225

7   Networking Opportunities For Improving Organizational Performance   265

8   Networking Opportunities for Improving Personal Performance   297

9   Determining Business Networking Requirements   319

10   Evaluation and Selection of Alternatives   353

11   Network Management and Security   379

12   Future Developments in Business Networking   431

Glossary   451
Index   465

CONTENTS

1 Strategic Planning and Network Technology   1

Introduction   1
Strategic Direction in Business through
  Networking   2
  The Process of Strategic Planning   4
  Integrating Strategic Planning with
  IT Planning   6
  The SWOT Method for Strategic
  Analysis   6
Achieving Competitive Advantage through
  Business Networking   11
  Five Key TBIT Developments   12
  Strategic Partnerships and Virtual
  Corporations   12
  Interorganizational Transaction
  Processing Systems   14
  Teamwork Enhanced by Cross-
  Functional Systems and
  Groupware   15
  Business Process Reengineering to
  Gain Quantum Improvements in
  Operations   15
  Location-Independent Work
  Processes   16
Enhancing Strengths and Overcoming
  Weaknesses through Networking   17
  Leveraging Strengths through TBIT   20

Conquering Weaknesses through
  TBIT   20
Applying IT to Increase
  Responsiveness   23
  Taking Advantage of Opportunities   25
  Defending against Threats   26
Summary   28

2 Networked Business Applications   33

Introduction   34
An Overview of Local and Wide Area
  Networks   34
Marketing Applications   36
  Order Entry Systems   36
  Point-of-Sale and Stock
  Management   37
  Reservation Systems   41
  Telemarketing   51
  Teleshopping   52
Financial Services   53
  Electronic Funds Transfer (EFT)   54
  Foreign Exchange and Investment
  Services   55
  Financing in Service Industries   61
Manufacturing Applications   64
  Just-in-Time and Stock Control
  Systems   64

Rapid Access to Up-to-Date
Organizational Information   65
Electronic Messaging and
Directories   68
Electronic Directories   69
Electronic Messaging   70
Electronic Diaries and
Calendaring   75
News Services, Bulletin Boards, and
Public/Corporate Databases   77
Electronic Data Interchange (EDI)   79
Teleconferencing   83
Benefits of Using Local and Wide Area
Networks in Business   84
Summary   86

3   **The Internet: A Global
Communications Resource   91**

Introduction   91
An Overview of the Internet   92
Internet Architecture and Protocols   95
Gaining Access to the Internet   96
Internet Services and Facilities   97
File Transfer Protocol (FTP)   98
Telnet: A Simple Remote Terminal
Protocol   99
Archie: An Archive of Archives   99
Gopher   100
Wide Area Information Server
(WAIS)   101
World Wide Web (WWW)   102
WWW Browsers   104
The Internet as a Business Tool   106
Why Get Involved?   107
Business Applications on the
Internet   111
A Few Commercial Examples   112
Operation and Performance   113
Security Issues in the Use of the
Internet   115
Router Filtering   116
Firewalls and Bastion Hosts   117
Application Layer Security   118
Summary   118

4   **Wide Area Networks (WANs):
Principles and Components   121**

Introduction   122
Major Functions of Wide Area
Networks   123
Communication Channels and Media   124
Bandwidth   125
Transmission Speeds   125
Twisted Pair Wire   126
Dial-up (Datel), Switched, and Leased
Circuits   127
Coaxial Cable   127
Optical Fiber Cable   127
Microwave and Satellite Systems   128
Summary   129
Network Components   129
Modems   130
Network Terminating Units (NTUs)   132
Multiplexers   133
Concentrators   135
Packet Assembler-Disassembler
(PAD)   138
Bridges and Routers   139
Software   139
Summary   140
Wide Area Network Environments   140
Public Switched Telephone Network
(PSTN)   141
Digital Data Network (DDN)   143
Packet Switching Network (PSN)   145
Integrated Services Digital Network
(ISDN)   145
Frame Relay   147
Consideration of Networking
Alternatives   149
Summary   149
Standards Used in Wide Area
Networking   151
ISO Model   152
CCITT and OSI Standards   154
International Standards Organization
(ISO)   155
American National Standards Institute
(ANSI)   155

Consultative Committee of the
Institute of Telegraph and Telephone
(CCITT)   155
De Facto Standards   156
Wide Area Network Topologies   157
Point-to-Point   157
Star   157
Multidrop or Multipoint   158
Mesh   159
Summary   161
Integration of Wide Area Network
Types   161
Cost of Acquiring and Using WANs   162
Summary   164

**5   Local Area Networks (LANs):
Principles and Components   167**

Introduction   168
Major Functions of Local Area
Networks   169
Local Area Network Functional
Principles   170
Communication Channels and Media:
Comparative Benefits and
Drawbacks   173
Popular Cabling Systems for Ethernet:
10BASE2, 10BASE5, 10BROAD36,
10BASE-T, and 10BASE-F   174
Local Area Network Standards   177
IEEE802 Local Area Network
Standards   177
Ethernet: Principles and Operation   181
Token Ring: Principles and
Operation   182
Local Area Network Hardware and
Connectivity   183
Terminals, PCs, Workstations, and
Microcomputers   183
Local Area Network Connectivity   184
Local Area Network Servers   186
Repeaters/Hubs, Bridges, Routers,
Brouters, and Gateways   188
Local Area Network Topologies   193
Star   194

Ring   194
Bus/Tree   195
Fiber Distributed Data Interface
(FDDI)   197
FDDI Architecture and
Applications   197
FDDI Technology   198
ISO Standards for FDDI   200
CDDI and TPDDI   201
High-Speed Local Area Networks
(100 Mbps)   202
Why 100 Mbps?   202
100 Mbps Standards   203
Summary   206
Client/Server Computing   208
Local Area Network Software
Components   209
Operating Systems in Local Area
Networks   210
Network Basic Input/Output Operating
System (NetBIOS)   211
TCP/IP Protocols   211
Novell NetWare   214
Microsoft Windows NT   214
Banyan VINES   214
Microsoft LAN Manager   214
Costs of Acquiring and Using Local
Area Networks   215
Acquisition and Usage Costs   215
Costs Associated with Local Area
Network Failure   217
Factors in Local Area Network
Selection   218
Summary   221

**6   Techniques for Analyzing and
Assessing Networking
Opportunities   225**

Introduction   226
Efficiency, Effectiveness, and Competitive
Advantage   226
Strategic Planning: A Foundation for
Analyzing Networking
Opportunities   231

The Benefits Cycle Model   231
Internal and External Factors: Their
   Impact on Competitiveness   234
A Combined Strategic Model   237
Critical Success Factors: Direction for
   Development   238
Analyzing the Organization for
   Networking Opportunities   240
   Models to Enhance Analysis of
   Business Networking
   Opportunities   243
   Function and Process Diagrams
   to Identify Networking
   Opportunities   248
   Association Matrices to Discover
   Networking Opportunities   250
   Data Models to Point Out Networking
   Opportunities   253
   Use of Rich Pictures to Analyze
   Network Needs   256
Summary   260

**7   Networking Opportunities for
   Improving Organizational
   Performance   265**

Introduction   266
Analyzing and Measuring Organizational
   Performance   266
   Organizational Analysis to Increase
   Efficiency through Networking   266
   Measuring Improvements in Resource
   Usage   269
   Cost-Saving Measures   275
Using Time and Risk to Gain Competitive
   Advantage   276
   Analyzing Time-Related Situations for
   TBIT Opportunities   277
   Networking Opportunities in Times of
   Uncertainty   282
Networked Applications to Support
   Organizational Groups   285
   Networked Groupware to Leverage
   Organizational Effort   285
   Workflow Applications   288

EDI: A Key to Trading Partner
   Effectiveness   289
Summary   292

**8   Networking Opportunities
   for Improving Personal
   Performance   297**

Introduction   298
Enhancing Personal Business
   Effectiveness   298
   A Communication Model   298
   Communication Effectiveness with
   Networks   299
   Research and Development   305
   Planning, Organizing, and
   Controlling   307
   Contact Management   308
Enhancing Personal Productivity   311
   Business Communications   311
   Electronic Filing and Document
   Retrieval   312
   Analyzing Situations and Making
   Decisions   315
Summary   315

**9   Determining Business Networking
   Requirements   319**

Introduction   320
Requirements Analysis for Network
   Solutions   320
   Internal and External
   Requirements   326
   Budgetary and Technical
   Requirements   330
   User Requirements   334
   Compatibility and Connectivity
   Requirements   335
Network Performance Standards
   and Fulfillment of User
   Requirements   337
   Response Time on the Network   337
   Reliability of the Network   338

Recoverability of the Network   341
Creating a Network Implementation
    Plan   343
Determining Sources of Network
    Components   347
Summary   348

10   Evaluation and Selection of Alternatives   353

Introduction   353
Cost-Benefit Analysis and Alternative
    Selection   354
    Alternative Solutions and Selection
        Concepts   354
    Cost-Benefit Analysis   357
Features Matrices and Min/Max Analysis
    for Alternative Selection   363
    Features Matrices   363
    Min/Max Analysis   364
    Spreadsheet to Combine Features
        Matrices with Cost-Effectiveness
        Ratio   364
Vendor-Related Characteristics Affecting
    Alternative Selection   368
Risk and Other Factors That Influence
    Alternative Choice   369
Alternative Financing Methods   370
    Purchasing   371
    Leasing   372
    Rental   372
Summary   373

11   Network Management and Security   379

Introduction   380
Management and Security Issues in
    Business Networks   381
    Distributed Network Management:
        Two Examples   381
    Network Intrusion: An Analysis   384
Change Management and Organizational
    Growth   387

Mixed-Vendor Network Management   389
    The Structure of Integrated Multivendor
        Network Management   391
    Multivendor Management
        Environments   392
    Operational Functions of a Management
        System   395
Open System and De Facto Network
    Management Protocols   396
    Simple Network Management Protocol
        (SNMP)   396
    Simple Network Management Protocol
        Version 2 (SNMP-2)   397
    Common Management Information
        Protocol (CMIP)   399
    Specialized Network Management
        Standards Activities   400
Distributed and Integrated Network
    Management   401
    Functional Management of Network
        Objects   401
Security Issues in Networking   403
    Costs versus Benefits   404
    Managing Security in the LAN   404
    Traditional Security Measures   405
    Structured Cabling and Building
        Security   406
    Security in the LAN Hardware   406
    Innovative Security Measures   410
    Verification and Audit Techniques   417
    Rating Security   423
    Summary of Security Measures   424
Backup and Disaster Recovery   425
Summary   427

12   Future Developments in Business Networking   431

Introduction   432
Change—A Driving Force for Future
    Telecommunications   433
Limitations on Networks and Future
    Developments   434
The Paperless Office and Its Effect on
    Business   436

Deregulation in the Telecommunications
    Industry   437
Important Technological Developments   438
ATM (Asynchronous Transfer Mode) and
    Multimedia Applications   439
Other Developing Technologies   442
    Building the Information Highways   442
    Personal Telephones   442
    Voice-Activated Computers   443
    Optical Computers   443
    Virtual Reality and
    Telecommunications   444
Seven Trends for an Electronic
    Future   444
    Increasing Miniaturization   445

Increasingly Powerful Systems   445
Increasing Digitization of
    Information   446
Increasing Digitization of Services   446
Increasingly Intelligent Systems   447
Increasing Integration of Business
    Organizations   447
Migration to Common Network
    Technology for LANs and
    WANs   448
Summary   449

Glossary of Terms   451
Index   465

1

STRATEGIC PLANNING AND NETWORK TECHNOLOGY

Chapter Outline

Introduction   1

Strategic Direction in Business through
Networking   2

Achieving Competitive Advantage
through Business Networking   11

Enhancing Strengths and Overcoming
Weaknesses through Networking
17

Applying IT to Increase
Responsiveness   23

Learning Objectives

By the end of Chapter 1, you should be able to

1. *Describe* how modern telecommunication systems can significantly support the organization's vision and **goals.**

2. *Identify* examples of leading-edge applications that have produced dynamic competitive advantage.

3. *Discuss* how networking the major functions can help an organization use its strengths and overcome its weaknesses.

4. *Explain* how the use of networks may increase an organization's responsiveness to opportunities and threats from the business environment.

Introduction

Appropriate application of **information technology (IT)** is one of the primary keys to efficient and effective business operation as we move into the 21st century. Yet merely having this technology is no guarantee of survival; the technology must be successfully integrated with the organization's strategic plan and diligently implemented in its daily operations. A structured procedure for discovering user and system requirements, analyzing system components, evaluating results and alternatives, and making recommendations to management should be followed. Many organizations are now nationally and globally based and thus require the appropriate use of computer networks and other telecommunications-based technologies. Both small and large firms are dealing with issues that demand better application of technology both internally and externally.

Chapter 1 looks at the **strategic leverage** a business may gain through the integration of network and IT planning with organization-wide strategy. Through the appropriate integration of information technology, organizations can successfully respond to customer needs with quality products and services in a competitive local and international marketplace. This area is further expanded in Chapter 6—Techniques for Analyzing and Assessing Network Opportunities—and Chapter 7—Networking Opportunities for Improving Organizational Performance.

Words that are printed in **boldface type** are listed at the end of each chapter and are defined in the Glossary at the end of this text. This method will be used to describe technical words and phrases that appear throughout this book.

Strategic Direction in Business through Networking

The following case, based on a real-life situation, illustrates the potential for integrating information technology planning with organizational **strategic planning**. In this case you will see how organizational goals can be achieved through telecommunications-based systems.

SMITH & JONES COMPANY

Frank Thomas, company comptroller, sat back in his desk chair, shaking his head as he thought over the events of the past four years. Smith & Jones Company(S&J), a manufacturer of wholesale and retail electronic products, had slowly lost market share and profitability up until four years ago. With the arrival of the new CEO, George Yeo, all that had changed. The first thing George did was call a staff meeting of all middle and top managers. He asked one question: "Why are you here?" On that one question hung the future of the company and the futures of many of the managers in the room. In the following weeks we met often, both formally and informally, to discuss that simple question. By the time we were finished, our conclusion was published as the "Smith & Jones Company **Mission Statement**." It consisted of one deceptively simple statement:

> Our business exists to provide quality electronic products to the wholesale and retail trade with the best service available and highly competitive prices, all in the best interests of our customers, employees, and shareholders.

After taking that first step, the company began a lengthy process of strategic planning to fulfill that statement of our purpose in the international economy. During meetings over the next nine months, all of the managers put forth their goals, **objectives,** and suggestions that would support the new direction. Some of the most surprising and profitable suggestions came from an unexpected source. The company had a small data processing (DP) facility, used primarily for transaction processing. Steve Case, a manager, had recently been hired to take over DP, but when George Yeo arrived, Steve's title was promptly changed to information systems & technology (IS&T) manager. Steve's promotion to the top management team injected a whole new perspective on the use of technology to enhance the organization. For example, one of the primary goals incorporated into the strategic plan was to improve customer service by reducing the time between when a customer places an order and when the customer receives the product. A week after the management team accepted this goal, Steve came back with two objectives intended to support and fulfill the goal:

1. Shorten time to acknowledge orders from nine days to one day by automating customer order entry via customer direct entry at in-store terminals. Terminals will communicate with the Smith & Jones Company IS&T computer systems over ordinary dial-up lines.
2. Shorten time to deliver order from six days to one day by expediting and automating order approval, warehouse notification, and shipping.

These two objectives combined would enable the company to deliver products to domestic customers within two days and a bit longer to international customers. This was 14 days faster than the current delivery time, and 10 days faster than the industry average! Both of these objectives would require substantial capital and development investments on the company's part. However, Steve was recommending a pilot project that he hoped would prove the effectiveness of the concept. If it produced the results he expected, there would be no problem getting both the company management and customers to agree to the changes required. Figure 1–1 shows a network diagram of the proposed system.

Within eight months, Steve Case and his development team had completed the advanced prototype software systems and were ready to test them with three customers located near S&J's head office that had agreed to act as test sites. After six months of operation and a number of modifications, the system was ready for full implementation

FIGURE 1–1

Simple network diagram for proposed Smith & Jones system

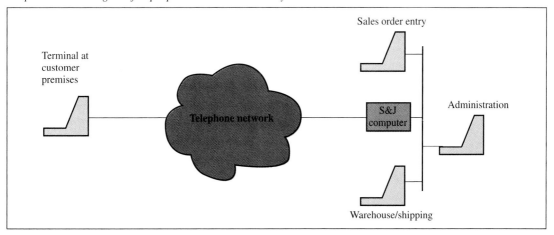

nationally and for international implementation a few months later. Modifications, primarily to improve ease of use, add functionality, and improve performance, were based on feedback from customers and IS&T operational staff. Test site results had shown that Steve had been accurate in his estimates of the potential, even erring on the conservative side. As it turned out, many customer orders were delivered within 24 hours of being placed by the client store. The customers were thrilled, since it meant that they would no longer need to carry as much stock as previously. The improvement was incredible. During the six-month test period the three customers saw their average stock holdings decline from $2.5 million to less than $1 million! In addition, the cost of order entry for Smith & Jones Company had declined on the test order system from $12 per order to only $2. This was because all data entry was performed and validated by customer personnel directly from in-store terminals using dial-up lines directly linked to the IS&T minicomputer.

When the company marketing people got hold of these statistics, it did not take them long to see the potential for selling customers on the idea. In-store terminals cost only $2,000, and the S&J salespeople guaranteed that customers would recoup that cost within the first month through stock reductions and did not have to pay for the terminals until that first month was over. This was an offer that could not be refused, and most of S&J's existing customers, and many new ones, accepted it. Sales began to skyrocket as customers found it was easier to place one automated order to Smith & Jones Company than multiple orders to the competition. Quick, accurate delivery, very competitive prices, and premier service strengthened S&J's position each month.

By the end of the first full year in operation, the new automated ordering system had fulfilled the original goal and objective beyond the wildest dreams of top management, and many new opportunities were arising each month thanks to the new relationship established with customers.

The Smith & Jones scenario points out some of the possibilities for enhancing and implementing corporate strategy using telecommunications-based information technology (TBIT). Successful implementation, however, requires more than just good technology. CEO commitment, realistic training budgets, and a change in corporate culture are often required as well.

The Process of Strategic Planning

What is strategic planning? What processes does it involve, and how can modern telecommunications systems help to support and achieve organizational strategy? The following pages will answer these important questions and more.

How to deal with strategic management

The process of strategic planning includes a hierarchy of purposes, including

1. Clearly defining the mission, or primary purpose, of the organization.
2. Describing the major overall goals that will help in achieving the mission.
3. Precisely listing the specific, realistic, and measurable objectives that will allow the organization to achieve its goals.

A visual illustration of this hierarchy appears in Figure 1–2.

The Smith & Jones Company case provides an example of this hierarchy. Here is S&J's mission statement, followed by a supporting goal, followed by an objective that supports the given goal:

FIGURE 1–2

The mission, goals, and objectives hierarchy

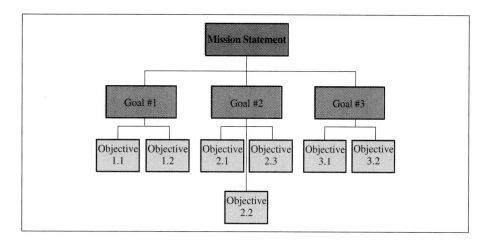

Mission statement: Our business exists to provide quality electronic products to the wholesale and retail trade with the best service available and highly competitive prices, all in the best interests of our customers, employees, and shareholders.

Goal: To improve customer service by reducing the time between when a customer places an order and when the customer receives the product.

Objective: Shorten time to acknowledge orders from nine days to one day by automating customer order entry via customer direct entry at in-store terminals. Terminals will communicate with the Smith & Jones Company IS&T computer systems over ordinary dial-up lines.

Each higher level is supported by increasing detail at the lower level, taking the organization from a broad statement of vision or mission to specific, achievable, and measurable objectives. The purpose of the strategic planning process is to efficiently direct the development of

- The goods and services provided by the organization.
- The functions and processes used in the organization.
- The people, finances, facilities, and other resources required.

To be successfully converted into action, a strategic plan must be combined with **tactical planning**. Tactical planning involves creating a blueprint to achieve the objectives. This blueprint should include the following key elements:

1. *What*: Steps of action to be performed.
2. *Who*: Person or persons responsible for achieving specific steps of action.
3. *When*: Specific target dates for achievement of the actions specified.
4. *How*: Resources required to support and achieve the steps of action.
5. *Where*: Place the action is to be performed; may be geographic or organizational.

When integrated with IT strategy, such organizational planning can maximize the leverage gained through investment in **telecommunications-based information**

technology (TBIT). Integrated planning can open up new business opportunities, gain an advantage over competitors, increase organizational responsiveness, enhance current strengths, and overcome existing weaknesses.

Integrating Strategic Planning with IT planning

Today, winning or losing in the commercial arena both locally and internationally depends on a number of major factors. One primary factor is the wise use of information technology (IT) in conjunction with telecommunications. Traditionally most organizations treated the "data processing department" as the "keepers of the mainframe" and received very little strategic input from this area. The primary function of data processing was just that: to process data and to keep the computer systems running properly. This attitude is rapidly giving way to the recognition that the appropriate use of IT can greatly enhance an organization's competitiveness, and that includes its competitors. If you do not gain the advantage, they might! This is clearly seen in the Smith & Jones Company case. As a result of this changing attitude, many organizations are moving the information systems department manager onto the top management team to enhance the process of aligning IT planning with overall organizational planning.

Managers of these functions need to be in tune with both the changing technology and the business needs of the organization. They need to be **hybrid managers**. These are managers who are capable of exercising skills in some functional area of the business (e.g., marketing, accounting, finance) and have a strong understanding of the appropriate use of IT. The additional control, application, and insight such managers can bring to the organization are greatly needed to put IT to its best use.

Managers not only need to successfully control information technology but also must use it to rethink new ways of doing business. The integration of IT strategy into the broader organizational goals and objectives can open up winning opportunities that will allow the organization to survive and thrive in the intensely competitive international marketplace (see Figure 1–3). There are various methods for performing strategic analysis. One very useful technique is the SWOT method, discussed next. Additional approaches are introduced in Chapters 6 and 7.

The SWOT Method for Strategic Analysis

With the highly competitive international marketplace exposing many previously "safe" markets to new competitors, telecommunications-based IT (TBIT) offers very real opportunities and threats to commercial organizations. This challenge has been compounded in the 1990s by the international economy, which is in the throes of a worldwide recession that is significantly reducing profitability. This situation has been caused by

1. Deregulation of many industries and globalization of both industries and organizations.
2. Service and Quality changes. In the past, customers paid for quality. Today, quality is the cost of getting into the game and not something customers expect to pay extra for.

FIGURE 1–3

Synergism between IT strategy and corporate strategy

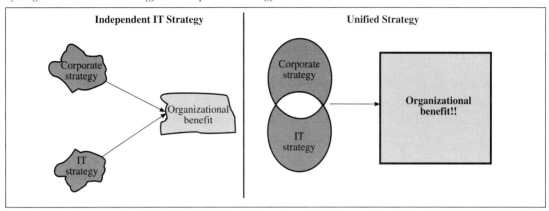

3. Global overcapacity in many industries, which has been assisted by IT. For example, airline computers have moved from being purely reservations based to being used for franchise, distribution, marketing, and customer contact. There are eight major airline computer systems in the world, each capable of performing around 2,000 **transactions per second (tps).** Therefore, capacity is around 16,000 transactions per second. The industry requirement, however, is only 6,000 transactions per second.[1]

4. A move from mass marketing–style production to mass-customized production, with even large organizations aiming at ever-smaller niche markets.

Given these and many other changes that are occurring, as well as rapid advances in computer hardware and telecommunications technology, the possibilities are immense if used wisely.

SWOT Analysis.   One particularly useful method is strengths, weaknesses, opportunities, and threats **(SWOT)** analysis. This approach presents a framework for considering the mission, goals, and objectives of the organization. Strengths and weaknesses are primarily *internal* considerations, that is, those within the company. These strengths and weaknesses may present opportunities and threats to the competition.

Strengths and Weaknesses.   When considering strengths and weaknesses, managers ask questions such as

- What strengths does our organization have that we can capitalize on, enhance, or use to improve our competitive position?

---

[1] P. G. W. Keen. *Competing in Time: Using Telecommunications for Competitive Advantage* (Ballinger Press, 1988), pp. 55–58.

- How can we use our strengths in new ways?
- What are the strong points about our current products or services?
- What new products or services may we develop based on our strengths?
- What weaknesses do we have that offer opportunities for improving efficiency or effectiveness?
- What new resources do we need to overcome existing weaknesses?
- What changes to existing functions or processes might help us overcome these weaknesses?
- How may existing weaknesses be turned into strengths?

When raising questions such as these, it must be considered how the answers will mold the mission statement, frame goals, or point to objectives. This approach will help to provide a solid future direction for improvement of the organization.

Another question to ask is "How can TBIT be used to enhance and leverage existing strengths or overcome existing weaknesses?" American Hospital Supply Corporation (AHS) is a good example.

AMERICAN HOSPITAL SUPPLY CORPORATION
A Classic Case

In the late 1970s, a company named American Hospital Supply (AHS) revolutionized its industry and provided a classic example of using TBIT to gain a strategic advantage. AHS made the decision to automate the process of making sales calls on its hospital customers by installing ordering terminals in each hospital. A basic principle in AHS's business was "the more sales calls, the more sales." It would always be difficult to make enough sales calls to meet every customer need, but AHS had a good working relationship with its existing customer base. The new terminal-based system was called Automated System for Analytical Purchasing (ASAP), and it would put a "salesperson" at the customer's fingertips! Training was provided to customers in placing orders and using the analytical features of the system. Following the training, hospital staff members were able to order items online rather than waiting for a salesperson to call. The result of this seemingly minor administrative change was an increase from an average of 2.4 items per customer order to 5.7 items (compared to an industry average of 1.7) and skyrocketing sales for AHS!

AHS's customers also benefited. The new system brought dramatic reductions in hospital inventory due to more accurate ordering, and much quicker order-cycle and delivery times. One hospital reduced inventory from an average of $700,000 to $250,000, and another saw an increase in stock turns from 8 times to 12 times per year. Such exceptional results allowed AHS to gain many new hospital accounts and become a dominant force in its industry. AHS was then in a position to offer special new services to existing customers, such as automated stock management and discounts for volume purchases. AHS also experienced significant cost reductions for order transaction entry, since the customers were doing most of the work.

Using its growing technology base, AHS automated its own purchase ordering system and integrated the system into its inventory management. Automatic purchase orders could be placed to the lowest-priced, highest-quality suppliers. AHS used its increased purchasing power to pressure key suppliers to increase quality and reduce prices to gain full AHS support. When Baxter Healthcare Corporation acquired AHS in the mid-1980s, it used the AHS innovation to capture over half of the hospital market.

In summary, AHS identified a weakness in the sales and distribution cycle: insufficient sales calls. It identified a strength to assist in overcoming the weakness: a good working relationship with hospitals. AHS management then proceeded to install a system to overcome the weakness and take advantage of the strength.

In the AHS case, note that after the successful installation of the new system, AHS used an existing *strength*, order terminals in hospitals, to open up new business opportunities and support the organization's strategic direction by providing information services to hospitals, providing discounts to hospitals, and improving prices and quality from its own suppliers.

The benefits gained by early application of technology to an old problem or early adoption of a new technology can be sustained by further strategic initiatives built on past successes. However, any **competitive advantage** can erode over time, and consistent effort, innovation, and successful implementation is required to remain competitive (see Figure 1–4).

Opportunities and Threats   Just as strengths and weaknesses can be viewed primarily as an *internal* consideration, opportunities and threats are chiefly *external* considerations, dealing with the marketplace in which business is conducted. These may represent strengths and weaknesses in the competition. When considering them, managers ask questions such as

- What opportunities or unfilled needs exist in our markets that we are currently not benefiting from?
- How may we best use our existing strengths to take advantage of these opportunities?

FIGURE 1–4

Natural cycle of creation, erosion, and reconstruction of a strategic advantage

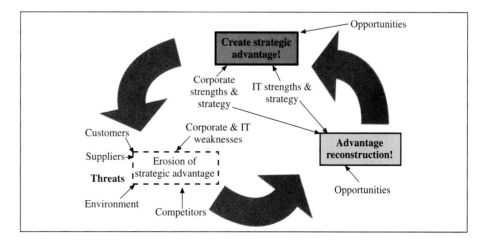

- How may we use or modify our existing products or services to gain from this opportunity?
- What new products or services do we need to benefit from these opportunities?
- What weaknesses in our competitors present new opportunities for us?
- What threats exist or may arise in our environment or markets?
- Which of our competitors present the greatest threat, and why?
- Which of our weaknesses may our competitors take advantage of?

Another question is, "How can we use TBIT to take advantage of opportunities or nullify threats?" The following Kangaroo Courier case provides a good example of taking advantage of an opportunity. In reading this case, note how Kangaroo Courier used telecommunications services that were readily available to all firms in the courier industry to gain a considerable advantage over competitors.

KANGAROO COURIER COMPANY
Speeding Parcel Delivery with Faster Communication

The courier business is highly competitive. The entry costs are low, and just about anyone who wants to can enter this industry. Staying ahead of the pack is no easy job. The Kangaroo Courier Company (KCC) of Australasia decided to make its key strategy "best service at a higher price." To demand even a marginally higher price would indeed require the best service. Like most courier services, KCC had used radio telephones to communicate pickup orders from the office to its vans. In 1989, KCC put in place a strategy to reduce costs yet increase service based on the application of existing telecommunications-based information technology. The company installed a computerized messaging system and a new **PABX** that allowed telephone operators to enter customer pickup requests directly into a computer database. Dispatchers could then forward these messages directly to the appropriate van drivers using an alphanumeric pager. Whereas an average of 8 minutes was previously required to reach drivers using the radio telephone, it took an average of just 20 seconds for a message to reach the driver on the pager. The new system meant no more multiple phone calls to catch drivers in their vans; fewer missed pickups, since the pagers could be reached even when the driver was in a building; and a more balanced workload on the telephone operators and dispatchers, since they all had access to the system at the same time. The system was further enhanced by the installation of an autocall facility, in which customers could dial in directly, interact with a voice-activated system using their touch-tone phones, and place their pickup orders without operator assistance. An operator-assisted order typically took 2 minutes of the customers' time, whereas the automated system typically required less than 20 seconds. Most of KCC's regular customers responded very positively to the new system.

Source: JV. Sheffield and M. D. Myers, *New Zealand Cases in Information Systems*, 2nd ed. (Auckland: Pagination Publishers, 1992) p. 156.

The results for KCC were impressive. Over the next two years KCC decreased the number of operators required to handle peak load demands from 17 to only 6. It was able to offer substantially improved service with a much larger percentage of pickups and deliveries occurring within the minimum amount of time. Overall costs were down, profits were up, and KCC had stolen the march on the competition.

Kangaroo Courier Company not only gained a competitive advantage through being able to deliver a faster, more reliable service but also achieved considerable **operational efficiency** through the application of TBIT.

Achieving Competitive Advantage through Business Networking

Information technology offers a wide range of capabilities to support organizational effort and provide a competitive advantage. The capabilities of these technologies to yield organization impact and benefit are listed in Figure 1–5.

When focusing on telecommunications-based IT, many of these capabilities are enhanced and extended. Examples of this can be seen in both the analytical and knowledge management capabilities, which may be considerably enhanced by a networked system's capability to bring multiple expert opinions to bear on a problem using conferencing and groupware. A number of key developments springing from these generic IT capabilities are leading edge concepts today, but may well be the standard for successful and surviving companies within a few years.

FIGURE 1–5

IT capabilities and organization impact

Capability	Organizational Impact or Benefit
Transactional	IT can transform unstructured processes into routinized transactions.
Geographical	IT can transfer information rapidly and easily across large distances, making processes independent of geography.
Automational	IT can replace or reduce human labor in a process.
Analytical	IT can apply complex analytical methods to a process.
Informational	IT can bring vast amounts of detailed information into a process.
Sequential	IT can enable changes in the sequence of tasks in a process, often allowing multiple tasks to be worked on simultaneously.
Knowledge management	IT allows the capture and dissemination of knowledge and expertise to improve a process.
Tracking	IT allows detailed tracking of task status, inputs, and outputs.
Disintermediation	IT can be used to connect two parties within a process that would otherwise communicate through an intermediary (internal or external).

Source: T. H. Davenport and J. E. Short, "The New Industrial Engineering: Information Technology and Business Process Redesign," *Sloan Management Review,* Summer 1990.

Five Key TBIT Developments

Technology alone will not produce a competitive advantage. Integration of the corporate vision, thorough analysis, the right corporate culture, and appropriate technology are required to establish a sustainable advantage. A number of key developments have opened the way for increasing applications of TBIT systems to enable competitive advancement. Among these key developments are

- Strategic partnerships and virtual corporations.
- Interorganizational transaction-processing systems to accelerate business cycles.
- Teamwork enhanced by cross-functional systems groupware.
- Business process reengineering to gain quantum improvements in operations.
- Location-independent work processes.

These developments have one thing in common: They all involve a cooperative effort that crosses departmental, organizational, and national boundaries and requires telecommunications-based information technology as a major enabling factor.

The close integration of the organization's IT strategy with its business strategy is often an overriding factor in many successful companies. Failure to do so can lead to costly mistakes. Increasingly, companies are finding that up to 50 percent of their capital investment is IT investment. If these major investments are poorly chosen and are not integrated with the business strategy, the best technology may produce the worst results.

Let's look at these five areas more closely, along with some leading-edge examples.

Strategic Partnerships and Virtual Corporations

With many organizations **downsizing** and retrenching into their **core competencies,** it is becoming increasingly necessary that they work cooperatively with other organizations to achieve market success. Two key concepts in this arena are strategic partnerships and virtual corporations.

Strategic partnerships include a wide range of interorganizational relationships, such as franchising, joint marketing, joint R&D, and cross-licensing agreements for technology. In many cases, a high degree of communication must accompany such arrangements, and often this involves various TBIT systems. An example of a strategic partnership is that between Ford Motor Company and Mazda of Japan. In a series of technology-sharing and joint marketing arrangements, these two automobile companies have supported each other through some difficult times and developed some very innovative manufacturing and marketing strategies. A key factor in the success of this strategic partnership has been the development of a strong trust relationship among key individuals in the two organizations. A primary factor in implementing this partnership has been the electronic messaging system put in place to support joint R&D, as well as administrative E-mail.

Because electronic partnerships allow rapid interaction between diverse companies, organizations can design and produce a wider range of products in far less time than ever before. For example, the time needed to launch a new car in the United States used to be seven years (from specification to design and manufacture). Japanese automakers initially reduced this time to 36 months, thus allowing them to introduce new models in half the time their competitors did. They saw a strategic opportunity and capitalized on it. They achieved substantial strategic advantage through reengineering their processes in cooperation with suppliers (see the following section) with the use of TBIT. The **chief executive officer (CEO)** must be committed to IT, not as a technology per se but as a basic methodology for doing business.

The **virtual corporation,** an outgrowth of the strategic partnership, is an organization that has been put together in a short time frame to achieve a specific purpose or capitalize on a market opportunity. For example, a virtual corporation could be a cooperative arrangement between an R&D lab and an independent technology manufacturer in conjunction with an expert marketing organization. This virtual corporation might exist for a period of years (or months) to market a new product. When the market has matured and the profit levels of the product range have dropped, the virtual corporation may dissolve even more quickly than it was formed (see Figure 1–6). As with strategic partnerships, trust is a key ingredient in the initial formation of a virtual corporation, and TBIT may be critical to the successful implementation of a conglomeration of commercially and perhaps geographically diverse organizations. An example of a virtual corporation is the arrangement among IBM (R&D), Mitsubishi Electronics (manufacturing), and BellSouth Corporation for development, manufacture, and marketing of the "Simon" **personal digital assistant (PDA)**.

FIGURE 1–6

Construction and dissolution of a virtual corporation

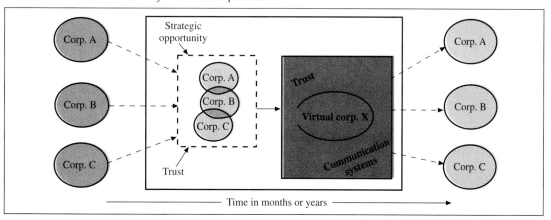

Interorganizational Transaction Processing Systems

A wide range of TBIT-based systems are beginning to have a significant impact on organizations and the ways organizations can work together. Some of these systems are especially potent in accelerating business cycles and thus assisting organizations in becoming more responsive to the marketplace. Applications of TBIT-based systems include the following:

- **Electronic funds transfer (EFT)** between companies in payment of invoices speeds the cash flow of the selling organization while reducing paperwork and errors for both companies.
- Electronic funds transfer at the point of sale **(EFT/POS),** which accelerates the cash flow of retailers by reducing administrative costs, bad debts, and uncertainty.
- **Electronic data interchange (EDI)** systems, which transfer electronic purchase and sales orders from one company to another as well as other electronic documents, thus accelerating the inventory replenishment cycle while reducing errors, out-of-stock conditions, inventory levels, and administrative costs.
- E-mail, fax, E-fax, voice mail, and bulletin board systems, which speed up communication while providing the accuracy of written correspondence. They also reduce communication cycle time "telephone tag," which is especially important when communicating internationally across different time zones. These systems are often used for placing orders and for accelerating feedback in market research and R&D.
- Airline computerized reservation systems (CRS's), which link travel agents and travelers with airlines and hotels to increase ease, efficiency, and variety in travel arrangements.

Consider Wal-Mart Stores, the giant retailer. A significant factor in Wal-Mart's continuing success is the company's major investment in the use of TBIT systems to accelerate its inventory replenishment cycle and optimize total inventory management. The most important single asset (apart from people) of a major retailer is inventory. The right inventory in the right quantities at the right prices and quality means strong sales, while the opposite can spell disaster. Wal-Mart installed a satellite-based network linking headquarters, regional warehouses, and all stores. Every store has a **point-of-sale (POS)** terminal system that records the item and quantity for each sale, and then maintains records showing the levels of inventory of every item in the store. The satellite network communicates automatically with each store every few hours to determine stock levels and the rate at which each inventory item is moving. This allows marketing staff at headquarters to discover slow-moving items that need to be put on sale. It also allows restocking of items that are moving rapidly so that the stores do not run out of stock and lose sales. In addition, this electronic communication network is linked to all of Wal-Mart's major suppliers using EDI, automatically placing orders on low-stock items. As a result of this system, Wal-Mart has reduced stock replenishment time to four or five days, compared to industry average of three to four weeks. The ongoing refinement of this system has sustained Wal-Mart's competitive advantage in conjunction with its basic strategy of everyday low prices (EDLP)[2]

Teamwork Enhanced by Cross-Functional Systems and Groupware

Teamwork and the concepts of empowering workers to be decision makers and continuously improving the way the organization works are critical success factors for many organizations. The development of cross-functional systems and **groupware** systems to support teams of workers in cooperative work has been an ongoing development in the use of TBIT. Using both local and wide area networks, these applications allow multiple individuals and groups to work on the same documents as though the documents resided on one local hard drive. The file, whether an electronic document, a spreadsheet, or a database file, may actually be located hundreds or even thousands of miles away, yet organizationally or geographically dispersed team members can share it in working on a joint project. Group schedulers, enhanced E-mail, and group-supported word processing and databases are all examples of this category of TBIT system. A related development is in the area of **workflow software**. This type of software provides for collaboration among systems, providing support for automated routing of documents among systems and people who need to complete various processes on related documents.

Frito-Lay, the snack food producer, illustrates the effectiveness that can be obtained by enabling business strategy with TBIT. This important market player recognized that to maintain and extend its position in the market, it needed to become more responsive to customer desires and market conditions. As a result, it developed a series of systems that strongly enhanced its marketing function. Cross-functional systems were developed that allowed access to current market research, product demand and market share, sales levels, and other key information. These systems were set up so that product managers, advertising, pricing, and field sales teams could all be in close communication via integrated WAN/LAN applications. The result is that Frito-Lay is able to respond to competitive changes, including test marketing of new products by competitors and development of new products in record time, within one to two days at the individual store level.

Business Process Reengineering to Gain Quantum Improvements in Operations

The area of business process reengineering is gaining momentum as organizations recognize the need for radical change in addition to ongoing improvements. **Business process reengineering** is fundamentally a total rethinking of how specific functions of a business are accomplished. The work is redesigned using information technology to gain a multifold increase in human resource productivity and cost reductions that will also yield a higher level of service to customers. For some

---

[2] "Wal-Mart's Advances in EDI,"*Discount Merchandiser*, September 1990, pp. 32–33; "EDI: Who's on First?," *Bobbin*, April 1992, pp. 22–24; "Going Beyond EDI," *Chainstore Age Executive*, March 1993, pp. 150–52; "What Came First: Productivity Loops or EDLP?," *Discount Merchandiser*, May 1993.

organizations, the concept might be phrased "don't automate, but obliterate."[3] In other words, the objective of business process reengineering is not simply to automate existing functionality but to redesign the process to gain optimal results. This may involve eliminating tasks that are not adding value to the final product or service, as well as reconstructing the remaining processes to flow more quickly, accurately, and efficiently. This approach often takes processes previously confined to individual departments of the organization and joins them with processes from other functions to remove time and cost bottlenecks and improve output quality.

Rank Xerox U.K. undertook a project to redesign its business in 1987 when it realized that poor business responsiveness and strategy were leading to stagnant growth. The new CEO, David O'Brien, took advantage of his "honeymoon" period to upgrade the company's competitive position by building cross-functional teams and then developing integrated information systems to support them. The combination of networked database applications and the new cooperative culture worked wonders for the company's operations. Results included a 20 percent growth in revenues, a reduction of staff not directly involved with customer contact from 1,100 to 800, and a reduction of order delivery time from 33 days to 6 days. This was not accomplished without some difficulties, as several top managers, unable to handle the change in organization culture and approach and a substantial investment in new technology, left during this time.[4]

Location-Independent Work Processes

A wide range of issues have begun to affect the ability of organizations to distribute the work to the workers rather than bringing the workers to the work. Most of these concepts are enabled by telecommunications-based information technology and include the following:

- Employees using **telecommuting** (working from an office at home or in a small branch linked to the head office E-mail and other systems via network technology) to do their work more effectively and efficiently without having to fight commuter traffic.
- Information-intensive businesses relocating to sources of cheap land and cheap labor. One major insurance company located its headquarters away from all major urban areas to keep overhead costs down. All services were provided using 800 numbers and networked information systems to provide up-to-the-minute, accurate information to support many innovative marketing and service approaches.
- Commodities and stockbrokers placing buy and sell orders across continents and time zones using telecommunications-based systems to support the transactions.

---

[3] M. Hammer and J. Champy. *Reengineering the Corporation: A Manifesto for Business Revolution*, (New York: HarperCollins, 1993).

[4] T. H. Davenport and J. E. Short. "The New Industrial Engineering: Information Technology and Business Process Redesigns," *Sloan Management Review*, Summer 1990.

- Software development organizations having high-quality code written by local programmers in India at one-third the cost of U.S. or European professionals.

All of these applications and others simply hint at the possibilities open to companies and individuals for the use of TBIT systems to enhance and enable new ways of working to provide cost-effective products and services to customers.

The insurance company USAA is a good example of this trend. Corporate headquarters are located in a nonurban area. The company has designed its main customer support systems around image technology applications. All incoming mail is digitally scanned and electronically stored; then the mail is burned! Conversion of all documents to electronic images makes the documents available to anyone in the organization without the time and paper costs of photocopying and the delays of mailing material. This approach has allowed USAA to increase the number of policies processed per employee by 500 percent! In addition, the electronic documents allow the company to cross-link policies, yielding a much higher level of policy customization to client needs. A company that has a policy allowing cross-linking of all document services has many more **degrees of freedom** and is in a stronger strategic position.

When documents and data are primarily stored physically, people who need to use them must have physical access to them. Workers need to be near the filing system. However, when documents and data are primarily or exclusively electronic, a worker has access to them no matter where she or he is located. Consider a well-known company that currently takes 24 days to issue a life insurance policy. Even a competitor that takes 16 days isn't a real threat. But what about a company that can do it in four hours, as does Mutual Benefits in the United States? Companies like USAA and Mutual Benefits are able to process policies more quickly and to locate workers wherever the best labor pool and living/cost conditions are. Competitors must respond, and those that cannot may be forced out of the business. IT is often one of the key factors determining success or failure.[5]

The impact of modern telecommunications systems on organizations can be immense. Those that make effective use of these new technologies gain a strategic advantage. Those that misuse or ignore the changing market incur a distinct disadvantage.

Enhancing Strengths and Overcoming Weaknesses through Networking

Earlier in this chapter, you learned about a strategic analysis technique called SWOT analysis. In the remainder of this chapter, you will see a number of direct applications of this concept. This section focuses on strengths and weaknesses of an organization. The following section looks at an organization's responsiveness to the competitive environment, particularly opportunities and threats.

---

[5] P. G. W. Keen. *Shaping the Future–Business Design Through Information Technology* (Cambridge, MA: Harvard Business School Press, 1991).

✶**FIGURE 1–7**

Graphical depiction of the SWOT analysis model

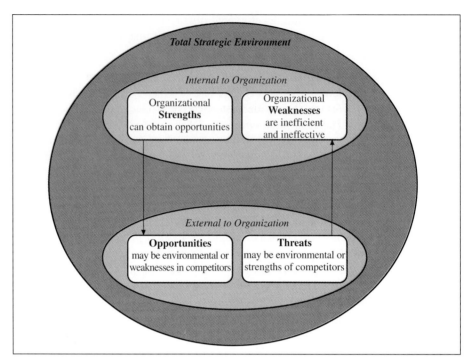

✶**FIGURE 1–7**

Graphical depiction of the SWOT analysis model

It is useful to view the SWOT model as a system in which the organization's strengths provide leverage to take advantage of opportunities that may arise from environmental factors or competitor weaknesses. On the other hand, the organization's weaknesses, which demonstrate inefficiencies or ineffectiveness, may provide a point of attack for competitors. A graphic depiction of this process appears in Figure 1–7.

The strengths of an organization are those special competencies or resources that currently give the organization an advantage in the marketplace. Its weaknesses are those areas where the organization shows a less than optimal performance and leaves room for improvement. Appropriate use of IT allows the organization to leverage its strengths and minimize the effects of its weaknesses.

The following hypothetical case illustrates what can happen using SWOT analysis and TBIT.

JELFAB, LTD.

Jim Clark is managing director of JELFAB, Ltd. (Hong Kong), a medium-size trading firm. The firm has its head office in Hong Kong and in recent years has gained a reputation for supplying quality products with good customer service and highly effective employees. As a result, the company has grown substantially and enjoys a high level of employee retention and increasing productivity as the well-trained employees take on more and more customers.

Recently Susie Yin, marketing director, raised an issue with Jim Clark. A number of customer service employees have complained about the slowness of correspondence between the head office and the branches as well as between locations when they try to find particular items of stock to complete customer orders. In addition, data entry operators often incorrectly key in information from customers' faxed orders, resulting in a number of embarrassing errors. Fortunately, customers have not complained about slowness of service yet, and employees have handled the errors in customer orders in such a professional manner that customers have been quite satisfied.

Currently all orders are received by the head office, keyed into the computer database and forwarded by mail to the appropriate branch to be filled. When an order is filled, the branch sends a copy of the packing slip to the head office for billing. If any problems occur with the order, the customer service people at the branch handle the query or problem. After the problem is resolved, branch personnel mail the head office a credit note request or other documentation as necessary. Then the head office issues a credit invoice or additional charges. This procedure works well, but it is slow. Often customers phone in to ask if their orders are ready, and the branch personnel have not even received the orders in the mail yet. Often an order doesn't arrive until three to five days after the head office receives the fax from the customer, with a two-day backlog in data entry and then one to three days in the mail.

In discussing this problem with Jim, Susie has suggested that a technology solution might prove to be effective, since the problem seems to involve an increasing workload on the staff rather than poor procedures. Susie recommends installation of an **electronic fax (E-fax)** and data modem on one PC each at the head office and the branches to replace the existing fax machine and provide E-mail capability at the same time. The electronic fax will allow immediate forwarding of an order via E-mail to the appropriate branch and instant acknowledgment in electronic form, providing automated data entry into the computer database. This will speed up order delivery to the branches as well as reduce order entry errors. With a modem for wide area E-mail and E-fax on at least one PC at each branch, customer service employees will be able to query all the branches and the head office at the same time when they are looking for a product to complete an unfilled order. Instead of having to phone each office, they can send the same E-mail request to all offices using a "mailing list" feature.

Following a formal analysis of the company's requirements and an evaluation of the technology, the recommended solution has been implemented with minimal problems and little retraining required. The results have been highly satisfactory, and have met everyone's expectations. The turnaround time from receipt of a fax at the head office to delivery of the fax to the branch has been reduced from approximately four days to less than one hour. The company is now retraining customer order data entry operators because they are no longer needed for that task. Responses to stock requests by customer service employees has improved markedly, resulting in much better inventory utilization.

The JELFAB case points out a number of ways TBIT can be used to leverage existing company strengths and overcome weaknesses that could become serious problems. An exercise at the end of this chapter allows you to analyze the JELFAB case using the techniques you have learned.

Leveraging Strengths through TBIT

In a physical sense, a lever is a device used to gain mechanical advantage, allowing individuals to move a greater weight than they would be able to without the lever. To **leverage** strengths through TBIT means to use IT to gain a greater advantage from organizational strengths than would be possible without the IT application. Strengths may range from good employee morale to high manufacturing productivity. Enhancing and increasing the scope of these strengths can strongly assist in the accomplishment of organizational strategy and provide greater strategic benefits (see Figure 1–8).

Having seen a sample case of how strengths can be enhanced and weaknesses overcome using TBIT in the JELFAB scenario, let's look at some examples. Figure 1–9 lists a variety of strengths, sample IT applications, and some of the benefits that might accrue to an organization. These applications may assist in integrating the organization and thus leveraging strengths into an even more productive position.

Figure 1–9 enumerates some of the possibilities inherent in TBIT but is not an exhaustive list by any means. The technology behind these applications, further detailed examples, and the principles underlying them are discussed in later chapters.

Conquering Weaknesses through TBIT

Weaknesses in an organization may range from slow loss of productivity to providing a major opportunity for a competitor. As the old saying goes, "A small leak can sink a big ship." Thus, conquering the small and large weaknesses can be very beneficial to an organization, even to the point of salvaging its existence. In some cases the weakness may be the technology itself, and appropriate protective strategies must be put in place. The following example illustrates this type of weakness:

> An increasing number of organizations are automating their **core logistics** (primary functions and transactions) and in many cases their cash flow is directly affected by these systems. Thus when an airline's Central Reservations System (CRS) is down the airline is non-functional and the competitive strategy becomes meaningless. For example in August 1991 fire took out the power supply to Cathay Pacific's computers

FIGURE 1–8

Leveraging corporate strengths with TBIT to gain organizational benefit

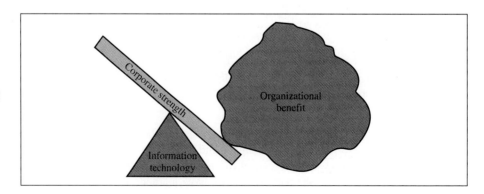

FIGURE 1-9

Sample strengths enhanced by TBIT

Strength	Sample TBIT Application	Benefit
Good communication with branches	E-mail or E-fax	24-hour availability, speed of communication, no need to rekey data
Good customer service	E-mail, E-fax, or voice mail/touchtone phone input Ordering terminals at customer office	Faster response to customer needs, higher staff morale, increased productivity
Low-cost structure	**Computer-integrated manufacturing (CIM)**	Higher profit, increased customizability, low-cost structure spread to product design and engineering
High-quality product design	CIM	Ensures conversion from design to final product, enhances the product development cycle, and speeds up **time to market**
Well-organized, goal-oriented management team	Electronic calendaring, E-mail, E-fax, external databases	Speeds up the process of meeting formation and facilitation, communication, and data gathering
Knowledgeable and motivated managers	Network workstation on each manager's desk with decision support system (DSS) software	Ready access to all pertinent management information
Well-educated and technically competent sales force	Laptop computers with modems and communications software for stock query, order entry, and market survey information, voice mail and touchtone information systems	Reduced data entry staff, fewer errors, motivated sales staff, better stock management, improved market research

which run 90 **mission critical applications** and process 40–50 transactions per second. It took 13 hours to bring the back up system into operation at Kai Tak airport and 3 additional Unisys 9740 disk drives had to be flown from the USA. The cost of this failure has not been estimated but could run into the tens of millions of dollars in lost revenues. Cathay Pacific was pleased that transfer of all mission critical applications was shifted so quickly from the main computer center in Quarry Bay to the back up site at Kai Tak airport, in line with their disaster recovery plan.[6]

Examples like this point out potential weaknesses in an organization's systems. These weaknesses are potential strategic obstacles and need to be addressed, as Cathay Pacific did with its disaster recovery plan. Such weaknesses also present strategic opportunities to competitors, which are only too happy to fill customer requirements when the organization's systems are out of action.

In comparing the use of TBIT to overcome organizational weaknesses with the approach used in leveraging strengths, a fundamental difference must be kept in mind. When using TBIT to leverage strengths to gain further advantage and productivity, there are good procedures that may be enhanced by technology. However,

---

[6] Hong Kong, *Computers and Technology Post of Hong Kong*, August 27, 1991.

in dealing with weaknesses, if the existing procedures are simply automated, the situation may get worse rather than better. If you had a problem you did not understand before automation, after automation you will have a high-tech problem that you understand even less. This problem will be moving at a higher rate of speed and be even more out of control than before. Therefore, when applying technology to conquer an organizational weakness, first analyze the weakness and discover what elements, procedures, and resources are causing the problem. Study the situation thoroughly until you can fix the problem without using technology. After you understand the situation sufficiently well, you will be in a position to implement a proposed TBIT solution. It is most important not to rely on the use of TBIT alone to improve effectiveness or efficiency. The technology must be applied in an appropriate way. In Chapter 6 we will look at some analysis techniques that will allow us to perform this deeper level of analysis.

Look closely at Figure 1–10, which shows possible weaknesses that may afflict an organization. The second column presents sample TBIT applications that may be used to overcome the weakness; the third column lists some of the benefits the

FIGURE 1–10

Sample weaknesses conquered by TBIT

Weakness	Sample TBIT Application	Benefit
High inventory levels and carrying costs	Online bar code receiving and order-filling system to maintain accurate, up-to-date records	Pinpoints obsolete and slow-moving inventory, faster inventory turnover, lower inventory levels
Frequent out-of-stock condition, resulting in customer dissatisfaction and lost sales	As above, plus automated reorder of low inventory using just-in-time (JIT) techniques and relationships with suppliers	Higher sales, more satisfied customers, higher employee morale, lower inventory levels, faster inventory turnover
Poor customer service, slow order filling	Online sales order entry, with automatic order-picking list and accounts notification	Rapid customer order turnaround, with fewer errors and lower inventory levels
Slow collection cycle on customer accounts receivable	Integrated billing system with invoices generated automatically on shipment of customer order, online credit check at sales order entry	Quicker invoicing, better cash flow, fewer bad debts, fewer invoicing errors and resulting collection delays
Misfiled records and records inaccessible to multiple people	Online electronic imaging system to scan and electronically file documents	Records available to multiple people at multiple sites in a controlled environment
Difficulty in hiring and retaining qualified employees	E-mail, E-fax, remote file access applications; automated data entry and online information access	Allows some employees to work productively from home or another remote site; increases employee productivity, so fewer employees needed
Poor quality control on manufactured products	CIM with integrated quality control feedback to design, engineering, and production	Higher-quality, more salable products, satisfied customers, higher employee productivity

organization may gain. As you can see, there are many areas in which organizational weakness can be addressed by TBIT solutions, keeping in mind the need to thoroughly understand the problem and design a nontechnology solution prior to attempting to implement an IT solution.

Applying IT to Increase Responsiveness

Many businesses today are reacting rather than responding to their environment. What is the difference? The following analogy can illustrate.

Suppose you are not feeling well and you go to see the doctor. The doctor prescribes medicine A, which you purchase at the pharmacy. You go home and take medicine A. After a short while, you begin to feel worse. You phone the doctor and describe how you are feeling. The doctor says, "You are reacting to the medicine—stop taking it! Try getting medicine B from your pharmacy." You purchase medicine B, go home, and take it. A short while later, you begin to feel better. You phone the doctor and tell him you are starting to feel better. He says, "That is good, you are responding to the medicine."

As this example illustrates, *reacting* is negative and *responding* is positive. A business that is reacting to its environment is on the defensive, acting only after a competitor has threatened or market conditions have changed. On the other hand, an organization that is responsive to its environment is anticipating changes, preparing for those changes, and perhaps even implementing changes that will make its competitors react. This is an aggressive, proactive style of management. Figure 1–11 gives a pictorial representation of the difference between reacting and responding. This section describes some concepts of an aggressive, responsive, proactive management style that can be implemented through networking technology. This responsiveness must consider both aggressive action—taking advantage of *opportunities* that present themselves—as well as defensive action—protecting against *threats* that arise. Consider the following case.

FIGURE 1–11

Reacting versus responding

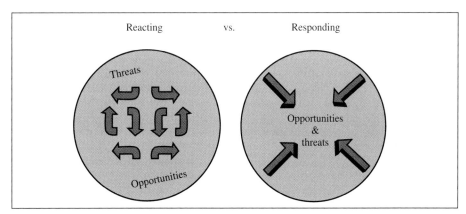

FAST CLOTHES COMPANY

James Low was feeling pretty good after his meeting with Erica Smith, vice president of marketing. They both knew that their employer, Fast Clothes Company (FCC), held a strong position in the market for discount ready-made clothes. But having a strong position and keeping that position were two different things.

James was part of the field sales force. The FCC sales force covered their areas in North America in large trucks stocked with the company's range of ready-made clothes. They took store orders and filled the orders at the same time by restocking the store shelves from the trucks. Any item that was out of stock would be back-ordered and delivered on the next trip, usually the following week.

Ten months ago, Erica had decided that the field salespeople needed notebook computers with modems to speed up store invoicing and back-order stock control. James was one of FCC's best salespeople and one of the first to get the new notebooks. Appropriate software had been acquired or written to meet the needs expressed by salespeople during analysis for the new system. The machines were set up with telecommunications, order entry input, E-mail, and database query software. All of these features tremendously boosted the salespeople's ability to respond to customer requests for product information. The new system also allowed the FCC sales force to respond to opportunities in the field. Previously, when a salesperson found a store that did not carry the FCC line of clothing, she or he had to first interview the store manager for credit information. Upon returning to the regional warehouse at the end of the week, the salesperson would turn in the credit information. The warehouse personnel then mailed the information to the head office. Once the head office gave approval, the salesperson could begin delivering product to the new store. This process usually took a couple of weeks, which meant the store would need to wait for product until then. With the new system, however, James Low and the other salespeople could interview store managers, dial up head office credit control directly through their notebook computers, and query the database for a credit check and authorization on the store. Response was usually immediate, and the salespeople could deliver product to the store during the current trip. The system had worked very well after some initial problems that were readily fixed by providing appropriate training for the sales force.

Two months ago, Erica Smith decided to start capturing market research information through the field sales force using the notebook computers. While implementing this process, an unusual thing happened. James Low was servicing one of his customer stores when he noted that a competitor was test marketing a new product that competed directly with an existing FCC product. The competitor's product was priced 15 percent lower. If the test marketing was successful, the competitor would undoubtedly launch the new product throughout North America.

James returned immediately to his motel and phoned the head office. Erica was in a meeting, so he dialed up the head office on his notebook computer and E-mailed Erica directly with this "market research information," including all product and pricing information. Then James continued with the remainder of his calls for the day. When he returned to his hotel that evening, Erica had replied to his E-mail message, saying that she had researched the matter further and that, after discussion with the general manager, they were authorizing James to put the competing FCC product on special at that store.

The next day, James went straight to a local sign writer, had a "Special" sign prepared, and returned to the store that was being used for the competitor's test market. James informed the store manager that certain products in the FCC line were being put on special for the following month. Then he put up a special product display, stocked it with extra product, and put up the signs reading "Special, 25% off, while stocks last." Finally, he authorized the appropriate credits to the store for the new, lower pricing.

At his meeting with Erica Smith, James learned the results of their competitor's test marketing of its new product. The demand for the product had been much lower than expected, and the competitor had decided not to launch the product and instead terminate development of that product line. Yes, James was feeling pretty good indeed!

As this case demonstrates, organizations that are responsive to the market environment are in a better position to aggressively take advantage of opportunities as well as to effectively defend themselves against threats from competitors.

Taking Advantage of Opportunities

Many opportunities arise for organizations, but some are passed over because they appear too costly, too risky, or just too hard to pursue. Regardless of whether the organization is a profit-making firm or a not-for-profit organization, TBIT systems can sometimes make the difference between taking the opportunity and letting it slip by. The following case describes a community need that could be met through innovative use of information technology.

SMALL TOWN HOSPITAL

Dr. Andrea Hull was a frustrated GP. She had been in practice for over 10 years, working in a medical clinic in a heavily populated urban area that had excellent hospitals and related clinics. What frustrated her was what she saw on her monthly visit to her parents, who lived in a small town two hours away by car. Here was a lovely rural town, with only a few GPs, one clinic, and no specialist support or hospital. Anyone requiring hospitalization or specialist care had to travel to the city, with attendant cost, discomfort, and danger. The local community had looked at building a small hospital capable of meeting the needs of 60 percent of the residents. The idea was dropped due to insufficient support from the big city hospital. However, Andrea had heard that the main hospital in the city was planning to provide a higher level of technical and specialist support for city clinics, and she wondered if that could be used as a springboard to open a small hospital in her parents' town.

After months of talks with doctors and administrators at the main hospital, a plan was established to test a new clinical information system, intended for smaller hospitals and clinics in the city, at the clinic in the small town where Andrea's parents lived. If this worked well, plans could be made to expand the service through a small hospital. The clinical information system would maintain a central record at the hospital on each patient of the clinic, including the patient's medical record, prescriptions, medical procedures undergone, and follow-up treatment needed. The system would require a leased line from the clinic to the city hospital, but the cost would be well worth it if the system worked. The new software was a client/server application; the client portion would be run on an existing Macintosh located at the clinic, while the server portion would be run at the main hospital. Additional features of the system included E-mail and electronic bulletin board services to allow clinic doctors to query hospital specialists on patient treatment and follow-up.

It was great to see her parents again, Andrea thought. Their health was good, but a friend of her mom had to go to the small local hospital each week for special outpatient treatment. She was pleased that she didn't have to go to the city for the weekly treatment anymore, and when she did have to go, the city doctors had easy access to her full medical records instead of asking her all those ridiculous questions each time..

Opportunities can be found in many industries and situations. Figure 1–12 lists some potential opportunities for an organization, together with sample TBIT applications that could help the organization take the opportunity. The last column lists some of the benefits that could be realized with a successful implementation of the technology.

Defending against Threats

Threats may come from various sources in the environment, in some cases due to weaknesses of the organization. Government, competitors, suppliers, and customers all have an influence on the organization's environment; the decisions they make can seriously threaten the organization's markets, its costs, and perhaps even its existence. Information technology can be a potent ally in defending against these threats and

FIGURE 1–12

Sample opportunities assisted by TBIT

Opportunity	Sample TBIT Application	Benefit
A major flood in the Near East creates a need for construction materials and expertise	E-mail and E-fax to all known international suppliers in the industry stating compliance with international EDI and quality standards	Availability and compliance with international standards are made known
Business demand for same-day national courier delivery	Voice-actuated/touchtone input network with alphanumeric pagers	Assured rapid pickup and delivery of letters and parcels, higher level of client communication
Telemarketing with assured employee productivity at lower wage scales	Use of integrated data and voice-over dedicated communication lines to offshore labor source	In areas with high labor costs or labor shortages, global telecommunications can provide an international, cost-effective labor market
Customer demand for products tailored to their unique needs	Use of CIM-based flexible manufacturing, integrated with JIT techniques and a marketing information system	Small production runs at highly competitive prices, inventory reductions, and higher profitability
Troubled competitor shutting down business	Use of current IT base to extend market share by integration of competitor's customer base into the existing systems	Increased market share, increased efficiency of IT resources, continuity of supply of service to customers
Short-term customer demand for fashion and fad products	Flexible manufacturing and JIT systems	Ability to produce low-quantity, cost-effective, high-quality products on short notice

blunting or turning away their attack. The increased responsiveness that well-designed and implemented network-based systems can offer may allow a more rapid response to unexpected threats as well as raise barriers to potential threats. The following case illustrates.

NICHOLLS FINE FURNITURE, INC.

Frank Nicholls, CEO and main shareholder of Nicholls Fine Furniture, Inc. (NFF), was pretty unhappy this morning. A few small competitors had begun importing less expensive furniture from Third World countries and then selling it locally at 15 percent below NFF's prices. They were just small fry, but last week Frank heard that one of his larger competitors was going to close its domestic factory and begin importing similar furniture. This really worried Frank. How was he going to compete against cut-rate imports without closing the factory and buying cheap overseas goods himself?

Later that day, Frank met with his top management team to consider strategies for responding to this new threat. Many ideas were tossed around, but the one that really caught his attention was the idea George Petkovic, IS manager, proposed. George pointed out that NFF carried large quantities of inventory, both in the factory warehouse and at the 20 company-run stores, and this inventory represented the single largest asset on the firm's balance sheet. In addition, the cost of storing all of this inventory was one of the largest expenses. George proposed that the firm move to a **just-in-time (JIT)** inventory management system that would link the stores with the factory.

Currently orders were hand written and mailed to NFF headquarters, where they were entered within a week and then forwarded to the warehouse. The warehouse filled the order within a week if it had the stock; otherwise, the order went to the factory for manufacture, which usually meant an additional two-week time lag. When the product was completed, the factory sent it to the warehouse, which then packed and shipped the furniture to the store for final customer delivery. The total process typically took four to eight weeks.

George's proposal involved adding a modem and additional software to the PCs that the individual stores already used for tracking customer orders and other administrative needs. New software for the headquarters' main computer would be needed to automatically receive orders from the store, log the orders, forward them directly to the factory, and print delivery notifications for the customers. The orders would be manufactured in a reengineered process designed to fill orders in one week maximum, with a reduction in factory space required. The furniture would then be shipped directly to customers. This process would allow NFF to close the warehouse and reassign staff to planned new stores. It would also allow stores to sublet half of their current floor space, since no room would be needed for storing customer orders before pickup or delivery.

The more Frank thought about the new proposal, the more excited he got. His financial controller had produced a cost-benefit analysis showing that some major outlays would be required for factory reorganization, software, staff training, and some new hardware, as well as operating costs for the communication lines. But the sale of the warehouse would more than pay for all of this. Furthermore, the impact on NFF's costs and profit would be sufficient to allow a 20 percent drop in prices across its product line, and still allow a higher profit!

Figure 1–13 gives additional examples of how some TBIT applications can be used to effectively deal with a range of threats.

FIGURE 1–13

Sample threats defended by TBIT

Threat	Sample TBIT Application	Benefit
Political unrest near a primary supplier threatens critically needed raw materials	Industry electronic forums/bulletin boards	Supply of raw materials assured through rapid location of new supplier with sufficient current capacity
A competitor launches a new, highly competitive product	Rapid response field sales and market research using communicating notebook computers or voice mail/touchtone input systems	Provides the ability to rapidly respond to particular market needs, reduce prices in target markets
The government removes tariffs that previously protected the firm's markets	Strategic partnership with an overseas producer, supported by an online inventory query system to still allow fast delivery to customers	Reduced product cost, access to new technology from partner, potential new overseas markets
An economic downturn in the major market creates excess capacity and burdensome overheads	Use of Internet Newsgroups and technical support makes the product line known beyond the traditional market	Increased market exposure opens new markets, soaking up excess capacity
An overseas competitor announces plans to enter the very profitable local market with a quality, low-priced product	Introduction of a JIT inventory system supported by online order entry from stores and customers	Reduction in inventory levels, more efficient production, reduced storage overhead

A useful point to keep in mind is that an organization's strengths open the way for aggressive action in taking opportunities as they become available. Conversely, threats from the marketplace are often most dangerous when they are targeted at the organization's weaknesses. The interaction among these four factors can provide many useful insights into the application of TBIT—applications in favor of the organization, as well as applications against it.

Summary

Telecommunications-based information technology (TBIT) is not a strategy in itself. However, in many cases it may hold the key to successful implementation of an organization's strategies. This chapter described how modern telecommunications systems can powerfully support an organization's vision and goals. The chapter outlined the process of strategic planning and defined a number of key terms, including mission, goal, objective, and tactical planning. It highlighted the need to integrate IT planning with organizationwide strategy and introduced the concept of telecommunications-based information technology and its central role. The chapter also introduced the SWOT technique for analyzing strategy. The material covered showed how effective use of TBIT can pave the way for successful implementation of the strategic plan and how inappropriate use can frustrate management in its attempts to employ the plan to advance the organization.

The chapter presented several examples, scenarios, and cases of leading-edge applications of TBIT that have produced a dynamic competitive advantage. The competitive leverage that can be gained through appropriate application of networking technology was identified as a key factor in establishing and sustaining competitive advantage. The chapter also identified five key developments that are opening up applications of TBIT to produce competitive opportunities.

The use of TBIT to capitalize on organizational strengths and overcome weaknesses was discussed, as well as the integration made possible through networking the major functions of a business enterprise. Telecommunications-based systems offer a unique opportunity for enhancing and leveraging the most useful strengths as well as alleviating or conquering the weaknesses.

In addition to providing an overall capacity for gaining a competitive advantage, networking provides the potential for utilizing opportunities that might otherwise be missed and avoiding threats that could do serious damage to the organization's ability to remain viable.

This chapter also explained how the use of networks may increase the organization's responsiveness to opportunities and threats from the business environment. It looked at specific opportunities as examples of how TBIT might be used to take advantage of their potential and gain real benefits for the organization.

Telecommunications-based information technology offers the potential to assist an organization in accomplishing its goals and objectives. Whether or not this potential is realized depends on a thorough understanding of the business climate, of appropriate application of the technology, and of the particular organization's strengths, weaknesses, opportunities, and threats. In the following chapters, you will gain familiarity with the technology and its application, as well as with the analytical tools necessary to gain the insight you need to successfully apply the technology.

Key Terms

Business process reengineering   15

CAD/CAM   31

Chief executive officer (CEO)   13

Competitive advantage   9

Computer-aided design and computer-aided
  manufacturing (CAD/CAM)   31

Computer-integrated manufacturing (CIM)   21

Core competencies   12

Core logistics   20

Degrees of freedom   17

Downsizing   12

EFT/POS   14

Electronic data interchange (EDI)   14

Electronic fax (E-fax)   19

Electronic funds transfer (EFT)   14

Goal   1

Groupware   15

Hybrid manager   6

Information technology (IT)   1

Just-in-time (JIT)   27

Leverage   20

Mission critical applications   21

Mission statement   2
Objective   3
Operational efficiency   11
PABX   10
Personal digital assistant (PDA)   13
Point of sale (POS)   14
Strategic leverage   2
Strategic partnerships   12
Strategic planning   2

SWOT analysis   7
Tactical planning   5
Telecommunications-based information technology
    (TBIT)   5–6
Telecommuting   16
Time to market   21
Transactions per second (TPS)   7
Virtual corporation   13
Workflow software   15

Questions for Discussion

1. Discuss the three major steps required by the strategic planning process and their importance for an organization.

2. Select a particular company or industry. Then describe and discuss a goal and/or an objective for each of the following areas.
   a. The goods and services provided by the organization.
   b. The functions and processes used.
   c. The people, finances, facilities, and other resources required.

3. How does tactical planning relate to strategic planning? Discuss the primary steps involved in this type of planning and why they are important.

4. Discuss the importance of having hybrid managers within an organization and how this would benefit the integration of strategic planning with IT planning.

5. Describe the benefits of using the SWOT analysis technique for strategic planning.

6. If an organization's strength is a well-educated and technically competent sales force, what IT applications could be used to take advantage of the strength? What potential benefits would the organization gain as a result of a successful implementation?

7. If one of an organization's weaknesses is poor quality control on manufactured products, what would be a useful application of TBIT to overcome the weakness? What benefits might be gained as a result of a successful implementation?

8. Many businesses react to their environment rather than respond to it. How can the use of TBIT solutions help an organization respond rather than react?

9. Describe how TBIT can be used in the form of notebook computers to gain or defend market share for an organization.

Case Discussion and Analysis

1. **Sing Lee Manufacturing**

   The Sing Lee Manufacturing Group (Hong Kong) has been conducting a strategic planning exercise. The company's primary products are children's toys, primarily for export. During the last five years, Sing Lee has developed some automated manufacturing techniques that have enabled it to reduce material wastage and labor costs and successfully compete in the international market. The result has been a 25 percent increase in sales. One difficulty, however, has been keeping the skilled workers who know the new techniques. After being trained, many of them stay only a short while and then leave the firm. The last six months have been particularly stressful because of increased competition from one Taiwanese manufacturer that is selling toys to a number of Sing Lee's traditional North American customers. The Taiwanese firm's success has been enhanced by using **computer-aided design and computer-aided manufacturing** (**CAD/CAM**) methods. Its CAD/CAM system downloads files directly from customers' computers anywhere in the world. The competitor then manufactures to these customers' CAD specifications. This has allowed the Taiwanese firm to shorten the delivery time for a new toy. The industry average for delivery of a new toy has been about 30 days. The Taiwanese firm is now delivering in less than 10 days.

Do a SWOT analysis for Sing Lee. Do you think TBIT applications could help this organization? Why or why not?

2. Carefully reread the **JELFAB** case and answer the following questions.
   a. List the strengths of the company that are illustrated in the case.
   b. List the weaknesses of the company that are described in the case.
   c. How was TBIT used to enhance JELFAB's strengths?
   d. How was TBIT used to overcome JELFAB's weaknesses?
   e. Were any other benefits gained through the implementation of E-mail via electronic fax? Explain.

3. **Marlborough Manufacturing Company**

   It had been a pretty typical month for the sales force of Marlborough Manufacturing Company, a producer of consumer electronics. As Shary Mace assessed her successes and near misses for the month of July, she was reminded of a comment she had heard as a sales trainee: "How much do you get paid for the sales you almost make? Nothing! How much do you get paid for the sales you barely succeed at? Full commission!" It was certainly true that even little things could make the big difference in closing a sale with a customer.

   The company had spent the last 18 months researching, designing, and producing a new product. It was a very good product, and the company's advertising agency had put together a tremendous launch campaign to announce it. The campaign drew the public's attention to the great opportunity it now had available to meet a

pressing need. The ad campaign which had covered television, radio, and all the major print media, was a real hit and had generated a large number of responses from the public. The sales office phone had been ringing off the hook for weeks with requests for more information, sales presentations, and even orders. The print media had also generated bags of reply cards. All of these raw opportunities had landed on Shary's desk (along with those of her sales colleagues) to be turned into increased sales and ultimately profits. Shary had taken her share of the leads and begun phoning them to find out if they wanted a product demonstration. Usually she would dial a number an average of four times before getting an answer. Sometimes it was busy, sometimes no one was there, and sometimes the person she needed to talk to wasn't there, so she would have to try again later. In many cases the lead simply wanted some literature first, and Shary would have to follow up the lead a week or two later to see if the person was still interested. Shary used her diary to keep track of leads she needed to call back as well as appointments made (or changed, or canceled), but keeping her diary straight was always a problem. Often, as she got near the bottom of the pile of follow-up cards and phone calls, she would find that the leads had "gone cold" and the people were no longer interested. That was understandable, but what irritated her was that she could see some of her sales colleagues taking long coffee breaks after they had finished their "quota" of calls. So she just had to throw out the "cold" leads. It was a bit "hit or miss" with such unqualified leads, but at least it gave her some prospects to work with. After days of phoning and mailing, she would gain a number of appointments to demonstrate the product, and would then spend a week or two in the field meeting those appointments and making sales.

   When Shary went to the prospect's home or office to demonstrate the product, she knew this was her best opportunity to gain the person's confidence, assess his or her real need, and meet that need by closing the sale. Naturally, before prospects would sign a formal order, they needed to have their questions answered. Shary was quite knowledgeable and was able to answer most questions confidently. Sometimes, however, even an interested prospect had questions that Shary could not answer immediately, such as

Can I buy on credit even if I am not a current credit customer of Marlborough's?

Can the product be manufactured in a nonstandard color?

If I order 100 of this product, when can you deliver and what discount can you give me?

Can this product be used under certain severe temperature and humidity conditions?

Most of these questions she needed advice or approval on from various people at the office, ranging from her sales manager to the technical support staff or the customer credit authorizers. Usually she tried to phone the office and get an answer the same day from the necessary people, but often they were out or busy in a meeting, and she would have to keep trying. Over the past month, this communication problem had cost her three sales. The first time, a competitor had closed a sale with her customer before she could get back with the appropriate answer. She was still mad about that one, but it seemed it was simply part of the game because it happened most months in such a competitive market. In addition, Shary had to fill in for Tom Lee, one of the other salespeople, for a couple of days because he had the flu. Generally the sales force tried to cover demonstration appointments for one another rather than postponing, because a postponement usually meant a lost prospect. Unfortunately, when Shary got Tom's prospects, she had little background on them because all the information was in Tom's diary, not on the prospect list Tom had left on her desk. But this too was pretty typical, and she just had to do the best she could.

In addition to all of this, competitors were not standing still in the marketplace. Six months after Marlborough announced its new product, a competitor announced a very similar product that competed directly with it. How the competitor had "cloned" the Marlborough product so quickly was a mystery to Shary, but she sure did not appreciate her customers reminding her that the competition could substitute its new product

if Marlborough could not deliver on time or if the quality was not up to par. She had in fact lost a sale this past month when a customer had canceled the order because the competition had promised an earlier delivery date than she was able to offer. Still, she knew that was the way it went in a competitive market, and she had made a good number of sales this month, so she shouldn't complain. However, Shary certainly wouldn't mind twice the sales for the same effort. Those sales she had "almost" made.

Shary Mace's experience at Marlborough Manufacturing is pretty typical. Everything does not always go right, and real life asserts itself in a host of unexpected and sometimes unpleasant ways, with the best of products and intentions not quite fulfilling their full potential. However, some of the glitches life offers can be eliminated through good planning and effective systems.

a. Write a mission statement for Marlborough Manufacturing Company.

b. Based on the mission statement, write three goals.

c. Write two or three objectives for each of the three goals.

d. Do you think TBIT applications can help Marlborough fulfill its goals and objectives? Why or why not?

2 NETWORKED BUSINESS APPLICATIONS

Chapter Outline

Introduction   34

An Overview of Local and Wide Area
   Networks   34

Marketing Applications   36

Financial Services   53

Manufacturing Applications   64

Electronic Messaging and
   Directories   68

Electronic Data Interchange (EDI)   79

Teleconferencing   83

Benefits of Using Local and Wide Area
   Networks in Business   84

Learning Objectives

By the end of Chapter 2, you should be able to

1. *Discuss* leading-edge marketing applications that have used networks to lock in customers and lock out competitors.

2. *Identify* benefits to financial services operations from the use of networks.

3. *Describe* benefits to manufacturing operations from the use of networks.

4. *Identify* key examples using electronic messaging, electronic scheduling, bulletin boards, and directories in business.

5. *Describe* the key uses of electronic data interchange (EDI) as a method of automating interbusiness document exchange.

6. *Explain* the benefits of using information databases and news services to gain rapid access to a wide variety of business information.

7. *Discuss* examples where cost savings result from the shared use of computer peripherals and from data sharing for improved decision making.

8. *Recognize* the strategic advantage of teleconferencing as an alternative to conventional long-distance communication methods, including meetings.

9. *Identify* the ways a manager can find out about new technologies and services and keep up to date with changing network services.

Introduction

In this chapter, we look at the applications in business that use local area networks (LANs) and wide area networks (WANs) and discuss how businesses use these networks to gain a competitive advantage. Some of the applications we will discuss primarily use wide area networks, while others focus on local area networks. In the majority of cases, however, a combination of the two is used.

This chapter covers applications of networks to (1) marketing, (2) financial services, (3) manufacturing, (4) electronic messaging and directories, (5) electronic diaries and calendaring, (6) news services, bulletin boards, and public/corporate databases, (7) electronic data interchange, and (8) teleconferencing.

These applications represent the key areas in which strategic advantage can be gained through the use of local and/or wide area networking. They are the most widely used applications and offer the greatest opportunities for cost-benefit analysis. The first three—marketing, financial services, and manufacturing—represent a wide penetration of the organization's present markets; the remainder represent important systems used to support common business practices.

It is important to remember that the success of an application depends on the ability of the technological solution to address the real business problem. These examples should not be considered as generally applicable to other business problems without careful and thorough analysis.

An Overview of Local and Wide Area Networks

The distinction between local and wide area network types is becoming increasingly blurred with new developments in networking technology. We can use an application in conjunction with a wide area network without a local area network, and vice versa, but this practice is becoming much less common. The building blocks for these networks and the technical aspects of how they work are presented in Chapters 4 and 5. In this chapter, we examine these applications to see the ways in which networking helps a business in its operations.

A **wide area network (WAN)** extends across streets, roads, cities, and even countries—in other words, outside the boundary of the individual property and into the public region, meaning those areas controlled by the government, regional authorities, or other public entities. The implication is that these networks are "public"; that is, anybody can subscribe to and use them in the same way they do a telephone network.

However, with deregulation occurring throughout the world, the boundaries of what is "public" and what is "private" are becoming somewhat blurred. A private network can be derived from a public network, meaning users have a totally secure and private network for their business applications at their disposal, while at the same time they are using a public service. This idea, called **virtual private networking,** has become very popular in the last few years and is further discussed in Chapters 11 and 12.

The most common example of a wide area network is the telephone system, something we use every day and usually take for granted (until it doesn't work). To communicate across these public regions, we usually need to employ the services of the local telephone company or network operator, such as AT&T, Bell, or Sprint, since it has the infrastructure (lines, cables, satellites, and other equipment) available to almost any location that might need to use its services. The national carriers also interconnect with telephone companies in other countries to form a worldwide communication system. Today it is possible to "connect" to almost every country of the world, although, as we shall see, the quality of the connection and what it is used for vary a great deal. Other companies provide paging and cellular phone services that interface with the wide area telephone network.

To communicate efficiently and effectively, businesses need different types of networks depending largely on the application. For example, the wide area network used to support telephone communication (known as the **PSTN,** or **public switched telephone network**) requires links of a certain capacity to support voice communication. If we replace people with computers at either end, things do not work so well, since the telephone network was designed for just that—telephones. Thus "data" networks are needed to support typical computer-to-computer applications such as those used in banking transactions and airline reservations. Further, the demands made by these computers vary a great deal. For example, the amount of information carried across a network to tell you how much money is in your bank account is very different from the amount of information carried across a network when the television news is transmitted from London to New York.

An important aspect of a **local area network (LAN)** is that it exists on the company's private property or land—for example, on an office floor, or in a building, hospital, airport, or factory. This means the interconnecting wiring of the local area network is not subject to the controls of the telephone company as is the case with wide area networks. Note that this freedom has a price! The need for complicated interconnection equipment to communicate in a distributed processing environment has resulted in incompatible local area networks. The interconnection of local area networks in different parts of the same city or in different cities or countries is a very important topic that we will discuss later in this chapter.

In contrast, wide area networks are "public," and usually anybody can connect to them. This is true in the same sense that anyone can obtain a connection to the telephone network. However, there is no conflict with privacy in that we have control over whom we call and, to some degree, who calls us (via answering machines, voice mail systems, call waiting, etc.).

To cope with the different demands made by the applications we will look at, different sizes of "pipes" are required to carry different volumes of information. A good analogy is water pipes. A large pipe is required to bring water to a suburb, a set of smaller pipes are needed to bring the water into individual streets, and still smaller pipes are required to bring the water to individual businesses and homes.

From the users' point of view, different networks are available for different business applications. Each application dictates the size of the "pipe" required. For instance, **fiber optic cable** between New York and London might carry data for such diverse applications as fax, voice mail, electronic funds transfer, and teleconferencing. The applications that use this fiber optic cable might emanate from the same company or from different companies and make use of quite diverse types of wide area networks (discussed further in Chapter 4).

Marketing Applications

The marketing applications discussed in this section represent those leading-edge and widely used systems that provide good cost benefits. This implies the use of networks for the provision of rapid access to data that has the potential to put a company in a competitive position.

In some cases a simple wide area network service such as the telephone or a fax system is quite adequate, and expenditure on sophisticated networking technology would give little advantage over the simpler services. Every case must be costed on its merits. Consumers in most countries spend significant portions of their disposable incomes on food, general merchandise, cars, and travel. Thus, marketing applications are frequently directed to those items.

As a result of automation in the telecommunications industry and the widespread use of computer technology, customers are becoming less tolerant of both delays in gaining information about products and in the delays associated with the delivery of the product. This is particularly important in areas such as supermarkets and general merchandise, travel (air, bus, and rail), and the automotive industry.

Order entry, point-of-sale, stock management systems, and other applications we will discuss are widely used in manufacturing, retail, and wholesale industries. Because of the scale of operations, there are many such systems used by small businesses for which a local area network is perfectly adequate. Reservation systems are applicable to a single industry: travel. The size of the travel industry makes this an important marketing application. Telemarketing and teleshopping are relatively recent marketing applications that are likely to increase in importance over the next decade.

Order Entry Systems, ⅊. *Dell*

Order entry (or order-processing) systems operate in one of three ways:

1. Customers phone in to confirm orders. (Note that even the use of the telephone in this situation is an example of an application over a wide area network.)
2. A computer terminal located on the business premises, such as a retail store, permits customers to place orders themselves. Often this simply involves scanning a product list from the database and indicating the item and the quantity required. This method gives customers greater access to product status and helps to reduce errors in communication.

3. Field sales staff can receive order data on a laptop computer and, with the use of a modem (discussed in Chapter 4), download orders over a dial-up telephone connection once they reach a motel or their homes.

The primary objectives of an order-processing system are to

- Provide accurate and timely recording of customers' orders.
- Initiate production of an order (if a manufacturer).
- Initiate the shipping of orders.
- Maintain a record of back-ordered items (items that are out of stock and will be shipped later).
- Produce sales analysis reports.

Shipping an order usually involves numerous documents that formerly had to be physically delivered but today can be transmitted across a network. These documents are normally issued in quadruplicate: A copy goes to the warehouse for shipping, a copy is sent with the goods, a copy is kept for record, and a copy goes to accounts to authorize customer invoicing. Some companies even use a fifth copy that serves as a customer acknowledgment and is sent to the customer when the shipping order is issued. Today this paper-intensive process can be carried out by electronic data interchange (EDI) (discussed later in this chapter). The use of a network has replaced the massive amount of paper shuffling that used to be required. The telephone network is frequently used in conjunction with these order entry systems. First, the agent receives a call from the customer by telephone. Following this, the agent accesses the computer (which may be part of a local area network) and takes the order directly, providing the supporting information as required.

Before producing a shipping order, many order entry systems access the inventory file to determine whether particular goods are available. If given items are not on hand, they are placed on back order (another example of the use of networks). The inventory file is updated to reflect the number of goods sent. Back orders remain on file so that when the goods are available, the order entry system can initiate a shipping order.

The daily orders-processed report can be used by management to monitor trends, the number of orders processed, and the level of back orders. If the quantity of back orders becomes excessive, customer relations may suffer. The weekly or monthly sales-by-item report is an example of the many types of sales analysis reports a network can produce. The rapid dispatch of these and associated documents, which is essential if a business is to maintain competitive advantage, depends on effective software and communication networks.

Point-of-Sale and Stock Management

ex. Wal-Mart In the last section, we saw how the ordering process can be automated. The next task is to automate the sales process, although the two activities are closely related. Many retail outlets have or are in the process of moving to point-of-sale and stock management systems. These systems offer a wide range of benefits:

- Stock levels can be kept to a minimum.

- Stores can gain better control over demand projections. Stores can be polled, data gathered, and profiles of products, customers, and financial information produced quickly.
- When combined with electronic funds transfer (EFT) (discussed in the section on financial services), these systems can help stores give better service to customers. Out-of-stock situations occur less often, and customer loss is minimized.

Point-of-sale (POS) data entry has given rise to point-of-sale equipment. In a typical POS configuration, cash registers are online to a minicomputer, usually by way of a local area network, which in turn is online to disk storage files containing data such as product descriptions, selling prices, and collected sales statistics. These files may be in a different location in a distant part of the city, thus requiring access to a wide area network.

When an item is sold, it is identified by its bar code. The POS terminal reads the bar code using either a reader embedded in the checkout counter or a light-wand reader. The information contained in the bar code is transmitted to the computer, which retrieves a description and selling price for the item and transmits them back to the POS terminal. Simultaneously, sales statistics are collected and the inventory files updated. For small businesses, bar code readers can be attached directly to microcomputers, allowing the same functions to be performed as with larger computers. POS equipment is used most extensively by supermarkets and chain stores, but it can be applied to any merchandising operation. In these cases, use of local and wide area networks is essential.

POS equipment also has other applications. For example, some libraries place bar code stickers on books and library cards. When books are checked out, the user's identification number on the card and the code of each book are read by a light wand. When books are returned, their codes are also read with a light wand. Files maintained by the computer contain book codes and the corresponding Library of Congress identification, titles, authors, and other information. Other files contain users' identification numbers, names, addresses, and information on checked-out books. Often another library's records in a different location are accessed by a wide area network.

Although supermarkets and libraries are situated in a variety of locations, all require the fast, efficient communication of data between sites, as though everybody were located in one place. Only through the use of local and wide area networks is this possible.

The next example describes an application that makes use of networks for a fast-food distributor. As such, it involves elements of order entry and point-of-sale stock management systems just discussed. This fast-food company operates in many states in the United States as well as in Canada. At this stage, do not be too concerned about the layout or topology of the network or the details of the equipment being used; we will cover these in Chapters 4 and 5. Rather, concentrate on how the network is used in conjunction with the truck distribution system to make the distribution process as efficient and competitive as possible. It is the application that is important here, not the technology.

FAST-FOOD DISTRIBUTOR DEPENDS ON NETWORKS FOR SWIFT SERVICE

Ex. American Airlines

The menu is about to change at a large distributor of fast foods. The company runs 25 regional distribution centers and owns more than 400 trucks that deliver food and paper products to over 5,000 fast-food restaurants.

The operations manager is a technical leader in the trucking industry with its use of automated routing systems and on-board computers that monitor the mechanical performance of each truck. Now it is on the verge of installing local area networks at each of its 25 regional distribution centers. The local area networks will be used to merge vehicle data with the transportation-routing database to further improve operational efficiency.

"The key to our business is on-time service," states the business distribution manager. "A restaurant manager typically schedules more employees to coincide with our deliveries to help unload the truck. If we say that we'll be there at 10 AM and don't show up until 1 PM, he's paying people to stand around." For this reason, delivery is promised within 15 minutes of the scheduled time. To help meet stringent schedules, the company has been using an automated routing system called Trucks. This system previously ran on the company mainframe, but recently it was switched to an IBM AS400 to take advantage of enhanced graphics capabilities with the latest version of the software. Instead of viewing a column of statistics, dispatchers can now see an onscreen video map of each delivery route.

Each of the 25 distribution centers uses a Trucks system. The databases at each center include street and highway maps of all possible road segments used by the trucks in that territory, as well as the location of each restaurant served by the distribution center.

Based on factors such as time commitments, available trucks, speed limits, distances, and what is being delivered, Trucks runs algorithms to plot the most efficient delivery route. Whereas it used to take two people 30 to 40 hours to develop a new set of route profiles using paper maps and calculators, Trucks can now build 100 routes in 15 minutes. The planning manager states, "We've been able to reduce our mileage by 10 percent to 15 percent while increasing our load factor on each truck by 10 percent." Although Trucks helps to improve operational efficiency, management has had no way to monitor how well drivers are actually meeting their delivery deadlines. To remedy this problem, the company is in the process of using its databases to compare and analyze data from vehicular-monitoring computers on its trucks with the information from the Trucks routing system at the various distribution centers.

Each truck is equipped with a "Vehicle Information System." The system monitors engine performance factors such as speed, rpm, and mileage. It also features an internal clock that times how long it takes to drive each road segment, as well as how long the driver spends at each stop. The driver activates the clock by entering a numerical code on the system's keyboard for each route and for each restaurant. The data are recorded on a cassette tape, and at the end of each day they are fed into a local area network–based PC at each distribution center for processing.

The company has been using this system for several years, but until now the data were used primarily to monitor driver performance and increase fuel efficiency. The company

Source: Adapted from J. O. Hicks, *Information Systems in Business: An Introduction* (St. Paul, MN: West Publishing Co., 1990), pp. 382–383.

now intends to further tighten its delivery schedule by combining the actual delivery information from the Vehicle Information System with the theoretical data from Trucks running on Novell local area networks with PC/Focus database management systems.

From these new combined data, the company has designed a special focus report called the Transportation Information System (TIS). This report compares the distances and times that Trucks predicts will be needed to complete a delivery route with the actual figures obtained from the Vehicle Information System. "We want to take the actual driving and unloading times and put them back into Trucks so that we can fine-tune that system and make it a more accurate transportation planning tool," said the planning manager.

In the initial tests, it was found that mileages and times on the Trucks system have been accurate to within 90 percent of the computed figures. But approaching 100 percent accuracy is still a corporate priority. "It's extremely advantageous to us in the budgeting process to be able to predict our operating expenses for the coming year," the planning manager said. "With TIS, we'll be able to adjust road speeds in the Trucks system to meet actual driving conditions and thus achieve greater accuracy with our routing system."

The PS/2 used for Trucks and the PCs running the Vehicle Information System will be the initial nodes on the local area networks, along with one each for the transportation and distribution manager at each distribution center. The operations manager expects that the number of network nodes on each local area network will eventually grow to about 10 to accommodate general business applications at the distribution centers. An IBM AS400 will act as the **file server** for the local area networks. "This AS400 was chosen as a file server because we needed the disk storage capacity and because we already have an AS400 at each site, we'll have a backup to run Trucks in a stand-alone mode if the file server ever goes down," he said.

The operations manager said that connecting the distribution local area networks to corporate headquarters will be vital in maintaining the Trucks automated routing system. As new restaurants are added to the distribution network, road segments necessary to service the new stops must be added to the database. A Trucks maintenance staff at corporate headquarters adds new roads to the system by tracing digitizers over paper maps and entering geographic coordinates for each new restaurant. Currently, updates to the Truck database are shipped to the centers on disks or magnetic tapes via overnight mail. "Our goal is to get the changes out to the distribution centers within one hour," said the operations manager. "Once all the networks are in place, we will send the changes electronically."

There are a number of points to note about this sample application:

- The system goes far beyond just implementing a database of products for distribution. It addresses distribution efficiency in great detail, even down to drivers' habits.

- The use of local area networks in the distribution centers is fundamental to the collection and provision of information for the distribution process.

- The local area networks are closely associated with the use of wide area networks, as is common practice in the industry today.

- The failure or success of such a situation depends on the very rapid inputting, processing, and availability of this processed information from any location on the network.

Reservation Systems *Ex. Reservations American Airlines*

In the last two sections, we looked at ways to automate the sale of products and maintain an accurate inventory for the purpose of reorder. Networks provide the high-speed links between the customer and the database that stores the information about the products. Reservation systems work on a similar principle. The product being sold is a seat on a boat, train, or airplane, or perhaps the booking of a rental car or a hotel room. A wide area network provides the link between customer and product.

Reservation systems are important applications because up-to-the-minute information needs to be provided to customers almost instantaneously from a single central database. Although the costs of providing a worldwide communications network are very high, the benefits are enormous. In fact, a company in the travel industry cannot remain competitive without access to networks. The intention is to lock customers in and keep competitors out. For example, many airlines have introduced a points or mileage system and offer special lounge facilities. These features make it attractive for customers to continue to deal with the same company.

Competitors can use networks for the same purpose. Therefore, it is imperative to use these systems in the most efficient manner possible. Remember, if you are running a business you do not have to be perfect—just better than your competitors!

We have all experienced the frustration of trying to get a seat on a train or an airplane at a busy time when stress levels are high. Conversely, we have marveled at being able to go into a United Airlines office, book a connecting flight from London to Zurich on Swiss Air, request a Chinese vegetarian meal and an aisle seat, reserve a hotel room at the destination, and have all of this confirmed within a minute. One airline has calculated that the last seat on an aircraft is often bought and sold electronically about six times. This means frequent cancellations and reservations occur during the period leading up to the aircraft's departure. Such information can be provided only by way of a communications network.

The airline reservation systems were the real pioneers of fast, efficient wide area network communications back in the 1960s, and we owe much to the joint work of IBM and British Airways in Europe and the American Airlines SABRE system in the United States. Basically the reservation systems are composed of interconnected computers over a wide area communications network. These are not telephone networks, which are designed primarily for communicating via the human voice over interconnected telephones; rather, reservation networks are based on pure data circuits. A number of networks can be used in this context; these will be discussed in Chapter 4.

It is necessary to provide customers with virtually instantaneous response, whether the terminal is connected to a computer in the next room or the next building via a local area network, or to a computer in a distant city or country via a wide area network (or some combination of the two). These systems pose difficult technical problems. A **passenger name record (PNR)** contains the travel details, frequently including flights on different airlines on different sectors, hotel reservations, and rental car reservations, all from different companies. Thus, your PNR may have to be linked to American Airlines, Singapore Airlines, British Airways, Hilton Hotels, and the Hertz agency. (If you are not so well off, your PNR may be linked to Air Garuda, Best Western Motels, and Rent-a-Wreck Car Company.) Further schedules can change by the minute, and only networks can make this information widely available.

Your PNR needs to be accessible to your local travel agent, the airline at your destination, your hotel at check-in, the car rental company when you arrive, and the "bag-track" system for any lost luggage. All of this would be impossible without the networks that have been put in place by the telephone companies in countries throughout the world.

This may all appear very obvious, but it is often not as simple as it seems. Until very recently, different computer terminals were commonly used to access different reservation systems. The interconnection of different vendors' computer equipment by competing airlines created enormous problems. To a large degree, these applications have solved the problems relating to reservations, meals, baggage, hotels, and rental cars. This means that aircraft can fly with more seats full, since with the use of telemarketing (see the next section), unsold seats can be marketed at reduced prices. An analysis of one flight between Chicago and New York showed that about 100 different fares had been paid depending largely on different marketing strategies. All of this has had the effect of shifting the bottleneck elsewhere. As anyone who has traveled recently knows, the bottleneck is now the check-in counter, and there lies the potential to automate this process by way of automated self-check-in.

We will now take a moment to capture some typical airline schedule and reservation information using a personal computer. This type of marketing information is used by hotels and travel agents for up-to-date information on flight arrivals and departures. You can do the following exercise if you have a PC, a modem, and a log-in to a **packet switching network (PSN)** which costs only a few dollars per month. First, we will connect to the flight control computer at Kai Tak Airport in Hong Kong. The packet switching address is 04545500550, and you can view the flight arrivals and departures.

%Call connected to Kai Tak Airport

Enquiry Service for On-line Flight Information

Please press [ENTER] to continue or enter [Q] to quit.

Welcome to Datapak ON-LINE FLIGHT INFORMATION ENQUIRY SERVICE

Hong Kong Telecom maintains a database of flight information provided by the Civil Aviation Department of Hong Kong. Datapak customers can access this database to retrieve the latest flight information.

continued

The following services are available :

Enquiry by   [1]   latest flight arrival information

[2]   latest flight departure information

[Q]   quit

Please enter your selection   **1**   *(Let's look at flight arrivals)*

15 OCT HONG KONG FLIGHT ARRIVALS - STATUS AS AT 11:40AM

Flight	From	Sch Time	Est Time	Status
CI 641	TAIPEI	10:35	10:38	ARRIVED
CA 161	SHENYANG	10:45	10:54	ARRIVED
CA 101	BEIJING	10:50	10:50	ARRIVED
CZ 3075	WUHAN	10:50	10:52	ARRIVED
CZ 303	GUANGZHOU	11:00	11:01	ARRIVED
MU 501	SHANGHAI	11:00	11:10	ARRIVED
KZ 201	TOKYO	11:20	11:58	
CZ 381	XIAMEN	11:25	11:18	ARRIVED
MU 503	HANGZHOU	11:30	11:24	ARRIVED
MU 505	FUZHOU	11:30	11:29	ARRIVED
OZ 301	SEOUL	11:30	11:47	
CI 603	TAIPEI	11:35	11:27	ARRIVED
MU 5003	NANJING	11:35	11:54	
MU 5011	QINGDAO	11:35	11:36	ARRIVED
UA 806	SINGAPORE	11:35	11:16	ARRIVED
KE 617	SEOUL	11:40	11:51	
AFR182	DELHI	11:50	11:52	
LH 736	FRANKFURT	12:00	11:52	
CP 8	BANGKOK	12:10	12:00	
CX 714	SINGAPORE	12:10	12:05	

concluded

Enquiry by **[1]** latest flight arrival information

[2] latest flight departure information

[Q] quit

Please enter your selection   2 *(Let's look at flight departures)*

15 OCT HONG KONG FLIGHT DEPARTURES - STATUS AS AT 11:42AM

Flight	To	Sch Time	Est Time	Gate	Status
CI 2610	TAIPEI	10:30	13:50		DELAYED
CI 602	TAIPEI	10:35	11:29	09	DEPARTED
CLX782	SAPPORO	10:45	11:19		DEPARTED
SQ 865	SINGAPORE	11:00	11:24	20	DEPARTED
PR 301	MANILA	11:05	11:15	07	CLOSED
CI 665	SINGAPORE	11:15	11:36	17	DEPARTED
MP 92	SEOUL	11:15			
SZ 4006	CHONGQING	11:20		15	CLOSED
JL 2	TOKYO	11:25		05	CLOSED
TG 605	CHINGMAI	11:25		24	CLOSED
CX 36	SEOUL	11:30			
CI 641	BANGKOK	11:35		27	BOARDING
CX 410	TAIPEI	11:35		21	CLOSED
KA 362	XIAMEN	11:35		12	CLOSED
CA 162	SHENYANG	11:45		16	CLOSED
CZ 3076	WUHAN	11:50		08	CLOSED
PRI787	SAPPORO	11:50			
UA 880	S FRANCISCO	11:55		20	BOARDING
MU 502	SHANGHAI	12:00		01	BOARDING
CZ 304	GUANGZHOU	12:10		08	BOARDING
KA 322	NANJING	12:15		11	BOARDING
CA 102	BEIJING	12:20		12	BOARDING
CZ 382	XIAMEN	12:25		24	

**** Please enter [M] to Main Menu or [Q] to quit :

Q

Another example of the use of a communications network for airline information is the Official Airlines Guide Database in the United States. This can be accessed from any public electronic mail service, such as the Dialcom System. If you have a user code for this service, connect to it and enter OAG (Official Airline Guide) to get connected to the database in Oak Brook, Illinois. (Of course, it doesn't really matter where the database is located.) If you do not have a user code or do not wish to pay the charges, a sample dialogue is given below. A brief example of reservations and flight schedules follows. We are interested in flights from Hong Kong to London on June 30, the availability of seats on a selected flight, the fares, and hotel accommodations in London.

OAG Database   **The Official Airlines Guide Database.**
For information, type INFO OAG at the system prompt.
To access this database, type OAG at the system prompt.

>OAG   *(Access the database)*

OFFICIAL AIRLINE GUIDES - OAG ELECTRONIC EDITION TRAVEL SERVICE ACCESS
Access to OAG is surcharged at $US.50 per minute.
OK to continue? Yes
WELCOME TO THE OAG ELECTRONIC EDITION TRAVEL SERVICE -

1	**OAG ELECTRONIC EDITION (R) - Flight Information & Reservations**
2	**Airport Arrivals, Departures & Gate Information**
3	**Accu-Weather Forecasts**
4	**Lodging & Dining**
5	**Worldwide Travel Facts**
6	**Travel Industry News**
7	**Frequent Traveller Programs**
8	**Leisure & Discount Travel**
9	**Cruises**
10	**What's New?**
11	**General & How-to-Use**
12	**User Comments & Suggestions**

continued

Don't pack too much—or too little! Check the weather forecast before your next business trip or getaway weekend. Access ACCU-WEATHER Forecasts, select #3

Enter a number, a /TO command, or   OFF = EXIT
X# for summary of contents (e.g., X1)

1   *(Let's look up flight information and reservations)*

==

WELCOME TO OFFICIAL AIRLINE GUIDES (OAG) ELECTRONIC EDITION
Official Airline Guides, Inc., Oak Brook, Illinois 60521

==

Enter /M = View List of OAG Electronic Edition commands, or
/S = View Schedules displays   /U = Send a message to OAG
/F = View Fares displays   /I = Information & Assistance
/H = View Hotel/Motel displays   /P = Set Airline Preference
/E = Enter/Exit Expert Mode   /Q = Exit OAG Electronic Edition
/S

ENTER DEPARTURE CITY NAME OR CODE

SINGLE LINE ENTRY EXAMPLE:
CHICAGO;NYC20JUN8A

HONG KONG;LONDON30JUNE   *(We want to go to London on June 30 next)*

YOUR DESTINATION CITY IS NOT UNIQUE. USE LINE NUMBER TO SELECT CITY NAME OR AIRPORT NAME FROM THE LIST BELOW.

1 LONDON, ONT, CANADA
2 LONDON, ENGLAND
3 LONDON, ENGLAND/CITY
4 LONDON, ENGLAND/GATWICK

continued

5 LONDON, ENGLAND/HEATHROW

6 LONDON, ENGLAND/LUTON

7 LONDON, ENGLAND/SOUTHEND

8 LONDON, ENGLAND/STANSTED

9 LONDON, KY, USA

ENTER +,-,LINE NUMBER OR CITY NAME. *(Lots of Londons—which one do we mean?)*

5

ENTER DEPARTURE TIME OR PRESS RETURN TO USE 6.00AM

10.00AM

================== **PREFERENCE STATUS: ALL** ==================

From: HONG KONG,HONG KONG   Departs: WED-JUNE 30

To: LONDON,ENGLAND/HEATHROW   Travel

#	Departs	Arrives	Flight Equip	Stops	Time
	No earlier direct flight service				
1	1015PM HKG	545AM+1 LHR	BA 032 747	0	14:30
2	1030PM HKG	600AM+1 LHR	BA 028 747	0	14:30
3	1130PM HKG	610AM+1 LHR	CX 251 747	0	14:40

(We can choose from British Airways or Cathay Pacific)

No later direct flight service

==

ENTER A COMMAND: (# = LINE NUMBER)   A# = seats available

RS = return schedules   CX = connecting flights   F# = fares

P = reset preferences   X# = expand flight

? = Help with Commands

continued

A3   *(We want to know if seats are available)*

PLEASE ENTER NUMBER OF SEATS REQUIRED UP TO A MAXIMUM OF 4.

2

TRIP TYPE MENU

1 ONE-WAY
2 ROUND-TRIP
3 ROUND-TRIP - RETURN DATE UNKNOWN

ENTER SELECTION NUMBER

1

CLASSES AVAILABLE ON WED - JUN 30 FOR HKG-CX 251-LHR

FIRST CLASS
BUSINESS CLASS
ECONOMY

/F   *(What are the fares?)*

FARE MENU

FARES FOR DIRECT FLIGHTS AND CONNECTIONS		**FARES FOR DIRECT FLIGHTS ONLY**
1 COACH AND BUSINESS CLASS FARES		**6**
2 FIRST CLASS AND EQUIVALENT FARES		**7**
3 COACH, BUSINESS AND FIRST CLASS		**8**
4 ADVANCE-PURCH AND EXCURSION FARES		**9**
5 ALL OF THE ABOVE FARES		**10**

PLEASE ENTER A NUMBER

10

continued

================= **PREFERENCE STATUS: ALL** ==================

Fares selected for: HKG-LHR   **Departs: WED - JUN 30**

Fares: HONG KONG DOLLAR   **Fare Restriction Summary:**

# No lower fares	One-way	Rnd-trp	Airline/ Class	Farecode	Cancel Penalty	Advance Purchase	Min. Stay
1	4160		BA	YLAPBO	25%	21 day	
2		8420	BA	YLPX	750*	21 day	3 day
3		8420	CX	YLPX	50*	21 day	3 day
4	4440		BA	YLIPO	100%	21 day	1 day
5	4610		BA	YKAPB	25%	21 day	
6	4630		BA	YLAP	750*	21 day	14 day
7	4630		CX	YLAP	25%	21 day	14 day

* Additional Restrictions apply

==

ENTER A COMMAND: (# = LINE NUMBER)   L# = fare restrictions

M = fares menu   + = higher fares   S# = schedules for fare

P = reset preferences   RF = return fares   X# = expand fare

O = original display

/H   *(What about hotels in London?)*

ENTER ANOTHER CITY NAME OR CODE OR PRESS RETURN TO USE - LONDON ENGLAND

HOTEL/MOTEL LOCATION MENU FOR - LONDON,ENGLAND

 1 CITY CENTER AND OTHER
 2 NEARBY LOCATIONS
 3 NEAR AIRPORT-Heathrow

concluded

4 NEAR AIRPORT-Gatwick
5 NEAR AIRPORT-Stansted

ENTER A LINE NUMBER

1

CITY CENTER # HOTEL/MOTEL	RATES

BEGINNING OF LISTINGS

1 The Abbey Court Hotel	
20 Pembridge Gardens	**$139-283**
TEL-71/2217518	
FAX-71/7920858	
2 Academy Hotel	
17-21 Gower St.	**$81-279**
TEL-71/6314115	
FAX-71/6363442	
3 Apollo Hotel	
18-22 Lexham Gardens	**$59-111**
TEL-71/8351133	
4 Aster House Hotel	
Sumner Place	**$99-172**
TEL-71/5815888	
FAX-71/5844925	
5 Athenaeum Hotel	
116 Piccadilly	**$309-444**
TEL-71/4993464	
FAX-71/4931860	

etc...

/Q

/OFF

**THANK YOU FOR USING THE OAG ELECTRONIC EDITION
TRAVEL SERVICE**

The use of this reservation system leads us to the next section on telemarketing, because this database is the basic tool from which to market these services.

Telemarketing

Telemarketing combines the use of computers with the telephone network. Its advantage is that you get the communication right at your home or office. You might not bother to go to a marketing presentation in the city, but you will almost always answer the telephone and at least listen to what the caller has to say. Once the caller has your attention, his or her success largely depends on the ability to capture your interest. Usually the caller already has some information about you and knows that you use a competitor's product or travel on a particular airline (or the product may be an everyday item that we all use). The caller may also have your name (perhaps from your friend) and invite you to pass on the name of one of your friends (for a discount).

You have probably received many sales calls from salespeople or people soliciting donations. Use of the telephone to sell products and services by use of telemarketing systems has become a common and important means by which organizations improve the productivity of their sales force. The telephone allows salespeople to initiate contacts, offer products and services, or follow up on sales calls without incurring travel costs or travel time. It also lets salespeople reach many more customers in a given time period than they could through other means. Some telemarketing systems include computer support for automatic dialing and delivering voice messages.

Thus, the *cost* of communicating with prospective customers is very small (the cost of a local telephone call is still free in the United States and a few other countries). Further, the marketing organization does not have to rent expensive office or store space. A good telemarketer can make many contacts per day and uses computers to cut the cost of sales prospecting and follow-up, making it possible to address the needs of a much larger market. The use of a network is central to the success of such a venture.

Consider the following example:

All businesses profit from promptness in connecting telephone callers with the right people, but sometimes the caller has to be put on hold. Then the caller must endure a period of either dead silence or music. Music may entertain the customer, but it does nothing for the company's business. A discreet and informative telemarketing message, on the other hand, makes a prospective client more fully acquainted with the company's range of services and more willing to do business by the time the call is completed.

In some countries, various telecommunications companies have recently begun providing the option of "advertising on hold" to its customers in association with independent advertising companies. Top copywriters and professional commercial voices produce the taped messages in cooperation with the customer, while the telephone company installs the digital announcer equipment on the customer's telephone system.

Recently one of these telecommunications companies quoted the following example:

Among 50 already satisfied users is R. Dickson and Co., Real Estate Agents, which has advertising on hold at a number of its main branches. A friendly voice runs through the services the company provides, assuring the client of Dickson's "energetic approach" and "capability to meet your needs." Background music complements the professional voice. Managing director Roger Dickson says auctions have been one particular service aired over the "hold" line, and this has coincided with a growing interest in selling by auction. "Last year, we held 200 auctions in total, while this year we've done more than that already." While he says the boom cannot be credited entirely to the new telemarketing medium, it has been a key factor. Advertising on hold maintains "top-of-the-mind recall" of the R. Dickson name and services among prospective customers, he says, "and it gives us a more professional image than silence or a tune." Advertising on hold is provided to customers on a one- or two-year agreement with a deposit and a small monthly payment.

Telemarketing Software.   Telemarketing software provides computer support for identifying customers and calling them from diskbased telephone directories or from customer files maintained on a database. The software company may provide the telemarketer with regularly updated telephone directories of major corporations or specialized lists of selected customer types. The packages may allow salespeople to make notes about telephone calls made, generate follow-up letters to customers, and view a customer file while a call to that customer is in progress.

Some software finds, dials, and connects salespeople automatically to people or companies listed in diskbased telephone directories. This software may then provide a digitized message about a product to people who answer the phone or permit the salesperson to answer the call. However, not all customers respond favorably to digitized messages, and this can sometimes have an adverse effect on sales.

Telemarketing software has allowed many firms to substantially increase sales while decreasing the costs per sale. This technology gives these firms great potential to increase market share over their competitors.

The costs of leasing or purchasing the software must be carefully assessed against the revenue earned. Frequently business needs are so specialized that specific software needs to be developed for individual companies' requirements.

Teleshopping

Teleshopping is similar in many ways to telemarketing in that both use a wide area telephone network. The applications differ somewhat, but the methodology and technology used to enable these applications are virtually identical. Teleshopping is still a developing application, but it is becoming increasingly common in North America. Variations of teleshopping are available in some other countries.

As the name implies, teleshopping means shopping from home. For example, you can fax grocery orders to some supermarkets, and they will deliver your orders to you. A disadvantage of teleshopping is that you cannot browse or compare prices, but if you know exactly what you want, it is often unnecessary to visit the store. Teleshopping usually means ordering items from a catalog (which may have been previously mailed to you) and then using the wide area telephone network. The TV is also becoming an important component in teleshopping. Customers can order directly from products displayed or advertised by using a toll-free number. A successful transaction requires that the customer receive a friendly and efficient response from the other end and usually entails the use of voice mail or recorded messaging systems so that the customer is not kept waiting. Fast and efficient delivery are also necessary for customer satisfaction.

Teleshopping is frequently used in conjunction with the **800 freefone** service. The customer can make a free long-distance call to the teleshopping data center without incurring any charges. Some businesses even provide this service on an international basis, although it is used mainly by high-profile and prestigious retail outlets. For example, Harrods, England's premier department store, attracts London visitors from all over the world. As a result of recent lulls in international tourism, particularly following the stock market crash in 1987 and the Gulf War in 1991, Harrods undertook a trial in which it promoted its products in New York state and provided a toll-free international service to Harrods in London. The trial was an instant success. Harrods captured a whole new market, and the service is now expanding to serve a growing customer base. The success of this teleshopping venture hinged on access to an international wide area telephone network.

The use of 800 freefone services allows customers to inquire about a product they have seen advertised in the newspaper, on television, or through the mail. Thus, product information can be made available 24 hours per day with the careful use of voice mail or call diversion systems, all made possible with a modern wide area telephone network. This service is particularly attractive in a large country or internationally, since customers do not have to pay long-distance charges.

Another practical example of teleshopping in action is the French Minitel system. In 1983 France Telecom introduced the idea of a small terminal in every home and business in France as an alternative to providing a telephone book. This had the added advantage of ensuring that customers had access to totally up-to-date records. Following the success of this single application, Minitel now offers around 12,000 different services and is an integral part of French society. It is a simple matter to browse the lastest movies or plays, read news, access financial information, and examine and order from a wide range of products for sale from stores and mail-order companies.

Financial Services

The financial services industry makes extensive use of networks. Indeed, without these networks, financial services would come to a halt all over the world. We use these services daily—withdrawing cash from an ATM (automatic teller machine), making an inquiry about a bank account, purchasing an item from a store where the payment is carried out electronically, and buying and selling securities. As in marketing applications, networks link the computers storing the relevant information. The applications differ, however.

Computerized communications systems allow transactions to be carried out in time-critical periods. For example, the stock exchanges around the world rely on wide area networks to convey data about share prices in a given country as that country's markets open for business. The electronic automation of the London stock exchange in the late 1980s and the efficiencies that quickly resulted have become a classic example. As another example, the Australian stock exchange opens two hours before the Hong Kong stock exchange and the trading that occurs in Australia during those two hours provides some important indicators to the Hong Kong market when it opens.

In this section, we look at EFT (electronic funds transfer), foreign exchange and investment services, and applications in other service industries. These applications represent a wide range of financial services and in fact form the basis of the world's financial processing. The use of local and wide area networks is integral to the operation of these applications.

Electronic Funds Transfer (EFT)

Electronic funds transfer (EFT) has been loosely described as a "paperless payment" system. Another important application is electronic funds transfer–point of sale (EFT–POS), which we discussed in the section on marketing applications. With EFT, payment instructions are sent over a wide area network. With EFT–POS, payment instructions are sent from the point of sale for goods or services provided to the individual consumer.

Electronic funds transfer covers a wide range of transaction services, including

- Banking services.
- Funds transfer between accounts at the same bank or at different banks.
- Stockbrokerage activities (e.g., placement of orders for stocks).
- Retail ATM (automatic teller machine) services.
- Business transactions involving funds transfer between accounts, short-term investments, and overdraft limit arrangements.

The potential advantages of EFT include

- Immediate or overnight transfer of funds from the consumer's bank account to the good or service provider's bank account, thereby improving company cash flow.
- Online credit authorization, hence reducing bad-debt and check problems.
- A reduced need for customers to carry cash or checks.

Banking organizations have been very quick to take advantage of the EFT environment, as evidenced from the growing number of ATM networks. The widespread acceptance of ATMs by the public as a means of doing banking transactions provides a major indicator of what customers want. The success of EFT depends heavily on networks to provide reliable and efficient interconnections.

ATMs are specialized terminals that dispense cash and require wide area network communication with the central banking computer. The volume of information flow is small; typically 20 to 40 characters each way are required to verify a customer's identity and debit the account. ATM terminals are often connected to a concentrator (see Chapter 4), which in turn is connected to the central banking computer. All of these interconnections require a highly reliable and secure data network.

Foreign Exchange and Investment Services

Foreign exchange and investment services cover a wide spectrum of common financial services. These include access to online databases for

- Interest rates for local, onshore, and offshore time deposits.
- Bond rates.
- Mortgage investment rates.
- Business investment rates and services.
- Foreign exchange rates and cross-rates.
- Stock market information.
- Online business news.
- Statistical information, financial analysis, and market trends.

Because access to up-to-the-minute interest and exchange rates is so widely needed, it is essential that these services be online via communication networks to remain competitive.

Hong Kong is a very important world financial market and is the first major international money market to open each day. It provides an excellent range of exchange rate and investment services, which can be accessed online via a wide area communication network. A particularly good example comes from the Dah Sing Bank. Its rates are accurate to the nearest minute, which would not be possible without the use of wide area networks. If you have access to a PC and a modem, try experimenting with a (free) connection to the database. The access number from any packet switching network connection is 04545340125. If this is not possible, look at the sample that follows,

```
* * * * * * * * * * * * * * * * * * * * * * * * * * * * * * * * * * * * * * * *
*DAH  SING  BANK            LTD  TEL : 2507 8811*
* * * * * * * * * * * * * * * * * * * * * * * * * * * * * * * * * * * * * * * *

29 NOV 09:47

FOREIGN EXCHANGE RATES
```

continued

------------------- (COMMERCIAL : AGAINST HKD) -------------------

	BANK BUY	BANK SELL			BANK BUY	BANK SELL
USD	7.734000	7.740000	*	GBP	14.920000	14.94500
DEM	5.247000	5.255000	*	JPY	0.060640	0.060720
CHF	5.930500	5.941000	*	AUD	5.747500	5.758000
NZD	4.219500	4.229500	*	CAD	6.507500	6.518000
XEU	10.705000	10.72000	*	FRF	1.552500	1.559000
SGD	4.793000	4.803500	*	MYR	3.090000	3.100000
ITL	0.006920	0.006950	*	SEK	1.444500	1.451500
NLG	4.651000	4.662500	*	NOK	1.333500	1.340500

----------- * RATES SHOWN ARE FOR INDICATION ONLY * -----------

DAH SING PHONE BANKING ALLOWS YOU TO MAKE TRANSFER, PAYMENT, ACCOUNT BALANCE ENQUIRY, INTEREST RATE & EXCHANGE RATE ENQUIRY CALL 25078811 FOR DETAILS

FOREIGN EXCHANGE RATES

------------------------------ (INTER-BANK) ------------------------------

	BANK SELL	BANK BUY			BANK SELL	BANK BUY
USD/HKD	7.736500	7.737500	*	GBP/USD	1.929000	1.930000
USD/DEM	1.473000	1.474000	*	USD/JPY	127.4500	127.5500
USD/CHF	1.303000	1.304000	*	AUD/USD	0.743000	0.744000
NZD/USD	0.545500	0.546500	*	USD/CAD	1.187500	1.188500
XEU/USD	1.383800	1.384800	*	USD/FRF	4.973000	4.975000
USD/SGD	1.612000	1.613000	*	USD/MYR	2.499000	2.501000
USD/ITL	1115.000000	1116.000	*	USD/SEK	5.342000	5.347000
USD/NLG	1.661000	1.662000	*	USD/NOK	5.785000	5.790000

----------- * RATES SHOWN ARE FOR INDICATION ONLY * -----------

concluded

FOREIGN EXCHANGE MARGIN TRADING ACCOUNT ALLOWS YOU TO LEVERAGE UP TO TEN TIMES OF YOUR MONEY AND HEDGE AGAINST EXCHANGE FLUCTUATION CALL 25078811 FOR DETAILS

DEPOSIT INTEREST RATE

	CALL	1 WEEK	1 MONTH	2 MONTHS	3 MONTHS	6 MONTHS
HKD	3.1250	3.2500	3.2500	3.2500	3.2500	6.5000
USD	3.2500	3.2500	3.2500	3.2500	3.3750	3.5000
GBP	8.5000	9.6250	9.8750	9.8750	10.000	10.000
DEM	8.0000	9.2500	9.5000	9.5000	9.5000	9.5000
JPY	3.0000	3.7500	3.8750	3.8750	3.8750	3.7500
CHF	6.7500	8.0000	8.1250	8.2500	8.2500	8.2500
AUD	4.0000	5.2500	5.2500	5.2500	5.1250	5.0000
NZD	4.2500	5.5000	5.5000	5.5000	5.5000	5.5000
CAD	3.8750	5.2500	5.2500	5.2500	5.1250	5.0000
XEU	9.0000	10.500	10.625	10.625	10.625	10.625

From this example, you can see that at the moment these data were transmitted to you, the best time deposit rates were in sterling (GBP), deutsche marks (DEM), or European Currency Units (XEU).

All major banks and financial institutions are linked to international networks, which facilitate the rapid exchange of financial information in the same way that all major airlines are linked via the French-based network SITA (Society for International Aeronautical Telecommunications). SWIFT (Society for Worldwide Interbank Financial Telecommunications) is a good example of a virtual private network used by the world's banks. It provides a value-added service directed primarily at the worldwide transfer of electronic funds transactions for banks and their clients. It is used mainly as a vehicle for interbank transfers and funds clearance. SWIFT is a nonprofit organization wholly owned and financed by the participating international banks. The tariff structure is based on a connection charge plus a per-transaction fee (a transaction is generally delivered to or from any international location in less than one minute). It is a message-switching network (discussed in Chapter 4) based on the use of a telecommunications company's data circuits.

Reuter's Telerate system is another example of a major international banking network. Reuters, which operates one of the biggest news and financial networks with around 150,000 connected terminals worldwide, provides information on stock prices, analysis of data, and trend forecasts.

The accompanying example illustrates how networks form the vital component of the effective operation of a brokerage firm. In this example, you will encounter terms such as *transmission media, multiplexer,* and *PBX* . The functions of these items are explained in Chapter 4. In this example, it is the *application* that is important rather than the details of how these devices actually operate.

DISTRIBUTED LOCAL AREA NETWORKS FORM THE TRADING NETWORK FOR A BROKERAGE COMPANY

Networking Requirements

A brokerage firm requires a trading network that will provide rapid access to the central computer file servers from a number of remote locations. These locations need to be able to share the data with the main center as well as peripheral equipment for functions such as remote printing. The firm also wants to provide its retail brokerage offices with economical yet highly reliable online access to securities quotations and client account information. A backup data center is also required, and the method of connectivity has to be determined.

The network designers want to accommodate all of these requirements in a consolidated network. But can they do it? The company profile and special requirements are described below.

Profile

- Require online electronic trading at three trading offices.
- Require online quotations and order placement applications from 16 retail brokerage offices.
- Local area networks at main data center and all remote locations.
- Require all local area networks to have connections to the backup data center for application security.

Special Requirements

- High reliability and network availability.
- Support for bulk file transfer application to backup data center.
- Network consolidation, if practical.
- Where possible, minimize communication costs.

Source: Adapted from R. Fardal, (1992) *Internetworking Success Stories: A Guide to Bridging and Routing Applications* (Retix, 1992), pp. 10–15.

By installing a variety of interconnection equipment, the brokerage firm created an extensive network of integrated local area networks that includes all of its remote locations and
satisfies all of its special requirements. Figure 2–1 provides an overview of the network
solution.

The network supports dual T1 links to each of the three trading offices, for an effective transfer rate of more than 3 Mbps in each direction. (In Chapter 4, we will define
two well-known transmission speed standards: T1 (1.544 Mbps) and E1 (2.048 Mbps).
Each of the retail offices is triangulated with another retail office and the main data center,
using 56 or 64 Kbps links, so that if one link fails, there is always an alternate path for
the data.

A pair of T1 multiplexers and a T1 link are used to connect the main data center to the
backup data center. This provides plenty of bandwidth for the interconnection of the two
multiplexers, as well as for digitized voice communication between the company's PBXs.
The benefits of this network solution include the ability to handle wide area networking,
support for all protocols, high-speed operation, automatic path selection, and rerouting, as
well as link efficiency. Let us now examine each of these benefits in detail.

FIGURE 2–1

*Distributed local
area networking
configuration for
brokerage firm*

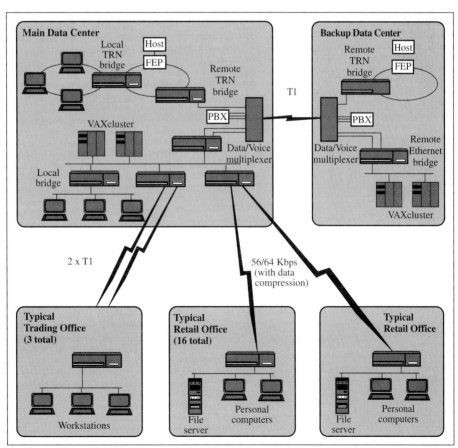

Interconnecting the Local Area Networks

In the retail trading offices, the PCs have shared data access to the database on the local file server. In addition, the same PCs can access the databases on the file server, entitled "VAXcluster," as well as the host computer at the main data center as shown in Figure 2–1. Also, the interconnection among the retail offices allows a "duplication" of the functions of one retail office with another in the same wide area network triangle. The backup data center is also accessible from all trading and retail offices. Thus, full data and peripheral sharing is supported.

The primary purpose of remote bridges (which we discuss in Chapter 5) is to support distributed local and wide area networking through the use of **(DDN) digital data network** links. Remote bridges or routers are used for applications in which the sites are too far apart to be connected with local bridges or for applications that require connections across a physical barrier such as a public road or private property.

T1 circuits are expensive to lease, but prices are falling, and for applications that require a great deal of bandwidth they are an effective solution. In this case, the backup data center is only a few miles away, and T1 multiplexers and a link are used to consolidate the local area network and voice traffic.

High-Speed Operation

Remote bridges or routers work very well in high-speed distributed applications. For example, the brokerage firm is using two T1 links in parallel to provide rapid access from its three trading offices. Remote bridges were selected for this application due to their ability to evenly load parallel links at high rates. In this case, they provide an effective transfer rate of more than 3 Mbps in each direction. Both T1 links can be fully utilized, and the remote users get virtually the same performance level that the local users do.

Link Efficiency through Data Compression

At 64 Kbps, the standard DDN circuits are adequate for normal loads, but during periods of active trading, the brokerage firm's retail offices require more than the usual amount of bandwidth. Data compression is used for these links so that a single circuit can carry the load of two or more regular circuits without the cost of installing additional circuits. The compression ratio for internetworking data is typically more than 2 to 1. If the data have a high degree of serial correlation —that is, a considerable degree of similarity between successive items—the ratio can be much greater.

Summary and Final Points

Remote bridges or routers provide excellent connectivity at any distance in this distributed environment, as well as the ability to share data and peripheral equipment at these remote locations. Rapid response times, support for all protocols, and other features and services provided on a distributed local area network can now be provided on a worldwide basis.

In summary, some of the important functions of remote bridges or routers in forming distributed local area networks are

- Wide area networking over any distance.
- Shared use of data and peripherals.

- The use of standard DDN circuits.
- Support for a number of protocols and architectures on the different local area networks.
- High-speed operation.
- Link efficiency through data compression.

Financing in Service Industries

The sharing of data implies two contradictory situations. First, the data must be accessible to a number of users on the interconnected networks. Second, the organization may wish to limit access to this information to authorized personnel. The result is often a matrix of information files and users that defines each user in terms of his or her access rights. Some of the equipment used to control access is described in the example below and is further discussed in Chapter 5, where we look at specific items of local area network interconnection equipment that support various access control measures.

The example below examines a hospital consisting of six independent departments, each with its own local area networks used to support accounting, patient, and other application systems. With the advent of integrated management information systems, it is now essential that patient files be accessible from any of the six departments. A similar situation exists in many large, structured organizations. For example, at Los Angeles Airport, independent local area networks serve specific work groups, but the users on one LAN sometimes need access to data and peripherals on other local area networks, but still with strict measures of access control.

As in the previous example, some new terms appear in this example, such as *bridge, file server, hub,* and *transmission media.* The functions of these devices are explained in Chapters 4 and 5.

CONNECTIVITY AND SECURITY AT A LARGE HOSPITAL COMPLEX

Functional Requirements

The staff at a hospital complex needs to access patient files from any of six buildings. For example, the accounting department needs access to patient files to process administrative information, and the emergency room doctors need to be able to quickly review a patient's medical history. How can the hospital provide such access to those who need it and still provide security for the accounting department? The networking requirements are highlighted below.

Profile

- Access required to accounting applications from all hospital departments.
- Frequent access needed to patient records applications database.

Source: Adapted from R. Fardal, *Internetworking Success Stories: A Guide to Bridging and Routing Applications,* (Retix, 1992), pp. 6–9.

- Personal computers and local area networks already in use.
- File server containing the patient records is the strategic source of information for all of the hospital's processing requirements.

Special Requirements

- Hospitalwide access.
- Prevent access by unauthorized users to specific applications.
- Isolate department traffic to individual local area networks.
- Protect the accounting department from outside access.
- Incorporate existing local area networks where possible.

Local Area Networking Solution to Support Access to Applications

This is a classic case where some applications are already running on existing local area networking equipment but access is required to these applications from other locations in the hospital complex. The hospital complex needs to expand and integrate already existing (legacy) local area network applications. The local area networking equipment supporting the records department application was expanded to serve as a center for the entire hospital complex, so that each department now has direct access to the file server supporting the patient records application (see Figure 2–2).

The various buildings were interconnected with bridging equipment (to be discussed in Chapter 5). A bridge connects two networks to allow access to an application on one local area network from a workstation on the other. The bridges provide *isolation of departmental traffic, security, transmission media conversion,* and *speed matching* to support access to the interconnected applications.

Traffic Isolation

When applications are interconnected via different local area networks, it is important to provide for isolation and security of departmental local area network traffic, thus ensuring that only authorized people have access to the records, accounting, or other appropriate applications. Bridges automatically learn the location of the end users by "listening" to the source addresses of regular traffic and building a table that lists where the appropriate devices are located in the interconnection of the local area networks.

If local segment traffic is a large proportion of the total traffic (as it usually is), bridges can dramatically increase the capacity of the entire network by isolating the majority of the traffic to individual departments and thus improving the performance of the applications for the users. In the hospital network, only the interdepartmental traffic leaves the local area network segment, as shown in Figure 2–2.

Another benefit of traffic isolation is improved network reliability, since malfunctioning devices on one segment can be shielded from devices on other network segments.

Security Filters

The hospital's accounting department applications are protected from all outside access by a bridge that is configured to filter all traffic except that from the patient records application file server. These filters bar all other departments from unauthorized use of the network by passing data to the required application only from the approved stations.

FIGURE 2–2

Interconnection of the hospital's departments using bridges for connectivity and security

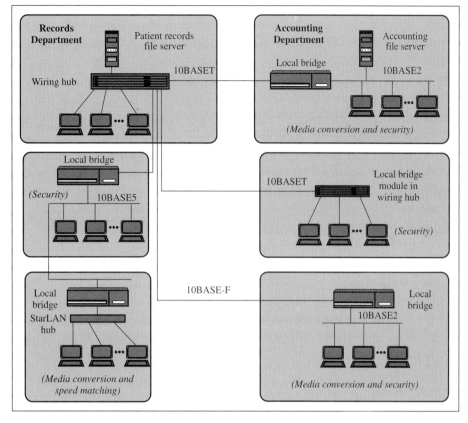

Media Conversion and Speed Matching to Support Integration of Applications

When the different departments are interconnected, the existing local area networks, each operating with its own wiring system and at its individual speed, require that various conversions be carried out. For example, twisted pair wiring in one building can be connected to coaxial cable in another via a third medium such as fiber optic cable. Further, an application running on a local area network that operates at one speed in one department of the hospital complex has to be connected to a local area network operating at a different speed in another department.

Summary and Final Points

Interconnection of applications in different work groups has enhanced the operation and productivity of this hospital by providing data sharing for more rapid decision making. Authorized users have rapid access to patient and accounting information from workstations in different buildings.

The hospital will realize overall cost savings through the shared use of computer peripheral equipment. For example, a user at a single workstation on one hospital ward has access to any of the authorized applications on the entire network, thus avoiding the use of different workstations for different applications that would be necessary without this integrated solution.

However, improved connectivity may make a network more accessible to unauthorized users. In most cases, the host applications are password-protected, but the bridges may also be used to provide the required network security and isolation of application traffic.

The networking solution developed for this hospital complex demonstrates how an organization can interconnect a number of departments without compromising network security and allow the applications on the overall network to be managed from a central location. Network administration can be centralized for better fault isolation or for downline loading of new software to distant workstations, file servers, and applications.

Manufacturing Applications

Manufacturing applications are important business systems that require access to networks for managing the design, manufacture, and delivery of goods. They are closely linked with the marketing applications discussed earlier, since information must flow from the stock levels through to the manufacturing process. This process involves ordering stock (often raw materials) and keeping stock levels to a minimum to avoid costs associated with holding excess inventory.

Sometimes redesign becomes an important component of the manufacturing process, necessitating the use of **computer-aided design and computer-aided manufacturing (CAD/CAM).** The documents related to ordering and payment can be electronic (discussed in the section on electronic data interchange). Thus, the network becomes the transport mechanism for marketing, manufacturing, and financial services.

Just-in-Time and Stock Control Systems

A manufacturing firm has three types of stock, or inventory: raw materials, work in process, and finished goods. A merchandising firm has only one type of stock or inventory: finished goods, or merchandise inventory. Since a service firm sells services rather than goods, it does not maintain an inventory system.

Regardless of the type of stock, an inventory system has two primary objectives: (1) to minimize loss of sales due to out-of-stock situations, and (2) to minimize inventory carrying costs. The two objectives often conflict. At the finished-goods level, out-of-stock situations can result in loss of sales; at the raw materials level, out-of-stock conditions can lead to unnecessary idling of production employees and facilities. However, a company cannot keep large quantities of stock on hand to avoid out-of-stock situations; such an approach would increase inventory carrying costs beyond acceptable levels.

Inventory carrying costs include such costs as interest, insurance costs, and warehousing costs. As the amount of stock increases, carrying costs also increase. Companies could minimize these costs by carrying no stock at all. However, out-of-stock

costs (loss of sales) would then be unacceptable. Inventory must be closely monitored to minimize both out-of-stock and inventory costs. Computer-based inventory
systems provide this close monitoring. Computers can be programmed to automatically make inventory reorder decisions that minimize these two costs. This
requires rapid communication with suppliers, again making the communications
network critical.

Techniques that minimize both out-of-stock and inventory costs are sometimes
called *just-in-time (JIT)* systems. The goal of these systems is to deliver inventory
to the firm just in time for use. Thus, both inventory on hand and out-of-stock situations are minimal. With just-in-time inventory systems, a firm shares production
information with suppliers by means of a network, enabling the suppliers to deliver
materials just as needed. The work-in-process stock or inventory system monitors
goods while they are being produced. This involves two additional objectives: (1)
to provide scheduling control over individual production jobs so that an accurate
prediction of their completion dates can be made, and (2) to accumulate the unit
costs of individual products. In large companies, these objectives are often met by
two separate applications: a scheduling system and a cost accounting system.

The two primary inputs that update the merchandise stock or inventory files are
quantities of goods shipped (input from the sales order processing system or shipping department) and quantities of goods received (input by the receiving department). The merchandise stock or inventory system produces outputs that update the
general ledger system in the areas of current inventory on hand and cost of goods
sold. The system also provides the purchasing department with a purchase order
notice. This notice identifies the items whose quantities are at or below the reorder
level. Many merchandise inventory systems produce a purchase order instead of a
purchase order notice. This purchase order, which may be in hard copy or electronic form, is again sent to the purchasing department (usually via the network)
for approval before being sent to a vendor.

The most familiar example of such a system is the automobile industry, where
stocks of parts for car assembly need to be kept as low as possible to save storage
and interest costs, yet efficient, just-in-time delivery is essential. This time-critical
communication, particularly with suppliers, is often best handled by computer networks.

Rapid Access to Up-to-Date Organizational Information

The following case illustrates how networks can be used to streamline the manufacturing procedures of a large factory that manufactures several lines of refrigerators, freezers, washing machines, and health care equipment. At this factory, networks
provide tremendous flexibility. For example, a retail store that has placed an order
for 20 combination fridge/freezers can alter the order—which is already on the production line—so that left- rather than right-opening doors are fitted to the last 5 in the
batch (assuming they have not already been completed). The ability to provide
customers with maximum flexibility is an enormous competitive advantage, especially when the end user is unwilling to wait more than the absolute minimum period
of time before delivery.

FISHER & PAYKEL INDUSTRIES LTD.

Can a small manufacturing company in a relatively unpopulated Pacific Rim country successfully compete against much larger, multinational companies in a wide-open commodity marketplace? Fisher & Paykel Industries Ltd. is doing just that, thanks to a data network that it has put in place.

A modern-day David, Fisher & Paykel is the envy of its Goliath competitors. Using technical innovation and human ingenuity as competitive advantages, the company builds high-quality major domestic appliances (refrigerators and washing machines), programmable controllers, and health care equipment. The factory floor and networks are so well integrated that each appliance is tested online, and the resulting data are fed into a company database.

Three years ago, Fisher & Paykel needed a network that would link its newly designed automated order entry, real-time manufacturing line information system, and automated distribution systems. Additional wide area connections were required to locations throughout New Zealand and Australia. "Sites and systems were operating in isolation," says Steve Shaw, communications manager. "Machines, devices, and people in different divisions weren't communicating. We wanted to integrate our information systems and our functional areas. An enterprise network was a key element to this plan."

Fisher & Paykel hired Kaon Technologies to design and implement a data network to meet its needs (see Figure 2–3). "The company wanted a scalable network that would accommodate new technology while preserving existing investment," explains Tony Krzyzewski, managing director for Kaon Technologies. "We designed a network with the latest and most critical technology implemented at the core; existing equipment is then migrated to the network periphery, protecting their technology investment."

Not surprisingly, when evaluating vendors, Fisher & Paykel looked for a company that would provide solid technological leadership as well as competitive products. 3Com outscored its other major network vendor suppliers and won the contract. "We gave 3Com the highest marks for supplier confidence and technical ability. They were also enthusiastic about our project and had strong technical edges in their equipment," observes Shaw.

The East Tamaki and Carbine Road site networks in Auckland, New Zealand, were designed as collapsed backbones, with each area star-wired into a LinkBuilder ECS/10 hub and then connected by Ethernet fiber to a central ECS/10 hub at each site. As bandwidth demand increased, the company installed high-performance NETBuilder II bridge/routers as the collapsed backbone. Local area network security architecture software installed on one LinkBuilder ECS hub prevents unauthorized access to the consumer finance division.

LinkBuilder hubs support product design departments that need dedicated fiber servers on the desktop for high-bandwidth CAD (computer-aided design) applications. These hubs are easily reconfigurable and can support multiple mixed Ethernet and token ring LANs today, but the hub's technology-independent passive bus will support emerging technologies as they become available. TCP/IP and Digital's LAT protocols are used for mainframe and server distributed database and production control traffic. Novell/NetWare IPX is used for desktop automation traffic.

Source: "Taking on Goliath," *LAN Asia Magazine,* September 1994, pp. 91–92

FIGURE 2–3

*Example of local
and wide area
networks used in
manufacturing*

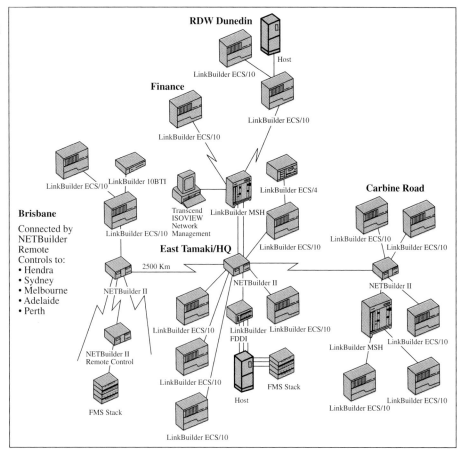

Fisher & Paykel uses Transcend ISOVIEW network management software on a Compaq PC platform. "ISOVIEW is our early warning system for network problems and serves as our main information source for fine-tuning and network improvement planning," says Shaw.

According to Fisher & Paykel's management information system (MIS) team, uptime is important. "Our mean time to repair is now less than 15 minutes," states Shaw. "We've purchased over $750,000 of 3Com equipment, and we've spent less than $1,000 on repairs in three years."

Connecting Offices to the Wide Area

Recently Fisher & Paykel connected remote sales offices throughout Australia to division headquarters in Brisbane using 3Com's Boundary Routing system architecture solution, which concentrates on speed, intelligence, and network management at the central router, and simpler, lower-cost routers at the branches. Each branch has a NETBuilder Remote

Control router attached to a LinkBuilder hub stack supporting remote office PCs and terminal servers. Each site connects over the **Integrated Services Digital Network (ISDN)** to the central NETBuilder II in Brisbane, which in turn is connected over ISDN to the backbone NETBuilder II at the East Tamaki headquarters.

Sales update information and network management data flow into the central division local area network, while software updates and engineering design changes flow out to the remote sites. Line charges are substantially reduced because compressed voice and data traffic share the same line.

"The network is the lifeline of our company system," emphasizes Shaw. "With our highly integrated information systems, we can meet customer demands more easily, evaluate and resolve areas prone to error, and retrieve information for an unlimited number of applications and users."

Electronic Messaging and Directories

Electronic mail has had a history of a disaster in the computer industry. The main reason was incompatible electronic mail systems from different vendors that simply could not interwork readily. Today, with the growth in the use of two widely used standards, X.400 and Internet, this problem has largely disappeared as far as text messaging is concerned. However, problems persist in the intercommunication of documents with formatting, various type fonts, and embedded pictures. To see what we mean, ask a colleague who uses a messaging system different than yours to send you a formatted document in exactly the same form as at the sender's end.

Many different and seemingly incompatible messaging systems (which now frequently form part of an office automation system) still exist. Examples include Dialcom, MCImail, Digital's All-in-One or PathWorks, IBM's PROFS and DISOSS, Lotus Notes, Data General's CEO, Novell's Da Vinci, and PCC/Systems CC: (Carbon Copy:) Mail. When it comes to intercompany communication, the most common form of electronic mail is really the fax (or more recently, perhaps, the Internet), but this can be an enormous waste of time, since the source for a fax is often computer-stored data. Further, once a fax arrives at the destination, it is frequently rekeyed back into another computer!

Electronic mail is used widely within work groups, for example, within an organization's sales or marketing offices. Problems can arise when users try to send formatted documents between different vendors' systems or between different (and incompatible) messaging application products, whether local or remote. To some degree, the Internet has become the lowest common denominator. Many companies are now interfacing their own electronic mail systems to the Internet, making a restricted form of communication possible.

The costs and benefits of electronic mail and news services are often difficult to quantify, but they need to be seen as appropriate and strategic ways to do business. Clearly, there is still a place for conventional mail via the postal system, fax, and various other types of communication services. If electronic mail and news services provide employees with information more rapidly than other means, it offers a definite business advantage.

Further, we need to see these systems as part of the entire automated office environment. In some cases, electronic mail and news services are provided as part of the local area network's operating system, although some of the enhanced services and interfaces (described shortly) need to be purchased. If electronic mail and news can be provided efficiently at a relatively small cost, it is clearly a worthwhile method of doing business.

In many businesses today, success depends on rapid access to, or exchange of, decision-critical information or information that needs to get to the customer rapidly so that the organization can remain competitive. For example, the success of a business such as a bank or an airline depends on rapid access to the relevant database, whether locally situated (local area network) or remotely located (wide area network).

Electronic Directories

Frequently, the volume of information that must be stored and accessed rapidly makes some form of terminal access to a central database essential. This does not mean, however, that a network is essential for such rapid access. All that is required is that a number of terminals be connected to the database. However, the reason a local area network is commonly used to achieve this objective is secondary. Frequently, once we have obtained this information, we want to process it further. For example, we may want to enter it into another computer, print it, send it as electronic mail, enter it into a letter via a word processor, or create a **multimedia** document. It is this subsequent *shared* activity that makes networks so attractive.

One of the best examples of small-scale access to an organization's information is the telephone White Pages. Some countries provide public online access to their telephone and fax directories. In the following case, we see how such a network-run application facilitates the rapid access to information.

ELECTRONIC WHITE PAGES: GOOD FOR BUSINESS

Have you ever tried to trace existing customers who have moved and not left an address? Thumbing through directories is a slow way to do it. With this customer need in mind, Telecom Directories (a subsidary of Telecom New Zealand) recently started a one-year trial of an Electronic White Pages service, and six major trial customers are already using the system. From workstations on their office local area networks, users have instant online access to over 2 million current listings on one phone company's local area network, which are updated every night with 2,000 to 3,000 listing amendments, says the information services manager for Telecom Directories.

The American Automobile Association (AAA) is one of the early users of Electronic White Pages. Previously, when an AAA magazine was returned marked "gone, no address," the AAA might have lost track of the member unless that member had reapplied directly. Now it can trace such members efficiently using a workstation on its local area network together with a wide area network link to the Electronic White Pages database.

Like many other organizations, the American Automobile Association knows it makes better sense to retain existing customers than to search for new ones to replace them. It helps maintain customer relations, and that has to be good for business.

The Electronic White Pages database enables name searching in small district groups. It is possible, for example, to find every establishment in a suburb with "pharmacy" or "restaurant" in its name. While this provides a basic market targeting capability, it is not a substitute for the Yellow Pages.

The Electronic White Pages database is entirely separate from the telephone company's mainstream directory production system, but the listing information is the same as that available for publication in the company's regional telephone directories.

The preceding case illustrates a number of important points. First, access to information is rapid and, since the database is up to date, the information obtained is totally current. Second, a local area network running in an office can have one of its workstations connected via a wide area network to access data for inputting to an application that is currently active on the first LAN. Thus, local and wide area networking are effectively integrated.

Seldom is a computer used solely for rapid access to databases. Increasingly, workstations are being used to *process* information obtained from a database. These subsequent processing activities and the sharing of the information obtained are greatly assisted by the use of a local area network. It is commonly thought that the local area network is a cheap way to connect terminals to a computer. This is sometimes true, but it is not the key issue; it is just a subsidiary benefit.

Electronic Messaging

Any data that traverse a network can be viewed as a message, as we saw in the discussions on marketing, financial, and manufacturing applications. In this section, electronic *messaging* refers to electronic communication among people rather than among databases, machines, or application programs. Electronic messaging significantly speeds up the day-to-day paper communication with which we have all become familiar. Sometimes the message is transferred between people (usually via an electronic mailbox); in other cases, somebody places the message or news item into a database for others to read.

Today messaging systems are increasingly becoming a part of integrated office or desktop systems, and electronic mail forms just one component of the integrated system. Example of such products include Digital's PathWorks and Lotus Notes. The generation, transmission, and storage of multimedia documents consisting of formatted text, embedded graphics, sound, and even video clips are becoming popular, but such systems will not realize their full potential until the underlying multimedia transmission and building-block technology is in place.

Consider the following example of electronic mail (which forms part of the office automation system) used by a specific professional group. As you study this case, think about the information lawyers need to access as part of their daily business and observe how electronic mail and related services provide an easy way for them to do this as well as gain rapid access to a wide range of information situated in various databases. Note also the use of desktop office automation facilities through the use of the same software package, since it is essential that electronic mail form a seamless interconnection with the other desktop functions.

THE LAWNET SYSTEM

In many countries, a system called *LawLink* allows lawyers to exchange information relating to clients, cases, court proceedings, and judgments. The system used to facilitate this communication within this professional group is called *LawNet*. It is an excellent example of electronic mail in action within both the local and wide area networking environments and provides convenient electronic mail and other office functions for LAN-based systems. Of course, the user interface is tailored to the needs of lawyers.

LawNet usually operates in conjunction with electronic mailboxes such as those provided by various telecommunications companies. The key services it provides to subscribers within a work group or local area network as well as via the wide area network services include

- Message services such as electronic mail to other LawNet subscribers, as well as fax, boxlink, and paging services.
- Database access to the Credit Reference databases for verification of bad debtors, Property Valuation databases, and the District Law Society bulletin boards.
- File transfer services among LawNet members.

While in theory a computer-literate LawNet member could make use of much of the LawNet system using standard communications software, a subscriber can be effectively shielded from the "nuts and bolts" of the computer systems involved with an appropriately designed communications package. A good example is the "Microtex LawNet" gateway, which is a package tailored to LawNet and has been chosen as the preferred communications system by many law firms. The Microtex LawNet gateway provides straightfoward, menu-driven access to LawNet services, along with the associated tools to prepare and process information and messages using a word processor.

Using this local area network interface in conjunction with a wide area network offers some important advantages. First, it brings access to both the local and wide area services into a common interface, thus avoiding the need for separate systems. In most business situations, office automation functions are carried out using a workstation that forms part of the local area network. Frequently, information generated at the workstation, such as mail, files, and database queries, traverses the local area into a wide area network. The Microtex LawNet approach is to automate many of the processes by, for example, preparing outgoing and reading incoming mail and news while not connected to wide area network services, thus keeping connect time charges to a minimum. Users can capture online information to local files for more leisurely examination later on the desktop system.

The actual sending and receiving of mail is an automatic process. Choosing a single menu option makes the connection to the telecommunications company's electronic mailbox, copies any waiting mail to a local file, transmits any prepared outgoing mail, saves the "news of the day," and signs off from LawNet without any further intervention by the user.

Similarly, searching the LawNet databases is a matter of making the appropriate menu selections and performing the search. Microtex automatically stores everything displayed on the screen in a local file. Again, the purpose is to minimize the time spent off the desktop. After completing a search, the user can log off from LawNet and examine, print, or edit this captured information at leisure.

The main advantages of the Microtex LawNet gateway on the local area network in conjunction with wide area network services are as follows:

- It is menu driven.

- It automates establishing contact with LawNet, sending and receiving mail covering both local and remote offices.

- It contains a flexible word processor for preparing all messaging and text file printing.

- It provides online help.

- It automatically captures all LawNet communications to local files.

- It can be easily extended to provide access to other, similar gateways.

The Desktop Concept

As Figure 2–4 shows, the Microtex LawNet system has two distinct aspects: (1) features that are local to the workstation and (2) features that manage communication with the wide area network messaging system and, through that process, interaction with the commercial database providers. The local services include configuring Microtex itself, preparing messages for transmission, and reading received messages or "captured" data from sessions on the Credit Reference and Property Valuation databases. Microtex calls these local functions "desktop services," since they take place offline entirely within the PC, workstation, or local area network. No LawNet charges are incurred with desktop functions.

Use of LawNet requires that at some point the user go online, that is, establish a network link with the telecommunications company's messaging system if communication is required with the wider community for the exchange of information with LawNet services. This is necessary for sending or receiving wide area network mail, reading the bulletin boards, and making searches on the available databases.

The LawNet gateway comes as part of the basic Microtex package for LawNet subscribers. It is, however, only one of a number of similar gateways marketed for Microtex to provide access to the increasing number of local and wide area electronic information services. Several of these gateways are also of interest to lawyers:

- LEXIS—a very large database of law reports from the United States and the United Kingdom, including information from some law journals.

- ABAnet—the American Bar Association's database for various banking services.

- TaxLink—the gateway to the Internal Revenue Service's E-File system for electronic filing of tax returns.

Additional gateways for these and future services are easily added to the Microtex LawNet system. Such additions are automatically included at the 'Gateway List' in the lower part of the Main screen.

FIGURE 2–4

*The Microtex
LawNet desktop
and electronic
messaging menu*

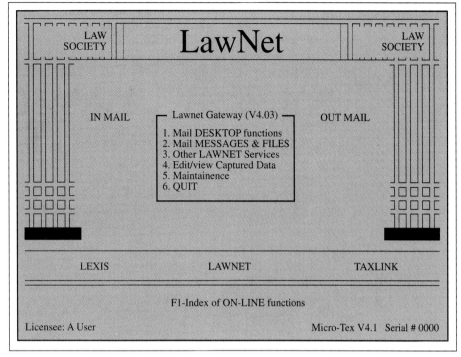

This case demonstrates the great benefits of a desktop system for a specific professional or industrial group as long as a "critical mass" of users exists within the group who agree that this will be the primary mode of communication. The only really successful way to enforce the use of systems such as electronic mail is for management to inform its staff that this will now be the preferred means of communication. When employees try to persuade management to use such tools, they are usually unsuccessful; there must be a commitment from management on down.

Electronic mail systems have the following advantages and disadvantages.

Benefits

- Telephone tag is reduced by eliminating the time spent trying and retrying to reach someone by telephone. Surveys carried out by a number of telephone companies as well as several large corporate organizations indicate that on average, 90 percent of calls to managers and 75 percent of calls to staff under these managers fail to reach the desired person the first time.
- The time spent in lengthy telephone conversations is reduced.
- Information is delivered rapidly so that it can be used proactively rather than reactively in a competitive business environment.
- Paper handling and the accompanying costs are reduced by decreasing the volume of print messages.
- The receiver is provided with a permanent record.

- Gateways are sometimes provided to other public and private electronic mail systems, which is particularly helpful when sender and receiver are each in a different time zone. For example, users can communicate across time zones when it may not be convenient to contact recipients by telephone.
- Immediate confirmation that the message was received can be provided.

Drawbacks

- Users often forget to check their electronic mail. Some systems provide reminders, such as an announcement across the screen while other applications are in process signaling the arrival of new mail.
- Some users dislike using a keyboard (see comments under voice mail to follow); others have difficulty learning and using the electronic mail system.
- Efficient message archiving software is necessary for back referral and cross-referencing of old messages.
- Message security can be a problem unless a password system is used.

Electronic Mail Standards.   One major difficulty with electronic mail systems is incompatibility among different vendors' systems. In fact, there are too many different standards. A more recent development is the CCITT X.400 mail standard. Although this was intended to be an electronic mail system on which everyone would standardize, it has now become a gateway product. This means it forms a link between specific vendors' mail systems and the outside world.

Internet is another example of a system that interconnects proprietary mail systems. For example, one Novell local area network may be running the Da Vinci mail system and need to send mail to a user on an IBM local area network running the PROFS mail system. The X.400 or Internet networks act as an interconnecting link. This is similar to the way X.25 packet switching forms a wide area network link among communicating systems (discussed in Chapter 4).

The X.400 messaging system also supports "communication" in its true form. Often a message consists of text, graphical, and voice components, but incompatibility among electronic mail systems makes it difficult or impossible to integrate these components. However, X.400 is now providing important links among otherwise incompatible electronic mail systems.

This standard is part of the model developed by the Consultative Committee for International Telegraphy and Telephony (CCITT) for communicating among dissimilar computer-based systems. It is designed for manufacturers to use in developing products that will allow incompatible computer-based messaging systems to communicate. The creation of the X.400 international messaging standard has made the concept of a global messaging network a reality. For example, the American Bar Association in Chicago relies on public electronic mail services to pass vital legal information among members nationwide. Without the X.400 standard, the various members' private systems would be unable to communicate. The X.400 standard defines the basic structure of an electronic mail message—its architecture, protocols, and formats—so that virtually all electronic mail users can exchange messages even if they do not use the same type of system.

Further developments in the standardization of multimedia electronic mail systems are under way. Soon it will be possible to send a message consisting of text, graphics, voice, and video components.

Voice Mail.   Since the human voice can be *digitized,* stored, and transmitted by computers, many firms have installed voice mail capabilities. Voice mail offers many of the same advantages as electronic mail. A voice message may be stored or routed to many people on a distribution list. Voice mail has one major advantage over electronic mail: It is easier to use because it does not require typing skills, and it is faster to talk than to type a message. However, voice mail cannot be printed, and documents cannot be attached to the voice message as is the case with electronic mail.

Although voice can be one part of the overall message discussed in relation to the X.400 messaging system, the actual transmission and storage of voice mail and electronic mail are the same, although, of course, voice mail requires more storage capacity. Many vendors are now providing voice mail application systems on their local area networks. Usually, however, these systems are incompatible with the voice mail systems provided by many telephone companies around the world.

As with electronic mail, "islands" of voice mail systems can result. Members within a work group can communicate effectively, but such systems are usually incompatible with other local area network voice mail and with many telephone companies' voice mail systems.

With some packages, such as Microsoft's Windows for Workgroups, it is easy to embed voice messages and graphics along with conventional text-based mail. However, it is very unlikely that such office automation desktop systems produced by different vendors can be interconnected easily.

Electronic Diaries and Calendaring

Earlier in this section we discussed electronic mail, which is an example of what is commonly called an *automated office* or *desktop* function. Now we look at two other commonly used automated office functions: electronic diaries and calendaring. A vast amount of user-friendly software has given users local processing power for these office automation functions.

The following example introduces the use of electronic diaries and calendaring.

GETTING THEM ALL TOGETHER FOR AN URGENT MEETING: EFFICIENCY AND CUSTOMER SATISFACTION

Recently an IBM applications client telephoned David Tan, its account manager at IBM in New York. The secretary checked and found that Mr. Tan was in Chicago until that evening. The client said, "But I need to meet with him tomorrow—will he be available then?" The secretary checked his diary by accessing the Microsoft Windows for Workgroups desktop software running on the local area network. "He has already scheduled a number of meetings for tomorrow, but he could meet with you at 2 pm tomorrow. Would that do?" "Sure," said the client, "but we will probably need to pull in the financial manager and systems manager for a group meeting." "Just a minute, I'll check their schedules," said the secretary. He electronically rescheduled a nonurgent meeting for one of the managers to a slot later in the same day and then confirmed the meeting time, date, and location for all three IBM managers with the client. All this was done with *one* telephone call and without having to contact Mr. Tan in Chicago or either of the other two managers, who at that stage had their telephones configured to voice mail answering so they wouldn't be interrupted.

Suppose the secretary had tried to contact the three IBM managers by telephone. AT&T claims that more than 90 % of all telephone calls to senior managers are unsuccessful because the managers are out of the office, out of town, in a meeting, or simply not available. The probability of reaching all three IBM managers with a single telephone call to each is about 10% times 10% times $10\% = .1\%$—in other words, very unlikely!

Scheduling a meeting by accessing electronic appointment calendars for the participants is becoming a strategic method for managing an office. The scheduling software chooses a time at which all participants are available. The attendees' calendars can be accessed over the network, a common convenient time determined, and appointments made in the calendars without having to contact each participant personally. This application is in fact a type of electronic mail directed to a very specific function.

By automating a diary electronically and specifying who may have access to it, bookings can be quickly and efficiently made. A manager can block off periods not to be scheduled. She or he can also access the diary from remote locations and permit other managers, systems people, and secretaries to make the appointments. Staff do not have to waste time chasing people, and ultimately this translates into customer satisfaction.

The concept of an electronic diary can be easily extended to allow bookings for resources such as meeting rooms, overhead projectors, and laptop computers. This concept is usually called **electronic calendaring**. It is another component of the overall office automation system that allows appointments to be made for employees and other resources. Through workstations on the local area network, designated personnel can then have access to these resources.

Electronic diaries and calendars are almost always embedded as part of an office automation system. For example, Microsoft's 'Windows for Workgroups' is often used in conjunction with Novell/NetWare local area networks. Such a system combines the familiar Windows operating system with easy-to-use networking, making it simple to send electronic mail, schedule group meetings, share files and printers, manage a calendar, or work with other applications. Microsoft promotes this package as a one-stop networking, electronic mail, and scheduling desktop system.

News Services, Bulletin Boards, and Public/Corporate Databases

News services, bulletin boards, and public and corporate databases have one key thing in common: They provide the user with information quickly and efficiently.

News Services. *News services* are considered one-way services; that is, the information is provided to the user. However, this is only partially true, since someone has to put the news or information into the database for others to be able to read it. Thus, most news networks, bulletin boards, and public/corporate databases provide a mechanism whereby the user can send information to the database (albeit with certain restrictions).

Infonet is a news network used in several countries and provides news in a variety of areas, including general and statistical government information, banking, shipping, transportation, and hotels. Other news services include Internet, CompuServe, The Source, US Sprint, and GE Information Services. There is often some overlap among these news services. Given the ease of international communications, the actual location of the database is not critical.

The most extensively used news service is USENET, which forms part of the Internet and will be discussed in the following chapter. USENET is effectively a worldwide bulletin board with hundreds of news groups on a very wide variety of topics from gardening to rock music groups. Most countries transmit and receive many megabytes a day through their gateways, and the news is then made available to various organizations, businesses, and educational institutions. Here are a few of the many hundreds of news groups on USENET:

clar.apbl.biz.headlines	Associated Press headlines of top business news
clar.apbl.briefs	Hourly Associated Press news briefs
clar.apbl.reports.commodity	Commodity news from the Chicago Board of Trade
clar.apbl.reports.dollar_gold	News about gold and dollar prices
clar.apbl.reports.economy	General economic reports
clar.apbl.reports.finance	Financial reports
clar.apbl.stocks	Stock market news and reports
clar.apbl.stocks.dow	Dow Jones averages
clar.apbl.movies	Movie and film news
rec.skiing	Recreation—skiing
rec.photo	Recreation—photography
talk.politics	Political discussion
sci.space.shuttle	Space shuttle science

Bulletin Boards. *Bulletin boards* are similar to news services, except they are smaller in scale and are often used for special-interest groups, buy/sell/exchange transactions, and computer clubs. They are usually accessible with just a PC and a modem, together with a dial-up telephone connection. A good example of a bulletin board is information provided to a class in a university. Information about a course, lectures, laboratories, assignments, and exams can be sent to the bulletin board, and only students in that class need to access the information.

Following is a list of the last six items found on a computer buy/sell bulletin board. To read these items, you select the number and the notice is displayed.

39   Wanted to buy modem 9600bps or 14,400bps

38   For sale Apple MAC SE with 80M hard disk

37   Sell front-end messaging software—runs on all PCs

36   6 Ethernet controller boards sell—suitable for PC 386s

35   Training courses on Novell/NetWare

34   LAN with file server, 6 PCs, printer and cabling—sell

Diamond retailers and wholesalers in California use a bulletin board to post requests for specific sizes and qualities of gems. A diamond cutter or wholesaler that has the required stone in stock will E-mail the requesting retailer. When a satisfactory price is agreed on, the stone is couriered to the retailer. The result for successful users of the service has been a reduction in diamond stock levels for the retailers. The retailers know they will not need to keep such large stocks to meet the needs of customers, yet they can get rapid access to the stones they need. Therefore, they are able to reduce prices and increase the level of service to customers.

In addition, many thousands of bulletin boards allow users to ask questions of other users and to share information about their special areas of interest. An example of such a bulletin board system is the Health Information Network, offered by U.S. Telecom, which provides 24-hour access to information on drugs, physical fitness, nutrition, and similar topics to physicians and dentists. It includes specialized databases and bulletin board systems from agencies such as the Centers for Disease Control and the Food and Drug Administration.

Public and Corporate Databases.   **Public** and **corporate databases** have recently become popular in recent times as a means of providing information to users about a company's products. These applications thus overlap with telemarketing. A wide area network is the essential component in providing the interconnection.

Some managers need to access information provided by commercial or online databases. Examples of diverse commercial databases include

- Dow Jones News/Retrieval Service, which provides stock and bond quotations and other types of financial information to subscribers.
- The Source, a 24-hour information service that provides stock quotes, performance reviews of companies, industry information, and U.S. and world news. The service also provides electronic mail and electronic conferencing services to subscribers.
- CompuServe, which provides services similar to those of The Source, including public domain software, games, and business software.

Other widely known databases include US Sprint, BIX (Byte Information Exchange), GE Information Services, and Dialcom. BIX is a corporate database run by McGraw-Hill. The access code on a packet switching network for BIX is 310600157878. The prefix 310 designates Tymnet's network. You may want to try browsing the huge variety of databases available. Once connected, you will be asked for your name; to register, you should enter *new*. After registering your name and a few other details, you will be asked for your credit card number—so be prepared!

Another example of the use of public/corporate databases occurs when telecommunications services are required internationally. For example, if a company in San Francisco requires links into Asia, it must be able to quickly and easily determine the cost of communication services in that part of the world. Hong Kong Telecom operates a well-known database in Hong Kong that provides information typical of that held in many databases around the world. With many of these databases, you do *not* have to be a registered user. The access code on a packet switching network is 04545500104. Here 0 is an international prefix (which varies from country to country) and 454 designates Hong Kong's Datapak network in the same way 310 designates Tymnet's network in the preceding example. You will be offered a menu that specifies a whole range of telecommunications services (directories, faxline, information on private circuits, and a number of other options, including their respective costs).

Electronic Data Interchange (EDI)

We have discussed EDI in terms of its business applications, costs, and benefits. EDI has been generally described as paperless trading or electronic trading. A more comprehensive description would be a direct computer-to-computer exchange of standard business forms. In fact, as mentioned in the preceding section, EDI is simply another type of electronic messaging. Most of the problems associated with EDI have been political rather than technical. The transfer of business documents (which implies the payment and receipt of vast amounts of money) must be carried out in a very secure and controlled manner. It is this concern that has frequently delayed the introduction of EDI services.

EDI has been slow to develop in many countries, but new efforts are being made to electronically automate the massive amount of paper that is currently handled physically. The problems to be solved are not technical; rather, they involve changes in thinking and the ways in which businesses have handled transactions for a very long time.

Figure 2–5 shows that once an electronic form has been designed (just as paper forms were designed), client data are entered into the form, encoded using the American (ANSI) or European (EDIFACT) standard, and transmitted through a security interface, which might encrypt the data before becoming an electronic mail message as previously described.

The basic principle of EDI is that computer-generated trading documents (e.g., purchase orders, invoices, remittance advices) are transmitted across

FIGURE 2–5

The EDI process

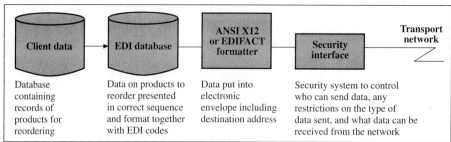

telecommunications networks, either directly or via an electronic clearinghouse, to the trading partners' computers. EDI makes it possible to

- Reduce costs in the ordering and delivery processes.
- Enhance the flow of information from company to company and hence facilitate closer relationships with trading partners.
- Decrease time delays through bypassing the postal/courier systems.
- Increase accuracy and hence provide tighter control by eliminating the duplication of data entry with its associated transcription errors.
- Reduce stock holdings through more efficient ordering procedures.

EDI trading has been made possible by the standardization of key document types by various standards organizations. The American National Standards Institute (ANSI) covers various industry groups in the United States and has defined the **ANSI X12** EDI standard. In an effort to facilitate world trading, the International Standards Organization (ISO) has defined and implemented the **EDIFACT** (Electronic Document Interchange for Administration, Commerce, and Transport) standards, which build on and enhance earlier standards. Examples of documents that can be handled via EDI are purchase orders, acknowledgments, delivery dockets, receipt notes, invoices, remittance advices, payments, schedules, manifests, and customs documentation. Figure 2–6 shows some of these transactions between a buyer and seller.

Companies can implement EDI in their networks in one of three possible ways:

1. They can create one-to-one or one-to-many direct links with their trading partners, as shown in Figure 2–7.
2. They can communicate with their trading partners via an electronic clearinghouse, which acts as a central mailbox, as shown in Figure 2–8.
3. As a logical extension, the central clearinghouse may also allow access to the information by other, related parties (e.g., transport companies, customs, financial institutions) (see Figure 2–9), which is advantageous when trading internationally. From the time the initial purchase order is sent to the manufacturer, all of the various organizations involved in getting the goods delivered and paid for can have access to that information electronically. In this environment, the new EDIFACT standards will become the dominant standard.

FIGURE 2–6

Typical EDI transactions between buyer and seller

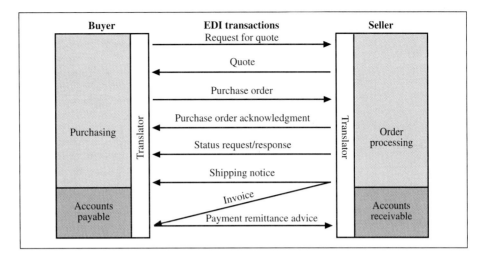

FIGURE 2–7

EDI network: direct trading partner links

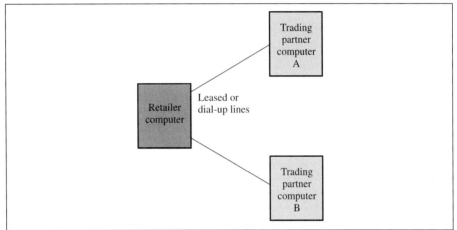

FIGURE 2–8

EDI network: via EDI clearinghouse

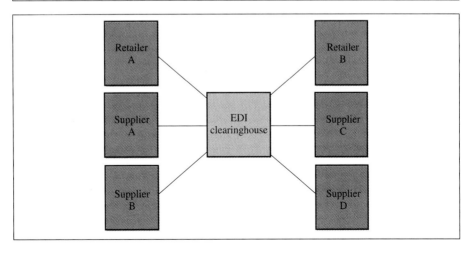

FIGURE 2–9

EDI network: international connections

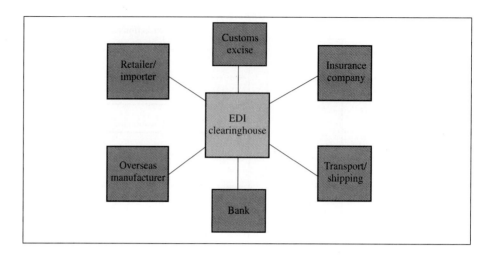

As discussed in Chapter 1, the growing interest in EDI over the past few years has led to an increase in the number of active users, particularly in countries such as Singapore. We also saw the way Wal-Mart Stores, Inc., does business using EDI. Unfortunately, the high entry costs—typically $5,000 to $10,000 for a small trader—have always been a disincentive to using EDI, particularly since the investment does not always yield immediate tangible benefits.

Recognition that EDI will have a major impact on the way companies do business is growing. This has led businesses in vertical markets (e.g., transportation, retailing) to form individual industry groups. These groups lobby for standardization within their market sector and provide a better bargaining position with potential EDI providers in what we can expect to become a high-volume transaction service. This grouping of otherwise highly competitive companies to facilitate a reduction in operating costs is rather unique and a very positive move that ensures the future successful implementation of EDI.

At first glance, it may seem difficult to distinguish EDI from electronic mail, since both involve the transmission of electronic messages among computer systems. But the internal structure and contents of the data message differentiate the two. The contents of electronic mail messages are not intended to be processed in any way by the receiving system. Apart from certain header information that defines the address, start, and end of the message and, in some systems, the type of data contained in the message (voice, image, character), E-mail systems pay no attention to the message contents. The contents of EDI messages, on the other hand, are intended to be processed automatically. They must be formatted so that the receiving application can read them. Although some EDI systems use electronic mail networks as the transmission medium, it is the structure and contents of the message that make one an E-mail message and another an EDI message.

EDI implies a degree of integration between the EDI application (or utility) and other computer applications from which data may be derived or that receive data from the data exchange. The level of integration between the EDI software and the various ledger and accounting applications companies use in their EDI transactions may vary greatly.

In the automotive industry, EDI allows companies to use business techniques such as just-in-time (JIT) inventory management (discussed under manufacturing applications), in which a manufacturer plans to receive parts from its suppliers just before it needs those parts on an assembly line. EDI provides the communications link JIT requires; it is a fast and accurate way for a manufacturer to send a supplier an order specifying what parts it needs, where, and at what time.

Because information is processed by computers and not people, EDI involves a high level of cooperation between partners such as buyers and sellers and even among competitors. No longer are humans there to interpret data and make corrections. Trading partners at all levels must cooperate to set up an EDI system, and at the very least they must agree on which items of data to exchange.

Teleconferencing

Recently IBM arranged for a notable visitor from Harvard Business School to give a presentation in Hong Kong. Other people in Singapore and Bangkok were not able to attend, but still wished to see the presentation. Hong Kong Telecom International provided the links to Singapore and Bangkok using Picturetel equipment, and the "participants" were able to sit in a room and watch the presentation on a large computer screen.

During the Gulf War in 1991, staff from many large companies were requested not to travel internationally. Yet life had to go on and business to proceed as far as possible. Various telecommunications companies provided the links to a number of countries, allowing meetings to be held using video cameras and large computer screens.

This technology, **teleconferencing**, ranges from simple text-based communication through audio- or voice-based conferencing, through still pictures to full-motion video. All forms make use of wide area communications networks, each using progressively more capacity from the wide area network with correspondingly higher costs:

- Text-based teleconferencing (also known as *computer teleconferencing*) uses a personal computer together with a modem, telephone line, and appropriate software.
- Audio-based or voice-based teleconferencing uses telephone facilities similar to those used for the common conference call (often likewise called a conference call).
- Audiographic teleconferencing uses audio exchanges and limited video or graphic visual support (conference call plus still pictures).
- Video-based teleconferencing uses equipment that allows participants to see as well as speak to one another.

A number of multinational construction firms use computer conferencing to assist in project management and control over the widely dispersed international projects they have under way. The use of the two-way bulletin boards allows headquarter managers, project designers, and field staff to keep in contact regarding the progress of the project, regardless of time zones and of proximity to a telephone.

Two forms of video conferencing are commonly used: still video and motion video. *Still video,* sometimes called *slow scan, freeze frame,* or *captured video,* is the simplest and least expensive form of videoconferencing. It transmits one single, motionless image at a time, although the audio can be continuous. Images can change throughout the videoconference, but each one is always motionless. This form of videoconferencing is basically an audioconference with a picture and, although sometimes used for transmitting pictures of people, it is more commonly used for transmitting photographs, documents, charts, or other graphic displays.

Motion video offers more features and capabilities and therefore is the more popular (and more expensive) option. In addition, nearly all motion videoconferencing systems can also send still-video images during a motion video transmission. Motion video varies in image quality depending on the coding algorithm and the data rate used. Motion video offers the ability to conduct an effective point-to-point meeting. Today many videoconferencing service companies offer a combined system whereby a still graphic display from a computer monitor can be sent in a window with full motion showing behind it.

Benefits of Using Local and Wide Area Networks in Business

Distributed networks are not new. For many years, terminals have accessed data at local and remote locations in typical financial, marketing, and reservations applications. Two main changes have occurred:

1. The terminal has become an intelligent workstation (e.g., PC or Mac) capable of handling both local and remote functions.
2. This intelligent workstation has become integrated into the local area network for the many reasons already discussed.

Distributed local area networks interconnected by wide area networks are important due to the need to exchange application information. Thus, interconnection is a vital issue, for many incompatibility problems need to be solved to facilitate integrated applications. For example, from a workstation in your brokerage company you need to run various desktop functions such as diaries and calendaring, as well as a word processor and spreadsheet program for preparing reports to management. In addition, you need to use the same workstation to access online securities quotations as well as international currency and investment rates from remote databases on other local area networks. This may seem fairly easy to do, but some difficult technological problems must be solved that are based on the problems associated with incompatible architectures. For example, your local workstation might be an

Apple Macintosh connected to an Appleshare local area network, whereas the remote databases to which you wish to connect and make inquiries is a Novell NetWare local area network.

These problems are not insurmountable, but the presence of different architectures in a distributed local area network environment often limit some of the functions that can be carried out. Further, the conversion processes necessary to achieve interconnectability can be obtained only at a price, usually in terms of cost and degraded performance resulting from complicated architectural software conversions needed to provide a transparent platform for the distributed application you want to use.

Nevertheless, numerous applications in business benefit from using networks. The telephone is, of course, the most extensively used wide area network and supports a variety of services, including voice communication, voice messaging, fax services, and cellular phone interconnections.

Financial transactions and airline reservations are the most high-profile examples of business applications. These can be easily carried out from terminals located in different countries. You can obtain your Citibank account balance in Los Angeles from countless locations around the world. Similarly, a passenger name record for a flight is accessible from many countries. The next time you request some information—for example, bank account balance, flight schedule, share prices, or interest rates—try to find out where the data is coming from. You may be surprised to find out that your agent or bank clerk does not know. In many cases, the information comes (seemingly instantaneously) from another city or country.

Studies carried out by the original local area network designers in California in the 1970s observed that 80 percent of all companies' documents travel only a short distance, making local area networks very important. The other 20 percent represent some very important applications in the way we live and do business. We already discussed examples from the financial and marketing industries.

The key benefit of a wide area network, therefore, is that it makes information stored in a computer in another location appear to be locally available, thus making the wide area network transparent. It matters little whether we move around the world and access centralized data from different locations or the data are stored in different locations and we access those data from a central point. For example, a number of U.S. telemarketing organizations have moved their customer interface function to the West Indies, where they have ready access to well-educated English speakers who can be employed as telemarketing agents.

The provision of large information databases offering public access, such as those discussed in the section on public and corporate databases, has become very important in recent years. It is also important that the cost of accessing the information be only a fraction of the value of the information accessed. If this figure becomes too high, competitive advantage is lost.

Networks also provide a business with the freedom to locate its operations in different places, while at the same time the business runs as an integrated unit (from the customer's point of view).

Finally, networks allow a business to locate a data center in a secure physical location (e.g., away from earthquake-prone areas) and to perform rapid backup of data files to alternative locations. (The issue of backup is discussed in the context of security in Chapter 11.) In general, these networks facilitate distributed processing in which the workload can be shared among different computers in different locations.

Summary

This chapter provided an overview of the business applications that benefit from the use of communication networks. One of the keys to business success today lies in being able to effectively market the product. This means both directing product information to appropriate groups and providing clients with relevant information from databases. Networks are a key to success in this respect, for they provide the links for the rapid dissemination of data. Companies that successfully use these systems can gain a competitive advantage and increase the opportunity to lock in their customers.

Of course, careful cost-benefit and strategic analysis must be carried out. The costs associated with purchase and rental of the marketing hardware and software systems and the rental of the communication links need to be carefully balanced against the benefits derived. Not every application benefits from such technology.

In this chapter, we first examined common types of networks: local and wide area networks, virtual private networks, and the telephone network, which is the most extensively used business network. We then studied a range of business applications that require the use of networks for successful functioning. These include marketing, financial services, and manufacturing applications. Marketing applications include telemarketing, teleshopping, reservation systems, order entry, and point-of-sale systems. The importance of the electronic movement of money was discussed and illustrated with a number of examples of electronic funds transfer, foreign exchange, and investment. Manufacturing network applications includes just-in-time and stock control systems.

Next, we covered electronic mail and news services, along with some of the problems associated with "islands of activity." We also discussed electronic diaries and calendaring within the overall framework of desktop office automation. These applications represent the key areas in which strategic advantage can be gained through the use of networks and include the most widely used applications and services that offer the greatest benefits. We also examined electronic bulletin boards and public and corporate databases.

Next, we looked at the use of electronic data interchange (EDI) to relieve the business world of the burden of paper shuffling and teleconferencing as a means to offer improved business communication and save travel costs.

Finally, we examined the benefits of using local and wide area networks for business applications.

Key Terms

ANSI X12   80

Bulletin boards   77

Computer-aided design computer-aided
  manufacturing (CAD/CAM)   64

Corporate database   78

Digital data network (DDN)   60

EDIFACT   80

Electronic funds transfer (EFT)   54

Electronic calendering   76

Fiber optic cable   35

File server   40

Integrated Services Digital Network (ISDN)   68

Local area network (LAN)   35

Multimedia   69

News services   77

Order entry   36

Packet switching network (PSN)   42

Passenger name record (PNR)   41

Public database   78

Public switched telephone network (PSTN)   35

Teleconferencing   83

Telemarketing   51

Teleshopping   52

Virtual private networking   34

Wide area network (WAN)   34

800 freefone   53

Questions for Discussion

1. "EDI requires more employees to process business documents." Is this statement true or false? Explain.

2. "EDI software translates data in a business document into a standard format suitable for data transmission." Is this statement true or false? Explain.

3. Name two widely used standards for exchanging electronic mail between companies or between countries.

4. Identify an organization that provides data for public access.

5. What is the most extensively used wide area network?

6. What is the difference between a public and a private wide area network?

7. What system can be used for electronically transmitting purchase orders, invoices, and customs documents?

8. Why is it not a good idea to connect two computers via the telephone network?

9. Match the items in column A with column B in the following groups.

A	**B**
a. (1) News service	(1) Buy and sell computers, cars, etc.
(2) Bulletin board	(2) What are the latest developments in electronic document transfer?
(3) Public/corporate database	(3) We need to know the costs associated with alternative network connections.
b. (1) Telemarketing	(1) A meeting is required among three people, one each in Hong Kong, Singapore, and Tokyo.
(2) Teleshopping	(2) You have a new style of jeans that you want to market.
(3) Teleconferencing	(3) You want to buy a pair of jeans from home.
(4) Telemarketing	(4) High-speed data network.
(5) Teleshopping	(5) Telephone network, possibly in conjunction with a data network.
(6) Teleconferencing	(6) Telephone network.

A *concluded*

c. (1) Voice teleconferencing

(2) Freeze-frame videoconferencing

(3) Full-motion videoconferencing

B *concluded*

(1) Meeting between board members in different cities.

(2) Conference call between two offices.

(3) Interpol needs to transfer a photograph rapidly.

---

10. Refer back to the "Fast Food" case on page 39 and answer the following questions:
    a. Does the fast-food Trucks system give the firm a competitive advantage? If so, what is this competitive advantage?
    b. Assume you are a competitor. What would you do to overcome your rival's competitive advantage?
    c. Are there any other types of business to which such a system could be applied? If so, what are they, and how would you apply the system?

11. a. Give three key reasons, along with a brief explanation of each, why local area networks are important for today's key applications that require rapid access to information.
    b. Describe three ways the use of a local area network can increase the productivity of a department.

12. a. Why is the use of electronic mail restricted in the business world today?
    b. It has often been said that rooms full of telex machines have been replaced with rooms full of fax machines, thus implying that today's messaging problems remain to be solved. Explain why such a replacement has not solved the real problems of document transfer.

c. Suppose you have a three-page formatted document including a couple of diagrams stored in your PC, which is connected to a local area network. You live in New York and wish to transmit this document to a colleague on her local area network in London. What problems must you solve to be able to transmit your document via electronic mail?

13. Suppose you wish to implement an electronic diary and scheduling system for your organization. What key issues must you address to ensure the successful implementation and operation of such a system?

14. When local area networks are interconnected through wide area networks, major difficulties often arise. Describe briefly the problems you might have to solve in implementing networks to support distributed business applications.

15. What benefits would you expect from connecting your local area network in your city to the company's host computer if it were located in
    a. The same building?
    b. The same city?
    c. A different city?

Case Discussion and Analysis

Do the following exercises based on your area of expertise.

1. Create a diagram that shows how some of the departments where you work are interconnected to permit sharing of data. If you do not work in such an organization, choose one with which you

are familiar. Suggestions might be departments at a college, university, airport, bank, department store, or large manufacturing center.

2. Based on a business in which you might soon work, list three ways you could keep up-to-date with emerging developments in wide area

network applications and services. Your answer should take particular account of the business activity in which you might become engaged.

3. Describe a business situation you have encountered recently where good computer communications via a local or wide area network have provided you with fast, efficient service that would not have been otherwise possible.

4. Discuss why EDI has been remarkably slow to receive acceptance in the marketplace even though it appears to be leading-edge technology.

5. It has often been said that single, unified terminals should be available to the public for financial processing. For example, from an ATM it should be possible to access a number of services in different banks without having to go to a specific bank's terminal to access its transactions. Discuss some of the problems associated with implementing such a unified system.

3

THE INTERNET: A GLOBAL COMMUNICATIONS RESOURCE

Chapter Outline

Introduction   91
An Overview of the Internet   92
Internet Architecture and Protocols   95
Gaining Access to the Internet   96
Internet Services and Facilities   97
The Internet as a Business Tool   106
Security Issues in the Use of the
     Internet   115

Learning Objectives

By the end of Chapter 3, you should be able to

1. *Describe* what the Internet is and why it is important to business networking.

2. *Identify* the primary architectures and protocols of the Internet.

3. *Explain* how to gain commercial access to the Internet.

4. *Describe* the primary services and facilities that are available for using the Internet.

5. *Discuss* current and future business applications as well as key issues in the commercial development of the Internet.

6. *Employ* various security and performance concepts to understand the needs of organizations that are considering use of the Internet.

Introduction

The Internet. It is like a name out of a science fiction novel. This term has seen a lot of media hype over the last few years, but what is it really? The Internet refers to a wide area network made up of tens of thousands of other computer networks using a common protocol to communicate with one another. The interconnected networks include UNIX, VAX, IBM, Novell, Apple, MS-Windows, and many other network and computer types. The Internet allows a wide range of data to be shared among the "Internet community," including text, databases, video, graphics, and other media types. Sometimes called "The Mother of All Networks," the Internet should be differentiated from the **National Information Infrastructure (NII).** The NII is a U.S. government-funded program to establish an integrated information highway that allows businesses to conduct electronic commerce more effectively. Electronic commerce includes EDI and other company-to-company commerce, as well as direct-to-the-customer commerce using concepts such as at-home shopping via interactive TV. Often referred to generically as the "information superhighway," the NII is still being designed, whereas the Internet operates actively now and has done so in one form or another for over 20 years. Ultimately the Internet may provide the foundation for the NII, but this is still speculation.

What is the Internet good for, how do you use it, and what tools are available to access it? This chapter addresses these questions and more, including the technology, tools, and business applications of the Internet. In this chapter, we will cover Internet services such as FTP, Telnet, and Archie, as well as the fastest-growing part of the Internet, the World Wide Web (WWW). We will discuss emerging business uses of the Internet, including steps an organization can take to prepare itself for productive use of this new electronic commerce environment. In an environment such as the Internet, security issues and performance are always concerns. We will look at the technology and processes available to provide a secure yet usable connection to the Internet.

An Overview of the Internet

Why is the Internet enjoying such a surge of popularity? The simplest explanation is that there is nothing else like it. Local area networks enable users to exchange data only with a select set of others. In contrast, the Internet is the largest wide area network in existence, with more than 2 million hosts and over 36,000 interconnected networks covering 83 countries. Currently it has over 20 million users, and this number is expected to grow to 100 million by the year 2000. The Internet now supports storage, searching, and transmission of full multimedia data, including audio, video, and formatted documents as well as conventional data. It allows local and wide area network users to communicate with more people in more ways and provides access to the largest range of database servers in the world, with an ever-growing range of **client/server** tools and graphical user interfaces.

The last two years have seen substantial changes in the availability of the Internet services. Not only has commercial access to the Internet been made available in many countries, but the range of services and facilities has increased markedly. Organizations worldwide now offer access to the Internet in a variety of ways. Much of this increase in commercial access has resulted from a more liberal interpretation of the **Acceptable Use Policy (AUP)** by the National Science Foundation (NSF) in the United States.

Although commercial access to the Internet has been available for many years, companies were expected to connect only for research and educational purposes. However, with the more liberal interpretation of the AUP, organizations such as the telecommunications authorities in various countries have taken on the responsibility for providing access to Internet, although the range of these services, their performance, and cost vary enormously.

For users, the Internet provides a wealth of technical information, databases, and software services, usually at minimal cost. The Internet is in a unique position in that it is not owned by any one organization. *All* users contribute to the Internet by making services available to other users on their own networks. It is a unique example of cooperation in a competitive world that benefits everybody provided basic rules and courtesies are respected.

No other network provides such a comprehensive range of facilities and services. Private networks enable users to communicate only with those in the same business. In fact, communication and information sharing between major networking players such as IBM and Digital are very limited unless the user has access to specific gateways, which these companies sometimes provide for their customers. Networks such as CompuServe, Sprint, BIX, and so on do provide a wide range of information services, but often at a higher cost than that available with the Internet.

A fundamental difference in philosophy concerning the use of the Internet still exists among its users, but there is every sign that these differences can be accommodated. The academic and research institutions and the government agencies that pioneered the use of the Internet made information freely available to the Internet community, usually at no cost, for the advancement of learning and research. Exchange of ideas and software was encouraged. Further, little attention was given to the security of information; rather, widespread dissemination of information was to be encouraged. Not until 1988, following a major security breach in Europe and the United States, as well as the release of the Internet "worm," was attention directed to issues of security. These security issues are vital to the growing number of commercial Internet users.

Finally, the manner in which the commercial sector engages in promotion, marketing, and advertising has been at odds with the AUP. The more liberal interpretation of this policy now accepts the provision of information services, but not the direct advertising of products.

The following case illustrates the benefits and opportunities available to businesses on the Internet.

THE THOMPSON REFRIGERATION COMPANY

Jack Thompson, founder and managing director of Thompson Refrigeration Company (TRC), finally got the breakthrough he needed. Jack had formed TRC four years ago to market a new aftermarket product for the refrigeration industry. The inventor had approached Jack to help him market the product, which was capable of producing 20 to 50 percent energy savings on all forms of existing refrigeration units, air conditioners, heat pumps, and freezers. The product applied to both commercial and residential equipment and offered a guaranteed payback period of two to three years, an excellent return on investment.

After much confirming research, Jack was finally convinced that the product and energy savings were real, and he agreed to start up TRC to market the product. Jack had thought it would be easy to sell a product that offered such great savings in running costs. Unfortunately, the economy had been sluggish, and the idea of adding this unit onto existing refrigeration equipment worried many business and private owners. Sales had gone up slowly, and Jack's finances had nearly hit rock bottom during the first two years.

All of that changed six months ago when Jack decided to hook up his PC to the Internet to access a refrigeration technical news group. Originally he thought he would simply be able to keep up-to-date with industry changes and maybe make a few new contacts. It would also be fun to exchange E-mail with his mother, father, and brother Joe, who had recently joined CompuServe, which had a gateway to the Internet. So he bought "Internet-in-a-Box" and a 14.4 Kbps modem, took a couple of hours to read the instructions, hooked up the modem, and established the dial-up connection with the Internet service provider. He enjoyed exchanging E-mail with his family and found the Internet refrigeration news group interesting, but that was only the beginning.

Things really opened up when Jack responded to a news group comment about energy conservation in an area where the local electricity provider had just announced a 10 percent increase in usage charges. He simply put a comment on the news group about the savings made possible with the technology TRC had available, including a few specific examples from some of TRC's customers. The floodgates burst wide open! First, he received 20 comments on the news group. After responding to these comments and including his E-mail address, he received 40 more requests for further information. Over the next six months, this snowballed into a 50 percent increase in sales and a 100 percent increase in referrals, mostly over the Internet. For once Jack was experiencing a business problem he liked: finding time to fill all the orders and bill his customers!

Last month someone on the news group suggested that interested small-business owners should begin using a commercial electronic software package that would allow the group to order, confirm, and pay for goods and services electronically, thus increasing their efficiency and keeping paperwork costs down. Jack thought this was such a good idea that he immediately contacted the software provider using Internet E-mail. Later in the day, the vendor responded with an invitation to download the necessary software for Jack's computer environment (Macintosh, UNIX, VAX, and MS-Windows versions were available). There would be no charge for 30 days, and if Jack was satisfied, he would authorize the billing through his Visa account at the end of that period. What could he lose?

The package included everything he needed, including an EDI standards–based purchase order (PO), a PO confirmation, sales order (SO), an SO confirmation, electronic receipts, and payments using his Visa account and the local bank of his choice. The program also included an excellent Internet/WWW browser and other utilities. Although swamped with the many new orders, contacts, and requests for information flowing in, Jack found he was able to make product information available and handle order and payment paperwork simply and easily using E-mail, a WWW home page, and his other software. It had taken him some time to learn the new software, but after extensive reading and practice, he had become adept at it. It hadn't taken him long to train his new assistant, now that he could afford some additional staff.

Many of his referrals used Prodigy, America Online, or CompuServe, in addition to direct users of the Internet. But all the information could be passed simply among these proprietary networks using Internet gateways. Jack didn't need to set anything up or even to understand the technicalities. The system simply worked, and worked great! Jack was overwhelmed by the opportunities he was experiencing, but he knew he needed to watch his cash flow and other important business indicators—now that he had a cash flow to watch!

Internet Architecture and Protocols

Internet is based on the UNIX architecture and the **TCP/IP (Transmission Control Protocol/Internet Protocol**) protocol suite, as shown in Figure 3–1. The lowest layer of the suite is called the *link layer* and contains specific protocols for LANs and other types of communications subnetworks, including serial routing protocols such as SLIP (Serial Line IP) and PPP (Point-to-Point Protocol). The next layer is the Internet layer, which provides routing and relaying between subnetworks in the Internet. The transport layer provides end-to-end communications links between systems. The application layer provides applications such as remote login and file transfer.

TCP/IP operates on the assumption that a common Internet layer service can be provided to support applications. The Internet layer provides a **connectionless** (datagram) service to the transport layer and operates directly over connectionless media such as ISO 8802-series LANs. The Internet Protocol (IP) provides routing and relaying among the various types of networks, whether they be connection-oriented, such as the X.25, or connectionless, as in the case of LANs. IP always operates in conjunction with the Internet Control Message Protocol (ICMP), which provides error reporting and congestion control facilities. The uniqueness of this architecture when it was invented was the ability to be used over *any* conceivable transmission medium.

The use of PPP or SLIP means the user's computer has full Internet connectivity permitting full client/server operation and graphical user interface applications to be used with native access to all Internet services. Both support asynchronous (transmission of one character at a time) dial-up and synchronous (transmission of a number of characters at a time) leased line operation. The terms *asynchronous* and *synchronous communication* are fully defined in the section entitled Packet

FIGURE 3–1

The four layers of the TCP/IP model

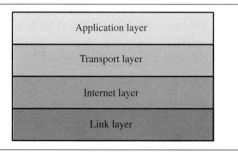

Assembler Disassembler (PAD) (including Figures 4–9 and 4–10) in Chapter 4. SLIP cannot support error detection or data compression (although one version, CSLIP, compresses the TCP/IP headers), but it is easy to configure and is included in most UNIX system architectures. PPP also offers a three-way hand-shaking security feature for dial-up connections.

The transport layer consists of two protocols. The Transmission Control Protocol (TCP) is **connection-oriented** and provides for reliable end-to-end transmission of long streams of bytes. The User Datagram Protocol (UDP) is connectionless and provides the ability to send short messages without the overhead of establishing an end-to-end connection. Several application layer protocols exist that use UDP and TCP to provide network services. Figure 3–2 shows a typical range of application protocols used on the Internet to support E-mail, file transfer, remote logins, network management, and other functions. This layered architecture is further discussed on p. 152–4.

Gaining Access to the Internet

Internet access providers offer the necessary hardware and software interface appropriate to the users' architecture (UNIX, PC, Macintosh, etc.). Physical access is available over dial-up and leased lines as well as over packet switched and frame relay networks. If the user already has a local area network, the usual approach is to install a router (either hardware-based or software on a PC) with a leased line connection to the provider's network. Users are provided with logical access via the allocation of Internet Protocol (IP) addresses.

If the user's network is entirely private, any unique allocation of IP addresses is adequate. However, almost all users wish to be part of the wider Internet and must therefore obtain addresses from the appropriate allocation authority. These are available in one of three classes (class A, B, or C), depending largely on the size of the network and the number of connected hosts. For the majority of organizations, Class B addresses are allocated. Access providers frequently obtain blocks of contiguous addresses and allocate them to subscribers as necessary. These addresses are actually numerical values; for example, a range of addresses allocated to one organization is 132.181.30 to 132.181.39. In practice, however, user-friendly addresses are used,

This layered architecture is further discussed on p. 152–4.

FIGURE 3–2

Sample protocol stack of the commonly used protocols from the TCP/IP suite

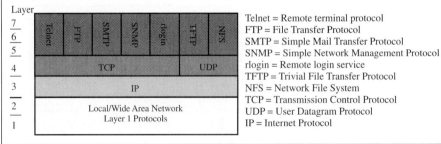

and these numerical values might become something like *ray@cosc.canterbury.ac.nz,* where *nz* represents the country (New Zealand), *ac* (academic) a domain name in that country, *canterbury* the name of the organization, *cosc* the abbreviated the name of a department in that organization, and *ray* a user in that department.

The software services available for running applications vary greatly. However, many Internet applications, such as online information services, mailing lists, and news group services, can be run using three main tools: E-mail, a file transfer protocol (FTP), and remote login (rlogin). Users with UNIX hosts are clearly in an excellent position to run these applications, since they form part of the TCP/IP protocol suite (see Figure 3–2). Commercial availability of WWW browsers, which combine some or all of these features in a graphical user environment, has created a major surge in Internet accessibility.

For other architectures, users can be provided with a direct line to either the user's UNIX host or the UNIX host of the network provider. Alternatively, software can be provided that makes DOS machines emulate a UNIX host, such as Chameleon and WinSock (these point-and-click interfaces require SLIP or PPP link layer protocol support). Packages are also available (e.g., by downloading directly from Internet) for PCs and Macs that implement file transfer, remote login, and other facilities. Here users log into the host and execute UNIX commands. Providers sometimes offer a menu-driven interface to assist users who are not familiar with UNIX commands. This is the most common way to connect a stand-alone, non-UNIX computer to the Internet. Thus, the PC essentially acts as a terminal connected to the provider's host.

Stand-alone UNIX computers can also be configured as hosts themselves. In this case, the machines have their own Internet addresses and communicate with the provider's router over a link using a serial routing protocol such as SLIP or PPP.

Most services that provide database, news, and other services in a proprietary environment (such as AT&T Mail, CompuServe, and MCI Mail) give users an account on a host machine that has an E-mail gateway to the Internet. This scheme is easy to use and to provide, but a user who has only E-mail access to the Internet cannot easily take advantage of Internet's power. In particular, such a user cannot connect to online information services, perform anonymous FTPs, or log into remote machines.

Internet Services and Facilities

The most attractive Internet facilities for commercial users include the ability to access information services, news, and mailing lists and to download files anonymously from remote locations. The Internet also provides access to other commercial online services such as Nexis/Lexis, Dow Jones News Retrieval, and CompuServe. Connecting to these services through the Internet can save access and usage costs, since users pay only for the Internet connection.

By joining more than 4,000 available mailing lists, Internet users can exchange electronic mail on topics ranging from aerospace engineering to X-Windows programming. Hobbies and special-interest groups also are amply represented; for example, there are separate mailings lists for wine making, child care, and bird-watching. Subscription to these lists is free, and the user pays only for Internet access.

In addition to electronic mail, users have access to technical reports, software documentation, and electronic copies of published papers. Many hosts allow remote users to log in anonymously and download these files; this process is called *anonymous FTP*. Sophisticated online information servers help users locate and download information.

A considerable amount of research and engineering work actually takes place on the Internet. Internet working standards are developed by the Internet Engineering Task Force (IETF) entirely on the network, and the most up-to-date copies of the specifications are usually available. Common network protocols, E-mail packages, and operating system extensions are also available. Internet users often test applications that will soon be available commercially. By participating in these tests, users can give input into the development of the products, as well as gain an understanding of future developments.

The primary purpose of the Internet is information sharing. However, because of the vast size and scope of this network, important tools have been and are still being developed to aid users in accessing this information. These tools go beyond the conventional E-mail, news, bulletin board, and directory services. They include powerful client/server and graphical user interfaces, discussed briefly next.

File Transfer Protocol (FTP)

File transfer protocol (FTP) allows users to transfer files quickly from machine to machine on the Internet. It is possible to transfer files in various formats, allowing one to retrieve software programs, graphic images, and other files that are not necessarily ASCII text.

Access to files posted to the Internet, such as directories, catalogs, and bibliographies, is an example of a research-related application of FTP. The Oxford Text Archive, a database of the full texts of books, plays, essays, and poetry, makes its updated catalog of materials available for capture with FTP. Also available via FTP are the full texts of electronic journals and copies of software packages.

As mentioned earlier, the Internet is a network of thousands of computers, and fortunately many of them provide public access via anonymous FTP. This means one can use the TCP/IP software and FTP to log into a remote computer with the user ID of *anonymous*. This restricted access to remote computers grants access to thousands of files that can be transferred to a local Internet computer. Text files, computer programs, and graphics are just a few types of files available through anonymous FTP.

A document on the Internet called *FTPsites* lists many of the remote computers that permit FTP access. This document includes explanations of what is available at FTP sites on the Internet. One can also use the Archie command *Archie FTPsites* (discussed shortly) to find out where the desired site is located.

Telnet: A Simple Remote Terminal Protocol

Telnet is the virtual terminal protocol that enables a user to simulate a direct connection from a terminal to a remote host on the Internet. This function is implemented by defining a standard character code, ASCII (the usual symbols plus a set of control codes), for the network. This standard code corresponds to a virtual terminal with which all the hosts should be able to interact. This interaction takes place by converting the characters sent by the actual terminal into the network standard. Similarly, the virtual terminal input is translated into the input expected by the host.

To permit the connection of more sophisticated terminals, Telnet has an *option negotiation* phase that allows users to agree on a set of options to be supported by the virtual terminal. For example, echo can be handled either locally or by the remote computer. The sizes of the output (line length, page size) can also be negotiated.

Archie: An Archive of Archives

Archie is a "search engine," or a collection of resource discovery tools that together provide an electronic directory service for locating information on the Internet. Originally created to track the contents of anonymous FTP archive sites, the Archie service now includes a variety of other online directories and resource listings. Thus, having become aware of the enormous volume of information and software that can be obtained via FTP on the Internet, the challenge is then how to find the item or file when it is needed.

Archie's primary use is to locate specific files that are available on the Internet via anonymous FTP. The number of FTP sites that are included in Archie's database is usually limited to a region or country; however, the database is extensive and indexes many of the most popular anonymous FTP locations.

Archie is not the only means for finding files that are available for anonymous FTP. Often electronic mailing lists and news groups can be good sources of FTP information related to a particular topic or computing system. However, these forums require that you either (1) happen to see a message about a particular piece of software or document that is available via anonymous FTP or (2) post an inquiry and hope that someone will reply. However, Archie has the advantage of being automated and immediately accessible, thus enabling you to carry out multiple searches for an item.

Archie is a good example of a client/server system in action whereby the local workstation runs the Archie client software, which in turn communicates with the Archie server in a remote location to accomplish the search. Access to Archie is also possible via Telnet or E-mail.

The heart of the Archie service is a database of the file systems of anonymous FTP sites that number in the thousands. Each server maintains its own database. Special resource discovery software runs each night to update about one-thirtieth of the database so that each file system image is updated approximately once a month.

The various Archie servers are obviously a very important part of the Archie service. Examples of some of the Archie servers throughout the world appear in

Figure 3–3. As you can see from this list, Archie is a worldwide service and any of the addresses shown can be specified as the primary server for an Archie client. These servers collect and maintain the anonymous FTP information and accept and process queries using the methods described above. The Archie servers are generally computers running on the UNIX operating system. These servers are maintained primarily by universities and network service organizations and are offered as a public resource to Internet users.

Gopher

Gopher is an extension of Archie and ties together a variety of systems on the Internet. Originally, Gopher was designed as a campuswide information system (CWIS) and document delivery system, but it has been expanded greatly over time. It is menu-driven, and menu items can be documents, menus, FTP sites, Archie searches, Telnets, a wide area information server (WAIS), or other kinds of information on the Internet.

The Internet provides access to terabytes of information, data, files, and programs on computer systems around the world. Archie provides a method for searching for basic files and programs, while Gopher is a more elaborate, worldwide client/server information retrieval tool. Although originally designed to be used for text only, Gopher has evolved into a full multimedia information retrieval tool, and new Gopher services offer the ability to retrieve plain text, formatted text images, sounds, and full-motion video.

The **Gopher client** is a program running on the local workstation (e.g., UNIX, Mac, DOS, Windows), which provides a connection to a **Gopher server**.

A short list of some Gopher sites in selected countries appears in Figure 3–4.

FIGURE 3–3

A sample of Archie servers in different countries

Server Address	IP Address	Area
archie.ans.net	147.225.1.10	ANS Server, New York
archie.au	139.130.4.6	Australia
archie.doc.ic.ac.uk	146.169.1.2	United Kingdom
archie.wide.ad.jp	133.4.3.6	Japan
archie.vuw.ac.nz	130.195.9.4	New Zealand
archie.mcgill.ca	192.77.55.2	Canada
archie.funet.fi	128.214.6.102	Finland

FIGURE 3–4

A sample of public Gopher sites in different countries

Host Name	IP Address	Log in as	Area
pandaa.uiowa.edu	128.2.19.92	panda	North America
gopher.sunet.se	192.36.125.10	gopher	Europe
info.aun.edu.au	150.203.84.20	info	Australia
gopher.denet.dk	129.142.6.66	gopher	Denmark
gopher.th.darmstadt.de	130.83.55.75	gopher	Germany
gopher.chalmers.se	129.16.221.40	gopher	Sweden
gopher.brad.ac.uk	143.53.2.5	info	United Kingdom

Wide Area Information Server (WAIS)

The **wide area information server**, or **WAIS** (pronounced *ways*), attempts to harness the vast data resources of the Internet by making it easy to search for and retrieve information from remote databases (called *sources* in WAIS terminology). WAIS servers not only help users to find the right source, but also handle access to it.

Like Gopher, WAIS uses the client/server model to make navigating data resources easy. Unlike Gopher, WAIS does the searching for the user. A WAIS client (run either on the user's workstation or on a remote system through Telnet) talks to a WAIS server and asks it to perform a search for data containing a specific text. WAIS uses an information retrieval language similar to Structured Query Language (SQL).

After doing a search to identify any documents, a list of *hits*, or ranked document titles, will be returned. The WAIS server ranks the hits from the most to least relevant document and also by the number of search words that occur in the document and the number of times those words appear.

Many documents can be accessed using a number of these tools, and Internet news groups have taken advantage of WAIS by making their archives available. The sources are as varied as the groups that communicate over the Internet, for example, software reviews, environmental reports, weather information, and chemistry abstracts.

As with other interfaces, such as Archie, access to WAIS can be obtained by running the WAIS software client on the local workstation. Alternatively, WAIS can be accessed via Telnet or Gopher. Once the WAIS server is accessed, the screen provides a reference number for each source, the location of the WAIS server, the name of the server, and the cost of the library search for each WAIS library source. A sample of WAIS servers is listed in Figure 3–5. The names of the servers do not necessarily describe what the servers contain, but a directory of servers containing short abstracts of the content of each server is available.

FIGURE 3–5

An example of the WAIS interface and directory

Number	Server	Source	Cost
001	archie.au	aarnet.resource.guide	Free
002	muin.ub2.lu.se	academic_email_cong	Free
003	wraith.cs.uow.edu.au	acronyms	Free
004	archive.orst.edu	aeronautics	Free
005	nostromo.oes.orst.ed	agricultural.market.news	Free
006	archive.orst.edu	alt.drugs	Free
007	coombs.anu.edu.au	ANU–Asian Computing	$x.xx/minute

World Wide Web (WWW)

The most recent and fastest-growing addition to the family of Internet tools is the **World Wide Web (WWW)** server hypermedia project, designed and prototyped at CERN (European Laboratory for Particle Physics) in Switzerland and known as CERN 3.0 HTTP (HyperText Transport Protocol). The CERN server software, as well as an alternative from NCSA (National Center for Supercomputing Applications), is available by anonymous FTP from *info.cern.ch*. WWW takes Internet usage a step forward by linking information globally via hypertext, alongside the ability to link with FTP sites, Gopher, WAIS, and news servers.

WWW is similar to Gopher, but instead of being menu-driven, it is hypertext-based. It appears to be a much better platform for multimedia documents than Gopher. Like Gopher, WWW can act as a front end for just about any piece of information on the Internet. The idea behind WWW is that all users should have access to any document, sound recording, or video image from their workstations. With the growth in processing power together with the scope of the Internet, the WWW project is close to achieving this goal. The WWW attempts to unify the huge amount of information available via the global networks and to do this using a simple client/server system. WWW can be seen as part of the move toward unifying network tools, thus negating the need to run several different pieces of software to make the best use of the network resources.

Anonymous FTP, still one of the most useful Internet facilities, provided the original archive facility, making it possible for sites to make files available across the world. The addition of a search engine, Archie, made it possible to find named files. However, Archie tells the user only about sites where the desired file resides; the user still needs to use an FTP client to obtain a copy. Gopher took a step toward remedying this problem by providing online viewing and retrieval facilities within the client package. WAIS brought the power of full text search and querying of resources.

Although these tools allow the searching of the Internet and the retrieval of information and resources, they generally exist independently of one another. Figure

3–6 shows some of the properties and relationships among these client/server systems used to assist in information retrieval on the Internet.

Gopher implemented the concept of *bookmarks,* which allows the marking of desirable sites or documents for future reference. WWW, on the other hand, is built on the concept of *links.* The underlying language is powerful yet extremely simple; any WWW document can contain links to other documents, links to marks within the same document, and links to other resources such as FTP sites, Gopher, WAIS servers, and news groups.

WWW relates to existing resources in a simple manner. Pointers can easily be built into text documents to specify the location of the target. The target can be a text file, an image, a Gopher server, an FTP site, or various other types of information. The work of locating and displaying the target information is done within the client application; all that is transferred across the network is the information, and this is displayed according to the built-in rules of the client browser. All formatting and layout information is constructed locally according to the software and preference settings. For this reason, WWW information can be constructed according to standard rules and WWW browsers (discussed next) return different results depending on their sophistication. WWW browsers will return information from FTP sites and from Gophers, but they are most effective when used in conjunction with Hyper-Text Markup Language (HTML) and the HyperText Transport Protocol (HTTP) servers, WWW's own server software.

FIGURE 3–6

Client/server systems used for Internet access

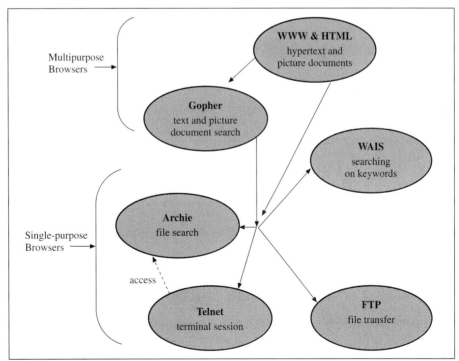

The user's view of the WWW depends heavily on the client software used. Most organizations now have a **home page** that represents details about the organization and provides links to departments or projects within it. For example, the WWW address of the home page for the University of Canterbury is shown in Figure 3–7 and a graphical view of a campus map appears in Figure 3–8. A link then connects the administration center with a home page. This is usually accessed by clicking on the building. Information about other departments is accessible through point-and-click methods.

WWW Browsers

Mosaic is the name of a software tool developed by the U.S. National Center for Supercomputer Applications (NCSA) and has been the most widely used graphics-based front-end client software for the World Wide Web. Mosaic is typically referred to as a **WWW browser**. However, a new company, Advanced Mosaic Communications, has continued the development of Mosaic under a new name, **Netscape**. Cello is a windows-based browser developed by the Cornell University Law School. Other independent browsers include Winweb, Macweb, and Lynx (text-based). These browsers usually operate on multiple platforms and are designed to be used in conjunction with the CERN or NCSA WWW server software to provide sophisticated graphics facilities that have the ability to display

- Hypertext and hypermedia documents.
- Electronic text in a variety of fonts.
- Text in bold and italic.
- Layout elements such as paragraphs, bulleted lists, and quoted paragraphs.

The ability to support hypermedia—sounds, movies, extended character sets, and interactive graphics—is fundamental to most WWW browsers. This is done by using external software. For example, the browser will fire up and use a known sound player when a sound link is clicked. The browser has the capability to support and make hypermedia links to FTP, Gopher, Telnet, NetNews, and WAIS servers.

FIGURE 3–7

Sample WWW sites

WWW Address	Organization
http://www.atmforum.com	ATM Forum
http://www.canterbury.ac.nz	Canterbury University
http://www.cpsr.org/dox/home.html	Computer Professionals for Social Responsibility
http://www.cam-orl.co.uk	Olivetti Research (UK)
http://wings.buffalo.edu/contest/awards	Interesting WWW sites for 1994
http://hpl33.na.infn.it	Physical Museum, Naples
http://galaxy.einet.net/galaxy.html	A comprehensive and easy-to-search index of WWW sites

FIGURE 3–8

Mosaic display of the University of Canterbury

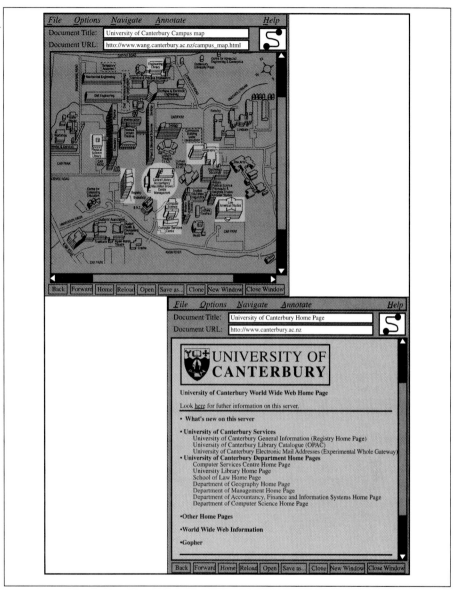

WWW browsers typically keep track of where the user has been, offering a list of previously visited pages or sites that enables quick backtracking—a very useful feature when the user has moved a long way down a branch and found a dead end. A browser offers *caching;* that is, it keeps a copy of pages that have been visited so that if a backtrack is necessary, information does not have to be downloaded all over again. This is similar to the way CompuServe operates. Caching is usually implemented by way of a proxy server.

A WWW browser is an interface to the WWW distributed information system. Like Gopher, WWW is functionally split into two parts, the server and the client. The server manages the data and answers requests from client applications. On the Internet, multiple servers and clients can run simultaneously. This arrangement enables the data to be distributed among many computers, and allows many users to access a particular server at the same time. The user works with the client application, which connects to all the servers, gathers the desired information, and presents it in a useful format. Other WWW client applications exist, but a browser such as Mosaic is distinguished by its support for multiple hardware platforms and the advanced features of the WWW HyperText Markup Language (HTML). HTML enables text formatting, embedded pictures, and hypertext links to other documents and different locations within documents. This format enables much more information to be conveyed in a document than the plain text files common in Gopher. HTML is based on the Standard Generalized Markup Language (SGML), which is used in many industries to create documentation in a device-independent format. An SGML document contains the text information along with *tags* that specify character formatting (boldface, underlining, etc.) and layout formatting (document title, section headings, bulleted lists, etc.).

One advantage of Mosaic and its progeny is that they support three major windowing platforms: Apple Macintosh, Microsoft Windows, and the X Window System. By abandoning the least common denominator VT100 platform, Mosaic is able to display all of the advanced formatting features available in WWW HTML documents. The addition of individual character formatting, inline pictures, and so on conveys considerably more information than just text files and hierarchical lists of information. With Mosaic, chapter titles can be highlighted in bold, lists of items can be identified by markers, and one can even view a map of a museum and then click on a room to see the exhibits in that room.

Mosaic and its descendants have some useful features that are common among each platform-specific version. One is support for annotations to documents. As a document is browsed, it can be annotated for future reference. The annotations appear at the bottom of the document and can be viewed and edited along with the original document. Future versions of these WWW browsers will allow annotations to be shared publicly or within a local group of users. WWW resources can be browsed and the most recent pages saved. This caching process makes backtracking much faster (and less costly) than reloading an entire document over the Internet. Finally, the list of documents that have been visited is saved on a *hot list* for rapid future reference.

The Internet as a Business Tool

An understanding of the Internet and the technologies that drive it provides a springboard for making productive business use of this increasingly popular communications network. Why would an organization want to get involved with the Internet, how can businesses use it productively, and what future developments and issues need to be addressed on the road to full commercial utilization of the Internet? In this section we consider these factors.

Why Get Involved?

The most fundamental reason to get commercially involved on the Internet is its rapid growth and the resulting customer markets. Other reasons include efficient interactive communication with large groups of people and the ability to provide timely customer support with limited effort.

The statistics relating to the Internet are phenomenal. Most demonstrate exponential growth, as shown in Figures 3–9 through 3–14. The number of Internet users is growing between 10 and 15 percent per month, with the business sector being the fastest-growing segment. These and other figures are available directly from the Internet and are constantly updated. For example, Figures 3–9, 3–10, and 3–11 show the growth in the number of interconnected networks, Internet hosts, and Internet domains, respectively. Figure 3–12 indicates the projected number of users of the Internet to be 100 million by the end of this decade.[1]

The largest growth segment of the Internet is the business sector. Based on statistics gathered by the National Science Foundation (NSF), commercial addresses comprise 51 percent of Internet network registrations. This percentage does not

_____

1. *The Internet Unleashed* (Indianapolis: Sams Publishing, 1994), pp. 23, 725–27.

FIGURE 3–9

Growth rate of interconnected networks, 1988–95

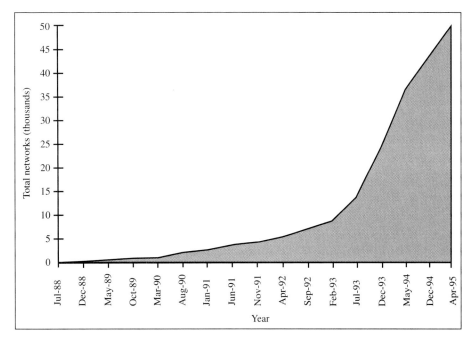

FIGURE 3–10

Growth rate of interconnected hosts 1987–95

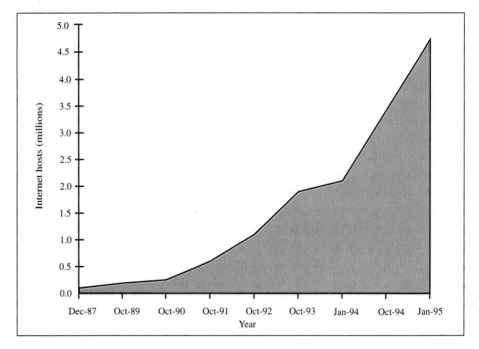

FIGURE 3–11

Growth rate of interconnected domains 1988–95

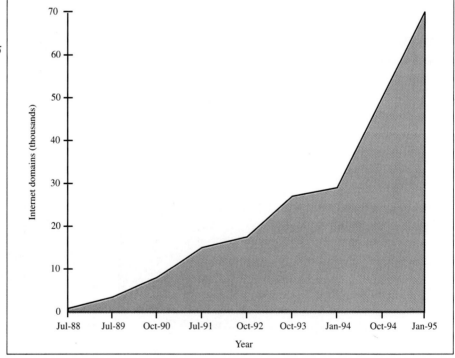

include companies that registered under some research-related functions. In contrast, defense is 7 percent, government is 9 percent, and education is just 4 percent, as shown in Figure 3–13.

FIGURE 3–12

Growth rate of Internet users (projected to year 2000)

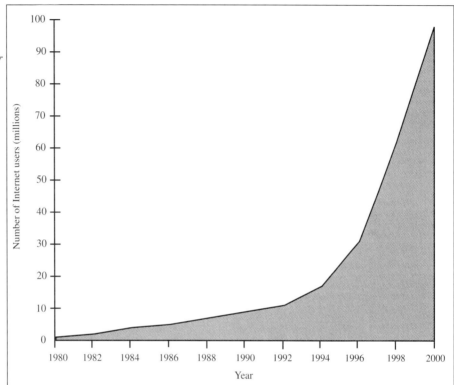

FIGURE 3–13

Distribution of industry categories by registration address

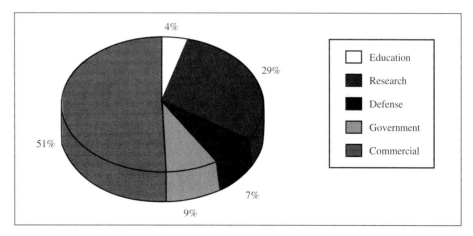

Similarly Figure 3–14 shows the distribution of Internet users by their top-level domain name—commercial (.com—42 percent), education (.edu—39 percent), government (.gov—8 percent), defense (.mil—6 percent), organizations (.org—3 percent), and networks (.net—2 percent). Clearly there is some overlap among these groupings. The *organizations* grouping is intended to include nonprofit groups such as the Internet Engineering Task Force (IETF), the Network Management Forum (NMF), the Desktop Management Task Force (DMTF), and the International Standards Organization (ISO). The *networks* grouping includes nonprofit network operators such as the International Airline Transport Association (IATA), the Society for Worldwide International Funds Transfer (SWIFT), and Usenet News Groups.

The Internet provides an environment for efficient interactive communication with large groups of potential customers. Easy-to-use WWW browsers require very little learning, yet allow the user to view advertising, read technical literature, give opinions on future releases, and order products. All of this can be provided with the most current information the organization has available. Compared to many of the alternatives, the Internet provides high leverage at low cost. Consider the cost of mailing tens of thousands of pieces of marketing literature to potential customers versus the cost of maintaining a home page on the World Wide Web. The Internet provides interactivity that the paper media do not. The Internet provides a capacity for information depth that the paper media can duplicate only at great cost in bulk paper and postage. Admittedly, the Internet version is available only to those who have an Internet connection and those who choose to look at the particular organization's home page, but the benefits to this group are great, and the number who meet this criteria is growing dramatically.

The above benefits apply in even greater measure to support of existing customers. Existing customers have a greater reason to contact the organization, and allowing them to make that contact as effectively and efficiently as possible is in the organization's best interest. The ability to provide the most up-to-date catalog of new products and prices, technical data, and fixes for known product defects allows customers to be better served without the high costs of toll calls, staff time, and unhappy customers.

FIGURE 3–14

Distribution of Internet users by top-level domain name

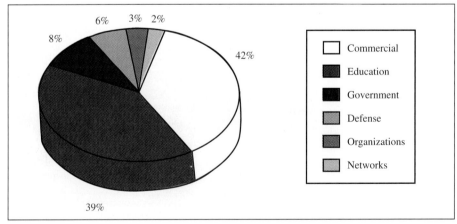

Business Applications on the Internet

Businesses of all types and sizes have found that the Internet can serve many of their needs, including marketing, customer and vendor support, exchange of information, and joint ventures for research and development. With the aid of the Internet, companies can also develop new products, take orders, receive electronic publications and documents, and retrieve data from specialty databases. Businesses can find technical advice, create and maintain business relationships, obtain market intelligence, search out good deals, locate people with needed skills, and even provide products directly. The possibilities are limited only by your imagination! Rapid development of new services means that full electronic commerce is quickly coming to the Internet. Order taking, order verification, invoicing, and electronic funds payments are becoming a reality for both large and small businesses. These advances offer great prospects for breaking the bottleneck that has hindered many companies from moving to EDI.

The following benefits may accrue from the commercial use of the Internet:

- Global communications. *AT+T*
- Corporate logistics.
- Competitive advantage.
- Information resources.
- Customer feedback and support.
- Marketing. *Coca-Cola*
- Collaboration and development.
- Vendor support and networking.

Internet's Acceptable Use Policy (AUP) currently prohibits unsolicited advertisements, but it does permit information-rich, value-added approaches to marketing. Although currently most marketing information is text-based, this is changing rapidly with use of the new tools. Internet marketing concentrates on providing valuable information and services as part of efforts to sell products and services. By creating an information service, businesses can very successfully market their products and services without contravening the AUP. In addition, with the development of full electronic catalogs, online ordering, and other basic business functions, interpretations of the AUP are becoming increasingly liberal. However, businesses venturing on the Internet are cautioned to follow the "rules of the road," and there is still no substitute for courtesy and quality service in building a business reputation.

Exploiting opportunities for information exchange and interaction is the key to creating a successful business presence on the Internet. The Internet offers several models for marketing, including Yellow Pages, billboard, and virtual storefront.

- *Yellow Pages*—As with the paper version of the Yellow Pages, you can participate in various ways, including FTP archives, Gopher server, Bulletin Board Service, Usenet News, WWW, WAIS, and E-mail.
- *Billboard*— includes Finger and Plan, Signature blocks (user information that appears at the end of a message), and E-mail. Finger allows you to find

out information about a local or remote user, such as whether the user has an E-mail account, is logged in, and so on. Plan permits you to make useful information available along with Finger.

- *Virtual storefront*—Combines some of the activities from both the Yellow Pages and billboard approach, but goes further by including the capability to deliver actual products and take orders.

A wide range of organizations from small to large have set up a presence on the Internet, most recently using WWW home pages as the presentation medium. Naturally, they include many computer technology firms, such as Microsoft (*http://www.microsoft.com*), Compaq (*http://www.compaq.com*), and Dell (*http://www.us.dell.com*).

A Few Commercial Examples

A description of a few direct business ventures on the Internet would be a valuable signpost on the road to the National Information Infrastructure (NII). We will focus on virtual storefront applications involving smaller specialty businesses (the big ones get enough advertising as it is!), since these incorporate a full range of other Internet services. We will look at three applications: a specialty garden furniture store, a virtual CD store, and a 21st-century wine merchant.

Using Mosaic, Netscape, or some other WWW browser, you can go shopping at any one of these "stores."

Example 1. How about looking for that special piece of teak garden furniture you have been promising yourself? Fire up your browser and enter this WWW site address:

http://www.spinners.com/garden/welcome.html

Welcome to the Garden Cottage! Browse through the catalog of beautiful teak garden furniture or other lovely items to grace your garden. The catalog includes full-color pictures of the various items, pricing, and delivery options. The folks at the Garden Cottage are very obliging; you can even order the furniture online. However, they do like to give a personal touch, so you must include your phone number and they will phone you back, verify your order, and receive your payment details (credit card number, expiration date, etc.).

Example 2. Next, you will order your favorite music at the local Internet CD shop. Enter this address:

http://cdnow.com:80

You now have been transported into the CD-Now virtual storefront, where you can browse through over 140,000 CDs, cassettes, and videos from classical or country to the latest rock titles. The initial home page presents basic information about the organization, the latest picks, and a button to take you straight into the store, where you can browse by musical category. This organization lets you order online using your credit card (just as you would with a phone order) and will ship your music selections anywhere in the world!

Example 3. The next stop is the 21st-Century wine shop. Enter the address:

http://www.virtualvin.com/

If you are a wine connoisseur and are having trouble locating a favorite vintage, here is the store for you! Run by one of the foremost wine experts in the United States, the store lets you search for that special vintage and order it by the bottle or the case; or you can order a sampler case with a range of wines to suit your taste. You can select from a wide range of wines and vineyards at special prices and view expert opinions on the wines. This virtual storefront not only will allow you to order online but will accept payment by credit card or Cybercash (an Internet form of payment that is still in the experimental stage). It is a secure site, using encryption and other features to secure your financial transactions.

As you can see, the potential for both large and small firms in manufacturing, retailing, wholesale, and service industries is unlimited. But is the Internet really ready for all that traffic? The next section addresses this issue.

Operation and Performance

The potential uses for the technology represented by the Internet are exciting, but the commercial applications are in the early stages of growth and a number of issues must be resolved before full utilization can become a reality. The Internet is a major new highway that is still under construction and as such is experiencing many traffic and security problems.

When you go browsing on the WWW, you will see much evidence of this. You may click on a hypertext link in a home page, only to find that the link has not been activated or that the document or home page to which it points is no longer available. Despite the increasing number of high-quality commercial organizations represented that deliver excellent goods and services, other members of the Internet community represent education, research, local clubs, and special-interest groups that are not really interested in the commercial aspects—and they were there first!

Probably the top two issues that concern organizations considering using the Internet for commercial applications are security and speed (or capacity). First, let's consider security. It is possible to "eavesdrop" on the Internet (as it is on the telephone system). For much of the traffic on the Internet, this is not really a problem. However, for financial transactions, passwords, and some commercially sensitive information, it is a very real concern. When you go into a "physical" shop and purchase something, personnel can see you, examine your credit card, check, or cash, verify your signature, and get your address and phone number. All of these procedures verify your identity and trustworthiness. However, given the level of anonymity provided by the Internet, identity becomes a serious issue. A number of technologies are being developed to provide a method of ID verification as well as protection of sensitive data, including electronic signatures and other forms of user authentication, encryption of user IDs, passwords, and data. Standards for Internet security are still being developed, but are rapidly being agreed upon and finding their way into user applications. Other security issues involving users who attempt to "break into" your electronic organization using the Internet are covered in the next section.

The second major issue for commercial users is Internet capacity and speed. With the exponential growth in Internet use described earlier in the chapter, the industry is encountering the traditional "freeway effect." As the highway is developed, more and more people see the potential and then want to use it themselves. The result is a dramatic increase in traffic, particularly during "rush hour." Adding additional carrying capacity takes time, and there never seems to be enough. A compounding factor is that multimedia has come of age, and everyone wants to use it on the Internet. Naturally, video and sound clips, graphic images, and other media put far more pressure on the system than do simple text documents. Hope is in sight, however. The National Science Foundation (NSF), the U.S. government-funded keeper of the Internet backbone, has been negotiating with a consortium of telecommunications providers, including the Baby Bells and cable TV providers, to make their excess capacity available to the Internet. The success or failure of this negotiation will be a major turning point for the development of the Internet. If the negotiation succeeds, the existing Internet will take a leap forward in carrying capacity and become the direct forerunner of the NII. If the negotiation fails, we can expect to see many competing organizations and consortiums vying to become leading NII contenders.

Future developments of the Internet (or NII) will include applications of full electronic commerce, electronic publishing, and myriad other applications. Full electronic commerce in a business-to-business setting will mean the ability to place orders, verify stock levels, invoice, and pay for products and services completely by electronic means, saving much effort, time, and paper. Finding the closest or lowest-priced supplier will become far easier and thus give a tremendous boost to free enterprise and competitive markets on an international basis. For individuals it will open up whole new methods of education, shopping, meeting people, and entertainment, including such services as interactive video and video-on-demand applications. Electronic publishing is likely to become a wide-scale reality in a very short time. Already some magazines and newspapers, as well as many research publications and academic journals, are appearing on the Internet. Two examples are *Time* magazine (*http://www.timeinc.com/time/universe.html*) and the *San Jose Mercury News* (*http://www.sjmercury.com*). Both of these publications are excellent examples of electronic publishing and are searchable. Past issues as well as the most recent issue are available via a WWW browser.

To keep up with these issues and to find out more about the developing field of electronic commerce, the information superhighway, and how to move in this direction, two good Internet/WWW sources are EINet Galaxy (*http://galaxy.einet.net/galaxy.html*) and CommerceNet (*http://www.commerce.net*). These sources represent major research projects funded by the U.S. government to develop the NII. EINet

Galaxy is affiliated with Microelectronic and Computer Technology Corporation (MCC) in Austin, Texas, a research and development consortium. CommerceNet is a similar development in California's Silicon Valley in conjunction with Stanford University.

EINet Galaxy is a comprehensive index of over 100,000 WWW home pages, articles, and resources organized topically. The graphical front end makes it very easy to use. To get to the electronic commerce material, follow this path:

1. After the EINet Galaxy home page comes up, go to the *Business and Commerce* major topic and select (click on) the *Electronic Commerce* item.

2. At the next page, select the *Commercial Use of the Net, Strategies* home page.

3. At the next page, select *Setting up Shop on the Internet.*

Browsing through these various sections will bring you up to speed on the latest developments. To see a list of the "50 most interesting" commercial sites and try them out, use this address:

http://www.rpt.edu/~okeefe/business.html

CommerceNet specifically focuses on research and development of the NII and provides many useful insights on current developments, tests, and technology that are being developed and tested. This WWW site also gives you the opportunity to become directly involved by becoming a "member" of CommerceNet.

Security Issues in the Use of the Internet

In the past, universities and other research organizations have been considerably more tolerant of poor performance than the commercial sector is expected to be, particularly since it pays real dollars for Internet access. This is due partly to the fact that until recently, the primary use of the Internet has been as a research and experimentation tool, and variable performance can naturally be expected. One of the key factors affecting Internet performance as seen by the users is dictated by the capacity of the access links to the interface router and the Internet backbone.

The requirement for multimedia applications is starting to place heavy demands on the Internet backbone links, and it is far from clear who will be responsible for providing adequate backbone capacity. Clearly a great deal of fine-tuning will be necessary to provide businesses with a reliable performance interface to the Internet.

Security was never a key design parameter of the original Internet. Many stories in the literature describe how the Internet was used either directly or indirectly to break into remote hosts.[2] Thus, attention needs to be given to security issues

---

2. Clifford Stoll, "Stalking the Wily Hacker," *Communication of the ACM* 31, No. 5 (1988), pp. 484–89.

at the network interface between the provider and the user. Several options now available include address filtering, access lists, encryption, and emergency disconnection facilities.

Address filtering permits routers to be programmed to control remote logins, file transfers, and other facilities. Another level of protection can be provided by the application layer package, which can operate user/host authentication, organization identification, and IP packet **encryption**. Emergency disconnection can be used to disconnect sites from the Internet in the event that a traveling virus, worm, or security breach in routers is detected.

An adequate level of security can be achieved by combining knowledge of computer security issues, the security features that a vendor can provide, public domain security software, and adequate user education. Figure 3–15 shows the relationship among various security devices in terms of cost and value. Some of these devices are discussed next.

Router Filtering

One of the simplest protection methods is to ensure that the boundary router or hub supports filtering that permits the specification of who can perform outbound remote logins or inbound file transfers. These routers are often called **screening routers**. Most of the popular routers support packet filtering at a host level, network level, and service (protocol) level. Each information packet carries a description of the source, destination, and service type (login, mail, etc.), which enables routers to selectively filter out unwanted data.

Routers can be configured to prohibit traffic going from the Internet to an internal host or internal subnet. Routers can also be configured to prohibit traffic that participates in dangerous services such as TFTP (Trivial File Transfer Protocol without passwords) and remote printing.

Filters can be set up to allow E-mail to reach only one host on the local area network. From there the specified host can distribute the mail internally, thus reducing the number of hosts that have E-mail contact with the Internet. The famous Internet worm exploited a bug in *sendmail* and used it to gain access to many hosts throughout the Internet.

FIGURE 3–15

Possible security devices for use on the Internet

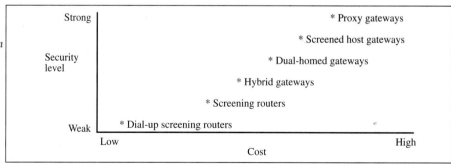

Firewalls and Bastion Hosts

Firewalls are a compromise between ease of use and security. The local network that is available to the Internet can be considered the *zone of risk*. Without a firewall, the entire local network becomes a zone of risk. A firewall reduces the zone of risk by defining a smaller area that is accessible to the Internet. By defining such a smaller zone of risk, the areas that need to be covered to detect an Internet intruder can be reduced. There are many configurations of firewalls using various components.

Two basic approaches exist: Either a firewall can be designed to prohibit any service that is not explicitly permitted or the firewall can permit access to all services except those expressly prohibited.

The **bastion host** is a practical implementation of a firewall that can provide many Internet services such as E-mail, FTP, and Gopher services. The bastion host usually receives extra security attention and is monitored more frequently than other network hosts and is often called a **proxy gateway** or *application-level gateway*. The bastion host runs software programs that act as forwarders for services such as E-mail or Usenet news. The services can also be interactive, such as FTP or Telnet. For example, Digital Equipment Corporation (DEC) operates bastion hosts that act as proxy gateways for FTP and Telnet. These hosts filter the FTP and Telnet packets transparently to the user between the Internet and the private DEC network. A bastion host may be connected to the Internet but accessible only to the local private network using protocols other than TCP/IP, such as with proprietary IBM/SNA or DECnet networks. An example of this appears in Figure 3–16 where the internal network users must Telnet to the terminal server and log into the bastion host before using the Internet. In the other direction, Internet users can log only into the bastion host and cannot access the private network.

These types of bastion hosts are also called **hybrid gateways** because they use a combination of protocols to limit Internet access to the private network. Access to the hybrid gateway can be made through serial lines or **IP tunneling**. A terminal server can be used to gain serial access to the hybrid gateway and then on to the Internet.

IP tunneling takes the Internet IP packet and encloses it in another protocol such as SNA or X.25. One example of a corporate firewall that uses a hybrid design is AT&T's connection to the Internet. This design prevented the famous Internet worm from infecting any of the AT&T computers during the 1988 Internet worm crisis.

Another example of a bastion host implementation is to install two network boards in the computer. One is connected to the Internet and the other to the private network. This approach is known as a **dual-homed gateway**. Yet another example uses the combination of a screening router and a bastion host to provide a *screened host gateway*. All of these devices are included in Figure 3–15.

A number of programs are available to enhance security on the Internet; some are in the public domain, and others are proprietary in nature. These are designed mostly for TCP/IP UNIX-based systems, but other system types are covered as well.

FIGURE 3–16

Bastion host used to provide firewall between Internet and private network

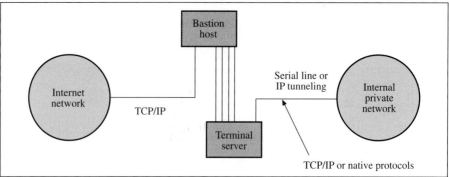

Security is undergoing rapid change. You may keep up with this critical area by reading on the Internet under topics such as "Internet Security" and "Electronic Commerce." Reading from EINet Galaxy and CommerceNet (see the WWW addresses on page 114) will provide excellent information on this topic.

Application Layer Security

Another layer of protection can be incorporated into the application layer package. This method can offer user authentication, origination, identification, and encryption. The user can set up such software to monitor incoming access and allow entry only to a predefined list of users or hosts, as well as provide encryption if required. The system also traces calls back to the originating system, preventing illegal users from logging into a system with another computer's privileges.

Summary

The demand for access to the Internet is growing at a phenomenal rate, and the range of tools associated with the use of the Internet is changing extremely rapidly. Much of this activity centers around the use of the World Wide Web (WWW). Many new web servers with their home pages are being added to the Internet daily. A considerable amount of software is available on the Internet itself, although the commercial products are usually superior and ongoing development and support are provided. The next few years will see the Internet grow in significance as a strategic resource for many sectors of our society. This chapter looked at how to gain access to the Internet through commercial providers. The services and facilities covered included FTP, Telnet, Archie, Gopher, WAIS, the World Wide Web, and WWW browsers such as Mosaic and Netscape. These facilities enable the user to access the Internet, locate information, communicate with other users, and navigate the ocean of information available.

The chapter also covered various aspects of commercial applications of the Internet. Due to the rapid increase in Internet users, this burgeoning marketplace offers vast marketing and commercial potential. Learning the ropes early to become well positioned as the NII develops is an important strategic issue for many firms. The chapter looked at a number of businesses that currently use the Internet, including their addresses so that readers can try it for themselves.

Because the Internet and the NII are still under construction, a number of issues with commercial implications are still being resolved. The two most important issues are security and the ability of the system to carry the potential communication load. These issues were discussed briefly, and a number of Internet/WWW addresses were provided to help readers keep up-to-date with these important developments.

The final section of the chapter covered issues of security and performance. Given the dramatic increase in Internet users and new demands being placed on the system by multimedia applications, performance is a serious concern for many users, especially for commercial users whose businesses may depend on Internet performance and reliability. The chapter concluded by discussing the alternatives and technology that are now available to provide secure access to the Internet.

Key Terms

Acceptable Use Policy (AUP) 92

Archie 99

Bastion host 117

Client/server 92

Connection-oriented 96

Connectionless 95

Dual-homed gateway 117

Encryption 116

Firewalls 117

File transfer protocol (FTP) 98

Gopher 100

Gopher client 100

Gopher server 100

Home page 104

Hybrid gateways 117

IP tunneling 117

Mosaic 104

National Information Infrastructure (NII) 92

Netscape 104

Proxy gateway 117

Screening routers 116

Telnet 99

Transmission Control Protocol/Internet Protocol (TCP/IP) 95

Wide area information server (WAIS) 101

World Wide Web (WWW) 102

WWW browser 104

Questions for Discussion

1. Describe what the Internet is and differentiate it from the National Information Infrastructure (NII).

2. How has a more liberal interpretation of the Internet Acceptable Use Policy (AUP) helped in commercializing the Internet?

3. Identify the four layers of the TCP/IP protocol, and compare this protocol to the OSI seven-layer communication model (Figure 4–17). How does the TCP/IP protocol help Internet provide almost universal connectivity among diverse networks?

4. Discuss how you could gain access to the Internet (*a*) if you work for a large business with an internal LAN and (*b*) if you run an office from home and want to connect to the Internet from there.

5. What Internet application would you use to run a program on a remote host computer?

6. Compare the Internet applications Gopher, FTP, and Archie. How do they differ, how do they complement one another?

7. Describe the function of the wide area information server (WAIS) software? How does it fit in with FTP, Gopher, and Archie?

8. How does the World Wide Web (WWW) relate to the Internet?

9. How do WWW browsers differ from other Internet tools, such as FTP or Gopher?

10. Discuss the implications of the rapid growth of the Internet for commercial markets.

11. List a number of key ways a commercial firm could establish a presence on the Internet, and describe the benefits that might accrue as a result.

12. Describe the two primary factors putting pressure on the Internet's carrying capacity.

13. Discuss the key security issues affecting commercial firms that are considering doing business on the Internet.

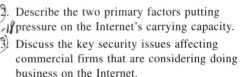

Case Discussion and Analysis

1. Reread the Thompson Refrigeration Company (TRC) case on page 93. Analyze the case to determine the Internet-related software applications that Jack Thompson used and the business benefits that he gained from accessing the Internet. Discuss the results of your analysis in light of the implications that the Internet has for TRC customer support and future growth. How do the security and Internet carrying capacity issues discussed in the chapter influence your views on TRC's commercial use of the Internet?

2. Levon Diamond Merchants Inc. is a wholesaler of fine gemstones to the retail jewelry trade. Levon creates a full-color catalog of the stones it has available and mails this catalog to hundreds of jewelry stores throughout its region four times a year. The company has always been praised for the quality of its catalog and of its stones. However, the catalog becomes increasingly out-of-date prior to publication of the next catalog, and retailers become dependent on using the phone and fax to determine whether the stones they need are available before actually placing orders. This has become such a problem for Levon that it is considering technological solutions. You have been hired as an IT consultant to advise Levon on potential solutions. What questions would you ask Levon's owner and staff to determine whether an Internet application might be suitable? What types of Internet solutions could benefit Levon given its situation?

WIDE AREA NETWORKS (WANS): PRINCIPLES AND COMPONENTS

Chapter Outline

Introduction   122

Major Functions of Wide Area
    Networks   123

Communication Channels and Media
    124

Network Components   129

Wide Area Network Environments
    140

Standards Used in Wide Area
    Networking   151

Wide Area Network Topologies   157

Integration of Wide Area Network
    Types   161

Cost of Acquiring and Using WANs
    162

Learning Objectives

By the end of chapter 4, you should be able to

1. *Identify* the important functions of a WAN in the business environment.
2. *Describe* the main transmission media used in data networks.
3. *Explain* the primary components of WANs and their software requirements.
4. *Discuss* the five main types of WANs used by telecommunications companies.
5. *Identify* the primary WAN industry standards.
6. *Analyze* the key WAN topologies and relate particular topologies to specific performance and operational requirements.
7. *Describe* how specific business requirements can be solved with a combination of the five main types of WANs.
8. *Analyze* cost factors associated with WANs.

Introduction

In Chapter 2 we examined some of the business applications that make use of networks, but did not look at the network technology that supports these applications. The topic of network components and equipment is a very technical one, so we have simplified some of the discussion. In this chapter, we present only the information that is needed from a manager's point of view. By the end of this chapter, you will be in a position to specify what equipment would be required for some of the applications discussed in Chapter 2. For example, you will be able to specify what a bank requires to provide online financial services in a variety of locations or what a marketing organization needs to implement a telemarketing application.

In general, this chapter looks at the equipment required to form a wide area network, together with the interconnecting links. These days it is unlikely that individual businesses will buy and install their own wide area network (this is not true of local area networks, which are covered in Chapter 5). Because of the highly specialized and technical nature of modern wide area networks, it is usually more appropriate to rent or lease the equipment and services from the network operators—usually the local telecommunications company—since they have the infrastructure to provide such expertise. In most countries, telecommunications is deregulated and a choice of network service providers is commonly available.

The distinction between a local and a wide area application, and therefore what constitutes appropriate equipment, is not always clear. As we will see in this and the following chapters, an integration of both local and wide area networks is becoming very common, and sometimes the distinction disappears entirely.

Although one may rent or lease wide area network services from a telecommunications company or some other network service provider, it is still necessary to understand the types of networks available, when to use them, their costs, and their advantages and disadvantages. When a service provider recommends that you lease $100,000 worth of packet switching equipment along with **Packet Assembler-Disassemblers (PADs)**, **multiplexers**, **concentrators**, **bridges**, and **routers**, you need to understand the functions of this equipment and why it is recommended rather than a different range of equipment and services.

Another complicating factor is the rapid change in technology. Equipment available three years ago may now be obsolete, and today there are more cost-effective ways to solve the same problem to maintain a competitive advantage. When carrying out a cost-benefit analysis, it is therefore important to allow an appropriate write-off period for your equipment. Three years is a common time span for much of the equipment we will discuss in this chapter. Alternatively, if you decide to lease services from a service provider, the charges may be based on an even shorter write-off period.

This does not mean you need to dump your network equipment after three years. It simply means that the equipment should not cost you anything in terms of borrowed capital and interest rates. Sometimes maintenance charges can become excessive. In one five-year-old network design recently, a communications processor had a *current* value of $10,000, but the supplier was charging an *annual* maintenance fee of $6,000. This is hardly good economics!

An expanding range of new networks with ever-increasing capacity is becoming available to meet our burgeoning demands, and the way telecommunications companies charge for all this equipment is changing rapidly. This chapter provides enough information for you to understand the basic technologies that support some of the networking applications discussed in Chapter 2. It does not deal with needs analysis, but merely with the supporting technology. Specifically, this chapter covers

- Major functions of wide area networks.
- Communication channels and media.
- Network components.
- Wide area network environments.
- Standards used in wide area networks.
- Wide area network topologies and their performance.
- Integration of wide area network types.
- Costs of acquiring and using wide area networks.

Major Functions of Wide Area Networks

In Chapter 2 we examined marketing, financial, and manufacturing applications of wide area networks, as well as supporting technologies such as EDI and teleconferencing that require the use of a wide area network for satisfactory operation in a distributed environment (within cities, between cities and/or countries). We saw what a wide area network is, but did not delve into the technicalities. Often a wide area network is described as a communications *cloud* that connects people and applications together. In this chapter we examine what this cloud is composed of.

In Chapter 2 we introduced the following relevant points, which we will discuss in more detail in this chapter:

- What is meant by a wide area network?
- Who is likely to provide these networks?
- What is the most widely used network in the world, and what is its function?
- Data networks are required to link computers together.
- Different business applications require networks of different capacities.
- Networks consist of different sizes of "pipes" in the same manner that a city's water system does.
- Some networks can be "public," while others can be "private."

Familiarity with these points will help you understand the functionality of wide area networks.

The most important function of a wide area network is to make the connected parties appear as though they were in the same room so that if the reply took three seconds from a computer in the same room, introducing a gap of 600 miles between the user and the computer should make little difference. Sometimes this goal is achieved and other times it is not, and by the end of this chapter you should understand why.

The next important function of a wide area network is **interface** standardization. One needs to be able to connect one's equipment to the network in a standardized way. For example, telephones commonly have two "male" plugs for connecting to "female" wall sockets. You no doubt have been frustrated by this difference between the European and American telephone standards at times. Further, the procedures for sending data into the network need to be standardized so that the sender and the receiver understand each other. Returning to the telephone analogy, three different types of sound are standardized and we all understand what they mean (a ringing tone, a busy signal, and an overload tone).

Protocols are rules that govern communication over a network. A protocol describes the timing, format content, and error control of messages. Low-level protocols encompass transmission rates, contention, physical interfaces, and data-encoding schemes. High-level protocols cover user-related functions such as file sharing, print spooling, and access to other shared resources. It is often said that there is no shortage of protocols to choose from! No doubt you are familiar with protocol problems in other areas of computing; for instance, a file created on a PC cannot easily be read by an Apple Macintosh.

The next issue is errors in data, security, and integrity. Clearly no network can be considered functional if it lacks in these areas, although they are not necessarily only network issues. The customer's equipment plays an important role in this respect.

As we mentioned in Chapter 2, the cost of moving information across a network should certainly be no more than a fraction of the value of the product. A network that allows users to connect to it in a standard way and exchange information rapidly and efficiently without errors, with security, and at a reasonable cost is a network that functions well.

Communication Channels and Media

In Chapter 2 we saw that a wide area network is used to link different parties together—within a city or between cities or countries. In this section we examine the different links, or *channels,* and discuss the physical media used to transfer the data.

Different applications discussed in Chapter 2 require different capacity links and different media. For example, the link capacity required to send an electronic mail or EDI message is very small compared to the capacity required for a teleconferencing session where full-color images must be transferred. Since the capacity of a link is closely related to its cost (which is not true of local area networks, as we shall see in Chapter 5), it is important to determine the appropriate capacity and medium for the link given the requirements of the particular application.

A channel is a path along which data flow. Frequently many channels simultaneously share the same physical medium, such as twisted pair wire, coaxial cable, fiber optic cable, microwave, or satellite circuit. For example, a single fiber optic cable, when used for voice communication, can support nearly 2,000 channels or simultaneous individual telephone communications. This process of sharing is achieved by the use of a *multiplexer* (discussed later in this chapter).

Bandwidth

The capacity of a communications channel is a measure of its **bandwidth**. A good analogy is a water pipeline. High-capacity water pipes are used to connect key locations with smaller water pipes connecting to the main arteries. Similar principles apply when we connect to networks; we have to ensure that bottlenecks do not occur in getting onto and within the network.

The unit of capacity used in the water pipe example is usually cubic meters per second. For a communications link, two units are used. The first is **hertz, or Hz** (also kilohertz or KHz, megahertz or MHz, gigahertz or GHz), which specifies the capacity or bandwidth of analog communication systems. For example, the bandwidth of a typical telephone circuit is around 3 KHz, and that of a color TV transmission is around 6 MHz. For a digital communications system, the unit used is **bits per second (bps)**. Increments of this unit include Kbps (thousands of bits per second), Mbps (millions of bits per second), Gbps (thousands of millions of bits per second), and Tbps (thousands of Gbps). The letters *K, M, G,* and *T* stand for *kilo, mega, giga,* and *tera,* respectively.

The capacity or bandwidth of communications media permits a very large number of channels to be multiplexed onto a single physical medium, although the bandwidth or transmission rate for each channel must be taken into consideration.

Transmission Speeds

Transmission speeds vary widely and depend on the application. Here are some typical examples:

Dial-up (datel) telephone connection: 2,400 bps, 9,600 bps, 14,400 bps, 28,800 bps, or even higher.

Leased data circuits with telephone wire for common computer applications (analog transmission): 9,600 bps, 14,800 bps, 19,200 bps, and 28,800 bps. (The last is possible only on very-high-quality telephone circuits.)

Leased data circuits for common computer applications (digital transmission): 2,400 bps, 4,800 bps, 9,600 bps, 48,000 bps, 56,000 bps, *n* x 64,000 bps, where *n* can be any value between 1 and 32. (Note that 2,400 bps = 2.4 Kbps, 64,000 bps = 64 Kbps, 10 Mbps = 10,000,000 bps, etc.)

Higher speeds are becoming popular for certain applications:

1.544 Mbps (T1 carrier and a Bell standard) 24 × 64 Kbps channels.

2.048 Mbps (E1 carrier and a CCITT standard) 32 × 64 Kbps channels.

Even higher speeds will be required in future wide area networks that will carry multimedia data. The capacity necessary to support voice and video media storage is vast by present-day standards. Some multimedia workstations currently under trial have 8 Gbytes (8,000 Mbytes) of local hard disk space.

To appreciate the significance of these speeds, consider how long it would take to transmit this book you are now reading, which is about 1.5 million characters (excluding diagrams). Note that 1.5 million characters is equivalent to about 12 million bits.

- At 2.4 Kbps (2,400 bps), it would take about 83 minutes.
- At 64 Kbps (64,000 bps), it would take about three minutes.
- At 2.048 Mbps, it would take about six seconds.

Note that these transmission times are indicative. The actual time taken will be longer due to protocol overhead such as packet control information, which must be transmitted, and also to retries if the transmission is not correctly received.

Twisted Pair Wire

Twisted pair wire is one of the oldest types of communications channel, but it is still commonly used. It was designed primarily for telephone systems, although it is now also widely used in local area networks. Pairs of wires are twisted together to minimize the interference created when adjacent pairs of wires are combined in multipair cables. One weakness of twisted pair wire is its susceptibility to interference and noise, including cross-talk from adjacent wiring. These effects can be minimized with appropriate twisting of the cables as well as by the choice of insulation material. Unshielded twisted pair (UTP) cable can be used at speeds of 100 Mbps in conjunction with the appropriate protocol, and shielded twisted pair (STP) is also used in specific situations. UTP is graded in five categories as follows:

Category 1	Standard telephone wire *Voice braid twisted Pair 56 Kbps*
Category 2	High-quality wide area network cabling used for speeds up to 2 Mbps (e.g., for T1/E1 and ISDN networks) *T/ line 1.544 Mbps*
Category 3	Used for most 10 Mbps local area networks *Ex. Ethernet*
Category 4	Used specifically for IBM token ring networks *16 Mbps*
Category 5	Used for 100 Mbps local area networks

used for WAN connections

7x faster

The last three categories are discussed further in Chapter 5.

The maximum speed of data transmission over this medium for a wide area network is about 28.8 Kbps when used in conjunction with **modems**, although higher speeds are possible when used with data compression and error correction devices. Otherwise, speeds of 2 Mbps are possible in a wide area network. When it is used in a local area network environment together with careful shielding from electrical interference, data transmission rates on the order of 100 Mbps are possible.

Twisted pair wire can be two-wire, four-wire, or six-wire. Telephone systems use a two-wire system. For almost every data application full-duplex or two-way communication is required. This can be achieved by using one pair for sending data and another pair for receiving data (four-pair system). Alternatively, two separate frequency bands are created, one for sending and one for receiving; this is common practice with some modems.

Dial-up (Datel), Switched, and Leased Circuits

Connections can be established between a terminal and a remote computer through the use of a *dial-up* or *datel* telephone call. Such a connection employs a procedure called *circuit switching,* in which a physical data path is established between the two end points. This is exactly how a telephone call operates. Use of such circuit-switched systems is usually very inefficient unless large volumes of data are transferred once the switched data path has been established. Fax transmission is an example of efficient use of such a system. Usually you pay for the length of time the circuit is established and not for the volume of data transferred.

A *leased circuit* works similarly, except that a fixed routing is established and no dialing is necessary. This means that higher speeds are possible and a fixed monthly charge is applied. Such circuits are for the dedicated users who are not part of the telephone system, even though the physical hardware used is frequently the same. Leased circuits can utilize analog (telephone) or digital signaling systems.

Coaxial Cable

A **coaxial cable** consists of a central copper conductor surrounded by an outer cylindrical metal shell or braided mesh of shielding wire. Insulators separate the central conductor from the shell. Coaxial cable offers large bandwidth and the ability to support high data transmission rates with high immunity to electrical interference and few errors. It is widely used in the telephone network to multiplex many calls onto one cable (typically 20,000 multiplexed data paths), particularly long-distance calls, and reduces the need for thousands of individual wires.

Coaxial cable is also used extensively by the CATV community antenna TV (better known as cable TV) industry, since it has the capacity to carry many television channels at once. Television channels require a high amount of bandwidth, typically 6 MHz (megahertz) for color TV signals. Coaxial cables usually have a single central conductor (coaxial) or twin central conductors (twin-axial, as used with some older IBM equipment).

This widespread use makes coaxial cable moderate in cost and readily available. In addition, the technology for installation, connection, and transmission control on coaxial cable is well developed. A variety of taps, controllers, splitters, couplers, and repeaters are available that allow the cable to be extended and branched to reach locations for connection of user devices.

Optical Fiber Cable

Fiber optic cables are made of plastic or glass and can serve as a very-high-performance transmission medium for many modern distributed applications. It has a higher potential capacity than coaxial cable and offers a number of advantages over both coaxial cable and twisted pair wire, including light weight, small diameter, low noise susceptibility, and practically no emissions. It has the following characteristics:

- Currently available fibers have usable bandwidths ranging from up to 10 Gbps over 100 kilometers to 10,000 Gbps over a few meters.
- Error rates are very low (one bit error per 10^9 bits); thus, most error detection and retransmission overhead can be eliminated.
- Fiber optic transmissions are not affected by electrical or electromagnetic interference and do not emit noise, making them inherently secure.
- Optical fibers are very small and light (since they are manufactured from plastic or glass), allowing space and weight savings.

In fiber optic communications, electrical signals are translated into light pulses by a modulator, transmitted over the fiber by a light source, and detected and converted back into electrical signals by photoelectric diodes.

Fibers are rated on a "graded index" scale that represents the degree of loss and relative bandwidth. Single or monomode fibers are now available with 10 to 20 times the bandwidth of multimode fibers, although they require laser diodes rather than light-emitting diodes (LEDs) as the light source. This allows substantially increased repeater spacing, up to 100 km. Fibers are specified by their size (inside and outside diameter in microns), as shown in Figure 4–1.

Fiber optic cable is now being widely used as manufacturing costs for both the cable and interfaces come down. Multipoint topologies such as the bus and the tree (discussed later in this chapter) are difficult to implement with optical fiber, because each tap imposes large power losses and causes optical reflections.

Microwave and Satellite Systems

A *microwave system* is a high-capacity facility that provides line-of-sight radio communications. Because the curvature of the earth limits the distance over which one can communicate, line-of-sight, repeater stations are installed approximately every 25 miles along the route.

FIGURE 4–1

Fiber sizes and bandwidth

Size	Numerical Aperture	Minimum Bandwidth (MHz.km)	Maximum Bandwidth (MHz.km)
50/125*	0.21	400	1000
62.5/125†	0.275	100	500
100/140	0.29	100	300

* This is an older fiber optic cable that is little used now.
† Probably 90 percent of the market uses this type (85/125 is also available).

The quality of transmission varies with the type of medium and the distance involved. Twisted pair wire provide quality communications over short distances, whereas coaxial cable, fiber optic cable, and microwave systems can provide high-capacity, high-quality communications over longer distances.

The advantage of satellite communications is that the satellite can provide very wide coverage on the ground, and, within the field of view of the satellite, you can set up an earth station and immediately get very high quality communications. This is of great value to developing countries and in areas that involve long terrestrial distances. Nevertheless, satellite systems suffer from an inherent disadvantage: A propagation delay of about 540 msec for the round trip, something familiar to all of us on long-distance calls where satellites are used. This is a particular disadvantage for time-dependent computer applications and is one reason so much effort is being made to provide fiber optic links around the world. Multiple satellite links can rapidly erode a user's response time.

Summary

Following is a summary of the key points relating to the communication channels and media discussed:

- Wide area networks can operate at a range of speeds that are closely linked to the costs of using them.
- Twisted pair wire still forms the basis of many networks, including parts of the telephone network.
- Dial-up, switched, and leased circuits represent ways to interconnect to the telephone network for data transmission.
- Coaxial cable allows for higher data transmission speeds and better immunity from noise than does twisted pair wire. Usually many applications share the use of this resource.
- Fiber optic cable is the latest technology in high-speed communication, allowing massive amounts of data to be transmitted very rapidly.
- Microwave and satellite systems are appropriate for situations where the positioning of fiber optic cable is not possible.

Figure 4–2 summarizes the key issues surrounding the different types of transmission media used in networks. Note that these transmission media apply equally to local area and wide area networks, which you should keep in mind when you read Chapter 5.

Network Components

In Chapter 2 we discussed marketing, financial, and manufacturing applications that require the use of a wide area network. In the previous section we discussed the links required to interconnect these systems. Now we discuss the equipment that inter-

FIGURE 4–2

Technical features and key characteristics of different transmission media

Medium	Signalling Technique	Maximum Data Rate	Maximum Range	Advantages	Disadvantages
Twisted pair (UTP & STP)	Digital	2 Mbps 100 Mbps	Few miles 300 feet	Widely used Cheap Inexpensive interfaces	Insecure
Coaxial (thick and thin)	Digital	10 Mbps	Few miles	Cheap Can attach multiple devices	Becoming superseded by fiber
Optical fiber	Modulated light	10 Gbps 10,000 Gbps	100 miles Few feet	Light High capacity Secure Immune from electrical interference	Interface equipment expensive
Microwave/ satellite	Wave modulation	Many Gbps	Up to 100 miles (microwave) Up to 5,000 miles (satellite)	Very high capacity	Very expensive

faces, or connects, the user's workstation or other equipment to the data communication links discussed in the previous section. This equipment varies depending on the type of transmission media used and the user equipment to which it is to be connected. This section also describes equipment that allows for the *sharing* of these transmission media among different users and applications, similar to the way many users share the use of telephone network equipment and interconnecting links.

When data are transmitted, there must be a means of interconnecting the transmitting and receiving devices with the transmission system. The choice of these devices depends heavily on the nature and purpose of the communication. Only devices used in the applications covered in Chapter 2 are covered here. These include devices needed to

- Interface to different types of networks. The necessary equipment includes the modem and the network terminating unit.
- Share the use of telecommunication resources. The required equipment includes multiplexers, concentrators, and PADs as well as the software used to operate these devices.

Modems

The Public Switched Telephone Network (PSTN) was designed to carry the human voice—**analog signals** in the frequency range of 300 to 3300 Hz—and such a system is not the best medium for data transmission. In most countries digital data networks (DDN) are now replacing the PSTN for data transmission. In fact, the DDN is now used to transmit both traditional data and digitized voice communication. Being a digital network, the DDN provides a much better service than do telephone networks, offering higher speeds, less interference through noise, and network management facilities. However, widespread use of the telephone network for data transmission continues, especially in the part of the network connecting the user's premises to the nearest switching exchange.

A modem takes the computer's **digital signals** and modulates them onto a carrier wave. A *carrier* is a wave that has a frequency much higher than the frequency of the digital signals. The modulated waveform is a smooth sine wave and can be transmitted over long distances without distortion. The process of modulating and demodulating the digital data is performed by a modem (*modem* is a contraction of *modulator/demodulator*). The analog communication link between the modems can be either two-wire (usually for **half-duplex** or take-it-in-turns communication) or **four-wire** (usually for **full-duplex** or simultaneous communication by both parties), as shown in Figure 4–3. Another term used occasionally is **simplex**, which implies that messages can be sent or received in one direction only, such as data being sent to a printer.

Modems are used in pairs, and a typical sequence of events is as follows:

1. Digital data from the source are modulated with the carrier signal by modem A.
2. Analog transmission to modem B.
3. Demodulation of the signal by modem B.
4. Digital transmission to the receiver.

To avoid incompatibility problems, some standardized interface specifications have been produced for connection of modems to end-user equipment. The most important specification is the CCITT (**Consultative Committee of the Institute of**

✕FIGURE 4–3

Simplex, half-duplex, and full-duplex transmission

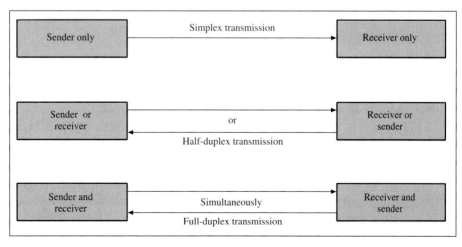

Telegraph and Telephone) V.24 or RS-232 interface specification. The CCITT (see pp. 154–6) has a series of recommendations with the prefix V that relate to data transmission over the public telephone network. (In the United States, the relevant body is the Electronic Industries Association (EIA); hence the equivalent of V.24 is RS-232). Modems are available in a variety of standard speeds—9,600 bps, 14,400 bps, 19,200 bps, 28,800 bps, or higher.

Following is a summary of the CCITT standard modems that can be used on telephone circuits:

Standard	Speed	Transmission
CCITT V.21	300	Full-duplex
CCITT V.22	1,200 or 600 bps	Full-duplex
CCITT V.22bis	2,400 or 1,200 bps	Full-duplex
CCITT V.23	1,200 or 600 bps	Half-duplex
CCITT V.26bis	2,400 or 1,200 bps	Half-duplex
CCITT V.26ter	2,400 or 1,200 bps	Full-duplex
CCITT V.27ter	4,800 or 2,400 bps	Half-duplex
CCITT V.32	9,600 or 4,800 bps	Full-duplex
CCITT V.32bis	14.4 Kbps	Full-duplex
CCITT V.33	14.4 Kbps	Full-duplex
CCITT V.34 (V.fast)	Up to 28.8 Kbps	Full-duplex
CCITT V.42*	Up to 38.4 Kbps	Full-duplex
CCITT V.42bis*	Up to 38.4 Kbps	Full-duplex

* These are recent modems that have the ability to correct errors (V.42) and compress data (V.42bis) for high-speed transmission.

Network Terminating Units (NTUs)

A network terminating unit (NTU) can be thought of as a "digital modem," even though it does not function like a modem. Different names are used in different countries for this device, although the term NTU is most common. Other terms are **channel service unit (CSU)** and **data service unit (DSU)**. The NTU is the interface between the data communications channel and the user's equipment as the modem is an interface between the PSTN and the user's equipment. The NTU takes one or more digital data streams and codes them for data transmission through the digital network. The coding technique commonly used is called *pulse code modulation (PCM)*.

The NTU can operate at speeds of from 2,400 bps to 2.048 Mbps (or higher in certain circumstances). It has a microprocessor that communicates directly with the digital data network (DDN) management system; hence, the signal quality is under constant surveillance. Further, within defined limits, the speed of the NTU can be changed by a command from the network management system. No physical device swapping is usually necessary to change speeds as is the case with modems.

Multiplexers

A *multiplexer* (often called a *mux*) is a device that is used to share communications circuits among a number of users. For example, a number of computer terminals used for telemarketing can be connected to a multiplexer. The multiplexer combines the data signals from two or more lower-speed circuits into a single data stream for transmission over a higher-speed circuit at the transmitting terminal and divides the single higher-speed circuit into the same number of lower-speed circuits at the receiving terminal (see Figure 4–4).

There are three basic methods of multiplexing:

- Time division multiplexing (TDM).
- Frequency division multiplexing (FDM).
- Statistical time division multiplexing (STDM).

In time division multiplexing (see Figure 4–5), the communications link is allocated to different users on a time-slice basis, whereas in frequency division multiplexing, each user gets a continuous share of only part of the bandwidth. Each method has advantages and disadvantages, but the main problem with either system is that when a user is not transmitting—the time slice in the case of time division multiplexing or bandwidth in the case of frequency division multiplexing—the capacity of the communications link is wasted.

Both of these multiplexing techniques have given way to a system called *statistical time division multiplexing (STDM)* (see Figure 4–6). STDM dynamically allocates the time slots (i.e., the bandwidth) among active devices; thus, dedicated subchannels (frequency division multiplexing) and dedicated time slots (time division multiplexing) are not provided for each port. As a result, idle device time does not waste the capacity of the link. Links using STDMs can often accommodate two to five times more traffic.

FIGURE 4–4

Multiplexing

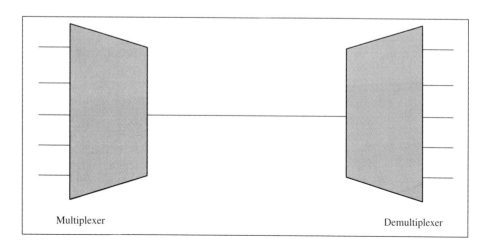

Multiplexer   Demultiplexer

FIGURE 4–5

*Time division
multiplexing
(TDM)*

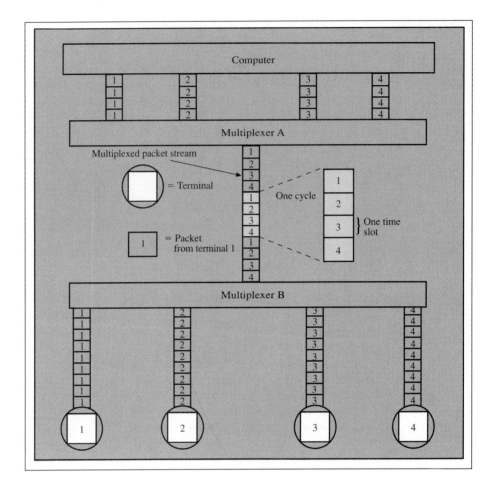

The data transmission rate of the output of STDM is less than the sum of the data transmission rates of the inputs. This results from the necessity for a small header to be associated with each block of data, which is required to specify the address of the transmitting device. In TDM each block of data lies in a specified position, but this is not the case with STDM (see Figure 4–6). The average amount of input is anticipated to be less than the capacity of the multiplexed link. The difficulty with this approach is that while the average aggregate input may be less than the multiplexed link capacity, there may be peak periods when the input exceeds capacity. The solution to this problem is to include a buffer in the multiplexer to hold temporary excess input or to control the flow of data so that it does not leave the workstation or computer. Either approach has a negative impact on performance.

Despite its shortcomings, TDM has recently become popular again. With the move to multimedia communication, time-sensitive data, such as data associated with voice and video applications, require that a constant bandwidth be available to

FIGURE 4–6

Standard time division multiplexing (TDM) compared with statistical time division multiplexing (STDM)

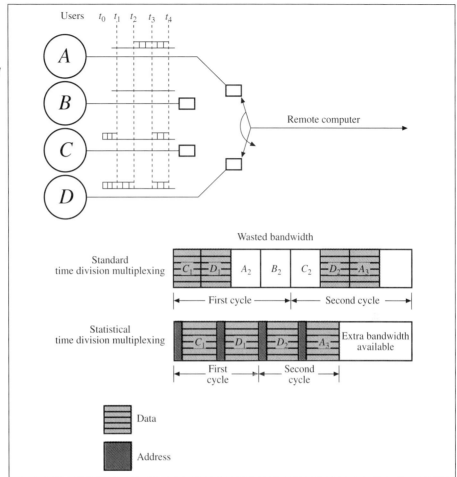

avoid the data encountering variable delays in buffers. Therefore, one or more channels of a TDM system is frequently dedicated to data, another to voice, and possibly another to video.

Concentrators

Concentrators are similar to multiplexers in that they permit the sharing of devices on a communications link and are thus appropriate for some of the applications discussed in Chapter 2. They take various forms depending frequently on whether they are associated with (1) the concentration of remote terminals into a cluster or (2) the concentration of a variety of link speeds and functional characteristics (e.g., code sets and protocols) adjacent to the host computer. Concentrators are called by a variety of names, many of them created by vendors. In the case of the concentration of remote terminals, the prime requirement is buffering, and a concentrator can be called a *cluster controller* (a term widely used to refer to IBM equipment), a *terminal concentrator*, a *terminal interface unit*, or a *control unit*. In the case of concentration of links at the host end, a concentrator is usually called a *front-end processor* (IBM terminology), a *data communications processor* (UNISYS terminology), a *communications control unit*, or a *line concentrator.*

A concentrator is frequently used to interconnect a group of terminals that carry out similar functions. The connection of the terminals to the concentrator is usually short distance via a standard CCITT V.24 interface, although distant terminal access via a leased circuit and modems or dial-up connections is possible. The concentrator has buffer space allocated to each terminal to hold data before their transmission into the network (see Figure 4–7).

Figure 4–8 shows how a concentrator associated with a host computer can interface a communication network to a computer. The concentrator itself is usually connected to the host computer by a high-speed link, and the terminal network is interfaced directly into the concentrator. In this diagram, a concentrator is interfacing a varied network ranging from low-speed asynchronous devices (one character at a time) to medium-speed synchronous (a block of characters at a time). The terms *asynchronous* and *synchronous* may be new to you. They are more commonly associated with PADs and are therefore defined in the following section.

FIGURE 4–7

*Concentration of
terminals at
remote end*

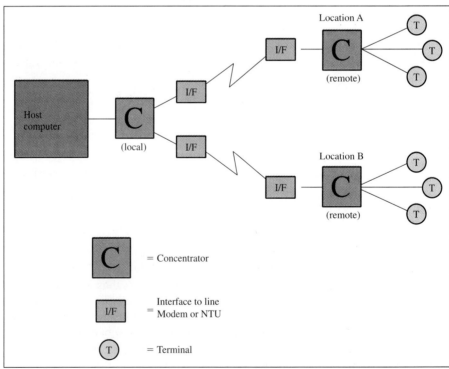

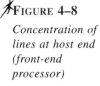

FIGURE 4–8

Concentration of lines at host end (front-end processor)

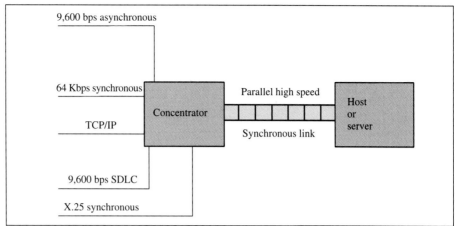

The concentrator is a very useful device for taking some load off the host computer. Communications processing is not a demanding task in that it does not require high-powered instructions to handle the links and the data. On the other hand, it is a time-consuming task because of the high interrupt rate required by the protocol mechanisms. This is particularly true for low-speed terminal traffic, which tends to have very little error-detecting capability.

If equipped with adequate memory, the concentrator can act as a store-and-forward device in that it will assemble complete messages or blocks of messages from the network terminals, store them in its memory, and then forward them to the host computer. This is particularly useful when low-speed terminal data comes from unbuffered terminals, because the concentrator can assemble a complete message and send it to the host in a standardized format at high speed. In essence, the concentrator performs code conversion, speed conversion, and format conversion. These functions are usually required if it is desirable to interface **dumb terminals**.

There is some overlap in the functions that multiplexers and concentrators can perform. The principal differences between the two devices are as follows:

- Multiplexers are used in pairs, whereas concentrators are used one at a time.
- Multiplexing involves multiple ports into the host computer, whereas with a concentrator there is usually a single link to the host computer, together with the capacity to support multiple connections or multiple drops over a wide geographical area.
- Multiplexers usually connect to terminals in a localized geographical area.
- In multiplexing, the sharing is a physical layer function carried out by TDM or STDM, although both cases still require a link-level protocol. (The characteristics of physical and link layers are discussed in the section on the ISO model.)

- The sharing of these multiple connections is carried out by the protocol at layer 2 (e.g., SDLC), which essentially time division multiplexes the link among the connections.
- The users of either system may not notice any difference in performance even though the configuration and sharing methodology are totally different.

Some manufacturers, such as IBM and UNISYS, use the term *multiplexer* to mean the same thing as *concentrator*. This implies only one device, whereas the strict definition of multiplexing, according to the previous section indicates that they operate in pairs. The IBM 3299 multiplexer, which connects to an IBM 3174 controller, is one such example.

Packet Assembler-Disassembler (PAD)

There are two key methods of transmitting data: either a character at a time (**asynchronous**), such as occurs when characters are typed on a keyboard, or a block at a time (**synchronous**), such as occurs in a packet switching network, in which a number of characters are grouped into a single block and transmitted in a packet.

Figure 4–9 shows asynchronous transmission in which the bits representing a single character are surrounded by start and stop bits (as well as an error-checking parity bit) and then transmitted off into the network as a unit.

Figure 4–10 depicts synchronous transmission in which a number of characters (often 128) are grouped together and represent the message. Some control information is added to the front and rear, and the complete unit is transmitted into the network.

Frequently it is necessary to convert from one type of transmission to the other, and this is the function of the *packet assembler-disassembler (PAD)*. It is very common to find a number of terminals, such as PCs, being used for data entry and connected

FIGURE 4–9

Asynchronous character transmission

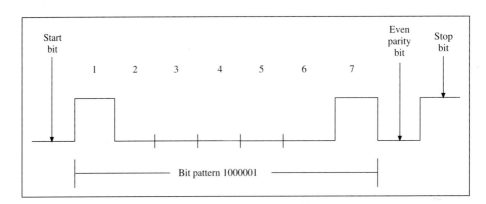

FIGURE 4–10

Synchronous character transmission

to a PAD using asynchronous transmission, which in turn is connected to a wide area network, such as a packet switching network, using synchronous transmission. The PAD is merely a small computer with memory that assembles characters into packets in one direction and disassembles them from packets into character streams in the other direction.

Usually a number of parameters can be set in the PAD that relate to the type of terminal equipment connected to it. Figure 4–11 shows a PAD used to interconnect asynchronous terminals to a wide area network.

Bridges and Routers

Bridges and routers form links between local and wide area networks and are also commonly used within interconnected local area networks. They will be discussed further in Chapter 5.

Software

All of the equipment described above comes with software. In fact, it would not be sensible to consider one without the other. The instructions governing the function of each item of equipment are controlled by the software. The functions carried out by this software include

- Error detection and correction.
- **Polling** (the messages controlling when the data are to be transmitted).
- Conversion from one speed to another.
- Buffering data for onward transmission.
- Conversion of one data format into another.

FIGURE 4–11

PAD used to interface asynchronous terminals to a network

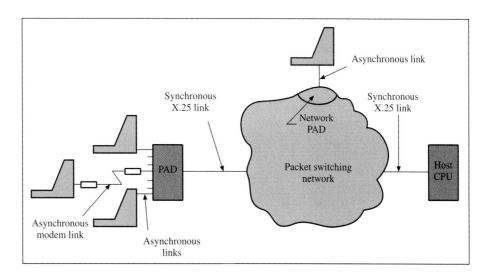

- Capabilities to handle different types of devices (e.g., workstations and printers).
- Data compression for controlling the volumes of data across networks.
- Automated dialing of stored telephone numbers (modems).
- Test routines and diagnostic programs.
- Statistical reports and network management routines.

In some situations the functions of the hardware described above can be performed by the software, although the performance will be degraded. For example, the functions performed by a PAD are sometimes run as software on a medium-speed to fast computer. In general, it is better not to separate the functions performed by the equipment or hardware described above and those performed by the software. More and more functions that were previously carried out by the software are now being performed by the hardware to reduce costs and increase performance speed. For example, IBM's System Network Architecture Software is a major software product used in conjunction with the network components (and the host computers) described in this chapter. Hardware and software should not be considered as separate purchases. Vendors' architecture software is very complicated and specific to the vendor, and the topic is too specialized and advanced to be discussed here.

Summary

Following is a summary of the key points relating to the network components discussed in this section:

- Modems connect users' equipment to the analog telephone network.
- Network terminating units (NTUs) connect users' equipment to the digital data network (DDN).
- Multiplexers allow users to share expensive communication links.
- Concentrators group terminals for connection to communication links and group communication links for connection to the host computer(s).
- PADs convert between asynchronous and synchronous communication protocols.
- Bridges and routers form the links between local and wide area networks.
- All of the equipment described operates under the control of some vendors' architecture software.

Wide Area Network Environments

In Chapter 2 we discussed a variety of applications that require the interconnection of workstations and related equipment to some host, mainframe computer, or file server in a different or distant location and saw that networks exist to facilitate such an interconnection. Earlier in this chapter, we looked at transmission media that make up these networks and the items most likely to be connected to them.

Wide area networks are very complex and expensive systems to operate and hence are usually under the control of the telecommunications companies. Normally users rent or lease only enough bandwidth on these networks for their application requirements; otherwise, the costs will start to outweigh the benefits. Today companies frequently combine or multiplex the voice and data applications discussed in Chapter 2 over the same circuits to use the capacity more economically.

Five types of wide area networks are in widespread use:

- Public switched telephone network (PSTN).
- Digital data network (DDN).
- Packet switching network (PSN).
- Integrated services digital network (ISDN).
- Frame relay.

The public switched telephone network (PSTN) has been in use for voice communication for most of this century. Only in recent years has data transmission between computers produced a new network requirement. At first, the only network available was the PSTN, and computer data had to be transformed at one end to resemble the human voice and transformed back again at the other. This is a cumbersome process, although modems that carry out this function have improved over the years.

What was required was a new wide area network suitable specifically for digital data transmission rather than the human voice. The digital data network (DDN) and packet switching network (PSN) were developed specifically for this purpose. Another type of data network is the integrated services digital network (ISDN), which has been around for a long time but has not been widely used until recently.

We will now examine each of these networks in turn.

Public Switched Telephone Network (PSTN)

The PSTN is the largest traffic network in terms of both equipment utilization and traffic volume. The PSTN consists of two interdependent parts, the "local loop" network being the links between the switching exchanges and the customers. It is often said that 60 percent of a telephone company's assets are copper wires buried under the ground. The other part is the long-distance network that includes coaxial, fiber optic, microwave, and satellite links, as well as switching equipment.

A switching system in a telecommunications network interconnects customers' telephones or other telecommunications terminals to provide rapid and efficient service. The local exchange interconnects local subscribers via the local loop and has trunks to other local exchanges. Some exchanges are called *tandem exchanges* since they function solely as switching points between other exchanges. In addition, each exchange has trunks to at least one toll or long-distance exchange that can handle national and international long-distance traffic.

A *private line* (also called a *dedicated* or *leased line*) is a dedicated transmission channel for the customer's exclusive use between two locations, usually between different cities in the same country. These private lines frequently carry a mix of data for a company (e.g., telephone, data, fax) via the use of multiplexers, as discussed in the previous section. These lines are used for voice and data when traffic patterns justify the cost. For example, a leased line can be less expensive than dial-up services when a significant amount of traffic is destined for one location.

Private lines can have certain drawbacks. First, private lines may be expensive to lease from the telecommunications company, so careful analysis of telecommunication costs must be carried out. Second, a private line may not be the total answer, since at peak times use will still have to be made of the PSTN, while at other times of the day the private line may be very underutilized. The latter point has contributed to the move to a more flexible tariff system whereby customers pay a monthly charge plus a tariff based on the bandwidth and time usage.

A *tie line* is a private leased or dedicated telephone circuit provided by a network operator that links two remote offices without using the PSTN. Each line supports only one call at a time. To access the tie line from either location, a user dials a specific number to connect to the tie line. Once the connection is made, the user can dial any extension at the remote location. A tie line makes it possible for distant locations to operate as though they were in the same building.

Another type of private line is a *foreign exchange* service. This enables a subscriber to be served by a distant or "foreign" exchange rather than by its own local exchange. With a foreign exchange line, the user's dedicated line ends in a local exchange that is outside, or foreign to, the company's local service area, usually in another city. For example, a subscriber leases a line from the local telephone company. One end terminates in the subscriber's own telephone equipment, while the other end terminates in an exchange of a distant city. A user in the subscriber's office who accesses this service receives a dial tone from the distant city. A subscriber's calls to customers in the distant exchange area are treated as local calls instead of long-distance calls.

Businesses that find it too costly to lease or purchase a **private branch-exchange (PBX)** can now lease such a service from the telephone company. This means that instead of the PBX being situated at the business's premises, the company leases a share of the phone company's PBX equipment, often referred to as **Centrex** or *centralized exchange*. This also has the advantage of avoiding the purchase of expensive PBX equipment that might become obsolete within a few years. Careful cost-benefit analysis must be carried out to make the best decision in this case.

The 800 freefone service has some similarities to the foreign exchange line concept, but it is a public service. The intention is that the company being called incurs the long-distance call charges. The service can operate between different cities or even different countries, as we saw in Chapter 2. It has become a very popular telemarketing service. You can see a product advertised on television and immediately dial an 800 number to find out more details or place an order. Many companies use 800 service to centralize their customer service offices and avoid duplicating office services in different cities.

Digital Data Network (DDN)

The digital data network (DDN) is a fully digital network used to interconnect computer equipment. The DDN provides dedicated synchronous services operating at speeds of 2,400, 9,600, 19,200, 48,000, 56,000, and multiples of 64,000 bps. Sometimes the term *digital data service* (DDS) is used to mean the same thing.

The DDN provides improvements over the PSTN for data transmission as follows:

- Improved transmission quality (error rate about 10 times lower).
- Improved reliability as a result of network management.
- Fast restoration of service following a fault.
- New network interfaces.
- Flexibility to reconfigure and extend networks to accommodate changing operational needs.

Network Interfaces.   The access circuit between the DDN and the customer's office terminates at the network terminating unit (NTU), which is provided by the telecommunications company; that is, the customer's equipment interfaces the DDN at the NTU. Simple interfaces that ensure compatibility between customer equipment and data communications networks have been defined and recommended by the CCITT. This organization will be discussed further in the following section.

We discussed NTUs in the previous section on network components, but it is worth noting again the functions they perform in this context when interfacing customers' equipment with the DDN:

- They eliminate the need to convert the digital output from a computer into analog form for transmission over the network, as is the case with the PSTN.
- They provide the control, timing, and data signals over the interface between the customer's equipment and the NTU.
- They transfer the original information stream from the customer's equipment into a format suitable for transport, control, and management through the network.
- They incorporate facilities that allow a customer to check the integrity of the total communication path as well as the local path. This can be done without the assistance of the telecommunications provider.
- They respond to network management commands for data looping and testing.

Network Management.   The DDN incorporates a centralized management system that provides the following facilities:

1. It provides means of isolating faults rapidly so that repair staff can be quickly directed to the problem. This results in improved availability and performance.

2. Central control means that many network configuration and service speed adjustments can be made from within the network, thus shortening the need to visit premises and shortening the delay in changing network configuration.

3. As an additional tool, data error rates and other parameters can be readily monitored over extended periods to confirm that performance objectives are being met or to locate difficult intermittent faults.

Point-to-Point and Multipoint Configurations.   The *point-to-point* service provides a dedicated synchronous circuit between two customers' premises. When a data processing center requires access to a number of remote locations, the **multipoint** service can be used as an alternative to many point-to-point services. A multipoint service enables two or more remote or tributary stations to be connected to the data processing center or control station.

The network simultaneously transmits the data over multiple paths to the remote terminals. The DDN provides only the communication path, and it is the function of each customer's equipment to identify its own message from the received data and signal to the NTU when to transmit data back to the control terminals.

Direct communication is possible only between the control station and the tributary terminals and not between the tributaries. In a multipoint service, all equipment must operate at the same speed. The maximum number of tributaries or remote terminals that can be connected to a particular control end terminal is limited only by operational considerations. Figure 4–12 shows equipment interconnections to a DDN.

Higher Speed Options for the DDN.   Different telecommunications companies define and specify the higher-speed end of the DDN spectrum in different ways. In general, however, the **wideband DDN** or **fractional T1/E1** service refers to a managed multiple 64 Kbps (up to 2 Mbps) point-to-point interconnection service, while

FIGURE 4–12

Equipment interconnection to the digital data network (DDN)

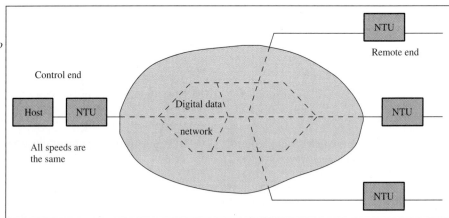

megalink or **T1/E1** refers to a simple point-to-point 2 Mbps interconnection service. These can be considered higher-speed extensions of the DDN and are shown in Figures 4–15 and 4–16 on pages 150 and 151.

Packet Switching Network (PSN)

By its very nature, a packet switching network (PSN) provides additional services over either the PSTN or the DDN. It is a highly efficient, reliable, and flexible method of transmitting data. Most data communication consists of short bursts of data with intervening spaces that are often of longer duration than the bursts of data. Packet switching takes advantage of this by interleaving (multiplexing) bursts of data from many different users so that maximum use can be made of the communications links.

This interleaving is achieved by assembling the bursts of data into packets, each containing address and control information as well as the user's data. These packets are then switched between users (hence the term *packet switching*). The process is strictly one of "statistical time division multiplexing" (STDM), and there are many similarities between a packet switching network and a private STDM network. However, in the case of an STDM network, the multiplexing function is carried out by the hardware, while with packet switching it is carried out by the software.

Packets are assembled and disassembled either by the subscriber's equipment or by a packet assembler-disassembler (PAD) facility that forms part of the packet switching network interface. In either case, the process is almost instantaneous and data are transmitted in an uninterrupted stream.

The widespread use of packet switching networks throughout the world, together with international agreement on the use of the CCITT **X.25** protocol, makes computer-to-computer communication relatively fast and simple. With public packet switching networks, users pay monthly rentals along with usage charges based on time and volume. In cases where large enterprises are transmitting vast volumes of data, or for certain security measures, it may be cost justified to set up a private packet switching network, sometimes called a virtual private network. This requires that an organization manage its own switches in conjunction with digital connecting links. The packet switching concept is shown in Figure 4–13.

Integrated Services Digital Network (ISDN)

Since its inception nearly two decades ago, interest in and expectations for the integrated services digital network (ISDN) have risen and waned on two occasions. The first occurred in the early 1980s and resulted from a push by the telephone companies to implement ISDN as a means of consolidating network resources and achieving savings in operating costs. Because the telephone companies attempted to go it alone without the understanding and support of the equipment vendors and end users, this attempt failed.

The second push for ISDN built up after 1985 and arose from a number of trials, again initiated by the telephone companies, which sought to implement proprietary

FIGURE 4–13

Equipment interconnections to the packet switching network (PSN)

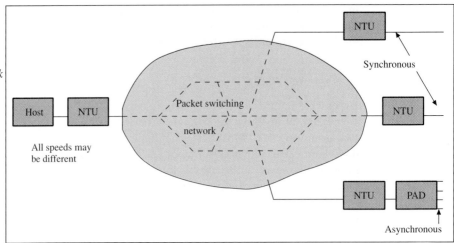

versions of ISDN interface standards, often supported by vendors. This failed to gain a significant presence for ISDN, because the end users had not been included in the development process.

Today ISDN has built up to a third wave of expectations, with the involvement of the telecommunications companies, terminal equipment manufacturers, and end users. Unlike the previous two attempts, this third effort has been much more successful. However, many consider ISDN to be "too little too late." Undoubtedly the speeds originally envisioned for ISDN are particularly undramatic by today's standards, especially with modern error-correcting compression modems pushing toward the 64 Kbps mark—the basic channel speed of ISDN.

The telecommunications companies do not intend for ISDN to encourage large-scale movement away from other network services. Its fundamental ability lies in providing *high-volume data transfer* capability where *short holding times* are common.

ISDN provides both basic rate and primary rate interfaces. *Basic rate* access provides two 64 Kbps channels. *Primary rate* access is capable of delivering up to 30 channels, each at 64 Kbps. Both basic and primary rate links support circuit-switched connections, where the user dials up a distant site on an as-required basis via a number of 64 Kbps channels.

ISDN has been defined variously as an *architecture*, a *technology*, a *network,* and a *service*. It is most suitable for users that need to transmit large quantities of data on an intermittent basis. Its potential is developing in areas such as interactive file transfer and image transmission and as a backup service for critical, leased data circuits. Thus, it does have application as a LAN-to-LAN interconnection service.

In summary, the advantages of ISDN as a LAN-to-LAN interconnection service are as follows:

- It provides dial-up service on an "as-required" basis.
- It provides a multiple 64 Kbps interconnection service.

• The flexibility of ISDN by virtue of its switched circuit capability enables the establishment of an efficient network among LANs when data transmission is required on a relatively infrequent basis.

The chief disadvantage is that high costs will result from long holding times, long distances, and high volumes of data transfer.

Frame Relay

Frame relay was launched in late 1990 in the United States and progressively over the last two years in the Asia-Pacific region. Its promoters have acclaimed it as being ideal for information system applications that require interconnected LANs, thus resulting in cost savings over the use of DDNs, particularly because of its elastic bandwidth. In very general terms, it seems that, at best, network costs can be reduced by around 50 percent and, at worst, it performs no differently than conventional X.25 packet switching networks. It is clear, however, that very careful design and application tuning is required if frame relay service is to reach its full potential.

In some ways, frame relay is of more significance to the telecommunications companies than to users, since 64 Kbps–2 Mbps point-to-point links have been widely available for many years. However, the provision of such bandwidth on a continuous basis is uneconomical for many applications, and a more flexible or elastic ("rubber") bandwidth system was needed. In most implementations of a public frame relay service, it is easy to budget for the communication charges since these are based on fixed costs such as the access rate and the committed information rate (CIR) for each virtual circuit in the interconnected mesh.

Frame relay is appropriate for major sites and networks requiring intermittent traffic flow among interconnected LANs. It is relatively cheap to implement on existing hardware; sometimes it merely requires a software upgrade to the existing CCITT X.21 interface on a bridge or router. However, it may also need to be seen as an interim solution until a new technology called **asynchronous transfer mode (ATM)** is fully developed. This topic is briefly discussed in Chapter 12 on new networking technologies.

The important differences between frame relay and X.25 packet switching are (1) more efficient use of digital bandwidth, leading to higher data rates, and (2) the absence of error checking. Frame relay's proponents argue that error checking at this level is not required, both because the error rates on modern digital leased lines are much lower than those on the analog lines that X.25 was designed to use and because error checking can still be implemented at a higher level by the system end points.

The Frame relay interface is thus designed to be simple, fast, and efficient and is optimized for reliable, digital communications lines. With today's low error rates, it is unnecessary and inefficient to manage acknowledgments and retransmissions at each segment of the network. If a frame is corrupted or lost, it is not retransmitted within the network, since all acknowledgments and retransmissions are handled by the end systems. Without this overhead, frame relay is able to run at very high speeds—up to 2 Mbps by today's specification, with higher speeds up to 34 Mbps (E3) and 45 Mbps (T3) demonstrated by vendors.

Virtual Circuits.   In principle, the frame relay standard allows use of either **permanent or switched virtual circuits** (**PVCs** or **SVCs**). Virtual circuits in the frame relay context are used for connectivity and addressing. All traffic for a particular virtual circuit uses the same path through the network. However, virtual circuits consume no resources when they are not active, but can (theoretically) instantaneously carry up to 2 Mbps of traffic.

The protocols for dynamically setting up SVCs are still under development, since they are more complicated than those used for PVCs, although SVCs will inevitably be required for international frame relay services. Today frame relay with PVCs allows any single device to communicate with hundreds of other devices directly by way of a single access port.

Once frames enter the frame relay network, they are forwarded along the PVC according to the connection identifier specified in the two bytes at the front of the frame. Data transmitted on a particular PVC are statistically multiplexed onto network trunks along with data from other users in a manner similar to X.25 packet switching. Since this statistical multiplexing process involves variable store-and-forward delays, the throughput for individual transactions will be variable and usually less than the access rate. (See Figure 4–14).

Committed Information Rate (CIR).   Nodes in a frame relay network are linked by PVCs, each with a *committed information rate (CIR),* which defines the bandwidth guaranteed to be available to the connection, although the maximum amount of bandwidth can be much higher if network capacity is available. This does not mean excess bandwidth is always available, since the network can supply bandwidth only up to the access rate of the connection to the network. If the network is congested, the bursts may not make it through the network and data can be discarded.

Typically the CIR can be set to a minimum value of 8 Kbps and then increased in blocks of 4 Kbps. However, this depends very much on the equipment supplier and network operator.

FIGURE 4–14

Frame relay interconnection using PVCs

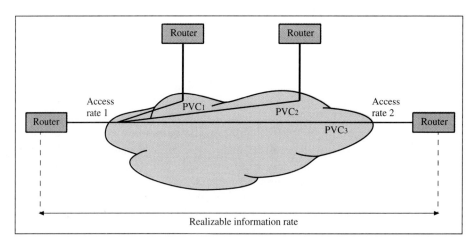

The advantages of frame relay are

- Higher network throughput capacity.
- Flexible bandwidth.
- Protocol transparency.
- Reduced network delay.
- Potential cost savings.

The main disadvantages of frame relay are as follows:

- Error protection must be provided at a higher level in the architecture.
- Frame relay is not suitable as a multimedia transport network.
- Difficult to obtain the optimum balance between the access speed to the network, the number of PVCs, and the CIR for each PVC.
- There is wide variation in vendors' implementations of congestion control systems.
- It is difficult to obtain accurate traffic profiles.

Consideration of Networking Alternatives

The network designer must carefully weigh individual requirements against the cost, facilities, and performance that each network service offers. Each network being considered for many of the applications discussed in Chapter 2 will need detailed analysis on a case-by-case basis. For example, sometimes a DDN will be the correct solution to provide interconnection for a financial application; at other times, a PSN will be the answer for the same application. Sometimes either the DDN or the frame relay network will be equally appropriate. Much depends on the manner in which service providers charge for use of these various networks.

Factors to be considered (not necessarily in order of importance) include

1. Installation and other initial "one-time" costs.
2. Rentals, including rental versus the total of maintenance, opportunity costs, finance charges, and amortization of any equipment purchases or other capital outlay.
3. Data speed, volume, and frequency of transactions with the computer.
4. Number of destinations and associated route lengths.
5. Network performance in terms of error rate, turnaround time, availability, and configuration flexibility.
6. The facilities provided in the customer's equipment.

Summary

The PSTN was originally designed for voice communication, and voice and fax remain the dominant applications. Limited access can be gained by way of a modem and dial-up connections.

The DDN provides dedicated access among a number of sites and is ideally suited to situations where there is a frequent need to exchange significant volumes of data. The rigid structure of the DDN makes it expensive for the intermittent traffic often associated with LAN-to-LAN communication, and therefore frame relay is sometimes a better alternative. For high volumes of data transfer and for short holding times typical of those found in videoconferencing applications, ISDN has become an attractive option.

DDN, packet switching, and now ISDN provide switched access to a virtually unlimited number of sites. In general, the packet switching network will be more economical when data communication must be established with a very large number of terminals and/or when data volumes are lower and the need for data exchange is less frequent. The packet switching network can also provide a level of privacy and security commensurate with that of a dedicated network.

Figure 4–15 shows these different wide area networking options for comparison purposes. The horizontal axis specifies a range of speeds appropriate for various applications, while the vertical axis specifies the loading or utilization needed to achieve economic usage of the particular service. The shapes of the "clouds" should not be taken too literally. They are intended to indicate the relative, rather than absolute, positions within the graph. Further, telecommunications companies frequently alter the range of speeds available for some of these services.

The one service we have not discussed so far is asynchronous transfer mode (ATM), which is very likely to be the key intercommunication technology supporting multimedia communications in the future and therefore is covered in Chapter 12.

Figure 4–15

Positioning of telecommunications interconnection services

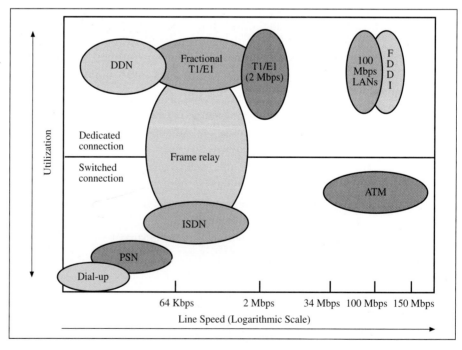

100 mbps LANs and **fiber distributed data interface (FDDI)** are specific to local area networks and will therefore be covered in Chapter 5. They are mentioned here merely for comparison purposes.

Figure 4–16 compares the key technical features of these wide area networking alternatives. Figures 4–15 and 4–16 indicate that overlap with other services does exist, and in some situations it may be difficult to choose among certain alternatives.

Standards Used in Wide Area Networking

To provide wide area network services for some of the applications discussed in Chapter 2, it is necessary to use the transmission media, network components, and various network types already discussed in this chapter. In the same way that nuts, bolts, taps, and tires come in standard sizes so that they can interface with one another, transmission media, network components, and network types require standards for interconnection. The lack of standardization with respect to power plugs and sockets and to the European and American telephone jacks is a good example of the

FIGURE 4–16

Comparison of WAN alternatives

	DDN T1/E1	Packet Switching X.25	Frame Relay	ISDN	ATM
Type of service	Circuit switched (leased circuit)	Packet switched over SVC and PVC	Frame over PVC (and SVC)	Circuit switched software	Cell switching
Public/private	Both	Both	Both	Public	Both
Maximum speed	1.5/2 Mbps, wideband	64 Kbps, low speed to wideband	2 Mbps (45 Mbps tested) wideband	2 Mbps, low speed to wideband	155 Mbps, broadband
Channel sharing	Fixed	Statistical	Statistical	Dynamic	Dynamic
Availability	Worldwide	Worldwide	Rapid growth worldwide	Limited	Experimental
Error control	None	Detection and correction	Detection	None	None
Transmission quality	—	Tolerant	Sensitive	Sensitive	Sensitive
Flow and congestion control	—	Local and end-to-end	Open and closed loop congestion control	—	Yes—under development
OSI layers	1	1–3	1–1.5	1	1–2
Data unit	Bit	Packet (variable size)	Frame (variable size)	Bit	Cell (fixed size)
Overhead	None	Moderate	Low	Low	High

lack of attention paid to the standardization process. Thus, we need standard ways to support our applications using various network components and types. These approaches are discussed in this section.

ISO Model

The purpose of the International Standards Reference Model of Open Systems Interconnection (now commonly called the *open system model*, *OSI model*, or **ISO model**) is to provide a common basis for the coordination of standards development for the purpose of systems interconnection. It was developed by the International Standards Organization (ISO 7498—basic reference model for OSI) and has now been adopted by the CCITT (X.200—basic reference model)

Many older networks were designed hierarchically—that is, as a series of layers, each layer building on the one below. At first, each network design team started out by choosing its own set of layers. With the advent of experimental packet switching data networks, the ISO recognized the urgent need to standardize the rules associated with such interconnections, and it began formulating the so-called ISO model. The ISO model was designed primarily for use in wide area networks although it is applicable to (and has been adapted for) local area networks as well.

The reference model contains seven layers as shown in Figure 4–17. With the exception of the application layer, each layer provides a number of services to support the layer above it. The upper three layers (application, presentation, and session) deal with information activities associated with host applications, while the lower three layers (network, data link, and physical) are concerned with the mechanisms of the communication network. The transport layer forms a bridge between the two and is relative to both host and network services.

Following is a brief summary of the services and facilities associated with each layer

Layer 7: Application Layer.   This layer provides the application services for many of the financial, marketing, and manufacturing examples previously discussed. Further, this layer includes support services for file transfer, electronic mail, terminal emulation, directory services, network management services, and many other facilities. In proprietary terms, Novell's NetWare, Microsoft's Windows NT, and Sun's Network File System fit into this layer, but also extend downward to include the presentation and session layers.

Layer 6: Presentation Layer.   This layer provides services permitting code conversion or data reformatting, including encryption and data compression required by application processes to shield them from inconsistencies in data storage methods. The vendors' architectures mentioned earlier all include the presentation layer.

Layer 5: Session Layer.   This layer provides services supporting the dialog among application processes. By monitoring data integrity and establishing restart or roll-

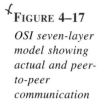

FIGURE 4–17

OSI seven-layer model showing actual and peer-to-peer communication

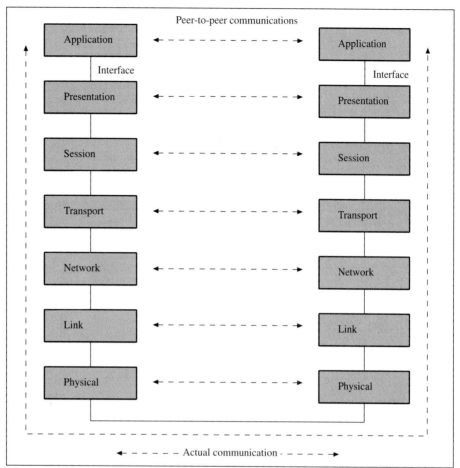

back points, the session layer ensures orderly transmission and recovery in the event of an underlying network failure. NetBIOS is perhaps the best-known session management software associated with local area network usage, although all of the vendors' architectures mentioned earlier include the session layer.

Layer 4: Transport Layer.   This layer provides services critical to the functioning of the overall system. Lower levels are concerned with the topology and physical structure, but the transport layer provides "pipes" for application-to-application communications. In addition, it provides services to maximize throughput by allocating resources and providing for priorities and multiplexing, as well as ensuring transmission integrity through comprehensive error detection and recovery procedures. Major specifications and protocols include the TCP part of the TCP/IP suite, CCITT X.224, and ISO 9602 (connectionless transport protocol).

Layer 3: Network Layer.   This layer provides services that allow data (packets) to be relayed, switched, and routed through networks and intermediate systems, depending on the precise network topology. Network conditions are monitored for use by the transport layer. Major specifications and protocols include CCITT X.25, the IP part of the TCP/IP suite, and Novell's IPX.

Packet (Router Device)

Layer 2: Data Link Layer.   This layer provides services that maintain communications between corresponding data link layers by processing requests to establish physical connections and by organizing data into standard message format (framing). Major specifications and protocols include HDLC, SDLC, LAP-B, LAP-D, IEEE802.3 (**Ethernet**), and 802.5 (token ring).

Frame (Bridge/Switch)

Layer 1: Physical Layer.   This layer enables the transmission of raw data and the handling of interfaces among the different media involved. This layer's function is to communicate bit streams among widely differing media and to handle clocking synchronization and modulation. Major specifications and protocols include ISO 8802.3 and 802.5, 10BASE-T, 100BASE-T, RS-232/V.24, RS-449/V.35, RS-422/3, X.21, FDDI, and many more.

ATM-Cell Repeater Connection Concentrator (Hub)

The way each layer communicates with its corresponding peer layer is governed by certain rules called *protocols*. In reality, data are not transmitted horizontally, that is, from machine to machine within a given layer, as the logical peer-to-peer communication might indicate; rather, they are passed vertically down the layers of the sending machine, across the interconnecting link, and up the layers of the receiving machine, as indicated in Figure 4–17. Only in layer 1 does actual inter-machine communication occur. The boundary between adjacent layers is called an *interface*.

Not all layers need be present in every application, and frequently the protocols associated with each layer form a suite of services from which applications select their services. Vendors such as IBM, Digital Equipment, Novell, and Microsoft have marketed layered architectures for many years (e.g., SNA and DECNET), but now there is a requirement to provide compatible communication among the different vendors' architectures.

CCITT and OSI Standards

The proliferation of different vendors' proprietary standards led to a situation where it was virtually impossible to interconnect different systems. The rapid growth in public networks made it essential to provide internationally accepted communication standards. However, many of the standards bodies took considerable time to produce working results, and in certain situations the industry could not wait. Hence, a number of de facto standards arrived in the market, some of which became incorporated into international standards. As the industry moved more toward interworking among different vendors' equipment, it was found that applications developed for one system could not be used on another. Thus, the CCITT and ISO stepped in to attempt to achieve some uniformity in data communications standardization. The result was that there has been, and will continue to be, much activity within the standards bodies, and the ongoing results of this work is of great importance to the computer communications industry.

Standardization is required at all levels of the ISO model. Initial effort went into the bottom three or four layers, since these were the most important as standards in this region that allowed interfacing with telecommunications companies' equipment, including voice, data, and packet switching networks. More recently, standardization efforts have addressed the upper layers of the OSI model to provide application-to-application communication involving a mix of both local and wide area networks as well as a variety of different vendors' equipment. Much recent work has also been done on standards to support multimedia communications.

Standards are evolving from a number of important organizations, the primary contributors being the ISO (International Standards Organization), the CCITT (Consultative Committee of the Institute of Telegraphy and Telephony), the ANSI (American National Standards Institute), and the IEEE (Institute of Electrical and Electronic Engineers). The IEEE standards organization is discussed in Chapter 5, p. 177–180.

International Standards Organization (ISO)

The ISO is a voluntary organization consisting of national standards committees from each member country. The ISO coordinates its activities with groups such as the CCITT and IEEE on common issues, and a number of its subcommittees are working with the CCITT and ANSI to develop standards for many interface and network applications, including circuit switched networks, public data networks, and integrated services digital networks. In particular, the ISO has made a significant contribution to the standardization of the ISO model of "open system interconnection."

American National Standards Institute (ANSI)

ANSI is a voluntary standards body in the United States and is a member of the ISO. It makes a very significant contribution to the ISO by developing standards itself as well as accepting standards proposals from other organizations in the United States. ANSI's activities are extensive. Its body, ANSC X3 (American National Standards Committee 3), and subcommittees provide the organization and mechanism for members to develop communications standards in conjunction with the ISO groups.

Consultative Committee of the Institute of Telegraph and Telephone (CCITT)

Telecommunications companies in most countries belong to the **International Telecommunications Union (ITU)**, which is managed by the United Nations. The primary purpose of the ITU (and its subgroups, such as the CCITT and CCIR) is to facilitate the creation of standards for public networks covering the full range of telecommunications services: telephone switching and signaling, digital transmission and multiplexing, integrated services digital networks, and data communications over telephone networks (the familiar V, X, and I series recommendations, for example).

To a large degree, this is a success story of compliance. Telecommunications companies around the world have developed and agreed on these standards through the CCITT, and thus interconnection to networks supported by these companies is relatively simple.

More recently the name CCITT has been dropped (although it will be widely used for many years yet) and renamed the ITU–TSS (International Telecommunications Union–Telecommunications Standards Sector).

✸*De Facto Standards*

De facto standards are industry or proprietary standards that evolve from vendors or specific industry groups. This occurs for two reasons. Either the regular standards of CCITT and ISO are not suitable for the particular industry or the CCITT and ISO take too long to agree on a standard. Frequently vendors are eager to see their products in the marketplace and do not want to be delayed unnecessarily by these bodies. The rapid development of the protocols used on the Internet (discussed in Chapter 3) is a good example of this. The organizations most involved in setting these de facto standards are

- Internet (TCP/IP for network interconnections, SNMP for network management).
- International Federation of Information Processing (IFIP).
- European Computer Manufacturers Association (ECMA).
- Electronic Industries Association (EIA) (U.S.).
- International Airline Transport Association (IATA).
- IBM (de facto standards, e.g., EBCDIC, SDLC, BSC, SNA).
- Society for Worldwide Interbank Financial Telecommunications (SWIFT).

The main conclusions to be drawn from these various standardizations is that interconnection of equipment at the bottom three layers of the ISO model is not difficult to achieve. Hence, interconnection to the PSTN, DDN, ISDN, PSN, and frame relay is well standardized.

The problems arise when particular vendors' equipment and accompanying software are interconnected across these networks. For example, interconnection of IBM's SNA architecture for one airline to Novell's NetWare architecture for a different airline is difficult to achieve. Another example occurs with E-mail, especially when formatted documents including graphics are attached. Often different standards are used to encode and decode these attachments. Sometimes a receiver who is running a different E-mail standard than that of the sender cannot decode the received documents. This results from the use of different standards by the various vendors at the upper four layers of the ISO model.

Ad hoc solutions exist at present, of which the Internet is a good example, but in general the problem is still largely unsolved. We address it again in Chapter 5, where we look at the interconnection of local and wide area networks.

Wide Area Network Topologies

In Chapter 2 when we discussed using a wide area network for the interconnection of the applications described, we did not consider factors such as reliability, alternative paths, or the economic aspects of different network layouts. A network designer can build up a network in different ways, and these alternatives are generally dependent not on the transmission media or components but on the specific requirements of the application system. The term **topology** in this context refers to the way in which multiple devices are interconnected via communication links.

Various structures are possible for the interconnection of nodes in a network. These structures relate to the way data are processed as well as the direction and nature of the data transmission. An enormous variety of physical structures are possible, but they can be broadly categorized as point-to-point, star, multidrop, multipoint, bus, tree, ring, and mesh. In the case of star, multidrop, and multipoint networks, the processing power is usually centered in one place; with bus, tree, ring, and mesh networks, the processing power is distributed among the nodes.

Another important property of these networks is related to "closed loops," which can offer an alternative path(s) in the event of failure. They fall into two groups: those for wide area networks (mesh) and those for local area networks (ring).

Certain topologies are specific to local area networks, others to wide area networks, and still others to both. In Chapter 5 we will discuss those topologies relevant to local area networks. In this section, we look at those specific to wide area networks: point-to-point, star, multidrop or multipoint, and mesh.

Point-to-Point

The simplest form of network is the *point-to-point* connection, shown in Figure 4–18. The connection can be short or long, simplex (one direction), half-duplex (one-way), or full-duplex (two-way), and it can operate asynchronously or synchronously. Note that the hardware (interfaces, modems, NTUs, or links) may permit full-duplex operation as seen from layer 1, but the application (e.g., transaction processing) may be only half-duplex as seen from the upper layers of the architecture.

Due to its simplicity, performance is not usually a problem in this type of topology. The main issue is to determine the appropriate capacity of the interconnecting link.

Star

The **star** network is an extension of the point-to-point configuration in which all communication links are connected to one central site as shown in Figure 4–19. The central node behaves like a switch, and each station in turn has dedicated access to a node; the reliability is a function of the switching node; the outlying nodes have no real control. This topology is simple and generally inexpensive, but a new link must be added for each new node. The star configuration has undergone a great deal

FIGURE 4–18

Point-to-point configuration: (a) half-duplex, (b) full-duplex

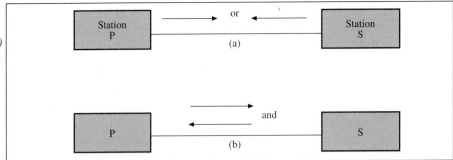

of development recently, and the term *hub* is now widely used to represent the implementation of a star topology—particularly in the LAN environment—and will be discussed further in Chapter 5.

    A star connection is common for applications where the central node serves as the time-sharing host or switch and is the basis of a private branch exchange (PBX). It is also used for small clusters of terminals carrying out applications such as word processing, spreadsheets, and other office applications. Sometimes advantage can be taken of an existing telephone exchange and its associated wiring. The main disadvantages of a star network are the large number of ports at the central computer, the high link cost in some situations, and the fact that reliability is a function of the central node. More recently these devices have become enhanced with network management and security software that serves to improve the overall performance of the network.

Multidrop or Multipoint

For wide area networks, a very common topology is a *multidrop* or *multipoint* network (also called a hierarchical network) shown in Figure 4–20. The terminals in a small area are terminated in a central switching station or concentrator rather than being connected to the main computer directly, as in the case of the star network. These concentrators are usually connected to the main computer by high-speed links. This type of network can considerably reduce line costs where large geographical areas are involved. The main drawback is the double handling of messages (terminal to concentrator and concentrator to main computer).

    In addition, each concentrator on the link must be polled by way of a short message from the main computer to indicate that it may now transmit its data and receive any data due for the terminals connected to it. The rate of polling, the number of concentrators on a link, and the number of terminals connected to each concentrator all have an important effect on the performance, particularly on response time. Usually each poll collects all buffered messages for the terminals connected to a concentrator and at the same time transmits the return messages from the main computer to the concentrator. It is often very difficult to determine the response

FIGURE 4–19

Star network

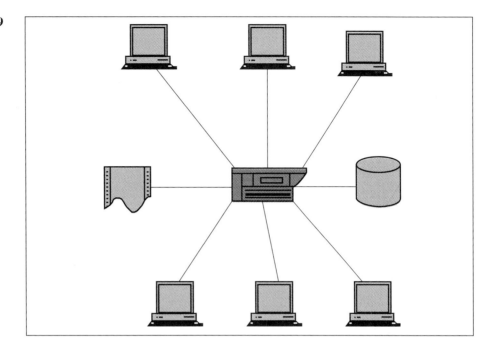

time due to the number of terminals active, input and output message sizes, the rate of polling, and host computer delays. Nevertheless, this type of topology is very widely used by many industries, including banking and airlines. In any situation where there are clusters of terminals in different parts of the city or in different cities and these terminals need to communicate with the main computer, this topology is ideal, since it saves on the line costs.

Figure 4–20 shows a typical multidrop or multipoint network such as that operated by a bank.

Mesh

The *mesh* network (also called an *interconnected plex network*) is found in many public and private packet switching and digital data networks and would be the option for any of the applications discussed in Chapter 2 that require international interconnection. The Internet is an example of this type of network. The node is an intelligent switch or router to which incoming and outgoing link(s) are connected. It has to be intelligent enough to manage routing as well as handle flow control, buffering, and protocols. There are often several pathways through the network, and the router or switching nodes (R) must determine the routing on a static basis when the call is set up or on a dynamic basis as the communication is in progress, a problem that in practice turns out to be difficult to solve efficiently.

Mesh networks involve sophisticated equipment and are generally operated only by the telecommunications companies or large corporate organizations. More often

FIGURE 4–20

*Multidrop or
multipoint
network*

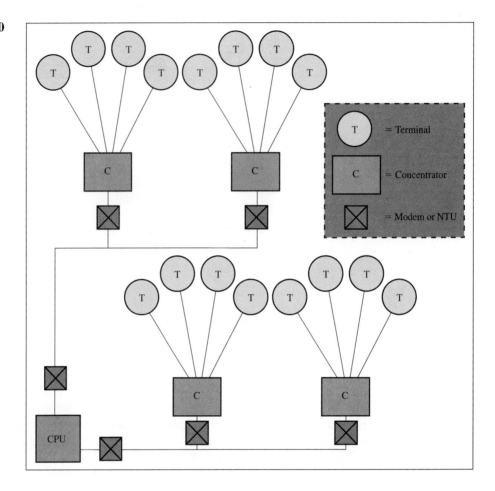

a subnetwork or virtual private network is made available to customer organizations from the larger network operated by the telecommunications company. Figure 4–21 shows an example of an interconnected mesh network.

Network reliability and capability increase as the network becomes more complex. In the centralized network, if the central site fails, the network ceases to exist. To guard against this type of failure, critical items such as modems, multiplexers, front-end processors, or routers can be duplicated at the central site. In the decentralized configuration, the failure of one center puts out of action only the terminals directly connected to the failed center, because the remaining sites can communicate by using other parts of the network. Similarly, the distributed network is more reliable, again due to the increased number of interconnections.

All of these networks involve different lengths of communication links and provide different degrees of reliability. In designing a network, trade-offs are usually made among reliability, efficiency, and costs, with the result that any one system may contain different types of networks based on a combination of the four types discussed above.

FIGURE 4–21

Mesh network

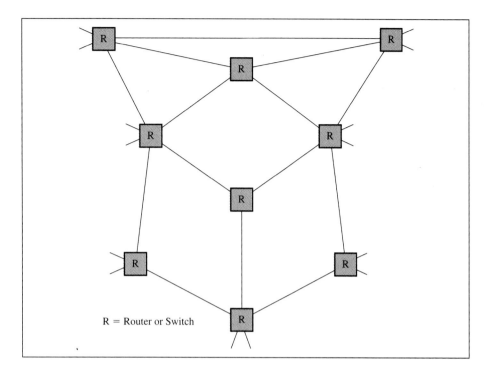

R = Router or Switch

Summary

The selection of a network topology typically entails a trade-off. Generally reliability is needed at minimum cost, but these criteria are often difficult to achieve together. Clearly, if your applications require reliability (and those described in Chapter 2 usually do), some form of redundant path is necessary, as would be found with a mesh network. Where groups of terminals need to be connected to a concentrator and then back to a data center, as is typical in financial and reservations applications, multidrop or multipoint options are desirable. When simplicity and low cost are important, point-to-point may be the best option. This can be extended to a star network (with many point-to-point links), although line costs may become prohibitive.

Integration of Wide Area Network Types

In Chapter 2, we saw that from the *user's* point of view, different networks are available to solve different interconnection requirements. From the network service provider's point of view, equipment and links carry users' data irrespective of the network from which the data originated.

As we have seen, different wide area networks are available for different business applications such as voice, electronic funds transfer, document transfer, and teleconferencing. These applications largely dictate the size of the network "pipes" required. One difficulty for businesses is that they end up with individual connections to different networks, that is, individual links for fax, telephone, data, and videoconferencing. These separate physical links create strategic problems for the service provider (in providing cables into the premises) as well as problems for the business (laying cables within the building).

This issue drove the evolution of the ISDN (integrated services digital network). The idea is for the customer to have a single network interface at its premises. To this single interface, the customer connects all of its equipment while the network operator (e.g., a telecommunications company) connects the interface box to the network via a single connection. Essentially the data from all of the applications are multiplexed within this interface and demultiplexed at the switching exchange end. Thus, this single connection will carry all multiplexed data.

Despite the many advantages of this idea, it has been slow to evolve, and the marketing push for ISDN is directed more toward the types of applications it can support (videoconferencing, high-speed fax, and as a backup network for disaster recovery) rather than being a "single hole in the wall" philosophy. In many ways, the applications customers now require have overtaken the facilities designed into the ISDN standards, and the 64 Kbps channel speed—once thought to be very fast—is now considered a rather moderate interconnection speed.

Among private companies or individual branches of the same company, it is common practice to integrate voice, data, and fax services. For example, a large bank in Los Angeles needs to communicate with its Singapore office by way of telephone, computer data, and fax. Leasing multiple connections from the various telecommunications companies is an expensive solution. Instead, by purchasing a pair of multiplexers or routers—one for the Los Angeles end and the other for the Singapore end—it is possible to multiplex the traffic from *all* of these applications on a single wide area network link.

This approach also offers cost advantages. The sum of the costs of separate links is usually far greater than the cost of a single higher-speed link together with the cost of the end equipment. As we will discuss in the next section, a nonlinear relationship exists between link capacity and cost. Naturally, each situation must be evaluated carefully since traffic volumes and time of day patterns can have a major influence on the solution.

In this respect, the move by telecommunications companies to provide "elastic" bandwidth, such as is found with frame relay, is very feasible. In other words, within certain limits they provide an elastic pipe to suit individual requirements. It is expected that in the future, ATM will offer one highly integrated networking service that is transparent to both the local and wide areas as well as to the applications they support. This is further discussed in Chapter 12.

Cost of Acquiring and Using WANs

In Chapter 2 we discussed the costs and benefits of various financial, marketing, and manufacturing applications. These are related to the costs and benefits of using the wide area network technologies.

Wide area network costs include network design, the purchase of hardware and software, usage fees for the network, administration, and maintenance. The benefits include the sharing of resources, direct data entry and retrieval, and reduction of staff costs. In fact, effective networking is a prerequisite to effective worldwide operations.

There are some very important considerations when it comes to wide area network costs. The issues affecting these costs fall into the following categories:

- Public versus private network.
- Deregulation and competition in the telecommunications industry.
- Changing tariff methods.
- Technological developments in network facilities.
- Growing demands in customers' requirements as a result of new applications.

The distinction between a public network and a private network is sometimes difficult to determine. One form of a so-called private network involves the company purchasing all nodal switching equipment (which can be very costly) and then leasing interconnecting links from the telecommunications company. Then all operation, maintenance, and network management become the responsibility of the company. However, some of the network components may be "private" while the interconnecting links belong to the "public" network. A solution such as this is applicable only to large organizations such as banks, airlines, and major manufacturers. One problem is that the organization must recover the capital cost of the nodal equipment within two to three years to keep up-to-date with new technological developments—a challenging and expensive undertaking.

For all but the large enterprises, switching equipment and links are leased from the telecommunications company and paid for on a monthly and/or usage volume basis. This permits a company to run a *virtual private network* as a subset of the overall network. Of course, the company can decide to open it up to public use, as is the case with a marketing information network, or limit access to only selected clients or certain staff from within the company, such as with an airline reservations network. The more complex and technical the wide area network facilities become, the more attractive this option becomes.

Deregulation is now commonplace in the telecommunications industry. There are pros and cons to deregulation, but one clear result is competitive pricing. Telecommunications companies must charge realistic prices for services, since cross-subsidy would allow competitors to get a foothold. The main areas of competition are

- Long-distance or toll circuits.
- Intercity data circuits.
- Wideband (high-volume) data circuits.
- Value-added services where the telecommunications company provides a full end-to-end service, not just the interconnecting links.

There is also some competition with respect to packet switching services. One area where little competition exists is in the local loop. Changes are also taking place in the way tariffs are applied. In the past, services at a fixed capacity were leased on a monthly basis, together with a one-time installation charge. Now tariffs are based much more heavily on traffic volume.

In general, more flexible tariffs are starting to be applied for the higher-speed services. These consist of a monthly connection charge along with a charge based on the peak data volume transferred. Sometimes peak data volume charges vary according to the time of the day. The term often used in this context is *flexible* or *elastic* bandwidth. Further, there is a highly nonlinear relationship between data rate and tariff. It is generally much more cost effective to lease one higher-speed circuit than a number of lower-speed circuits. This makes the economics of multiplexing application data over a single high-speed circuit most attractive.

New technological developments with respect to both switching equipment and interconnecting links are occurring all the time. It is therefore becoming more and more difficult for businesses to keep up to date with these changes. The general tendency is to concentrate on the company's *primary* business—for example, selling banking services or airline seats—and buy in the expertise from the local telecommunications company (for which telecommunications is their primary business). This is not to say that the company can neglect to be aware of and understand the principles of the new technology. You can understand the workings of a car engine and be familiar with new developments in the automotive industry without having to do the repairs or maintenance yourself.

One of the driving forces for wide area network providers is customer demand. As users demand high-speed networks for teleconferencing, distributed window applications, distributed graphical user interfaces, computer-aided design across a network, and so on, network designers and network operators labor to keep abreast with new switching and circuit interconnection equipment. This never-ending spiral has gone on for the last 10 years and is likely to continue for the next 10 years as the following examples demonstrate.

Singapore Telecom plans to provide a fiber optic connection to every business and home by the year 2000. This is a remarkable goal by any standard, and it is by no means clear how these services should be charged. A further example can be seen in the ongoing development of the Internet. Recently the National Science Foundation (NSF) upgraded major parts of the Internet backbone with fiber optic links. The older coaxial cable links were severely limiting the network's capacity, which is shown in Figures 3–10 and 3–11. The graphs flatten off around the October 93–January 94 period, demonstrating the bottlenecks at that time.

Summary

In Chapter 2 we introduced a variety of networking applications from a number of industries. In this chapter we explained the components of the wide area network necessary to provide for some of the interconnected applications discussed in Chapter 2. This chapter should have given you a good understanding of the wide area network components that are used to support these business applications. You need only know enough to be able to discuss different options with your telecommunications consultants. You do not need to know the details of how these network building blocks work, but you should understand their basic advantages and disadvantages.

After introducing the major functions of wide area networks, we examined the various communications channels and media in common use, how to choose among them, and why selecting the correct speed is important. Next, we looked at the network components that provide access and links to the shared network resources. Then we introduced the five main types of wide area networks—PSTN, DDN, PSN, ISDN, and frame relay—as well as the different topologies and discussed why a company would choose a particular one. We also examined the standards that are important for interconnection.

Finally, we covered aspects of wide area network integration, costs, and performance. Cost factors and performance are most important in considering various business options.

In Chapter 5 you will learn about the technical aspects of local area networks that are required to support some of the distributed applications discussed in Chapter 2. There is some overlap in some of the transmission media and interfacing equipment used in both local and wide area networks, and we will refer back to this chapter where appropriate.

Key Terms

Analog signals   130
Asynchronous   138
Asynchronous transfer mode (ATM)   147
Bandwidth   125
Bits per second (bps)   125
Bridges   122
Centrex   142
Channel service unit (CSU)   132
Coaxial cable   127
Concentrators   122
Consultative Committee of the Institute of Telegraph and Telephone (CCITT)   131
Data service unit (DSU)   132
Digital signals   131
Dumb terminals   137
Ethernet   154
Fiber distributed data interface (FDDI)   151
Frame relay   147
Full-duplex   131
Half-duplex   131
Hertz (Hz)   125

ISO model   152
Interface   124
Megalink (T1/E1)   145
Modems   126
Multiplexers   122
Multipoint   144
Packet Assembler-Disassemblers (PADs)   122
Permanent virtual circuits (PVCs)   148
Polling   139
Private branch exchange (PBX)   142
Protocols   124
Routers   122
Simplex   131
Star   157
Switched virtual circuits (SVCs)   148
Synchronous   138
Topology   157
V.24/RS-232   132
Wideband DDN (fractional T1/E1)   144
X.25   145

Questions for Discussion

1. What network device could you use for each of the following requirements?

   a. A number of terminals are to be connected to this device for linking into a multidrop network.

   b. A number of lines are to be connected to this device, which is then directly connected to the computer.

   c. A number of dumb terminals need to be connected to this device so that the data can be built up into packets and transmitted across a packet switching network.

   d. To save line costs, these devices on either end of the line allow the data from different applications to be shared.

   e. This device is needed to connect your PC to the telephone network to convert computer data to resemble human voice signals.

   f. This device is needed to connect your computer equipment to the digital data network.

2. What type of network (circuit, message, or packet switching) would each of the following be?

   a. Telephone network.

   b. Digital data network.

   c. Frame relay network.

   d. Integrated services digital network.

   e. The SWIFT banking network.

3. A synchronous online inquiry terminal sends a 200-character input message to a host computer and receives a 700-character output message in reply. Host processing takes 1.55 msecs. What minimum standard line speed would you use to obtain a response time of 2 secs at the terminal? Assume 8-bit characters and ignore any protocol overhead and line/modem turnaround times.

4. Identify the seven layers that comprise the ISO model, and give an example of a protocol with which you are familiar for each layer.

5. To what layer(s) of the ISO model do the following networks apply?

   a. Circuit switching network.

   b. Packet switching network.

   c. Message switching network.

6. What type of transmission media would you be likely to use for each of the following applications? Give a reason for your choice.

   a. To connect your telephone to the nearest exchange.

   b. To connect two telephone exchanges.

   c. To interconnect two telecommunications companies in different countries.

   d. To interconnect two buildings by line of sight where cables are not possible.

   e. Where isolation from electrical interference is required.

7. Match the most appropriate circuit speeds in column B with the applications in column A.

Column A	Column B
(a) Telex	(a) 2 Mbps
(b) Electronic mail messaging	(b) 2,400 bps
(c) Videoconferencing	(c) 50 bps
(d) Terminal cluster connected to a bank	(d) 9,600 bps

8. What topology best fits each of the following network scenarios?

   a. Four branches of a bank in midtown Manhattan are to be connected to the main office in the same region of New York City.

   b. A videoconferencing session is to be set up between the Los Angeles and Singapore offices.

   c. A PBX is to be installed for a company and telephones and data terminals connected.

   d. Six new routers are to be added to enhance the Internet.

5 LOCAL AREA NETWORKS (LANS): PRINCIPLES AND COMPONENTS

Chapter Outline

Introduction   168

Major Functions of Local Area
   Networks   169

Communication Channels and Media:
   Comparative Benefits and
   Drawbacks   173

Local Area Network Standards   177

Local Area Network Hardware and
   Connectivity   183

Local Area Network Topologies   193

Fiber Distributed Data Interface
   (FDDI)   197

High-Speed Local Area Networks
   (100 Mbps)   202

Client/Server Computing   208

Local Area Network Software
   Components   209

Operating Systems in Local Area
   Networks   210

Costs of Acquiring and Using Local
   Area Networks   215

Factors in Local Area Network
   Selection   218

Learning Objectives

By the end of chapter 5, you should be
able to

1. *Explain* the significant functions
   of a local area network in the
   business environment.

2. *Describe* the main transmission
   media used in local area
   networks.

3. *Discuss* the primary local area
   network industry standards.

4. *Describe* the main hardware
   components and identify the key
   difficulties associated with
   interconnecting local and wide
   area networks.

5. *Explain* the primary software
   components and functions used
   in local area networks.

6. *Describe* the main network
   topologies used in local area
   networks.

7. *Analyze* cost factors associated
   with local area networks.

8. *Identify* important factors in
   selecting a local area
   network.

Introduction

In Chapter 2 we examined some of the business applications that use local area networks together with various office automation functions. In this chapter, we look at the details of LANs and the equipment that supports these applications. By the end of this chapter, you will know what is required to implement a financial service for a bank and for the associated office automation functions such as electronic mail and calendaring. You will also be able to specify the wiring or cabling systems that need to be installed in various office or factory environments to support these various applications.

Remember that local and wide area networks seldom exist in isolation. Increasingly, an *integrated* solution is required. Thus, this chapter focuses primarily on the equipment that allows you to interconnect these two different types of networks. As we saw in Chapter 4, some equipment and associated software are specific to local area networks, while other equipment and software apply to wide area networks. From the user's point of view, however, there is no difference; no clear boundary exists designating that this is a *local* and that is a *wide* area piece of networking equipment.

In general, this section covers the building blocks required to form a local area network, together with the associated cabling. We look briefly at how local area networks operate; sufficient detail is provided to allow a manager to distinguish among the main types and understand why a specific type of local area networking equipment or architecture is used in a certain environment or why a particular type of cabling system is used in an office. Generally, managers are supported by technicians who understand the finer details about hardware issues such as pins, plugs, and the specifics of the local area network **operating systems**. This area is so highly technical that technicians generally specialize in one or two types of local area networks.

Probably in no other area of communications has so much change taken place so rapidly. Along with these changes have come many new technological terms. Cabling systems that were considered state-of-the-art a few years ago have now been replaced by new systems. Once unprecedented network speeds are now found in everyday local area networks, and even higher speeds are being proposed. Equipment available three years ago may be obsolete today, and there are now more cost-effective ways to solve the same problems to maintain a competitive advantage. Therefore, as mentioned in Chapter 4, it is important to allow an appropriate write-off period for your equipment, typically three years. It is also important to keep up to date with network software. It is often difficult to support modern applications and connectivity to other networks without using the latest version of the software operating system.

Although some of the basic technology and standards, such as twisted pair, Ethernet, and packet switching, remain largely unchanged, new ways are being found to operate these basic technologies to provide enhanced facilities—particularly in the areas of network security and management. We address these topics in more detail in Chapter 11.

In Chapter 4 we saw that because of the size and complexity of wide area network equipment and the associated links, it is customary to lease access to these networks from the local telecommunications company. In the case of local area networks, however, the entire network of equipment and interconnecting links is under the control and management of the office, company, or factory that purchased it. No regulations govern the type of equipment, cabling, or use of this equipment. However, many de facto standards have emerged, making interconnections of both local and wide area networks difficult in many situations. The need to interconnect local and wide area components has brought a whole range of interconnection equipment onto the market, such as **hubs**, bridges, routers, and **gateways**. We discuss some of these devices later in this chapter.

The bulk of this chapter covers the principles and components of local area networks as follows:

- Major functions of local area networks.
- Communication channels and media.
- Local area network standards.
- Local area network hardware and connectivity.
- Local area network topologies and network interconnections.
- Local area network software architecture.

The final sections discuss cost issues associated with local area network purchase and operation and factors relating to the selection of LANs.

Major Functions of Local Area Networks

Organizations are acquiring an ever-increasing variety of information technology systems: personal computers, word processors, intelligent terminals, workstations, high-capacity floppy and hard disk systems, private branch exchanges (PBXs), and enterprise systems. At the same time, demands on functionality are growing rapidly. Formerly, an organization's most difficult problem in using these new technologies effectively stemmed from the absence of equipment interconnection standards and the inability of traditional computer architectures to offer any flexible solution.

Chapter 2 looked at a variety of local area network applications, including

- Terminal-to-host connectivity.
- Increased processing power as a result of distributed processors.
- Sharing of a printer or hard disk in a workstation cluster.
- Access to a variety of wide area network services.
- Control of equipment in a manufacturing environment.

Although applications differ in their particular needs, all applications require the ability to exchange information among various computer-related devices in a local area, whether a room, an office, factory, or a warehouse. This functional requirement for communication, both among multiple computer systems within an organization and between those systems and shared resources, is met by the local area network, which can be defined as follows:

A *local area network* is a communications network that provides interconnection of a variety of data communication devices within a limited geographical area.

The geographical scope of a local area network is small, most commonly a single building, although increased functionality now requires local and wide area networks to be interconnected—a requirement that can cause considerable difficulty.

Another distinguishing feature of a local area network is that it is generally a privately owned rather than a public or commercially available system. Usually a single organization owns both the network and the attached devices.

Local Area Network Functional Principles

Compared to terminal-like devices, a local area network generally has an inexpensive communications medium and high data rates. Every node on the network can communicate with every other node, and the network requires no central node or processor. Messages are "broadcast" over the communications medium, with a destination address included. Only the intended receiver is expected to respond, although other stations have the capability to "listen in." Thus, a high level of security, such as that found in point-to-point networks, is not present unless security techniques are used, as we discuss in Chapter 11. Local area networks are meant to be highly reliable so that if a station fails, it will simply be unavailable without interrupting communications among the remaining stations. Similarly, it is possible to add new stations without disrupting the ongoing communications flow.

Due to the limited-distance nature of local area networks, another standard feature is the ability to interconnect multiple networks. The internetwork link, usually called a *bridge, router,* or *gateway,* may form a high-speed interface for closely coupled networks, or it may depend on a more conventional telecommunications network, such as one of those discussed in Chapter 4, for reliably transmitting data from city to city or around the world.

One of the most important potential benefits of a local area network relates to system evolution. In a nonnetworked installation such as a time-sharing center, all processing power exists in one or a few systems. To upgrade hardware, existing applications software must be either converted to new hardware or reprogrammed, introducing the risk of error in either case. Even adding new applications on the same hardware or enhancing existing applications can introduce errors and reduce the performance of the entire system.

With a local area network, it is possible to gradually replace applications or systems, thus avoiding the "all-or-nothing" approach. In addition, older but still useful (now referred to as "legacy") equipment can be left in the system to run a single application if the cost of moving that application to a new system is not justified. A local area network also provides the potential to connect devices from multiple vendors, giving users greater flexibility.

One of the significant benefits of a local area network lies in the potential to connect devices from multiple vendors. However, the local area network does not guarantee interoperability and that these devices can interoperate seamlessly. Two word processors from different vendors can be attached to a local area network, but will most likely use different file formats and control characters. Some form of format-conversion software will be required to take a file from one system and edit it on the other.

In summary, local area networks offer the following advantages over centralized processing systems:

- Control is distributed, thus increasing reliability.
- Use is made of the significant processing power of PCs (and of the low cost per PC relative to mainframe or minicomputer systems).
- Equipment from multiple vendors can be interconnected.
- Better sharing of resources is possible.

A local area network has potential pitfalls as well. First, data are usually *distributed* in a local area network to allow the various resources to be shared among multiple users or at least ensure that access to data will be possible from multiple sources. Distributed systems imply some loss of control; it is difficult to manage this resource, enforce standards for software and data, and control the information available through a network. Thus, the primary benefit of networking distributed systems also incorporates the primary pitfall!

Second, distributed systems introduce the problems of data integrity (e.g., two users trying to update a database at the same time), security and management of data, and privacy.

As we indicated a number of times in earlier chapters, local area networks seldom function in isolation from other local or wide area networks. Therefore, the major functions cannot be seen in isolation either. Undoubtedly the major function of local area networks today is *sharing*—sharing data on the file servers as well as sharing expensive peripheral devices such as laser printers, plotters, gateways, and so on, along with the interconnecting cable systems. This idea was introduced in the application examples in Chapter 2; in this chapter we will focus on the equipment used to carry out these sharing processes.

The second major function of the local area network is *connectivity*, which provides users with access to a range of applications and services. We address this topic in the next section.

The workstation, which is the focus of a user's activity, must be able to operate as a stand-alone device without connection to the network. All of the applications usually associated with it, such as word processing and spreadsheets, need to be able to function without access to the network. Connectivity to the local area network therefore *enhances* the functionality by providing shared access to the file servers, gateway servers, and other peripheral equipment for a number of users. Further, connectivity to a wide area network to gain access to other local area networks and to public and corporate databases further enhances the functionality for the user.

Following are important issues relating to local area network functionality:

1. The local area network boom has resulted from lower hardware costs, availability of network and application software, and the use of workstations in the workplace.

2. When large volumes of data need to be transferred, local area networks provide much improved functionality over the use of magnetic tapes or the use of highly specific vendor protocols such as those associated with the early IBM mainframe systems.

3. Substantial speed is available for data transfer. Local area network speeds of 10 to 100 Mbps are 200 to 2,000 times faster than the link speeds typically used in earlier mainframe networks.

4. Data transfer is under program control and therefore offers greater efficiency than is possible with operator intervention.

5. Resource sharing is a most important function because of the high cost of peripheral equipment, which includes hard disks, laser printers, and software (it is cheaper to purchase a license for a *network* version of the and software than to purchase individual copies).

6. Disk sharing has given way to file sharing, which offers better use of the hardware resources and lower software costs. However, shared access to files creates a number of problems that have to be carefully solved by concurrency-driven operating system programs.

7. Functionality can be improved by offering the user access to a **structured query language (SQL)** for making standard requests to databases.

8. The local area network can be used to share other devices such as fax machines, modems, gateways to wide area networks, and a variety of special-purpose equipment and associated software. This capability, however, introduces problems of resource allocation, since users' needs are rarely evenly distributed in time. Note that the intention is that use of the network facility (e.g., a laser printer) should be no more difficult than use of the same dedicated facility.

9. Functionality should remain simple; for example, starting an application from a file server should be no more difficult than starting it from a local hard disk.

10. With the evolution of local area networks, individual productivity applications have become work group applications. Work group productivity tools are collectively referred to as groupware, which allows users to communicate and coordinate activities such as those discussed in Chapter 2 (e.g., electronic mail, bulletin boards, calendaring, project management, decision support systems).

11. Local area network functionality has moved from simple hardware resource sharing through data and application sharing and to idea sharing and personnel coordination.

Communication Channels and Media: Comparative Benefits and Drawbacks

A local area network can be described as a communications network that covers a limited geographical area, typically in the range of .1 to 1 miles. Data rates on a local area network also vary. In general, most local area networks operate at 10 or 16 Mbps, although there is now a move to 100 Mbps "switched" or "dedicated" connections. To put local area networks into perspective, the following table shows the relationship among a number of different local and wide area network categories, some of which were discussed in Chapter 4:

Type of Network	Typical Speed	Typical Distance
LAN (standard Ethernet or token ring)	10–16 Mbps	.1–1 miles
LAN (high-speed Ethernet)	100 Mbps	.1–1 miles
LAN (FDDI interconnection network)	100 Mbps	1–100 miles
WAN (DDN)	2.4 Kbps–2 Mbps	1–10,000 miles
WAN (PSN)	2.4 Kbps–64 Kbps	1–10,000 miles
WAN (frame relay network)	9.6 Kbps—2 Mbps	1–10,000 miles
WAN (ISDN)	64 Kbps–2 Mbps	1–10,000 miles
LAN and WAN (ATM network)	25–622 Mbps	any distance

Abbreviations:

DDN   digital data network
PSN   packet switching network
ISDN   integrated services digital network
FDDI   fiber distributed data interface
ATM   asynchronous transfer mode (multimedia)

Local area networks generally experience fewer data transmission errors and lower communications costs than do wide area networks, and cost-performance trade-offs therefore differ significantly. Also, it is possible to achieve greater integration between the local area network and the attached devices, since they are generally owned by the same organization.

Local and wide area networks can vary in other characteristics. For example, the protocols used in each case are entirely different. The error rate on local area networks is usually much lower than that on wide area networks, although this is changing as a result of the widespread use of fiber in wide area networks. The "loading" or usage of local area network channels is often only about 5 percent, whereas with the high cost of communication channels for wide area networks, a loading of up to 70 to 80 percent is common. As we will see later in this chapter, the topologies also vary widely.

In Chapter 4 we examined the key characteristics of the well-known transmission media: twisted pair wire, coaxial cable, and fiber optic cable. The characteristics of these media are largely the same whether they are used in a local or wide area network. Therefore, you should refer to the section "Communication Channels and Media" in Chapter 4.

Popular Cabling Systems for Ethernet: 10BASE2, 10BASE5, 10BROAD36, 10BASE-T, and 10BASE-F

Since Ethernet local area networks occupy about 90 percent of the market, it is important to discuss the characteristics of the five cabling systems shown in Figure 5–1, which are built from segments of coaxial cable, twisted wire pairs, or optical fibers. In these five designations, the first number (*1* or *10*) indicates the transmission rate in megabits per second. *BASE* indicates that the computer data utilize the full bandwidth of the cable and that the nodes transmit the information in baseband by using a special encoding technique called **Manchester encoding**. *BROAD* identifies a broadband network in which a number of channels are employed for different types of applications and the bits are encoded using a different encoding technique called *differential phase shift keying* (DPSK). The number at the end of the designation (*5, 2,* or *36*) is the maximum length of a segment of the network as a multiple of 100 meters.

10BASE-T designates a 10 Mbps baseband network that uses twisted wire pairs as the transmission medium. Twisted pair cable has undergone much development recently. When used to interconnect peripheral equipment to hubs, it is called *data grade* cable. As noted in Chapter 4, it is available in two commonly used groupings: category 3 (for transmission of data at up to 10 Mbps or possibly 100 Mbps if four instead of two pairs are used) and category 5 (for transmission of data at up to 100 Mbps).

The 10BASE-F standard is a cheaper method of fiber-based transmission than the FDDI standard (to be discussed later in this chapter) and replaces the older FOIRL (fiber optic inter-repeater link) standard. It is particularly useful for point-to-point connection among buildings where electrical isolation is necessary. There are three versions of 10BASE-F. The best-known form is 10BASE-FL (up to 2 km) for point-to-point links, as shown in Figure 5–1. It replaces the older FOIRL, which had a distance limitation of only 1 km. 10BASE-FP is a passive hub of fused glass fiber which divides input power to all outputs. 10BASE-FB is a backbone system for use in situations where many **repeaters** are needed end to end. This protocol minimizes interpacket gap, which can often affect network size when very short distances are required between repeaters.

The **medium access control (MAC)** protocol specified by these five standards is the **CSMA/CD** Ethernet protocol, both of which are described later in this chapter. The nodes on a 10BASE5 or 10BASE2 network detect a collision when they measure a large current on the cable. Collisions on 10BASE-T are detected by the **medium access unit (MAU)** when it locates activity on both the transmitter and receiver lines. The repeater unit then transmits a special signal that informs the nodes of the collision. The nodes on the 10BROAD36 network detect collisions by comparing what they transmit on one frequency with what a head-end station repeats on another frequency. 10BROAD36 will soon be replaced by ATM protocols, which are described in Chapter 12.

It is important not to view the transmission media in isolation from the transmission standards to be used in conjunction with them (to be discussed in the following section) or from the applications and environments in which they are to be used.

There is considerable overlap in the use of these cabling systems. Rapid changes are taking place in this area, and the benefits and drawbacks are constantly changing. Clearly the use of **unshielded twisted pair (UTP)** is now extremely important as a result of standardization of various categories of cables in use together with their various electrical and transmission properties.

Many installations still use both thick and thin coaxial cable since they provide excellent immunity from interference, although there are no specifications suitable for transmission speeds of 100 Mbps. Fiber optic cable is excellent for interconnecting buildings where electrical isolation is necessary and for the interconnecting floors in a building, although coaxial cable is also commonly used for this purpose. For wiring on floors, UTP has now become the popular standard. In special cases requiring high data rates, fiber optic cable can be used right up to the user's workstation, as might be the case with distributed CAD/CAM applications (such situations are still rare, however).

Due to the requirements for local area network security, individual workstations are now wired directly to the distribution boxes (or hubs, and concentrators, as they are called) discussed later in this chapter. Therefore, UTP has become a cheap and popular transmission medium for meeting these requirements.

Local area network cabling has given rise to the term **intelligent building**. This does not mean that the building can talk; rather, it means that it is wired for local area network equipment interconnection so that when a business moves in with its

FIGURE 5–1

Twisted pair and coaxial cable systems

	10BASE5 Ethernet	10BASE2 Cheapernet	10BROAD36 Broadband	10BASE-T Twisted Pair	10BASE-F Fiber Optic
Medium	Coaxial cable, 50 ohms–10 mm	Coaxial cable, 50 ohms–5 mm	Coaxial cable, 75 ohms	Unshielded twisted pair	Fiber optic cable
Signals	10 Mbps— Manchester encoding	10 Mbps— Manchester encoding	10Mbps—DPSK	10 Mbps— Manchester encoding	10 Mbps— Manchester encoding
Maximum segment	500 m	185 m	1,800 m*	100 m	2.0 km
Maximum distance	2.5 km	.925 km	3.6 km	1 km	2.0 km
Nodes per segment	100	30		2	2
Topology	Bus	Bus	Bus	Star (hub)	Point-to-point

Note: slot time = 512 bits; gap time = 96 bits; jam time = 32–48 bits.
        * send and receive cables required, hence, $1,800 \times 2 = 3600$ meters.

computer equipment, connection can be readily made and the applications run. After all, when a building is constructed or renovated, it would be unthinkable to install electrical wiring, air conditioning, and plumbing after the building is completed. In the same way, local area network cabling needs to be put in place at an appropriate time.

Sometimes computer equipment is connected to this wiring to monitor and control services for the building rather than just for the business unit located in the building. In this way, air conditioning, heating, lighting, telephone, and other services within the building are centrally monitored and controlled by a computer.

The installation of local area network cabling, particularly for voice and data services, is an essential prerequisite for the successful operation of the various local and wide area network applications we discuss here. Consider the following branch of a bank in Seattle.

INTELLIGENT BUILDING FOR THE FUTURE

When a new branch of a well-known bank was built in downtown Seattle last year, the telecommunications channels for local area network applications and voice services needed to support a wide range of financial application requirements were installed as part of the project, together with a large amount of flexibility for potential expansion."Voice and several kinds of data are intermingled on miles of copper wire around each floor, together with a high-capacity fiber optic backbone traveling up the building and linking the workstations on different floors via a local area network," states Peter Stewart, the bank's systems manager.

"The most important benefit is flexibility, since in our old building, every time someone wanted to move a workstation, we had to get our engineering people to run new cables. Now it's just a matter of moving the workstation and patching it into the local area network hub at the new location."

A lot of this activity happens at the bank anyway, he says. "People are always forming and reforming into new groups and subgroups—it's part of the business of a modern bank. We need flexibility to meet customer demands and the demands of the market and also to be able to introduce new financial applications without rewiring and installing a new local area network cabling system. Telecommunications is thus critically linked to the bank's success."

All telephone traffic for the building's PBX and all computer traffic to and from the mainframe computers and over local area networks is carried over structured cabling. Ethernet, voice extension lines, and X.25 links all travel over the same wires with transport conversion provided by adaptors and transceivers. The treasury department's Reuters and Telerate terminals, with their high-bandwidth demand, are supported with optical fiber right up to the point of connection.

"Structured local area network cabling has saved us, and should continue to save us, significant time and money," says Peter Stewart. "Without it, we would have had to employ a full-time cabling technician just for recabling."

We can see from the above example that to support the business applications on the local area network, flexible cabling systems must be in place that are not dependent upon a particular vendor's local area network architecture, such as Novell, IBM, Digital, or 3Com.

Local Area Network Standards

Standards benefit vendors as well as users. Designing, manufacturing, and maintaining proprietary local area networks is expensive, and as standards become popular, components become cheaper.

The key to the development of the local area network market is the availability of a low-cost interface; the cost of connecting equipment to a local area network must be much lower than the cost of the actual equipment. However, chip manufacturers were reluctant to commit the necessary resources unless there was potential for a high-volume market. A local area network standard ensures that volume, and also enables equipment from a variety of manufacturers to intercommunicate.

IEEE802 Local Area Network Standards

The main body responsible for most of the local area network standards in use today is the **IEEE802** standards committee. Its goal was to set standards so that different manufacturers' equipment could be plug-compatible on the same network in the same way many manufacturers are providing X.25-compatible equipment to interface with PSNs. IEEE802 undertook to standardize the bottom two layers of the OSI model (discussed in Chapter 4) as the CCITT originally did for the bottom three layers (X.25) and the ISO did for the bottom two layers of the data link layer protocol called HDLC and used by X.25. The bottom two layers were chosen because they have the greatest impact on semiconductor manufacturing of local area network chips.

A three-layer reference model incorporating the following technological specifications was required (see Figure 5–2):

- A physical layer (to define the cabling and plug standards).
- A medium access control (MAC) layer to define the access mechanism to the physical layer.
- A **logical link control (LLC)** layer to provide end-to-end services independently of the underlying MAC and physical layers.

These three layers perform the following basic functions:

1. The logical link control (LLC) layer is responsible for data transfer, sequencing, flow control, and error recovery.
2. The medium access control (MAC) layer is responsible for delimitation of frames, frame check sequencing, station selection, and access control.

FIGURE 5–2

Correspondence between ISO Model and IEEE802 LAN/RM

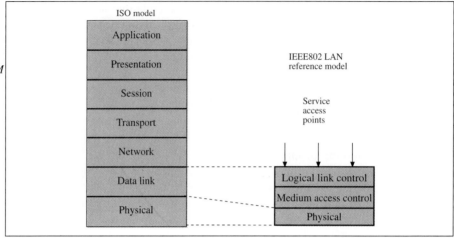

3. The physical layer is responsible for signalling, bit encoding, and medium handling.

The functions of the LLC layer are now often performed by IP (Internet protocol) as part of the TCP/IP protocol suite. At the MAC layer, there are three standards. First, CSMA/CD has converged with the Ethernet specification, which is well suited to typical office applications. Also, two forms of token access have been standardized (although only token ring is normally used in practice) for time-critical applications, such as process control, as well as for office applications. At the physical layer, changes are occurring constantly, mainly as a result of new developments in signaling standards associated with twisted pair and fiber optic cables as previously discussed.

The IEEE802 local area network standards have been formally adopted by the ISO and are shown in Figure 5–3.

Another view of the IEEE802 standards and their relationship to the ISO model are shown in Figure 5–4.

Logical Link Control (LLC) Layer. The logical link control layer provides for the exchange of data between service access points (SAPs), which are multiplexed over a single physical connection to the local area network. The LLC provides for both a connectionless, datagramlike service and a connection-oriented, virtual circuit–like service.

In the connectionless or datagram service (type 1), frames are transmitted with source and destination addresses but without the need for establishing a logical link. In this mode, frames are not acknowledged and there are no flow control or error recovery procedures. Since a session does not exist, there is no guarantee that frames sent will be received by the destination. Therefore, the higher layers of the architecture must provide the recovery and frame sequencing. This implies that the intelligence needed to recover from these errors must reside in the end stations, since

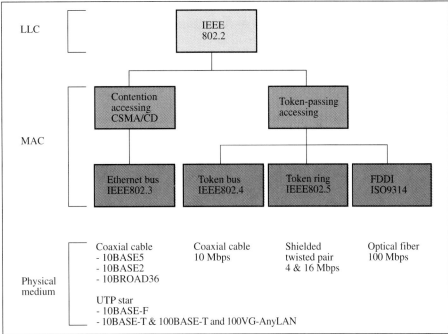

FIGURE 5–3

The IEEE802 local area network standards

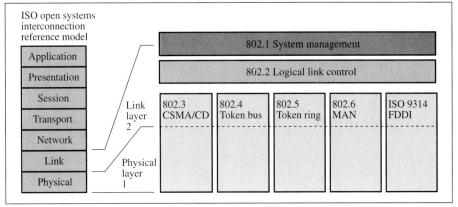

FIGURE 5–4

IEEE802 standards and their relationship to the ISO model

the network itself offers no ability to recover from errors. In this way, it resembles the conventional postal system, where once a letter is posted there is normally no absolute guarantee that it will not be lost in the system. An acknowledgment sent back to the sender to indicate that the letter has arrived is equivalent to an upper layer architectural function. The Internet protocol (IP) of the TCP/IP suite is an example of a connectionless protocol.

In the connection-oriented or virtual circuit service (type 2), a logical link is established prior to any exchange of user data, and the services provided include sequenced delivery of frames, error detection and correction, and flow control. Hence, connection-oriented services provide a reliable end-to-end service capable of supporting high traffic rates, with minimal impact on the processing capacities of the individual devices being served. This implies that the intelligence resides in the network, since it has the ability to recover from errors. In this way, it is comparable to existing data link control protocols such as HDLC, SDLC, and TCP of the TCP/IP suite or the X.25 packet switching network.

Medium Access Control (MAC) Layer.   The MAC layer contains the mechanisms to control transmissions on the local area network so that two or more stations do not try to transmit at the same time, and, if they do, the contention resulting from the collision of packets is resolved in a satisfactory manner. It also provides station-to-station addressing, start and end frame delimiters, error control, and a priority mechanism (token ring only). The two main mechanisms now widely used on the market are CSMA/CD (Ethernet), a probabilistic technique, and token ring, a deterministic technique. Thus in the case of Ethernet there is a high probability (but no absolute guarantee) that a message will arrive within a specified time. In the case of token rings it is possible to determine the worst response time under a defined load.

Physical Layer.   The physical layer specifies the mechanical, electrical, and functional procedures and provides the capability to transmit and receive bits. Other characteristics specified by the physical layer include cable connectors, cable characteristics, signaling schemes, and encoding schemes such as Biphase-M and Differential Manchester. Recent developments with standards in this layer now enable transmission speeds of 100 Mbps over twisted pair cable and almost unlimited capacity with fiber optic cable.

Other Ongoing IEEE Local Area Network Standards Developments

IEEE802.1b	Network management
IEEE802.1d	Bridges
IEEE802.1e	Software distribution
IEEE802.2	Logical link control
IEEE802.6	Metropolitan area networks (MAN)—designed to provide a "ring or bus main" within a city area similar to the way water or electricity is distributed
IEEE802.7	Broadband LANs
IEEE802.8	Fiber optic media
IEEE802.9	LANs and integrated services digital networks (ISDNs)
IEEE802.10	LLC/MAC layer security system
IEEE802.11	Wireless LANs, including infrared, microwave, and spread spectrum transmission systems
IEEE802.12	100VG–AnyLAN four-pair category 3 cable for 100 Mbps Ethernet

Ethernet: Principles and Operation

CSMA/CD (carrier sense multiple access/collision detect) (IEEE802.3, ISO 8802/3).   To transmit data, a station first listens to the medium to determine if another station is transmitting. If there is no "carrier," the station may transmit. Since the protocol is multiple access, two stations could start to transmit at the same time, causing a collision. The collision is detected as the station listens to the medium *while* it is transmitting. Both stations then stop transmitting and try again.

Carrier sense (CS) is the ability of each node to detect any traffic on the channel (called *listen-before-talking*—see Figure 5–5). Nodes defer transmitting whenever they sense traffic on the channel. However, because of the time it takes for a signal to travel across the network (called the *propagation delay*), two nodes could detect that the channel is free either exactly at or close to the same time, since each will not yet have detected the other's signal. In such a situation, a collision between the two messages will occur.

The *multiple access (MA)* feature of CSMA/CD lets any node send a message immediately upon sensing that the channel is free of traffic. Thus, a substantial portion of the waiting that is characteristic of noncontention techniques is eliminated. In token passing, a node that wishes to transmit must wait for the token to circulate to all nodes that precede it on the channel. CSMA/CD contains no such delays, and can allow quicker access to and greater utilization of the channel.

Collision detection (CD) is carried out by nodes while they are transmitting by monitoring the energy level (i.e., the electrical signal level) of the channel (called *listen-while-talking*—see Figure 5–6). Message collisions change the energy level on the channel. Collision detect is the ability of a transmitting node to sense a change in the energy level of the channel and interpret it as a collision. Upon detecting a collision, each node involved backs off and abandons its transmission, waits for a brief interval, and attempts to transmit again. The period before retransmitting is either fixed (at a unique interval for each station) or random. The selection of random intervals is more effective in avoiding further collisions. If successive collisions occur, the nodes back off and wait a longer period each time. The nodes also emit a short burst of noise, called a *jam* (32 to 48 bits in length), to ensure that all other nodes involved have detected the collision.

FIGURE 5–5

Carrier sense multiple access (listen before talking to avoid collisions)

Figure 5–6

*Collision detect
(listen while
talking to detect
collisions)*

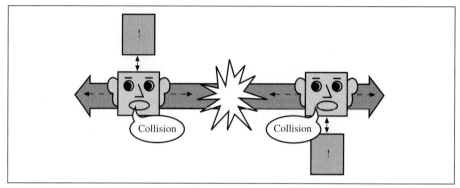

To ensure that all nodes, including the transmitting node, are able to hear a collision on the channel, packets must be of a certain minimum length. That size is called the *slot time* ($64 \times 8 = 512$ bits in length), which is slightly greater than the round-trip propagation delay time between the network's two most distant nodes.

The fewer collisions that occur on the channel, the more efficient is the use of the network, since less retransmission is required and the channel will be less busy and more available overall. The efficiency of the CSMA/CD mechanism is related to the ratio of the slot time to the average duration of transmitted packets. Once the slot time has passed in the transmission of a packet, the node is said to have *acquired* the channel; at this point, the possibility for collision no longer exists, since all nodes will have had the chance to detect traffic on the channel and defer to the transmitting node. The remainder of the packet is sent in the most efficient manner possible, contention free. It follows, then, that the CSMA/CD mechanism is used most efficiently when packets are larger; the longer the packets that are broadcast, the fewer collisions will occur relative to the total time the channel is used.

Due to the ability to listen before and during transmission, the number of collisions can be quite low, and successive collisions between nodes are rare. Thus, CSMA/CD is a highly efficient form of distributed access. In addition, since any remaining portion of a message that has been in a collision is not sent, no time or channel capacity is wasted. This enhances the already low-delay nature of CSMA/CD.

Because there is no predetermined order of access by nodes in CSMA/CD, no guarantee exists of a maximum wait time before getting access to the channel. However, since each node randomly bids for the channel, a statistical guarantee can be calculated.

Token Ring: Principles and Operation

Token Ring Architecture (IEEE802.5, ISO8802/5).   With a token ring system, when a station wishes to transmit, it captures the token and transmits the frame of data onto the ring. This frame is then copied by the receiving station but continues to circulate around the ring until it is removed by the transmitting station and checked for verification. The transmitting station then puts the free token back onto the ring for another station to use.

Token rings guarantee a minimum and maximum response time and are therefore effective when the load is high and a guaranteed minimum access time is required. The total delay on the ring equals the sum of the delay at each station (about 1 microsecond) plus the propagation delay. Rings do not suffer attenuation as Ethernet CSMA/CD networks do, and the use of several interconnected rings may be preferable to one large ring in which failure of one node can cause a major problem.

In Figure 5–7, diagram (*a*) shows the sending station (node A) looking for a free token. When it finds one, it changes the free token to busy and adds the data. In diagram (*b*) if the destination station (node C) is active, it will copy the frame and set the *frame-copied* and *address-recognized* bits. This lets the transmitting station (node A) know that the frame was received. The sending station (node A) then removes the frame and releases a new token onto the ring.

Local Area Network Hardware and Connectivity

In this section, we address the actual physical units that are connected to a local area network and the devices that permit local and wide area networks to be interconnected. Although we focus on the hardware devices, these are supplied by the vendors with the appropriate software to operate and interconnect them.

Terminals, PCs, Workstations, and Microcomputers

Much confusion surrounds the terms *terminal, PC, workstation,* and *microcomputer,* and all are used interchangeably. It does not matter which term you use as long as it is clear what function(s) is being specified.

Terminal usually means simply a keyboard and screen without the hardware or software used to operate as a stand-alone computer. Sometimes it is called a *dumb terminal,* in contrast to an *intelligent terminal,* a term that is synonymous with *PC.* Dumb terminals are connected to a device that has the communications intelligence needed to access the local area network. This type of device is also called by different names, including *controller, concentrator, hub, repeater,* and *server.* Clearly the

FIGURE 5–7

Token ring: (a) free token; (b) frame in transmission; (c) frame being removed and free token issued

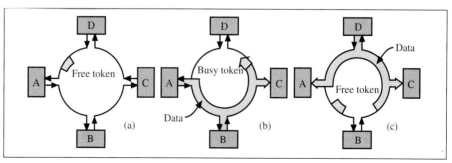

advantage here is that the hardware and software for communication with the local area network need only be purchased once and its use is shared by the dumb terminals. The three terminals connected to the controller labeled C in Figure 5–10 (p. 186) is an example of such a configuration.

The term *PC (personal computer)* implies a device that has its own main memory and microprocessor that can function in stand-alone mode. In addition, it may have floppy and hard disk drives. The term *PC* usually implies any compatible PC clone, but is sometimes extended to include an Apple Macintosh which is certainly an example of a PC. However, the IBM compatible PC and the Apple Macintosh cannot be interconnected without special software.

Once a network communications card and appropriate software are loaded into the PC, the unit is usually referred to as a *workstation* because it becomes a device for use on a local area network. Strictly speaking, a workstation can be thought of as identical to a PC, but usually the implication is that it can be connected to the network. High-end workstations such as CAD systems can be standalone.

The terms *microcomputer* and *PC* are often used interchangeably. Again, the implication is that the microcomputer becomes a workstation once the necessary local area network communications hardware card and software have been added.

Local Area Network Connectivity

A PC may be connected to other PCs and to host computers in a variety of ways. These types of connections offer some of the facilities discussed in Chapter 2, including data sharing, device sharing, remote operation, access to wide area network services, electronic mail, backup facilities, file transfer, host access, and **terminal emulation** (discussed shortly).

PC-to-PC Direct Connection.   Two PCs can be connected with a simple crossover cable, typically using the standard RS-232/V.24 interface plugs and the PC's asynchronous port as shown in Figure 5–8. The main use for this type of connection is to exchange data used in applications such as files, spreadsheets, and databases. However, the methods by which data can be exchanged are severely limited, as is the distance between PCs.

PC-to-PC Connection via a Dial-up or Leased Line.   When two PCs are *remote* from each other, a connection can be formed by way of a dial-up or leased line, again using the PC's asynchronous port as shown in Figure 5–9. This implies the use of

FIGURE 5–8

Direct PC-to-PC connection

modems for an analog connection (e.g., a datel or dial-up connection) or network terminating units (NTUs) (or CSU/DSUs in the case of a digital link; refer back to Chapter 4).

PC-to-Host-Connection.   PCs can replace dumb terminals in mainframe networks as well as perform independent processing tasks. This enables a user to share centrally stored files and utilize the powerful processing facilities of a host computer in addition to normal PC operation.

Connecting a PC to a host may require the addition of PC-to-host hardware and possibly software depending on whether a basic asynchronous connection or a full terminal emulation is required. The hardware usually consists of either an interface board that fits into the PC's expansion slot or an external protocol conversion box that acts as an interface (protocol converter) between the PC and the host. Such an interface must perform layer 1 conversions involving electrical connections, as well as layer 2 conversions relating to data link control (frame format, headers, asynchronous/synchronous methods, character conversion, link setup, and error control). If the PC is to emulate a terminal, it must appear to have the characteristics of a terminal expected by the host mainframe. This is called terminal emulation. A terminal emulator must be able to reformat data generated on the PC so that the host receives the data in a form that it recognizes. Many PC-to-host communications products emulate IBM 3270 terminals.

This form of PC-to-host communication has been a stepping stone to a fully integrated local area network. It does have a benefit for users who require access to both types of computers. Hosts are relieved of chores that burden a large system, and the PC users can make the best use of both the host and the PC when they combine the freedom and flexibility of independent processing with the central storage and processing power of host computers. The various options for PC-to-host connectivity are shown in Figure 5–10.

PC Local Area Networks.   A PC-based local area network consists of PCs, interface cards that let the PCs communicate with one another, one or more hard disks for mass data storage, peripherals such as printers, interconnection cables, and software that manages the network. A PC local area network must provide

- Device sharing (disks, printers, etc.).
- Record locking (to avoid more than one user modifying a record at a time).
- Multitasking (to allow multiple users access to a single device).

FIGURE 5–9

PC-to-PC connection via a wide area network link

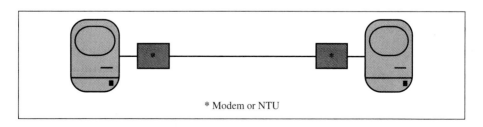

* Modem or NTU

FIGURE 5–10

Different PC interconnections to a host computer

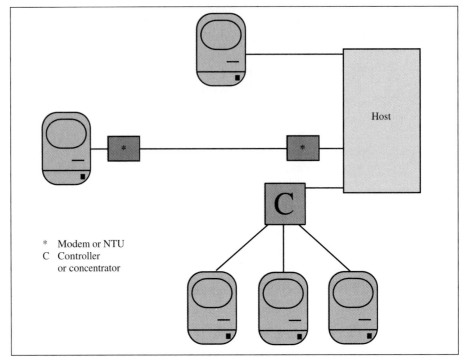

*   Modem or NTU
C   Controller
      or concentrator

Features that are important to managing multiuser networks, such as record locking and security (which ensure that only authorized users have access to data), are not part of a basic PC operating system. As a result, manufacturers have enhanced the basic operating system to permit these facilities.

Networks by their nature present problems. What happens when two users attempt to modify a spreadsheet file or update an inventory file at the same time? Obviously, concurrent data sharing requires a means of locking files so that they can be accessed by only one user at a time. Local area network vendors provide such facilities as part of the network operating system. The key to successful networking lies not only in the appropriate hardware but also in the availability and usefulness of PC software, much of which needs to be adapted for multiuser environments.

Local Area Network Servers

A variety of servers can be attached to local area networks, as shown in Figure 5–11.

File Server.   The primary use of a local area network is the sharing of files among multiple users. The **file server** is usually a fast PC, such as a Pentium, with a large-capacity disk with high-speed access of less than 10 msec and disk capacity ranging from around 1 to 10 Gbytes as well as 16 to 32 Mbytes of RAM. In spite of these parameters, disk access speed, size of RAM, and transaction processing rates at the file server account for the single biggest factor in poor local area network performance.

Incorrect cabling can be another problem. Even though most PCs have a local hard disk, access to a few processor and disk-hungry applications on the file server can cause major problems.

Print Server.   The print server is usually a low-end PC running a special program to store and queue the spooled print tasks for the printers attached to the print server. Thus, expensive peripherals such as laser printers and color dot matrix printers can be shared by users on the local area network.

Terminal Server.   Terminal servers provide a cost-effective and flexible way to connect (usually at speeds up to 64 Kbps) cheaper asynchronous terminals to hosts in a local area network. Each terminal connected to a terminal server can access services running on service nodes connected to the same local area network. For example, a Digital Server 500 is a network terminal switch for Ethernet local area networks and supports the simultaneous operation of up to 128 terminals at speeds up to 64 Kbps.

Host Server.   This term is less commonly used and refers to a host or "enterprise" system that acts as the server. Typically a host server has aproximately the speed and capacity of a Digital 8350/8800 or an IBM 3080/3090.

Gateway Server.   This is a generic term that is used to mean a bridge or a router (or some combination of the two) that provides connections to wide area networks such as a digital data network (DDN), a packet switching network (PSN), an integrated services digital network (ISDN), or a frame relay network.

FIGURE 5–11

Types of servers attached to a local area network

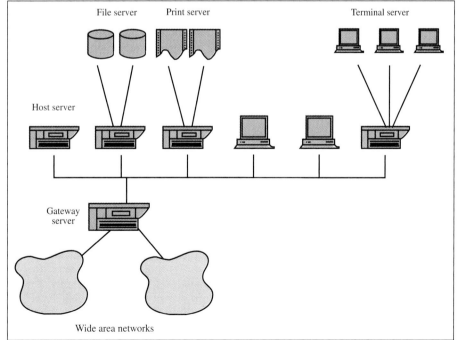

Repeaters/Hubs, Bridges, Routers, Brouters, and Gateways

Repeaters/hubs, bridges, and gateways provide for the interconnection of networks. As Figure 5–12 shows, a variety of products are available to suit topology, distance, and other configuration needs.

Networks A and B are homogeneous and might be, for example, Ethernet cable segments from the same vendor to be interconnected. Networks D and E may also be Ethernet cable segments from the same vendor to be interconnected, but the number of PCs connected may make it strategic to subdivide the network into manageable sections. Networks E and C may be two local area networks from different suppliers (e.g., IBM token ring and Novell NetWare bus systems). In this case, a considerable amount of data must be reformatted; in fact, full conversion of the communication protocols is required, as well as interconnection to a variety of both local and wide area networks running different architectures. Networks D and B have incompatible architectures requiring conversation at many layers (e.g., Novell NetWare and Microsoft **Windows NT** systems).

Repeater and Hub.   A *repeater* is used to extend the length of a cable segment. It retimes, amplifies, and repeats all signals it receives from one segment and passes the signal to the next segment(s). This device implements layer 1 of the OSI model and merely regenerates the original signal and permits extension of the network topology, particularly to a variety of cable media. The signal is reformatted, and no

FIGURE 5–12

*Local area
network
interconnection
devices*

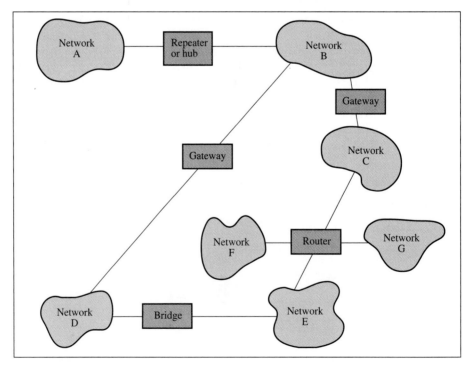

filtering or isolation of the messages occurs (as occurs with bridges). Repeaters are useful in extending the Ethernet local area network beyond the 100-meter UTP, 185-meter thin Ethernet, or 500-meter thick Ethernet recommended maximum cable segment lengths.

Repeaters are now most commonly used to interconnect different cable types, such as fiber optic, thin and thick Ethernet, and UTP (unshielded twisted pair) cables. Examples include the Digital Ethernet Repeater (DECRepeater 900TM—a multiport repeater consisting of thin-wire Ethernet on one side and 32 UTP ports on the other) or the DECRepeater 90FA (interconnects fiber with thick or thin Ethernet cable). Many of these devices have an attached unit interface (AUI) port that provides connection to a transceiver, which in turn offers interfaces to thick or thin Ethernet, fiber, and most other physical cable types (see Figure 5–13).

A **hub** (sometimes called a *multiport repeater*) carries out the same functions a repeater does, but is usually associated with the connection of workstations in a star topology. Software is now added to the hub to provide for network management and security. A common configuration is a single cabinet with connections for about 16 devices. Hubs usually lack internal expansion capability.

Another, similar device consists of a modular cabinet with a common back-plane and slots that can accept various plug-in hardware modules for different wiring connections, management modules, and devices such as bridges (see the following section). This type of flexible and expandable device is commonly called an *intelligent concentrator*, *wiring concentrator,* or simply *concentrator.*

The distinctions between repeater/hub, and concentrator are not clear cut. Both terms are often used interchangeably in the network industry, and both devices are commonly used in conjunction with 10BASE-T cabling.

The main advantage of a concentrator over a hub is its ability not only to link different media types, such as UTP, thin Ethernet, thick Ethernet, and fiber optic cable, but also to manage all the nodes individually on those attached cables.

Bridge.   *Bridges* segment local area networks when there is too much traffic on a single bus or ring segment. It provides a means for filtering traffic local to a particular segment, work group, floor, and so on. For example, the DECbridge 90FL segments the local area network and also provides a physical interconnection for different media types (e.g., 10BASE-FL and 10BASE2).

FIGURE 5–13

Single and multiport repeaters/hubs

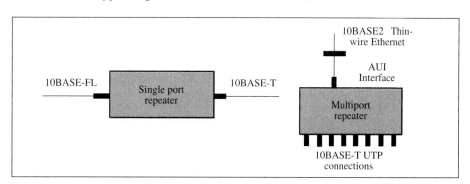

Bridges utilize a store-and-forward feature to receive, regenerate, and transmit frames. They do not retransmit all frames as a repeater or a hub does, but receive all frames on the local area network segment. They filter (discard) frames that are destined for the local side and forward (regenerate) only those frames that are destined for the remote side. In this way, bridges route frames based strictly on the destination address and do not depend on any routing protocol. Network devices on each side of a bridge simply address the frames to other devices as though they were on the same local area network and thus never address the bridge. Bridges do not depend on any other protocol beyond the link layer addresses and are therefore independent of the upper-layer protocols such as TCP/IP, IPX, AppleTalk, and DECnet.

A bridge allows a configuration of extended local area networks several times larger than the original Ethernet guidelines permitted. It improves network performance by dynamically managing the data traffic flow. Organizations can increase bandwidth efficiency by isolating traffic on heavily loaded segments from the rest of the network. Traffic management is done automatically while still providing full network connectivity. The locally destined traffic remains local. The remote traffic is forwarded to the specified destination.

A bridge only passes frames bound for stations beyond a particular subnet. For example, a large Ethernet local area network might be subdivided into three subnets (e.g., marketing, sales, personnel, etc.) and each subnet interconnected with a bridge. Bridges can also connect local area networks to wide area networks. In terms of the OSI model, the segments have separate MAC sublayers but a common IP or LLC sublayer. Most bridges are used to interconnect network segments of the same architecture or from the same vendor. However, the Multigate bridge interconnects two Ethernet technologies from different manufacturers: Apple's local area network (.254 Mbps CSMA/CA, twisted pair network) and Digital's local area network (10 Mbps, CSMA/CD network). A variety of special-purpose bridges are available; for example, some bridges can be used to interconnect a pair of local area networks over a wide area network link (e.g., DEC TRANSLAN), interconnect to microwave transmitters, and so on.

Figure 5–14 shows examples of bridges used to isolate departmental traffic from one another, yet provide connectivity for traffic addressed to other departmental groups. Figure 5–15 shows a similar arrangement to interconnect floors, but this time by using an FDDI ring in conjunction with bridges for high security and reliability. FDDI is discussed later in this chapter.

Router.   Local area networks joined by a *router* are physically and logically separate networks, whereas local area networks connected by a bridge are physically different but logically the same; that is, they share the same network address space. Unlike local area networks that are interconnected with bridges, routers are not transparent and are addressable by other devices on the local area network by the higher-layer protocols.

Routers specify the destination and route for each packet. The MAC and IP or LLC layers are different in the two subnetworks. For example, a Windows for Workgroups PC LAN, a Novell/NetWare Ethernet, and a Digital DECnet Ethernet can be interconnected via a router. Routers can therefore be used to direct packets and thus interconnect a variety of network architectures. An important distinction between a bridge and a router is that the bridge filters frames only by source and destination address, whereas a router can also filter by protocol type. A router can be specifically addressed in the network and can be instructed to filter traffic by layer 3 protocol type (e.g., TCP/IP, IPX, AppleTalk). Routers provide a considerable degree of management in the network and for the interfaces to wide area networks such as frame relay, digital data, and packet switching services. Routers are therefore used in applications somewhat different from those for bridges, although some new bridge products are adding routerlike functionality. Generally, each technology provides an interconnection of local area networks at a different level and with different inherent capabilities, but practical distinctions often become blurred.

FIGURE 5–14

Bridges interconnected via a backbone

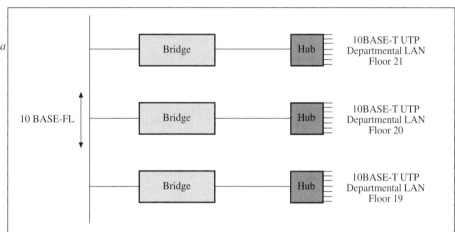

FIGURE 5–15

FDDI backbone with links to floors

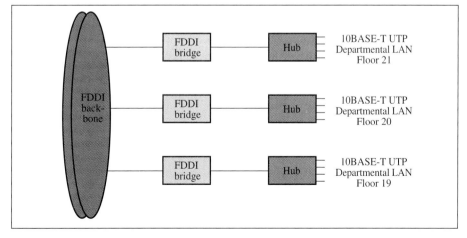

Well-known suppliers of routers include CISCO, 3Com, Baynet, Digital, Retix, and HP. Examples of routers include 3Com's Netbuilder and Digital's DECNIS600, DEC WANrouter250/500, and DEC WANrouter 90. These support interconnection of and conversion among a wide variety of layered architectures, including the following:

Layer 1	Layer 2	Layer 3
IEEE802.3/802.5	HDLC/SDLC	X.25
T1/E1	PPP/SLIP	TCP/IP
FDDI/T3	Frame relay	NetWare IPX
X.21	DDCMP	AppleTalk
	ISDN	DECnet
		Banyan VINES
		OSI

An important aspect of routers is the interconnection protocol used for routing the traffic flow among various nodes. Examples employed by these routers include OSPF (open shortest path first), IGP (interior gateway protocol), RIP (routing information protocol), and IS–IS (intermediate system–intermediate system). Figure 5–16 shows an example of structured wiring in a building using a router in conjunction with **collapsed backbone** cabling and hubs on each floor for specific departmental work groups.

Brouter.   A *brouter* is a term used less often now to represent combined bridge and router functions. It can control packet flow on selected packet types—for example, TCP/IP, IPX, and X.25—as well as filtering by frame address as defined for bridges. Generally, a brouter bridges where bridging is most appropriate and routes where routing is most appropriate. For example, some protocols, such as Digital's LAT, NetBIOS, and LU6.2, are nonroutable because they lack an address layer; thus, they can benefit from the use of a brouter.

Today organizations commonly buy interconnection equipment that is highly configurable. Depending on location, a unit might consist of some bridging cards, some router cards, and perhaps a hub card.

Gateway.   The term *gateway* is often used in its generic sense to designate some form of network interconnection that is often implemented by way of a bridge or a gateway. Frequently *gateway* implies a connection between a local and wide area network, and a gateway server provides such interconnection via a bridge or router. In its strict definition, a gateway totally rebuilds packets and provides full protocol conversion at all seven layers of the architecture. This function will allow two completely incompatible architectures, such as NetWare and UNIX, to communicate. This is usually an expensive option in terms of hardware and software costs as well as performance.

FIGURE 5–16

*Collapsed
backbone wiring
with router*

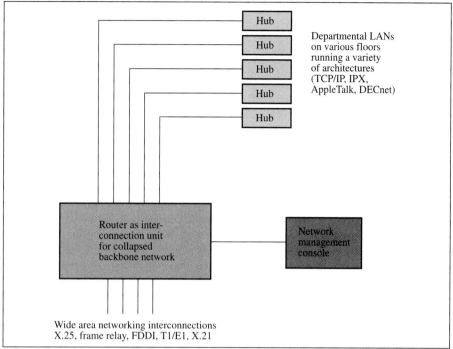

Figure 5–17 summarizes the key features of repeaters/hubs, bridges, routers, and gateways.

Local Area Network Topologies

In Chapter 4 we introduced the idea of topology with respect to wide area networks. Topology refers to the way multiple devices are interconnected via communication links. Various structures are possible for the interconnection of nodes in a local area network. These structures relate to the way data are processed as well as the direction and nature of the data transmission. An enormous variety of physical structures are possible and can be broadly categorized as point-to-point, star, multidrop, multipoint, bus, tree, ring, and mesh. With the star, multidrop, and multipoint networks, the processing power is usually centered in one place; with the bus, tree, ring, and mesh networks, the processing power is distributed among the nodes.

Another important property of these networks is related to "closed loops," which can offer an alternative path(s) in the event of failure. They fall into two groups: those for wide area networks (mesh), and those for local area networks (ring).

Two principal features that determine the nature of a local area network are its topology and transmission medium, which affect the type of data that may be transmitted, the speed and efficiency of communications, and even the kinds of applications the network may support.

FIGURE 5–17

Features of repeaters/hubs, bridges, routers, and gateways

Feature	Repeater/Hub	Bridge	Router	Gateway
ISO layer	Physical	Data link	Network	Up to 7
Forwarding capability	Forwards bits	Forwards frames	Forwards packets	Translation at all 7 layers of the ISO model
Addressing functions	No address	MAC address (IEEE802.3 format)	Network address	
Network extension	Yes	Yes	Yes	Yes
Frame/packet filtering	No	Yes	Yes	Yes
Network management	Repeater—no; hub—optional	Yes	Yes	Yes
Performance/throughput	High	Medium	Low	Low
Cost	Repeater—low; hub—varies	Medium	High	High
Transparent to upper-level protocols (> L2)	Yes	Yes	No	No
Connection to WANs	No	Yes/no	Yes	Yes

Certain topologies are specific to local area networks, others apply to wide area networks, and still others are common to both. In this section we discuss those topologies relevant to local area networks. Local area networks are often characterized in terms of the star, ring, and bus/tree topologies.

Star

In the early days, the PBX telephone wiring was used for local area network interconnection mainly because it was inexpensive and already in place. Later the bus topology became popular because of its flexibility. More recently, the emphasis on structured wiring using hubs and concentrators, particularly to improve network management and security, has brought a move back to the star topology. Further, the use of the popular wiring standards discussed earlier, particularly 10BASE-T, has been combined with hub technology to produce the very widely used star topology shown in Figure 5–18.

Ring

The ring topology consists of a closed loop, with each node attached to a repeater station. Data circulate around the ring on a series of point-to-point data links between repeaters. A station that wishes to transmit waits for its next turn and then sends the data out onto the ring in the form of a packet, which contains both the source and

FIGURE 5–18

Star network commonly used in local area networks

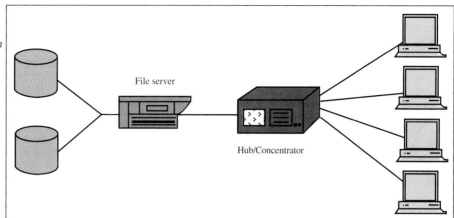

File server

Hub/Concentrator

destination addresses as well as the data. As the packet circulates, the destination node copies the data into a local buffer. The packet continues to circulate until it returns to the source node, providing a form of acknowledgment.

Sometimes it is difficult to connect a new node to an existing ring. Failure of a node or an active component (such as a repeater), adding a new node, or any other break in the ring configuration will usually cause network failure unless special measures are taken.

Ring-based local area networks are used where performance must be guaranteed. Since it is possible to calculate the worst response time from the number of stations and the maximum amount of data that each station can transmit, it is easy to determine the worst-case performance. Hence ring topologies are sometimes used in manufacturing and industrial situations where machine tools or robotics equipment is being controlled.

Token ring systems that use this topology were discussed earlier in this chapter. Another ring topology is fiber distributed data interface (FDDI), which is discussed later in this chapter. FDDI is used as a backbone link for connecting many local area networks, for example, in the case of a large factory, hospital, airport, or university campus. These networks incorporate twin rings to ensure maximum reliability in the event of link failure.

Figure 5–7 (p. 183) illustrates the ring concept. Figure 5–19 shows a combination of a star and ring topology used in some local area networks to gain the benefits of both types of topologies.

Bus/Tree

The bus topology is characterized by the use of a multiple-access, broadcast medium. Nodes share a physical channel by way of cable taps or connectors as shown in Figure 5–20. Like the ring, the bus topology is most frequently used for distributing control in local area networks. Messages placed on a bus are broadcast to all nodes.

FIGURE 5–19

Star–ring combination used in many IBM local area network configurations

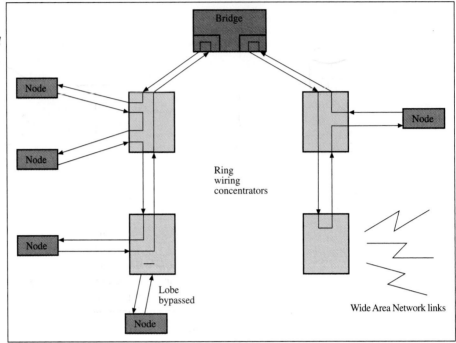

Because all devices share a common communications medium, only one device can transmit at a time. As with the ring, transmission involves a packet containing source and destination addresses and data. Each station monitors the medium and copies packets addressed to itself. However, unlike the ring nodes, they do not have to repeat and forward messages intended for other nodes. Thus, no delay or overhead is associated with retransmitting messages at each intervening node. Since nodes are passive, the network can continue to operate if one node fails.

Because it is possible for data packets to collide on bus networks, as we saw in the section on Ethernet, it is not possible to determine precisely the worst response time for the user. Hence, these networks are not used in industrial environments that require an absolute guarantee of response time. They are, however, very commonly used as the basis for many commercial and financial local area networks, including many of those discussed in Chapter 2.

Bus networks are easily expandable; an interconnection of two or more buses is called a *tree*.

Local area networks are seldom selected on the basis of their topology alone. Issues such as Ethernet versus token passing systems, types of transmission media, and the networking software must all be taken into account when considering the choice of a local area network. Later in this chapter, we will examine these issues further.

FIGURE 5–20

Bus topology commonly used in local area networks

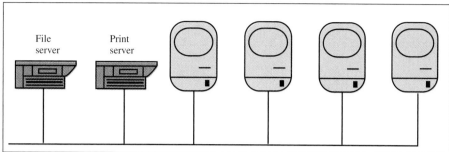

Fiber Distributed Data Interface (FDDI)

Fiber distributed data interface (FDDI) plays an important role in the area of LAN-to-LAN interconnection. The FDDI standard has been available for a number of years and offers an interconnection service at 100 Mbps. High purchase costs (more than 10 times that of 10BASE-T) as well as the need to install fiber optic cable hurt FDDI's potential. More recent technologies offering the same speed at lower costs have relegated FDDI to the role of a high-speed backbone network. FDDI bridges used to connect departmental LANs can cost as much as $10,000 each, and this is the main reason FDDI has not become an important standard for 100 Mbps LANs to the desktop. With its growing popularity, however, the costs are decreasing.

Nevertheless, FDDI has provided, and is likely to continue to provide, an excellent high-speed *interconnection highway* within limited geographical areas such as between buildings in a campus, factory, or airport environment. Remarkably, it is one of the few practical networking architectures that is both multivendor provided and has consistent standards defined from the outset. Equally important, the real-life solutions and products became available slightly ahead of users' needs, rather than lagging behind them, which has too often been the case with networking in the past (ISDN, for example).

To some degree, FDDI is being overtaken by new developments. For example, 100 Mbps to the desktop is now most likely to be provided via the 100BASE-T and 100VG-AnyLAN standards (discussed in the following section). Further, LAN hubs and their interconnection to the wide area are likely to be achieved by way of the ATM (asynchronous transfer mode) standard in the near future (discussed in Chapter 12).

Thus, FDDI has provided an important interconnection tool and is likely to continue to do so for some years to come. With the growing popularity of ATM, however, it is unlikely that major investments in FDDI will continue in the distant future.

FDDI Architecture and Applications

The basic architectural structure of FDDI is a ring of stations operating as equal peers without the need for a central master station, hence the inclusion of the word *distributed*. Specially authorized stations may carry out network management functions.

The term *FDDI* has gained very wide acceptance.

- In general, it implies a high-speed, high-capacity, and highly resilient fiber network.
- It is based on token passing protocols and utilizes a dual counter-rotating ring topology.
- It is capable of supporting several hundred stations.
- Transmission rates of 100 Mbps over a total ring distance of up to 100 km are possible.

FDDI has an enormous capacity for data transmission. In fact, it is often stated that Ethernet LANs use only a small fraction of their 10 Mbps nominal capacity as it is. One almost equally often hears the reply that it is the constraining nature of the Ethernet protocols that prevents them from loading the network more heavily with applications! But to emphasize utilization of bandwidth capacity alone is to miss the whole point. FDDI's advantages come from its high performance, its wide geographic coverage, some new types of applications that it enables, and, in particular, its use as a LAN interconnection system.

FDDI applications include the following:

- FDDI as a backbone "LAN of LANs" linking different communities of users across sites such as factories, airports, universities, and business complexes previously supported only by disparate LANs.
- High-rise buildings being cabled for FDDI in the vertical risers; thus, FDDI acts as a backbone for individual horizontal LANs, which in turn support individual floors and departments.
- Concentration of lower-speed devices and bridging of LANs from different vendors onto an FDDI network for connectivity and multiprotocol interconnection benefits.
- Direct dual attachment of high-performance devices (e.g., CAD/CAM, high-resolution color graphics, and other multimedia devices) onto the backbone network to obtain the speed and performance it provides.
- The basis for cooperative, distributed data processing systems.
- Support for new high-bandwidth applications such as medical imaging, engineering graphics, and document image processing.

FDDI Technology

FDDI is a high performance fiber optic *token ring* LAN running at 100 Mbps over distances of up to 100 km. It offers the potential to connect several hundred devices to the ring, although it has been more common to connect departmental LANs to the FDDI ring rather than individual devices, as shown in Figure 5–21.

The basic FDDI protocols are closely modeled on the IEEE 802.5 protocols. To transmit data, a station must first capture the token. Then it transmits a frame and removes it when it comes around again. One difference between FDDI and IEEE

FIGURE 5–21

An FDDI ring used as a backbone to connect LANs

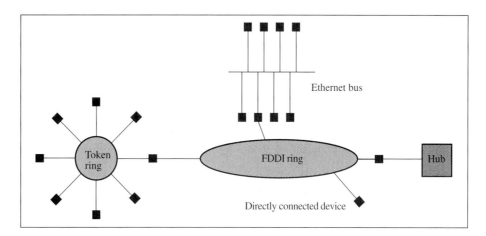

802.5 is that in the latter case, a station may not generate a new token until its frame has returned. In FDDI, with potentially 1,000 stations and 100 miles of fiber, the amount of time wasted waiting for the frame to circumnavigate the ring could be substantial. For this reason, it was decided to allow a station to put a new token back onto the ring as soon as it has finished transmitting its frames. In a large ring, several frames may be on the ring at the same time.

FDDI-II, the successor to FDDI, has been modified to handle synchronous circuit switched PCM data for voice or ISDN traffic. However, it is more likely that ATM will be the technology for multimedia communications.

FDDI uses multimode fibers because the additional expense of single-mode fibers is not needed for networks running at only 100 Mbps. It also uses LEDs rather than lasers, since they are cheaper and provide less risk for stations which could be directly connected to the FDDI ring.

The FDDI cabling consists of two fiber rings, one transmitting counterclockwise and the other transmitting clockwise. When FDDI is used in local metropolitan networks as a ring around central business districts, it provides fault tolerance in the event of disaster. If either ring breaks, the other can be used as a backup. If both break at the same point, which might occur when the FDDI cable is cut, the two rings are automatically joined into a single ring. The two devices nearest the break will operate their *optical bypass relays*, thus interconnecting the two rings or, alternatively, bypassing the faulty station in the event of problems (see Figure 5–22).

FDDI defines two classes of stations, A and B. Class A stations connect to both rings as shown in Figure 5–23. The cheaper class B stations connect to only one ring. Depending on how important fault tolerance is, an installation can choose class A or class B station, or some of each. With these two counter-rotating rings, failure of both rings at one point means the two rings can be joined to form a single long ring.

An FDDI bridge (such as the DECbridge 900) can filter around 15,000 packets per second on each Ethernet port and has a corresponding forwarding rate of 60,000 packets per second. It is important, therefore, that the attached LANs be able to handle packets at this rate; otherwise, there is little point in using FDDI.

FIGURE 5–22

FDDI acts as a fault-tolerant network, even when both paths are broken

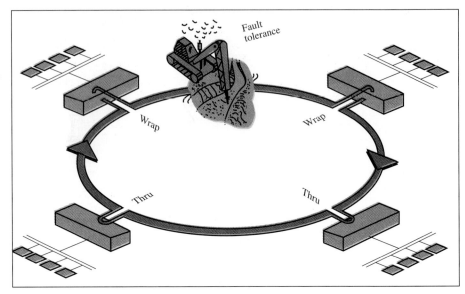

Direct connection of hosts and high-speed servers to the FDDI network has been quite rare. However, as the cost of the interface continues to fall and the demand for individual device access data rates in excess of 10 Mbps increases (e.g., graphical user interfaces [GUIs]), this type of connection is becoming more common.

ISO Standards for FDDI

FDDI has been defined as ISO 9314 (ANSI X3T9.5) and incorporates the physical media-dependent layer ISO 9314/3, the physical layer ISO 9314/1, the medium access control layer ISO 9314/2, and the logical link control layer ISO 8802/2. Further, the FDDI SMT (station management) standard was included from the outset, as it was realized that such a technology could not operate in a satisfactory manner without network management. This FDDI standard has gained wide acceptance from the major vendors such as IBM, Digital, UNISYS, AT&T, and Hewlett-Packard (HP). It is defined as follows (see also Figure 5–24):

- PMD (physical media dependent layer): ISO 9314/3.
- PHY (physical layer): ISO 9314/1.
- MAC (medium access control layer): ISO 9314/2.
- LLC (logical link control layer): ISO 8802/2.
- SMT (station management): network management, configuration, and control.
- SM-PMD: single-mode fiber physical medium dependent.
- HRC: hybrid ring control (for isochronous applications such as voice).

FIGURE 5–23

Dual attached devices to an FDDI ring can continue to operate even after a cable break

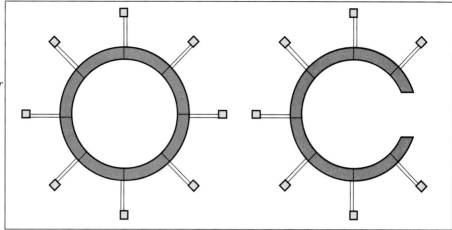

FIGURE 5–24

ISO standards for FDDI, including station management

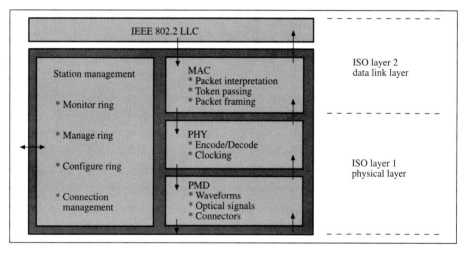

CDDI and TPDDI

As the term implies, FDDI was originally envisioned as being "fiber" based, although the use of traditional copper wiring in the form of either shielded (STP) or unshielded twisted pairs (UTP) within FDDI networks has increased. These are Copper Distributed Data Interface (CDDI) and Twisted Pair Distributed Data Interface (TPDDI). These alternatives to fiber-based FDDI offer a number of benefits, including lower-cost copper cable and interface components. However, CDDI and TPDDI are still expensive relative to 10BASE-T and require installation of category 5 UTP cabling.

These alternatives are applicable only where there is no specific requirement for fiber. In most cases, the interconnection of buildings and electrical interference require that fiber optic–based protocols be used. 10BASE-F is also a fiber-based protocol, but is applicable for point-to-point operation and does not possess the fault-tolerant capabilities of FDDI.

High Speed Local Area Networks (100 Mbps)

Why 100 Mbps?

Ever since computers started arriving on desktops, demands for higher speeds have increased. Over the past 10 years, desktop PC processing power has increased over a hundredfold from the Intel 8088–based IBM PC to today's Intel Pentium–based microprocessors. Over the same period, software applications have grown in sophistication and information content to the point where routine information items such as a business letter or presentation graphic require more than 100 times more storage space than items used 10 years ago. Over the same 10-year period, however, the data transmission speed of Ethernet local area networks has remained constant at 10 Mbps. Network speed is now becoming a critical issue in a variety of key business application areas, including database management, imaging, computer-aided design, desktop publishing, and network printing. Emerging applications will put even more strain on networks over the next few years.

Applications Drive the Need for 100 Mbps.   Many of the aforementioned data-intensive applications require that very large amounts of data be moved from one location to another (server to client or client to printer) in a single burst. For example, a desktop publishing document with multiple typefaces, a bit-mapped logo, four-color graphics, and other features may consume as much as 1 Mbyte of storage space for a single page. On a typical Ethernet or token ring network, it can take as long as 20 seconds to retrieve that one page, depending on network traffic; retrieving multiple-page documents can take a minute or more. If 100 Mbps networks were available, the transfers would take one to two seconds per page, dramatically changing the way users can work with data.

Another emerging application area that will require higher-speed networking in the future is multimedia, particularly in the use of real-time audio and video for videoconferencing and interactive video, typical of those discussed in Chapter 2. Current trials under way in Cambridge (UK) with video messaging have created the requirement for 8 Gbytes of local disk storage for the client workstation to allow storing of multiple video streams associated with a single video-mail message.

Unlike most current applications, which simply move entire files from one location to another, these applications require that packets be transferred on a routine basis. For example, they might paint a moving image at 30 frames per second or fill in a portion of a voice conversation. These applications cannot afford to have a packet of data delayed or dropped due to collision or congestion on the network. These application needs are not being met by existing 10 Mbps Ethernet or 4/16 Mbps token ring networks.

Examples of applications that currently place a heavy load on the network are computer-aided design, desktop publishing, and network printing. The network utilization of these applications will continue to grow. Future applications such as database management, image processing, videoconferencing, and multimedia will also require large amounts of bandwidth.

Increasing the Speed Is Not the Only Requirement.   Increased network speed is not the only requirement, however. Technologies such as FDDI have offered 100 Mbps speed for several years. However, these technologies have not caught on in the mainstream marketplace because they have failed to address other needs, such as low costs and the provision of a migration path from an organization's existing network infrastructure. Implementing a network implies a number of costs, including cabling, network adapters on each network client desktop, and a concentrator or hub in the building wiring closet. To date FDDI has been too expensive to support communications to the desktop. The electronics required to implement an FDDI network are very expensive: about $2,000 for each client adapter and another $2,000 to $3,000 for the necessary share of a concentrator or hub. A 10 Mbps Ethernet network, in contrast, costs about $100 per connection. Use of FDDI implies more than 20 times the cost for 10 times the performance.

An easy migration path also entails both monetary and organizational costs of disruption and training. With the cost of labor rising and the costs of network components (bridges, hubs, routers, and LAN adapters) falling, a significant percentage of the replacement value of an existing 10BASE-T network is in the cabling. If migrating to a higher-speed network means replacing cabling, additional costs will be incurred. The cost of installing new cabling can run as high as $1,000 per desktop for installation alone, especially in older buildings. Most of this cost is in the labor required to pull and terminate the cabling; the actual cost of the cable is comparatively small. Obviously, any networking technology that lets organizations keep their existing cabling would be preferable to one that required them to install new cabling.

Two standards that can provide the required bandwidth are receiving much attention at the present time: 100BASE-T and 100VG-AnyLAN.

100 Mbps Standards

100BASE-T.   The IEEE committee for 100BASE-T is IEEE802.3u. Also known as *100BASE-X, 4TPlus,* and *Fast Ethernet*, the specification for this standard was created by the Fast Ethernet Alliance and then given to the IEEE to be incorporated into the IEEE802.3 standard. Members of this alliance include 3Com, AT&T, Grand Junction, Cabletron, Cray Communications, Data General, Digital, IBM, Intel Corporation, National Semiconductor, Novell, Racal Datacom, Sun Microsystems, Unisys, and Wellfleet. It is hoped that by using the same access method, companies will be able to build on their existing Ethernets without the need for major reeducation.

Access Methods : CSMA/CD (Ethernet)

Advantages

- Cabling—category 3, 4 (100BASE-T4, or four pairs), or 5 (100BASE-TX, or two pairs) UTP, STP, and 100BASE-FX fiber.
- No change in access method.
- Suitable for video and multimedia.

Disadvantages

- Need to replace hubs, network interface cards (NICs), and drivers.
- Category 3 and 4 UTP use four pairs.

To give easy backward compatibility, the use of the access method CSMA/CD (carrier sense multiple access/collision detect) has been retained and is shown in Figure 5–25.

All common cabling types are supported, including category 3, 4, and 5 UTP, STP, and fiber. The fiber can be used between hubs to extend the diameter of the network. This has been achieved by creating the 100BASE-FX standard (two pairs of multimode fiber). If Category 5 UTP or STP is being utilized, two-pair cable is sufficient since the increased bandwidth is provided by faster transmission speeds.

Despite claims to the contrary, nothing prevents the running of new applications such as video and multimedia. However, it is necessary to ensure that the network is not overloaded in an effort to maintain satisfactory performance.

To implement a 100BASE-T network, it is necessary to replace the hubs, the LAN adapters, and their drivers with 100 Mbps–capable equipment. Current cabling should not need to be replaced.

The category 3 and category 4 UTP cable has four pairs. The encoding scheme for these types of cables uses four pairs to run 100 Mbps without exceeding Federal Communications Commission (FCC) electromagnetic radiation limits.

FIGURE 5–25

100BASE-T Ethernet hub for 100 Mbps LAN

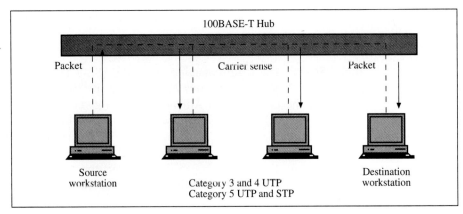

100VG-AnyLAN.   The IEEE committee for 100VG-AnyLAN, previously called *100BASE-VG*, is IEEE802.12. The specification was created by Hewlett-Packard and AT&T. Companies backing this standard include AT&T, Hewlett-Packard, IBM, CISCO, Apple, Microsoft, Proteon, Kalpana, and Ungermann Bass.

Access Methods: Demand Priority Protocol

Advantages

Cabling—category 3, 4, or 5 UTP.
* Supports both Ethernet and token ring.
* Suitable for voice, video, and multimedia.
* Deterministic protocol, providing security and priorities.

Disadvantages

* Need to replace hubs, NICs, and drivers.
* Needs four-pair cable.
* Change in protocol.

To provide the faster speeds over the lower-category UTP cables, a new media access control protocol has been designed called the *demand priority protocol*. This is a frame switching technique that is controlled by the hub and is shown in Figure 5–26.

A wide range of cable types are supported, including category 3, 4, or 5 UTP, with STP and fiber support in the future. Existing Ethernet and token ring networks can also be connected. It is possible to run time-dependent applications such as voice, multimedia, video, and videoconferencing, although care will probably be needed to maintain good performance, possibly by limiting the number of users.

With the current Ethernet media access method (CSMA/CD), it is not possible to predict the maximum length of time a device may have to wait to send a packet. Demand priority protocol does enable these predictions to be made if the number of workstations in the network is known. Demand priority protocol provides some

FIGURE 5–26

100VG-AnyLAN hub for 100 Mbps LAN

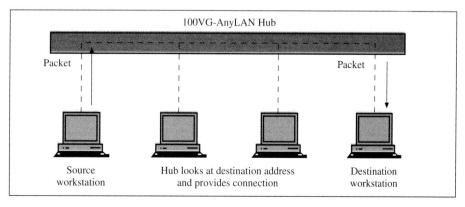

built-in security that was not in CSMA/CD. This protocol also enables traffic to be prioritized, meaning that time-critical applications such as video can be given high-priority access to the network.

Due to the nature of the access method, it is necessary to replace the hub as well as the LAN adapters and their drivers. The cable must consist of four pairs; two pairs are insufficient for the media access method.

The demand priority protocol permits 100 Mbps running over UTP cable without exceeding the FCC electromagnetic radiation limit. The distance from the hub to the device is 100 m on category 3 UTP and 200 m on category 5 UTP. The maximum end-to-end distances (the cabling distance between devices without using repeaters) are 600 m with category 3 UTP and 1,200 m with category 5 UTP.

The hub controls access to the media. Access requests from workstations are forwarded to the hub. The hub answers each request using a round-robin method. There are two priority levels, high and normal; these can be used if the packet being sent is time sensitive (e.g., interactive voice or video) or of a higher priority in some other way. High-priority requests will be serviced before normal-priority requests. After 250 milliseconds, a normal priority packet is made high priority to enable it to be serviced. The hub then decodes the destination address and passes the packet on to the destination device. A root hub is designated so that if the destination is not on the local hub, it can be passed on. The connection between the source and destination devices is effectively a point-to-point connection. This provides security that is not available with CSMA/CD, since the other devices on the network do not see the signal that is being transmitted (see Figure 5–27).

Summary

A business's current situation will affect the alternatives. If category 5 (four-wire) UTP cabling is already in use, together with existing hubs, upgrading the system will be relatively easy. If not, recabling may be necessary—not an easy task. As with

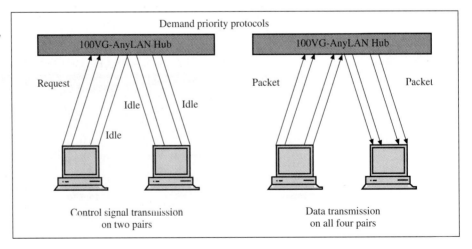

FIGURE 5–27

Demand priority protocol operation used with 100VG-AnyLAN

implementing any new system, the cost is an important factor. The minimum equipment to be replaced will be adapter cards and hubs.

Besides these two new 100 Mbps protocols, the other alternatives are therefore

- 100BASE-T.
- 100VG-AnyLAN.
- Full-duplex Ethernet.
- Switched Ethernet hubs.
- FDDI.
- ATM.
- Fiber channel.

Full-Duplex Ethernet.   This enables each workstation to transmit at 10 Mbps while receiving at 10 Mbps, effectively doubling existing Ethernet speed. This also avoids the collision problem with CSMA/CD. However, it does not represent a significant increase in local area network speed.

Switched Ethernet Hubs.   Switching hubs enable 10 Mbps to be dedicated to each workstation. Since this requires very little change in equipment, it is cheap and quick to implement and may well satisfy short-term requirements. It means that the hub provides *parallel* switching, that is, 10 Mbps for each pair of interconnected workstations or interconnected bus/ring systems.

FDDI.   FDDI was already discussed as an established 100 Mbps networking standard that uses multimode fiber optic cabling. However, high purchase costs (more than 10 times those of 10BASE-T) and the need to install expensive cabling hurt FDDI's potential. More recent technologies offering the same speed at much lower costs have relegated FDDI to the role of a high-speed backbone network connecting LANs.

Copper-based FDDI (CDDI) is one alternative to the FDDI transmission scheme, which can also be used over lower-cost copper cabling. Operating at 100 Mbps, CDDI promised many of the benefits of FDDI at lower electronic component costs and lower cabling costs. However, CDDI is still expensive compared to 10BASE-T and requires new higher-level (category 5) unshielded twisted pair (UTP) cabling. Another option is TPDDI (Twisted Pair Distributed Data Interface).

Asynchronous Transfer Mode (ATM).   ATM is a packet switching technology that bears much similarity to a high-speed telephone switch. Intended primarily for high-end clients, ATM will support complex multimedia applications, bringing switched, dedicated bandwidth directly to the desktop over existing UTP or fiber optic cabling at rates of 155 Mbps. ATM is also well-suited to backbone implementations by providing true multiplexing (as opposed to dedicated bandwidth and thus providing effective point-to-point throughput at speeds of 155 Mbps). Further, ATM can offer unique scalability and seamless integration of campus LAN backbones with the wide area network. ATM is discussed in more detail in Chapter 12.

Fiber Channel.   Fiber channel, a recent initiative among HP, IBM, and Sun Microsystems, is designed primarily for high-speed mass storage and clustered computing, and is based on an extremely high-speed/low-delay switching system. Using fiber optic cabling, fiber channel will switch dedicated circuits at rates of from 266 Mbps to multigigabits/sec. Fiber channel will also be an optimal choice for connecting high-end workstations to supercomputers.

Figure 5–28 provides a comparison of some of the more popular of these technologies, along with the applications they support and their availability.

Client/Server Computing

Client/server computing is a relatively new term and is usually defined as the ability of an application to run on any of several networked computer systems in such a way that any processing that must be done is done on the most appropriate server. PCs or workstations cooperate with one or more servers to accomplish whatever tasks need to be done in a coordinated manner also limiting the volumes of network traffic. Client/server is a new and important concept in the industry.

Structured query language (SQL) is a good example of software that enhances the user's capabilities. For example, in an SQL environment records may be sorted on the file server running SQL server database software and then sent to a workstation or *client* running a different version of the same database software or another application program such as a spreadsheet. Sometimes the term *back-end* processing refers to the server computing component and the term *front-end* computing refers to the client computing component.

In a client/server environment, the file server running the appropriate software, such as that for the SQL server database discussed above, provides access to the database and a variety of database services such as remote connectivity, data integrity, and data security. The client software running on the workstation provides data entry and data validation, as well as formatting and displaying the data appropriately. Both the server and the client software may perform operations on the data such as sorting and calculating.

FIGURE 5–28

Comparison of the main high-speed LAN alternatives

Technology	Application	Availability
FDDI/CDDI/TPDDI	Long-distance backbone	Today
100 Mbps Ethernet	Server	Today
Switched Ethernet	Backbone, server, client	Today
ATM	Backbone, server, client	Emerging

✴ Client/server computing is not limited to a single local area network. The client/server software is usually permitted to access data wherever it is located and to have many processors perform whatever processing needs to be done, according to their availability and capability. Thus, the client/server model includes both local and wide area networks, together with a range of attached host computers. Examples of client/server systems in popular use are Gopher and WWW (World Wide Web), which are used on the Internet and discussed in Chapter 3.

In such an environment, mainframe computers can be used to perform large, repetitive processing operations such as sorting, and the mini- or microcomputers handle the formatting and display of the results, which usually implies user-friendly software. For example, a database might be searched for specific records using a relational database management system on a server while the final results of the search are displayed on a workstation system running a graphical user interface spreadsheet package.

The main idea of client/server computing, therefore, is to make all data in all databases for an organization available to any user at a workstation who has the authority to use the data. It also permits the most appropriate computing resource on the network to perform the processing so that each of the network's computing resources is used to its best advantage. In other words, client/server computing is *intelligent distributed processing.*

Local Area Network Software Components

Earlier we discussed Ethernet and token ring systems, as well as the cabling used to interconnect these local area networks. However, these topics refer to the bottom *two* layers of the ISO model discussed in Chapter 4. To operate satisfactorily, a local area network needs upper-layer software to provide the types of activities discussed in Chapter 2, for example, electronic mail, news services, diaries, and calendaring, as well as many database services such as those provided by client/server computing. Even some of the hardware components introduced earlier, including bridges, routers, and gateways, require certain layers of software to operate satisfactorily.

Many local area network vendors now exist, and virtually all of them support either Ethernet or token ring systems. However, the software at the upper layers that allows users to perform the many functions possible with local area networks varies a great deal as each vendor attempts to gain market share and a competitive edge by claiming to offer more user-friendly and efficient ways to run local area network applications. Frequently it is far from clear which option is the best. In fact, there are many satisfactory ways to implement these various upper-layer software–based application functions.

Some of the functions local area network software can be required to perform include

- Shared access to devices, file transfer, and logical connection among users, usually provided by the software.

- File server functions—concurrent access for multiple users, naming conventions for temporary files.
- License agreements for multiuser software.
- Fault tolerance, file recovery, disk caching for commonly accessed records and multiple file servers processing.
- Transparent access so that users need not be concerned about the architecture or location of data; this is usually provided via a graphical user interface.
- Performing presentation and session layer functions at both client and server locations in the network, but needs to be able to handle multiple users at the server.
- Network management and security functions (discussed in detail in Chapter 11).
- Application program interface, such as IBM's NetBIOS, Novell's Internetwork Packet Exchange (IPX) and Sequenced Packet Exchange (SPX) (see Figure 5–29).
- Management functions associated with print servers.

Operating Systems in Local Area Networks

Vendor architectures change rapidly as new versions of the systems are released. This section does not attempt to explain how each of these operates, since a great deal of experience and knowledge are necessary to become familiar with even one of them. The objective is to introduce and briefly describe the key software systems on the market.

A variety of well-known local area network operating systems are on the market, including NetWare (Novell), Windows NT, and Advanced Server (Microsoft), LAN Server (IBM), LAN Manager (Microsoft), Banyan (VINES), and Appleshare (Apple), as well as a variety of DOS-based local area networks and TCP/IP systems designed mainly for the UNIX environment. There are a number of important facets of local area network operating systems to note. The NOS (network operating system) is a group of distributed programs used to manage the local area network's resources, including communication between the PCs and various servers (file, print, mail, and gateway).

Local area network operating systems have three primary components:

- The *disk operating system* runs in each PC and server attached to the network, managing the device and providing a standard interface to the network hardware (e.g., NetBIOS). Versions of DOS from 3.1 on provide multiuser facilities.
- The *file server software* manages the network resources, particularly the servers. It permits access to a file by multiple users in the same way multiprogram operating systems have done for many years.

- The *redirector* runs in each workstation on the local area network and directs the requests to appropriate network devices, including various servers.

The ISO model discussed in Chapter 4 was intended to be a common base for architecture and interconnection among different vendors' equipment. However, this has largely been superceded by de facto standards such as NetBIOS and TCP/IP.

Figure 5–29 shows the software components for six of the main local area network architectures on the market. These software components exist at layers 3 and above of the OSI model. As you can see, each vendor provides very different software, making interconnectability quite difficult. However, new ways are being found to offer limited functionality with interconnected local area networks from different vendors.

The following sections describe these six operating systems in turn.

Network Basic Input/Output Operating System (NetBIOS)

In the early days of local area network development, DOS had little network support until the release of DOS 3.1. Up until that time, vendors had to provide their own proprietary interfaces, as well as record- and file-locking mechanisms. NetBIOS was developed as an interface between the local area network hardware—that is, the network interface card implementing Ethernet or token ring—and the DOS operating system. Its functions are to

1. Allow interchange (session layer communication) among users on the local area network.
2. Send and receive broadcast information to and from other network nodes.
3. Allow for the establishment of multiple user names within one node (session layer function).
4. Interface with the network interface card and perform basic control and management functions.

Figure 5–30 shows the key hardware and software elements for a workstation and a server. These include the workstation, file server, network interface cards (token ring or Ethernet), the DOS (disk operating system), the BIOS (basic input/output operating system), the redirector, and NetBIOS.

TCP/IP Protocols

This protocol suite was introduced in Chapter 3 as the basis for the Internet. It was developed by the U.S. Department of Defense and used as the basis of the world-wide Advanced Research Projects Agency Network (ARPANET). Subsequently these protocols became synonymous with the use of UNIX-based architecture and Sun systems as well as the Internet. More recently they have been used as a link between incompatible local area networks. Most vendors now implement the TCP/IP

FIGURE 5–29

A sample of vendors' local area network operating systems

OSI Model	DOS-based LANs	TCP/IP Protocols	NetWare	LAN Manager	VINES	Windows NT (Standalone and Advanced Server)
Layer 7 Application	DOS and redirector		NetWare Core Protocols (NCP)	Server Message Block (SMB)	VINES Remote Procedure Calls	Telnet, FTP, Client/server, Chat and other applications.
Layer 6 Presentation	Windows		NetBIOS emulator			Windows NT and Windows for Work Groups – Peer to peer
Layer 5 Session	Network Basic Input/Output System (NetBIOS)	Simple Mail Transfer Protocol (SMTP); File Transfer Protocol (FTP); TELNET virtual terminal protocol; Simple Network Management Protocol; Network File System (NFS)	NetWare Sequenced Package exchange (SPX)	NetBIOS Extended User Interface (NetBEUI)	VINES Interprocess Com's Protocol (VICP)	TCP/IP; NetBEUI; SPX IPX; Ethertalk
Layer 4 Transport		Transmission Control Protocol (TCP); User Datagram Protocol (UDP)	NetWare Internetwork Packet exchange (IPX)		VINES Internet Protocol (VIP)	
Layer 3 Network	Network driver	Internet Protocol (IP); Network Driver	Open Data-link Interface (ODI)	NDIS	Network driver; NDIS	Hardware Data Definition
Layer 2 Data Link						
Layer 1 Physical			IEEE 802.3 Ethernet; 10BASE-T; 10BASE2; 10BASE5; 100BASE-F; 100BASE-T	IEEE 802.2 logical link control (LLC); IEEE 802.5 Token-ring; Fiber Distributed Data Interface (FDDI)		

Unshielded Twisted-Pair (UTP); Shielded Twisted-Pair (STP); Single-mode fiber; Multi-mode fiber

FIGURE 5–30

Configuration of workstation and server showing key hardware and software components

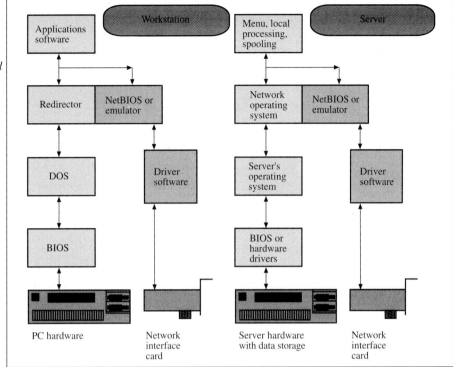

protocols to provide interoperability among different vendors' local area networks. They are also widely implemented on local area network routers. Following are the key components of the TCP/IP suite as shown in Figure 5–29:

TCP—a protocol that organizes packets, manages transmission, and ensures accurate delivery.

IP—a protocol that manages the routing of data packets among stations on the same or different networks.

UDP—a protocol that determines the final route for messages reaching applications programs. It has less overhead than TCP, but is less reliable.

SMTP—the UNIX-based electronic mail system, similar to X.400 but less functional.

FTP—a protocol for exchanging files across a TCP/IP-based network.

TELNET virtual terminal protocol—a terminal emulation protocol for TCP/IP-based networks.

SNMP—a protocol that collects and reports network management information (see Chapter 11).

NFS—a distributed file system originally developed by Sun Microsystems but now licensed to dozens of UNIX vendors.

Novell NetWare

Novell software, NetWare 3.x and 4.1, will run on almost any compatible PC and supports an enormous range of applications software. Currently, it is the largest local area network supplier worldwide, with around 2.5 million nodes and over 70 percent of the world market. It can interwork with most hardware suppliers and can operate in conjunction with both token ring and Ethernet systems.

In Figure 5–29, NCP is the naming service used by NetWare. SPX is a set of commands that provides guaranteed data delivery somewhat like TCP. IPX is NetWare's network protocol for transmitting data among applications in a manner similar to IP.

One of the important advantages of Novell's NetWare local area network lies in the enormous range of application software which can be run on these networks.

Microsoft Windows NT

Windows NT is a full 32-bit, preemptive multitasking operating system and is designed to be easily ported to many hardware platforms. It supports multiple-processor machines and several popular networking protocols and has security and data protection features associated mainly with workstations and minicomputers. Windows NT incorporates the popular graphical user interface of Microsoft Windows 3.1 and **Windows 95**. In addition, it includes the functionality of Windows for Workgroups (peer-to-peer networking and work group scheduling), and has additional features expected of modern client/server architectures. Its excellent security features and ease of network management make it a strong competitor of UNIX and NetWare 4.1.

Banyan VINES

VINES integrates the entire suite of enterprise network services with its UNIX-based network operating system (NOS) into one package. VINES installs on PC servers and clients and permits users of the leading PC desktop systems—DOS, OS/2, Windows NT, and Macintosh—to share information and computing resources with each other and with host computing environments throughout the enterprise.

VINES supports a wide range of hardware peripherals, including printers, RAID Adapters, SCSI devices, tape drives, and LAN cards from leading hardware vendors. To meet the needs of organizations that maintain a variety of network types throughout the enterprise, Banyan also offers its enterprise network services for other popular operating environments, including NetWare and UNIX.

Microsoft LAN Manager

In Figure 5–29, the Server Message Block (SMB) is a distributed file system developed by IBM, Intel, and Microsoft that enables an application on one PC to call a file elsewhere on the network as though the file resided on the PC's hard disk. SMB is very similar to NetWare's NCP and NFS, and it operates on top of an extended version of NetBIOS, all of which were previously described.

Vendors' operating systems change regularly; thus, a specific description of one such system would be out-of-date in a year or so. Further, the systems just described are only a sample; there are many more important local area network systems on the market that cannot be discussed in the space available here but nevertheless are very important in the industry. Market competition among these vendors' systems is fierce. Some of the important points to look for in selecting a local area network system are discussed later in this chapter.

Costs of Acquiring and Using Local Area Networks

The area of costs presents some very important and often overlooked issues. First, one can easily be misled by local area network vendors if one believes that the cost of a local area network lies merely in the initial purchase of hardware and software. These are the immediate and visible costs at the time that a local area network is being purchased and installed. However, there are other very important—and expensive—issues to consider.

Like an automobile, a local area network involves many ongoing expenses. These costs will depend on the type of local area network chosen and will have to be calculated individually for each configuration.

Standardization has had an important influence on local area network costs. For example, a few years ago an Ethernet interface board for a PC cost over $800. Now they can be purchased for about $80. This dramatic decrease has resulted mainly from standardization and mass production. Hardware costs, particularly for PC workstations, have come down in spite of the enhanced capabilities of modern microprocessors and the increased functionality resulting from mass storage and high-speed memory. Like hardware, software costs have also passed through a peak and are now declining.

Acquisition and Usage Costs

The costs of acquisition and usage will vary from installation to installation. Some of the more important costs include the following.

Workstation Hardware Costs.   These costs include the purchase of workstations and associated local peripherals such as local floppy and hard disks, additional primary memory, and interface cards to connect to the network. In his video *Getting Value from Information Technology*, Peter Keen states that only 20 percent of information technology costs are visible (the "iceberg problem"). For example, a $2,000 PC requires education, training, installation, maintenance agreements, spare equipment, data storage management, communications, and many other items. The real cost may well be in the range of $2,000 to $8,000 per year for support, consultants, hot-line services, and the like. Such figures can vary enormously, but the important thing is to take these issues into account so that no nasty surprises come later.

Workstation Software Costs.   Purchase of the above hardware usually entails a software cost for a very basic operating system. Frequently the user will require software for client/server computing, file transfer, electronic mail, electronic diaries, and calendaring. Although some of these software items may be purchased to run on the file server, their cost is usually related to the number of workstations or the number of users who will simultaneously access this software.

Further, new versions of the operating system are released from time to time. Even if the existing version of the operating system software seems to be quite adequate for your needs, your new application software may be supported only by the latest version of the operating system, thus forcing you to upgrade. Often these enhanced software facilities impinge on the hardware, and additional primary memory and hard disk capacity will frequently have to be purchased as well.

Server Software Costs.   The initial costs associated with file, print, host, terminal, and gateway servers cannot be separated from the workstation software costs discussed above. For most local area networks today, an enormous amount of third-party software is constantly coming onto the market, providing users with faster and more efficient ways of working. It is often difficult to sort out what is essential and what is novel. Nevertheless, software costs are ongoing, and an annual budget must be set aside for this software.

Bridging, Routing, and Wide Area Network Connection Costs.   Today local area networks frequently require interconnection to other local area networks, either directly as in the same building or adjacent buildings or through wide area networks. To facilitate these interconnections, bridges, routers, and gateways must be purchased. This means costs for these hardware devices as well as for the software to operate them. Routers and gateways will require additional protocols such as DECnet, TCP/IP, or X.25, implying capital purchase or leasing arrangements for these software protocols. The equipment to provide these interconnections can range from $1,000 for a simple bridge to $10,000 for a high-performance, multi-protocol router.

Cable Costs.   Not too long ago, when an older building was wired for a local area network, the cost of installing the cable was 100 times the cost of the cable and its interface equipment. The costs of installing cables into an existing building (particularly if it is made of concrete!) are usually enormous. Today there is a strong move toward installing cabling in buildings at the time of construction or modification, but often this does not happen.

The cost of the twisted pair, coaxial, or fiber optic cable is not usually significant. It is the connectors and interface cards required to connect the peripheral equipment that often hikes up the cost.

Adding extra wiring for expansion during the initial cable installation is always a good investment. Planning is important when wiring for expansion because distances between future workstations and wiring must be considered.

Installation Costs.   Unlike with wide area networks, where installation costs are clearly specified by the local telecommunications company, in the case of local area networks these costs depend largely on the environment in which the network is being installed. In many commercial organizations where the local area network is located on a single floor, as in some of the examples in Chapter 2, these costs are not significant. Issues associated with cabling through walls and ceilings were identified under cable costs above. Further, cabling up the riser or elevator shaft in a building can increase these installation costs greatly; this is also the case when buildings are interconnected by fiber optic links.

It is important to make arrangements with the equipment vendor at installation time to demonstrate the local area network in operation. In fact, this should be part of the contractual agreement.

Administration and Technical Support   It would be foolish to think you could buy a car and never need the support and advice of an auto mechanic. The same is true with a local area network. Users are not interested in fault finding and diagnosis. Hardware problems with workstations and servers, installing new versions of the operating system and applications software, checking for cable faults, reorganizing work groups of activity, and providing training and education are all essential support services that must be costed into the overall operation of a local area network. For example, one small local area network running 50 workstations in a small-business environment has one-half of a full-time person dedicated to these activities, whereas a large set of local area networks with 200 major nodes running with interconnected bridges together with routers to wide area network services has three full-time staff members dedicated to these activities.

Costs Associated with Local Area Network Failure

Once all of the local area network equipment is installed and operating satisfactorily and your business operations are running on the network, you must ask a very important question: What will it cost if the local area network fails for 1 minute, 15 minutes, 1 hour, 1 day, and so on? Few organizations consider this very important issue until the day the network actually fails. It is difficult to give precise figures for this type of situation, but usually the local area network will be operating in conjunction with a wide area network and providing a wide variety of services. When the Cathay Pacific Airlines computer system failed in August 1991, it was running 90 user applications simultaneously and processing around 40 to 50 transactions per second. There was a 13-hour delay before all systems were operating satisfactorily again. Although only part of this total network failure affected the local area network, the overall impact was dramatic.

The Peter Keen video states that "today information technology represents 50 percent of large firms' capital investment, and now up to 80 percent of a company's cash flow is online." As you might expect, the costs associated with network failure are devastating. Consider these examples:

- Federal Express quotes a loss of $200,000 per minute of network failure.
- One hotel chain quotes $200,000 per hour for its network failure.
- Even medium-size companies report $5,000 to $55,000 per hour.

In the old days, if the system was down in the morning, it was rerun in the afternoon. Now the afternoon is often too late.

In summary, local area network configurations often need to be dynamic. Existing nodes may receive hardware and software upgrades, new workstations may be needed, printers and servers may be added, and new functions such as fax or a database server may be included. The local area network must be able to accommodate these changes without incurring a large additional cost for the upgrade.

It may be more expensive to provide for expansion initially, but it is usually worthwhile in the long run. Adding a new workstation to a fully configured local area network will require substantial reorganization. Similarly, purchasing a single protocol router simply because only one protocol currently needs to be routed is a very shortsighted approach that usually results in higher overall costs in the long term. Thus, when evaluating local area network costs, you need to look at the future as well as the immediate costs.

Factors in Local Area Network Selection

To determine whether you need a local area network or an alternative to an existing network, consider the following questions:

- What are your present networking requirements? To what extent do employees need to share peripherals and data files?
- What must you do to satisfy your current business requirements so that you will be able to operate in a competitive environment and gain a competitive edge over your rivals?
- What do you anticipate your requirements to be three to five years from now?
- How can you satisfy both your present and future requirements?

The answer to any of these questions is seldom to purchase one vendor's local area network in preference to another. Rather, you need to aquire a good knowledge of your own business requirements. Once you do so, the issues relating to transmission media, baseband/broadband, Ethernet or token ring become quite easy to solve.

The common trap is that businesses call in a local area network vendor to tell them what they need. But if you do not understand your own business needs, it is most unlikely that a vendor who is not familiar with your organization will understand it either. There is no alternative to becoming familiar with your own business requirements such as required user response time, traffic profiles, usage, and application growth.

The following questions should be addressed when selecting a local area network. Not all of these issues are important in every case; you must decide which apply to your particular environment.

1. *Should you standardize on one type of local area network?* This is a desirable objective, but it is difficult to achieve in a multifunctional environment. Often a variety of local area networks have already been purchased, so the issue then becomes interconnectability. However, using a single major vendor for the backbone systems and main architectural components is likely to avoid many problems in the long run.

2. *Can products from different vendors be selected?* The answer to this relates to question 1. Some products cannot be interconnected. IBM's SNA equipment is a good example. Other products are specifically designed to be connected to other vendors' products. Various bridges and routers and associated software make this possible. However, there will always be some limits on interconnectivity.

3. *Will the local area network interoperate with remote networks?* Here the issue is to decide which functions must be performed from a workstation on one local area network in conjunction with the servers on the remote networks. Frequently, users require only a subset of the full functionality required on the main local area network. Examples of these functions are electronic mail transfer, file transfer, and record processing.

4. *Will the local area network reduce costs and provide flexibility of operations?* This is always a difficult question to answer, particularly since computer communication costs are often a significant portion of many companies' budgets. The answer lies more in the requirement to introduce local area networks to provide efficient functioning, which in turn allows the company to compete in the marketplace. After all, a bank that lacks a local and wide area network system ceases to be a viable business very quickly.

5. *Is use of the local area network transparent to the user?* Users have little interest in operating systems, bridges, routers, and transmission media. Generally, a user requires simple access to data wherever they are stored on the local or wide area network combination. Simple menu or icon systems are required to identify the appropriate data. If the user has to log in to successive servers on different local area networks, access is not transparent. Similarly, if a user has to deal with incompatible software systems for electronic mail, file structures, and print devices, the local area network lacks the desired transparency.

6. *Does the local area network provide users with sufficient device speed and capacity to avoid bottlenecks?* Access to file servers by multiple users is probably the single most common reason for poor local area network performance. Adequate channel speed to support multiple-user access, as well as adequate RAM and disk storage for file, print, and gateway servers, must be considered carefully when choosing an appropriate local area network configuration.

7. *Does the selected local area network's operational characteristics meet the user's service-level agreement?* In the service contract, users will have specified performance characteristics such as response time for selected transaction rates,

throughput for applications such as file transfer, mean and maximum times for accessing records in a database, and many others. It is essential to see these performance standards demonstrated on the selected local area network.

8. *Is the local area network's transmission speed appropriate for the users' applications?* With the growing use of multimedia applications today, the demand made on interconnecting links is considerable. For example, some twisted pair cables are now capable of transmitting 100 Mbps to the user's workstation, as is the case with sophisticated graphics terminals and CAD/CAM applications. Generally, any video or graphics application will make significant demands on the local area network's bandwidth. It is important to be aware of these needs at the time the local area network configuration is selected.

9. *What are the maximum cable lengths and station separation distances allowed?* Most local area network cabling systems require strict distance limitations for satisfactory operation. For example, token ring stations must be within 100 meters of the medium access unit; thin Ethernet cable cannot be longer than 185 meters, with a maximum of 30 attached stations; thick Ethernet cable cannot be longer than 500 meters, with a maximum of 100 attached stations; UTP runs must be no more than 100 meters; and so on. While these restrictions may not pose problems initially, once network expansion is required, difficulties can arise if adequate allowance has not been made.

10. *What is the availability of access points to the local area network?* Just as a building needs an adequate number and distribution of electrical power points, a similar situation applies to local area network connections. Allowance must be made for the mobility of users and their terminals, as well as for the reorganization of work groups.

11. *Does the local area network provide facilities for the interconnection of routers and gateways to interconnect with other networks?* If connection is required to a service provider's digital data, packet switching, frame relay, or integrated services digital networks for onward connection to other local area networks and remote databases, bridge or router equipment will be required. Sometimes these can be very expensive.

12. *Does the selected local area network vendor offer support for TCP/IP protocols to interconnect with different vendors' local area networks?* Interconnection of different vendors' local area networks is virtually mandatory today as organizations interconnect various departments and mergers between organizations necessitate the interconnection of their local area networks. At the present time, the most common way to achieve this aim is to use the TCP/IP protocol suite. It is essential to ensure that the chosen vendor supports these protocols; in other words, is multivendor communication possible?

13. *What maintenance agreement is in place from the local area network vendor?* Maintenance of both hardware and software is essential to avoid downtime. This may be carried out by the vendor, in-house by the technical staff, or by a third party.

14. *Is the local area network vendor a reputable supplier?* The buyer should carefully consider the reputation of the vendor before making the purchase. Purchasing from an unreliable supplier could cause the user to lose not only the investment in the local area network but also customers who become dissatisfied with poor service.

15. Does the selected local area network adequately address issues of security and management? User requirements for data security and network management are becoming increasingly stringent, and local area networks are now being designed with security and management in mind. These two topics are addressed in detail in Chapter 11.

The issues relating to local area network selection will vary in every environment. Therefore, you must base your selection criteria on the needs of your organization.

Summary

Chapter 2 introduced you to a variety of local area networking applications for different types of industries and businesses. In this chapter we looked at the components of the local area network necessary to support these applications. We examined the functions a local area network must perform and saw why the development of local area networks over older methods of networking has become important today.

We also discussed standards for local area networks and why they are important to vendors and users. We then briefly examined the main IEEE802 standards as well as the Ethernet, token ring, and cabling standards.

Next, we examined the devices actually used on the local area network, together with their software components. We also considered the equipment used to interconnect local area networks with the wide area network components discussed in Chapter 4 and examined the main topologies along with their distinguishing characteristics. In addition, we discussed some of the better-known architectures.

Next, we considered the factors affecting the cost of acquiring and operating local area networks. Finally, we examined the factors that influence local area network selection for particular environments.

Key Terms

Carrier sense multiple access/collision detect (CSMA/CD)   174
Collapsed backbone   192
Fiber distributed data interface (FDDI)   197
File server   186
Gateway   169
Hub   189
IEEE802   177
Intelligent building   175
Logical link control (LLC)   177
Manchester encoding   174

Medium access control (MAC)   174
Medium access unit (MAU)   174
Operating systems   168
Repeaters   174
Structured query language (SQL)   172
Terminal emulation   184
Unshielded twisted pair (UTP) categories 2, 3, and 5   175
Windows NT   188
Windows 95   214

Questions for Discussion

1. Indicate whether the following statements are true or false.

   a. Dumb terminals connected to a host computer in a star configuration are an example of a local area network. *T*

   b. The basic functions of a local area network are determined by the network's operating system. *F*

   c. A server that handles only communication tasks is classified as a specialized rather than a general-purpose server. *T*

   d. A network access method that is designed so that no collisions of packets occur among the nodes wishing to transmit is called token passing. *F*

   e. The bus topology is an example of a multipoint connection. *T*

   f. A large local area network can be subdivided into sections that are connected by a bridge. *T*

   g. Fiber optic cable has become an important medium for interconnecting workstations in a local area network because it is very fast and inexpensive. *T*

   h. Ethernet is an example of a standard used at the LLC (logical link control) layer of the OSI model. *F*

   i. Baseband cable transmission systems are now widely used to support multimedia local area network applications. *T*

   j. The bus topology, although widely used, cannot provide good security in local area network design. *T*

2. Complete each of the following statements.

   a. The transmission method that devotes its entire bandwidth to a single channel in order to carry one signal at a time is called _____.

   b. The local area network transmission medium that is most susceptible to noise from outside sources is _____.

   c. The local area network transmission medium with the largest bandwidth is _____.

   d. A PC or microcomputer becomes a workstation when _____.

   e. The ability of all system elements to exchange information between equipment from the same or different vendors is called _____.

   f. The MAC (medium access control) protocol that provides an absolute guarantee of performance is called _____.

   g. The device used to interconnect a local area network to a variety of wide area networks is called a(n) _____.

   h. The device used to extend the maximum allowable cable run is called a(n) _____.

   i. The name of the widely used software protocol suite that allows interworking among different vendors' local area networks is called *Internet*

   j. Bottlenecks and poor local area network performance are most likely to occur as a result of _____.

3. Reread the section on the major functions of local area networks at the beginning of this chapter. Then make a list of the three major functions that a local area network in your working environment is required to perform, and give a short explanation of each item. If you do not have a local area network where you work, choose an environment with which you are familiar.

4. List and briefly describe the key characteristics that differentiate local area networks from wide area networks.

5. Describe some of the changing requirements in the ways we use local area networks that affect the communications channels necessary to provide interconnection.

6. Standards benefit vendors as well as users because they allow for mass production of hardware chips and interface boards for connecting equipment to a local area network. Since standards seem to be so desirable, why do we have so many incompatible standards that make it difficult to interconnect local area networks?

7. Explain the main reasons single-user operating system software that runs on stand-alone PCs is

unsatisfactory when run in a local area network environment.

8. When using a printer in a local area network, why is it necessary to spool the printer files?

9. Consider the environment where you work. If there is not a local area network already operating, propose one based on the business needs of your organization. From the topics discussed in this chapter, list what you consider to be the *six* most pertinent issues affecting the selection of this local area network and explain how they apply to your environment.

10. Although local area networks are vital in today's workplace, a number of significant problems remain that local area network designers have to solve. From your own experience and your reading of this textbook so far, describe *two* of these problem areas.

CHAPTER

6

TECHNIQUES FOR ANALYZING AND ASSESSING NETWORKING OPPORTUNITIES

Chapter Outline

Introduction   226

Efficiency, Effectiveness, and
Competitive Advantage   226

Strategic Planning: A Foundation for
Analyzing Networking
Opportunities   231

Analyzing the Organization for
Networking Opportunities   240

Learning Objectives

By the end of Chapter 6, you should be able to

1. *Explain* the differences and overlap among efficiency, effectiveness, and competitive advantage as they apply to alignment of organizational strategy and IT strategy as carried out by TBIT applications.

2. *Employ* a strategic planning process to establish organizational purpose and action.

3. *Analyze* internal and external factors that affect an organization's competitiveness.

4. *Identify* critical success factors in an organization's use of networks.

5. *Use* various models to enhance analysis of business networking opportunities.

6. *Identify* networking opportunities using function and process diagrams and association matrices.

7. *Use* a data model to point out potential applications for networking.

8. *Create* a rich picture diagram to analyze network needs.

Introduction

Chapter 1 introduced you to some of the concepts of strategic planning and the appropriate applications of telecommunications-based information technology (TBIT). Chapters 2, 3, 4, and 5 gave you the opportunity to learn more about specific networking technologies and their application to the commercial environment. Before an individual company can begin to successfully apply these modern technologies, it must first analyze its existing situation and the situation in which it would like to be. This analysis is needed to

1. Understand the organization: its goals and objectives, organizational structure, processes and procedures, data, and interrelationships among people and other components of the overall system.
2. Discover opportunities to gain competitive advantage, improve business effectiveness, or strengthen organizational efficiency. These opportunities may be strategic, tactical, or operational in nature.
3. Determine problems within the organization that need solutions.

In this chapter you will learn the tools and techniques you need to analyze a wide range of business situations. In doing so, you will gain insight into potential applications of networking technologies and procedures to meet organizational needs and requirements.

Efficiency, Effectiveness, and Competitive Advantage

Efficiency, effectiveness, and competitive advantage are three related ways of looking at business improvement—specifically, to find TBIT applications that will improve the organization's operations. What do we mean by these terms? Why are they important? How can networks help in these areas? This chapter addresses these questions and more. First, let's look at some definitions.

internal   **Efficiency** is that characteristic of an organization that permits it to produce the maximum quantity of outputs of a specified quality from a minimum of materials and human and organizational effort. In short, it means maximizing productivity by doing things right. To detect efficiency in operation, ask this question: Are we producing the most output from the least input, given our quality goals?

internal and external   **Effectiveness** is that characteristic of an organization that permits it to have the intended effect in the marketplace, producing the desired result in carrying out its processes—in short, doing the right things to produce the right results. To detect effectiveness in operation, ask this question: Are we producing the desired result?

external   To gain a **competitive advantage** means to get an edge on competitors in the marketing of the organization's goods and services by making those products more desirable or the competitors' products less desirable. This advantage may be short term, medium term, long term, or indefinite. It may be established through cost leadership, quality and service leadership, product differentiation, **niche market-ing,** customer or supplier relationships, **strategic partnerships,** or a variety of other approaches.

The use of TBIT systems to leverage the effort of people to produce more and higher-quality products is becoming a necessity in highly competitive markets. Gaining the benefits is not simply a matter of purchasing new hardware and software; rather, it is part of a system that includes people and their attitudes, organizations and their cultures. These three critical characteristics—efficiency, effectiveness, and competitive advantage—are often enmeshed in an organization. Consider the following scenarios, which will strengthen your understanding of these concepts and set the stage for the remainder of the chapter.

COLE & SONS MANUFACTURING COMPANY

Tom Lee, assistant marketing manager in charge of new-business development at Cole & Sons Manufacturing Company, arrived at the office early Monday morning to find the usual piles of work strewn about his desk since Saturday morning. What would he do first? He knew he had to make an important proposal to a new client today, but he couldn't complete the proposal without the appropriate information from manufacturing and pricing information from the new-products section of marketing. He would have to wait to talk to them when they came in.

At least he could get through his mail, before the others arrived. As Tom opened his mail, it was the usual story. Some was junk and went right into the trash; some he needed further information about, so it went on one pile on a corner of his desk; other items needed urgent attention, so he put them on another pile; and so it went. By the time he had finished going through the mail, it was already 9:05. Picking up the phone, he dialed manufacturing to talk to George Yancey, the supervisor in charge of production, about details of the proposal. "Yes," said the voice on the other end, "Mr. Yancey came in at 8:30, but he'll be in a meeting until about 10:00. Could you call back then?" As he hung up, Tom felt a bit irritated, but it couldn't be helped; he would have to call back later.

Next, he called the new-products section of marketing and spoke with Sue Powell. Sue was both competent and friendly. After the usual social chat, they discussed the important proposal for the new client. Sue said that she, Tom, and George Yancey would have to meet together to discuss the key issues.

Hanging up the phone, Tom sat back in his chair. He was frustrated because George was both busy and worked in a different building halfway across town. Now it was coffee break time. He read through a supplier's price list and brochure to kill a bit of time and then went down the hall to the cafeteria. He would call George when he got back.

Upon returning from coffee break, Tom saw the note from his secretary sitting on top of the pile in the middle of his desk—the urgent pile: "George Yancey called, please call back." Dialing the manufacturing supervisor's number, Tom thought, maybe we'll get somewhere finally. George's secretary answered and informed Tom that George had not come back from coffee break yet, but should be back in a few minutes. Tom sat back, drafted a response in longhand to one of the urgent items on his pile, and took it down the hall to his secretary for entry onto her word processor. He went on to a colleague's office to see how her weekend had gone. After a brief chat, he returned past his secretary's desk. As she handed the word-processed document to Tom, she said that Mr. Yancey had returned his call again, but would be out of the office for the remainder of the day at a meeting with a key supplier. Tom walked back to his office and sat down to proofread his reply to the urgent request for information he had drafted. After only a few minor changes, it was finished. He returned the document to his secretary for corrections and mailing.

Tom finally caught up with George Yancey late the following day and set up a meeting between them for Friday morning at Tom's office regarding the important proposal for the new client. At last, some progress! Next, Tom phoned Sue Powell to confirm that this was a suitable time for her. Unfortunately, Sue could not come on Friday morning, since she had a prior important meeting. How about Monday morning? Yes, that was OK with Tom; he would phone George to verify that it was OK with him. Finally, two hours and many phone calls later, Tom found a time on Wednesday of the following week that was suitable for all three of them.

The meeting on Wednesday went very well. All of the major items were sorted out, and Tom got all the information he needed to complete the proposal. He spent all of the next day finishing the documentation. Since the proposal due date was in three days, there wasn't time to run it past George and Sue for a final reading, so he just put it in the mail.

Two weeks later, Tom received a form letter from the important new client:

Dear Mr. Lee: We are very sorry, but since Cole & Sons' proposal has arrived after the closing date, the proposal has been disqualified and is being returned.

This was disastrous! What would his boss say? Tom had done his best, but it had been so hard to communicate with everyone, it had all dragged out so long. Now they had missed the opportunity.

Tom Lee and his colleagues paint a picture of an organization that is doing its best, but is ineffective and inefficient in accomplishing its goals. Let's look at another scenario where better procedures and appropriate technology enhance organizational efficiency, effectiveness, and competitive advantage.

ACD MANUFACTURING GROUP

James Davis arrived at the ACD Manufacturing Group headquarters offices at 8:15 AM. To James, to be on time meant to be a little bit early, and good quality meant to produce a little bit better than expected. First, he switched on his networked PC and then thought about what priorities he had for the day. He had received a request for proposal (RFP) from a potential customer, and ACD wanted all the new customers it could get. The economy was tough, and ACD intended to be both a survivor and a leader. James made a short list of tasks he needed to do today to make progress on this proposal. First, he had to talk to manufacturing regarding potential production turnaround and costs. Then he had to talk to the new-products department of marketing to see about prices and terms.

James phoned Lyn Snyder, the manufacturing supervisor. Unfortunately, she was in a meeting. When he hung up, he immediately sent an E-mail message to Lyn describing the request for proposal and asking for some information. Then he called Mary Manthei, pricing manager over in marketing. Mary answered the phone in her usual positive fashion, and after a short chat about the weekend, James brought up the RFP. Mary said that to really make rapid progress on this, the two of them and Lyn Snyder needed to meet, discuss the main issues, and gather the facts. Then the proposal documentation could be prepared.

When James got off the phone with Mary he thought about where to go from here. He could try phoning Lyn back for a possible meeting time, but Lyn might still be in her other meeting. No, the best thing to do was to look at the online electronic diary that was part of the company's groupware networked office system and see when Lyn, Mary, and he were all free and book the meeting that way. The system would post it, and then, out of courtesy, James could E-mail the two of them and ask if that was a suitable time. James clicked on the electronic diary icon on his computer screen and was immediately in the application. He called up his own diary as well as Mary's and Lyn's for the next couple of days to find a block of two to three hours when they could meet. Tuesday afternoon at 2 PM was the first slot, so James booked it onscreen in each of their diaries. After leaving the electronic diary, James sent an E-mail message to each of them to check if the booked time was OK.

Next, James word-processed a couple of urgent requests for information from some customers. He proofread and spell-checked them, printed them, and dropped them off at his secretary's desk for envelopes and mailing on his way to coffee break. When he returned from coffee break, he had a brief chat with his secretary and then returned to his office. He saw that he had some new E-mail, so he opened his electronic mailbox and read the messages. One required a reply, two were general broadcast notices, and the last two were from Mary and Lyn. They both said the time he had chosen was OK for them and they would look forward to the meeting the next day. James replied to the messages, thanked them, provided them with a bit of additional information about the proposal request, and asked them to bring any appropriate information so they could get the job done during the meeting.

The meeting the next day went very smoothly, and James got the answers he needed to complete the proposal documentation. He spent most of Wednesday preparing the documentation on his word processor. By the end of the day, he had it pretty well wrapped up. He checked the RFP and saw that he had four more days before proposals were due and that they could be submitted by regular mail or E-mail to the requesting organization. That meant James had a few days left, so he sent an electronic copy of the proposal to Mary and Lyn for their comments and corrections. He received replies from each of his team members late the next day. After incorporating their comments, he read through the document one last time, polishing a sentence here and there, and making sure the proposal conveyed an aura of authority and responsiveness. Then he sent the document electronically, printed it out, and sent a second hard copy by mail. He realized that not everybody was used to electronic communications of this sort, and he didn't want to take the chance with this particular company's employees. They might not all be properly trained, and he wanted to make sure that the proposal got to them on time. In fact, it got there a little early.

Four weeks later, James received a letter addressed to him from the company that had requested the proposal. After considerable evaluation, they had concluded that ACD Manufacturing Group offered the best combination of price and quality, and therefore it was to be awarded the contract.

The above examples illustrate efficiency, effectiveness, and competitive advantage—and the lack thereof and the overlap among them. Consider the second scenario.

Efficiency:

- James's use of the word processor to reply to a couple of urgent requests required less time than handwriting the replies and having the secretary type them, proofread them, make the corrections, do a final proofread, and then mail them. James gets more work done in less time; he makes economical use of his time resources.

Effectiveness:

- James establishes priorities; this helps him do the right things.
- James' decision to E-mail Lyn and Mary about the meeting time demonstrates courtesy and helps build a team atmosphere of respect.

Competitive Advantage:

- ACD Manufacturing Group ends up with new business and an ongoing competitive advantage due to its ability to respond quickly and effectively to proposal requests.

Overlap:

- When James calls Lyn Snyder and fails to reach her, he immediately sends an E-mail message explaining the situation. This is more effective, since it will assist in getting out the proposal on time. It is also more efficient because it reduces "telephone tag" and the resulting waste of time.
- James uses the online electronic diary to book a meeting among Lyn, Mary, and himself. This is effective in that the meeting is booked and not postponed, allowing progressive action toward the goal of a timely proposal submission. It is also efficient since it requires less time than phoning back and forth between the two other participants to find a free meeting time.
- After receiving Lyn's and Mary's E-mail messages saying they can come to the meeting, James sends them additional information and asks them to bring what they need to make the meeting a success. This is effective communication, providing additional planning and organization. At the same time, James has to compose and send only one message because E-mail is able to send the same message to more than one person. This is efficient because fewer time, paper, and mail resources are used to accomplish the communication.
- James prepares the proposal on a word processor and E-mails it to Lyn and Mary for feedback. The feedback cycle produces a more accurate, higher-quality document. This is effective. The process also uses fewer time, paper, and mail resources than traditional report preparation methods, photocopying, addressing envelopes, and mailing; thus, it is efficient.

Efficiency, effectiveness, and competitive advantage may benefit from the application of TBIT systems, and a model called the *benefits cycle model* will be covered in the next section with this view in mind. The remainder of this chapter looks at models, techniques, and tools to assist in analyzing an organization for TBIT opportunities that can enhance efficiency, effectiveness, and competitive advantage.

Strategic Planning: A Foundation for Analyzing Networking Opportunities

In Chapter 1 we looked at a basic strategic planning process and the need to integrate IS planning with the overall organization strategy. In this section we first review the material from Chapter 1, adding some additional strategic modeling methods to enhance the strategic planning process. We also cover internal and external factors that affect the organization's competitiveness and examine a technique called *critical success factors (CSF)* for assisting in the strategic planning process.

Recall from Chapter 1 that strategic planning is a process used to establish organizational purpose, direction, and action. This includes

1. A three-step process involving the management team in the cooperative development of a mission statement, supporting goals, and detailed objectives.
2. The concept of tactical planning to assist in carrying out the organization's strategic plan.
3. The integration of strategic planning with IS planning through investment in TBIT.
4. The use of the SWOT method of strategic analysis.

Other approaches can be used in conjunction with the SWOT method to gain additional insight. Approaches we will look at include (1) the benefits cycle model, (2) internal and external factors, (3) a combined strategic model, and (4) critical success factors.

The Benefits Cycle Model

In the process of planning and using TBIT systems, various types of benefits may accrue to the organization. These benefits may be internal or external, incorporating various elements of the SWOT model, and fall into the three major categories discussed earlier:

1. Gaining competitive advantage (external—taking opportunities and overcoming threats).
2. Increasing business effectiveness (internal and external—full range of SWOT).
3. Improving organizational efficiency (internal—using strengths to better advantage and overcoming weaknesses).

Figure 6–1 illustrates this *benefits cycle model* and shows the interaction among the three broad categories of benefits. In this model, we see that attempts to gain competitive advantage through TBIT provide a strong sense of strategic direction for the organization and motivation to increase organizational effectiveness. A desire to increase organizational effectiveness will drive a demand to improve organizational efficiency, which in turn will provide a productivity foundation from which to gain competitive advantage. Gains in competitive advantage will generate **economies of scale** and **economies of scope,** which will lead to further opportunities to increase organizational effectiveness and improve organizational efficiency. The dynamic, interactive nature of these benefits can provide for sustained growth and competitive advantage if integrated effectively with the organization as a whole and successfully implemented.

Let's look at the use of this model in conjunction with SWOT analysis. The Sing Lee Manufacturing Group case, introduced in Chapter 1, is reproduced below, together with a brief SWOT analysis.

SING LEE MANUFACTURING GROUP

The Sing Lee Manufacturing Group (Hong Kong) has been conducting a strategic planning exercise. The company's primary products are children's toys, primarily for export. During the last five years, Sing Lee has built a local area network and developed some automated

FIGURE 6–1

The benefits cycle model

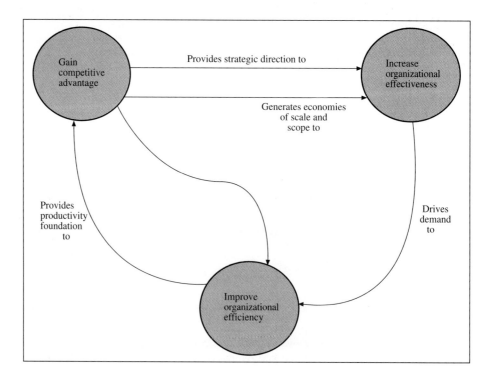

manufacturing techniques that have enabled it to reduce material wastage and labor costs and successfully compete in the international market. The result has been a 25 percent increase in sales. One difficulty, however, has been keeping the skilled workers who understand the network and know the new techniques. After being trained, many of them stay only a short while and then leave the firm. The last six months have been particularly stressful because of increased competition from one Taiwanese manufacturer that is selling toys to a number of Sing Lee's traditional North American customers. The Taiwanese firm's success has been enhanced by using computer-aided design and computer-aided manufacturing (CAD/CAM) methods. Its CAD/CAM system downloads files directly from customers' computers anywhere in the world. The competitor then manufactures to these customers' CAD specifications. This has allowed the Taiwanese firm to shorten the delivery time for a new toy. The industry average for delivery of a new toy has been about 30 days. The Taiwanese firm is now delivering in less than 10 days.

SWOT Analysis.   A SWOT analysis applied to the Sing Lee Manufacturing Group could produce the following results:

> *Strength*: The company has developed a local area network and refined its manufacturing process. This increase in cost effectiveness may be used to market its products more aggressively.
>
> *Weakness*: The turnover of experienced staff suggests that the company culture lacks loyalty and sufficient motivation to succeed.
>
> *Opportunity*: The company may integrate its new strength in flexible manufacturing and automation with CAD/CAM and electronic file transfer to gain a cost and price advantage over competitors. This is a good example of competitive necessity. This upgrade path will move the firm to full Computer Integrated Manufacturing (CIM).
>
> *Threat*: The Taiwanese competitor has used CAD/CAM technology with electronic file transfer to tie into customer product specifications, thereby improving service and speed. Already there has been a negative impact on Sing Lee's sales and customer base.

Benefits Cycle Model.   Now let us apply the benefits cycle model to this situation to gain further insight into strategic planning to establish organizational purpose and action. The following cycle steps might be followed in the case of Sing Lee. This example begins with a company strength that happens to be an improvement in organizational efficiency and therefore begins at the efficiency portion of the cycle model.

1. First, Sing Lee has a notable strength in having developed expertise in flexible manufacturing, which has helped reduce costs and increase flexibility. This improvement in organizational efficiency provides a productivity foundation on which the company can build a competitive advantage.
2. Sing Lee has already shown a gain in competitive advantage as a result of this technology: a 25 percent increase in sales.

3. How can this strength be further leveraged to gain more competitive advantage? The company has an opportunity to integrate its cost-effective manufacturing process with CAD/CAM and electronic file transfer technology. This will allow it to deliver high-quality products at lower prices more quickly, thus retaining and consolidating its existing customer base and expanding into competitors' markets.

4. The opportunity to gain competitive advantage provides the strategic direction the company needs to follow through with further innovations that will increase its organizational effectiveness. Sing Lee will be more effective if it can reduce its time to deliver a new toy to the same level (10 days) as the Taiwanese competitor. In fact, given its flexible manufacturing expertise, Sing Lee could even improve on the 10 days! This will result in increased effectiveness with customers.

5. This increased effectiveness can drive the demand for even more efficient operations. Potential TBIT applications could include the use of EDI to speed up delivery of materials and reduce the costs of paperwork, data entry, and data error.

6. These increased organizational efficiencies will allow Sing Lee to further reduce costs and provide cash flow for further investment, setting the stage for additional sustained competitive advantage.

7. These gains in competitive advantage will provide opportunities for further increases in organizational effectiveness through economies of scale such as a more dynamic, higher-paid, and more stable working environment that will assist in staff retention.

8. Increases in effectiveness could also be available through economies of scope: for example, being able to offer a wider range of products, styles, and materials, reaching a wider range of customers.

9. These increased economies of scale and scope would also open up further opportunities for improved organizational efficiency, such as better utilization of workshop space, less machine idle time, and more line items per order and per invoice, resulting in higher cash flow and profit for the order-processing operation.

The benefits cycle model can be used as a way to view the opportunities an organization faces in a stimulating and creative way, thus enhancing its current competitive position and establishing direction and action for the future.

Internal and External Factors: Their Impact on Competitiveness

A wide range of **internal** and **external factors** may affect an organization's competitiveness. Many of these factors will also influence the development of TBIT applications and their successful implementation. Figure 6–2 illustrates the impact of these internal and external factors on the organization and its future success.

FIGURE 6–2

*Impact of internal
and external
factors on the
organization*

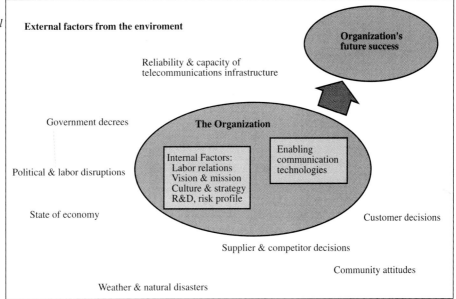

Following are some of the key factors that may increase an organization's competitiveness and enhance its ability to improve that competitiveness through TBIT. Some of these items will be discussed below. Others will be looked at more closely in the section on critical success factors; these are indicated with the designation *CSF*.

Internal Factors

• Labor relations: If the relationship between the company and its people is positive, cooperative, and supportive, the organization is in a position to implement changes in technology, job functions, and procedures that can improve its competitive position. If labor relations are poor, however, management may find that no matter how exciting the opportunities and how dynamic the technology, implementation is always flawed and results are less than expected or even disastrous.

• Vision of top management: If top management has a strong vision, with specific goals and objectives, it can set a platform for sustained strategic gain. This must be coupled with the ability to create a corporate culture that will motivate employees to higher levels of creativity, productivity, and loyalty.

• Corporate culture: A culture of creativity and responsibility will stimulate new ideas and applications, with many of them coming from front-line employees who deal directly with customers and products. In this type of environment, communicating information about new technologies and initiatives is important to stimulate other people in the organization.

• Level of staff motivation: The extent to which staff are highly motivated and enthusiastic about the company, its direction, and their functions within the organization will influence the design and execution of new strategies and TBIT initiatives.

- Competitive strategy (CSF).
- Level of dialogue and integration of IST with the CEO and other top managers: When the IST manager is a hybrid manager and part of the top management team, there is more likely to be an effective communication of strategic TBIT opportunities. Top managers will readily see the business impact of the new initiatives rather than just the obscuring "techno-talk."
- Cash flow and capitalization: A well-managed company that is solidly capitalized and has a good cash flow is in a position to take advantage of opportunities as they arise rather than passing them by because of insufficient funds. Tight management control over costs, close attention to profitability and quality of individual product lines, and caution regarding **overtrading** (when a business grows so fast that its capital is exhausted and the business moves into a cash flow crisis) will assist tremendously in this regard.
- R&D commitment: This internal factor is somewhat industry dependent, but in most cases a corporate culture of creativity and responsibility will foster commitment to product and process improvements.
- Risk profile: The willingness to take risks, or the desire to avoid risk, sets the risk profile of the organization. This usually reflects the attitudes toward risk of the CEO and other top managers and is a critical variable in highly competitive markets. Risk management is therefore an important function in the organization.
- IT platform consistency: The **IT platform** may well require some rationalization following the rapid change and growth in competition of the 1980s. Many organizations introduced microcomputers and local area networks alongside their mini or mainframe computer systems. There may even be a diversity of microworkstations, including Apple Macintosh, PC-compatible machines, and UNIX workstations, in the same organization, with some networked and others not. The extent to which such incompatibilities prevent the widest access to the most data possible is the extent to which the organization limits the strategic application of its existing systems.
- Centralization versus decentralization of decision making and IST: Either centralization or decentralization can be a useful strategy provided that it is in line with the corporate culture and motivating to people in the organization. Many organizations are downsizing their systems and moving to a **distributed processing** environment. Other organizations are closely integrating previous stand-alone PCs and isolated networks into their centralized mainframe environments.

External Factors

- Government actions (CSF).
- Level of the general economy (CSF).
- Attitude of community toward the industry and company: The attitude of the local and wider community will have obvious effects on the industry's and the individual organization's competitive position. A strong reputation for service, quality, and concern for employees and community will add immeasurably to the industry's and individual companies' ability to compete. This general goodwill sets a background of confidence in which an organization can venture into new strategies.

• Community attitude toward work and quality: If the general community has an attitude that mediocrity is good enough and that one should do as little work for as much pay as possible, this will hinder the competitive efforts of individual companies, even if their own internal cultures are moving in the opposite direction. Employees hired from the general community will be far more productive if they come from a background that values excellence and hard work for a fair wage.

• Weather patterns: Changing global or local weather patterns can have a substantial impact on a company's success and therefore on its ability to institute new TBIT initiatives. A particularly mild winter in the Northern Hemisphere would have a very detrimental impact on a company that manufactures primarily winter clothing.

• Natural disasters: Major earthquakes, floods, volcanic eruptions, hurricanes, and other natural disasters can greatly disrupt an organization's strategy and its ability to maintain the flow of goods and services. For example, a hurricane could disrupt telecommunications service and prevent the ongoing operation of an organization's EDI links with overseas customers and suppliers.

• Wars and political disruptions: Where political instability exists, such as in some parts of the former Soviet Union, local organizations' efforts to compete locally or internationally can be severely hampered.

• Reliability of communication links: An organization that is dependent on public telecommunications service providers must be concerned about the reliability of this service. In most Western countries, the performances of public telecommunications providers are highly reliable. However, a company that deals with organizations in countries where political instability, general infrastructure weakness, or other cultural factors may influence the reliability of the communication links may need to consider other alternatives.

• Actions of competitors (CSF).

• Current competitive positioning in the industry (CSF).

• Geographical location (CSF).

• Flow of raw materials, energy, and other key resources (CSF).

• Time-related factors (CSF).

A Combined Strategic Model

Support for the view that external factors affect competitiveness is found in the work done by Porter, McFarlan, and Parsons, all of Harvard University. They have conceived a variety of models and methods that can assist in evaluating certain external forces and their impact on TBIT decisions.[1]

Michael Porter's *competitive forces model*[2] describes five forces that affect competition in a marketplace:

1. The threat of new entrants.

---

1 B. Ives and G. P. Learmonth, "The Information System as a Competitive Weapon," *Communications of the ACM,* 27 (December 1984), pp. 1193–1201.

2 Michael Porter, *Competitive Strategy,* The Free Press (New York: 1980).

2. The intensity of rivalry among existing competitors.

3. Pressure from substitute products.

4. The bargaining power of buyers.

5. The bargaining power of suppliers.

Following from Porter's work, McFarlan raises five questions to aid in applying Porter's model to information systems and technology (IST) situations: [3]

1. Can IST be used to build barriers against new entrants?

2. Can IST change the basis of competition?

3. Can IST be used to generate new products?

4. Can IST be used to build in **switching costs**?

5. Can IST change the balance of power in supplier relationships?

In the context of Porter's model, Parsons indicates that a solid understanding of the impact IST will have on an organization's strategy may be gained by asking *how, when,* and *where* IST will affect a firm.[4]

An additional way to look at the strategic opportunities is from a cooperative (rather than a competitive) point of view. In what ways can IST be used to enhance cooperation with suppliers, or even domestic competitors, to gain a competitive advantage in the international arena?

These various approaches need not be treated separately. They can be used together to broaden the scope of our competitive analysis. Look at the model shown in Figure 6–3.

Information technology is not a total solution, and it does not always yield a competitive advantage. As was stated in Chapter 1, planning for TBIT must be integrated with organizational goals and objectives. Changes and opportunities in the business environment should give rise to a range of organizational, process, and IT changes working together to gain advantage.[5] The model in Figure 6–3 may be used to gain insight into how to apply TBIT effectively, but solid managerial control over such projects still must be exercised.

Critical Success Factors: Direction for Development

In preparing plans for developing TBIT applications, another tool that can be used for analyzing an organization's broad needs is the **critical success factors (CSF)** method. In this method, interviews are conducted with top managers to determine the factors they believe are critical to the success of the organization. These are

3 F. W. McFarlan, *IS and Competitive Strategy*, Note 0-184-055 (Cambridge, MA: Harvard Business School, 1983).

4 G. L. Parsons, *Information Technology: A New Competitive Weapon*, Note 0-183-121 (Cambridge, MA: Harvard Business School, 1983).

5 M. J. Earl, "Putting IT in Its Place: A Polemic for the Nineties," *Journal of Information Technology* 7 (1992), pp. 100–8.

FIGURE 6–3

A combined TBIT strategic model

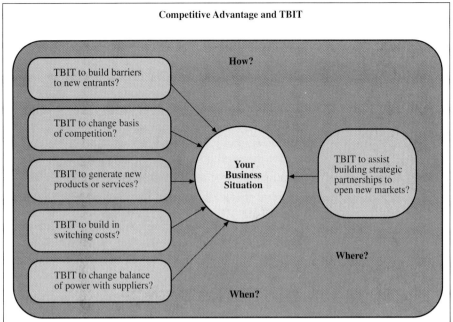

"the limited number of areas in which results, if they are satisfactory, will ensure successful competitive performance for the organization. They are the few key areas where things must go right for the business to flourish."[6] The method was originally developed to assist in discovering managers' business data needs; however, it can highlight opportunities for the application of networks to business situations. For example, the CSFs for the auto industry might include (1) styling, (2) a quality dealer system, (3) cost control, and (4) time to market.

Some or all of these CSFs may suggest network-based applications to assist in the successful conduct of the organization's business. To illustrate, let us take each of these CSFs and look at some appropriate TBIT applications.

- Styling: To measure the success of styling, a market survey may be used during the initial body design. Gathering responses, feeding them back to designers, changing design, and gaining additional feedback from potential customers will all assist in producing a more acceptable and marketable design. The use of notebook computers to capture responses, E-mail to give feedback to designers, CAD for design changes, and electronic file transfer to send a changed vehicle design to market research people could all be used to speed turnaround in evaluating responses to the survey. This could

---

6 J. F. Rockart, "Chief Executives Define Their Own Data Needs," *Harvard Business Review*, March–April 1979, pp. 81–93.

increase the number of iterations and increase the validity and marketability of the design.

- Quality dealer system: Having an online order entry system for new car orders would help dealers deliver better service to customers, assist dealers in managing their stocks of new cars, and assist the manufacturer in maintaining JIT manufacturing coordination.

- Cost control: A networked system of data terminals on the assembly line could assist in tracking individual vehicle orders as they proceed through the manufacturing process, thereby monitoring the timeliness, the cost, and ultimately the profitability of each vehicle sold.

- Time to market: Use of CAD systems networked to market research people (as noted above) could shorten the design cycle. Communication of CAD specifications to suppliers and subcontractors would speed up both the design cycle and the supplier setup cycle. The extension of CAD through networks to automated manufacturing systems and data entry and analysis systems in a computer-integrated manufacturing (CIM) system could shorten the manufacturing cycle.

As you can see, the CSF method can be very useful for uncovering additional TBIT application opportunities.

According to John Rockart, CSFs have a number of prime sources, including

1. The structure of the particular industry.
2. Competitive strategy, industry position, and geographic location.
3. Environmental factors.
4. Time-related factors.[7]

Figure 6–4 takes a closer look at some of these sources of CSFs and shows how they may highlight TBIT needs or opportunities for an organization. The items given cover Rockart's primary sources, expanded to include the CSF items mentioned in the previous section on internal and external factors.

Critical success factors are just that: factors critical to the organization's ongoing ability to compete successfully. As we have seen, CSFs can point out new and creative ways to view IS strategy and the potential to put TBIT to beneficial use in the organization.

Analyzing the Organization for Networking Opportunities

Up to this point, we have focused on the use of strategic planning methods to uncover TBIT application possibilities. This type of broad strategic analysis can be very beneficial in establishing direction and action for an organization in the medium- to long-term time horizon.

---

7 Ibid.

FIGURE 6–4

CSF implications for TBIT applications

Critical Success Factor	Implications for TBIT
Structure of the industry	The set of CSFs that are determined by the structure of the industry require close attention. For example, CSFs for the supermarket industry include product mix, inventory levels, sales promotion, and price. The use of in-store point-of-sale terminals connected with a LAN to a sales, stock management, and replenishment system could greatly improve stock management, maintain a proper product mix, and point to particular sales promotion ideas.
Competitive strategy	If a company's strategy is "lowest price," a high level of cost control will be necessary. This cost control could be enhanced by an electronic distribution system using EDI. Labor for data entry, mailing, data correction, and file maintenance could be considerably reduced as a result of electronic transaction communication and processing.
Current competitive positioning in industry	If your company is a small firm in a service industry, the use of alphanumeric pagers in conjunction with voice mail systems may allow you to provide a higher level of service to your clients and therefore strengthen your ability to compete with the bigger firms in the industry.
Actions of competitors	If a competing firm in your industry successfully implements a new TBIT system, this success will very likely begin to change the way business is conducted in the industry. Often a key factor that differentiates successful companies is being one of the early followers of successful innovators.[*]
Geographical location	Geographical location can offer both competitve advantages and disadvantages to companies. If your organization is at a considerable distance from some of your key customers or potential customers, this apparent disadvantage can be turned around through the appropriate use of communications technology. Applications such as E-fax, E-mail, voice mail, videoconferencing, file transfer, or EDI can help to build a long-distance relationship that is stronger than those of some local firms that didn't feel they needed to use such "high-tech" with close neighbors.
Level of general economy	When the local or international economy is good, most firms will do well. However, it is during difficult times that innovations and creativity sort out the winners from the losers. In every recession or depression there are still firms that grow and prosper, often at the expense of more complacent firms. For example, even in the travel downturn that resulted from the poor international economy in the late 1980s to early 1990s American Airlines and British Airways continued to prosper, largely due to their electronic reservation system, while many other international carriers went bankrupt.
Government actions	Government actions on a wide range of issues may affect a firm's competitiveness and therefore be a CSF for the firms involved. For example, an increase in local income taxes for companies may be just the catalyst a company needs to move some of its operations offshore to a lower-tax and lower-wage country. An appropriate use of TBIT can assist in building solid centralized control of overseas subsidiaries, even for firms new to this type of venture.
Flow of raw materials, energy, and other key resources	As John Rockart points out, "at the beginning of 1973, virtually no chief executive in the United States would have listed 'energy supply availability' as a critical success factor. Following the oil embargo, however, for a considerable period of time this factor was monitored closely by many executives."[†] Fundamental raw materials, energy, and other key resources may be more readily and accurately monitored in volatile markets using international databases and bulletin boards.

continued

FIGURE 6–4 *(concluded)*

CSF implications for TBIT applications

Critical Success Factor	Implications for TBIT
Time-related factors	Some CSFs are important only for a short time, and some opportunities are available only for a limited period. The organizations that successfully monitor the marketplace, changing customer tastes and international trends, and respond to them more quickly will be the ones to gain advantage. TBIT applications such as automatic database monitoring, electronic review of online news services, and real-time market research via data entry terminals (laptops or hand-held devices) and modems leverage this capability.

[*] Management Science America Ltd., "Excellence and the IT Factor: Information Technology Inside Excellent Companies in Britain," *Journal of Information Technology* 5 (1990), pp. 41–48.
[†] John F. Rockart, "Chief Executives Define Their Own Data Needs," *Harvard Business Review*, March–April 1979, pp.81–93.

In the remainder of this chapter, we will apply methods for analyzing the organization in a more detailed way. We will highlight additional, and more specific, ways in which networking can be applied to the organization. These methods are often used in analyzing organizational information systems. We will use the methods in a more narrow way, however, focusing specifically on networking opportunities. The following background case will be used and expanded throughout the remainder of this chapter to illustrate the techniques you will learn about.

RAPID DELIVERY COURIERS CORPORATION

Rapid Delivery Couriers Corporation (RDC) is a medium-size firm in the international courier market. RDC is considering how it can protect and expand its market share in this lucrative but intensely competitive industry. John Tomas, the manager in charge of IST, has had an ongoing dialogue with Mary Kong, CEO of RDC, concerning areas where the company could profitably use telecommunications-based systems to enhance customer service and keep costs under control so that prices can remain competitive. Ms. Kong asked John to analyze the company's operations and prepare a report showing areas in which communication and networking technology could be applied.

John knew his analysis needed to take into account a range of factors so that decisions that were ultimately made would have a solid foundation in reality. Sufficient detail and a variety of viewpoints would be necessary to prevent presumptuous mistakes and erroneous omissions. He remembered the various models he had studied. One of them, the five-component model of information systems development, would be useful to lend balance to the overall analysis so that key components did not get left out of the picture. Another model, the stages of growth model, would help him assess the extent to which the organization was ready for certain types of innovation and point out areas where it might need outside expertise.

Naturally, he would have to take a very close look at what people actually did in the organization. This type of functional and process analysis would point out areas where the work performed could be enhanced, customer service improved, and costs saved through greater efficiency—in short, give John and his team a clear view of how to improve what RDC did. He had heard of a technique called *association matrix analysis* that would allow them to relate various processes performed in the organization to a range of network applications. The resulting matrix would highlight the processes most affected by certain possible network applications and thereby point out the applications that offered the most promise for a given investment.

Knowing George Young, one of John's senior analysts, they would inevitably end up doing a data model of the organization as well. Since George had come back from that IS conference in Australia, he had been raving about "data models" and the need to build a solid data infrastructure on which the organization could then rapidly build the applications it needed to compete. John was not totally sold on the concept, but he was open to persuasion.

A critical factor in the success of the overall analysis and the ultimate implementation of their recommendations was going to be the "people" component of the system. John was well aware of the importance of systems acceptance by the users and of the "soft analysis" that was needed to discover some of the less evident requirements. When he was a senior analyst for another company a few years ago, John had overseen the development and implementation of a network for data entry. The chaos that followed the initial introduction of that system was overcome only after a grueling six months of recoding and retraining. The system's ultimate success was considered miraculous under the circumstances and more a measure of the flexibility of the data entry operators than of the user friendliness of the system. John did not want to repeat that mistake for sure. Recently John had come across a British analysis concept that he thought he would try out. It was called the *rich picture* method. Based on the project that he had seen using it, it looked more like a third-rate artist's sketches, but he could see some potential in it and was prepared to give it a try. He had heard of a number of organizations that had had some success with this soft analysis method, especially in the area of the people and procedural aspects of the system.

John believed in his team and looked forward to the challenge of this project. He trusted Mary Kong's intuition that this could be an area of great benefit to the company if they did their homework thoroughly. He was indeed looking forward to the months of work they would have with this tremendous opportunity.

Models to Enhance Analysis of Business Networking Opportunities

A number of models, or viewpoints, can be used to enhance our analysis of networking opportunities and situations. One of these models is often referred to as the *five-component model*.[8] As the name implies, this model views an information system as consisting of five major components: (1) hardware, (2) software, (3) data, (4) people, and (5) procedures. Figure 6–5 depicts the relationship among these components.

---

8 D. M. Kroenke and K. A. Dolan, *Business Computer Systems: An Introduction* (Santa Cruz, CA: Mitchell Publishing, 1987), pp. 33–60.

FIGURE 6–5

*The five-
component
model of a TBIT
system*

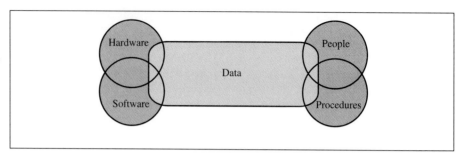

The software is the instructions that tell the hardware what to do. The procedures are the instructions that tell the people what to do. The data are what the people and hardware communicate and process using instructions from the procedures and software. The five components fit the simple definition of a system: a group of components working together to achieve a common goal.

This model is very useful for several reasons. First, the model prevents the analyst from focusing on the hardware, software, and data to the exclusion of the very important people and the procedures the people must follow. This balance is often necessary to maintain a proper perspective among computing systems professionals who tend to emphasize the more technical aspects of systems work.

Second, the model provides a framework to assist in planning for costs. In many situations, the decision to proceed with a networking project is based on a cost analysis that encompasses only 20 percent of the full costs involved. This 20 percent may be the hardware and direct software acquisition or development costs for the project. However, this costing approach often completely ignores factors such as training, hiring new personnel, data conversion or acquisition, and design and dissemination of procedural aspects of the system. It also frequently ignores the issues of operation and maintenance of the new system. In many cases, these costs may amount to four times the initial estimates on which the decision was based.[9] The five-component model provides a framework in which these other costs can be more readily and properly assessed. Consider how this model might be applied to the Rapid Delivery Couriers Corporation case.

John Tomas had assigned a team member named Frank Ohono to do a brief five-component model analysis of the existing telecommunications-based systems in use at RDC. During his analysis Frank discovered the following:

- Hardware consisted of

  A four-year-old PABX that handled the company's telephone system, routing incoming client calls to operators as well as handling general incoming and outgoing phone calls.

9 P. G. W. Keen, *Shaping the Future: Business Design through Information Technology* (Cambridge, MA: Harvard Business School Press, 1991), pp. 141–178.

Five multiband radiotelephone transmitter/receivers for use by the dispatchers in communicating with the pickup drivers.

45 mobile radiotelephone transmitter/receivers located in the vans used by the drivers.

- The software component currently was nonexistent for telecommunications-based systems, since all of the systems were voice and manually based.
- Data used in the systems under consideration included

Customer name and address to allow proper pickup of courier packs. These data were transmitted verbally by the customer to a company operator.

Delivery name, address, and phone number, as well as the customer name, address, and phone number. These data were recorded on the package to be delivered.

Service slips turned in by the drivers to the head office. These were used to validate the pickups and deliveries the drivers made and were the basis for wage payments.

- People involved in the system were noted above and included drivers, telephone operators, dispatchers, and customers.
- Procedures the people followed included the following:

Customers prepared prepaid courier packages, recording the delivery name, address, and phone number on one side of the package and their own name, address, and phone number on the other side. They then placed the article or document to be couriered inside the package and sealed it.

Customers telephoned RDC and gave their name, address, and where they wanted the package delivered to (locally, out of the central city but in the area, intercity, interstate, or internationally) and indicated that it was a prepaid package.

An operator received the customer's call and wrote the details on a slip of paper.

The operator passed the slip of paper to one of the dispatchers. Currently, a group of two or three operators worked with a specific dispatcher.

The dispatcher passed the data to the area driver via the radiotelephone.

The driver picked up the package.

The driver tore off a perforated portion of the service slip attached to the prepaid package.

The driver either (1) delivered the package to the address on the package if it was within the area, (2) brought it to the central station for transfer to another courier for delivery within another area in the city, or (3) brought it to the central station for transfer to the intercity, interstate, or international section for overseas delivery.

The driver submitted all of the service slips at the central station.

Service slips were entered into the payroll system to authorize weekly payments to the drivers.

After John had reviewed this initial analysis, he was satisfied with the work Frank had done and could see that it laid the groundwork for future analysis.

The five-component model will be used on a number of occasions in the remainder of this book and should be considered as a fundamental model for viewing the work carried out.

Another useful model is the *stages of growth model.* [10] This model proposes that an organization goes through the following four stages in developing information systems.

1. *Initiation:* The first stage is the introduction of a new concept or technology, or even the initiation of computer-based information systems within the organization. The initiation stage is often characterized by a considerable amount of experimentation, discovery, and attendant trial and error.

2. *Expansion or proliferation:* If the initiation stage is successful, the organization will move into the expansion stage, where widespread use of the new systems is a characteristic. A significant proliferation of additional applications and systems may be proposed and implemented during this phase, with costs spiraling upward and a sense of being almost out of control.

3. *Formalization or control:* The almost unchecked growth during the expansion stage typically leads to the control stage, where management demands stronger controls over new developments. The lack of integration

---

10 C. F. Gibson and R. L. Nolan, "Managing the Four Stages of EDP Growth," *Harvard Business Review,* January–February 1974, pp. 76–88; W. S. Humphrey, *Managing the Software Process* (Reading, MA: Addison-Wesley, 1989); C. S. Parker and T. Case, *Management Information Systems: Strategy and Action,* 2nd ed. (New York: McGraw-Hill, 1993), pp.123–26.

FIGURE 6–6

Technology stages of growth model

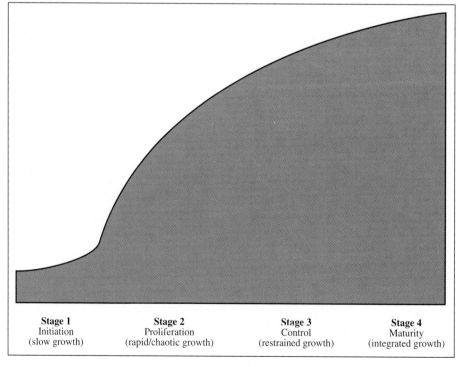

| **Stage 1**
Initiation
(slow growth) | **Stage 2**
Proliferation
(rapid/chaotic growth) | **Stage 3**
Control
(restrained growth) | **Stage 4**
Maturity
(integrated growth) |

and security that often accompanies the proliferation stage has to be addressed at this time as well. Often requirements for financial justification (net present value, payback, cost-benefit analysis, etc.) of new systems become very stringent, as do formal project control requirements to bring costs under control.

4. *Maturity:* As the systems come under control and are integrated with overall company strategy, the organization moves into the maturity phase. Often new innovations may be proposed that will shift the organization back into the initiation stage, and the cycle will start again.[11]

This model is very general and may be applied in a variety of ways. One particularly useful application is to assist in making decisions on how to proceed with TBIT developments and to determine the least risky approach to take. Often outside assistance may be necessary to avoid certain pitfalls if the necessary expertise is not available from within the organization. Let us look at the RDC case and see how this model may be applied.

According to the stages of growth model John Tomas had studied, it looked like RDC was in the initiation stage of TBIT. Therefore, John could see there were a number of pitfalls that might become a problem if they were not careful. John was pretty sure that more experienced companies, consultants, and vendors could save them much trial and error through their expertise. He certainly did not want to move into the proliferation stage unprepared, with all the chaos that could result from insufficient control. John could also anticipate some benefits during the later stages of growth that RDC could reap if it accelerated the process with sound planning and strong controls at the beginning. He and his team wanted to foster an environment of innovation without all the attendant problems that the stages of growth model implied could be part of the process. He could see real value in this model as an early warning system. Forewarned was truly forearmed.

A third useful model is the *value chain model*. Every organization delivers products or services to customers. To retain those customers, the value of those products or services must be sufficient to persuade them to continue buying from the organization. Porter and Millar call the process of value creation in products or services a value chain.[12] In their model (see Figure 6–7), they innumerate nine generic activities that create value in an organization. The primary activities focus on acquisition and production of goods together with the sales, delivery, and servicing of those goods. The support activities include procurement of inputs, technology support, staffing, and provision of the firm's infrastructure of legal, accounting, and other firmwide services. The enhancement of these activities with TBIT can create additional value through process improvement, cost reduction, or value enhancement through greater effectiveness.

By analyzing the organization in the light of this model, supplemented by other models such as SWOT, key areas for network technology enhancement can

---

11 Gibson and Nolan, "Managing the Four Stages of EDP Growth."

12 M. E. Porter and V. E. Millar, "How Information Gives You Competitive Advantage," *Harvard Business Review*, July–August 1985, pp.149–60.

FIGURE 6–7

*Value chain
model*

Support Activities						
	Firm infrastructure					
	Human resource management					
	Technology development					
	Procurement					
		Inbound logistics	Operations	Outbound logistics	Marketing & sales	Service
	Primary activities					

Facilitate primary activities to accomplish its goals

leads to profit margin increase

Source: Adapted from M. E. Porter and V. E. Millar, "How Information Gives You Competitive Advantage," *Harvard Business Review*, July–August 1985, pp.149–60.

be spotted. By raising questions of strengths, weaknesses, opportunities, and threats and by questioning what are the "best" business practices in each of these nine areas, considerable insight can be gained.

Using this broad value chain model as a background model, it is possible to develop various value-adding activities. The RDC case illustrates how this model might be employed in a broad way.

The real key to RDC's long-term success was going to be adding value to its parcel delivery services without adding cost. This would involve new efficiencies that would help to maintain RDC's competitive position and hopefully make its services more effective from the customer's viewpoint. John Tomas was familiar with the value chain model and knew that he could use it in his analysis. Given that communication was a major recurring issue in the analysis, he could see that the support activities at RDC involving technology development could be combined to provide a more efficient and effective communication infrastructure using a combination of WAN and LAN communication technologies. These technologies could especially affect customer order placement and collection of parcels (inbound logistics), processing and tracking of parcels (operations), final delivery (outbound logistics), and processing of driver payments (operations). Naturally, RDC would have to take a closer look at the processes involved and the competing technologies that could enable this more efficient communication system.

Function and Process Diagrams to Identify Networking Opportunities

One area that analysis must cover is the functions and processes that are performed within the organization. In the context of the five-component model, these functions and processes represent the software and procedures components. These are the two components that represent what is to be done. This analysis serves a three-fold purpose:

1. To document the analysis team's understanding of the system operations.
2. To act as a communication device between users and analysts for clarifying system requirements.
3. To act as a planning support document and a bridge to designing and implementing the final TBIT system.

The type of diagram you will learn to use in this section is referred to as a *function* or *process decomposition diagram*. Some professionals also refer to it as a *hierarchical diagram*, although the term is typically used to refer to program module decomposition. The terms *function* and *process* will be treated as interchangeable, even though *function* refers to higher-level and more encompassing activity, whereas *process* may be used in the context of a more detailed, lower-level activity.

To illustrate the use of this graphical modeling tool, let's take another look at the brief five-component model analysis conducted by Frank Ohono of RDC. Figure 6-8 presents a decomposition diagram of the list of procedures in RDC's telecommunications-related area on page 250. Procedures and software are the processes of this decomposition diagram.

A few rules should be followed in preparing such a diagram:

1. Decompose the processes from the most general to increasingly specific processes. In Figure 6-8, the most general and encompassing process, "pickup and delivery of customer parcel," is at the top of diagram. At the next level down are the activities of the the major people involved, followed by specific activities under each category.
2. Group processes in a natural way.
3. Begin the process description with a verb (action): for example, "Pickup (verb) . . . parcel (noun)."
4. Include in the process description a noun (an object that may reflect data need): for example, "Receive (verb) . . . message (noun)."

This type of diagram offers a number of benefits. First, the diagram is very easy to construct and read. Therefore, users are more likely to really understand what it portrays and in turn are far more likely to give useful feedback on the accuracy of the model, since they have a thorough working knowledge of the existing system. Second, the style of the diagram naturally highlights the relationships among different processes in a way that the list of processes originally prepared by Frank Ohono does not show directly.

Now that we have done this decomposition diagram, have any TBIT opportunities come to light in the process? TBIT systems offer a number of benefits. By their nature they are aimed at the process of communication and provide opportunities for faster and more accurate communication. What communication aspects are taking place in Figure 6–8? The following list includes five processes involving communication:

FIGURE 6–8

Decomposition diagram of RDC parcel pickup and delivery

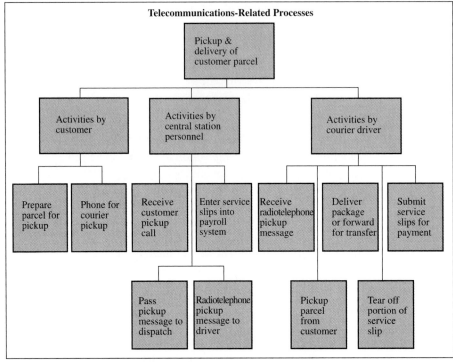

1. Customers telephone RDC and give their name, address, and where they want the package delivered to (locally, out of the central city, intercity, interstate, or international) and indicate that it is a prepaid package.
2. An operator receives the customer's call and writes the details on a slip of paper.
3. The operator passes the slip of paper to one of the dispatchers.
4. The dispatcher passes the data to the driver via the radiotelephone.
5. The driver submits all of the service slips at the central station.

Under the current system, items 1, 2, and 4 involve some use of telecommunications, specifically the telephone or radiotelephone. Items 2, 3, and 5 involve some communication that is manual in nature.

Association Matrices to Discover Networking Opportunities

In this section you will learn about association matrices. An *association matrix* highlights relationships among groups of objects. We will see how potential TBIT applications can be associated with processes to highlight applications that have the greatest organizational impact. Let's look again at the RDC case.

The project was proceeding nicely. John Tomas, Frank Ohono, and the rest of the team were making real progress in discovering where the company could profitably use telecommunications-based systems to enhance customer service and keep costs under control. The initial five-component analysis done by Frank had been converted to a decomposition diagram, and that diagram had been shared with a group of users to determine its accuracy. That discussion had brought to the surface a number of additional processes and problems that the analysis would need to address. The whole area of receiving customer calls and passing pickup messages on to the drivers had become a hot topic of discussion during the review session. Frank Ohono had modified the decomposition diagram to reflect those concerns. The portion of the modified diagram reflecting the area of concern, "activities by central station personnel," is reproduced in Figure 6-9.

The quality service provided by RDC had been in increasing demand by customers, and this growth had put a strain on the staff as management tried to keep costs under control. Cost control in this case generally meant operators, dispatchers, and drivers working harder. A study had been done on the proportion of customer calls that were of a routine nature. The company had found that nearly 60 percent of all incoming calls were the standard "I am from XYZ company. I have a prepaid courier package to go to ABC location." As John and Frank discussed the matter, they **brainstormed** TBIT applications that could improve the situation. During their brainstorming session, they came up with the following potentially applicable items:

LAN based:	*WAN based:*
Electronic mail	Alphanumeric pager
Multiuser database	Voice-activated network
Barcode data capture	800 toll-free service
Image-processing system	

After they finished brainstorming, John said he would prepare an association matrix. The matrix would associate the processes under consideration with potential TBIT applications that could help them to enhance their customer service and keep costs under control.

✗ **FIGURE 6–9**

Decomposition diagram of RDC central station personnel

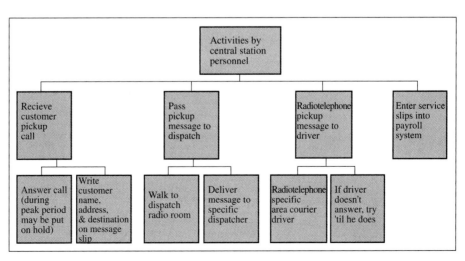

An association matrix is a simple table consisting of column headings and row labels. Where a row and a column intersect, an *X* is placed for all combinations where a meaningful or useful association exists. Let's continue with the Rapid Delivery Couriers case.

After completing the association matrix (see Figure 6–10), John and Frank met again to discuss the results. John had designated the processes from Frank's decomposition diagram as the row labels and the potential TBIT applications as the column headings. The results were quite exciting, pointing very strongly to a combination of technologies that could have a dramatic impact on company service and cost structures.

Initially the team concluded that the barcoding and 800 service would have no effect on the processes currently under analysis. The barcoding technology might have some benefits in package tracking, but this would be for a future development. The use of the 800 toll-free service would not alleviate the current operator bottleneck at peak times and would have only a small cost benefit for the customer, but they concluded that the benefit would not influence customer loyalty or perception of service.

In further narrowing down the choices, the team determined that both the E-mail and image-processing applications, although potentially useful, were a distant second to the voice-activated network system. This narrowed the possible applications down to the three remaining, interrelated applications: (1) multiuser database, (2) alphanumeric pager, and (3) voice-activated network. Both Frank and John had read about the use of these technologies in various types of applications. Now they would have to do a bit more research to find out the details of their interaction and function.

To effectively use the association matrix model, you need to understand both the business processes being looked at and the TBIT applications that offer solutions or enhancements to those processes.

✗ FIGURE 6–10

Association matrix of processes with TBIT applications

	Electronic mail	Database	Barcode	Image processing	Alphanumeric pager	Voice-activated network	800 toll-free service
Answer call, on hold						X	
Write message slip	X	X		X		X	
Walk to dispatch radio room	X	X		X		X	
Deliver message to specific dispatcher	X	X		X		X	
Radiotelephone specific area driver		X			X	X	
Repeat RT call until answered					X	X	

Having covered decomposition diagrams and association matrices, it is time to round out our system analysis tools with a data-oriented model. The next part discusses a method of data modeling referred to as entity-relationship modeling.

Data Models to Point Out Networking Opportunities

Keep in mind that in the context of the five-component model, the data are the connecting point between the hardware and the software, and between the people and the procedures. Data are what the system communicates and processes. Because the data are so central to the system, it is beneficial to do a thorough analysis so that their impact can be clearly seen. This analysis can fill a strategic role as well, enhancing previous strategic planning techniques.

The *entity-relationship (E-R)* model describes the primary items of data with which an organization deals and the relationships among those items of data. The **E-R diagram** represents data as they are stored; it does not represent flows of data or the ways in which data are processed. An E-R diagram is read not like a data flow diagram but as "data at rest."[13] The diagram is constructed using the following steps:

1. List the **entities**, that is, anything that can be described by data. Entities typically fall into four categories: persons, objects, locations, and events. They are usually named with nouns, often the nouns used in constructing the process decomposition diagrams.

2. Draw a rough first draft of the diagram, indicating the **relationships** with single lines connecting entities together, and using a few simple words to describe the relationships.

3. Indicate the numeric portion of the relationship as either one-to-one, one-to-many, or many-to-many.

4. Once the first draft is satisfactory, consider how it might be reorganized to clarify any relationships or present them in a more orderly fashion.

5. Under the name of each entity in the final list of entities, list the **attributes** or data elements of each entity and indicate the **primary key** for each entity by underlining the key attribute. This listing is often called a **data dictionary** and may have other characteristics added to it later, such as the length of the data field in the database or whether the data are alphabetic, numeric, date, or logical.

Let's look again at the RDC case to see the process in action.

John Tomas sat down with George Young to review the data-modeling analysis George was going to do for the current project. George would use the initial five-component analysis that Frank Ohono had performed. Initial data discovered were as follows:

---

13 Whitten, Bentley, and Barlow, *System Analysis and Design Methods* (Homewood, IL: Richard D. Irwin, 1989), pp.228–66.

Customer name and address to ensure proper pickup of courier packs. These data were transmitted verbally by the customer to a company operator.

Delivery name, address, and phone number, as well as customer name, address, and phone number. These data were recorded on the package to be delivered.

Service slips turned in by the drivers to the head office. These were used to validate the pickups and deliveries the drivers had made and were the basis for wage payments.

George followed the steps he had learned in data modeling with entity-relationship (E-R) diagrams. First, he listed the entities (people, objects, locations, or events) involved in the area under study as nouns:

Customer.
Package.
Destination.
Driver.
Service slip.

Then George prepared a rough first draft of the E-R diagram, including a first pass at establishing the numeric portion of the relationship, as shown in Figure 6–11.

✗ FIGURE 6–11

An entity-relationship (E-R) diagram for RDC pickup and delivery service

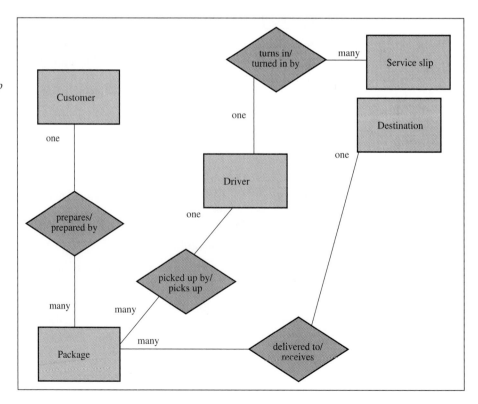

John Tomas had to admit he didn't really understand these E-R diagrams and wasn't too sure how they were going to benefit this project, but George offered to explain it to him. George said, "You read the diagram as simple sentences—for example, 'A given customer prepares many packages' or, reading in the other direction, 'A given package is prepared by one customer.'" George explained how the procedures followed by the staff and any programs that might be written for the computer would all have to use the data. Data to be transmitted over the WAN needed to be identified and quantities determined in order to size transmission capacities. The right data had to be captured, or certain information would be omitted and possibly strategic needs would remain unmet. Also, if the data were not organized properly, both the performance of the system and the reliability of the data could be negatively affected. That did make sense to John; he was beginning to see how this data modeling could provide for a more reliable system as well as a more responsive and cost-effective system.

Next, George redrew the E-R diagram so that it was more readable and better organized. The results of his effort appear in Figure 6–12.

As John reviewed the updated E-R diagram, he could see that the package entity had been moved so that the other entities to which it was related projected from it like the spokes of a wheel. This showed that the package, as an item of data, was central to current and future applications in this area. This was very interesting indeed. In fact, John could now see why RDC had difficulty tracking missing packages. Currently, the only data actually captured were customer, driver, and service slip data. No package or destination data were captured or kept, so naturally it was difficult to manage this part of the business when errors occurred.

When George came in later that day, he had the data dictionary with him. It looked like this (entity name in all capital letters, primary key attribute underlined):

CUSTOMER	DRIVER
<u>Customer number</u>	<u>Employee number</u>
Customer name	Name
Pickup area	Truck ID
Customer address	Address
Customer phone	Phone
Customer fax	Pickup area
Contact person	Radiotelephone frequency number
Current balance	

PACKAGE	SERVICE SLIP
<u>Service slip ID</u>	<u>Service slip ID</u>
Customer name	Driver's employee number
Customer address	
Customer phone	DESTINATION
Delivery name	<u>Delivery ID</u>
Delivery address	Delivery name
Delivery phone	Delivery address
	Delivery phone

As John went over the data dictionary with George, he could see the need for close attention to detail in preparing this data model. George had certainly included the data that were currently captured and used by the organization and, as noted earlier, he had also added a number of entities that were part of the business but currently were not captured and used, and were creating problems: specifically, the package entity. They could begin capturing data

FIGURE 6–12

Reorganized E-R diagram for RDC

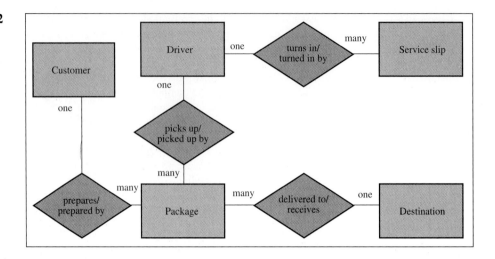

on the package and even automate the process. Certainly some work would be required to implement a barcode system to capture the service slip ID from the package at first pickup. Drivers would have to be equipped with portable data terminals and modems. They would also need to be trained to scan the packages and then key in the driver's employee number and the customer number. These data could be downloaded from the portable data terminals to the main computer via modem. This would save clerical data entry time from the service slips turned in by the drivers to determine their pay. In addition, it would save data entry errors, and speed up complaint resolution with the drivers for underpayments that absorbed so much of payroll staff time. From an operational standpoint, there were some very real benefits. But the potential strategic benefits were even greater. If the package was scanned at each transfer point, the organization would know where each individual package was within minutes of its arrival. This had the potential to resolve the late delivery and lost package problems. George explained to John that the data model still required some technical refinements, but was in pretty good shape from a general management standpoint.

As they finished their discussion, John and George set a meeting date for the following week. They would meet with the team and users to review the results so far and plan the details of the next stage of the project.

Thorough data modeling helps to establish a reliable data foundation on which to build TBIT applications, as well as offering insight into problem resolution and business enhancement. However, it does not address the people, procedural, or organizational context of the situation under study. The next method to be covered, called the *rich picture diagram*, focuses on the people portion of the five-component model and the related organizational context.

Use of Rich Pictures to Analyze Network Needs

The models we have examined so far in this chapter aim more at the "hard" components of the system than the "soft" components. Models such as decomposition diagrams, association matrices, and E-R diagrams tend to focus on the hardware, software, data, and procedural aspects. In this section we look at another technique for representing the organizational situation. This technique, called a *rich picture diagram*, borrows from the "soft systems" methodology developed by Checkland and others.[14] The major contribution this approach makes to the area of information systems analysis "is that it emphasizes the people in organizational systems and their perceptions of these systems."[15] Given the considerable impact people have on the successful operation of TBIT systems, this technique adds considerable balance and breadth to the analysis tools we have been developing. Although this technique is being introduced last (being the most different of the approaches introduced in this chapter), it could well be applied first in practice, since it gives the broadest and "richest" view of the organization.

A rich picture diagram is a way of viewing the system under analysis in its broad organizational setting. It is a visual representation of the system under study. As the rich picture diagram takes shape, it can be tested for "richness" by taking into consideration six key elements that comprise the acronym CATWOE:

C stands for *customers*. These are the people who consume the outputs of the system. They are outside the system; they are in the *environment*.

A stands for *actors*. These are the people who transform the inputs of the system into outputs that will be consumed by the *customers*.

T stands for *transformation*. This is the process performed by the *actors* to change the inputs into outputs. It is the process of throughput.

W stands for *Weltanschauung*. This German word essentially means "world view." This is the set of assumptions through which the *environment* is viewed.

O stands for *owners*. These are the people who live in the *environment* but for whom the system exists.

E stands for *environment*. The environment is the set of external factors that place constraints on the system; however, it is fundamentally unaffected by the system.

The process is typically a participative one, with analysts working together with the "actors" involved to discover as much as possible about the organization and its environment and then expressing this understanding as a rich picture diagram. Although not a "requirement" of the soft-systems methodology of Checkland, it is a widely used technique for expressing and communicating the group understanding of the situation.

The soft-systems method attempts to discover these six elements and their relation to one another, building up a "rich picture" to highlight problems and generate discussion toward the goal of improving the situation. The rich picture diagram is a

---

14 P. Checkland, *Systems Thinking, Systems Practice* (New York: John Wiley & Sons, 1981), pp. 224–27.

15 M. Sager, *Managing Advanced Information Systems* (Englewood Cliffs, NJ: Prentice Hall, 1990), pp.7–8.

literal picture that may be hand drawn or created using a drawing program or a **computer-aided systems engineering (CASE)** tool when such a device becomes available for this diagram type. It is intended to be not a work of art but a work of communication and insight to gain understanding of the system of people interactions that need to be changed in some way.

Let us go back to the RDC case and see this technique in action.

Having started with the five-component model, John Tomas was increasingly satisfied that they had a good grasp of the pickup and delivery system from the viewpoint of four of the components. They had analyzed the procedures and data, looked at the existing hardware and software, and considered some options for each of these components. However, John felt a bit uneasy about the people and organizational part of the analysis. He realized how important that component was. He and his team could do a brilliant job of analyzing, designing, acquiring, and implementing a top-rate telecommunications and information system, but if the people involved reacted negatively to some part of it, misused it, or were disrupted by it, the system could fail no matter how excellent it was. Simply put, the people were part of the system. If that part did not fit right, the common goal of the components in the system might not be achieved.

John met with the rest of the team, George, Frank, and Maria, as well as a couple of key users and a representative of the top management IST steering committee. Their goal was to develop a model of the people within the context of the organization. At the meeting, John asked them to join him in brainstorming in the context of the CATWOE model to produce a rich picture of the people context of the organization. He explained how they would first list the items they could think of in each category of the model. As they worked through that morning, they came up with the following items:

- *Customers*: This obviously included RDC's regular courier customers, but the team concluded that it should also include the people and organizations to which the packages were delivered.
- *Actors*: This included those directly involved in the pickup and delivery process: the operators, the dispatchers, the drivers, and the supervisors of these people.
- *Transformation*: The process of taking inputs (phone calls, actors' time and talents, system resources such as phones and computers, packages to be delivered) and producing outputs: safely and quickly delivered packages.
- *Weltanschauung*: This proved to be the hardest yet one of the most valuable parts of the exercise. The basic world views or assumptions the team came up with included the following:

  RDC executives assumed that better service to customers produced more loyal customers, and good service was dependent on enthusiastic employees.

  RDC operators and dispatchers assumed the company had a responsibility to not put them out of work with new technology.

  Drivers want to make as much money with as little hassle as possible.

  The IST team assumed that better technology produces better service.

  Customers assumed that they deserved error-free service at the standard price—quality with no price premium.

- *Owners*: The shareholders of the company.
- *Environment*: This included the general state of the economy, decisions of competitors and suppliers, and decisions made by the government.

Based on this initial listing of items, John attempted to draw a rich picture of this organizational situation. Naturally, this initial attempt would probably need to go through an iterative process of refinement as the group communicated further. John's first attempt is illustrated in Figure 6–13.

The current "hard" analysis pointed to the possible application of a voice-activated network with alphanumeric pagers to ensure rapid message transmission and keep costs under control as the business grew. As the team discussed this rich picture, they perceived a number of problems that had not been evident to them during the earlier portion of their analysis. For example,

- The potential application envisioned could put operators and dispatchers out of jobs.
- Customers probably would not pay more for the improved service, so improvements would have to be funded by cost savings.
- Drivers wanted to be as efficient as possible, not missing customer calls because the radiotelephone could not reach them, as was often the case (radiotelephone in the van, but the driver in a building picking up packages).

✻ FIGURE 6–13

A rich picture of the RDC situation

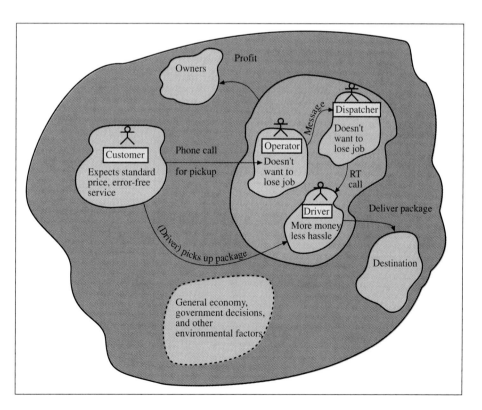

- Government decisions, such as deregulating the telecommunications industry, could affect the long-term usefulness of new TBIT applications.

To John, this further analysis pointed to the human needs of the system and requirements for retraining of staff, promotion of the idea to customers, and a solid financial analysis to support the decision to move to this new system.

In using the rich picture model, the key to remember is that the attitudes, assumptions, and interactions among people in the system affect the system's success in the long run. Many of the environmental items described in the analysis are the same as those we looked at earlier in the sections on critical success factors and internal and external factors.

Summary

This chapter covered strategic planning as a foundation for analyzing network opportunities. It also covered the process of analyzing an organizational situation to discover potential networking applications.

The coverage of strategic planning built on the concepts introduced in Chapter 1. We reviewed the material in Chapter 1 and then enhanced it with additional methods and concepts. To the general strategic model and SWOT analysis discussed in Chapter 1, we added a benefits cycle model showing the interaction among the primary benefits that may arise through the application of TBIT systems. These three major types of benefits included gaining competitive advantage, increasing organizational effectiveness, and improving organizational efficiency.

In building on the strategic planning process, we took a closer look at internal and external factors that might affect the organization and its ability to implement its strategy. Internal factors such as labor relations, vision of top management, and the general corporate culture are factors over which management has some direct control. Management can make specific plans to modify these factors to assist change and TBIT implementation as necessary. However, the organization has little or no influence over such external factors as government actions, the level of the general economy, community attitudes toward work, and natural disasters. These internal and external factors have profound implications for the organization's planning and its ability to change competitive direction and can suggest areas in which TBIT could be profitably implemented.

Next, we looked at a combined strategic model. This model considers five competitive forces at work in the marketplace and how TBIT could be applied to each area with the proper timing and geographical emphasis. Included in the model is the concept of cooperation using TBIT to enhance competitiveness. To this model we added the concept of critical success factors (CSF), which picks up the concept of internal and external factors in some specific ways and suggests a limited number of areas in which satisfactory results will ensure successful competitive performance for the organization. Discovering and then analyzing these CSFs may suggest network-based applications to assist in the successful conduct of the organization's business.

Next, we turned to a specific analysis of the organization to discover networking opportunities, using an ongoing case to tie together the diverse models that would be used. The Rapid Delivery Couriers (RDC) case illustrated a number of key points in the context of a service-based company. First, we introduced an overview modeling technique. The five-component model of an information system was used throughout the remainder of the chapter to maintain a balanced view of the whole system being assessed. This model consists of hardware, software, data, people, and procedures. We also reviewed the stages of growth model, which can help the organization anticipate problems as it grows and changes. The model also points to potential opportunities to gain assistance from outside consultants in areas where the internal organization is not yet competent. We also covered the value chain model, which can help the organization pinpoint activities that will add value to its products.

Specific analysis techniques discussed included process decomposition diagrams, association matrices, and entity-relationship (E-R) diagrams. A process decomposition diagram is a graphical modeling technique for analyzing the functions and processes an organization follows. This area encompasses the software and procedures portions of the five-component model. Among the benefits of this model are its ease of construction, which allows for a very effective communication device between analyst and users. The model also shows the natural associations among the processes within the organization.

The association matrix was introduced as a method for highlighting latent but undiscovered associations between objects, such as between organizational processes and potential TBIT applications. Using the RDC case as a background, various telecommunications-related applications were listed and then associated with the processes highlighted in the decomposition diagrams. The analysis showed that certain potential applications can affect a wide range of processes, therefore offering a greater range of improvements.

The final model discussed was the data modeling technique of E-R diagrams. This model focuses on the data component of the five-component model, which is the pivotal element of that model. The process consists of listing entities on which the organization wants to keep data, creating a rough draft of the diagram, and then refining it.

The last area covered in the chapter was rich pictures, a modeling technique that emphasizes the people component of the five-component model. This technique focuses on the associations among the people inside and outside the organization. The acronym CATWOE was introduced as a way of recalling the six key elements of the method: customers, actors, transformation, weltanschauung, owners, and environment. A useful rich picture diagram was developed to highlight the interactions among these elements, bringing a human balance to the previous analysis.

The concepts and techniques for analyzing an organization's opportunities to apply networking technology introduced in this chapter provide a foundation for Chapter 7, "Networking Opportunities for Improving Organizational Performance."

Key Terms

Attribute   253
Brainstorming   251
Competitive advantage   226
Computer-aided systems engineering (CASE)   258
Critical success factors (CSF)   238
Data dictionary   253
Distributed processing   236
E-R diagram   253
Economies of scale   232
Economies of scope   232
Effectiveness   226

Efficiency   226
Entity   253
External factors   234
Internal factors   234
IT platform   236
Niche marketing   227
Overtrading   236
Primary key   253
Relationships   253
Strategic partnerships   227
Switching costs   238

Questions for Discussion

✗1. Differentiate among the terms *efficiency*, *effectiveness,* and *competitive advantage*. Give a few examples where telecommunications-based applications would yield each of these qualities for an organization.

2. Using the benefits cycle model, describe how efficiency, effectiveness, and competitive advantage can support and enhance one another. Give a few illustrations from your reading in IT publications such as *Datamation* or *Computerworld*.

3. Various internal and external factors affect an organization's competitive position. Discuss whether each of the following items is internal or external and the impact it might have on an organization's competitiveness. Would the industry make a difference?

    a. Reliability of communication links.

    b. Labor relations.

    c. R&D commitment.

    d. Level of general economy.

    e. Vision of top management.

    f. Community attitude toward work and quality.

    g. Geographical location.

    h. IT platform consistency.

4. Discuss the four prime sources of critical success factors, and give examples of each factor for *(a)* a regional wholesaler, *(b)* a multinational manufacturer, and *(c)* a national financial institution.

✗5. The five-component model provides a useful approach for viewing a technology situation in broad terms. Identify and discuss the primary elements that would make up the five-component model for a small local area network used for word processing.

6. Describe how the stages of growth model can be used to assist an organization in controlling risk when considering a new, network-based system.

✗7. Using the value chain model, discuss the value-adding activities that are affected by a point-of-sale system such as that used in a supermarket.

8. Compare and contrast a process decomposition diagram and an entity-relationship diagram. Are there any points of overlap between these two modeling techniques?

9. What are the primary purposes of developing models such as the process/function decomposition diagram?

Case Discussion and Analysis

1. Young & Company Manufacturing is in the process of developing its strategic plan. The managing director together with the manufacturing, marketing, finance, and IS managers have been working on this project for the past four weeks. As the IS manager, you believe your contribution has been insufficient, and you have been doing additional research to discover some methods, models, or concepts that would help you think more strategically. Your managing director is especially interested in the strategic implications of networking systems, both local and wide area networks.

   Young & Company, which produces children's clothing to order, has been in business for over 30 years and is a medium-size firm in an intensely competitive market. Its customers include both Hong Kong and other Asian companies, as well as some other Pacific Rim countries such as Australia and New Zealand. Currently, customers fax their orders to Young & Company's manufacturing facility. The fax contains data such as customer name, customer number, address, and fax number, as well as a description and quantity of the clothing item desired. If the item is a standard item from the catalog, an item number is also included. Very often, however, customers want a modification to a standard item or want a new design altogether. In the case of modifications and new designs, the fax will include artwork showing various views of the garment, which will allow Young & Company pattern makers to create a pattern for the garment. Patterns are drawn manually and then used in the cutting room to cut out portions of the garments before they go to the sewing room for assembly. When the full number of garments has been cut and sewn, they are moved to the quality inspection and packaging room prior to shipping to the customer. Finally, a shipping notice is written up and a copy is placed in the package before it is sealed for shipment.

   You have been thinking about how you might use telecommunications-based information technology to benefit Young & Company.

   Analyze the Young & Company situation using the benefits cycle model.

2. John Tomas has asked Maria Grieg to do an analysis of the parcel pickup and delivery area of RDC's business. RDC generally does a very good job of safely and quickly delivering customers' packages. In a recent quality study, the company found it had averaged only 3 unresolved errors in every 1,000 deliveries over the most recent three months; however, even those 3 per 1,000 were an embarrassment to the organization. CEO Mary Kong had asked the IST team to look into how they might resolve those errors and reduce the error rate to zero per 1,000. The errors usually consisted of packages that went astray and were not delivered on a timely basis. The problem was that after the pickup driver collected the package from the customer's address, RDC did not know for sure where the package was located until it was actually delivered. Currently there was no way to track the movement of packages through the multiple hands and locations they might go through before final delivery. As a result, if a package was not delivered, it was very difficult to tell where it had been lost. This was hardly a satisfactory response to the customer. Often the package turned up and was delivered, but later than normal. On some occasions it never turned up, and an insurance claim had to be filed for the loss.

   Maria took Frank Ohono's original analysis, which overlapped her assigned area. After further discussions with staff, she modified Frank's original list, and came up with the following processes that described the area of parcel pickup and delivery:

   The driver picks up the package from the customer.

   The driver either (1) delivers the package to the address on the package if it is within the area, (2) brings it to the central station for transfer to another courier for delivery within another area in the territory, or (3) brings it to the central station for transfer to the international section for overseas delivery.

If the package is destined for another area in the territory, when the pickup driver arrives back at the central station, he or she takes all such packages and sorts them into mobile bins allocated and marked for the other areas within the territory.

Each driver collects all packages for delivery from his or her mobile bin, and places them in the van.

Each driver delivers packages to customers in his or her area.

If the package is destined for overseas, the pickup driver places it in the international bin.

International packages are sorted by destination and then delivered to the airport for overseas shipment.

Upon arrival at the international destination, the packages are collected by the local RDC agent and delivered to the appropriate addresses.

John, Maria, and Frank conducted a brainstorming session to come up with potential TBIT applications. The outcome of that session was the following list of potential applications:

LAN based:	*WAN based*
Electronic mail	E-fax
Multiuser database	Alphanumeric page
Barcode data capture	Voice-activated network

Based on the above information and the background of the RDC case in the text, prepare a process decomposition diagram and an association matrix. The decomposition diagram should include all of the above processes. The association matrix should compare the processes with potential TBIT applications, similar to the one done by John Tomas earlier.

3. Kennedy Wholesalers markets electronic goods. It carries a wide range of products with a total of over 30,000 unique parts and finished products. Over the last two years, as unique items in stock have proliferated, the company has had continuing problems controlling inventory with the computer system it has been using for the last eight years. As a result, the total value of inventory on hand has grown from $20 million to over $35 million, and product sales have increased by 25 percent during the same period. Currently, when an item is low in stock, the inventory manager reports this to the purchase order supervisor. The purchase order supervisor adds the item to an open purchase order for one of the company's vendors; purchase orders are sent on a two-week cycle. When the items arrive from the vendor, they are unpacked, inspected, and compared to the accompanying packing slip. This packing slip is annotated and used as a receiving document. Then it is sent to data entry for recording of the new inventory.

Complete the five steps in the data modeling technique for Kennedy Wholesalers.

4. A university is considering implementing a new, automated student enrollment system. In this system, students would use networked terminals available on campus to specify the courses they plan to take for each term. The system would verify that the appropriate course prerequisites had been taken and that there were no conflicts with lectures or exams. Then it would automatically charge the student's bank account (specified by the student when first enrolled) for the computed level of fees.

Assess this situation in light of the CATWOE characteristics. Then create a rich picture for it, making whatever assumptions seem reasonable.

7

NETWORKING OPPORTUNITIES FOR IMPROVING ORGANIZATIONAL PERFORMANCE

Chapter Outline

Introduction   266

Analyzing and Measuring
   Organizational Performance   266

Using Time and Risk to Gain
   Competitive Advantage   276

Networked Applications to Support
   Organizational Groups   285

Learning Objectives

By the end of Chapter 7, you should be able to

1. *Define* a process for measuring efficiency and apply network systems to improve organizational efficiency.

2. *Measure* improvements in resource usage resulting from the use of telecommunications-based systems.

3. *Demonstrate* the use of networks to implement cost-saving measures.

4. *Utilize* aspects of change and risk to find strategic applications of network technology.

5. *Define groupware* and demonstrate effectiveness benefits that can be derived from its use.

6. *Describe* the application of workflow systems to streamline document processing within an organization.

7. *Use* the features of electronic data interchange (EDI) to enhance interbusiness effectiveness.

Introduction

To maintain and strengthen its competitive position, an organization must rely on both individual and group performance to achieve the necessary effectiveness and gain the needed efficiencies. This chapter focuses on TBIT application opportunities to improve organizational performance, with an emphasis on the organization as a whole or on groups within the organization. Chapter 8 focuses more on the impact TBIT applications can have for individual performance within the context of the larger organization.

In this chapter we will apply techniques and concepts learned in prior chapters to discover ways TBIT applications can enhance organizational efficiency, effectiveness, and competitive advantage. We will see how networked systems can help in the analysis and measurement of organizational efficiency and the implementation of various cost-saving measures.

Many business opportunities today are short term in nature or arise from the highly competitive and risky markets that are typical of the international arena. This environment of rapid change and risk can provide some unprecedented opportunities for those organizations capable of flexible and rapid response. TBIT applications offer much support in this type of marketplace, and we will discuss some of these opportunities and applications.

Finally, we will look at group-related network applications, including groupware support systems for team effort, workflow applications to streamline document process control, and EDI as a means of support for building trading partner effectiveness.

Analyzing and Measuring Organizational Performance

Before we look further into the various ways networking can enhance efficiency, it will be useful to use some of the analytical tools we learned about in Chapter 6 to gain insight into the organization, focusing on areas that are inefficient or where TBIT systems could enhance current performance. Following that, we will examine and apply some methods of measuring improvements in productivity.

Organizational Analysis to Increase Efficiency through Networking

This section will demonstrate how the tools introduced in Chapter 6 may be used to highlight efficiency improvement opportunities within the organization. Data modeling using entity-relationship (E-R) diagrams will be used here, while the end-of-chapter case studies will allow you to apply process decomposition diagrams and association matrices. In using this technique, we will focus on the first four steps of the data-modeling process involving the diagram, more so than on the data dictionary of step 5. The following scenario sets the stage and provides us with an organizational environment to work with.

BEST MANUFACTURING COMPANY

Thomas Chambers had worked for Best Manufacturing Company for over 30 years and had seen many changes, both in the company and in the economy. For most of that time the company had been quite prosperous, producing an up-to-date line of products that were generally well received in the marketplace. Over the last couple of years, however, Thomas suspected that something had begun to slip. Last week was a good example. As shipping and receiving manager, he saw what came and went at Best and managed to keep up with the latest happenings in the firm. On Monday morning of last week, an order of materials had arrived from a supplier that Thomas learned were destined for production of a large rush order received from an important customer. When his receiving clerks inspected the materials, they found that some of them were damaged and would need to be replaced.

Thomas rang purchasing to clear a return of the damaged materials to the supplier and get replacements "ASAP." Unfortunately, he was unable to reach Mike Nair, the purchasing officer, for most of the day. By the time he got hold of Mike, it was too late to do anything, so they would have to wait until the next day to return the materials and order replacements. Meanwhile, the 10 crates of defective materials had to be moved out of the way while other shipments were sent or received during the day. In fact, they had to shift the crates three times that day.

The next day, they finally got authorization to return the materials, but would have to wait two more days for the replacements. This would naturally hold up production of the "rush" job for the important customer. The job had been scheduled for this week, and the delay meant that some of the factory workers would be underutilized during this time because not all of the other jobs could be readily rescheduled.

Three days later, the replacements finally arrived and production was cranked up to produce the rush order as quickly as possible. The factory got the order through in record time, disrupting the production schedule for a number of other jobs in the process, but that was the way it went sometimes. When the factory sent the product to Thomas's area, his people immediately crated and shipped it to the customer; then they notified marketing and accounting that the order had been sent.

On Monday of this week, Thomas received an angry phone call from marketing. The sales account manager wanted to know why shipping had not been more careful in handling the product, because the important customer claimed that fully 20 percent of the order had arrived in a damaged or low-quality condition and would have to be returned and reworked. Thomas was naturally a bit defensive. His people always handled orders carefully, and he didn't believe the damage was caused by shipping. They would have to sort out whose fault it was when the product came back later in the day. In the meantime, they had a dissatisfied customer on their hands. Last month the company had lost one very good customer to the competition over poor-quality product.

When the defective product came in late on Monday, Thomas took a close look at the "damage." As it turned out, the damage had occurred because factory workers handled the product before the paint was totally dry. This type of damage had become increasingly common over the last year or two due to some jobs being held up and then "rushed," as this job had been. They were all working hard, but Thomas knew that some improvements in efficiency were needed.

To construct our E-R diagram for Best Manufacturing, we need to identify the relevant data entities. The following nouns represent data entities (persons, objects, locations, and events) for Best:

Products

An order (purchase order)

Materials (or parts)

Supplier

Large rush order (sales order)

Customer

Figure 7–1 shows a draft of an E-R diagram, including the numeric relationships among the entities.

Our primary focus in using this technique is to ask questions about the entities and the relationships among them that might highlight efficiency opportunities. This approach might be used in a group meeting with knowledgeable users and management asking questions such as

- How can cost-saving measures related to *parts* be implemented with networks?
- In what way does *sales order* involve the management of user time? How can staff make more efficient use of time through network applications?
- In what way is the *purchase order* communicated internally or externally? How can the efficiency of this communication be improved through networks?
- How are *product* data used in manufacturing, and how can manufacturing efficiency be amplified through network use of these data?

A sample of the results of such a session appears in Figure 7–2. In this figure showing the results of an analysis session with users, each question has been applied to only one of the data entities. In reality, however, each question would be

FIGURE 7 1

E-R diagram for Best Manufacturing

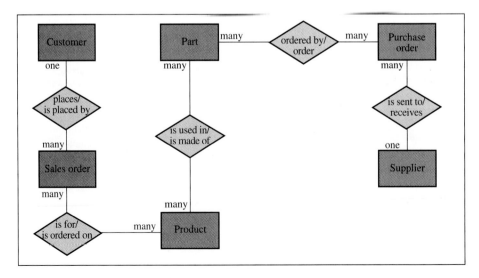

asked regarding each entity to see if a potential improvement in efficiency existed. Once this analysis is completed, measurement of resource usage will establish a benchmark against which efficiency improvements through TBIT can be measured.

Measuring Improvements in Resource Usage

To determine whether any real efficiency benefits can be gained from changes made in an organization, there must be a basis for measuring productivity or efficiency gains. In this section, we explore concepts and methods of measuring efficiency

FIGURE 7–2

Results of sample efficiency analysis

Question	Efficiency Opportunity
• How can cost-saving measures related to *parts* be implemented with networks?	*Part* costs involve the raw cost from the supplier and the holding cost involved in keeping an inventory of the parts. If the time between discovering a low-stock condition and receipt of the stock from a supplier can be shortened, the holding cost can be reduced. EDI allows the automation of stock maintenance and order placement, thus shortening the order cycle time.
• In what way does *sales order* involve the management of user time? How can staff make more efficient use of time through network applications?	The fact that a *sales order* initiates a chain of data and action indicates that it will affect a number of people within the organization. The chain of data and events following the placement of a sales order by a customer involves the time of many users in the system. The use of a networked database system allows the order clerk to verify the production schedule quickly for the customer, allows the purchasing agent rapid access to material stock levels to determine need for purchase orders, and allows ready notification of shipping and receiving of incoming or outgoing orders. This type of network support also speeds up the movement of goods related to the data, allowing a more efficient use of time.
• In what way is the *purchase order* communicated internally or externally? How can the efficiency of this be improved through networks?	The *purchase order* is communicated internally to shipping, accounting, and possibly manufacturing. Speeding this communication via E-mail will increase the efficiency of the company's internal mail system and eliminate wasteful paper shuffling, thus involving less effort and faster communication. The *purchase order* is also communicated externally to the supplier. The use of EDI to place the order increases the speed of communication, reduces errors in orders, and increases the supplier's efficiency by automating the order-filling process.
• How are *product* data used in manufacturing, and how can manufacturing efficiency be amplified through network use of these data?	*Product* data are the basis for the manufacturing process. The *product* determines which *parts* will be needed and what manufacturing process will be used. If an automated MRP (materials requirements planning) system is used in conjunction with an automated shop floor control program, both of these systems will be driven by the product. In a larger organization, these systems are dependent on a networked environment to tie the diverse functions of stock management, manufacturing, purchasing, and sales together. Faster, smoother production with fewer errors and less stock holding could result.

improvements made through the use of TBIT systems. To gain an understanding of efficiency measurement concepts and methods, we first need to review the basic model of a system as well as our definition of efficiency. A variety of definitions and models of a system exist. The model that best suits our current purposes is sometimes referred to as the *input-process-output* model and is depicted in Figure 7–3. This simple model illustrates the action of converting inputs into outputs through a process. It involves feedback to ensure that the process is producing the type, quantity, and quality of output required and also involves storage of resources and intermediate outputs. Figure 7–4 applies this model to the production of goods and services.

In the context of discussing and analyzing efficiency, the model is readily applicable. This is clearly seen on closer inspection of our definition of efficiency from Chapter 6:

> **Efficiency:** That characteristic of an organization that permits it to produce the maximum quantity of outputs of a specified quality from a minimum of materials, and human and organizational effort. In short, it means maximizing productivity by doing things right. To detect efficiency in operation, ask this question: Are we producing the most output from the least input, given our quality goals?

The primary components of our definition are much the same as the primary components of the systems model. The key measurable items drawn from the definition are

Quantity of outputs.
Quality of outputs.
Material inputs.
People input.
Organizational input.
Productivity (process).
Minimizing resource waste.

FIGURE 7–3

A system model

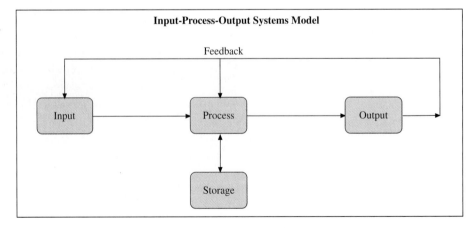

FIGURE 7–4

System model applied to producing goods and services

Model Component	Manufactured Goods	Services
Input	Materials, labor, and overhead such as machine time, electricity, organization and supervision, building environment, etc.	Information workers' time, data capture, computing, and other equipment time, organization and supervision, building environment, etc.
Process	Assembly, fabrication, welding, fastening, shaping, painting, packaging, etc.	Analysis, summarization, classification, meetings, interviews
Output	Toys, clothing, equipment, furniture, etc.	Reports, policies, presentations, tickets and bookings, etc.
Storage	Raw materials, factory productive capacity, in-process product partially completed, and finished product	Data and files that are the basis for outputs, either awaiting processing, partially complete, or finished
Feedback	Quality control reports, assembly-line inspections, comparisons to original production order	Changes and corrections to data from clients, co-workers, and managers

In comparing the definition of efficiency with the model of a system, we can create a new model: The process of measuring improvements in efficiency. This model appears in Figure 7–5.

Now let's apply this model to a practical scenario to see how it works. We'll go back to the efficiency analysis of Best Manufacturing Company that was done earlier using the data-modeling technique of E-R diagrams. In that analysis four sample questions were asked, each highlighting one or more possible areas of efficiency improvement using networked applications. A list of the possible improvements using networks from that analysis might include

1. Use of EDI to shorten the purchase order (PO) cycle: low-stock discovery–produce PO–receive materials–restock.

2. Use of EDI to reduce stock-holding costs.

3. Use of a networked database to speed up sales order processing, production, shipping, and customer billing.

4. Use of E-mail to increase efficient processing of purchase orders through the full cycle.

5. Networked manufacturing system to speed up and smooth production with fewer errors and lower stock-holding costs.

Let's use these five opportunities to illustrate the process of measuring efficiency improvements as described in Figure 7–6. First, look at the application of the model to item 1 on the list. Following this process through the purchasing cycle, the hypothetical data in Figure 7–7 may be generated during the initial stages of the model.

FIGURE 7–5

*Measuring
efficiency
improvements*

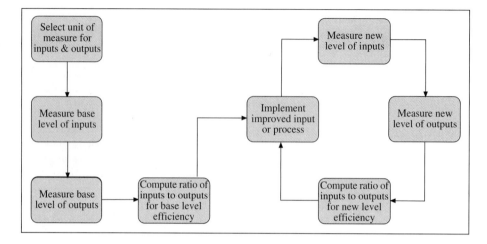

FIGURE 7–6

*Using EDI
to improve
purchase order
efficiency*

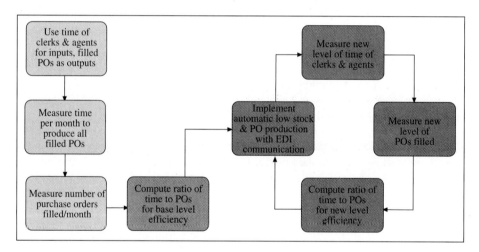

After designing and implementing the new networked system, it is necessary to continue measuring the monthly inputs and outputs to determine whether the new system has had any beneficial effect on efficiency. The hypothetical results over the first three months of operation of the new system are presented in Figure 7–8. In the first month of operation, the new system does not seem to boost efficiency; rather, efficiency deteriorates from 1.23 hours to 1.31 hours per PO. However, this is not unusual in the early stages of implementation, when the users are just learning the system, and it takes longer to carry out tasks due to unfamiliarity with new procedures. In addition, some of the functionality of the new system may go unused due to insufficient training on the system. If, however, a satisfactory budget has been established for training users, the benefits of the new system should begin to be evident in the following months. This can be seen in Figure 7–8 during months 2 and 3 following implementation of the new system. In month 2 there is a significant gain in efficiency according to the measure established, and a further major gain occurs in month 3; thus, by the end of the third month, efficiency has improved from 1.23 to .72 hours per PO. This amounts to a cumulative efficiency gain of 42 percent $(1.23 - .72)/1.23$.

In our example, the primary resource of concern has been the time of service employees, who convert that resource into filled purchase orders. Among the list of possible improvements using networks as a result of the efficiency analysis of Best Manufacturing Company were examples involving (1) stock-holding costs; (2) employee time in sales order processing, production, shipping, and customer billing; and (3) employee time, stock-holding costs, and material usage in manufacturing systems.

It would be useful to look at some of the methods of measurement for these factors to see how to establish the measurement process. Figure 7–9 shows a comparison of the various inputs, outputs, and the units of measure that might be appropriate. Measuring efficiency is a process of establishing a benchmark ratio of current inputs to current outputs and then comparing the changes in these ratios over time as improvements in the networked support systems are made.

FIGURE 7–7

Efficiency measurement process illustration

Example of Measurement Process at Best Manufacturing	
Step of Model	*Measured Result*
Establish units of measure: *time* per month of stock clerks, purchasing agents, and receiving clerks to discover low-stock condition, prepare and send PO, receive stock, and put in warehouse as *inputs, number of filled POs* per month as *outputs*.	N/A
Measure time of employees involved in cycle	Stock clerk: 5 hours per month phoning purchasing with low-stock notices
	Purchasing agent: 30 hours per month preparing purchase orders
	Purchasing agent: 25 hours per month phoning suppliers with urgent orders and expediting orders
	Receiving clerk: 17 hours per month communicating with purchasing regarding partial shipments and expected receiving times and handling receiving paperwork
	Stock clerk: 15 hours per month restocking shelves and handling receiving paperwork
	Total hours invested in cycle: 92 hours/month
Measure number of POs filled per month	75 POs filled in initial month
Compute ratio of time to POs filled	92 hours/75 POs = 1.23 hours per PO
Implement networked stock management and EDI purchasing system	N/A

FIGURE 7–8

Results of efficiency analysis

Step of Model	Hypothetical Monthly Results of System Installation					
	Month 1 Results		Month 2 Results		Month 3 Results	
Measure time	Low stock:	6 hr.	Low stock:	4 hr.	Low stock:	2 hr.
of employees	PO preparation:	28 hr.	PO preparation:	20 hr.	PO preparation:	12 hr.
	Urgent PO and		Urgent PO and		Urgent PO and	
	expediting:	27 hr.	expediting:	19 hr.	expediting:	17 hr.
	Receiving:	16 hr.	Receiving:	14 hr.	Receiving:	12 hr.
	Stock shelves, etc.:	16 hr.	Stock shelves, etc.:	13 hr.	Stock shelves, etc.:	13 hr.
	Total hours:	93 hr.	Total hours:	70 hr.	Total hours:	56 hr.
Measure number	Total POs filled:	71 hr.	Total POs filled:	69 hr.	Total POs filled:	78 hr.
of POs filled						
Compute ratio of	93 hr./71 PO = 1.31		70 hr./69 PO = 1.02		56 hr./78 PO = .72	
time to POs filled						

FIGURE 7–9

Units of measure for various inputs and outputs

Example	Input or Output	Unit of Measure
Stock-holding costs	Input: storage space	Square feet of warehouse
	Input: heating, light, etc.	Kilowatts of electricity per month
	Output: shipments of product from warehouse	Dollars of sales per month
Sales order processing	Input: employees' time	Hours per month
	Output: number of sales orders processed	Number of sales orders per month
Manufacturing efficiency	Input: employees' time	Direct labor hours
	Input: quantity of material used	Pounds, yards, tons, etc.
	Input: cost of overheads	Dollars of overhead
	Output: manufactured product	Units produced of particular product

The next section looks at some of the areas in which efficiency can be enhanced through TBIT applications and to which the preceding methods of analysis and measurement could be applied.

Cost-Saving Measures

A major area in which efficiency gains can be realized is that of cost-saving measures. Reducing the costs of current operations and production can give an organization the cost advantage that will allow it to compete and maintain profitability. The desire to improve efficiencies is driven by the organization's plans to gain competitive advantage and increase organizational effectiveness, each of which is part of an overall interdependent process.

In the area of cost savings, a methodology that might be employed to discover opportunities using TBIT applications includes the following steps:

1. List and analyze the costs of the organization under consideration, using functional decomposition, budgets, or data modeling to discover costs.

2. Develop a list of possible TBIT applications that might reduce the costs discovered in step 1 without reducing quantity or quality of production or service.

3. Create an association matrix of costs and TBIT applications to determine which applications apply to which costs.

4. Prioritize the list of TBIT applications based on maximum cost savings in maximum cost categories.

5. Develop measurement devices (in line with Figures 7–5 through 7–9 earlier in this chapter) to allow comparison of efficiency before and after changes.

The above steps incorporate portions of the feasibility study for a system development project, but are not intended to fully illustrate that process. Additional concepts, such as cost-benefit analysis and project justification, will be covered in greater detail in Chapter 10.

Let's look at some cost types and categories and then consider how LAN and WAN systems can be applied to some of these costs. Think of the various ways an organization may save costs in the context of the system model covered earlier in this chapter (see Figure 7–3). The cost categories that could be considered are (1) inputs, (2) processes, (3) storage, or (4) feedback. All of these cost categories are used to produce the outputs. Given that we are discussing efficiency, we assume the objective is to reduce costs (or increase outputs with no cost increases) and at the same time maintain the quantity and quality of output. Figure 7–10 shows some examples of costs that might fall into the four categories. In discovering which of these costs are actually involved in a particular organization's operation, functional and data analysis are both beneficial tools.

How might TBIT applications, both LAN and WAN systems, be applied to reducing some of these costs? Figure 7–11 shows but a few examples, including some covered in the section "EDI: A Key to Trading Partner Effectiveness" later in this chapter.

The next section balances the areas of efficiency and cost savings with other organizational performance issues of concern in times of uncertainty.

FIGURE 7–10

Cost categories and examples

Cost Category	Examples
Inputs	Assembly worker's direct labor
	Knowledge worker's direct or indirect labor
	Direct materials such as multipart paper forms and other office supplies, metal, timber, paint, wire, plastic, subassemblies, nuts and bolts, and other manufacturing materials
	Indirect materials such as machine repair parts, cleaning fluids, toner for laser printer, lubricants for machines
	Other overhead costs such as heating and electricity, building and machinery rent or depreciation, landscape maintenance
Processes	Manufacturing processes such as drilling, welding, bolting, riveting, sewing, painting, nailing, and gluing
	Service processes such as data entry, ticket issuing, insurance policy review, auditing of accounts, preparation of legal contracts, analysis of software requirements, response to requests for proposals and bids, room and flight bookings
	Planning, organizing, and control processes such as conduct of meetings, communication of decisions, creation of budgets, review of operating results, hiring, review, and promotion of employees
Storage	Storage of raw materials for production, payroll and employee data, work-in-progress product during manufacturing, client files for an insurance company or bank stored electronically or on paper forms, finished product awaiting orders or shipping, database, word processing, and spreadsheet files
Feedback	Report design and generation manually or by a computer system
	Conduct of review meetings for weekly or monthly production quality results
	Sales manager's time in analyzing and reporting on the monthly performance of salespeople toward sales quotas
	Computer system resource usage in measuring and reporting production quantity and quality information

Using Time and Risk to Gain Competitive Advantage

In his book *Thriving on Chaos*, Thomas J. Peters (co-author of *In Search of Excellence*) makes this statement:

> Most fundamentally, the times demand that flexibility and love of change replace our long standing penchant for mass production and mass markets, based as it is upon a relatively predictable environment now vanished....The true objective is to take the chaos as given and learn to thrive on it. The winners of tomorrow will deal proactively with chaos, will look at the chaos per se as the source of market advantage, not as a problem to be got around. Chaos and fleeting market anomalies will be the successful business's greatest accomplishment. It is with that in mind that we must proceed.[1]

---

1 Thomas J. Peters, *Thriving on Chaos* (New York: Knopf, 1987), p. xi.

FIGURE 7–11

Examples of cost savings from TBIT applications

Cost Savings	TBIT Application
Reduced wages of in-house mail staff	Use of in-house E-mail rather than traditional interoffice mail system
Reduced stock-holding costs	Use of JIT networked system to reduce overall stock levels, including order placement by EDI, E-mail, or E-fax
Reduced material wastage	Use of shop floor control system in conjunction with online sales order maintenance to reduce errors on production runs
Reduced cost of travel for sales, research and development people, and executives	Use of computer conferencing, E-mail, and groupware products
Elimination of paperwork related to business documents transfer such as purchase orders, order confirmations, invoices, remittance notices, and paper checks	Use of workflow EDI, E-mail, or E-fax for document
Elimination of errors arising from reentry of data from paper documents	Use of workflow EDI, E-mail, or E-fax for document transfer
Automation of document processing, thus eliminating costly manual handling	Use of workflow EDI, E-mail, or E-fax for document transfer
Increased efficiency in order filling with automated picking lists and back ordering	Use of EDI and networked databases
Reduced stationery and postage costs	Use of EDI with high-speed transmission
Reduced purchasing personnel wages	Use of networked stock management system with automatic purchase orders and EDI communication
Reduced obsolete stock	Use of networked JIT manufacturing system to allow production on demand rather than production for stock, which may later become obsolete

In essence, Peters is saying that many of the best opportunities organizations will face in the future will arise out of the chaotic marketplaces in which firms must operate. Most companies would traditionally view such change as a problem to be solved or managed, as a source of risk to be reduced or removed. However, the organizations that come to realize that such change is most likely to accelerate and that if the right set of attitudes, people, and technology are put in place, these organizations can flourish on the many short-term opportunities presented in such a fast-paced market.

Analyzing Time-Related Situations for TBIT Opportunities

When we speak of *time-related situations*, we refer to the niche and short-term opportunities that may present themselves to an organization. To take advantage of these opportunities, the organization must prepare to move quickly, innovate rapidly, and deliver the best service in the shortest time to the most diverse range of customers possible. This is a tall order for any organization, and a few key skills and attitudes that must be implemented before an organization can begin to fill it. Basically, it means viewing rapid change over time as a resource—as an asset rather than a liability. Before we look at the ways TBIT may assist in developing and supporting such an organization, let us first consider some of these key skills and attitudes. They include

1. A "prototyping" attitude toward everything.
2. An environment of creativity, responsibility, and cooperation.
3. Self-managing teams.
4. A reward structure for successful risk taking and "change production."

We will now take a closer look at each of these skills or attitudes, see what they mean, and consider how TBIT can be used to assist in implementing them.

A "Prototyping" Attitude toward Everything.   A **prototype** is a working model of the "real thing" and is used for testing and refinement purposes. This means the organization must recognize that every process, person, product, and customer need is in a constant state of testing and refinement, a continuous state of change. If this attitude is accepted as the status quo in the organization, the people within the organization can work proactively on changing themselves, their products, and their manufacturing, marketing, and other processes for the better. Companies cannot afford to allow them to remain at the same mediocre level or deteriorate into a worse condition. An organization must discover its customers' new or changed needs quickly so that it can meet them with new products and services rather than assuming the same old products will be good enough. This process and attitude can be supported by TBIT using a variety of applications discussed earlier in this book. Use of CAD/CAM and CIM provide a platform for rapid development, production, and redevelopment of products in a flexible and cost-effective manner. The use of notebook computers by salespeople in the field allows gathering of data on customer needs and changing requirements quickly and feeding them back to the product design team almost instantaneously. The use of networked, integrated databases encourages innovation in process design. This technology smooths the communication of such changes to other team members and affected parties and provides for rapid feedback to gain the maximum benefit with minimum mistakes at each iteration.

An Environment of creativity, responsibility, and cooperation.   Integral with having a prototyping attitude toward everything must be an environment created by top management that fosters creativity, responsibility, and cooperation. Naturally, training is required to promote this concept and to provide the skills for successful implementation. This type of environment permits mistakes to be made while experimenting creatively with a new prototype. The prototype may be a new way to maintain contact with customers by a salesperson, a change in the current manufacturing process, or a new idea for a product or service. Mistakes are not viewed negatively but are encouraged, because they are seen as being necessary to discover a better way to do something or serve someone. In conjunction with this environment must be a sense of personal responsibility for decisions made in cooperation with colleagues who are also responsible for the outcomes of change. This balance will lend a stability to the process of change so that it doesn't get out of control but achieves its goal: A positive, continuous improvement in service to customers. The following case illustrates this point.

VENTURE MANUFACTURING

After attending a seminar by management aimed at motivating all employees to look for and implement improvements in their work, a production team discussed the possibility of performing their own quality inspection instead of leaving it to the inspectors at the end of the assembly process. For this idea to benefit the team and the organization, the team had to gain direct access to defect information from the inspectors to see if any real improvement had occurred. The team knew that if they could produce the same number of units per hour but at the same time reduce their defect rate, the change was worthwhile. The quality control (QC) inspectors and the factory manager agreed to go along with the experiment. The application was implemented by simply installing a networked PC in the production area that reported the results in real time from the quality inspectors' defect capture and reporting application. At the end of the first week of the change, the team's productivity had decreased by 10 percent and the number of defects in their production had gone up by 5 percent. The factory manager met with them and said, "Well, the experiment is working— we are seeing change!" Everyone laughed, mostly in embarrassment, but took her point. "Give it another week and see how it goes," she said.

   The following week, the team spent Monday morning with the inspectors going over the types of defects that were being found so that they would be better able to spot them and change their production process to prevent them. As the second week progressed, they began to spot the defects and discover the things they were doing that were causing them. Changes to the process were applied, some things worked and some didn't, and they kept doing the things that did work. By the end of the second week, the team's productivity had remained the same as the previous week—down 10 percent on average—but the number of defects had declined, with an overall reduction in defects of 10 percent compared to normal levels. "Well, change is still happening, but now it's in the right direction!" said the factory manager. Everyone laughed again, but this time from relief.

   During week three, the team began to spot defects with increasing accuracy and also began to see ways to simplify their work. They found that simplification produced fewer defects and also helped them to perform their work faster. The week's statistics supported their prediction of improvement. Productivity was 5 percent better than normal, and defects were down 30 percent. Now that was more like it! Over the next five weeks, the team brought their portion of the manufacturing process to a 40 percent productivity improvement and an 80 percent reduction in defects. The factory manager was thrilled, and the customers were even more pleased.

   TBIT may be used to support this environment of creativity, responsibility, and cooperation in a variety of ways. As noted in the example, a networked production database with workstations on the factory floor at the various production team areas, along with QC inspection stations could provide the production team with continuous feedback from the QC inspectors on defect levels rather than making them wait for the weekly production review meeting. Such an integrated production database tied into the product costing and sales system could also produce rapid feedback on improvements in sales, customer satisfaction, and cost savings, all useful information for fueling the process of continuous improvement and staff motivation. Other technologies, such as voice-activated data capture, could allow the production team members to record production information such as product quantity, type and quantity of defects, production lot numbers, and so forth through a microphone directly into the database while keeping their hands free to continue working. This use of technology leverages productivity as well as quality, both key factors in gaining competitive advantage.

Self-Managing Teams.   For the organization to respond quickly to changing environments and markets, organization structures must be in place that allow rapid and accurate decision making where it counts: at the work floor. Empowering the front-line workers to make decisions and implement them is an important part of this process. As the preceding scenario indicates, the production team conceived of the changes, got the agreement of others who would be affected (inspectors and factory manager), and implemented the changes. Regular feedback maintained open communication among the various parties. Even when things appeared to be going poorly at the beginning, the team had the support of the organization, because mistakes were seen as a path to useful change. The final results were very positive. Self-managing teams remove the need for multilevel management hierarchies, which act primarily as information filters and slow down the organization's responsiveness considerably.

The application of networked and integrated databases can allow higher-level managers to keep abreast of the impact of ongoing changes and the effects those changes are having on production quantity, product quality, customer satisfaction, sales levels, costs, and profits. This high level of centralized control accompanied by the self-managing teams' decentralized decision making is directly supported by sophisticated, networked information systems. Such applications of TBIT reduce the cost of managing an organization while accelerating the responsiveness and control levels within the organization.

FIGURE 7–12

Organizational characteristics to take advantage of short-term opportunities

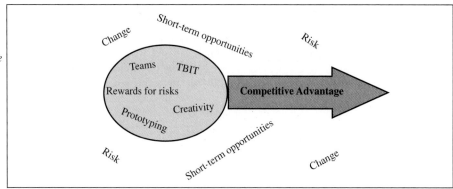

A Reward Structure for Successful Risk Taking and "Change Production."   People are generally motivated by a variety of things, two of the most common and persistent being: the hope for reward and the threat of punishment. Of these two factors, the more positive reward system offers the longer-term benefits. Let's look again at the Venture Manufacturing case.

The tremendously positive results of the production team's efforts to take responsibility for the quality of their production through self-management and continuous improvement of their production process caught on with many of the other production groups in the factory. They had also captured the attention of the factory supervisor and the quality control (QC) inspectors, but for very different reasons. The factory manager believed the team should be rewarded for being prepared to take the risk and producing such outstanding results. She also wanted the process to continue and to spread to the other production groups. At the same time, the QC inspectors could see they would be out of a job pretty quickly with the defect rate falling all over the factory! Fortunately, the factory manager was a perceptive person, and before tempers could flare up she called together the successful production team and the QC inspectors. At the meeting, she explained to all of them how proud she was of both groups for their team effort and cooperation. She told the QC inspectors they would be rewarded as well as the production team by sharing 20 percent of the cost savings as a result of increased productivity and reduced QC inspection costs. Needless to say, both the production team and the QC inspectors were pleased. The factory manager also stated that sales were rising as a result of the improved product quality and that she would be forming a new production team of the QC inspectors who were no longer needed in that function.

As you can see, such an environment must reward the people who take the risks and choose to innovate and change if the process of positive change and innovation is to be sustained. A paradox of this process is that the organization as a whole must establish a policy of stable employment to sustain rapid, continuous change. The reason is that employees will be unwilling to take the risks of innovation if they believe their jobs will be at risk too. In the above scenario, the factory manager intended to retain her redundant QC inspectors in more productive roles; she did not intend to let those valuable, trained, and innovative team players get away from her organization!

Examples of TBIT Applications.   How might a highly responsive and innovative organization further use TBIT to take advantage of short-term and niche opportunities? Here are a variety of examples that may spark further ideas:

• Have field salespeople and other employees scan the news regularly for potential opportunities and place brief summaries of the opportunities on an electronic bulletin board (EBB) for broader organizational dissemination, discussion, and action. Such items might include new product announcements by competitors to which the organization can respond by being an early follower, government initiatives that could open new niche markets, and international or local problems that suggest needs the organization can meet with its existing or new products. Regardless of whether the employees are located in the home office or in a branch office thousands of miles away, they can all participate in adding to the EBB, reading and commenting on the items posted.

• Have public relations employees who handle complaints from customers enter the nature of the complaints onto a database to which production teams have direct access. The production teams can use this information as stimulus for improving their production process, techniques, and technology to provide a better-quality product and service to customers.

• Have product design people, manufacturing engineers, and production teams networked to share production information. In so doing, product designers and engineers can learn what works best along with the production teams. Future product designs and manufacturing layouts will benefit from this continuous learning, so the production teams won't need to be continually fixing the same product and engineering design defects.

Networking Opportunities in Times of Uncertainty

According to the *American Heritage Dictionary* (from Houghton, Mifflin Company in Microsoft Bookshelf, 1993), risk is "(1) The possibility of suffering harm or loss; danger. (2) A factor, element, or course involving uncertain danger; hazard." This is certainly a good description of the economic environment in which most commercial organizations have to compete. The key words in this definition are "loss" and "uncertain." To the extent that the organization can reduce the uncertainty in a situation, it can reduce the risk or chance of loss. Consider the following scenario.

W. B. Bentley Company, Inc.

James Rahrig is employed as finance manager for W. B. Bentley Company, Inc. During the 10 years he has worked there, the company has maintained a strong, profitable position in an increasingly competitive industry. Normally the company sells its products on a wholesale basis to other manufacturers on terms of net 30 days, with a 2 percent discount for payment within 10 days, and customers have usually placed relatively large orders every two to three months. Over the past two years, however, the company has converted its manufacturing over to a more flexible manufacturing system, together with JIT concepts to reduce its stock holdings and improve responsiveness to customer needs. The international economy has become increasingly unstable, and the top management of W. B. Bentley believes that such an environment of uncertainty offers an opportunity to gain competitive advantage by helping customers to reduce their risk. The company plans to do this by helping customers place many small orders rather than a few large orders. This will allow customers to reduce their inventory of Bentley products by as much as 60 to 80 percent. In exchange for this assistance, they will need to place their orders using EDI, which will allow Bentley to automatically process the orders, manufacture the goods, and ship them within just a few days. In addition, the customers who take advantage of this new system must pay for the goods upon arrival of the shipment using electronic funds transfer (EFT) so that Bentley has access to the funds that day. The entire process will be automated, so that when the customer records acceptance of the shipment, the customer's computer system will automatically issue an electronic payment to Bentley. Naturally, the customer will receive the 2 percent discount as before, as well as benefit from the massive reduction in its inventory.

Of course, the benefits of this new system do not accrue just to the customers, James Rahrig thought. Already the company had begun to realize the benefits of the reduced uncertainty. Because customer orders came in more frequently, the production manager was much more certain about each week's production schedule, which reduced the need to keep larger stocks of raw materials on hand. Since the company was more current on its material and labor requirements, it could place smaller orders for materials and hire and train additional staff without the risk of the staff having insufficient work to do. There was also less risk involved in accounts receivable collection—a much shorter collection period and no **check float.**

Most of the customers could see the significant benefits in the new system, with reductions in stock amounting to $200,000 for the average customer and much more for many others. Further, if they bought a larger proportion of their material requirements from Bentley, they would leverage their investment in the new system and obtain even greater reductions in inventory holdings. As a result, more than 75 percent of all customers were converting over to the new system.

This competitive advantage was doing wonderful things for the company's sales and profits, as well as reducing the risk from bad debts and excessive or obsolete stock. The company had already seen a 20 percent increase in sales and a 25 percent reduction in accounts receivable, and the process of changeover had begun only three months ago.

As you can see the JIT, EDI, and EFT system installed in the above scenario reduces uncertainty for both the initiating company and the customers taking advantage of the new system. As a result of the reduced risk, a stronger relationship is built between the company and customers, leading customers to desire making additional purchases from the company, with a further benefit to both parties.

When assessing an organization and its environment of risk and uncertainty, a variety of factors must be looked at and techniques used, including some of the modeling techniques introduced in Chapter 6. For example, consider the simple functional decomposition diagram of a manufacturing company depicted in Figure 7–13. In viewing this diagram, what questions could we ask that would highlight issues of risk or uncertainty? Here are a few:

- What new products, services, or competitors may enter our existing markets?
- How quickly do we need to design and release a new product to effectively counter introduction of a new product from a competitor?
- How much inventory of raw materials is safe to keep on hand for meeting expected product demand?
- How will the current economic slowdown affect our customers' ability to pay us on a timely basis?
- Are there new accounting methods that would help us to determine our product costs more accurately and quickly?

FIGURE 7–13

*Functional
decomposition
diagram for a
manufacturer*

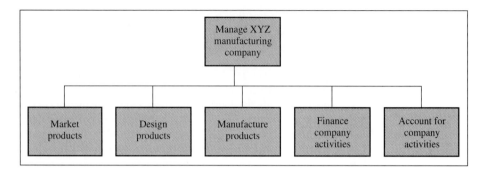

These questions and more may be raised while viewing an organizational decomposition diagram or a data model, especially if used as a brainstorming technique with organization staff.

What are some specific areas of risk or uncertainty that organizations face, and how can TBIT be used to reduce the uncertainty, and therefore the risk, and gain a competitive advantage? An exhaustive list would be too long for the space available here, but the risks and uncertainties would certainly include the following:

• *Excess capacity and excess inventory*: The risk of excess capacity may be reduced in a variety of ways. By using JIT systems, including integration of networked systems, the organization can move to smaller production lots, gain rapid throughput (thus reducing work in progress), eliminate finished goods, and gain significant reductions of raw materials. During times of excess capacity, it may be able to sell the capacity to other organizations. For example, a rental car dealer could establish an electronic "partnership" with a travel wholesaler using E-mail and electronic bulletin board (EBB) technology. Using this system, the rental car dealer could offer large discounts on excess cars when it knows it will be overstocked. The EBB could be updated daily for the various locations, allowing the excess cars to be rented and yielding a much higher utilization rate.

• *Obsolete stock*: The risk of obsolete inventory is largely eliminated using JIT systems, as noted earlier.

• *Nonpaying creditors (bad debts)*: Automated EFT greatly reduces this risk, thus eliminating bounced checks, check float, and **mail float**. Also, the organization can use WAN connections to credit bureau service providers, linking credit information to online order entry. In this way, it can avoid credit-risky customers at the beginning of the process rather than having to fix the problem after it arises.

• *Competitor release of new products*: This significant risk in highly innovative, open international markets can be effectively countered by implementing the environment of creativity, responsibility, and cooperation discussed earlier in this chapter. When supported by appropriate TBIT, such an environment will allow an organization to release new products and upgrades to existing products regularly. It will also help the organization respond quickly to threats from new products.

• *New competitors entering the market from the international arena:* An organization that keeps up-to-date on the state of competition in its industry is unlikely to be taken totally by surprise. Use of electronic news services and bulletin boards, Internet news groups, and online newsheets electronically tailored to the organization's industry and company profile can greatly assist the organization in keeping abreast of the competitive ebb and flow on the international markets.

• *Existing markets shrinking due to an unfavorable local economic environment*: The risk of shrinking local markets can be alleviated to a certain extent by being aware of international opportunities, creating partnerships with other organizations in other markets, and being increasingly aggressive in the local market by offering better products and services at more competitive prices. Creation and penetration of niche markets offer additional opportunities. Each of these strategies can be assisted with TBIT to speed up communication, increase innovation, modify cost structures, support reward systems, and inform management of changing situations.

Uncertainty and risk are an integral part of today's business environment. In the past, these characteristics were viewed as problems to be surmounted. Today they may offer unparalleled opportunities for those firms that are prepared to face the challenge.

Networked Applications to Support Organizational Groups

Organizations are made up of groups that need to communicate with one another. Intergroup and intragroup communication may consist of informal communication or formal business documents, and this communication is the lifeblood of any organization. This section looks at three key technologies designed to specifically support group effort: groupware to support teamwork and creativity, workflow systems to speed up the flow of documents within an organization, and EDI to facilitate the flow of interorganizational documents.

Networked Groupware to Leverage Organizational Effort

In earlier sections of this chapter, you saw various applications intended to assist people in organizations to work better, communicate better, and be more effective in the conduct of their work. These applications include E-mail, computer conferencing, bulletin boards, and others. This section consolidates and expands this area of cooperative work under the label *groupware*.

The literature on general management, quality management, and various technical areas has abounded in recent years with articles about the need to build organizational environments of teamwork to effectively implement total quality management systems (TQM) in organizations.[2] These articles emphasize that technology alone will

---

[2] For examples, see C. McKinnis and R. Brusch, "Convair Goes Concurrent," *Computer Aided Engineering*, February 1991; J. Phelps-Kearn, "The QIS/TQM Balancing Act," *Quality*, December 1991; R. M. Stair, *Principles of Information Systems* (Boston: Boyd & Fraser Publishing 1992), pp. 40–43; and L. M. Tobin, "The New Quality Landscape: Total Quality Management," *Journal of Systems Management*, November 1990.

not make organizations more effective and competitive; organizational change is needed as well. Concepts such as "empowering the workers," "teamwork," "flattening the organizational pyramid," and "downsizing the organization" are all aimed at creating organizational structures that are more efficient, responsive, and effective.

Information workers are the largest class of workers in industrialized nations. The professionals, managers, and other workers that make up this segment of the working population often spend between 30 percent and 80 percent of their time working in collaboration with other colleagues.[3] Activities include meetings and conferences, reports requiring input from multiple people, budgets that require decisions from a team of workers, and departmental decisions needing informed consent from a variety of workers. The combination of traditional work patterns of information workers and the strong move toward teamwork concepts adds up to more cooperative work and the need to provide technology that can assist this process.

In what ways can networked applications provide this assistance? What is groupware, and how can it help increase teamwork effectiveness? Groupware is the integrated use of networked application software to allow shared access to files needed for group communication, joint planning, joint decision making, and other collaborative efforts. Groupware includes

- Networked word processing with collaborative features such as shared files, revision marks, and version control.
- Networked electronic spreadsheets with collaborative features such as shared multiple access to spreadsheet files so that changes made by one user will be immediately updated on other users' screens.
- Joint calendaring and scheduling to assist in establishing meeting and appointment times.
- E-mail with mailing list and broadcast features so that messages can be communicated to entire groups with a single action.
- Electronic bulletin boards (EBBs) for one-way communication of a broadcast nature, such as news updates.
- Computer conferencing built on the EBB system to facilitate multiway group communication.
- Online, **concurrent access** to databases via user-friendly front ends, **E-mail enabled applications**, or Graphical User Interface (GUI) access applications.
- Group decision-making aids such as electronic white boards, shared access outliners, online brainstorming support, and group consensus (voting) support.

Figure 7–14 lists examples of activities that may need to be performed by groups, together with some of the groupware applications that might assist in these activities.

---

[3] E. W. Martin, D. W. Dehayes, J. A. Hoffer, and W. C. Perkins, *Managing Information Technology: What Managers Need to Know* (New York: Macmillan, 1991), p.25.

FIGURE 7–14

Groupware applications to assist teamwork

Activity	Groupware Applications
Report preparation by a management group	Communicating word processors with group access to common files. The word processing package must have the ability to track changes made by various authors and the dates of changes via version control.
Joint pricing decisions for new-product release involving marketing, manufacturing, and cost accounting	Communicating spreadsheets allowing multiple users access to common spreadsheet files. This allows changes to be made by the various departments in a controlled fashion, with all parties having access to the changes and being able to perform "what if" analysis to see the impact of changes.
Technical problem resolution of product design for manufacturing by a geographically dispersed group of design engineers	Computer conferencing supported by communicating word processor, file transfer of technical CAD files, video- and audioconferencing.
Creation of annual corporation budget	E-mail and group access to budget database and reporting software to allow group design and decision making to take place as the budget numbers and assumptions take shape.
Project control of a large manufacturing project involving multiple departments in multiple companies across several countries	Group access to project control application software and shared access to related project data files. Communicating word processors, computer conferencing, and/or E-mail to assist communication and coordination across time zones, company, and departmental boundaries. This may be via Internet-based applications such as World Wide Web and Mosaic or through systems provided by other commercial network providers.
Design of an important modular application package by a team of software engineers	Networked computer-aided systems engineering (CASE) software to allow multiple engineers to work simultaneously on various parts of the project, yet maintaining consistency of quality, user interface, and other software features. This also allows the project supervisor to readily review and communicate with team members.
Implementation of a just-in-time (JIT) manufacturing system	EDI for high-speed communication and coordination of sales orders and purchase orders, in conjunction with multidepartmental access to online sales order, inventory, and manufacturing data.

Improvements in team performance through the use of groupware might include the following:

- More timely decisions can be made due to rapid communication and more readily achieved consensus.
- More appropriate and higher-quality decisions can be made due to better and quicker joint access to needed data and improved opportunities to analyze data in a rapid feedback team effort.
- Group-based decisions will tend to bring higher levels of commitment and action from the team, yielding higher quality and quantity outputs.
- Thorough and open communication and rapid joint access to current data will enhance teams' ability to adapt to changes in the competitive environment.

Another category of support software can enhance the work of organizational groups, often groups in cross-functional areas. This category is referred to as *workflow software* and is covered in the next section.

Workflow Applications

Consider an insurance organization. The typical life insurance application is handled by the insurance agent, then by the front office, then by auditing for verification, and finally by a manager for approval. Next, the application goes to the policy department for final checking and issuance of the policy, and then to records for storage. Such a business situation can benefit from workflow networked applications. Workflow applications use a variety of technology platforms and software tools to accomplish a basic business function more efficiently and effectively. Documents can be routed quickly and automatically through the network of people who must handle various aspects of a business process. This involves automating tasks, routing documents, and tracking the status of activities necessary to complete the process. Figure 7–15 illustrates a document being routed from a field sales branch to a regional office and finally to the head office for various processes.

The technology of workflow applications may involve configurations based on imaging systems, large servers with optical storage, or client/server configurations with GUI-based user PCs as clients. Software components include database systems capable of handling a range of data types, often including document

FIGURE 7–15

A workflow application routing a document

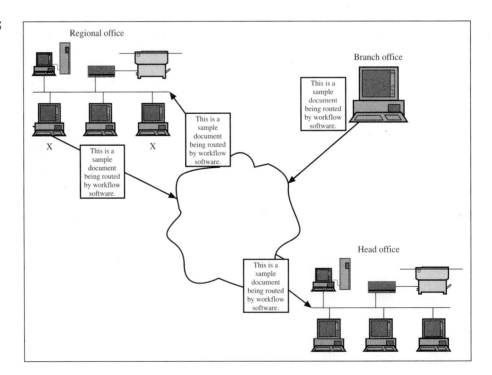

images that have been scanned into the system when the document first arrived at the organization. Naturally, workflow tools must be available to allow the developer to determine the routing of the documents, as well as measurement tools to track the status of the documents and report on delays, rerouting the document when an employee is overloaded. All of this must be transportable over a network, often LAN and WAN based, with documents flowing between offices in a building and between locations across state or even international boundaries.

The concepts of business process reengineering[4] as implemented through workflow systems are seen as being the key that allows many organizations to gain the productivity improvements promised by information system vendors. Although they may not be the "Holy Grail," these concepts do appear to yield significant benefits for those organizations that apply them to core business functions that deal with the customer.

The range of organizational situations that can benefit from workflow applications are many and varied, from insurance applications to university student enrollments, from a manufacturing customer job order to tracking the warranty history of an automobile. A common thread among many workflow applications is that the application or business process crosses functional boundaries and is often in the process of being reorganized as part of a business process reengineering project for the organization.

The benefits from workflow applications typically result from breaking the inertia created when physical documents must be moved from one desktop to another. Often such a document may sit on a desk for hours or even days when it requires only a few minutes of processing before being moved on to the next stop on the chain; then more hours or days may go by until the document is transported to the next stop. These hours/days spent sitting on different desks often add up to weeks of delay in processing, excess inventories, wasted resources, and unsatisfied customers. Workflow applications can considerably enhance many of the support and primary activities of the value chain introduced in Chapter 6. Some examples appear in Figure 7–16.

Note that many of the applications in Figure 7–16 overlap. This is typical of workflow applications, since many of the processes being automated are cross-functional processes. It is also important to realize that workflow applications need to be aimed at the bottom line. To gain the real benefits available, an organization must focus on applications that will make a real difference in value to the customer.

The next section addresses electronic data interchange (EDI), a technology directly related to workflow that deals with interorganizational document transfer and routing.

EDI: A Key to Trading Partner Effectiveness

In modern commercial operations, the relationship between trading partners is increasingly determining the competitive positions of individual companies. This is clearly seen in the widely accepted competitive forces model proposed by Michael Porter

---

[4] T. H. Davenport and J. E. Short, "The New Industrial Engineering: Information Technology and Business Process Redesign," *Sloan Management Review*, Summer 1990, pp. 11–27.

FIGURE 7–16

Workflow applications to enhance value chain activities

Value Chain Activity	Workflow Example
1. Firm infrastructure	Automatic routing and matching of purchase orders, invoices and receiving documents, approval for payment and check generation and posting.
2. Human resource management	Automated support for new-applicant interview scheduling, routing of applicant résumés, routing of follow-up evaluation forms, and summarizing of multiple interviewers' results.
3. Technology development	Routing and support for patent application and tracking through to final approval and dissemination.
4. Procurement	Support for automatic purchase order generation based on low-stock position with routing through purchasing, EDI support direct to supplier, receiving notification to tie into 1 above.
5. Inbound logistics	Automatic EDI notification of product shipment/delivery, receiving notification routed to inventory control, automatic update of inventory levels and manufacturing notification of restocked items that were backordered. Could be further linked to sales/customer service notification of order availability for delivery.
6. Operations	Insurance claim routing through agent, claims department, disbursements/treasury function, and customer file update.
7. Outbound logistics	Automatic routing of shipping notification to shipping department, customer, and invoicing as well as production management and customer service.
8. Marketing and sales	Automatic tracking of hot sales leads generated by an advertising campaign through original acquisition of the telephone lead, follow-up by telemarketing, person-to-person demonstration of product, and final sales contract.
9. Service	Support for warranty tracking on new-product sales through to manufacturing defect management and assembly-line engineering design.

of the Harvard Business School, which was discussed in Chapter 6. The five forces of the Porter model are

1. The threat of new entrants.
2. The intensity of rivalry among existing competitors.
3. Pressure from substitute products.
4. The bargaining power of buyers.
5. The bargaining power of suppliers.[5]

Two of the five forces involve a company's trading partners—customers and suppliers—rather than the direct competition. One application that is being increasingly used to strengthen the relationship with trading partners is EDI. How can this electronic method of sending and receiving business documents affect trading partner effectiveness?

---

[5] Michael Porter, *Competitive Strategy* (New York: The Free Press, 1980).

Direct and potential benefits of EDI include

1. Elimination of paperwork related to business documents such as purchase orders, order confirmations, invoices, remittance notices, and paper checks.

2. Elimination of errors from reentry of data for paper documents.

3. Reduction in stock levels due to shortened order cycles.

4. Automation of document processing, thus eliminating costly manual handling.

5. Increased efficiency in order filling with automated picking lists and back ordering.

6. More current and complete information on order status and stock levels.

7. Superior sales analysis and forecasting based on up-to-date customer order profiles.

8. Improved customer service with faster delivery of product and better information regarding expected delivery times, out-of-stock conditions, stock availability, and pricing.

9. A higher level of cooperation within the organization due to the integration of data dependencies, as illustrated by the following:

   - A sales order triggers an automatic recording of a back-order situation.
   - Which causes the generation of an EDI purchase order (PO) for a low-stock item.
   - Which causes the reception of an EDI PO acknowledgment from the supplier.
   - Which is followed by an EDI notification of shipment.
   - Which is followed by a barcode input of goods received, which generates a notification of receipt of goods.
   - Which is followed by receipt of an EDI invoice.
   - Which is followed by the generation of a payment check or an EDI automatic electronic funds transfer to the supplier's bank account.
   - Which is followed by the generation of an automatic picking slip for back-ordered goods.
   - Which is followed by an automatic invoice to the customer.
   - Which is followed by an automatic transfer of funds or generation of a check payable to the company's bank account.

These items are a combination of efficiency and effectiveness benefits, which set the stage for enhanced organizational performance and competitiveness. The application of EDI has become such an important strategic issue for some organizations that they require suppliers to move to EDI or risk being discontinued as an authorized supplier. The benefits of this level of integration are so substantial that these companies demand the responsiveness that this system offers. Companies such as Kmart, R. J. Reynolds, Wal-Mart, Ford Motor Company, and many others are taking advantage of the benefits and encouraging suppliers and larger customers to gain the same advantages.

In most locations, however, EDI documents currently are not normally accepted as legally binding contracts. The trading partners must establish a contract that accepts EDI documents as legally binding on each party. This issue is being worked on by both the legal profession and industry forces to gain general legal acceptance of EDI documents under specified, controlled circumstances.

Throughout this chapter, we have seen primarily positive examples of TBIT applications. However, not all applications produce a positive result. Some TBIT projects fail to produce the promised results for a variety of reasons, including insufficient analysis, poor implementation, changing markets, and selection of inappropriate technology for the situation. Difficulties may also arise from environmental factors such as competitor actions, government decisions, and the general state of the economy. Some of these factors may be assessed and planned for using risk analysis techniques, which are beyond the scope of this book. Such risk analysis and planning can increase the potential for successful TBIT implementation.

Summary

This chapter looked at various aspects of improving organizational performance through the use of networked systems. The primary focus was on the overall organization and groups within the organization. Analyzing organizational efficiency and applying TBIT systems to improve the efficient functioning of the organization were considered. With a general system model as the background, the chapter introduced a process to measure resource usage to assist in discovering performance improvement after the implementation of a new telecommunications-based system.

A major aspect of efficiency improvement involves saving costs to maximize productivity. The chapter discussed a process to assess improvement in efficiency, along with a range of cost-saving measures that might benefit from the application of telecommunications-based information systems.

An organization must become adept at taking advantage of opportunities in a rapidly changing market environment. Recognizing that rapid change is fundamental to the modern marketplace and developing an organization that is highly responsive to this type of environment may well be a key to long-term success. Four key organizational characteristics that are supported by TBIT applications were considered. Organizations that will succeed in this environment have

1. A "prototyping" attitude toward everything.
2. An environment of creativity, responsibility, and cooperation.
3. Self-managing teams.
4. A reward structure for successful risk taking and "change production."

Related to rapid change are the many uncertainties and risks that such change brings. Taking advantage of these uncertainties and risks and alleviating the accompanying pitfalls provides significant opportunities for the effective application of TBIT systems. The chapter provided a number of examples applying TBIT to this important area.

Communication within groups of workers and among groups was the focus of the last section of this chapter. Groupware, workflow systems, and EDI all have the potential to enhance organizational performance. Groupware is the integrated use of networked application software to allow shared access to files needed for collaborative activities. Its benefits include more timely and higher-quality decisions, higher levels of commitment and action from team members, and enhanced ability to adapt to changes in the competitive environment. Workflow systems are designed to streamline the document-processing functions of organizations. The ability to quickly and accurately transmit and track electronic documents can lead to reduced costs, better customer service, and greater organizational responsiveness. Finally, the use of EDI can strengthen trading partner effectiveness. This electronic document transfer technology may be used to assist companies in better serving customers and help gain the most for the company and its suppliers in the integrated process of serving the marketplace.

Key Terms

Check float   283
Concurrent access   286
E-mail enabled applications   286

Mail float   284
Prototype   278

Questions for Discussion

1. Describe how the basic system input-process-output model can be used to assist in measuring efficiency improvements.

2. What are the key characteristics of efficiency?

3. What are some examples of TBIT-enhanced efficiency?

4. Using the model in Figure 7–5 for measuring efficiency improvements, give two examples of its application in a manufacturing firm.

5. Describe how EDI can be used to improve the efficiency of the purchase order cycle.

6. Why does Tom Peters say that many of the best opportunities that organizations will face in the future will arise out of the chaotic marketplaces in which firms must work? Give three examples.

7. Discuss the four organizational characteristics that will help an organization take advantage of opportunities arising from rapid market changes. Give an example of each.

8. Uncertainty in business creates difficulties for organizations. How can TBIT applications be used to reduce uncertainty and help organizations gain competitive advantage?

9. Describe what groupware is, and give two examples of groupware applications. What are the organizational benefits of using these two groupware examples?

10. Contrast workflow applications with groupware.

11. What are the primary benefits of workflow applications?

12. How is EDI related to workflow? What are the benefits of EDI applications?

Case Discussion and Analysis

1. **Efficiency Analysis for Best Manufacturing Company**

   Using the background information from the Best Manufacturing Company case on pages 267–274 do the following.

   a. Prepare a decomposition diagram of Best's shipping and receiving function.

   b. Using the decomposition diagram from part *a* and the data model given in the chapter, create a table of cost items for Best.

   c. Prepare a list of potential TBIT applications that could be used in the Best shipping and receiving function.

   d. Create an association matrix comparing the cost items from part *b* and the list of potential TBIT applications from part *c*.

2. **Improving Organizational Effectiveness with TBIT at the Magna Plastics Company**

   For over 25 years, Magna Plastics Manufacturing Company has produced plastics products to customer design specifications. During that time the company has had considerable success. However, over the last three or four years, it has experienced increasing pressure from both local and overseas competitors. Top management is looking for ways to increase the organization's effectiveness so that it can respond to these competitive pressures.

   Andrew Chow has worked for Magna Plastics as customer liaison manager for the last two years; prior to that, he worked in the product design department. Typically a customer couriers an order, with a product design attached, to the company. The product design must be agreed on with the customer prior to acceptance of the order. The product design department reviews the design for completeness and any specifications that are not clear; often it is necessary to correspond with the customer to clarify questionable specifications. The customer is often in a rush to get the product, but the company's policy is to make sure the design is right before accepting the order and going to production. In the past, the design engineers bowed to pressure from the customer to get on with the job and get the order produced and into the customer's hands. This usually turned into a serious customer relations problem, because often some aspect of the product was wrong and the customer refused to accept it, returned the shipment, and refused to pay for it. So now the design has to be right first! This ordinarily means doing full technical drawings of the product design as sent by the customer and annotating questions about unclear specifications. These drawings are then circulated through interoffice mail to the production supervisor (located in a different building a few blocks away) to ensure that the product can be manufactured with existing equipment as designed on a timely basis. Sometimes the supervisor annotates suggested changes to the design to make it easier to manufacture and attaches estimated costs to produce. Finally, the drawings go to the pricing department (in the same building as the design department) to set the product price based on the estimated costs, current market pricing, and past experience with this particular customer. Sometimes, after design or production sees the drawings and passes them on to the next department, they will think of a change that could be useful. Usually they phone the next department and give them the suggestion verbally, and the other department will annotate the change to the drawings or documents. This entire process ordinarily takes about a week to complete.

   Because of the time constraints and customer demands, the departments concerned rarely have the opportunity to meet and verify that everybody agrees on the the design changes and suggestions, so the full annotated drawings are couriered from the pricing department to the customer, together with proposed pricing and delivery details. The customer will either agree that everything is fine as is or will amend the drawings and other details as necessary. The drawings and details are then couriered back to Magna Plastics. Most of the time this process is completed in one cycle, but about 25 percent of orders require further modifications to the drawings, pricing, or delivery details, and everything may need to go back and forth from company to customer a few more times until everyone is satisfied. This can add one to three weeks of telephone and courier communication. Often the final design will require special fittings for the product that are not ordinarily kept in stock and must be ordered as needed. A purchase order is prepared and sent to an appropriate supplier; the supplier acknowledges receipt of the order, verifies prices and delivery dates, and then ships the goods. This process typically takes another week.

Although Magna Plastics' customers would like to receive their products in one to two weeks after first contact, the best the company can normally deliver is three to four weeks. Some orders, however, take up to six weeks or more. The company knows that customers sometimes

go to competitors for future orders because they offer more timely delivery. Further, despite Magna Plastics' efforts to ensure that the design is right before production begins, customer satisfaction is sometimes less than ideal because the process has to be rushed and sufficient feedback has not been allowed for.

a. Magna Plastics obviously has some communication problems. Describe how TBIT applications could improve the company's effectiveness, both internally and externally.

b. Compare and contrast workflow applications with groupware applications, and specify how these TBIT applications could benefit Magna Plastics.

c. Can EDI be used to enhance Magna Plastics' effectiveness in this situation? Justify your answer.

NETWORKING OPPORTUNITIES FOR IMPROVING PERSONAL PERFORMANCE

Chapter Outline

Introduction   298
Enhancing Personal Business
    Effectiveness   298
Enhancing Personal Productivity   311

Learning Objectives

By the end of Chapter 8, you should be able to

1. *Apply* the communication model to the use of TBIT applications to enhance effective personal business communication.

2. *Discuss* how networked systems can improve the process of personal research and development.

3. *Describe* the use of telecommunications systems to carry out management tasks involved in planning, organizing, and controlling a business unit.

4. *Explain* how networked systems can enhance the process of contact management for businesspeople.

5. *Apply* network applications to enhance personal productivity in document creation and retrieval.

6. *Discuss* how the use of TBIT can improve business analysis and decision-making processes.

7. *Employ* networks to improve efficient internal and external communications.

Introduction

Organizations consist of people fulfilling their individual and group responsibilities and the tasks needed to carry out the organization's purpose. Enhancing organizational performance with telecommunications-based information technology was the focus of Chapter 7. This chapter focuses on personal effectiveness and productivity. Telecommunications-based applications can be used to improve and support individual communication effectiveness, personal research, management responsibilities, and managing the important contacts businesspeople must make and foster to maximize their effectiveness. Increasing personal productivity in such important areas as document and report creation, filing and retrieval of electronic documents, analyzing situations, making business decisions, and maintaining efficient internal and external communications are all covered in this chapter.

Enhancing Personal Business Effectiveness

Telecommunications—this one word says it all. An industry built around electronic technology, telecommunications is designed to enhance human and organizational communication. Because this chapter focuses on improving personal performance, we begin by looking at improving interpersonal communication and the benefits that modern networks can contribute to this area.

A Communication Model

Communication is the lifeblood of all relationships, whether friend-friend, employer-employee, husband-wife, customer-supplier, or any other type of relationship. Communication will either strengthen and feed or weaken and starve a relationship. The accuracy, timeliness, and quality of communication are critical to the survival of the relationship, and in many circumstances networked applications can assist in improving that communication.

When we speak of communication in this section, we are focusing on the *sending* and *receiving* of personal messages, documents and reports, appointments, creative ideas, supporting information, encouragement, discipline, congratulations, and other positive messages to colleagues within the organization, as well as to customers, suppliers, and others outside the organization.

We tend to think that communication is a simple process of sending a message, believing that the person with whom we are communicating will understand the message just as we intended it. However, a wide range of factors can prevent the message from being sent or interpreted correctly. The **communication model** in Figure 8–1 illustrates the process of effective communication and will lay the foundation for further discussion in this section.

Figure 8–1 shows a sender with her own point of view (*I*) who wants to communicate with a receiver with a different point of view (*I*) through a **communication channel**. The channel is the means by which the message is passed. The most typical communication channels and a description of their level of timeliness versus media richness are shown in Figure 8–2. Timeliness, or immediacy of communication, ranges from days or weeks for regular mail to immediate delivery of the message for telephone, videoconferencing, and face-to-face meetings. Media richness ranges from simple to complex. On the simple end of the scale we have telephone, voice mail, text-based documents, and E-mail. All of these exhibit a single media characteristic (voice or text). On the complex end of the media richness scale we have videoconferencing and face-to-face meetings that allow many media types, including sound, motion, text, graphics, and interactive computing. All of the media shown permit two-way communication. Other communication media, such as television and radio (not shown), permit only one-way communication.

The effectiveness of the communication process can be considerably enhanced through the use of networked applications, especially in terms of increasing the clarity of the initial message, reducing channel noise, and improving feedback. We will look at these aspects of the communication model in the next section.

Communication Effectiveness with Networks

How can networks assist in increasing the clarity of the initial message, reducing channel noise, and improving feedback? In this section we will focus on these questions as we look at the communication model and assess network applications that can increase personal communication effectiveness.

FIGURE 8–1

A communication model

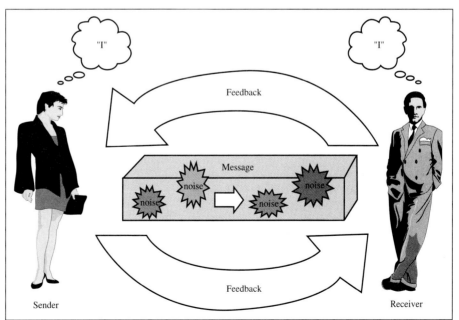

FIGURE 8–2

Communication channels and their timeliness versus media richness

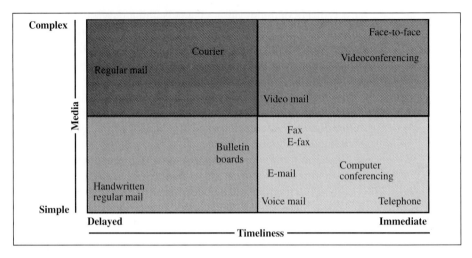

Increasing the Clarity of the Initial Message.   One of the great benefits of the telephone is the speed and directness of the communication. However, in many situations, the use of the telephone actually *reduces* the effectiveness of the communication. These include situations where

1. A record of the communication or reference to a specific document is needed.
2. Data such as numbers, diagrams, or other graphics are included in the communication.
3. Face-to-face contact is needed to establish or renew a relationship or to deal with a complex or unstructured situation.

Under these circumstances electronic means of communication may substitute for traditional communication vehicles such as mail, courier services, or meetings. Let's look at a few examples in these three categories.

The first category is situations that require a record of the communication or reference to specific documents. These might include the following:

• *Placing orders.* Purchase and sales orders are often placed over the telephone. Sometimes a phone call is sufficient for small details of an order, but most telephone orders should be confirmed with a written order. Items such as the terms and conditions of the order, discount rates, quantity, size, or quality may all end up in dispute if the order is based exclusively on a phone conversation. Ordinary mail or courier services may be used to transfer written documentation. These services, however, vary in speed and are often used in conjunction with a telephone call, so that two processes are used. However, if fax or E-mail is used, the speed of delivery is nearly the same as that with a phone call, and written documentation is provided at the same time, doing away with the need for further confirmation. E-mail with file transfer or E-fax offer additional advantages over standard fax. With an ordinary fax, the document must first be produced in paper form, physically fed through the fax machine, transmitted and printed at the receiving end, possibly entered through a keyboard into a computerized order entry system, and finally processed. Whenever pieces of paper are generated, the paper document may end up sitting on a pile on someone's desk. E-mail and E-fax, however, both offer speedy delivery, with no need for paper generation, and automated handling of the document, thus significantly increasing the accuracy, timeliness, and quality of the transaction. EDI offers all of these benefits as well, with even more automation possible in order preparation and delivery.

- *Conversations regarding an agreement or contract terms*: E-fax or E-mail can be used in conjunction with the telephone to negotiate details of a contract or an agreement.

- *Communicating changes to a document*: A conference phone call to discuss a document such as a report is beneficial only if all parties have a current copy of it. Electronic networked communication allows the most recent version of a report to be in the hands of all conference call participants. Changes agreed to during the conference call can be made immediately to the electronic version and then broadcast to all concerned parties using the mail list feature of E-mail or E-fax. Use of videoconferencing supported by groupware may also be an effective application for this purpose.

- *Transmission of documents for legal purposes*: Purchase and sales orders, invoices, and other legal documents are typically sent by regular mail or courier rather than by electronic means due to a lack of acceptance of an electronic document (such as a fax) as legal evidence of a contract. Formation of an EDI agreement between cooperating parties can overcome this hurdle until the courts and legal professionals settle this issue.

The second category is situations where data such as numbers, diagrams, or other graphics are needed as part of the communication. Such situations include the following:

- *Technical drawings of new or modified parts or products and building plans, as well as other architectural or engineering drawings*: In communicating technical drawings, excellent resolution and accurate scaling are often critical, which creates problems for ordinary fax. In addition, these drawings are often produced using CAD packages and may need to be scanned back into computer form at the receiving end if they are sent by mail or courier. Using E-mail with file transfer is an excellent alternative to ordinary mail and international courier, since it provides fast transfer of electronic files that can be used immediately in the receiver's CAD package (provided the CAD packages and file formats used are compatible).

- *Business graphics and electronic spreadsheets*: In situations where business graphics or spreadsheets are needed at a distance, an electronic version is often far more useful than a paper copy, as it can be modified instantaneously if assumptions change. A diskette containing the files can be sent by mail or courier, but the use of E-mail file transfer—or, even better, groupware applications for multiple users— offers much more rapid turnaround.

Finally, circumstances that require face-to-face contact to establish or renew a relationship or to deal with a complex or unstructured situation could include the following:

- *Business meetings with staff or clients*: When business meetings are intended primarily for review and decision making rather than relationship building, video-conferencing or voice conferencing can be successfully substituted in some circumstances. "Electronic" meetings can enhance overall effectiveness, since participants work in familiar surroundings without the need to travel.
- *Technical design and/or analysis meetings*: Use of electronic meeting technology for video or voice conferencing, as well as E-mail and file transfer, can effectively substitute for some meetings, as well as lay the groundwork for more productive face-to-face meetings.

In the next section we will see how TBIT applications can alleviate some of the noise that is inherent in most communication channels.

Reducing Channel Noise.   Channel noise refers to the environmental disturbances that may disrupt the flow of communication, cause the message to arrive in a distorted fashion, or prevent delivery of the message altogether. Figure 8–3 shows an excerpt from the communication model in which various types of noise disrupt the flow of communication through the channel.

Channel noise may fall into a variety of categories:

- *Audio*: This includes noise such as traffic blaring, a radio blasting, or someone else trying to talk at the same time. An example of using TBIT applications to alleviate audio noise is the use of E-mail chat mode or E-fax, which offer the speed advantages of the phone without a noisy environment.

FIGURE 8–3

Illustration of channel noise

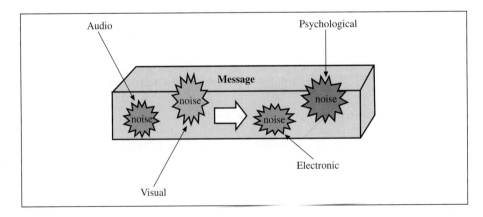

- *Visual*: Examples include trying to communicate with the TV going, a poor-quality video signal disrupting an otherwise good audio track, or a fax image that is unreadable. The use of current technologies such as error-correcting modems and ISDN lines to send a fax or for file transfer will improve the quality of the final image, CAD file, video, or other visual element.

- *Psychological*: Psychological noise includes emotions such as anger, anxiety, irritation, or stress that can interfere with the communication of a message. The use of E-mail, E-fax, voice mail, and other electronic communication technologies permits a fast turnaround of information requests, avoids telephone tag, and reduces the paper-based inertia of ordinary telephone and fax, thus reducing some of the causes of psychological noise. When using videoconferencing and other teleconferencing techniques, however, the lack of a personal presence may make some psychological noise worse due to the absence of the damping effects of social interchanges that tend to accompany face-to-face meetings.

- *Electronic*: Electronic noise occurs when a transmission signal (audio, video, E-mail, telephone, fax) is disrupted for any reason, such as a lightning storm, failure of wiring insulation, electronic equipment failure, or static in the line. Where transmission line quality is poor, an ordinary fax transmission may produce a very poor copy, especially of diagrams and graphics. Many E-mail, E-fax, and EDI applications use error correction methods to prevent such problems.

Another important factor in better communication is improving feedback in the communication process. In the next section we will look at how networked applications may help increase communication effectiveness by improving feedback speed and quality.

Improving Feedback.   In the communication model shown in Figure 8–1, notice the two large arrows labeled "Feedback." **Feedback** simply means testing the received message with the sender to see if it was received accurately or providing additional information about the subject of the message. Feedback allows you to verify accuracy and improve the overall quality of the communication. Methods of feedback include

- Paraphrasing the message as received.
- Asking questions about the message to clarify its content.
- Asking questions about the message to clarify any underlying messages (those not stated directly in the message but implied by the tone of voice).
- Comments and suggestions about the message (such as when a co-worker asks for feedback on a report or document).

Networked applications such as networked word processors and other groupware, E-mail, and E-fax, as well as video and voice conferencing, can improve both the speed and quality of feedback, which in turn can enhance the overall effectiveness of communication, boosting accuracy and sharpening the content of documents and reports.

Feedback is a major factor in overcoming channel noise and producing a high-quality communication, because the process of iteration that is inherent in feedback allows sender and receiver to build and shape the communication until both agree on the content and intent of the message. The following scenarios illustrate the benefits of feedback.

SUPERIOR TOY MANUFACTURING COMPANY

As Joe Case read through his morning mail, he heard the fax machine start to print. The message unrolled, and Joe took it from the tray. It read, "Joe, could you send me 200 large red fire engines as soon as possible? Thanks. Tom Smith, Smith & Co. Toy Retailers." After reading the message, Joe thought, I wonder if he means last year's model, which is being discounted 40 percent, or the new model. Joe thought of the bother of typing up a reply and faxing Tom to query the order, and then reconsidered: I guess he must have gotten our promotional brochure and wanted to take advantage of the good deal. Immediately Joe rang the warehouse and asked them to ship 200 of the old red toy fire engines to Tom Smith. Unfortunately, the warehouse clerk wrote down "Joe Smith," who was also a regular customer, and shipped the 200 red fire engines to him.

A week later, both Tom Smith and Joe Smith were on the phone to Joe Case, demanding to know what was going on. After Joe finally straightened out the mess, he authorized Joe Smith to return the goods and gave the warehouse clerk a piece of his mind for shipping to the wrong customer. The clerk finally sent 200 more old red toy fire engines to the right customer.

A week later, Tom Smith again called Joe Case, wanting to know why he had sent him the old-style fire engine when he wanted the new model. Embarrassed, Joe Case looked again at the fax Tom had originally sent and said to Tom, "Well, your original fax, which I have in front of me, doesn't actually say whether you want the old or the new model, so I just assumed you wanted the old one at the 40 percent discount." Tom's reply was blistering: "You assumed wrong, and now the sale that I had advertised has turned into a promotional nightmare. Many customers are coming in to buy the new model, only to find that I don't have any. What a mess! Cancel the order, I'm sending these old ones back!" As Tom slammed the phone down in Joe's ear, Joe thought, Oh well, things don't always go according to plan. Months later, the thought crossed his mind: I wonder why we haven't gotten an order from Tom Smith recently. He was such a good customer.

QUALITY TOYS COMPANY

Mary Lim sat planning the next toy promotional brochure for the last week in June when she heard her E-fax application beep. She double-clicked on the *fax* icon to read the message. It was from a Tom Smith of Smith & Co. Toy Retailers. He wanted 200 large, red toy fire engines as soon as possible. Mary wasn't too sure if he meant the large wooden ones, which were very popular and discounted this month only, or the standard red steel ones. Immediately she clicked on the *Reply* icon, and a window popped up that asked if she wanted to annotate the fax received and send it back or format a new message. She clicked the *Annotate* button, annotated Tom Smith's fax message on the computer screen with a question about whether he wanted wooden or metal engines, added the prices and terms, and clicked the *Send* button. Then she went back to work on the promotional brochure.

About 45 minutes later, the computer beeped again to say that a fax had been received. Mary double-clicked on the *fax* icon to read the message. It was Tom Smith again, confirming the order and saying that he wanted the more modern wooden engines and that the price and terms were fine. Please ship as soon as possible, and how soon could he have them?

Mary clicked on the database icon on her screen, and a menu of applications popped up. She clicked on the *Inventory* selection and then queried the database to check the stock levels for the red wooden engine. Yes, they were in sufficient supply. Mary annotated the order with a "ship today" message, clicked on the *Forward* icon, and entered "shipping, accounting" in the destination box. Immediately a copy of the order was forwarded to the shipping department, which would fill the order and send it to Smith, as well as a copy to accounting for control and billing purposes. When she finished forwarding the order, she further annotated it, saying that Tom should have the toys in two days or less, and double-clicked on the *fax* icon. Mary turned back to her promotional brochure, feeling glad that she could meet that customer's need and hoping he would be satisfied with the excellent quality of the toys.

Which of these two scenarios represents the more effective communication? Obviously, the first scenario points out some of the problems and the second points out some solutions. As you can see, networked applications can help improve communication effectiveness and thereby customer service. Also, note that the earlier an error in communication is discovered, the better, since an error discovered later will typically be more costly to fix.

Using networked applications for communication often permits more frequent and more rapid iterations of the feedback cycle. The result is higher-quality communication with fewer errors and more rapid turnaround time, allowing a higher level of responsiveness to customer needs and generally increasing effectiveness.

Research and Development

Research is the process of exploration, investigation, and discovery with the purpose of developing new or improved products and services. The products and services may be internal and indirect, such as preparing a report or a speech, or more direct, such as a new financial service, electronic device, or automobile. Figure 8–4 illustrates how telecommunications-based applications can support research in four ways:

1. Readier access to a variety of information resources.
2. Support for collaborative research.
3. Support for iterative quality processes.
4. More rapid access to information, customers, and colleagues.

Here are some examples of TBIT applications in these four categories.

FIGURE 8–4

*TBIT support for
research*

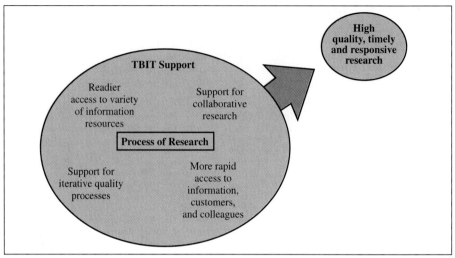

Readier Access to a Variety of Information Resources

- Network access to integrated company databases of market research data, using a statistical package to analyze the data, allows cross-tabulation of different data sources and surveys over time. This offers the potential to uncover trends that might be missed in cases where paper summaries, nonintegrated databases, and isolated product managers lack access to integrated data.

- Networked database of references to periodicals, books, and other printed matter are maintained by the organization in a library of support materials for its products and industry, or access to outside third-party databases.

- Internet/WWW access to news groups and discussion forums gives ready access to up-to-date technical and market information within an industry.

Support for Collaborative Research

- A shared file of famous quotes and humorous anecdotes maintained by staff members who need to make public presentations increases the effectiveness of speeches and other presentations and reduces stress on staff during preparation.

- Shared access to company proposals previously submitted, supported by a network search facility based on keyword summary data, allows rapid retrieval of similar or related proposals. Used to support client proposal preparation by both groups and individuals.

- Use of electronic mail and bulletin boards to enhance communication between scientific and technical researchers in developing new products or manufacturing processes allows rapid problem solution.

Support for Iterative Quality Processes

- Using groupware applications, E-mail, and file sharing, marketing may be involved in drafting the initial specifications for new products or changes to existing products. This information may be communicated to the engineering or product design department, which then creates the technical specifications, drawings, manufacturing requirements, and so on. This information may then be communicated back to marketing for verification and recommendations, perhaps including communication with the potential customers for feedback before manufacturing begins.

- When researching and developing reports or proposals, the responsible person can use E-mail, groupware, and other networked applications to readily communicate with colleagues and customers to gain feedback that will allow fine-tuning of the report or proposal. The rapid turnaround of electronic documents allows for multiple iterations that increase the quality of the final document.

More Rapid Access to Information, Customers, and Colleagues

- An executive may use an Internet news service set up with a personal profile search facility to automatically notify them of news articles on the industry or key competitors to allow a rapid response to changing market conditions.

- As part of market research, field salespeople can use notebook computers with modems to discover customer preferences on a proposed new product line, and automatically process and forward results to the home office via dial-up E-mail or file transfer.

Access to such networked research support facilities can add significant value to the processes being supported as well as speed up the process of research, allowing office and technical workers more time for other activities such as client and customer support. The result is an excellent synergism of effectiveness and efficiency.

Planning, Organizing, and Controlling

A major movement within competitive organizations in recent years has been "downsizing" the organizational pyramid. Essentially this involves reducing the number of managers and layers of management that separate top management from line workers. A major influence supporting this move toward more effective management has been the use of networked systems to automate the information assimilation and dissemination functions performed by management, thus allowing fewer managers to better manage more employees.

The processes that most managers administer involve a combination of individual activities and joint activities involving communication. Figure 8–5 presents some typical management activities and ways in which TBIT systems can help increase their effectiveness. Another major source of improved effectiveness in the use of management's and decision makers' time is the use of TBIT applications to eliminate unnecessary travel time and the attendant fatigue, as well as the associated travel and accommodations costs.

The use of telecommunications-based applications can greatly assist managers in maintaining the flow of information necessary to plan, organize, and control their business units. However, the modern manager must also be aware that this technology must be used to enhance, and not cause deterioration of, interpersonal and team-related relationships. The whole area of relationship management can be enhanced using networked contact management applications, especially in dealing with the many new business contacts that are so crucial to the success of a business.

Contact Management

Contact management refers to the process of following up the many new contacts all businesspeople make through both formal and informal channels. The exchange of business cards is a commercial ritual that often triggers the process of contact management. However, many new contacts are not followed up and maintained but are lost due to poor personal systems and habits. The use of network-based contact management applications can alleviate this ongoing problem by providing automated support for follow-up and maintenance of new contacts. We will look at this area of contact management in terms of two groups of individuals: marketing staff and managers and other staff.

FIGURE 8–5

TBIT applications to support management processes

Management Process	TBIT Application
Planning departmental and organizational activities, programs, product launches, proposal development, employee review, etc.	Networked calendering, project control applications, E-mail, and electronic bulletin boards; WAN access to external databases for statistics, foreign exchange, interest rates, and news services; videoconferencing, teleconferencing, and voice messaging applications
Organizing resources necessary to carry out planned activities	EDI for material ordering, networked calendering, project control applications, E-mail and electronic bulletin boards, and other groupware; workflow applications to ensure quality and smooth out process flow; use of voice messaging applications to assist timely communication
Controlling resources and planned activities so that they produce the desired outcomes	Networked databases, analysis and reporting applications to support the control function (such as EIS and DSS), networked calendering, project control applications, E-mail and electronic bulletin boards, videoconferencing and teleconferencing

Marketing Staff.   Marketing staff are the professionals of contact management. Their primary job is to reach new customers and keep old ones. Thus, good contact management is the heart of their function. From receiving leads on advertising to following up those leads to produce new sales, contact management can help them in this important task.

Receiving Leads from Advertising.   The purpose of advertising is to increase existing and potential customer awareness of the organization's goods and services and to persuade these people to buy the products or seek further information. A *lead* refers to a person who is a potential customer and is often generated by a reply card, a letter, or a phone call from print, radio, TV, or other advertising. Once leads have been generated from the advertising, they need to be followed up. If the raw leads are left in paper form (reply cards, letters, or phone messages), they can be lost or ignored, and they are accessible only to one salesperson or analyst to work on. Creating an integrated database that is networked for access by data entry operators, managers, analysts, and salespeople can increase the speed of response to the leads (while they are still hot), as well as provide historical information about the effectiveness of advertising and lead profiles for increased selling success.

Analyzing and Qualifying Leads.   Once leads are received, they need to be analyzed and qualified. This may involve a variety of activities, including

1. Tracking response rates from various types of advertising to obtain information for planning future advertising campaigns.
2. Analyzing leads to discover the characteristics most likely to result in a sale.
3. Phoning leads to see if they would like a salesperson to call on them.
4. Generally discovering whether the lead is worth following up or is a dead end.

This process of analyzing and qualifying can be considerably enhanced using the integrated database discussed earlier, together with statistical packages and other software for analyzing the data. Also useful in qualifying leads is autodial software, which will dial the prospect's phone number from the database while the analyst or qualifier is working on something else. This software will repeatedly dial the lead's number until the lead is reached. Database and autodial software increase both effectiveness and the efficiency by automating the repetitive task of dialing and redialing a phone number because the line is busy or the lead is not at home.

Following Up Qualified Leads.   A *qualified* lead is a lead that is more likely to result in a sale and therefore warrants more follow-up effort. This follow-up process may involve

1. Phoning the lead to make an appointment.
2. Sending a literature pack to the lead.

3. Following up a literature pack with a phone call a week later to make an appointment.

4. Making an in-person presentation to a lead to demonstrate the product or respond to specific questions or objections.

All of these tasks may be supported by an integrated database in one way or another. Autodial software can be used to assist in making initial contact as well as follow-up phone calls. Data may also be appended to the lead's data file so that if a different salesperson conducts the follow-up, consistency and coordination will be maintained and no critical information will be lost. Selection of appropriate literature for mailing can be automated based on the lead's characteristics so that leads are sent only the literature that is most useful to them. In-person presentations may be supported by modem links to field sales notebook computers. The notebook may be used to access special demonstration files, updated lead profiles, and other current and pertinent data that may assist the salesperson in effectively showing the product in the field and responding to the lead's questions or objections. For example, an electronic bulletin board may be used for posting questions or objections that a salesperson may be unable to answer effectively, and other salespeople or managers can place suggested responses onto the bulletin board. In this way, the original salesperson and other salespeople will all profit from the learning process.

Managers and Other Staff.   Obviously, the above marketing-related contact management systems can be modified for use with nonmarketing processes and people. Examples of the need for general contact management include the following:

- Purchasing staff need to keep track of suppliers.
- Managers of downsized organizations want to maintain the personal touch with their many employees.
- Manufacturing technical staff would like to keep in touch with professional colleagues so that they can help one another in solving mutual manufacturing process problems.
- Partners in accounting, engineering, law, and other professional firms need to maintain relationships with clients and new contacts made in the course of business.

The use of networked database applications allow staff and managers to share information about contacts as well as send electronic messages to those contacts that are accessible by E-mail, fax, and voice mail. Applications such as sending congratulations on the birth of a new child, happy birthday wishes, bon voyage messages, holiday greetings, and condolence messages all add a personal touch and can enhance the business relationships and strengthen individual workers' network of contacts with customers and colleagues.

This section focused primarily on issues of enhancing personal business effectiveness using TBIT applications. The next section addresses issues of productivity, recognizing that there is significant overlap between these two areas.

Enhancing Personal Productivity

Personal productivity means getting the most output from the limited time we have available. The previous section of this chapter looked at some implications of efficiency for personal effectiveness. This section examines the flip side of the coin.

The human effort invested in most organizations and in their services and products is the single largest cost incurred. Getting the most from that effort is critical to the success and even the survival of many organizations. How can networked applications assist in enhancing personal productivity? We will look at three areas:

1. Business communications.
2. Filing documents and locating files.
3. Analyzing situations and making decisions.

Business Communications

Because communication is such a pervasive feature of the modern workplace, telecommunications-based applications can assist in enhancing personal communication productivity. Types of communication in this area include

- Correspondence such as letters and requests for information.
- Brief messages such as instructions to a subordinate or a request for a meeting.
- Larger documents that need to be conveyed to co-workers, such as reports.
- Business documents such as invoices and purchase orders.
- Meetings.
- Feedback such as recommended changes to a document, requests for clarification to correct data errors, or feedback between collaborative researchers.
- Informal communication that strengthens relationships and transmits information through personal contact.

Networked applications may be used to increase the speed of or reduce the effort involved in a number of these communication types. Figure 8–6 presents some TBIT applications that can enhance these forms of communication. Productivity enhancements include

- Preparation of more documents in a given time period.
- Quicker completion of documents, leaving time for other tasks.
- Production of an equal number of documents of a higher quality (a combination of efficiency and effectiveness).

It must be cautioned, however, that productivity gains have not always been forthcoming[1] for a variety of reasons, including undue emphasis on presentation of the document, such as adding unnecessary graphics and varying typeface size and style; insufficient training on the system; and excessive perfectionism in writing multiple drafts of documents simply because it is easy to make changes. The development of workflow applications (covered in Chapter 7) has further enhanced this area.

In each of the examples in Figure 8–6, an analysis of potential additional telecommunications and system costs would need to be compared to the cost savings and efficiency improvements to determine the expected net realizable benefits. However, the strategic benefits often are the deciding factor in the implementation of such communication applications. Gaining long-term efficiency often depends on effective training of staff to gain the maximum benefits.

Electronic Filing and Document Retrieval

Efficient filing and retrieval of documents is a necessary and time-consuming task. Lost or misfiled records not only take a lot of time to locate or recreate, thereby reducing efficiency, but have a very negative impact on the organization's effectiveness in serving clients and customers. The use of sophisticated network filing systems, modern word processors, automated search facilities, and sound procedures can go a long way toward streamlining this important business process.

Electronic filing and retrieval systems provide the following benefits, among others:

- The ability to create a directory tree structure of files, making it easier to store files in an organized manner.
- The ability to establish a range of search criteria to locate a document, including date created, date last edited, author of document, person who last edited (if a shared file), title of document, content of document, size of file, keywords, and subject.
- The ability to specify a search for one disk drive only (for example, a local hard drive) or across multiple hard drives in a networked environment by specifying the path or paths to search.

Well-organized files created according to organizational standards of directory structure and file-naming conventions, together with automated search and retrieval systems, provide a solid foundation on which to build efficient filing systems. Figure 8–7 provides an example of such standards. This approach to directory and file naming standards is not a prescription for every organization. Each organization is unique and should establish standards that suit its industry and environment.

---

1 T. H. Davenport and J. E. Short, "The New Industrial Engineering: Information Technology and Business Process Redesign," *Sloan Management Review,* Summer 1990, pp. 11–27.

FIGURE 8–6

Productivity enhancement of personal communications

Communication Type	TBIT Application	Productivity Enhancement
Correspondence	E-mail, E-fax, electronic bulletin board	For mailing lists, labor would be considerably reduced, with no envelopes, stamps, or paper to handle. The same would be true for a single letter. In the case of internal mail, there could be reduced mailroom staff where E-mail is widely adopted.
Brief messages	E-mail, voice mail, electronic calendering	Reduced time wastage due to telephone tag, less time spent in organizing meetings.
Reports	Networked word processors and other work group applications, file transfer, workflow applications	Use of a word processor for original report creation can reduce production and modification time. Spell-check features can also reduce proofreading time. File transfer, perhaps using workflow applications, can speed up communication of the document to interested people and may reduce waiting and start-stop time for individuals (the time involved in following up and starting and stopping unfinished tasks).
Business documents	EDI, E-mail, E-fax, workflow applications, POS automation	The use of electronically transmitted documents allows automation of the document cycle, eliminating the paperwork, handling, postage, errors, and error correction required by manual systems.
Meetings	E-mail, file transfer, electronic calendering, and other workgroup applications; videoconferencing and teleconferencing	Travel cost reductions and elimination of wasted travel time, as well as improving preparation for physical meetings to allow greater productivity at actual meetings.
Business presentations	Networked presentation software; E-mail link to graphic artist; access to presenter database of anecdotes, examples, and jokes	Professional presentation software and access to tailored clip-art files make development of business presentations faster and more professional. E-mail access, groupware, or workflow applications linked to a graphic artist in the organization can increase productivity of both the artist and presenters. Access to a database of tailored anecdotes, examples, news clippings, and jokes reduces development effort and increases the effectiveness of presenters.
Feedback	E-mail, E-fax, electronic bulletin board, and workgroup applications; videoconferencing and teleconferencing; workflow applications	Rapid annotation of a document using communicating word processors reduces paper-handling time; where feedback is required by a group, use of a bulletin board or mail list message over E-mail or E-fax reduces the need to send individual paper messages. Market research conducted by field sales personnel may use electronic forms instead of paper ones, with electronic transmission of the results, thus saving keying of data and attendant errors later on. Feedback among collaborative researchers is greatly facilitated, reducing the need for many face-to-face meetings and leveraging the time spent in face-to-face meetings into more productive results.
Informal communications	E-mail, voice mail, electronic bulletin board	Most informal communication traditionally occurs over the telephone or in informal meetings such as morning or afternoon coffee breaks. However, E-mail and voice mail may be used to maintain more frequent and less costly informal communication, especially with colleagues who reside in different buildings or cities.

FIGURE 8–7

Sample system filing standards

Standard Type	Example
Directory structure	F:\(all network applications and shared files)
	\Network & operating system utilities
	\Application software
	\Accounting package
	\Presentation package
	\Wordprocessor
	\Spreadsheet
	\Shared data files
	\Correspondence
	\Proposals
	\Reports
	\Meeting minutes
	\General spreadsheet models
	P:\(all personal files and private applications)
	\Nonshared data files
	\Correspondence
	\Proposals
	\Client name
	\Client name
	\Client name
	\Client name
	\Reports
	\Meeting minutes
	\Committee name
	\Committee name
	\Committee name
	\General spreadsheet models
File naming	Correspondence: <4 character client name+ 2 char. month+2 char. day>.doc; e.g. yung0209.doc
	Proposals: <4 char. client name+2 char. month+2 char. day>.doc; e.g. yeel0511.doc
	Reports: <4 character description or client name+ 2 char. month+2 char. day>.doc; e.g. edi_0627.doc
	Meeting minutes: <4 char. committee name+ 2 char. month+2 char. day>.doc; e.g. mfg_1017.doc
	All word-processed documents will include summary information as provided by the word-processor search facilities, including author name, date created (auto), keywords, including full client name, committee, or report name.
	Spreadsheet models: <8 char. description>.xls; e.g. dcfpymnt.xls

Analyzing Situations and Making Decisions

For many managers and professionals, analysis and decision making in various situations are not only among the most time-consuming activities but are also among the most important. Carrying out these tasks successfully requires rapid access to appropriate analytical tools, current information, and concise communication. Productivity improvements may be gained through TBIT applications, including rapid access to networked decision support systems (DSSs) or executive information systems (EISs). These systems provide features such as

- Online database of foreign exchange rates.
- Online database of current interest rates.
- Online current news service, including highlights for the user's particular focus.
- Online access to company databases to obtain current company information.
- Network access to spreadsheet templates, shared with co-workers.
- Network access to other analysis and decision support models.
- "Drill down" facilities, which present highly summarized data first, with the option to access increasing levels of detail as necessary.

To enhance efficiency, these features must provide faster access than alternative sources such as newspapers and printed reports, particularly in cases where information is changing rapidly and daily or weekly reports are not sufficiently current. This may be enhanced through the use of "executive profiles," which provide a description of the interests and needs of a given executive and yield key words that are used by automated search facilities to access and summarize news articles and data of interest. Productivity may also be enhanced by the automated capture of electronic data from databases (internal or external) and automatic feeding of these data into spreadsheets or other models to assist in analysis and decision making.

Summary

This chapter focused on the improvement of personal performance through the use of networked systems. The discussion centered on two perspectives: enhancing personal business effectiveness and enhancing personal productivity.

The chapter opened with the introduction of an interpersonal communication model that set the stage for further discussion on this vital topic. The model included concepts of sender and receiver, a communication channel, channel noise, and the process of feedback to improve the quality and flow of communication. Various forms of electronic communication media and related aspects of speed of communication versus richness of the media were also covered.

Personal research is an important task in competitive organizations. Telecommunications-based systems can support this effort by providing (1) readier access to a variety of information resources, (2) support for collaborative research, (3) support for iterative quality processes, and (4) more rapid access to information, customers, and colleagues.

Next, the chapter discussed the application of TBIT systems to enhance the effectiveness of managers in planning, organizing, and controlling their business units. Then it discussed how contact management applications can assist marketing personnel, managers, and other staff in acquiring, following up, and maintaining business prospects.

The chapter then moved into the area of productivity enhancement. The process of creating business documents can be considerably enhanced by using networked systems. Directly linked to document creation is the filing and retrieval of documents. A process for setting up system filing standards and the use of automated tools to assist in retrieval of electronic documents was described.

Finally, the chapter discussed how TBIT applications can support the processes of analysis and decision making. Decision support systems provide access to the information managers need to perform these critical tasks.

Key Terms

Channel noise   302
Communication channel   298
Communication model   298

Contact management   308
Feedback   303
Personal productivity   311

Questions for Discussion

1. Describe the primary components of the communication model covered at the beginning of the chapter.

2. What electronic communication channels are most media rich and at the same time most immediate in the speed of communication? What are the benefits from the use of these channels? What are the drawbacks of their use, if any?

3. In what ways are TBIT applications able to enhance the clarity of the initial message in the communication process? Give a few examples.

4. What is communication channel noise? How does it impair the communication of a message, and how can networked applications alleviate this problem?

5. What is feedback, and why is it important to the communication process? Give a couple of examples of feedback.

6. In what ways can TBIT applications improve the feedback process? What effect does such improvement have on the quality of the communication?

7. What are the four ways in which networked applications are able to support the personal research process? Give an example of how each benefit might apply to research you have done.

8. Planning, organizing, and controlling are the primary functions of management. How can TBIT applications assist managers in carrying out these functions effectively?

9. Maintaining business contacts is an important task. Describe how you could use telecommunications-based systems to facilitate this process.

10. Give three examples of how marketing staff could enhance their performance by using networked contact management applications.

11. Describe how TBIT applications can help businesspeople create higher-quality and a larger quantity of business documents and reports.

12. Describe four ways in which networked applications are able to enhance the processes of analysis and decision making.

Case Discussion and Analysis

1. **Network File Search Facilities**

   Use the search facilities of your networked word processor to locate a file you have created. If shared file access is available on your system, save the file in the shared space and then ask another student to locate the file based on summary data that you provide. Experiment with the search facilities to discover the full range of features provided.

2. **Create a System Filing Standard**

   Based on your own work patterns and information needs—personal, work-related, and course-related—create a system filing standard for your own personal use, including personal correspondence and address book, class projects and essays, spreadsheets and database application files, and so on.

3. **Productivity Measurement**

   In groups of three, carry out the following experiment. Assign roles to various group members as follows: manager, secretary, observer/recorder.

   a. The manager hand-writes a short letter (100 to 200 words), and gives it to the secretary, who then types the letter and prints it out. The secretary gives the printed letter to the manager, who proofreads the letter and returns it to the secretary for corrections. The secretary makes the corrections, prints out the revised letter, and gives it to the manager for final approval. The manager signs the letter and gives it back to the secretary, who prepares an envelope with a stamp, folds the letter, inserts it in the envelope, seals it, and places it in the out-basket. The observer/recorder's job is to time each of these activities and record the time involved.

   b. The manager types a letter directly on a word processor and sends it via E-mail. The observer/recorder times and records the effort involved.

   c. Compare parts a and b in terms of effects on the productivity and on the effectiveness of the individuals and the organization.

9

DETERMINING BUSINESS NETWORKING REQUIREMENTS

Chapter Outline

Introduction   320

Requirements Analysis for Network
    Solutions   320

Network Performance Standards and
    Fulfillment of User Requirements
    337

Creating a Network Implementation
    Plan   343

Determining Sources of Network
    Components   347

Learning Objectives

By the end of Chapter 9, you should be able to

1. *Determine* an organization's internal and external requirements that network systems can meet in a cost-effective way.

2. *Establish* budgetary requirements and technical constraints.

3. *Determine* user requirements.

4. Assess requirements for connectivity and compatibility with current network solutions.

5. *Identify* the key performance standards in business networks and relate them to user requirements.

6. *Produce* a plan of network systems to be implemented by evaluating requirements and specifications in light of the organization's internal and external priorities and strategic plan.

7. *Use* a request for proposal to determine sources of network components.

Introduction

Clearly establishing the environmental, organizational, user, and technical requirements of a new network installation is critical to the successful implementation of a project. Clear communication, documentation, and follow-through on these requirements set a solid foundation for a network that will deliver the promises it makes.

In earlier chapters you learned about the applications of TBIT to business environments, how to analyze an organization for TBIT opportunities, and how to discover the benefits that can be gained from such applications. In this chapter you will learn how to ascertain and document the specific requirements of a new network system. You will also learn how to build a network implementation plan to carry the project through to successful completion.

Requirements Analysis for Network Solutions

What is requirements analysis? How does it affect the construction of network solutions? How should the users' view of network systems influence the design of the final system? This section will answer these questions and more.

Requirements analysis is the process of discovering, documenting, and communicating the needs of the organization regarding a proposed network system. The needs, or requirements, may fall into a variety of categories, including

- Internal, organizational requirements (e.g., "The network must provide an easy-to-learn system (low learning curve) for new users of the application software").

- External, environmental requirements ("This is a mission-critical network that will aid us in preventing further erosion of our customer base by competing suppliers").

- Budgetary requirements ("When estimating network system costs, full costs over the expected life of the system must be included").

- Technical requirements ("The communication network must be able to handle binary file transfer of CAD/CAM files between our international offices").

- General user requirements ("The electronic calendaring system must be able to allow me to E-mail my colleagues as a group and automatically book the meeting time on the calendars of all staff who respond that the time suits them"; "The EDI system must return a confirmation to us when the supplier has successfully received our purchase order").

- Compatibility requirements ("We are currently using a UNIX mail system, and the new PC-based mail system on the new network must be able to successfully and transparently exchange mail with the existing UNIX network").

FIGURE 9–1

*Networked
system
requirements*

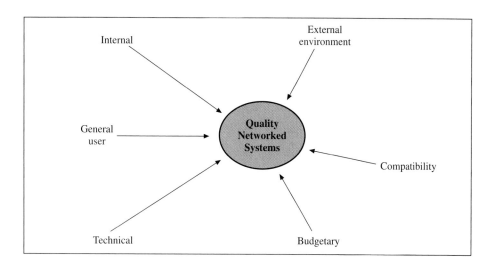

Simply put, system requirements are those characteristics that the new system must contain. Figure 9–1 summarizes these requirements. A number of concepts and techniques introduced in earlier chapters will be used in this chapter, and specific references to those concepts and techniques will be given as necessary.

The concepts we will cover in this chapter are a subset of the phases of a **systems development life cycle (SDLC)**. The full cycle moves through a process of

1. Problem investigation. *scope*
2. Analysis of system requirements. *business requirements*
3. Design of the proposed system. *Technical specs*
4. Implementation of the designed system. *architecture + infrastructure are built*
5. Operation and maintenance of the system. *feedback loop Evaluate + Revise*

In this chapter we will focus on the second phase, the analysis of system requirements. We will also look at portions of phase 4, the implementation phase, specifically procurement of hardware and software.

Since requirements analysis is the process of discovering, documenting, and communicating the network requirements, it is important that you review some previous models that will assist you in this process. Fundamentally, the process is one of communication, so first you should review the communication model covered in Chapter 8. Although this model was discussed in the context of improving communication effectiveness in the organization, it is very useful for discovering system requirements. In discovering the requirements of the proposed system a variety of methods may be used, including

1. Interviews with individual users and management.
2. Joint application design (JAD) with groups of users and management.
3. Distribution and analysis of questionnaires.

4. Gathering of pertinent organizational documents and discussing them with users and management.

5. Personal observation and discussions with staff.

In each of these cases, communication is an essential element in successfully uncovering the requirements of the proposed system. Each method will be used in some way in this chapter to assist in communicating requirements of a proposed network system.

Some key points to remember when reviewing the communication model are as follows:

- Be aware of noise in the communication: audio, visual, psychological, and electronic noise can all hinder the process of discovering and clarifying requirements.
- Watch out for differing viewpoints among participants in an interview or discussion, whether with an individual or in a group; self-centered viewpoints can be a real hindrance to effective communication of needs and requirements. In a group, the interaction among participants can be either a help or a hindrance in documenting needs of the system.
- Take advantage of the beneficial effects of feedback to clarify the communication and ensure the accuracy of the requirements discovered. Feedback may include

    Paraphrasing statements made by interview participants to verify understanding.

    Asking questions to request feedback when reviewing requirements documented by function decomposition diagrams, data models, and other methods.

    Asking questions about comments or statements made to clarify any underlying messages (those not stated directly in the message but implied by the tone of voice or hinted at).

    Written comments and suggestions on requirements documentation made by users and management.

Two of the methods mentioned earlier need further explanation: interviewing and JAD.

Interviewing.   *Interviewing* consists of structured discussion between the network system analyst/designer and users or managers of the organization. Often the interview is a one-on-one communication situation, although it may involve multiple users and/or analysts. A well-structured interviewing process should include the following major stages:

1. Preinterview preparation.
2. Introductions and overview.
3. Body of interview with questions, recording, and feedback.

4. Conclusion of the interview.

5. Review and follow-through after the interview.

Each of these stages has an important function in the process of requirements discovery, documentation, and communication.

The preinterview preparation is especially important, because it sets the stage and determines how effective the interview will be. If the analyst is well-prepared in advance, he or she will be able to conduct the interview with confidence. This, in turn, will tend to give users confidence in the process and make them more enthusiastic and cooperative. Some important steps to include in the preinterview preparation are as follows:

- Determine the objective of the interview, and communicate it clearly to the other participants.
- Arrange the schedule with the other participants, establishing the time, place, and duration of the meeting.
- Book the needed rooms and any required equipment.
- Prepare questions and recording instruments in advance.
- Decide in advance how you will approach feedback.
- Plan the environment for privacy, comfort, quiet, and effective use of appropriate equipment.
- Plan to dress appropriately for the meeting.

At the time of the meeting, the initial introductions and overview are key to establishing an appropriate atmosphere of friendliness and confidence. Greet the participant(s) and have a friendly but brief "ice breaker" conversation. Remind them about the objectives of the interview, the duration, and tasks to be covered.

During the body of the interview, control the direction by using appropriate questions and providing opportunities for clarification through feedback. Two major types of questions can be asked: open- and closed-end questions.

Open-end questions tend to produce lengthier responses and are useful for discovering opinions and attitudes or to lend a flow to the interview. Open-end questions may begin with *what*, *how*, and *why*. *Closed-end* questions tend to elicit very brief answers and are useful when simple facts are required. Such questions often begin with *who*, *when*, and *where* or with phrases such as "Do you...." or "Did they....," which often produce a simple *yes* or *no* answer. Keep in mind that the listener—the interviewer—controls the direction of the conversation. Most of the time, the analyst wants to discover the user's or manager's desires, needs, and requirements, not to express his or her own opinions or viewpoints.

Recording and feedback need to be planned in advance as well. The methods chosen will establish the type and quality of documentation produced from the process. Recording methods may include the following:

- *Questionnaires* can be sent to the users in advance and their responses clarified during the interview.

- *Data modeling techniques* such as E-R diagrams give a pictorial representation of the data requirements of the network applications. The user can more easily understand diagrams and provide effective feedback on them.

- *Decomposition diagrams* provide a good graphical representation of the functional requirements of the proposed system.

- *Annotated LAN and WAN network diagrams* are useful for capturing hardware and other technical requirements.

- Additional methods that have not been covered in this text include data flow diagrams (DFDs), action diagrams, and other tools used by systems analysts.

Try to avoid taking lengthy notes while the user is talking, since this will tend to hinder the flow of the interview. The diagramming techniques just listed tend to capture more information in a more structured way, thus providing greater opportunities for feedback than straight note-taking.

At the conclusion of the interview, you should follow a few key steps:

- Review the tasks accomplished and compare them to the agenda and objectives established at the beginning of the interview.

- If a follow-up interview is necessary, establish a date and a time.

FIGURE 9–2

The interviewing process

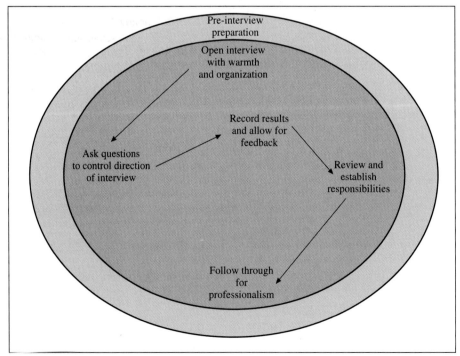

- If any tasks need to be completed before the next meeting, clearly establish responsibilities among the participants.
- Thank everyone for contributing their valuable time and talents to a successful meeting.

After the interview is completed, it is important to review the results and follow through on agreed-on tasks.

1. Review all documentation from the interview and edit it to include corrections and modifications made as a result of feedback from participants. If diagrams were hand-drawn during the meeting, convert them into machine-supportable form using appropriate CASE tools or diagramming application software. This should be done within 24 hours, while information is still fresh in your mind.

2. Complete all items agreed to as soon as possible.

3. Communicate with participants in writing, providing them with any material promised during the meeting. This communication should also be used to document the results of the meeting and remind everyone of their responsibilities as well as the time, place, purpose, and duration of the next meeting. Thank everyone again for their valuable participation.

Jod facilitator is key component for succeeding or failing

Joint Application Design (JAD). **Joint application design (JAD)** is a method that is typically used to compress the calendar time involved in analysis of requirements and design of the system. The approach uses group sessions in place of conducting multiple interviews with individual users. JAD is fundamentally a structured group interview that typically consists of a trained JAD facilitator, multiple users and managers, and support analyst(s) to capture and display requirements on CASE tools during the meeting.

The JAD approach typically speeds up the final development and implementation of the proposed system, while at the same time providing considerable user input in a way that reduces errors arising from the different viewpoints of the various stakeholders in the proposed system. Having the group sessions allows users to state their viewpoints while encouraging other users to clarify different and sometimes contradictory needs. It is important that the participants in the JAD session(s) have both the authority to decide on system requirements and the detailed knowledge to make informed decisions. This method tends to remove ambiguous requirements, produce more clearly stated and organizationally appropriate requirements, and produce group consensus on the overall needs of the system.

JAD sessions require a trained facilitator to handle the group dynamics that can produce negative results if not successfully managed. Group dynamics can lead to the following problems:

- The group makes decisions without reference to outside sources of information, believing their own judgment is infallible.

- Groups tend to make riskier decisions than the individual members would make if they were exclusively responsible for the outcomes of the decisions. Groups allow diffusion of blame for negative outcomes.
- Individuals may tend to remain silent even when they disagree due to apparent consensus, with other participants also remaining silent over disputed points or requirements. This is especially a problem when one strong individual dominates the group.
- Individuals may agree to accept requirements or perform tasks because of fear of embarrassment, peer pressure, or loss of face even though they do not really want to.[1]

A trained and experienced JAD facilitator is often able to overcome some of these difficulties by moderating strong individuals, keeping the meeting on the task at hand, drawing out the shier group members, and generally maintaining an open and honest atmosphere.

In addition to the facilitator, the JAD method relies on informed and responsible users who are willing and able to discuss their requirements with other users and managers and to reach consensus. JAD may not succeed in a situation where users are unable to meet these criteria.

The remainder of this section covers specific system requirements. As we discuss these areas, keep in mind the communications skills just covered. Note that specification of requirements is undertaken after a problem has been identified and investigated or in response to a specific strategic requirement that is part of the corporate strategic plan.

Internal and External Requirements

Internal and external requirements apply to the general environment in which the proposed network system will be installed. Internal requirements deal with the organization's policies and practices and the concerns of management. External requirements involve the factors outside the organization such as competitors, customers, suppliers, the general economy, and government decisions. A variety of methods are helpful in uncovering these requirements. In this section we review two methods: SWOT analysis from Chapter 1 and critical success factors from Chapter 6.

Recall that SWOT analysis involves strengths and weaknesses, which are basically internal considerations, and opportunities and threats, which are basically external considerations. This technique can highlight environmental requirements for the proposed network. The SWOT analysis technique may be applied in a group meeting with management or users to discover requirements for the proposed network system. Figure 9–3 shows a series of questions and possible requirements that might come to light as a result of using this technique.

---

[1] M. C. Kettelhut, "JAD Methodology and Group Dynamics," *Information Systems Management*, Winter 1993, pp. 46–53.

FIGURE 9–3

SWOT analysis for discovering internal and external requirements

SWOT	Questions	Possible Requirements
Strengths	How can our reputation for quality products be enhanced by the new network system? How can we use the new network system to capitalize on our good customer relations?	The proposed system must provide online defect information capture on the factory floor, with this information being made available to quality, design, and manufacturing engineers. The new system must be able to give customers dial-up, secure, read-only access to our inventory system to assist them in sales planning.
Weaknesses	In what ways can our poor employee relations be improved by the new network? Can the proposed network help lower our traditionally high manufacturing costs without lowering quality?	An intuitive GUI is required of the new system to provide a low learning curve for staff. Easy group access to standard document templates to reduce staff workload is required of the networked word processor chosen. The proposed system must provide an integrated system for sales order processing, manufacture to order, raw material stock control, and rapid purchase ordering to support a JIT system.
Opportunities	In what ways may the new network be used to take advantage of the increasingly open border with Canada and Mexico? How will the proposed network system help us take advantage of a competitor's slower than average delivery to customers?	The new system must provide transparent WAN and LAN communication for E-mail and file transfer across multiple hardware platforms, including PCs and UNIX networks, which are proliferating in Canada and Mexico. The proposed system must allow telephone orders to input directly to the computer with online verification of creditworthiness and inventory availability. Automatic picking lists must be generated by the system, with a maximum 24-hour turnaround from order reception to order shipment.
Threats	How can the network system assist in dealing with the recent merger of two major competitiors? In what ways can the network be used to combat the higher-quality, lower-priced products coming from a Japanese competitor?	The new system must be built on international standards and be sufficiently flexible to allow ready data transfer with potential strategic partners in North America, Europe, or Australasia. The new network must actively support automation and dissemination of existing quality programs aimed at continuous improvement of flexible manufacturing processes.

The types of requirements SWOT analysis can reveal may vary quite markedly from precise detailed requirements on the use of data and functionality to very general statements of desire for improvement. To directly benefit the final design and implementation of the proposed system, the requirements will ultimately need to be rather detailed. Requirements that are too general will need to be clarified through additional analysis, questions, and refinement.

A second useful method for discovering internal and external requirements is the use of critical success factors (CSFs), first introduced in conjunction with internal and external factors in Chapter 6. This method may be used in a variety of ways to discover and document requirements. One way is to list the CSFs of the organization as a whole and then, in a fashion similar to the SWOT analysis, ask what network system requirements are brought to light as a result of the CSFs. A second approach is to ask, "What factors are critical to the success of the proposed network system internally and externally?" We will use both of these approaches to demonstrate the usefulness of this method.

Building on the strategic analysis viewpoint presented in Chapter 6, an organization may have CSFs arising from various areas, including

- The structure of the industry.
- The competitive strategy of the firm.
- The company's current competitive positioning in the industry.
- Actions of competitors.
- Geographical location.
- The level of the general economy.
- Government actions.
- Flow of raw materials, energy, and other key resources.
- Time-related factors.

Figure 9–4 lists various CSFs relating to a range of companies and industries, together with network system requirements that could arise as a result of these CSFs. These examples are largely drawn from Figure 6–4 in Chapter 6.

As mentioned earlier, the second approach to using CSFs is to ask, "What factors are critical to the success of the proposed network system internally and externally?" The following scenario illustrates this approach.

RICHEY MANUFACTURING COMPANY, INC.

Richey Manufacturing Company, Inc., has been operating successfully for over 40 years. The company's growth was slow during most of that time, but over the last five years growth has been spectacular, including the takeover last year of two competitors (now subsidiaries) who had gotten into difficulties. To accommodate future growth, Richey's managing director has decided that a networked system must be implemented to strengthen

FIGURE 9–4

Network requirements to meet organizational CSFs

Critical Success Factor	Network System Requirement
Two CSFs for the supermarket industry are product mix and inventory levels.	The proposed system must ensure rapid, error-free data input via POS terminals with barcode readers connected with a LAN to a stock management and replenishment system to allow improved stock management and maintenance of a proper product mix.
A company's competitive strategy may be "lowest price," so a CSF will be a high level of cost control.	The new networked system must provide automatic generation of purchase orders and sales invoices with electronic delivery (EDI) whenever possible to reduce costly manual processing and errors.
A small firm in a service industry competing against larger firms may have very high-quality service at very competitive prices as a CSF.	The proposed system must allow direct organizational contact with field service personnel via alphanumeric pagers and voice mail to allow more timely, quality service while enhancing staff productivity.
A company participating in an industry characterized by rapid innovation may have the need to be highly sensitive to customers' changing product needs as a CSF.	The new networked system must provide field salespeople with the capability to survey customer preferences on a continuous basis and electronically communicate these data to the marketing department on a daily basis in machine-readable form.

communications with over 20 branch stores, three manufacturing facilities, and the head office. The system must also be able to facilitate communication and control of the two new subsidiaries. One subsidiary has a UNIX network in place to support a range of functions in the organization. The other subsidiary has a Novell network of PCs running various applications under Microsoft Windows. In addition, the system must maintain and strengthen the existing good relationships with the many small suppliers, many of whom use PCs in their business but are relatively unsophisticated computer users.

What are the critical success factors of the proposed system for Richey? A number of CSFs are evident in the above scenario, each pointing to requirements that should be incorporated into the system:

- The system must incorporate WAN facilities to allow data access among stores, factory facilities, the head office, and the two new subsidiaries.
- The system must support cross-platform communication since the two subsidiaries have diverse hardware and software platforms in place (UNIX in one and Novell/Windows/PCs in the other).
- Since communication is a key factor mentioned, cross-platform E-mail is one important application to consider.
- The importance of supplier relationships indicates that another factor critical to the success of the system would be the provision of a user-friendly GUI for supplier interaction.

The next section focuses on budgetary and technical requirements that need to be included in the proposed system to ensure satisfactory performance of the system in its intended function and over its useful life.

Budgetary and Technical Requirements

Two major stumbling blocks that sometimes cause network and other system projects to fail to deliver the benefits promised are budgetary and technical requirements. Inadequate budgetary controls over the development and acquisition of TBIT systems can cause serious cost overruns with no perceived increase in projected benefits. Such inattention to budgetary requirements and failure to deliver promised benefits has caused some CEOs to demand reorganization of the IT function in their firms and enforcement of management and cost controls in the IT function.[2] At the same time, with the increased emphasis on user requirements, the technical requirements of the system may be overshadowed. Requirements analysis must consider each major category to ensure success of the final delivered system.

Budgetary Requirements.   Establishing budgetary requirements may include the following approaches:

- Estimating techniques to determine the expected costs of the system.
- Control techniques to measure progress of the project on a budget versus actual basis as development and implementation proceed.
- Analysis methods for establishing priority among projects competing for limited capital investment dollars and for selecting among alternative vendor proposals.

This section focuses on the first two approaches, estimating and control techniques. The third approach, analysis methods for setting priorities and selecting vendors, will be addressed in Chapter 10.

The most obvious budgetary requirement is to establish a budget, or an estimate of the costs involved in the proposed project. A number of modeling techniques used in earlier chapters are useful in discussing and analyzing this area as well. It has been estimated that for major new projects, many large organizations consider only 25 percent of the total costs of the system. The remaining 75 percent are hidden costs, which, if known in advance, may cause management to reconsider the nature or scope of the system project.[3] Use of the five-component model, functional decomposition, and association matrices can be quite helpful in covering the major cost components. In determining user requirements (discussed later in this chapter) and proposed system functionality, decomposition diagrams may be used to document explicit hierarchical relationships in the proposed system and provide a basis for assessing the hardware, software, data, people, and procedural costs involved in delivering the system. These costs should be budgeted over the expected useful life of the system, typically three to five years in today's rapidly changing business environment. A table comparing expected user functional requirements to the five-component model, such as that in Figure 9–5, allows establishment of the major elements and cost categories involved.

---

[2] M. J. Earl, "Putting IT in Its Place: A Polemic for the Nineties," *Journal of Information Technology* 7 (1992), pp. 100–8.

[3] P. G. W. Keen, *Shaping the Future: Business Design through Information Technology* (Cambridge, MA: Harvard Business School Press, 1991), pp. 141–78.

FIGURE 9–5

Network functionality and the five-component model

User Functional Requirements	Five-Component Model Elements
1. The system must provide transparent and low learning curve internal E-mail to every user's desk. A total of 25 information workers will be users.	Hardware: 25 Windows-capable workstations/terminals with appropriate network electronics. Network cabling and installation. Network file server. Appropriate printing facilities. There must also be an allowance for growth. Software: E-mail software running in a Windows environment under Microsoft Windows NT, Apple Macintosh System 7.0, or a UNIX-based windowing environment. Data: Data are user created, with no additional costs beyond those of the existing manual system. People: No additional staff will be required beyond the existing system support staff now employed. Procedures: All staff will need to attend two half-day training seminars. Costs of seminar and loss of staff time must be included in costing. Systems operations staff estimate that 40 labor hours will be required, spread over one month to learn, install, and make operational the E-mail system. It is further estimated that another 40 labor hours will be used in responding to user queries over the first month of training.
2. The proposed network system must provide external E-mail, E-fax, file transfer, and access to external foreign exchange and news service databases.	Hardware: In addition to the 25 workstations and file server mentioned in item 1, a high-speed modem or X.25 connection will be required. Traffic levels must be established to determine number and type of modems or connections needed. Software: Server software to provide multiuser external access to databases as well as store and forward server software for E-mail, E-fax, and file transfer. Data: Data are user created with no additional costs beyond those of the existing manual system. People: No additional staff will be required beyond the existing system support staff now employed. Procedures: In addition to procedural costs of item 1, all staff will need to attend three half-day training seminars. Costs of seminar and loss of staff time must be included in costing. Systems operations staff estimate that 50 labor hours will be required, spread over two months to learn, install, and make operational the external E-mail, E-fax, file transfer, and access to external databases. It is further estimated that another 30 labor hours will be used in responding to user queries over the first month of training. This is on the assumption that the E-mail system of item 1 is installed first and staff has the experience with it to build on.
3. The proposed system must provide an inventory control system, giving appropriate access to all 25 users for response to customer and supplier queries as well as purchasing, shipping, receiving, and stock control needs.	Hardware: No additional hardware is required beyond the requirements of items 1 and 2. Care must be given, however, to appropriate configuration of network file server for disk size, backup requirements, memory, and response time. There must be an appropriate allowance for future growth. Software: Multiuser inventory control software capable of delivering needed functionality and security control. An off-the-shelf package is preferred, if available; otherwise a modified package or custom software is necessary. Data: All existing manual inventory data will need to be converted to electronic data, and temporary staff will need to be hired to key and verify data. People: One additional staff member will be needed to oversee the inventory control system, with hiring, salary, and benefits costs over the life of the system included in the costing. Procedures: Staff will need to attend two half-day training seminars. Costs of seminar and loss of staff time must be included in costing. Systems operations staff estimate that 60 labor hours will be required, spread over one month to learn, install, test, and make operational an off-the-shelf inventory control package. An additional 40 labor hours should be budgeted for conversion of existing manual records. It is further estimated that another 30 labor hours will be used in responding to user queries over the first three months of use.

The second approach is the use of control techniques to measure progress of the project on a budget versus actual basis as development and implementation proceed. These techniques are typically referred to as *project control techniques* and will be discussed only briefly here, with further consideration in the section "Creating a Network Implementation Plan." The primary techniques are (1) budgeting reports of estimated versus actual costs, (2) the project evaluation and review technique (PERT) method, (3) the critical path method (CPM), and (4) Gantt charts. All four of these approaches may be used to help control a project, and software products are available that will integrate all or some of the features of these methods under both text-based operating environments and GUIs. In dealing directly with budgetary requirements, however, the budget reporting and CPM techniques are probably the most useful where a direct relationship between resource expenditures and tasks can be established.[4]

In budgetary reporting, categories of costs are established and amounts and dates of disbursements are estimated using techniques such as the five-component model discussed earlier. In an automated budgeting system, actual amounts and dates would be input as data to the system and regular reports would be generated to determine variations from the budget. For items that cost more than projected, adjustments might be made in other cost categories to bring the project back into line with the overall budget. As the project proceeds, the project manager will continually monitor both the resource usage and time to keep the project within the budget originally approved by management.

Technical Requirements.   Technical requirements of the proposed network system may fall into a variety of categories, including

- Compatibility and connectivity requirements for interface with existing systems.
- Network traffic loading requirements, which will affect the response time and costs of operating the network.
- System storage requirements, disk sizes, and memory requirements.
- System expandability or scalability.

We will look at the first of the above technical requirements categories later in this chapter. The remaining items are discussed next.

One area of technical requirements is network traffic loading. This involves both the LAN and WAN traffic that may occur over the network. In the case of the LAN, consideration of the type of data being transported over the network will indicate the amount of traffic likely to occur. Where large quantities of graphical data will be transported, or where a large number of workstations with multiple file servers will be running, the traffic may prove to be sufficiently high to require a bridge, a router, or other hardware to separate the LAN into multiple logical LANs, with

---

[4] M. J. Power, P. H. Cheney, and G. Crow, *Structured Systems Development* (Boston: Boyd and Fraser Publishing, 1990), pp. 59–74.

traffic crossing only from one to the other where the data are specifically addressed to a workstation on the other side of the bridge. Such technical requirements should be considered in advance so that all components of the LAN can be appropriately budgeted for. In the case of WAN traffic, a consideration is the number of incoming/outgoing lines and the nature of those lines. The cost varies among dial-up, X.25 packet switching, leased data lines, frame relay, and ISDN lines. The type of data, quantity of data, distance over which data are to be transported, and the frequency of use of the lines will all affect the cost and choice of appropriate media. If multiple real-time connections will be needed—for example, access to external databases or real-time teleconferencing—multiple lines or multiplexed lines may be necessary. This is less likely if the WAN is being used only for E-fax, E-mail, or file transfer, since these applications typically work in a "store-and-forward" mode, in which data are sent when the line becomes free.

Another area of technical requirements is system data storage. This is especially crucial when configuring the network file server in a LAN. When deciding on the size of the disk drives for the system, consideration must be given to storage of system files, application program files, and data files. Given the increasing use of windows- and graphics-based applications, where the files sizes are quite large, it is now common for even small LAN disk drives to be 1 to 2 gigabytes or larger. When calculating the size of drives necessary, it is important to allow for considerable space capacity, since the demands on the system once it is in use will tend to be considerably higher than original estimates.

Because of this tendency toward growing usage once the system is operational, the scalability of the system is another important technical consideration. Essentially *scalability* refers to the ability of the system to grow with the organization's needs. In its simplest form, this means the ability to add additional disk drives and RAM to an existing network file server. Beyond that, it could include such options as

- Adding a dedicated database server to remove this function from the general-purpose file server.
- Upgrading the CPU in the file server to a faster processor or multiple processors, if this is where bottlenecks occur.
- Adding additional file servers to the network to partition the workload along departmental lines using bridges/routers to control interserver traffic across the network.
- Upgrading the file server to a high-powered, multiprocessor superserver without needing to change the other system components (software, data, people, or procedures).

Each of these technical considerations may have a marked effect on the system's performance and needs to be given sufficient attention so that the technical aspects of the system do not become a failure point for the system as a whole.

The technical requirements also provide a foundation on which to successfully deliver the functionality the users require of the system, the topic of the next section.

User Requirements

Discovering, documenting, and communicating the needs of the organization involve both the somewhat broader issues previously addressed on internal and external requirements as well as the details that affect individual users. The specific requirements of users may be discovered using a more traditional, very structured approach or a more iterative prototyping approach. In either case, the methods used to discover, document, and communicate the users' needs will involve the communication skills discussed at the beginning of the chapter. The more traditional approach is often used in larger projects where the analyst conducts a thorough study of the existing system to gain an understanding of the current environment. Then interviews are conducted with users to find out weaknesses in the existing system and additional requirements desired in the new or modified system. This more traditional approach is useful if the existing system is doing a fairly good job already but requires enhancement. However, if the existing system is totally failing to deliver the expected results, it may be a waste of time to do a thorough study of the existing system, and the time may be better spent finding out what users want in a new system.[5]

The prototyping method is more often used with smaller systems and involves an iterative approach, creating a working model of the system to assist in obtaining user feedback. Then the prototype is quickly modified to meet the new requirements. Because the prototype is a working model, users can sit down at a computer or terminal and try the system out to see how it fits their needs, test input and output formats, test dialogues, and generally determine whether the analyst has accurately converted the users' requirements into the working model. With some prototyping tools, the working model may ultimately become part of the delivered system; this is the "keep" type of prototype. With other prototyping tools, the prototype may serve its purpose by accurately capturing user needs and feedback. Such a prototype is used to provide information for the design of the system, but is not used as part of the system; instead, it is disposed of after design. Caution is necessary when using the prototyping approach to ensure that sufficient controls are implemented in the development process to prevent the addition of unplanned enhancements and functionality that were not approved or budgeted for simply because "it is so easy to do." Such uncontrolled development and multiple iterations can make a project run considerably over budget without management approval.

Often a valuable hybrid of these two methods, together with JAD sessions, can shorten the development time and increase the accuracy of the requirements discovered. With the hybrid method, user requirements are discovered using modeling techniques such as data modeling, decomposition diagrams, DFDs, and other tools. The first prototypes are built based on the requirements discovered during the modeling exercise and then act as a basis for further refinement of the users' requirements.

Regardless of the general approach taken, some of the key requirements that need to be gathered from the users will include

---

[5] C. S. Parker and T. Case, *Management Information Systems—Strategy and Action* (New York: McGraw-Hill,1993), pp. 598–642.

- Fundamental outputs required of the system: report formats, online queries, format of display for E-mail, and the ability to send a copy to the printer. Documentation may use decomposition diagrams, prototypes, report layout forms, and detailed functional descriptions.

- Inputs to the system: documentation may consist of data models, screen layout forms, prototypes, and decomposition diagrams, as well as copies of existing paper forms.

- User interfaces: documentation may include menu hierarchies, user prompts, description of help facilities, prototypes, mouse support descriptions, and function key standards for use of applications.

- Processes and functionality required: additional requirements may be documented for processes and further functionality, including action diagrams, data flow diagrams, process flow diagrams, and/or association matrices to establish security-level access to different applications by various staff members.

In the process of discovering user requirements, it is important for the analyst to interview a wide cross-section of the user community. If only a few users give input to the requirements, even if they are knowledgeable users, the system may omit important requirements of some groups of stakeholders. It is equally important that the user requirements be measured against some standard so that the system that is delivered actually meets the requirements of the business! A good standard against which to measure detailed user requirements are the objectives and CSFs of the business. If the requirements being specified by the users are on target toward fulfilling those objectives and CSFs, those requirements are on track.[6] If this standard of comparison is not followed, the system may fail to meet the organization's needs.

Often users' viewpoints will conflict. Such conflicts are a natural outgrowth of the users' differing tasks and responsibilities and will need to be resolved through discussion, hopefully resulting in a more comprehensive view of the requirements. If this approach doesn't work, the analysis team may need to appeal to higher management for resolution.

Compatibility and Connectivity Requirements

If the organization already has some networked systems in place, compatibility and connectivity requirements need to be addressed. Both of these concepts deal with the ability of the proposed systems or enhancements to be integrated with the existing networks. The level of integration required determines whether the focus is on compatibility or connectivity.

Compatibility is the ability of the proposed system to work directly with the existing system without special attention or modification. An example of a compatibility requirement is: "The proposed JIT system must be deliverable over our existing

---

[6] J. L. Whitten, L. D. Bentley, and V. M. Barlow, *Systems Analysis and Design Methods* (Homewood, IL: Richard D. Irwin, 1989), pp. 136–66.

Novell/Ethernet network using existing PCs as user workstations." This statement makes it clear that the software acquired for the JIT function must be compatible with the existing software and hardware base.

Connectivity is the ability of the proposed system to communicate with existing systems, but not necessarily be compatible with them. For example, an organization may have an existing UNIX network in place at the head office, and a new departmental network is being proposed for a sales office some miles away from the head office. The proposed network is based on a peer-to-peer network system using Microsoft Windows 95 and Ethernet hardware configuration. A connectivity requirement raised by head office systems staff might be: "The proposed sales office network must be able to communicate effectively with the head office UNIX mail system." The question of connectivity has several dimensions. It may be concluded that the proposed system will have gateway software that will allow satisfactory E-mail communication between the two systems. However, the head office systems staff may also require that the proposed system "make it possible for a workstation on the sales office system to sign on as a dial-up client to the UNIX system and act as a fully supported terminal at the home office." Here we see two levels of connectivity, one possibly being harder to achieve than the other.

Figure 9–6 uses the Open Systems Interconnect (OSI) seven-layer model to compare the issues of compatibility and connectivity. Compatibility typically encompasses a broader range and is more difficult to achieve than connectivity, which may encompass only five or fewer layers of the model.

Beyond understanding the requirements for compatibility and connectivity is the issue of the desired level of integration. It is one thing to say that there should be a minimum level of connectivity for all new systems and another thing to say that all new systems must be compatible with existing systems. Organizationwide issues such as the following need to be considered:

FIGURE 9–6

Using the OSI model to illustrate connectivity versus compatibility

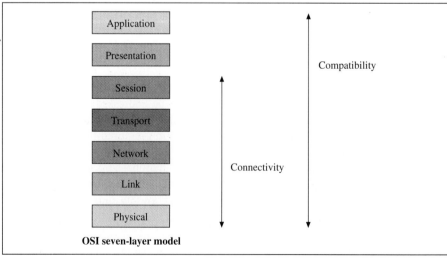

  × 1. Development of a strategic hardware/software platform to allow a high
      level of organizational integration, cross-functional training, and
      maximization of staff training and transfer opportunities.

  × 2. Staying with a standard configuration for all new systems when that
      configuration has become dated and is no longer able to serve
      organizational needs.

  × 3. Centralization versus decentralization of decision making for
      information systems and its impact on the competitive position of the
      organization.

Requirements of compatibility and connectivity are both organizational and technical requirements that affect the maintenance cost structures of network systems and the integration of organizational functions. These requirements can significantly affect the overall performance of the networked systems and the fulfillment of user requirements, which is the focus of the next section.

Network Performance Standards and Fulfillment of User Requirements

A major area of concern for users is the requirements regarding performance of the network system. Performance from the users' viewpoint is often measured by *response time*, system *reliability*, and system *recoverability*. This section addresses these three aspects of network performance and the standards needed to fulfill user requirements in these areas.

Response Time on the Network *client-to-server-to-client*

Bandwidth measures Response time w/ an inverse ratio

Response time refers to the time a user must wait when making a request, typing a character, or sending a command to the system until the system responds. Response times over LANs may vary from sub-one-second times under normal conditions to tens of minutes on an overloaded system. Response times over WANs will also vary depending on the nature of the communication, distance to the host, host loadings, and transaction levels. *How long it takes for client to receive answer*

User performance standards in the area of response time can be identified in a similar fashion to other requirements: using interviews, conducting JAD sessions, working with prototypes, observing existing systems, and asking questions about expectations regarding the new system. To be meaningful, the concept of response time must be used in conjunction with specific applications. Figure 9–7 lists some examples of response time performance standards for specific applications. The standards are intended as examples and are not necessarily prescriptive for every organization. Some users may insist on sub-one-second response time from transaction-processing systems and require "chat mode" from E-mail, which provides "instant E-mail" rather than the more typical "store-and-forward" variety.

FIGURE 9–7

Potential response times for specific network applications

Specific Application	Potential Response Time Standard
Networked word processor run from a PC workstation on a LAN	Sub-one-second response
Online transaction-processing system run from a terminal on a centralized system	Multisecond response
E-mail run over a LAN with WAN connections	Sub-one-second response to accept the message
	Multisecond to minutes response to deliver mail to addressee (typical store-and-forward E-mail is delivered when the system has a break, having low priority in the processing queue). However, the sender may not be aware of any delay unless waiting for a reply.
	Multisecond to hours or days for response from addressee, depending on when addressee checks his or her mail.
External database located on another continent	Multisecond response time due to distance and possible system loading

Estimating response time for individual transaction and application types and then investigating ways to improve the anticipated performance in those areas where it falls below the standard are important parts of the process of gathering requirements and ensuring that they are met. The major elements in estimating response time are (1) the time required to process a transaction, (2) disk access time, (3) CPU time, and (4) data communications time. Each of these elements may be modified to improve system performance. The automated procedure used to process the transaction and the efficiency of the computer code may be modified to enhance performance. Installing faster disk drives or running a defragmentation program to make the disk more efficient could relieve a bottleneck at this point. Acquiring a faster processor for the file server or moving from a slow 2,400 bps dial-up modem to a high-speed X.25 packet-switched or ISDN communications line is another way to improve response time when it appears that the response time in the proposed system will be below user requirements.

Reliability of the Network

Reliability standards for a network deal with the extent to which users can rely on the system to be functional when they need it. Even if all of the user's functional requirements are met, if the system is "down" frequently, overall user requirements will not be fulfilled. In situations where the system may be down occasionally, manual procedures must be in place to allow the organization to continue to function while the system is out of operation. Consider the following scenario.

FIGURE 9–8

On target to network performance standards

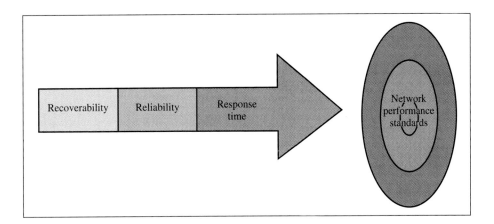

WORLD WIDE AIRLINES

As Tom Krantz stood in line at the airport ticket counter waiting to check in and get his boarding pass, he was thinking about the business meeting he would be attending that afternoon. Finally, it was his turn. The agent took Tom's ticket and began to key in a few details. Then she said, "Oh, we'll have to wait a moment, the system is down. This doesn't happen very often anymore, maybe once every few months." A minute later the agent said, "There we go," and finished issuing Tom's boarding pass.

As Tom walked away from the ticket counter, he recalled a similar incident about five years ago. On that occasion, the agent had announced to everyone on line, "You had all better come back in 15 minutes, the system is down again." Then he passed out numbers to allow the passengers to regain their proper place in line. As Tom left to get a cup of coffee, he overheard the exasperated agent muttering that this was the second time this week. When Tom returned 15 minutes later, the system was still down and didn't begin to function normally for another 10 minutes on that occasion. Advancing technology has resolved one more of life's little hassles, Tom thought as he headed for gate 17 and his important business meeting.

In the above scenario, the airline has clearly made considerable progress in the reliability of its system. It has implemented manual procedures to allow the system to continue operating, notifying the passengers affected of the likely duration of the delay in processing, and providing a procedure to minimize their inconvenience. In five years, system failures have dropped from several times per week lasting 15 to 30 minutes to only once every few months for only a minute or so. The difference in passenger inconvenience (and therefore the airline's market share) must be substantial.

What are key performance standards in this area of reliability? Figure 9–9 lists some of the more failure-prone components, useful performance standards that an organization might use for those components, and system requirements to assist in achieving the standards. Many of the key aspects of network reliability are related to mechanical components of the system as well as to electrical conditions around the network. A reliable power source also needs to be considered as a system component. This is especially important for international networks to countries that lack reliable power supplies.

In recent years, the reliability of networks has improved for a variety of reasons:

- Higher levels of miniaturization of electronic components means fewer connections between the chips and boards that make up the electronics of the system. This results in fewer failure points and much improved reliability.
- Underground cabling to replace cables suspended on poles prevents wind and storm damage as well as accidental damage from vehicles. (However, line failures can still occur if construction equipment cuts through an underground cable.)
- Better shielding for cabling protects data signals from electrical disturbances in the environment.
- Longer-life disk drives with fault-tolerant, disk-mirroring, or **redundant array of inexpensive disks** (RAID) technology can help overcome individual disk failures.
- "Smarter" operating systems can support the hardware improvements noted above.

The final area of network performance that we will discuss is recoverability of the network. This area is very closely related to reliability, and concepts applicable to one area may be readily applied to the other.

FIGURE 9–9

Network reliability performance standards

System Component	Performance Standard	System Requirements to Achieve Standard
WAN communication lines	The WAN lines are required to be available 100 percent of the time.	Multiple leased lines or sharing arrangements with a number of other companies to share one another's leased lines if there is a line failure.
Hard disk drives	The LAN network file server disk drives must be available 100 percent of the time.	The use of disk mirroring (using two sets of hard disks), one being backed up to the other on a real-time basis. If one fails the other takes over immediately, and the system notifies the network administrator.
		The use of RAID (Redundant Array of Inexpensive Disks) technology accomplishes a similar task to disk mirroring at a lower cost.
Network file server	The network file server must be able to be replaced within five minutes of failure.	The use of a backup server that is maintained in a ready state with disk drives and is updated regularly with current data. If the main server fails, it is a simple matter of unplugging a master cable from the main server and plugging into the backup server to reboot the system. It may be necessary for users to login to the system over again.

Recoverability of the Network

Even when network system standards are established to ensure reliability and fulfillment of technical requirements, it is still necessary to make provision for worst-case scenarios. Disasters do strike companies, cities, and countries. It is important that some provision be made to recover from a disaster, be it a localized fire or a regional hurricane or earthquake. Designing standards and requirements for **recoverability** help to ensure organizational survival, whereas the lack of such standards may doom the organization. Recoverability standards are closely related to reliability standards and have much in common with them.

The primary focus for recoverability is the process of system backup. *Backup* basically refers to making copies of the organization's data and of systems and applications software and then storing the copies in a disaster-proof vault in a different location. If the company headquarters, including the computers and network components, are destroyed by fire, the company can begin to operate out of temporary facilities as soon as it can acquire backup hardware. Assuming key employees are still available, it is then a matter of loading the software and data onto the hardware and starting up the operation. Many organizations operate network systems that are referred to as "mission critical." This means that without the system the organization cannot operate, and the longer the system is out of action, the less likely it is that the organization will recover. Under these circumstances, it may be necessary to provide complete backup facilities, including trained personnel, computer hardware and network components, software, and data, all ready to go in case of disaster. A good example of this is the Cathay Pacific example from Chapter 1, which is replicated below.

> Thus, when an airline's central reservations system (CRS) is down, the airline is nonfunctional and the competitive strategy becomes meaningless. For example, in August 1991, fire took out the power supply to Cathay Pacific's computers, which run 90 mission-critical applications and process 40 to 50 transactions per second. It took 13 hours to bring the backup system into operation at Kai Tak airport, and three additional Unisys 9740 disk drives had to be flown from the United States. The cost of this failure has not been estimated, but could run into tens of millions of dollars in lost revenues. Cathay Pacific was pleased that all mission-critical applications were shifted so quickly from the main computer center in Quarry Bay to the backup site at Kai Tak airport, in line with its disaster recovery plan.

Even though Cathay Pacific had a disaster recovery plan, it incurred a significant cost. However, it did recover from this disaster, and in only 13 hours! The provision of a backup site provides the ultimate in backup. In most smaller organizations, which may run a LAN with 5 to 20 PCs and some external WAN communications, the organization's data are what must be protected to allow recovery. Key performance standards for recoverability might include those listed in Figure 9–10.

When considering the areas of reliability and recoverability, keep in mind that the steps involved must be taken in context. The costs of the measures must be compared to the risks involved. Where the risk of loss is low or the results of loss of data would not be catastrophic, less costly procedures may prove sufficiently effective.

FIGURE 9–10

Network recoverability standards

Type of Disaster	Performance Standard	System Requirements to Achieve Standard
Hard disk failure	Ability to recover from a disaster within 24 hours.	Regular backup procedures with tested restoration procedures Offsite storage of data on a regular basis Three-generation backup process
Failure of external power supply due to severed cable or storm damage to main power supply	In the event of a local or major power failure, the system must be able to continue in operation for a half-hour and to shut down in a controlled fashion if necessary.	Use of an uninterruptible power supply (UPS) to ensure availability of power for a limited period. A UPS consists of a line voltage smoothing device and a large, rechargeable battery. The computer system is plugged into the UPS all the time, and if the power fails the UPS continues to supply electricity until the battery runs flat. Depending on the UPS, this may be 10 minutes or up to hours unless a backup power generator is available.
Failure of telecommunications lines due to construction workers severing cable	Ability to reestablish telecommunications functions within two hours.	This could include arranging for shared use of another company's leased line on an emergency basis, installation of a second (possibly redundant) leased line, or arrangement for use of a microwave or satellite connection in emergencies.
Destruction of total information center or computing facilities due to fire, storm, explosion, or other uncontrollable event	Ability to restore information system to functionality on critical applications within 12 hours.	This would require a comprehensive plan, including requirements for effective data backup with offsite storage; available backup hardware of same configuration as main system, perhaps used for noncritical applications at another company site, with appropriate telecommunications facilities; cross-trained personnel able to perform duties effectively for critical applications.
System software corrupted by a computer virus	The system software must be effectively protected from corruption electronically or by computer virus.	Requirements could include provision of a UPS that also "conditions" the incoming power, preventing damage by power surges, etc.; real-time virus detection and correction software that is updated regularly for new strains of virus.

However, where the risk of loss is high and loss could mean the termination of the company, considerably more stringent precautions are justified. Other precautions that can be taken to assist in this area are

- Physical security for the organization's computing facilities, including appropriate locks, identification of employees, fire sprinklers, waterproof file and data storage areas, and possibly even blastproof doors in some areas.

- Insurance for data loss, facilities damage, and business interruption coverage, which may provide additional protection from financial loss and badly needed cash flow during a disaster.
- A thorough and tested disaster recovery plan.

Disaster recovery and risk assessment are covered in further detail in Chapter 11.

Creating a Network Implementation Plan

In this section, we will cover the process of creating a plan to implement a network system and how to justify the plan in terms of organizational priorities and strategic plans. The concepts of creating a plan were first introduced in Chapter 1 when we looked at the process of strategic planning. We noted that the organization must create a tactical plan, or blueprint, to actually achieve its stated goals and objectives. This blueprint should include the following key elements:

1. *What*: Steps of action that need to be taken.
2. *Who*: Person or persons responsible for achieving specific steps of action.
3. *When*: Specific target dates for achievement of the actions specified.
4. *How*: Resources required to support and achieve the steps of action.
5. *Where*: Place action is to be performed (may be geographic or organizational).

In addition to these general elements of a tactical plan, it is often beneficial to add estimated costs at each step. Project control techniques such as PERT, CPM, and Gantt charts may be used to monitor progress of the project once it is under way, but the plan must be established first.

The system requirements established as a result of the systems analysis, design, and construction process will determine the basis for the system's functionality and performance. This will be followed by a determination of system details such as the approach to detailed design and construction, including options such as off-the-shelf, modified off-the-shelf, or custom hardware and software components for the system. Once the approach is established and the requirements detailed, estimations of costs and service levels can be obtained from potential vendors. We will look at this process more closely in the section entitled "Determining Sources of Network Components."

The process of implementing a networked system can be considered in the context of the five-component model, as we did earlier in the section on budgetary requirements. Look at the sample implementation plan shown in Figure 9–11, based on an off-the-shelf hardware and software approach, to see the major elements to be considered. This plan may be supported by an electronic spreadsheet of detailed costs together with the detailed system requirements.

An important part of the implementation plan is providing for maintenance of any existing systems that the new system may replace. Four general approaches can be taken, each with certain benefits and drawbacks:

FIGURE 9–11

Sample network implementation plan

What	Who	When	How and cost	Where
Hardware				
Acquire system hardware components, including 10 workstations, file server, UPS, WAN connections, routers, and cabling	Network supervisor	6/5/96	Acquire from system integrator; cost: $30,000 (see spreadsheet for details)	Server and 5 workstations at head office, 5 workstations at sales office
Software				
Acquire operating system, work group package, including word processor, spreadsheet, E-mail, and integrated order entry/ inventory control software, all preinstalled on server	System integrator to provide and preinstall	6/5/96	Software to be preinstalled and tested by system integrator prior to delivery and installation; cost: $30,000	As noted above
Data				
All inventory, customer, and purchasing data to be keyed into new system	Existing staff working overtime as necessary	6/26/96	Key all manual data into new system using batch and other control totals to verify accuracy; cost: $2,500	All work to be done at head office
People				
All existing staff to attend three half-day training seminars during first two weeks after system installation	All existing staff	6/8/96 to 6/22/96	Training provided by outside consultants under supervision of system integrator; cost: $5,000	All training to take place at head office on newly installed network
Network supervisor and inventory control staff to receive additional three half-day seminars of training	Network supervisor and inventory control staff	By arrangement		
Procedures				
Install hardware components and test for functionality and reliability	System integrator	6/5/96	As noted above under hardware and software	As noted above
All staff to learn appropriate procedures for system functionality during mandatory training sessions noted above	All staff	As noted above	As noted above	As noted above

- A *pilot* implementation involves installing the entire new system, but in only one part of the organization to determine its effectiveness before installing it in the entire organization. The existing system is kept operational at the sites that are not yet using the new system. For example, in an organization with multiple branches around the country, the new system may be installed at only one branch for the first three months. Once the system has proven its reliability and functionality at the one branch and any problems discovered have been fixed, the system can be installed at the remaining branches.

- The *phased* implementation approach involves implementing only certain functions at one time and phasing in other functions by sections. For example, in Figure 9–11, all of the hardware but only the groupware software may be installed for the first two months. Once all staff are familiar with the general operation of the network and groupware software and the network supervisor is comfortable with the system, the integrated order entry/inventory control software can be installed. During this phased implementation, the existing manual systems are replaced as the new systems are installed.

- The *parallel* implementation approach involves running both the new system and the old system in parallel for a time until the organization is satisfied that the new system is sufficiently reliable and functional to allow risk-free termination of the old system. A parallel approach could be used in the context of the integrated order entry/inventory control software. Even after the new software is installed, the old manual systems can continue to be operated in parallel with the new networked system for an established period of time.

- The *plunge* approach implements the complete new system throughout the entire organization, without taking any of the above precautions, and terminating any existing systems immediately. This approach is not recommended except in a new startup situation or when new functions are being implemented that did not exist previously.[7]

Often a hybrid approach incorporating features from some or all of the four methods may be used. For example, an organization may combine the parallel, pilot, and phased approaches by installing the new system at only one branch, while the existing manual systems are operated in parallel at that branch. Figure 9–12 illustrates these five implementation approaches.

After a network implementation plan and implementation process have been established, it may still be necessary to justify the plan in the light of the organization's strategic direction. A simple and straightforward approach to reconciling the implementation and strategic plans is to create an association matrix that compares organizational strategic goals and objectives to requirements of the system as specified in the implementation plan and requirements document. Figure 9–13 shows an

---

[7] D. M. Kroenke and K. A. Nolan, *Business Computer Systems—An Introduction* (Santa Cruz: Mitchell Publishing, 1987), pp. 160–62.

FIGURE 9–12

*Five
implementation
approaches*

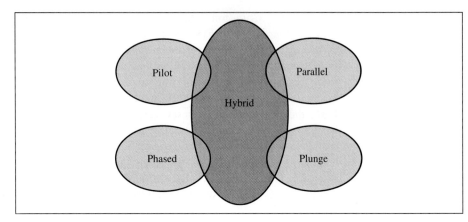

FIGURE 9–13

Sample association matrix to justify network plan

	Strategic Goals and Objectives of Organization				
Requirements	*Improve Efficiency of Organizational Communication*	*Provide for Business Expansion without Disruption to Customer Service Levels*	*Increase Customer Service Levels*	*Ensure Continuance of Service in Face of Natural or Political Disaster*	*Improve Efficiency of All Staff*
LAN with WAN connections supporting groupware software	✔		✔		
Integrated sales order/entry inventory control networked software	✔		✔		✔
Daily system backup with offsite data storage in disaster-proof vault				✔	
Windows-based applications software	✔		✔		✔
LAN system based on an open systems hardware configuration with X.25 WAN connection		✔		✔	

example of such an association matrix. By demonstrating the relationship between the organization's goals/objectives and the requirements of the proposed network system, the process of justifying the new system is well on its way. This process of justification can be readily supported by the budget for the proposed system as well as by any association with the organization's CSFs.

It is important to note that justification of a proposed network should *not* assume that a network is the best or even the only solution available. Alternative ways to meet the organization's strategic goals and objectives need to be considered, along with their costs and benefits compared to the networking option.

The entire process described so far in this chapter is aimed primarily at establishing the organization's requirements for the networked system. This process should be completed before contacting potential system vendors for prices and services. First, this gives the organization a better understanding of what it really wants out of the proposed system, putting the organization in a far better position to negotiate with potential vendors. Clear communication will significantly increase the likelihood of a successful system implementation and user satisfaction with the final system. Second, this process will help to weed out vendors that attempt to sell what they have rather than what the organization needs. If the company knows what it needs, it will be much more likely to find the best vendor to meet those needs rather than be sold by the first eager salesperson contacted.

Once the requirements analysis is completed and the implementation plan established, it is time to find out what various vendors can offer and what their service and products will cost. The next section addresses the process of using a request for proposal (RFP) to discover sources of network components.

Determining Sources of Network Components

Vendors of network systems and system components are an important source of service and information for the company moving to implement TBIT within the organization. This section discusses the use of the **request for proposal (RFP)** (sometimes called a *request for quotation (RFQ)*) to gather information and proposals from a range of vendors. The actual process of selecting vendors is covered in Chapter 10.

The RFP is a document created by the organization and sent to all vendors that are potential sources of the proposed system or components of the system. The purpose of the RFP is to communicate the organization's needs in a consistent fashion, provide a consistent basis for evaluating vendor proposals, and save time in the process of discovering sources of network systems and/or components. The RFP should include the following elements:

1. Cover letter introducing the organization's need and deadline for response.
2. Table of contents.
3. Overview of the organization and reasons for the system request.
4. List of system and user requirements and user characteristics.
5. Response ground rules and schedule.
6. Detailed evaluation criteria and required format.

The RFP may vary in length from perhaps 10 pages to a few hundred pages depending on the needs of the company and the complexity of the situation being addressed.

RFPs are typically used for larger systems and government organizations. However, the concepts may be applied to control and protect smaller network installation projects. Often a more informal process may be followed for small systems, for example, contacting a few vendors with which the organization is already familiar and asking them to submit proposals based on an abbreviated RFP.

The user(s) who put the RFP together need to give the vendors enough information to allow them to respond to the RFP in a thorough manner. The requirements discovered during the requirements analysis should be stated in the RFP, giving the needed information without biasing the responses. Thus, a statement such as "an X.25 packet-switched connection must be provided" might be inappropriate, whereas "a WAN connection capable of supporting 20 simultaneous external connections should be provided" would be quite useful. The more structured and specific the RFP is, the more structured and specific the vendor proposals will be, and the easier it will be to objectively and fairly evaluate those proposals.

Once the RFP is assembled, to whom should the company send it? There are a variety of ways to discover potential vendors for a given system need, including

- Contacting vendors known to the organization's technical staff.
- Asking the opinions of a few reputable systems consultants who deal with a wide variety of vendors.
- Asking the local branch of a computer society for a list of reputable system vendors.
- Advertising in trade and technical publications.
- Obtaining references from customers and suppliers of the organization.
- The Yellow Pages.

After the RFPs are mailed out to the potential vendors, the organization's network steering committee must prepare to objectively and fairly evaluate vendor proposals when they are received. Once the deadline for proposal submissions has passed, each will first undergo an initial evaluation to determine if it is a serious contender for the system. In some cases, it will be immediately evident that the "proposal" is really a request for an opportunity to sell something that may only partly meet the needs of the system. This screening process is especially important when there are many responses to the RFP. Chapter 10 gives more details about the process of evaluating vendor proposals.

Summary

This chapter covered requirements analysis, the process of discovering, documenting, and communicating the needs of the organization regarding a proposed network system. These requirements include internal, external, budgetary, technical, general user, compatibility, and performance requirements.

A variety of views on the communication process in requirements analysis were covered, including a review of the general communication model introduced in Chapter 8. Also covered was the process of interviewing organizational users and managers, including a particular type of group interview called joint application design (JAD).

Both the SWOT analysis method and the critical success factors (CSF) method are capable of discovering the organization's internal and external requirements for a network. The five-component model can be used to discover, document, and communicate the costs of a proposed network system, and budgeting and regular reporting methods can help to control costs. Technical requirements of a network relate to network traffic and response, system storage needs, and the expandability of the system as the organization grows. Documenting general user requirements is very important to the ultimate success of the proposed network system. Two general approaches to discovering those requirements are the more traditional highly structured approach and the less structured, iterative prototyping approach.

The ability of the proposed system to work with existing systems was discussed next, including issues of compatibility and connectivity. Compatibility is the ability of the proposed system to work directly with the existing system without special attention or modification. Connectivity is the ability of the proposed system to communicate with existing systems, but not necessarily be compatible with them.

Requirements in the area of system performance are an important factor in overall acceptability and functionality of the system. Performance characteristics include response time, system reliability, and system recoverability. Standards of response time can be established for various applications; methods of improving response time where it falls short of the standards include more memory for the file server, bridges to reduce network traffic, and faster leased lines. Network reliability refers to the assurance of availability of the network by limiting downtime. Recoverability refers to the extent to which a system can be brought back into operation if it fails. System backup is at the heart of recoverability. Physical security at the network site, appropriate insurance coverage, and a thorough and tested disaster recovery plan are also important.

Once the requirements for the system have been established, it is necessary to create a system implementation plan. This plan includes (1) *what* (steps of action need to be taken), (2) *who* (person or persons responsible for achieving specific steps of action), (3) *when* (specific target dates for achievement of the actions specified), (4) *how* (resources required to support and carry out the steps of action), and (5) *where* (place action is to be performed). Approaches to system implementation include: pilot, phased, parallel, or plunge implementation or a hybrid of these methods. Once the implementation plan has been created, it may be necessary to justify the plan before final approval is given.

Once the organization has clearly established its requirements, it can contact potential system vendors for specific information and costs. One method of contacting vendors is the request for proposal (RFP). The purpose of the RFP is to communicate the organization's needs in a consistent fashion, provide a consistent basis for evaluating vendor proposals, and save time in the process of discovering sources of network systems and/or components.

Key Terms

Joint application design (JAD) 325
Recoverability 341
Redundant array of inexpensive disks (RAID) 340
Reliability 338

Request for proposal (RFP) 347
Requirements analysis 320
Response time 337
Systems development life cycle (SDLC) 321

Questions for Discussion

1. What are the six areas of network requirements? Which of these areas do you think are most important?

2. What particular phase of the system development life cycle (SDLC) is the focus of this chapter? Why is this area important?

3. Describe the interview process, and discuss the importance of preinterview preparation.

4. Explain two methods for discovering the internal and external requirements that may affect the design of an organization's networked systems.

5. What are the key factors when establishing budgetary requirements? How can the five-component model help uncover the full costs of a networked system?

6. What are some of the technical factors that must be considered in looking at the system requirements for a new network? Give three examples of such technical requirements.

7. Identify the four areas of user requirements, and give an example of each.

8. Differentiate between compatibility and connectivity. Which is more important? Why?

9. Why are network performance standards important when considering network system requirements?

10. Contrast reliability and recoverability, and give an example of a network standard for each.

11. What is a network implementation plan? Why is the implementation plan important to an organization?

12. Describe the key elements you would include in a network implementation plan.

13. If you were required to justify your network implementation plan to a planning or steering committee, what are some of the key approaches you would take?

14. Describe what an RFP is, and explain how it can be used by an organization to both collect information on network vendors and streamline the process of deciding among alternative vendors.

Case Discussion and Analysis

1. **System Requirements at United Children's Clothes**

Anna Mironski had worked for United Children's Clothes (UCC) for over 10 years, first as a programmer and then as a systems analyst. The company is a manufacturer and wholesaler of children's clothing, and its competitive strategy is to be the low-cost producer in the market. For the past 10 years, UCC has used a computerized production management system to carry out this strategy. However, in the last year or two, the company has found it difficult to keep its prices down far enough and still show sufficient profit.

Anna became the network supervisor about 18 months ago, with the plan to update the company's networked systems. When Anna arrived, UCC was using an IBM System 34 minicomputer with four data terminals at the head office and four more terminals one at each sales office and two at the factory, working over 2,400 bps leased lines. About five years ago UCC upgraded to an A/S400, running with the same terminals as before. This system has continued to meet the organization's needs in the area of basic data processing for general accounting, production management, and sales forecasting, which the system had originally been designed for. However, as the company has grown, so has the proliferation of stand-alone PCs, ranging from a few old 8088 processors, some 80286 ATs and mostly 386s and 486s, with two Macintoshes in the advertising department. These personal computers are being put to varied uses in different departments using word processing, spreadsheets, desktop publishing, and personal databases, but they are unable to communicate with one another, requiring the old "floppy disk shuffle" to share files. The A/S400 is also unable to communicate with the PCs. A few of the more powerful computers have gone to the Microsoft Windows environment, since some managers found it easier to learn. However, less powerful PCs cannot support the Windows environment.

This is where Anna came in. The new position of network supervisor was created to focus attention on the growing need to network these computers. Top management also wants to give users, especially managers, readier access to important company information stored on the A/S400 databases. These data are often ignored because by the time reports are printed and read, the information is out-of-date and the business opportunity has passed. To compound the problem, most of the managers are very busy and have little time to learn new systems.

A number of other factors are increasing the company's need for more networking. A major competitor has begun guaranteeing delivery of product to most customers within 24 hours of ordering. UCC's customers have begun pressuring the company to reduce their delivery times as well. Normally it takes UCC five days to process sales orders, verify availability of stock, generate a picking list, and finally fill a customer order. Most of this time is spent in moving the various documents from sales offices to head office and among different departments for approval, typing picking lists, shipping documents, and so on. The best the company has been able to manage with the existing system is to reduce the time to four days by couriering sales orders from the sales offices to the head office rather than relying on the traditional postal system. This is still a long way from 24 hours!

Anna has looked into installing an Ethernet network to connect all of the PCs at the head office, the factory, and the two sales offices.

a. List three CSFs for UCC, and indicate what internal or external requirements they bring to light.

b. Discuss UCC's budgetary requirements, and explain how you would create a budget for the proposed system.

c. Design four interview questions to use in discovering user requirements for UCC. Also, indicate any company documents you would want to review in preparation for the interviews. Your questions should include two open-end and two closed-end questions. Restrict your analysis to the sales order processing and inventory control area.

d. Discuss the compatibility and connectivity issues raised in the case.

2. **Performance Standards and Implementation Planning at Universal Electronics Manufacturing**

Universal Electronics Manufacturing (UEM) is a manufacturer of high-tech electronic components that are used in a range of other manufacturers' products. The company has created a strategic plan to help maintain its leadership role in the industry. The strategic plan outlines the following organizational goals:

- The company will deliver the most reliable electronic components of their type in the industry.
- Customer service support will be highly responsive to customer quality and technical needs.
- Innovation will be a hallmark of the company's range of products.
- The company will foster an environment of creativity that will enhance product quality, innovation, and cost control.

One key area highlighted during the strategic planning process was the technical support for customers. Technical support engineers respond to customers' technical questions, mostly over the phone. The inquiries vary and include complaints about faulty products, questions about the best product to use for a particular application, new ideas for product applications, and new ideas for products. This function provides a major source of market information, new sales, innovative ideas, and manufacturing problems. UEM is planning to install a network to strengthen the overall organization, with initial installation to support the customer technical assistance function. Over the last three months, it has conducted a requirements analysis for the 24-hour technical hotline, the main point of contact for customer technical support. Among the requirements discovered were the following:

- The system must be able to support four engineers simultaneously in answering customers' technical questions over the 24-hour technical hotline.
- The system must be highly reliable due to the importance of this customer support function.
- The system must be expandable to support a number of other key functions within the organization.
- The system must be able to capture details about existing and potential customers, together with the nature of their phone calls (complaint about functionality or defect in a product, request for information on the application of particular components, innovative application of the company's products or new, related products). This information must be sharable among all of the engineers so that if a customer calls back later,

she or he won't need to repeat any of the information other than personal identification and a different engineer can respond to customer needs in an informed fashion.

- The system must provide quick online access to all product technical bulletins and product descriptions to assist engineers in responding to customer questions on the telephone.

Company management is now wondering how to go about identifying potential vendors of systems that might meet their requirements.

a. Describe four network performance standards that apply to UEM. You should have at least one in each of the primary areas of response time, reliability, and recoverability. How would you suggest that each performance standard be achieved?

b. Assume UEM has created a network implementation plan and you have been asked to justify the plan. Create an association matrix comparing the organization's goals from its strategic plan with the requirements of the system noted in the case. Briefly comment on the results of the association matrix.

c. Explain how UEM management can identify potential vendors of systems to meet its requirements and how an RFP can assist in this process.

10

EVALUATION AND SELECTION OF ALTERNATIVES

Chapter Outline

Introduction   353
Cost-Benefit Analysis and Alternative
    Selection   354
Features Matrices and Min/Max
    Analysis for Alternative Selection
    363
Vendor-Related Characteristics
    Affecting Alternative Selection
    368
Risk and Other Factors That Influence
    Alternative Choice   369
Alternative Financing Methods   370

Learning Objectives

By the end of Chapter 10, you should
be able to

1. *Use* cost-benefit analysis to
   differentiate among vendor proposals.
2. *Compare* alternatives using features
   matrices and min/max analysis.
3. *Evaluate* vendor factors affecting
   the choice of alternatives.
4. *Evaluate* risk and other factors
   affecting the choice of alternatives.
5. *Compare* the alternative acquisition
   methods of purchase, rent, and
   lease.

Introduction

This chapter concludes our discussion of strategy, organizational analysis, specific
requirements determination, and selection of a system to meet those requirements.
Once the organization has established requirements and has put out an RFP to discover
potential vendors, it will need to compare the alternatives presented by various
vendors. This chapter focuses on the issues related to comparing alternatives, especially vendor-related alternatives, and deciding which option best suits the organization. A number of methods will be used, including cost-benefit analysis, features
matrices, and risk factors. By using a range of methods, the organization can gain
a balanced view of the alternatives that will enable it to make informed choices based
on a number of criteria.

Cost-Benefit Analysis and Alternative Selection

In selecting among alternative approaches to delivering a networked system or solving an existing network problem, various approaches can be used. This section looks briefly at the concepts behind alternative selection and discusses a number of selection approaches; then it focuses on one particular approach called *cost-benefit analysis*. The methods introduced here may be used early in the analysis of alternatives, such as when comparing general approaches to problem solution and network design or evaluating specific vendor proposals.

Alternative Solutions and Selection Concepts

Any problem may have a range of alternative solutions, and network systems are no exception. There are alternative hardware platforms, alternative operating systems, alternative applications software, and alternative WAN configurations, to name just a few. For each given organizational situation, the range of alternative options will contain some options that are better than others. What are some of the criteria for differentiating the good alternatives from the bad ones? The following scenario describes an organization that is presented with a range of alternatives.

WILTON MANUFACTURING COMPANY

Wilton Manufacturing Company had finally decided to proceed with the installation of a network solution to resolve its communication and turnaround problems among the central office, three sales offices scattered throughout the country, the factory located a few blocks away, and the two warehouses, which were geographically dispersed. However, the best network configuration to meet its needs wasn't clear yet. The company had performed a thorough requirements analysis and thus had a very clear idea of what its needs were, but there were several approaches that could meet that need, some more costly and some more beneficial than others. The company had carried out a feasibility assessment of the proposed network, and in so doing had compared a couple of possible configurations.

The first approach involved a peer-to-peer network called Windows for Workgroups from Microsoft, which would allow E-mail, file sharing, and program sharing of Windows-based spreadsheet, word processing and other applications among the staff at a particular office, together with a modem and communication software to connect to the other offices for E-mail, file transfer, and database access. Database applications to support stock control and other transaction-processing applications were considered using Microsoft Access, a new database management system (DBMS) for Windows. This approach looked very economical, with rapid application development and ease of access to data and files offered by the Windows environment.

The second approach involved the use of a client/server network from Novell, with a compatible E-mail package, and network versions of DOS spreadsheet and word processing applications that the company already used. The database applications would be based on Oracle, a DBMS that had been ported down to the micro network environment from the mainframe and minicomputer environment. The central office would be connected to the WAN by a dedicated X.25 packet-switched network connection, while the other offices would connect to the central office and to one another via a dial-in connection to the X.25 network.

Both of these potential network configurations looked like they would do the job, with each having some advantages and disadvantages. But which one was better for Wilton Manufacturing?

What are some techniques that can assist Wilton Manufacturing in considering which approach would be more beneficial? First, and most important, the company must make a direct comparison of the alternatives to the network system requirements discovered during the requirements analysis phase. Does the alternative fulfill the internal and external requirements? What about budgetary constraints and technical requirements? How do the various options meet the needs expressed by prospective users of the proposed system? What about compatibility, connectivity, and performance? All of these issues, which were covered in Chapter 9, should be considered in evaluating the available options. These requirements give rise to the question of general feasibility in five key areas:

1. *Schedule feasibility*: Can the system be installed within the required time frame? Are there elements that might slow down implementation of one approach more than another, such as potential incompatibilities or unknown functionality due to the newness of a product?

2. *Technical feasibility:* This needs to be addressed in line with the technical requirements discovered during requirements analysis. Can each alternative actually deliver the required functionality and performance, or can some options be eliminated due to lack of technical feasibility? How does the alternative fit technically with the other systems in the organization with which it may have to interface?

3. *Organizational feasibility:* Does the given alternative fit the organizational culture and structure? If the organization is highly decentralized, does the alternative fit that structure or should it be eliminated from further consideration because it requires a centralized MIS department to manage it? If the organization is relatively unsophisticated in its computer use but the requirements are for widespread use of the new system, does the alternative under consideration provide a low learning curve for new users? Such organizational considerations and requirements can be used to eliminate some alternatives and strengthen the case for other alternatives.

4. *Cost feasibility:* Do the anticipated benefits of the alternative outweigh the expected costs over the life of the system? We will look at this issue more closely in the next section.

5. *Strategic feasibility:* Will the proposed alternative meet the strategic plans of the organization, or will it hinder those strategic initiatives that are being put in place? This area must be given close attention and in some

cases may become an overriding factor, even when the alternative fails certain other feasibility criteria such as cost or schedule. Chapters 1 and 6 covered some of these concepts.

It is not necessary that an alternative rank first in all of the above feasibility areas to be considered the best option. A points matrix may help in this type of feasibility comparison of alternatives, as illustrated in Figure 10–1. This technique first requires that management and users agree on the level of importance of each major aspect of feasibility. In Figure 10–1, a maximum total of 1,000 points was selected, out of which a portion was assigned to each aspect. In this hypothetical case, management and users believed strategic issues were most important and schedule feasibility issues least important. It is critical that the relative weightings of the feasibility areas be determined and approved by management and users *before* the evaluation of alternatives begins. Otherwise, people will argue for weightings that promote their preferred alternatives' scores. Then each alternative is evaluated to assign point values to each category for each alternative. This assigning of points may be done in various ways, including

- Formal evaluation of alternatives by a team that includes technical and user staff.
- General group consensus in a meeting.
- Secret ballot value assignment by managers and users, with an average of the points assigned by each participant being used as the final values.
- Obtaining opinion ratings from a range of consulting experts, and then averaging their scores.
- Some combination of the above methods.

As you can see in Figure 10–1, alternative 1 scores highest overall, with a total of 800 points against the other two alternatives with 700 points each. However, alternative 1 has two notable weaknesses: (1) It is weak in the technical feasibility area, and (2) it is the most costly of the alternatives (and therefore has the lowest number of points for cost). Assuming the organization can handle the additional costs involved, it will still be important to assess whether the technical weaknesses

FIGURE 10–1

Sample feasibility comparison matrix

Feasibility Area	Maximum Points	Alternative 1	Alternative 2	Alternative 3
Schedule	50	50	50	50
Technical	150	100	150	100
Organizational	150	150	50	100
Cost	250	150	200	250
Strategic	400	350	250	200
Total	1,000	800	700	700

indicated by the score of 100 out of a maximum of 150 can be overcome before proceeding with that alternative approach to the network system.

The areas of schedule, technical, and organizational feasibility are reasonably straightforward. Strategic requirements is a complex area; it was covered in Chapters 1 and 6 and may be covered in other specialty textbooks and courses on management policy and strategy and information systems strategic planning. Many techniques exist for determining cost feasibility. In the next section, we will take a closer look at the area of cost feasibility using an approach called *cost-benefit analysis.*

Cost-Benefit Analysis

A valuable method for discovering whether or not an alternative approach to solving the network problem or fulfilling the network requirements is cost feasible is cost-benefit analysis. This approach incorporates **discounted cash flow (DCF)** techniques as well as the concept of the **payback period**. The general concept of cost-benefit analysis is quite simple: Compare the anticipated costs of the proposed alternative to the anticipated benefits. If the benefits exceed the costs, the alternative is cost feasible.

When considering the costs, it is necessary to keep in mind the material on budgetary requirements in Chapter 9. There we used the five-component model to highlight the costs associated with fulfilling the requirements of the proposed network system. In addition to the five-component model, the costs should be considered in terms of

1. The full expected life of the proposed network system (typically three to seven years, depending on the nature of the system being installed).

2. The *initial* costs of setting up the system for all five components.

3. The *recurring* costs of operating the system over its useful life.

This approach will help to avoid the "hidden cost" syndrome mentioned in Chapter 9.

Similarly, the five-component model can be used to assess the benefits over the expected life of the system, again considering initial and recurring benefits. In addition, it is worth taking time with management and users to discuss potential benefits that may come to light by analyzing the organization's balance sheet and income statement. For example, implementation of a networked system could result in a 10 percent reduction in inventory held by the organization. This is not a five-component benefit; rather, it arises from considering the balance sheet for potential benefits. Figure 10–2 gives a partial listing of the costs and benefits that may be involved in this type of analysis.

In addition to the tangible costs and benefits listed in Figure 10–2, consideration should be given to intangible costs and benefits[1]. Intangible costs could include such things as[1]

---

[1] R. M. Stair, *Principles of Information Systems: A Managerial Approach* (Boyd and Fraser Publishing: 1992), pp. 438–41.

- Opportunities forgone because the investment dollars were not put into other areas of the organization.
- Impact in terms of organizational change, including organizational culture. (For example, the benefit of improved team creativity may bring the cost of lost interpersonal contact with the implementation of a videoconferencing system.)

Intangible benefits might include

- Improved public image.
- Higher morale of employees.
- Increased quality of service to customers.
- Higher industry profile.
- Improved ability to hire better employees.

FIGURE 10–2

Sample costs and benefits

Type of Cost or Benefit	Costs	Benefits
Hardware	Workstations, file servers, modems, hubs, routers, NTUs, cabling, printers, plotters, mice, scanners, fax boards	Salvage value of old hardware
Software	Network system software, off-the-shelf applications software, custom-written software, utilities for network management, systems development software such as DBMS, CASE, etc.	Resale value of existing software (if any residual value)
Data	Conversion of existing manual or electronic data into new formats	May free up physical file drawers for resale or other beneficial use
People	New operations staff to oversee network; cost of advertising and hiring new staff; time existing staff requires to learn and manage new systems; training costs and staff time for training; redundancy payments to staff who lose jobs	Savings on redundant staff salaries that are no longer necessary due to increased efficiencies
Procedures	Preparation of user and technical manuals; preparation of training materials	Improved efficiency in procedures, freeing up staff for other duties
Balance sheet	Associated asset costs such as office space, air conditioning (in case of mainframe computer installation), building alterations	Reduction in inventory holdings, warehouse and office space, and accounts receivable
Income statement	Operating costs such as additional telecommunication costs, new staff, and administrative costs	Reduction in travel, fax, and telephone costs; reduction in advertising and other selling or administrative expenses; increase in sales due to better information, lower out-of-stock ratios, etc. (only the gross profit portion of the sales increase should be included as a benefit, however)

It is difficult to assign a dollar value to such intangible costs and benefits, but keeping them in mind can strengthen or weaken a case for a particular alternative.

Once costs and benefits have been estimated for the various alternatives, an electronic spreadsheet can be used to evaluate the alternatives. In constructing the spreadsheet, two discounted cash flow (DCF) techniques will be beneficial to evaluate the costs and benefits over the useful life of the project. These two methods are known as **net present value (NPV)** and **internal rate of return (IRR).** Both methods can normally be calculated using a built-in function on the spreadsheet.

DCF techniques, like NPV and IRR, are intended to consider the time value of money, similar to that used in compound interest computations. NPV and IRR differ from compound interest in that they work in reverse, as shown in Figure 10–3. Compound interest calculations compute the accumulating value of an investment's cash flows over time to arrive at a *future value*, whereas NPV involves calculating the value of the future cash flows in today's dollars to arrive at an expected *present value*. All of these methods depend on the determination of a discount rate. The *discount rate* is the minimum acceptable rate of return on investments made by the organization. The higher the discount rate, the lower the present value of future cash flows. IRR calculations compute the expected rate of return on the investment in the project. The IRR is the discount rate at which the NPV of all future cash flows will be equal to zero. The following example should clarify this process.

An organization expects to invest $100,000 in a new network system, and it anticipates the benefits to amount to $30,000 per year over the five-year life of the system. The minimum rate of return the organization will accept on an investment in such a system is 20 percent. The discounted cash flow analysis would be as follows:

FIGURE 10–3

Compound interest versus present value

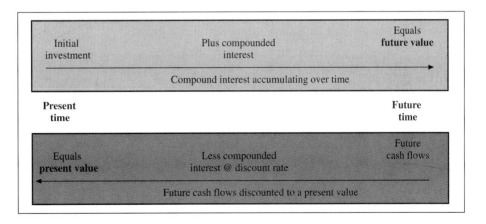

	Year 0	*Year 1*	*Year 2*	*Year 3*	*Year 4*	*Year 5*
Initial cost	− 100,000					
Recurring benefits		30,000	30,000	30,000	30,000	30,000
Total net cash flow	− 100,000	30,000	30,000	30,000	30,000	30,000
Discount rate	20.00 %					
NPV	− 10281.64					
IRR	15.24%					
Payback period (100,000/ 30,000)	3.33 years					

In the above spreadsheet, the expected formula (using EXCEL) for NPV is @NPV(B6,C5:G5)+B5 and the expected formula for IRR is @IRR(B5:G5, B6).

This spreadsheet analysis shows that the proposed network would not be cost feasible at a discount rate of 20 percent, since this produces a negative NPV. A factor to remember about the NPV method is that if it yields a negative value, the investment or project will give a return on investment lower than the discount rate. This is evident in the above example because the IRR computation shows that the expected rate of return for the project would be 15.24 percent. If this were used as the discount rate, the NPV would be zero.

An additional technique that does not require the discounting process is the payback period, which simply compares the original investment with the annual cash flows to determine how long it will take to pay back the original investment. In the above illustration, the payback period is 3.33 years ($100,000 divided by $30,000).

Based on this introduction to cost-benefit analysis and discounted cash flow techniques, let's look at a more in-depth illustration. Figure 10–4 shows the final spreadsheet for a cost-benefit exercise for G. Adrian Company, which is investigating the installation of an integrated LAN system for automating the sales order entry, order-filling, and invoicing processes. The spreadsheet has been designed to allow the analyst to enter the results of different alternatives, thus producing comparative cost-benefit results across the alternatives. The spreadsheet shown in Figure 10–4 is for the first alternative only.

Although the initial total cost of this alternative for a new system amounts to $370,000, this is offset to a considerable extent by the $253,000 in initial benefits that accrue primarily from improved management of inventory and better turnaround time in accounts receivable. In the five years following the implementation of the system, the expected cash flows generate a positive $43,000 each year. The overall results, shown in the box at the top of the spreadsheet, yield a positive NPV at a 20 percent discount rate, with an IRR of 24.43 percent and a payback period of 2.72 years. This same spreadsheet could then be used to enter the costs and benefits of the various other alternatives and compare the results. Figure 10–5 shows a summary of a hypothetical comparison among three alternative network solutions for G. Adrian Company.

Sample cost-benefit analysis

G. Adrian Company Cost-Benefit Analysis Spreadsheet						
	Analysis for Alternative 1					
Control panel						
Hardware maintenance costs	5%		NPV		11596	
Software maintenance costs	5%		IRR		24.43%	
Discount rate	20%		Payback		2.72 yrs	
	Initial					
	Period	Year 1	Year 2	Year 3	Year 4	Year 5
Initial Costs						
Hardware: wrkstns, file server, printers	− 145,000					
Software: Netw. oper. syst., custom softw.	− 95,000					
Data: Conversion of all manual data	− 30,000					
People: Hiring fee for netw. supervisor,	− 40,000					
training costs for all staff	− 60,000					
Procedures: included in software	0					
Recurring Costs						
Hardware maintenance		− 7,250	− 7,250	− 7,250	− 7,250	− 7,250
Software maintenance		− 4,750	− 4,750	− 4,750	− 4,750	− 4,750
People: network supervisor salary		− 120,000	− 120,000	− 120,000	− 120,000	− 120,000
Training for staff		− 10,000	− 10,000	− 10,000	− 10,000	− 10,000
TOTAL COSTS	− 370,000	− 142,000	− 142,000	− 142,000	− 142,000	− 142,000
Initial Benefits						
Salvage value of stand-alone computer	2,000					
Salvage value of 3 file cabinets	1,000					
Inventory reductions	150,000					
Accounts receivable reductions	100,000					
Recurring Benefits						
Savings of warehouse rent		50,000	50,000	50,000	50,000	50,000
Wage savings: two staff transferred		135,000	135,000	135,000	135,000	135,000
TOTAL BENEFITS	253,000	185,000	185,000	185,000	185,000	185,000
NET CASH FLOWS	− 117,000	43,000	43,000	43,000	43,000	43,000

The comparative results shown in Figure 10–5 point out that alternative 2 is the best of the three options, with alternative 1 being an acceptable choice. Alternative 3 is clearly unacceptable on a cost feasibility basis since it yields a negative NPV at the 20 percent discount rate, with an anticipated IRR of -2 percent. Keep in mind two things, however. First, we are working with estimates of the future, not facts. The numbers used for each alternative are the best estimates of the future. These numbers generally do not represent current facts as much as assumed results. Poor assumptions produce poor estimates, so it is always valuable to go over the results of a cost-benefit analysis with a group of knowledgeable managers and users to verify the accuracy of assumptions made. Figure 10–6 illustrates this dependency of the cost-benefit outputs on the inputs.

Second, cost feasibility is only one area of feasibility that needs to be investigated, and other areas, such as strategic feasibility, may cause a different alternative to be chosen than the one that is most cost feasible. In fact, in projects such as network infrastructure systems, strategic issues may result in alternatives that are clearly not cost feasible, such as alternative 3 in Figure 10–5. Although cost-benefit analysis is a useful tool, it must be balanced with the other issues concerned.

FIGURE 10–5

Comparison of cost-benefit results for three alternatives

Comparative Factors	Alternative 1		Alternative 2		Alternative 3	
	Initial	*Recurring*	*Initial*	*Recurring*	*Initial*	*Recurring*
Total costs	$370,000	$142,000	$270,000	$130,000	$430,000	$152,000
Total benefits	$253,000	$185,000	$253,000	$185,000	$253,000	$185,000
Net cash flows	−$117,000	$ 43,000	−$ 17,000	$ 43,000	−$177,000	$ 33,000
NPV	$ 11,596		$111,596		−$ 78,310	
IRR	24.43%		252%		−2%	
Payback period	2.72 years		0.40 years		5.36 years	

FIGURE 10–6

Cost-benefit analysis: outputs only as good as inputs

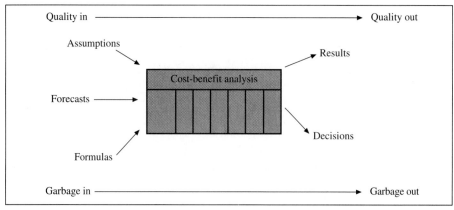

Other methods for evaluating alternatives may also shed light on which alternative offers the best prospects for the organization. Features matrices and min/max analysis, the methods we will look at next, are especially applicable to comparing vendor proposals.

Features Matrices and Min/Max Analysis for Alternative Selection

As we saw in the previous section, cost-benefit analysis is a very useful method for comparing alternatives, but it should be balanced with other methods. This section focuses on two related methods that are especially useful for comparing alternative vendor proposals. The first method involves the use of a **features matrix**, which is an extension of the concept introduced in Figure 10–1 involving the assignment of points for various levels of functionality. The second method is a simple approach for determining if an alternative is in the general range of suitability and is referred to as **min/max analysis**.

Features Matrices

Creating a features matrix is quite simple. The necessary steps may be accomplished at a network steering committee meeting of management decision makers and knowledgeable users. The steps would include the following:

1. Agree on the major categories in which alternative vendor proposals should be compared, typically based directly on the requirements analysis and RFP.

2. Distribute a total of 1,000 points across these major categories in terms of the importance of each category in the overall decision-making process; this establishes the maximum number of points any given alternative may gain during analysis. We chose 1,000 points simply because it is a round number large enough to be readily divided among the relatively large number of requirements.

3. List the individual features, or requirements, the system should contain in each category based on the requirements analysis conducted earlier, and assign a portion of the category's points to each feature.

The features matrix is best designed in conjunction with the design of the RFP, if one is used, so that vendor responses to the RFP can be easily analyzed. Once the features matrix is set up, each vendor alternative can be assessed and points assigned to determine how well each alternative matches the organization's needs. Figure 10–7 shows a features matrix incorporating steps 1 and 2 above, based on the five-component model together with other features.

Once general agreement has been reached on the overall categories and their relative importance, the detailed requirements in each category can be added and points distributed to them. This expansion of Figure 10–7 is shown in Figure 10–8.

FIGURE 10–7

Sample first draft of features matrix

Features	Maximum Points	Vendor 1 Alternative	Vendor 2 Alternative	Vendor 3 Alternative
Hardware performance	100			
Software functionality	300			
Data	100			
People	100			
Procedures	50			
Strategic platform issues	250			
Vendor-related issues	100			
Total Points	**1,000**			

The actual analysis of the individual vendor proposals should be done by a number of employees, and their results should be compared and justified in a steering committee meeting to provide as objective an analysis as possible. We will look at a completed features matrix after we discuss min/max analysis.

Min/Max Analysis

Min/max analysis is especially useful when dealing with a large number of vendor responses to an RFP. In a situation like this, the organization wants to do justice to the vendor proposals but at the same time not waste effort on proposals that are clearly outside the bounds of the minimum requirements and maximum financial resources of the organization.

Min/max analysis involves determining the features that *must* be part of the network system under consideration; this is the minimum configuration. Next, the organization, perhaps represented by the networking steering committee, must determine the maximum price it can afford for the proposed system, apart from cost feasibility considerations. This establishes the maximum over which a vendor proposal will simply not be considered. Having established these boundaries, a first pass of all vendor proposals is made to eliminate any proposals that do not fall within them. The result is a list of truly viable vendor alternatives, which can then be analyzed more closely using some of the other techniques discussed in this chapter. Care must be taken in setting financial boundaries in evaluations to ensure that essential solution requirements are not discarded due to their cost. Refer to Figure 10–9 for an illustration of min/max analysis.

Spreadsheet to Combine Features Matrices with Cost-Effectiveness Ratio

The features matrix may be effectively enhanced by the computation of a cost effectiveness ratio based on the total points accumulated by a vendor proposed alternative and the full price of the system configuration. Naturally, care must be

FIGURE 10–8

Sample second draft of features matrix

Features	Maximum Points	Vendor 1 Alternative	Vendor 2 Alternative	Vendor 3 Alternative
Hardware performance	**100**			
Large-screen color graphics capability	25			
Sub-one-second response time	50			
Typesetting-quality color printing	25			
Software functionality	**300**			
Desktop publishing with full multimedia Windows-based extensions	100			
Integrated order entry and inventory management system	150			
E-mail compatible with CC: mail system at primary customer	50			
Data	**100**			
Capable of automatic transfer from existing Harvard Graphics DTP system	50			
Order entry, etc. capable of high level of data integrity and reliability	50			
People	**100**			
System must provide for very low learning curve due to high employee turnover	50			
Network administration should be at a minimum, not requiring highly technical personnel	50			
Procedures	**50**			
Backup and recovery systems must be highly intuitive, easily learned, and easily executed	50			
Strategic platform issues	**250**			
Platform must be highly scalable to handle dramatic current and future growth	125			
Platform must be mainstream and easily integrated into WAN infrastructure and growing electronic trading networks, including voice/multimedia features	75			
Must readily accommodate move to EDI during next three years	50			
Vendor-related issues	**100**			
Experience with proposed system type	50			
Ability to provide local hardware & software support	50			
Total points	**1,000**			

FIGURE 10–9

Using min/max analysis to filter many proposals into a short list

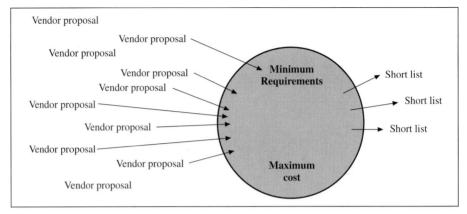

taken to ensure that the various vendor proposals are comparable, and the cost-benefit analysis used earlier can assist in this process. The total system cost will reflect the assumption that the recurring costs and benefits as well as the initial benefits are comparable across the final list of competing vendor proposals and will focus on the full initial cost section. Figure 10–10 shows a completed features matrix for a finalized list of three vendor proposals, complete with computed cost effectiveness ratios. This method somewhat overlaps, and is complementary to, cost-benefit analysis. However, it takes a different approach and does not involve any discounted cash flow (DCF) methods.

If you look closely at Figure 10–10, you will see a number of interesting points. The highest-scoring alternative on a cost effectiveness basis is alternative 3, with a ratio of 3.17. The primary reason for its high score is its low price. Essentially, what we see in the cost effectiveness ratio is a computation of value for money: The amount of effectiveness purchased for the given dollar. Alternative 2, which scored highest on total points, is noticeably more expensive than the other systems, and therefore its cost effectiveness ratio is the lowest. However, keep in mind the warning given earlier regarding cost-benefit analysis: Each technique needs to be balanced by the overall needs of the organization. Each technique yields a different view of the network system alternatives, and management ultimately needs to balance one view against another before coming to a final conclusion as to which alternative is best.

Figure 10–10 illustrates this balanced view. Alternative 3 is clearly the most cost effective; however, its low score on the integrated order entry system software may make the system functionally unfeasible and therefore rule it out. On the other hand, alternative 2 is clearly the superior system from an overall functionality and quality standpoint, but its price tag may be beyond the maximum budgeted; therefore, this alternative may also be ruled out. This is a good example of the use of min/max analysis to balance cost effectiveness.

Figure 10–10 includes vendor-related issues as a category worthy of including in the overall point evaluation. Vendor characteristics and how they can affect alternative selection are covered in the next section.

FIGURE 10–10

Completed features matrix with cost-effectiveness ratio

Features	Maximum Points	Vendor 1 Alternative	Vendor 2 Alternative	Vendor 3 Alternative
Hardware performance	**100**	**75**	**100**	**60**
Large-screen color graphics capability	25	20	25	15
Sub-one-second response time	50	40	50	30
Typesetting-quality color printing	25	15	25	15
Software functionality	**300**	**255**	**265**	**150**
Desktop publishing with full multimedia Windows-based extensions	100	85	85	75
Integrated order entry and inventory management system	150	120	130	25
E-mail compatible with CC: mail system at primary customer	50	50	50	50
Data	**100**	**80**	**90**	**40**
Capable of automatic transfer from existing Harvard Graphics DTP system	50	40	40	25
Order entry, etc. capable of high level of data integrity and reliability	50	40	50	15
People	**100**	**85**	**75**	**100**
System must provide for very low learning curve due to high employee turnover	50	50	50	50
Network administration should be at a minimum, not requiring highly technical personnel	50	35	25	50
Procedures	**50**	**35**	**25**	**50**
Backup and recovery systems must be highly intuitive, easily learned, and easily executed	50	35	25	50
Strategic platform issues	**250**	**190**	**250**	**185**
Platform must be highly scalable to handle dramatic current and future growth	125	100	125	100
Platform must be mainstream and easily integrated into WAN infrastructure and growing electronic trading networks, including voice/multimedia features	75	55	75	55
Must readily accommodate move to EDI during next three years	50	35	50	30
Vendor-related issues	**100**	**60**	**90**	**50**
Experience with proposed system type	50	30	40	20
Ability to provide local hardware and software support	50	30	50	30
Total points	**1,000**	**780**	**895**	**635**
System cost		$320,000	$450,000	$200,000
Cost effectiveness ratio (points/cost × 1,000)		2.43	1.99	3.17

Vendor-Related Characteristics Affecting Alternative Selection

When comparing alternatives, more than the price or the functionality must be considered. The ability of vendors to deliver on their promises, their reliability, and their technical competence all affect the final delivered solution. A number of questions concerning vendor characteristics should be asked when deciding among the final list of vendors, including the following:

1. What is the reputation of the vendor in the industry? Ask several respected consultants in the field; ask the vendor for a list of existing clients, and interview some of them.

2. How long has the vendor been in business, and is the vendor financially stable? A vendor that has been in business for only a few years may be a bit risky to buy from. Will the vendor still be there to support the organization over the life of the system?

3. Is the vendor experienced in the field in which the organization is asking it to work? For example, if the vendor is proposing a UNIX network, how many has it installed previously? If writing a custom multiuser inventory package, has the vendor done this before, and how successful was the implementation according to the customer? Talk to a few customers to get some idea of the vendor's competence.

4. Will the vendor be able to provide technical and training support locally? Or will it be necessary to send malfunctioning system components to another country for diagnosis and repair or for staff to travel to receive training?

5. What type of after-sales service will be provided? Will a technical hotline be provided to answer questions? Is the vendor's staff trained and authorized to maintain the systems? Will there be a cost for after-sales service? If the file server fails, what will be the expected turnaround time for repair or replacement? Are replacement components stored locally, or will they have to be sent from overseas?

6. Will the vendor provide the full system, or will the organization have to acquire some components from a third party and integrate them internally? Third-party involvement can create a real problem if the system malfunctions, since the primary vendor may blame the use of the third-party component for the failure. Responsibility is more readily established if the entire system comes from one vendor or system integrator. This particular area is becoming less problematic as industry standards become more strictly enforced. However, it is still a problem in many situations and should be watched carefully.

7. To what extent does the vendor guarantee its systems? Does it include delivery of backup systems if a failure occurs during the warranty period? Does the vendor offer extended service contracts to provide ongoing support beyond the warranty period?

Questions such as these can yield considerable insight into the competence and reliability of the final candidates. These points can be incorporated into a features matrix, with points assigned to each question, to allow a more direct and objective comparison among the vendors. Remember, when you choose the vendor, you are selecting more than a just a TBIT system. You are choosing a business relationship that may last over several years. Therefore, you want the relationship to be with someone whom you trust and who is capable of providing a valuable service over time.

In addition to the risks related to the choice of vendor, other uncertainties are involved in the selection of an alternative. The next section describes these risks and some ways to alleviate them.

Risk and Other Factors That Influence Alternative Choice

Uncertainty is an inevitable part of everyday life. The risks that attend uncertainty should be managed wherever possible to reduce their potential impact. The choice among alternative networking solutions should be assessed for risks and provisions made to minimize those risks as far as possible.

The risks an organization faces in the selection among alternative vendor proposals include

- *Vendor risks* (discussed earlier).
- *Technology risks.* These include choosing a technology that is not mainstream or is unproven, only to find that the technology becomes a tangent to the rest of the industry and is no longer supported by the manufacturer. Conversely, there is the risk of staying with a proven but increasingly obsolete technology and then moving to more modern systems too late.
- *Trading partner risks.* A risk arises when a major trading partner, such as a customer, chooses a communication technology that is significantly different from your choice, making it more difficult to work with them efficiently. An example would be your organization choosing an EDI software package based on the ANSI X.12 standard and your biggest customer selecting a system based on the EDIFAC standard. The problem is probably solvable, but trading partner decisions present uncertainty and associated risk to an organization.
- *Other external factors, such as market changes or governmental decisions.* For example, an organization may decide to wire a new building with fiber optic cable for an FDDI-based network, believing the local telecommunications supplier will soon be installing an FDDI loop through the local business district. However, after the expensive cabling has been installed, the telecommunications company announces that it has decided not to install FDDI after all but to wait for the development of another emerging international technology standard.

What are some methods for alleviating the types of risks just described? A number of approaches may prove valuable in reducing the level of risk in one or more of these areas, including

- Interviews with customers of potential vendors to determine their level of confidence in and satisfaction with the vendor and the type of system being proposed.
- A legally binding contract with the vendor, including performance and timeliness standards.
- System selection based on international standards and mainstream technology.
- Good communication with key trading partners and industry information sources.
- Keeping abreast of the facts concerning technology changes and international standards by reading technology-related articles in newspapers, magazines, and trade journals.
- Staying knowledgeable regarding government and telecommunications industry decisions that might affect the organization's network decisions by reading newspaper articles, newsmagazines, and government publications.
- Employment of a knowledgeable consultant in the field to advise management on risk-related issues.
- An insurance policy to cover business interruptation or other risks arising from the installation or failure of the system.

Figure 10–11 shows an association matrix of risk types, along with methods for alleviating these risks.

As you can see, the selection of a system based on international standards and mainstream technology, together with the use of a knowledgeable consultant, affect the widest range of risk types and are therefore the most broadly applicable methods. However, application of all of the methods will certainly assist in reducing the overall levels of risk.

Alternative Financing Methods

Once the choice of alternative vendor proposals has been made, the new network system needs to be financed. A package that includes the hardware, the software, and some training may be negotiated with the vendor(s) involved. Three basic methods may be used to finance the network system: purchasing, leasing, and rental.[2] Not all vendors will make all three options available, but it is worth being aware of these

---

[2] J. O. Hicks, *Information Systems in Business: An Introduction* (St. Paul, MN: West Publishing, 1990), pp. 503–6.

FIGURE 10–11

Risk association matrix

Methods for Alleviating Risk	Vendor-Related Risks	Technology-Related Risks	Trading Partner-Related Risks	Other External Related Risks
Interview with customers of potential vendors	✔	✔		
A legally binding contract with the vendor, including performances and timeliness standards	✔			
Systems selection based on international standards and mainstream technology	✔	✔	✔	✔
Good communication with key trading partners and industry information sources		✔	✔	
Keeping abreast of the facts concerning technology changes and international standards		✔	✔	
Staying knowledgeable regarding government and industry decisions that might affect the organization's network decisions		✔		✔
Employment of a knowledgeable consultant in the field to advise management on risk-related issues	✔	✔	✔	✔
Insurance policy to cover business interruption or other risks arising from the installation or failure of the system	✔			✔

alternatives. Note that financing major equipment purchases is a specialized task that often requires considerable expertise in financing. This section describes these options in a simplified form so that they will be clearly understood.

Purchasing

Direct purchase of the system by the organization is the most straightforward financing option. There are some advantages and disadvantages to purchasing the system. On the one hand, purchasing is typically the least expensive financing option if the system is kept for its full economic life (normally three to six years). Also, ownership of the system will give the organization the right to depreciate it as an asset, making it tax deductible. The disadvantages of purchasing include the risk of obsolescence of the system and less flexibility in upgrading the system. The organization must also consider the cost of maintaining the system. Finally, the organization will have to make a large capital outlay for the system, which may require borrowing additional funds.

Leasing

Leasing the new network system provides an alternative financing arrangement. With a lease, the organization does not have to make a large capital outlay and the lease payments are normally fully tax deductible. It is also possible to transfer some of the risk of obsolescence to the lessor by limiting the length of the lease. In addition, maintenance costs can be fixed by including them in the lease contract. However, most lease arrangements are for longer terms (two to four years), which means the organization is still locked into the existing system and thus has less flexibility and carries some of the risk of obsolescence. Leasing typically costs more than purchasing over the long run, because the vendor or a bank typically provides the financing and the lease therefore tends to carry a higher interest rate.

Rental

Renting the system provides maximum flexibility and freedom from risk of obsolescence because the rental agreement is typically for shorter periods, such as one month at a time, although there may be a minimum initial period such as six months. Also, the rental payments are tax deductible. No capital outlay is involved, and therefore no risk of loss of a capital sum. However, the cost of these benefits is that renting is the most expensive option.

Figure 10–12 shows a hypothetical example for comparison of the three financing alternatives. The costs represent a networked system with a total hardware and software cost of $200,000 financed over three years. The purchase option assumes the organization must borrow the money for the investment at the organization's cost of capital of 12 percent

As you can see, renting is the most costly option over the three-year life of the system. In most cases an organization probably would not rent over the full life, but over the rental period, this option is more costly. Cost of funds and opportunity costs have not been calculated for the purchase option.

FIGURE 10–12

Cost comparison of three financing options

	Purchase	Lease	Rental
Initial outlay	$200,000	$0.00	$0.00
Monthly payment	$6,600.00	$8,000	$9,000
Total of monthly payments over 36 months	$237,600.00	$288,000	$324,000
Total cost of system over three-year life	$237,600	$288,000	$324,000
Implicit interest rate	12%	26%	35%

Figure 10–13 summarizes the advantages and disadvantages of the three major financing options.

Figures 10–12 to 10–14 make it clear that purchase of the system is typically the least expensive alternative, but is also the least flexible and carries the highest risk of obsolescence. Rental is typically the most expensive option over the life of the system, but offers the greatest flexibility and the lowest risk of obsolescence. The leasing method tends to be a compromise between purchasing and renting.

Summary

Once the organization has clearly established its needs for a networked system, it will be necessary to select among alternative vendor proposals. This chapter covered a number of methods and factors that may be used in performing alternatives analysis and selection.

FIGURE 10–13

Advantages and disadvantages of three financing options

	Purchase	*Lease*	*Rental*
Flexibility to change the system in the near future	Least flexible	Average flexibility	Most flexible
Risk of obsolescence	Highest risk	Medium risk	Lowest risk
Cost over the life of the system	Lowest cost	Medium cost	Highest cost

FIGURE 10–14

Cost versus risk of obsolescence for financing choices

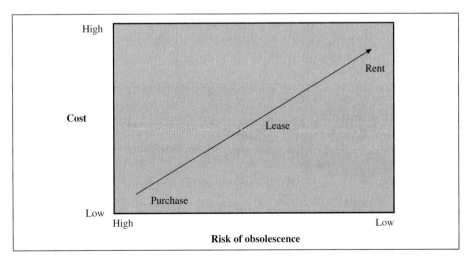

General concepts of feasibility were covered in the context of comparison of alternatives. Feasibility is concerned with reasonable expectations of success in five main areas, including schedule, technical, organizational, cost, and strategic feasibility. Each of these areas needs to be considered when comparing alternatives to maintain a balance in the overall network requirements of the organization. A point-scoring matrix is useful for considering the relative importance of each area to the organization and then scoring vendor proposals or alternative solutions on the basis of the matrix.

Cost-benefit analysis is a method of determining cost feasibility by comparing the costs of the proposed networked system to the expected benefits. The full range of costs and benefits over the total life of the proposed system can be determined using the five-component model and time value of money concepts. An electronic spreadsheet can be very useful in this analysis, allowing ready comparison of alternatives. Compound interest–related concepts of net present value and internal rate of return can also allow easy comparison of estimated costs and benefits from different time periods over the life of the system.

Two methods useful for comparing alternative proposals are the features matrix and min/max analysis. A features matrix distributes a total of 1,000 points among the required features of the system, representing the level of importance of each. Then the alternative vendor proposals are scored with respect to each feature. Min/max analysis is useful for weeding out proposals that are clearly unfeasible. The result is a shortened list of truly viable proposals.

In addition to comparing the feasibility of the various proposals of potential vendors, it is necessary to compare the vendors themselves. The choice of vendor is more than a decision on hardware and software; it is a decision on an ongoing business relationship. The chapter examined several important vendor characteristics.

The choice of a network alternative also requires considering various types of risk. Risk-related areas include vendor risks, technology risks, trading partner risks, and other external risks based on factors such as market changes and government decisions. A number of methods of reducing these risks were discussed.

Finally, the chapter considered alternative methods of financing the network system. The three primary methods—purchase, lease, and rental—were examined, along with the impact of each on the cost, flexibility, and risk of obsolescence of the network system. Purchase of the system is typically the least expensive option, but is also least flexible and carries the highest risk of obsolescence. Rental is typically the most expensive method over the life of the system, but offers the greatest flexibility and the lowest risk of obsolescence. Leasing tends to be a compromise between purchasing and renting.

Key Terms

Discounted cash flow (DCF) 357	Min/max analysis 363
Features matrix 363	Net present value (NPV) 359
Internal rate of return (IRR) 359	Payback period 357

Questions for Discussion

⋆1. Describe the five areas of feasibility, and give an example of each.   *P. 355*

2. Identify and describe a process that allows an organization to compare alternatives across the five feasibility areas.

3. What is cost-benefit analysis? How can it be used to help differentiate among vendor proposals?

4. Discuss the benefits of using discounted cash flow methods in doing cost-benefit analysis.

⋆5. When looking for costs and benefits of a network system proposal, what categories of costs and benefits should be considered? *PP 357-362*

6. What cautions must be kept in mind when using cost-benefit analysis to avoid misinterpreting the information generated?

⋆7. Compare and contrast a features matrix with min/max analysis. In what situations and processes is each used?   *PP 363-364*

8. What is a cost-effectiveness ratio, and how does it enhance the features matrix analysis?

9. What cautions must be kept in mind when assessing the results of a features matrix with a cost-effectiveness ratio?

⋆10. Why is it important to include vendor-related characteristics in the assessment of network alternatives? What are some vendor *P. 368* characteristics that should be considered?

⋆11. What are some of the risk factors in making a choice among network proposals? What are some ways to alleviate these risks? *PP. 369-370*

⋆12. Describe the pros and cons of the three financing methods for acquisition of a network alternative. *PP 370-372*

Case Discussion and Analysis

⋆1. **Cost-Benefit Analysis for Long Engineering Company** *PP 357-361*

Long Engineering Company (LEC) has decided to install a network system to help its technical support engineers (five of whom earn an average of $100,000 each per year) deliver better customer service, including mailing out sales and other literature, answering phone calls for technical assistance, and logging and forwarding repair requests using an alphanumeric paging system that will be part of the new network system. Currently all company technical manuals and literature are in paper format, but will need to be scanned and converted to electronic-readable form; there are about 3,000 pages of such literature. The initial feasibility study estimated savings in various areas, including (1) a reduction in clerical staff from four to two people (each earning $60,000), and (2) reduced telephone bills of $1,500 per month for calls to field support staff regarding repair requests. The study also estimated an increase in sales of $400,000 per year due to improved customer service, for a gross profit rate of 40 percent (the company typically requires a minimum return on

investment of 20 percent). After sending out an RFP to a number of vendors, LEC received responses from seven vendors. Two of the responses were simply advertising and not viable proposals. Of the remaining five proposals, three either did not meet the minimum requirements or were much too expensive. The remaining two proposals included the following information covering the expected five-year useful life of the proposed system.

Vendor 1.   Our system will provide a full LAN configuration for your customer support services area covering the major areas of functionality required, including call logging by customer or inquirer, recording of nature of request and nature of response, access to all company technical literature online, and automatic message forwarding to alphanumeric pagers of field service persons where necessary. The cost of the system includes the required file server and six workstations, a laser printer, and a WAN X.25 communications adapter ($150,000). The software provided will include the necessary LAN operating system (Windows NT) and applications software to meet the functionality requirements mentioned above ($175,000). Existing staff should be able to handle the new system with additional training, as the entire system will be very user-friendly, with a low learning curve, and should be easily administered by one of the existing engineers, absorbing only 20 percent of his or her time. We do recommend that you budget for at least one week of training for each of your employees each year to gain and maintain the skills necessary to achieve full benefit from this system. It will also be necessary to budget for conversion of your technical literature at an estimated cost of $5 per page. If you wish, a maintenance contract is available at a cost of 5 percent of the initial cost of the hardware, and a similar contract is available for the software.

Vendor 2.   The system we are proposing is established and has been found to be highly reliable by existing users. It consists of six terminals running off of a UNIX server capable of readily supporting all the functions required in your RFP, including mailing out of sales and other literature, answering phone calls for technical assistance with online access to all company technical literature, and logging and forwarding of repair requests using an alphanumeric paging system. The hardware costs total $175,000. Other costs include an X.25 WAN adapter ($15,000) and a laser printer ($12,000). Software costs, including the UNIX operating system and applications software, amounts to $200,000. Naturally, a maintenance contract is available at the rate of 5 percent of the hardware and software costs. We believe your existing staff will be able to quickly learn the new system and be functioning effectively after a two-week training course. It will be necessary to hire a system administrator to oversee the system; we estimate the annual salary of such an employee to be approximately $120,000 per year, with an estimated hiring fee of 50 percent of annual salary. We believe this would allow an additional saving of one further

clerical staff member. It is also recommended that you budget for one additional week per year of training for all employees using the system. Training costs typically amount to $2,500 per week per employee.

a. Prepare a cost-benefit analysis for LEC, using an electronic spreadsheet to assist in the computations. Use the same spreadsheet to compute the second vendor's results as well. You should also present a summary table of the results of the analysis. Where information is missing from one vendor's proposal, you may use the equivalent information from the other vendor's proposal to make the analysis comparable.

b. Based on the results of your cost-benefit analysis, what other factors should be considered when comparing the two proposals? What further information would you require to make the additional comparisons?

2. A Features Matrix for G & L Manufacturing Company

George Lim has worked for G & L Manufacturing Company (GLM) for over 20 years as chief programmer. Originally, GLM used a minicomputer for its needs, but with the proliferation of PCs within the organization, the mini had lost the technology edge and many staff members are now dissatisfied with the performance and user interface the system offers. In addition, a number of the company's key customers have begun suggesting that GLM move to an electronic data interchange system (EDI) to help speed up delivery and service. Two years ago, George and the others in the DP group began to talk about either upgrading to a more powerful mid-range computer system or converting all of the company's systems over to a PC-based LAN. After a year of going back and forth over the issue, they finally took the plunge and settled on a LAN, primarily for cost reasons. After months of analysis, the organization issued an RFP to the primary vendors of LAN systems and ended up with a short list of two companies from the six responses they received. Both of these vendors look promising, and GLM obtained the following information from the proposals, discussions with existing customers of the vendors, and other industry sources.

Vendor 1.   This company has been in business for 10 years and has installed 50 networked systems over the past five years similar to the one proposed for GLM. Existing customers confirmed that the company has an excellent reputation for competent and timely delivery of contracted systems and service. It is a fairly large organization, employing 25 people, including four programmers and five technical service people in the territory. Its proposal includes the full hardware configuration, as well as the systems and applications software modified by the vendor to suit the company's needs. Training will be provided by a firm the vendor works with regularly. The proposal also includes a full one-year warranty for the entire system, hardware and software, with the option of a maintenance contract to cover hardware and software after the warranty period runs out. Both the initial warranty and the extended maintenance contract include 4-hour turnaround on malfunctioning system hardware components and a 24-hour technical help hotline for telephone assistance. Total initial cost of the system is $350,000.

Vendor 2.   The second vendor is a very aggressive firm in the network market and has been in business for three-and-a-half years. It has installed a variety of networks in different sites, and its customers are generally satisfied with the results. This vendor likes to use the latest technology and network operating system software. Being a growing firm, it has gone from 3 to 10 employees, including one full-time and one part-time technician. It provides training with excellent in-house trainers to meet customer needs. Its proposal covers the full hardware configuration for the network, and the vendor subcontracts all the software to another company it has been dealing with for the last two years. A full warranty on the system hardware and software is provided for one year, with a maintenance contract available following the warranty period. The warranty and the maintenance contract both provide for 24-hour turnaround of damaged or misfunctioning hardware components and a business hours (nine hours per day, five days per week) technical hotline to give telephone assistance with system technical and operational queries. Total initial cost of the system is $290,000.

Now it's analysis time for George and his team so that they will know how to advise top management, and the company's current shortage of investment capital only makes the decision more difficult.

a. Create a features matrix for GLM focusing on the vendor characteristics. Compute a cost-effectiveness ratio as part of your matrix. Comment briefly on your results.

b. List the areas of risk that are evident in the scenario, identifying whether the risk is related to a particular vendor or is a general risk.

c. Given the facts of the situation, how would you advise the company to finance the new network system investment?

Chapter Outline

Introduction   380

Management and Security Issues in
    Business Networks   381

Change Management and
    Organizational Growth   387

Mixed-Vendor Network Management
    389

Open System and De Facto Network
    Management Protocols   396

Distributed and Integrated Network
    Management   401

Security Issues in Networking   403

Backup and Disaster Recovery   425

Learning Objectives

By the end of Chapter 11, you should
be able to

1. *Analyze* network management,
   security, and data integrity issues
   associated with both local and
   wide area business networks.

2. *Identify* and *discuss* factors in
   change management and
   organizational growth and explain
   how they can be managed.

3. *Analyze* mixed-vendor situations and
   the problems they can create.

4. *Explain* the concepts and benefits
   of open system management and
   compare them to de facto
   solutions.

5. *Describe* and *compare* the
   concepts of distributed and
   integrated network management
   as well as the areas that require
   management.

6 *Analyze* some existing networks
   to demonstrate how managers can
   achieve cost effectiveness, network
   maintenance, and related issues.

7. *Describe* security issues, including
   costs and benefits; network
   vulnerability; backup and disaster
   recovery; risk analysis; data
   encryption; and Trojan horses,
   viruses, and worms.

8. *Explain* network management and
   security issues raised in using PCs
   and PC-based LANs.

9. *Identify* innovative approaches,
   styles, and strategies of network
   security for both LANs and
   WANs.

Introduction

We have seen that computer networks play a very important role in many businesses. Dependence on these networks is increasing rapidly, and business success is now frequently linked to the reliability of the networks and the security of the data transmitted. Consider the telephone network, a vital link for many business operations. As technology has improved, organizations have come to expect better service from the telephone companies and are becoming less tolerant of faults and delays. Further, deregulation of the telecommunications industry means that many competing companies now tout quality service. As a result, network management and data security have become key selling points and critical success factors for these companies in the same way that accident-free records of new aircraft become selling points and CSFs for the airlines. Nevertheless, these areas are fraught with problems, which this chapter will address.

The problem of managing hardware on a single network is a relatively easy one to solve. It becomes more difficult, however, when hardware components, system software, and applications programs operate together over an interconnected system of local and wide area networks that in turn are managed by different companies (sometimes in different countries) and with different architectures. At this writing, only partial solutions to the problem of network management exist. Thus, it is not possible, for example, to purchase a single system that provides these requirements across such a diverse platform.

Telecommunications companies are now moving into this area and starting to offer "customer-to-customer" and "application-to-application" management. However, the products that enable this to be done are not yet mature, and individually tailored solutions are still required. Network management has not reached the stage where one can buy hardware and software equipment from virtually any vendor and expect it to operate on these networks. Although progress is being made, it is not keeping pace with customers' expectations of these networks!

Closely related to network management is the issue of security. Network management systems presently address issues such as fault determination, configuration and change, performance and accounting, and, to a lesser degree, security. In principle, security is a management issue, but solutions for security of data are often ad hoc and vendor specific and thus are usually not part of the network management software systems.

Some vendors attempt to solve the security issues at the lowest level of the OSI model (see Chapter 4) in the design of their hardware equipment. This can be seen in hardware encryption devices commonly used by banks and the military or with LAN equipment such as that currently marketed by 3Com. Other vendors direct their efforts to the upper layers of the OSI model and offer complex software security systems. In addition, a host of special software analysis programs are designed to look for **viruses**, **Trojan horses**, and **worms**.

Some people believe that if the security of a system can be breached and data accessed by an unauthorized party, the fault lies with the system designer and/or the systems manager; the intruder is often hailed as a hero. It has often been stated that high-quality, expert hackers are prized on the job market. These are moral issues worthy of thought and discussion.

There is little doubt that network management and security will continue to be important issues in the years to come. We can expect to see much progress in both standards development and the products that implement these standards. In the sections that follow, we will look at current issues and problems and describe the solutions that exist at present but also indicate the likely directions over the next few years.

Management and Security Issues in Business Networks

In this section, we will look at a number of examples that demonstrate the vital importance of network management and security in today's networks.

Distributed Network Management: Two Examples

The computer network is such an important part of many businesses' operations that network failure and loss of access by the users to many applications may well cost a business its very survival. The following two examples demonstrate how a well-managed network can provide cost effectiveness and competitive advantage for an organization.

IKEA

IKEA is a company specializing in the manufacture and sale of high-quality furniture, textiles, and other home products. The head office is in Sweden, with major operations in Germany and Switzerland, but the center of IKEA's Asia operations is in Hong Kong. IKEA has a total of seven warehouses, 20 purchasing offices, and 80 retail outlets. As IKEA grew, it became clear that a centralized system of applications and management was not meeting its primary needs; the company needed an integrated, worldwide system. The system that evolved is run on Digital VAX and IBM RS6000 servers using the Oracle Relational Database Management System but with Digital's MicroVAXs running in each regional office, thus supporting an integrated management system.

The problems that evolved as a result of the distributed geographical environment were more organizational than technical. Organizational problems related to the requirement to support complex systems in the regions (see Figure 11–1), where there were no technical staff. Retraining of existing staff in these regions and recruiting of individual staff members for these offices were largely impractical. The approach was to create Hong Kong as the regional system and management center to cover India, Thailand, Taiwan, and Korea as well as Hong Kong itself.

The overall support and management was divided into hardware, system software, network, electronic mail, and file transfer. IKEA developed applications and specialized databases for purchasing, distribution, retail processing, and quality control. For the regional hardware and software, Digital Equipment was contracted to provide normal maintenance and management support. Internally developed applications were maintained and managed in-house.

The network required specialized staff who could not be fully employed; thus, Digital was also contracted to provide for this network's support and management. This involved cooperating with the network management already provided by the communication carriers, including Hong Kong Telecom, the Communications Authority of Thailand, and the other Asian operators. To provide these services, Digital installed a network maintenance and management server at IKEA's offices in Hong Kong. By outsourcing the management, IKEA freed itself to carry out its primary function and specialization. Digital, on the other hand, was able to manage the network for the remote locations from Hong Kong by using its network specialist, who had contacts with Digital's staff in New Delhi, Bangkok, Taipei, and Seoul as well as in Sweden, where IKEA has its head office.

Management of the network requires ongoing monitoring of the cost structure of the leased data and packet-switching tariffs from the telecommunications companies as they move away from monthly billing to volume-related tariffs. Special management tools were developed to activate and deactivate circuits within the region in accordance with the daily business requirements, to provide strategic cost savings.

A variety of difficulties occurred, primarily due to the use of incompatible vendors' equipment (Digital and IBM) on the same international network. For example, at that time IBM's and Digital's messaging systems were incompatible. Further, problems were associated with the use of certain applications over packet-based networks compared with leased line data networks.

One part of the management system installed in Hong Kong includes a distributed electronic directory that enables the Asian offices to see the mail locations and addresses for the rest of IKEA. Also, the electronic mail system is linked to a distributed relational database system for the management of IKEA's suppliers. This database contains delivery schedules and delivery locations in the form of graphics files as well as appropriate E-mail and fax addresses.

As the IKEA case shows, the process of management has many facets. These range from managing the hardware components of the network (possibly provided by the telecommunications companies) through accounting for the various regional users, change and reconfiguration, and performance of the various applications. In fact, it is very unlikely that a single off-the-shelf management system will fulfill an individual company's requirements. It is also clear that close cooperation is required among the hardware and software vendor(s), the telecommunications companies, and the organization, including its various remotely located offices.

A further complication in this example is the fact that solutions developed in Sweden and widely used in Switzerland and Germany in conjunction with the telecommunications companies were not suitable for use in the Asian region without modification. This was due to two main factors: incompatibility between the IBM and Digital equipment and the different charging schemes of the telecommunications companies.

The second example comes from one of Hong Kong's largest operations, the Royal Hong Kong Jockey Club. We cannot describe all the aspects of the management systems for this organization; rather, we give an overview of its operations to demonstrate how important a network management system is for an organization of this complexity.

FIGURE 11–1

IKEA's Asian regional data network

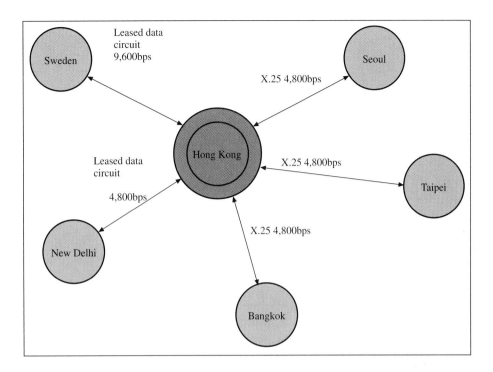

ROYAL HONG KONG JOCKEY CLUB

The Royal Hong Kong Jockey Club operates a very extensive network of over 32,000 terminals based out of two key locations, Happy Valley and Sha Tin. Its policy is to base information technology facilities on a preferred vendor—in this case Digital Equipment, which provides computing resources, bulk storage devices, LANs, and system software. Products from other vendors are installed only where their offerings complement the Digital architecture or where Digital lacks an equivalent or sufficiently competitive product. This policy simplifies the overall management of the computer-communications network.

With central sites at the Happy Valley and Sha Tin racecourses, the organization has implemented a management strategy of full cross-site redundancy for all critical systems. In the event of a disaster at one site, the other location can be switched to fully support the operations under the control of the management system. The sites are not mirror images of each other, since most development work takes place at Happy Valley, whereas Sha Tin is the test bed for the Telebet operation.

To further support reliability, the organization configures computer processors in clusters with common access to disk drives and the network. There are six such clusters at Happy Valley and four at Sha Tin. The overall management system can then allocate resources in a strategic manner given the amount of redundancy. It is interesting to note the size and complexity of some of these systems that must come under the control of the management system. These include about 132 Digital VAX 6000, 8000, and Micro VAX 3000 series processors, a dual fiber optic ring system between Happy Valley and Sha Tin, more than 32,000 terminals, numerous LANs, and about 200 Gbytes of disk storage (as discussed in Chapter 4, 1 Gbyte = 1 billion bytes!).

Management of this complex telecommunications network is critical, and currently it is being streamlined to provide a more integrated, resilient, and cost-effective communications system. Within the two main sites, communication is based on Digital LANs, with each cluster of processors linked to dual LANs to provide for reliability. The management system's task is therefore to monitor these systems and to switch to different configurations in times of disaster.

LAN segments are separated by bridges (see Chapter 5) for data security and load sharing. A dual fiber distributed data interface (FDDI) ring operates at 100 Mbps among Happy Valley, Sha Tin, and Tsing Yi Island (the location of the telephone telebetting system) and links the various LANs at these locations.

At a later stage, this network will be enhanced to support voice and video communications in addition to conventional data, thus making even greater demands on the management system. The 2,600 telephone lines into Sha Tin and Tsing Yi Island have recently been replaced by an optical fiber link directly to Hong Kong Telecom.

This example shows that the task for the management system of a computer-communications operation with more than 32,000 terminals and over 130 computer systems is particularly critical. It is Hong Kong's largest and most complex network (although it does not operate internationally, as do Reuters, the banks, and the airlines). One advantage is that Digital Equipment provides the management system as well as the vast majority of the equipment. Other businesses, because of integration and cooperation requirements, often do not have the advantages of being able to purchase from a single vendor.

These examples illustrate some of the complexities involved in managing networks, particularly mixed-vendor environments where products are far from mature. The issues to be resolved and further discussed in this chapter include

- Configuration and change management.
- Fault management.
- Performance monitoring.
- Accounting and security.

Network Intrusion: An Analysis

This section presents three progressively dramatic examples in which security was breached and data were exposed.

The first example will be familiar to many readers.

LAPTOPS—A POTENTIAL SECURITY RISK

Joe Adams works in the personnel section of a police department. He therefore has access to files on staff, including salaries, addresses, and many personal details. One day he was running late on updating some of the records, so he decided to take his laptop computer and disks home and finish the job in the evening. He had a modem and could dial up the office host computer via the telephone network. Just before he left, his wife called and asked him to pick up some items at the nearby supermarket. He was away from his car for only 10 minutes, but when he returned the laptop was gone, including the disks with the current updates.

There are a number of points to note in this example:

- A laptop computer frequently holds much sensitive information, yet is extremely insecure because it can be moved so easily. Today's laptops store the equivalent amount of data that many companies' multinational mainframes held 10 to 15 years ago!
- Laptop data are often backed up infrequently. Hence, recovery can be extremely time consuming.
- If the laptop is insured, probably only the hardware is covered (which can be replaced within a day). However, the *software* and *data* are the most valuable components. Recovery is often very expensive (and, for Joe Adams, most embarrassing).

The second example involves a bank, but it could happen in many other organizations.

How Secure Is Your Secure Network?

In late 1994, the manager of a major international computer company visited the IT manager of a large bank. In the discussions that followed, the computer company manager asked the bank's IT manager about the security of the bank's local area network. (Recall from Chapter 5 that a LAN consists of workstations, cables, file servers, print servers, etc.). The IT manager replied that he was in charge of "possibly one of the most secure LANs in town."

The computer company manager then asked if he could wander around the various floors of the bank, carrying his standard laptop computer and wearing a white coat to make himself look like a technician. "No problem at all," said the IT manager. "After all, we have a totally secure network that only fully authorized staff know how to access."

For the next 10 minutes, the computer manager wandered around until he saw a LAN wall socket (of which there were many in various offices). Then he plugged in his *standard* laptop with a *standard* cable into this *standard* socket. (We discussed these standard devices in Chapter 5.) Nobody asked him what he was doing; in fact, bank staff standing next to him took absolutely no notice at all. Over the next few minutes, the computer manager captured a highly secure and confidential file that just happened to be transmitted around the LAN at that time. After editing it, he printed a copy, returned to the IT manager's office, and handed him a copy of the confidential file. "I do not believe this—it is not possible!" exclaimed the IT manager, paling as he realized what had happened.

Note the following key issues in this example:

- The IT manager has since implemented a full review of security at the bank and undertaken a thorough risk analysis of the bank's operations. However, this review took place *after* the security breach occured. Sometimes companies are put out of business by security breaches—information stolen by competitors, corruption of data files, introduction of viruses, and so on.

- Nobody in the bank asked the computer manager what he was doing there (the "it's not my problem" syndrome).
- The computer manager used a standard PC (with a standard Ethernet card), a standard cable, and a connection to a standard wall plug—as easy as plugging in any electrical device.
- The network itself did not check to see who was connected to the wall plug. With many standard LANs on the market, it is not necessary to have an ID and password to log in to the network to capture the data. Thus, the design of the network itself was at fault as well.
- In most LANs, all connected devices receive all data from a device that transmits similarly to the way TV signals are transmitted. This method, of course, is fast and efficient. For security purposes, however, modern LAN design requires that only the *intended* recipient receive the data and that all other users receive unintelligible versions of the data. This, of course, requires more sophisticated and more expensive equipment.
- The cost of implementing a secure network must be compared with the benefits that accrue from such a system, since every business will have different requirements in this respect.

The third example occurred in 1986, when a major breach of security occurred that involved the use of international networks. This event became a landmark and triggered many advances in security around the world. It also became possibly the most widely reported security breach in the history of computers. Following is a brief summary.

STALKING THE WILY HACKER

In August 1986, a persistent computer intruder attacked the Lawrence Berkeley Laboratory (LBL) in California. Though not known at the time, the intruder was not even a U. S. resident. The authorities took a novel approach: The intruder was allowed to continue while his activities were traced. This process took *nearly* a year even with the cooperation of many international organizations.

It became apparent that the intruder was using LBL as a hub for accessing many other installations, including several military and defense establishments, universities, and research organizations. Over a 10-month period, he attacked 450 computers and successfully entered more than 30. The intruder used no new methods. Instead, he repeatedly applied techniques documented elsewhere: bugs in operating systems, exploiting blunders resulting from vendors, users, and system managers.

Sources: Clifford Stoll, "Stalking the Wily Hacker," *Communications of the ACM* 31, no. 5, (May 1988), (pp. 484–89); *The Cuckoo's Egg* (New York: Doubleday, 1989).

The first clue came when LBL noticed that a new account had been created without a corresponding billing address. Then a report came from the National Computer Security Center that someone at LBL had attempted to break into one of the military computers through a military network. (The intruder was not at LBL but was merely using it as a gateway.) After some time, it was found that the intruder was entering through an X.25 public packet-switching connection (we discussed this type of public network in Chapter 4). He guessed at passwords and managed to represent himself as a systems manager on a number of computers, gaining the accompanying operating privileges. The intruder downloaded encrypted password files into his own computer, cracking the codes and returning a week later to log in using these IDs and passwords. He even managed to connect to a computer running real-time support for a medical patient.

With the cooperation of the international telecommunications operators, the caller was eventually traced to the universities of Karlsruhe and Bremen in Germany. Yet the trail did not stop here.

The important point to note from these examples is that it is extremely difficult to differentiate between valid access to the network by an authorized systems manager or technician and an intruder. We will see later in this chapter that new design techniques are now finding their way into local and wide area networking equipment, offering much better security to users of these networks.

At the same time, however, the volume of information being stored and transmitted across these networks is growing at astounding rates. Organizations depend so heavily on this information that loss of access to it from security breaches can put a company out of business overnight. In Chapter 1, we looked at some examples of this. For instance, Cathay Pacific Airlines of Hong Kong lost access to data for 13 hours as a result of a security breach. Whether the breach was caused by an intruder or some other external source (as was the case in this example), the result for the business was the same. Other examples discussed in Chapter 1 demonstrated that loss of access to data can spell total catastrophe for the company.

Later in this chapter, we will look at a variety of network management tools and security systems that can assist in maintaining network operations and keeping the data secure. We will also see how networks are being designed and configured to achieve these objectives of management and security. No system can ever guarantee faultless management and security of data, but great strides are being made.

Change Management and Organizational Growth

The local and wide area networks that support the applications discussed in earlier chapters are in a constant state of change. It is most unlikely that a network you are using in your work has the same configuration that it did six months ago. In fact, the area of computer-communications changes so rapidly that the constant need to learn new procedures, document the location of equipment, and grapple with new releases of software (often after mastering the previous version) can be frustrating. However, tools are available to assist us in coping with these changes. These tools are referred to as *management systems*. This concept of *managing* the network has many implications, for example,

- Keeping a log of all equipment on the network, including location, serial number, value, and maintenance information.
- Monitoring all the equipment on the network (voltage levels, temperature levels, error rates, etc.).
- Keeping track of who is using the various items of equipment to ensure that unauthorized persons are not using the network.
- Maintaining an accounting log of equipment usage to bill users or customers for the use of resources.
- Monitoring the performance of the network and its applications from a user's viewpoint (e.g., monitoring response times for access to applications and availability of access to the networks and applications).

These issues become further complicated when we ask what we need from the IT platform:

1. To whom do we need to connect our business processes—the local office, the regional office, or worldwide customers and suppliers? This is often called the *reach*.

2. What information do we need to share? This is often called the *range*.

Reach and range are important issues in strategic business networking. Having one without the other can cause real problems, and one fundamental error is to establish *connection* rather than *communication*. The inability to manage a satisfactory IT platform has disabled many business strategies.

Achieving the reach may require interconnecting a number of LANs and WANs. Some of these networks will be private, while others will be owned and operated by the telecommunications companies. Each network is likely to come with its own management system. Today the telecommunications companies make a great deal of their *managed* networks. This implies that any component malfunction or failure on their networks is picked up virtually instantaneously. Similarly, a LAN may have its own management system, which unfortunately is still vendor specific.

The matter is further complicated by the requirements of the company with respect to recovering from a fault. For example, consider a company running a distributed network throughout the United States. If the central management system exists in New York and a device such as a workstation or modem fails in Seattle, to where should this fault be reported? It may well be that certain faults need to be reported and rectified locally, others reported to and rectified from the central management system, or even a combination of both.

To take this example even further, suppose the LAN and its associated management system running in New York is from a different vendor than the LAN and its associated management system running in Seattle. Also, each of the interconnecting networks (e.g., AT&T and Sprint) has its own management system. Reporting network faults can become a very difficult task in such a distributed environment.

The real problem today is that it is very difficult to integrate and communicate management information among these different management systems, since each system is usually a proprietary one. Later in this chapter we discuss *open systems,* which represent an ongoing attempt to solve this dilemma.

The important issue to be noted at this stage is what functions need to be managed in a changing environment. Once we understand what we are trying to do, the process of searching for and obtaining network management products becomes much easier, even if we do not obtain the total solution at this stage.

These functional requirements are as follows:

- *Problem or fault management*: handling errors within the network from initial detection to resolution. This involves fault detection and diagnosis, followed by procedures to repair or bypass the problem, as well as reporting the network equipment and service failures to a management database.

- *Accounting management*: determining costs for usage of resources and the assignment of corresponding charges.

- *Configuration management*: maintaining an inventory of network equipment software and circuits through facilities that control network resource interrelationships, set or change configuration parameters, and collect status information.

- *Performance management*: determining and reporting the network performance statistics in such areas as user response time, network availability, network resource utilization, and throughput. This encompasses network tuning and adjustment, bottleneck detection, and avoidance.

- *Change management*: planning, control, and application of changes to the network (the least defined yet one of the most important areas of network management).

- *Security management*: incorporating access control for the network via authentication, provision of encryption for stored and transmitted data, as well as a variety of verification and auditing techniques.

Mixed-Vendor Network Management

The explosion in the size and complexity of today's local and wide area networks, coupled with the ever-increasing demands businesses place on them for their strategic resources, means that management is a critical factor. To further complicate matters, the idea of a single vendor network has all but vanished. Even if a company's total networking solution is supplied by a single vendor, the requirement to interconnect with related companies via or in conjunction with public or private networks makes this objective unrealistic.

Many companies now place great strategic importance on their networks such that failure of the network is tantamount to failure of the business, or at least a failure to maintain market share. Even some medium-size businesses rate the cost of network failure around tens of thousands of dollars per hour.[1]

Users are increasingly becoming concerned about fault management as the strategic value of networks increases, due to migration following downsizing as well as the support required for mission-critical applications in a distributed environment. This concern, coupled with increased corporate globalization, often leads users to require constant network availability as the network becomes the primary strategic resource.

Most networks in organizations today consist of a relatively heterogeneous collection of components from various manufacturers, where every manufacturer would like to believe that its own network management system is the preferred choice. Although manufacturer-specific management systems have been used in the past, there is now considerable activity with the implementation of two specific management protocol suites. Therefore, some form of multivendor network is now thought to be inevitable. This, of course, is a difficult goal to achieve, since many companies employ the services of public network carriers to derive a virtual private network for national or international operation. Thus, it becomes very difficult to define the management boundaries of such interconnected networks.

The primary objective of network management has traditionally been fault detection and restoration to meet the requirements of the end user. While this is an admirable objective, network management encompasses a great deal more. As we will see later in this chapter, the development of **CMIP (Common Management Information Protocol)**—the ISO management protocols—has made the industry aware of the full range of management objectives, which include problem or fault management, accounting management, configuration management, performance management, change management and, more recently, security management. In the past, some of these management functions were carried out in an ad hoc, informal manner, with little or no attention given to the integration of these individual management components. One important management suite that evolved out of work with TCP/IP (Transmission Control Protocol/Internet Protocol) and the Internet was **SNMP (Simple Network Management Protocol)**. However, SNMP initially addressed only fault management, although significant changes have occurred as a result of the development of both CMIP and **SNMP-2** (version 2).

The primary characteristic of an integrated network management system is the ability to manage all parts of a multiproduct, multivendor, multicarrier communications network from one or more centralized or distributed points. Vendors now accept that independent systems that manage only a portion of the network are no longer acceptable.

---

[1] In a recent business video-conferencing presentation, Peter Keen reported network failures costing medium-size U. S. companies $5,000 to $50,000 per hour.

The Structure of Integrated Multivendor Network Management

The notion of *what* is to be managed in a network varies according to the specific interests and responsibilities of those involved (see Figure 11–2). For example, those involved in providing the transmission services (such as a telecommunications company) are *primarily* interested in the monitoring and management of the central telecommunications cloud. Others primarily concerned only with the provision of a transport service to the application systems tend to view the *physical* network. Finally, an end-to-end view is taken by those concerned with the delivery of service to the end users. They encounter situations where the physical network is fully operational but the application cannot be accessed for a variety of reasons, such as operator actions, user mistakes, misunderstandings, and upper-layer protocol violations. This group takes an end-to-end, *logical* view of the network. Network management systems can be implemented to accommodate each of these views, or they can be combined to form open system integrated network management.

The management system needs to include the *user* aspects of the network, that is, application functionality, performance parameters such as response time, and availability. What is required, therefore, is an integrated management system that provides supervision and control of *all* the elements and resources involved in the distributed application systems: communications services, attached devices, and users. The management system should also provide services that assist in the long-term planning, management, and changes to the network for the expansion and modification of the overall business.

There are a number of new and important aspects to network management development. The key issues concern

- The functional standards, as well as the modeling concepts, and how they relate to an open system multivendor framework.
- The use of object-oriented programming for the representation of the various management processes.
- Administrative requirements (maintenance, forward planning, historical summaries and analysis, and billing) and operational requirements (day-to-day fault analysis, restoration of services, real-time monitoring, bandwidth management, and alarm processing).

FIGURE 11–2

Views of the scope of open system network management

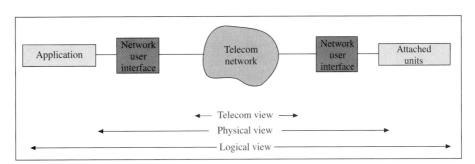

As open system management evolves and related products become widely available, computers can be interconnected more readily, thus reducing the costs of the management interconnectivity. Also, management support systems should be specified to improve the overall administration of the information system.

Management support systems take many forms, including

- Fault and audit trail archiving.
- Inventory control.
- Trouble ticket and spares ordering systems.
- User help desks.
- Network directories.
- Relational databases for statistical data analysis.
- Graphics devices for operator access.
- Automatic configuration file backups.
- Network software distribution.
- Report generators.
- Integrated mailing and bulletin systems.

This list is not meant to be exhaustive, but such mechanisms should be inspected against the overall operational cost-benefit criteria.

Multivendor Management Environments

There are four basic approaches to integrated network management:

- A universal interface to a standardized manager directly from all devices or subnetworks (see Figure 11–3).
- An integrated manager (general manager) with a uniform interface to element managers, which themselves possess standardized or specific interfaces to the network elements (see Figure 11–4).
- A management network in which the element managers are linked among themselves to several integrated managers rather than one (see Figure 11–5).
- The platform approach, in which the network elements use various protocols to access a multivendor network manager platform, which itself provides a universal **application program interface (API)**, on which standardized and manufacturer-specific network management applications can run (possibly from different manufacturers that have nothing to do with the network elements—see Figure 11–6).

The first alternative above (see Figure 11–3) requires a truly uniform network management standard. If every system in the network supported protocols and data structures based on this standard, a uniform general manager could be used. But currently, because of the enormous installed base, this approach is unrealistic. It would be impossible to replace all devices to the extent that they could conform to a new, uniform standard.

Manufacturers such as IBM have decided to continue using their own existing management interfaces for monitoring and controlling their own products. In a few areas there are standards, for example, with some LANs, TCP/IP networks, OSI networks, and **UNIX** systems. For example the common standard for TCP/IP network management, SNMP (discussed shortly), has become a de facto standard that permits the implementation of powerful manufacturer-independent network managers, even for the broad area of hubs, switches, bridges, and routers. Although such a de facto standard is extremely popular, whether the current euphoria will hold out in the long term is open to debate.

The second option, the integrated general manager (see Figure 11–4) is a much more likely scenario, since it requires only relatively few standardized interfaces to link the element managers with the integrated general manager. Because of the modular software design, element managers are easy to equip with these interfaces. Moreover, the element managers filter out important details for the integrated general manager and carry out element-specific tasks on their own. In the previous example, the standardized manager has to take on all the fine control tasks. The installed base of network elements can therefore remain untouched.

FIGURE 11–3

Multivendor management (universal interface)

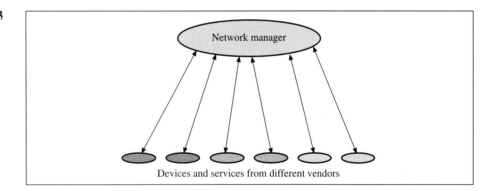

FIGURE 11–4

Multivendor management (single integrated manager)

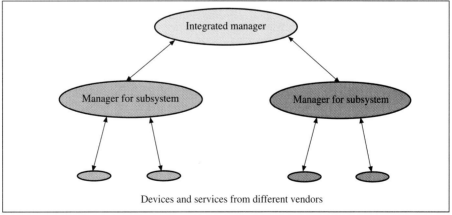

The third option (Figure 11–5) comes close to the recommendations of the OSI network management forum and offers considerable flexibility. From a practical point of view, this is clearly the most robust approach, since failure of the integrated general manager could sooner or later have far-reaching consequences for the network. However, the failure of a component has less serious consequences in this network. A hierarchically organized management network with few restrictions could lead to an unnecessary growth increase in management installations, more expensive and more frequent redundancy than desired, and even arguments over the capabilities of the various components (probably from different vendors).

The fourth option, the platform approach (see Figure 11–6), offers a real possibility for reducing the number of management systems. A management platform forms a standardized environment for the implementation of network and system management applications. The management platform defines a set of open application program interfaces that allows many vendors, software developers, and companies to generate high-quality, modern management software without having to struggle with the details of management protocols, management data definitions, or peculiarities of the user interfaces. The platform supplier would implement a set of tools and services to take over these functions.

A number of vendors' systems attempt to provide a multivendor network management system by implementing one of these strategies. These include IBM (NetView/6000), Hewlett-Packard (OpenView), and vendors such as cisco, Digital

FIGURE 11–5

Multivendor management (multiple integrated managers)

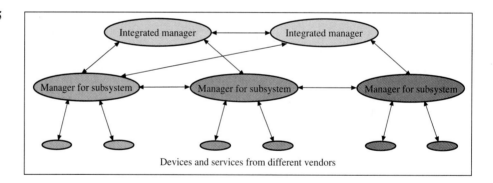

FIGURE 11–6

Multivendor management (platform strategy)

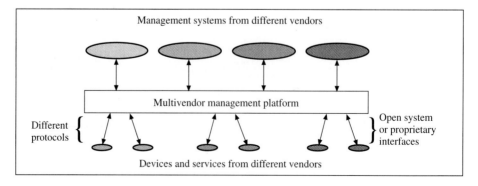

Equipment, Newbridge, and Telematics. SNMP is used very widely with UNIX architecture and on many of the world's large networks such as the Internet (see Chapter 3). Since this is a very important option affecting the multivendor situation, it is described next.

Operational Functions of a Management System

The interface between a device or software in the network and the management system is often called the *manager-agent interface*, because for each device or software suite involved, there is an agent that collects information for the management system and executes the management commands. Management information flows in both directions across this interface. To work together, both manager and agent must implement the same management information protocol and agree on a particular presentation of the management information to be carried by this protocol. This agreement over syntax (the protocol) and semantics (the data definitions) must be adhered to before a management system can work with a particular device.

CMIP and SNMP share important concepts. These are shown in Figure 11–7, which illustrates a typical management interaction. The managed resources shown can include protocol stacks, bridges, routers, modems, computer systems, applications programs, disk files, and so on. These resources are represented by managed objects, and all managed objects are stored in a conceptual repository called the **management information base (MIB)**. This MIB is made visible to managers by the agent, which is typically a management station or application program. The manager and agent communicate using a management protocol (e.g., CMIP or SNMP). The agent's job is to receive management protocol operations from the manager and to map from the operations on the conceptual managed objects to operations on the actual underlying system resources. For example, a management request to get the number of packets received on a network interface might involve a simple lookup by the agent or may require communication between the agent and an interface card to retrieve information.

FIGURE 11–7

Example of management interaction with resources using MIB, agent, and protocols

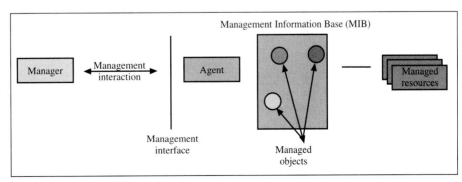

Open System and De Facto Network Management Protocols

The concept of open systems was introduced in the section on ISO (International Standards Organization) in Chapter 4. Standardization is a very important issue in networking, as we saw in many of the examples discussed in earlier chapters. Most of the public data networks around the world rely on the use of open system standards; previous examples include X.25 packet switching and RS-232/V.24 connector plugs. Many of these open system standards refer to the *lower* layers of the ISO model, but important developments are occurring at the *upper* layers. For example, X.400 electronic mail (discussed in Chapter 2 under electronic directories and messaging), EDI (also discussed in Chapter 2), X.500 directories, and various file transfer standards for intervendor communication have all been defined and accepted by the industry in recent years. Numerous examples of the use of these mail, EDI, directory, and file systems exist in practice.

The key management standard protocols are discussed next.

Simple Network Management Protocol (SNMP)

In an attempt to manage the different network topologies of complex internetwork systems, the U.S. Department of Defense and the commercial developers of TCP/IP released SNMP. Since then SNMP has grown into a widely accepted network management protocol, not just for connected networks but also for smaller LANs that use the same technology and topology.

Basically, SNMP defines a set of network management variables and the protocols used to exchange this network management information. In other words, SNMP provides a common format for network devices and equipment, such as modems, hubs, switches, concentrators, bridges, and routers, to exchange management data via an agent with the network management station. One or more of these management stations controls the network or internetwork through agents located in different pieces of network equipment. SNMP uses a simple scheme whereby the network management software (usually run from a central network management workstation) routinely polls for status information from an SNMP agent module installed on each network component. Figure 11–8 shows the typical protocol configuration used in the SNMP platform.

One problem with SNMP, as with any protocol implemented by many companies, is *compliance* versus *compatibility*. Although the standard was developed to enhance interoperability, the reality is often quite different. Some vendors provide proprietary information, called *extensions*. Software from other companies cannot read these extensions, and errors can result. Similarly, management software that is looking for proprietary extensions cannot effectively display another vendor's agent equipment.

Although some SNMP products offer better interoperability and more flexibility than others, most SNMP-equipped products are able to effectively exchange management and agent tasks between different vendors' systems. Clearly, SNMP is a popular and important development in network management and can now be

FIGURE 11–8

*Network
management
protocol
environment
for SNMP*

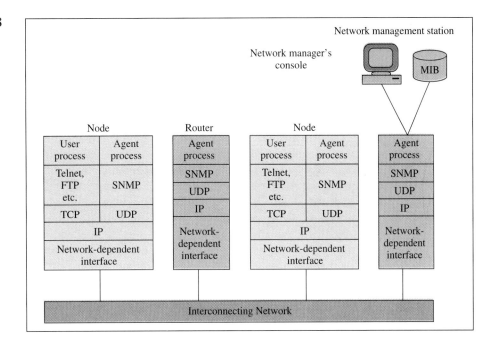

viewed as the de facto network management standard. However, it is very important to check for interoperability among the products before making any major purchasing decision.

Simplicity can also be a drawback, because it invites elaboration. Even when standards are created, they are violated as soon as a vendor adds a new feature. In SNMP, this violation takes the form of private extensions to MIBs and incomplete standard MIBs. These MIBs can also be used to specify other objects that require monitoring, such as network interfaces and traffic flows.

SNMP defines a standard MIB that, in theory, lets any network management console work with any agent and MIB. But vendors routinely omit parts of the standard MIB or use extensions that other vendors cannot support.

Perhaps the biggest problem with SNMP is its lack of security. Passwords for configuring routers, hubs, and servers are passed across the network in a single, unprotected packet. Another limitation of SNMP is that it currently includes support only for TCP/IP networks, although vendors have now modified SNMP to run on other network platforms, notably Novell's IPX and AppleTalk.

Simple Network Management Protocol Version 2 (SNMP-2)

Standard SNMP is suitable for simple tasks such as permitting network administrators to monitor remote hubs, switches, bridges, and routers. SNMP-2, on the other hand, is designed to extend management to applications and systems and to provide a path for manager-to-manager communication—the very features provided by CMIP.

Version 2 of SNMP was released in late 1993. A set of 12 **RFCs (requests for comments)** generated by the SNMP-2 and SNMP security working groups were approved by the Internet Engineering Steering Group (IESG). The release of the RFCs came only 13 months after the IESG issued a call for proposals on evolving the SNMP network management framework. A proposal called the Simple Management Protocol (SMP) was quickly developed by the original authors of SNMP and was pushed through the Internet standards structure.

SNMP-2 is an update of SNMP that is currently in use. The new standard enhances features and addresses faults found in the original version. It also draws from the five years of experience with SNMP and incorporates some of the features found in CMIP. It also reflects the need for the efficient and secure management of modern large distributed and integrated multivendor networks.

Mappings for several transport services are defined for SNMP-2. Additional data types based on implementation experience were also added, and coexistence with the existing SNMP framework has been of paramount importance. SNMP-2 is backward-compatible with SNMP devices through the use of proxy agents.

The general features of SNMP-2 include

- Security of management data between managing and managed devices, including encrypted password transfer, user authentication (discussed later in this chapter), and secure remote configuration capabilities.

- Faster collection and transfer of bulk management data.

- Peer-to-peer communications among different network management domains and remote management standards for manager-to-manager MIB operation.

- Operation over a variety of transports, including AppleTalk, Novell's IPX, OSI networks, as well as TCP/IP.

- More efficient SNMP applications through the extended command set, which provides functions that previously needed laborious hand coding.

- Other new features such as alarm correlation, distributed rule-based expert system, object-type definitions, report generation, improvement over SNMP's cryptic error codes, and procedures for adding rows to a network management table are included.

A further enhancement of SNMP that is closely related to SNMP-2 is the **remote monitoring (RMON) MIB**. RMON defines an MIB that lets active network monitors continuously feed information about network health and traffic into an SNMP-based console without waiting for a request. The RMON MIB consists of nine distinct groups, including statistics, history, alarms, filters, packet capture, events, host, and others. However, the RMON agent needs to implement only one of these functions. A single management station can therefore observe and manage a large network with many segments.

Common Management Information Protocol (CMIP)

CMIP is designed for networks based on the OSI model. It is an object-oriented protocol that keeps a database of objects, each of which represents an actual network device such as a workstation, bridge, or router. The database also defines the relationships among the objects. Network management software, in turn, makes use of the data stored in the CMIP database.

A CMIP console can also establish a session with a device and download many different pieces of information—all error statistics, for example—with one command. In contrast, SNMP must query for each piece of information.

Despite the appeal of its features, CMIP has so far found limited acceptance among vendors and users. One reason is that the specification is very broad and leaves considerable room for interpretation when it comes time to implement the protocol. This has resulted in difficulties in achieving interworking among different implementations of CMIP.

One reason for SNMP's continued dominance over CMIP lies in its flexibility. Missing features can be added to SNMP through a standards process that typically takes a year or two. Changes to the core CMIP specifications, on the other hand, must wait on OSI's approval cycles, which takes up to five years.

CMIP is more suitable for managing in-depth hierarchical information (such as complex error messages and some remote procedures). It uses a more intelligent, report-oriented method for gathering data on network components. It is frequently necessary to see more than just alarms and events when faults occur in the network. With SNMP, it is necessary to go through several procedural steps to configure a parameter on a device. In CMIP, a remote connection is established with the device, and one command can implement several actions.

SNMP can be used to gather data on individual network components, which can then be routed via CMIP to other network management programs. In such a scheme, CMIP becomes the common communications protocol among network management systems.

With CMIP, managers can operate a network of multiple devices, keeping the databases of individual management systems in synchronization, and easily issue commands to the management systems. CMIP is also concerned with other types of information, such as statistics on network performance, security, configuration, and accounting, in addition to fault detection. CMIP automatically updates the various management systems when changes are made in the network's configuration. These tasks are not possible in SNMP. For the management of complicated enterprise networks, CMIP is the preferred option, while for LANs and internetworking, SNMP is preferred. Figure 11–9 shows CMIP's specific management functional areas together with the system management functions and services required to support them.

CMIP specifications have recently gained support from critical vendors, including IBM and Hewlett-Packard. Users and vendors have found that CMIP is a better option than SNMP for enterprise management because it supports peer-to-peer interactions across numerous management domains. CMIP has greater reliability and is better suited for umbrella management systems that provide a centralized perspective of enterprise networks.

FIGURE 11–9

*CMIP's system
management
functions and
services*

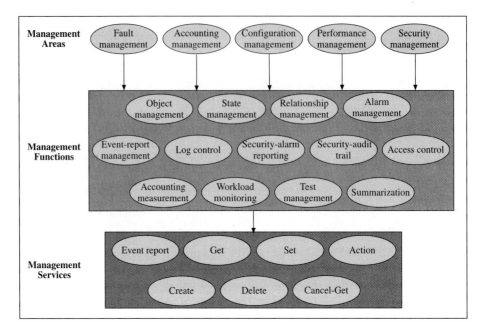

Specialized Network Management Standards Activities

Other specialized management standards are also emerging. One industry group, the Desktop Management Task Force (DMTF), has produced standards for managing PC applications and desktop systems for auditing, messaging, and other office automation products. The DMTF, a consortium that includes Microsoft, Apple, Compaq, and AST, has also produced MIB-like agents that will run on PCs and allow network managers to configure and control attached devices such as faxes, printers, and disks.

Another development lies in the cooperation and interworking of CMIP and SNMP as discussed earlier but is formalized under the Network Management Forum's project as the Distributed Management Environment (DME). The aim is to develop a platform that essentially resolves the debate over SNMP versus CMIP by allowing both protocols to exist within one framework. However, it actually goes far beyond that and proposes to cover everything from user interfaces to hierarchical management system communications. The practical result is that DME, if successful, will erase the differences among existing management systems. IBM, Microsoft, and Hewlett-Packard (HP), among others, have announced their support for DME. In fact, HP's OpenView network management platform is partly based on DME. DME-compliant products are unlikely to be available for some time. In the meantime, vendors will have to cooperate to make their platforms more interoperable.

Distributed and Integrated Network Management

The concepts of distributed and centralized or integrated network management were introduced earlier in this chapter. Ideally, a single focal point for the management of the entire network and applications appears desirable. In practice, this may be difficult to achieve. Consider the following scenarios.

> A large building had wiring and LAN equipment installed at the time it was constructed. From one point of view, it would be ideal if all of the equipment could be managed from a single focal point for all tenants in the building. However, consider a single tenant, such as a company that has a number of offices scattered around a city such as Los Angeles. This company would like to manage its distributed offices from a single focal point, which may well be different from the focal point for all of the building's tenants.
>
> Now suppose this company has offices in other parts of California as well as a number of other states. Interconnection to these other locations takes place via other agencies' networks (such as AT&T or Sprint), each of which manages its network from its own focal point. If our company is a multinational one, there may be good reason to carry out the management from the head office in Paris or New York so that the company will have overall management control. But would this be the optimal approach? Does the New York head office really want to know if the Anaheim branch of the Los Angeles operations goes down? In some cases yes, and in other cases no.

This example illustrates the need to define *what* information must be managed and *where* it is best managed from. Thus, these issues must be thoroughly analyzed before any thought is given to the purchase of a management system. This analysis alone will place a company in a better position to fully understanding these issues; it can only improve the company's mission. It is clearly foolish to purchase and install a management system and then say, "Well, now that we have it, what can we manage?"

Systems management is applicable to a wide range of distributed processing and communications environments, ranging from local area networks interconnecting small systems to interconnected corporate and national networks on a global scale.

Functional Management of Network Objects

Again we come back to the essential issues of *what it means to manage the objects in a network*. This time we look at it in terms of distributed versus centralized management control. The requirements to be satisfied by systems management activities can be categorized into the five functional areas of management: fault, accounting, configuration, performance, and security management.

Fault Management.   Fault management encompasses fault detection, isolation, and the correction of an abnormal operation. However, this is generally carried out on a local or regional basis. The New York management center may not want to know about a line dropout today but does want to know that it has occurred 20 times in the last three months.

Faults cause systems to fail to meet their operational objectives. They may be persistent or transient. Faults manifest themselves as events (e.g., errors) in the operation of a system. Error detection provides a means of recognizing faults. It includes functions to

- Maintain and examine error logs.
- Accept and act on error detection notifications.
- Trace and identify faults.
- Carry out sequences of diagnostic tests.
- Correct faults.

Careful analysis is required to ensure that a fault is reported to the location that can best respond to the problem.

Accounting Management.   Accounting management enables charges and costs to be established for the use of resources. It includes functions to

- Inform users of costs incurred or resources consumed.
- Enable accounting limits and tariff schedules to be set for the use of resources.
- Enable costs to be combined, where multiple resources are invoked, to achieve a given communication objective.

Generally, account reporting is carried out on a local or regional basis but with periodic accounting summaries to be reported to central management, usually the head office.

Configuration Management.   Networks are in a continual state of change. Users move locations, software is upgraded, applications are made available to different user groups, and cable types and routes are subject to change. Keeping track of these details is often so complex that a CAD (computer-aided design) system such as AutoCAD is required. Such a system includes features to

- Set the parameters that control the routine operation of the systems.
- Associate names with, initialize, and close down managed objects.
- Collect information on demand about the current condition of the system.
- Obtain announcements of significant changes in the condition of the system.
- Change the configuration as needed.

Again, certain configuration changes will need to be carried out at the local or regional level, while others will need to be reported to a central management center.

Performance Management.   Performance management enables the behavior of resources and the effectiveness of communication activities to be evaluated. It is closely linked to the competitiveness of an organization, since poor performance in the network frequently means poor performance overall. It includes functions to

- Gather statistical information.
- Maintain and examine system logs.
- Maintain state histories.
- Determine system performance under various conditions.
- Alter system modes of operation for the purpose of conducting performance management activities.

Some of these activities relate to equipment installed locally, but frequently the overall network design is at fault, demonstrating how important centralized management can become.

Security Management.   Security management supports the application of security policies by means of functions that include

- Creation, deletion, and control of security services and mechanisms.
- Distribution of and reporting on security-relevant information.

These five areas of functional management may or may not be handled by the same group within a business organization. For example, we may not want the technical people who are responsible for network design and fault resolution to be responsible for the accounting, billing, and financial functions of the network. Also, these functional areas can be decomposed into regional groups, with the appropriate regional staff responsible for each group's operation.

Security Issues in Networking

The most secure system is unusable, and the most usable system is insecure.

A fundamental paradox exists in networking between the need to *share* information and resources across distributed systems and at the same time *control access* to them. Networks are implemented to provide local and wide area access, resource sharing, information sharing, application sharing, and other shared services, but security features attempt to restrict and mediate users' actions and the information and services that they access. The problem is complex, and in many cases underlines the common belief that "networks should always be considered insecure." This notion can be overcome through sound network management practices.

The primary objectives for networks are to reduce costs by sharing equipment and thus foster cooperation among computing entities and make access to information-processing resources easy and flexible. This usually involves increasing access and removing barriers and restrictions. Security, on the other hand, normally involves limited cooperation, confinement of users and data, and limitation of access to resources.

Security should be considered very early in a network's life cycle and not as a knee-jerk reaction to a catastrophic event. Retrofitting a LAN with security once it is operational will almost certainly be more expensive and less effective than incorporating security measures as part of the initial design and of the network administration policy.

An organization incurs costs for network security features not only as a direct cost for equipment but in terms of performance limitations. The costs of network security are incurred immediately, but the benefits may be intangible. How can an organization quantify the cost savings for events that might have occurred if a security mechanism were not in place? Thus, the four key goals of network security are to

1. Maintain *confidentiality* of data as they are stored, processed, or transmitted.
2. Maintain the *integrity* of data as they are stored, processed, or transmitted.
3. Maintain the *availability* of stored data.
4. Ensure the *identity* of the sender and the receiver of a communication.

All security efforts are directed at implementing systems that meet these four objectives.

Costs versus Benefits

It is never possible to ensure that a network is 100 percent secure. The greater the level of security, the more costly it will be. However, it is necessary to find a level of security appropriate for the particular organization. For a military establishment, this level might be rated at 99.99 percent and its implementation will cost much more than for another organization that is rated at 95 percent.

Typically, security is associated with the protection of classified information. In the commercial environment, information that could have harmed an organization if accessed improperly includes personnel data, strategic information, and various other types of proprietary information. Disclosure of protected commercial information could cause a loss of competitive edge and thus represents a real financial loss for the organization. In this section, we examine why networks are vulnerable to security breaches although the cost associated with measures to rectify these breaches will depend very much on the techniques used.

Managing Security in the LAN

The threats to LAN security can be categorized as follows.

The User.   The greatest threat is from the users themselves. Choosing obvious passwords, leaving systems turned on with applications running, lack of modem access control, use of broadcast protocols, and insecure cabling can all lead to security breaches that are common in many organizations.

The PC.   The PCs were originally designed for single-user, autonomous operation, and security within the operating system was hardly even considered. DOS, for example, has no concept of either multiple users or security.

Change.   Change is a major threat for network managers. In many companies, more than 30 percent of staff change location annually. Job functions and responsibilities change regularly, yet few organizations alter access rights to information to match employees' new job specifications.

Growth.   Since networks grow rapidly, the network manager frequently lacks sufficient knowledge of where and when new equipment is being added. This is further complicated by issues such as global networking, multivendor systems, and constantly changing technology.

Control.   Few network managers have the level of control they really need, and few know exactly who is connected to their multivendor network.

Lack of Resilience.   The nature of growth means that legacy LANs have not been designed to be resilient to security breaches. As the LAN becomes a fundamental part of a corporate structure, more and more staff are dependent on the LAN providing the operational tools for strategic information access.

LAN Broadcasts.   The dominant LANs of today, Ethernet and token ring, both use a broadcast technique. The information packets being sent between two devices are also sent to all other nodes on the network. An economical way to ensure that only the addressee sees the information is needed.

Server Access.   In most LAN systems, the user first makes a connection to a server and only then is asked for identification in the form of a login and password. The fact that the user has gotten this far is already a threat to security.

Inconvenience.   Unless the security measures are simple to use, they will fall into disuse.

Traditional Security Measures

There are a number of traditional approaches to LAN security, all of which have limitations.

Physical Security.   Where possible, key network devices should be locked away. However, with the growth of office automation, the server and printer are often freely accessible to users.

Passwords.   To get around the choice of obvious passwords, security software such as Password Coach can now enforce regular password changes and also ensure that passwords will be difficult to guess.

Timeouts.   Some workstations have inactivity timeout implemented whereby the workstation suspends operation if no data are entered for a specified period of time.

Encryption.   Organizations that have very sensitive information protect their networks with devices that encrypt the data. Encryption devices tend to be expensive and also demand a high degree of administration.

Structured Cabling and Building Security

In recent years, a major revolution in building cabling has occurred that has enabled security to be implemented at the lowest level of the LAN architecture. Legacy LAN configuration via coaxial bus cabling meant that it was impossible to control service and security to individual users. The move by many companies toward a structured network has allowed them to exercise individual control over users, if desired. As hub-based LANs, combined with category 3–5 UTP cabling, gradually replace the older coaxial bus systems, the services and security to individual users and devices can be greatly enhanced. Thus, by installing intelligent network hubs in the wiring closet, the monitoring of individual user levels is now feasible.

The backbone connecting individual subnetworks on different floors or between departmental work groups is another vital area where security needs to be addressed. This backbone should consist of at least coaxial cable and preferably optical fiber. Fiber is almost impossible to tap into without detection; it can support high-speed networks and is immune to electrical interference.

Further, the use of managed bridges to control access to the backbone ensures that only authorized traffic is transmitted between subnetworks. The use of closed user groups within these bridges can control access to the backbone even further by ensuring that traffic is controlled among individual groups of users.

In addition, the use of wiring closets ensures that the network equipment is locked away and may be accessed only by authorized personnel. Figure 11–10 shows three examples of departmental LANs on separate floors or work groups within a building being interconnected by secure structured cabling, preferably optical fiber. The backbone and equipment rooms should also be physically secure. Bridges with closed user groups protect the entrance to each department. The intelligent hubs enforce a level of security that is discussed in the following section.

Security in the LAN Hardware

The *structured cabling* approach is generally accepted as the best way to cable modern buildings, thus implementing cabling as a physical star. The irony is that these organizations are so close to achieving the security benefits of point-to-point conversations, but currently use the dominant LAN protocols of today—Ethernet and token ring—which send *everything to everyone*! The benefits of staying with these standard protocols is overwhelming. They are supported by all the major vendors, interworking is already proven, pricing is competitive, a wide choice of products is available, and businesses have a very large existing investment in these standard products.

FIGURE 11–10

Examples of structured wiring and backbone security in interconnected LANs

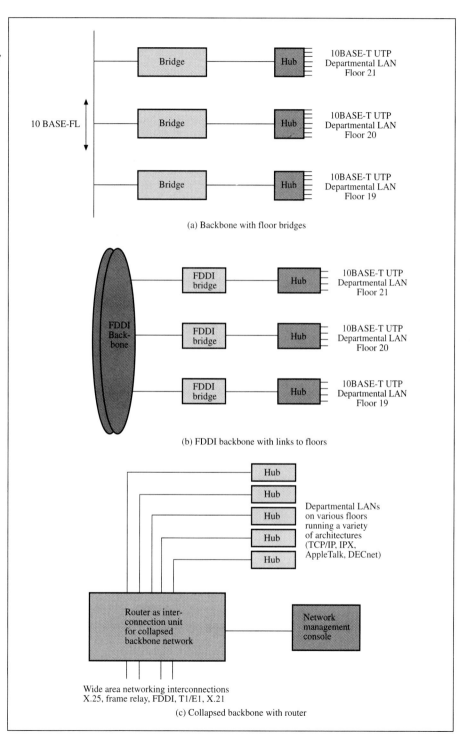

(a) Backbone with floor bridges

(b) FDDI backbone with links to floors

(c) Collapsed backbone with router

"Need to Know" Hubs.   An important principle of security is the need to know. In relation to LANs, this means sending the information only to the device and person to which the information is addressed. It is not necessary, and is not desirable from a security viewpoint, that all stations see the contents of every packet. Therefore, this ensures that only the addressed station sees the original packet and all other stations see a packet with the contents overwritten. This approach satisfies the rules of Ethernet while providing point-to-point security.

Figure 11–11 shows how this can be implemented in a star-wired Ethernet network. A normal Ethernet hub receives, retimes, and transmits the received packet out to all of its ports. If intelligence is added to this device, it can check each port before transmitting the packet. If the addressed device is known to be at the end of that connection, the packet is transmitted intact. On all ports connected to other devices, the information in the packet is overwritten.

The net effect of adding this intelligence to the hub is that only the addressee sees the information in the packet. In a sense, one has all the benefits of a LAN together with the security benefits of a point-to-point network available for every packet. This conformance to the Ethernet standard means that all existing Ethernet workstations, mini and mainframe network interface cards, terminal servers, and other Ethernet devices will work, unaltered, with this intelligent hub. Similar functionality can be added to a bridge.

Disconnecting Unknown and Unexpected Devices.   As the number of devices connected to the network grows, the challenge of knowing who is connected to the LAN increases. A way to restrict access to only known devices at known floor or wall sockets is required. This can be achieved by adding a functionality to the intelligent hub. As a packet is received from a port, its source MAC address can be checked against the expected MAC address for that port. If it does not match,

FIGURE 11–11

Implementing point-to-point security with an intelligent hub

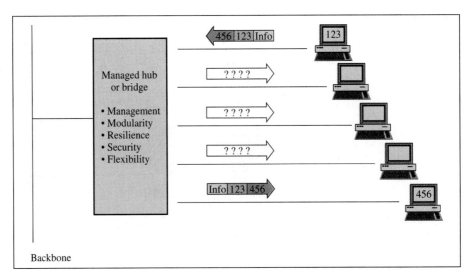

the port can be automatically disconnected, a warning sent to the management station, the event logged in a database for audit, and the packet destroyed, as shown in Figure 11–12.

Closed User Groups (CUGs).   CUG security has been part of wide area packet-based networks for many years but has only recently become part of the security philosophy in LANs. By adding intelligence to the hub or bridge, every packet can be examined to ensure that both the sending and addressed devices belong to the same CUG. Figure 11–13 shows how certain network devices, such as file or data-base servers, in the accounts, personnel, and inventory control departments are protected by CUGs. While Ray has access to the accounts server, he cannot access either the personnel or the inventory file server. Biddy can access two groups, accounts

FIGURE 11–12

Disconnection of unknown devices

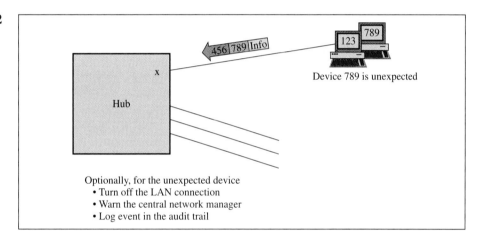

FIGURE 11–13

Closed user groups

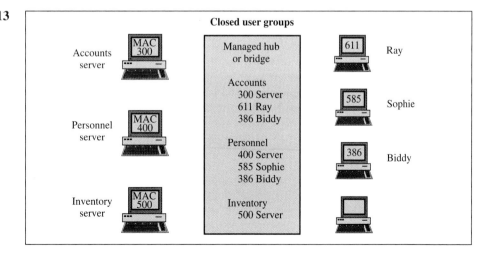

and personnel. The benefit is that the managed hub or bridge can restrict access to private conversations between authorized devices and prevent unauthorized (wandering around) conversations.

Access Servers.   The lack of security imposed by conventional password systems has led to the development of access servers, which provide a high level of security control. They are discussed in the following section.

Innovative Security Measures

In this section we look at new approaches to security that build on the features discussed in the previous sections and are receiving considerable attention in the literature as well as from the manufacturers. In particular, this section examines authentication techniques, encryption, and firewalls.

Passwords.   When it comes to choosing passwords, users show a dangerous lack of imagination. That plays right into the hands of hackers who take advantage of easy-to-guess passwords to gain entry to a network with at most a few attempts, even in spite of features such as user notification of "last successful login" and "number of login failures." Password capture and playback is a trivial task.

Users often base their passwords on their IDs, which are publicly known. A recent study found that 30 percent of the systems on the Internet could be penetrated by guessing a password that was a form of a user's ID or login, such as the ID itself or the ID spelled backwards. Robert Morris, who created the computer virus that brought down the Internet in November 1988, exploited this weakness to break into various computer systems. On his first attempt to access a system, Morris used a list of 73 words that included common names and words that Internet users frequently encountered. A study conducted after the virus attack found that more than 90 percent of the systems on the Internet had at least one user whose password was on Morris's list. If his list did not come up with a viable password, Morris resorted to the standard method used by hackers: using an online dictionary to try every word as a password. In most networking environments, dictionary attacks are very successful. A Syracuse University study found that 45 percent of the passwords on large computer systems were English words and 60 percent of users chose a password based on a word in a dictionary, a geographic location, or a proper name.

Message Authentication and Spoofing.   Message authentication, or nonrepudiation, allows users to determine (1) whether a received message is identical to the one transmitted from the origin, (2) if errors were introduced by accident or design, and (3) that no messages have disappeared and no new ones have been introduced. Authentication provides *integrity* but not *confidentiality*. It simply proves that the message originated from its proper source and that the source is authorized to issue the instructions that were received.

Spoofing refers to the unauthorized modification of traffic such that (1) either the contents of the message have been tampered with or (2) the message does not originate from the apparent sender's address (sometimes called *IP spoofing*). These problems can result from transmitting traffic in plaintext, lack of a date/time stamp on the message, lack of a message authentication code or digital signature, or lack of a real-time verification mechanism (to use against playback).

Token Authentication. In addition to conventional physical and software-controlled locks on hardware connectors, interface cables, and disks are token access systems. These include magnetic swipe cards, **smart cards**, and active badge readers, which have become popular as the limitations of pure password-based systems are fully realized. This is indicative of the move away from passwords (what the user can remember) to tokens (what the user can carry).

Active badge readers operate by use of an infrared transmitter and receiver that operate from the wearer's badge (or pager) and the workstation. Encrypted challenge/responses are handed between the two. Active badge systems have other benefits as well. They can provide hands-free access through security doors, activate secure printing only when the wearer is near the printer, provide a linkage to the UNIX finger command to assist with an individual's location, provide workstation lockout when the wearer leaves the room, and assist in the general location of personnel in or around a building.

Magnetic swipe cards and their personal identification numbers (PINs) can often be stolen, and therefore smart cards have been developed in conjunction with conventional password control. A smart card contains a chip that generates encrypted random numbers with a lifetime of around one minute. The user enables the token by entering a PIN. The smart card then accepts a challenge from the workstation or a similar device and generates a response or one-time password. This response is calculated from the challenge using data encryption. A cryptographic key is stored inside the token, and the PIN personalizes the token to its user; the same key, which is stored at the workstation, enables the system to establish the validity of the user. Since a different challenge is issued at each access attempt, even if someone is monitoring the communications channel, no information can be gained that would allow impersonation of the valid user. Examples of smart card products in this category include Racal's DynPass (used mainly for NetWare) and the Guardata WatchWord II Token.

Biometrics. **Biometrics** are techniques used for determining the way a person acts when using the system. For instance, it is possible to discriminate among users by observing the timing patterns of individual keystrokes for each user. Like a fingerprint, this timing pattern is usually unique to each person, and it is possible to accurately determine whether or not a person at a keyboard is who he or she claims to be. Other biometrics techniques are based on unique personal characteristics such as fingerprint recognition, retina scan, or **digital signature recognition** (to be discussed later).

Kerberos Security Access Server.   *Kerberos* is a security system developed as part of the Massachusetts Institute of Technology's Project Athena.[2] It is an add-on authentication system that delivers a higher level of security than those afforded by passwords and access control. In effect, Kerberos authenticates *every* user for *every* application. Kerberos is commonly used on the Internet and has been adopted by the Open Software Foundation (OSF) as part of its distributed computing environment (DCE). In addition, a number of vendors, including IBM, Digital Equipment, Hewlett-Packard, and Sun Microsystems, plan to make Kerberos part of their UNIX operating systems.

Kerberos, named for the three-headed watchdog that guarded the gates of Hades in Greek mythology, relies on three components to watch over network security: a *database*, an *authentication server*, and a *ticket-granting server*. All three components sit on a single, physically secured server that is connected to the network as shown in Figure 11–14.

The Kerberos database contains all network user names, their passwords, the network services to which each user has access, and an encryption key associated with each service. (In Kerberos terminology, a service can be an application on a host or something as simple as permission to look at a directory of files on a system.) The database is the only place on the network where passwords are stored. The **Kerberos authentication server** ensures that the persons requesting a network service, such as access to an application on a host, are actually who they say they are. The ticket-granting server, as its name suggests, issues tickets to the user once the authentication server has verified the user's identity. To access an application, a user needs both a ticket and a second credential, called an *authenticator*, which is issued by the client workstation. An authenticator consists of the user's name, the IP address of a workstation, and the time a request originates. In order to work with Kerberos, the PC operating system must be modified to process tickets and issue authenticators.

The Kerberos authentication process begins when a user logs onto a workstation and requests to be connected to an application. This request is sent to the authentication server, which determines whether the user has been granted access rights. The user name, not the password, is sent to the authentication server. Thus, if hackers are listening in, they are not given the opportunity to breach system security.

If the authentication server verifies that the user is allowed access to an application, it creates a ticket containing the client's name, the name of the target application server, the current time, the time for which the ticket is valid, and the client's IP address. (This ticket is good until the time limit is reached and can be reused for each request.) The authentication server also generates a random string of code, called a *session key*, which is appended to the ticket. Once the ticket has been written, it is encrypted using a key known only to the ticket-granting server and the authentication server. The authentication server takes the encrypted ticket and the session key and encrypts them a second time, using a private key derived from the user's

---

[2] J. I. Schiller, "Secure Distributed Computing," *Scientific American*, November 1994.

FIGURE 11–14

Ticket-granting authentication server

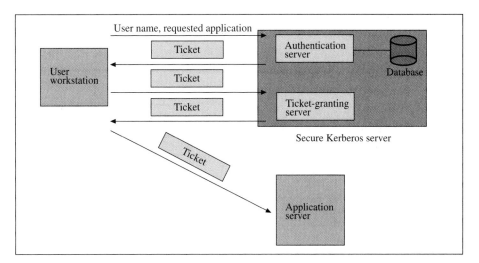

password (which is known only to the user and the authentication server). The output of this final encryption is sent back to the user, who decodes it with his or her private key (derived from the password) to recover the session key and the encrypted ticket. The authenticator is then encoded using the session key, combined with the encrypted ticket, and sent to the ticket-granting server. Here the ticket is decrypted (using the key sent from the authentication server previously) to recover the session key. It then uses the session key to decrypt the authenticator, which yields the time the authenticator was produced and the IP address of the client. If this information matches the IP address, user name, and time coded into the ticket, access to the application is granted. The time check is crucial because it prevents a hacker from capturing authenticators and tickets and reusing them.

Data Encryption.   Data encryption devices secure sensitive information while it is electronically transmitted, stored, or processed. Encryption systems, which include both hardware devices and software packages, employ a mathematical algorithm to scramble plaintext, rendering it unintelligible until it is unscrambled through the use of a special key. Used primarily by government agencies, encryption is becoming increasingly popular with businesses to protect confidential information and assets. Traditionally used to secure data transmissions, encryption is also capable of securing voice[3] and facsimile transmissions.

   Within the business community, encryption is used extensively by the banking and financial sectors for the transmission of financial reports, banking statistics, electronic money transfers, and other sensitive information. Unlike the government, businesses have the choice of whether to use an encryption device based on the **Data**

---

[3] Voice encryption is commonly achieved by the use of "clipper chips," which employ a proprietary split-key encryption algorithm called "shipjack."

Encryption Standard (DES) algorithm or use one of the proprietary algorithms. Businesses can also freely adopt improvements such as smartcard portable encryptors and downline key loading.

The use of hardware DES devices must be authorized by the U.S. government (sometimes in conjunction with other governments), although its use is accepted for the banking industry. DES is a symmetric algorithm in which both the sender and the receiver use the same (private) key. These keys are usually controlled and issued by a government agency. DES has a 56-bit key, but messages can be made more secure by repeated applications of DES (three passes of DES form the equivalent of a 128-bit key).

The alternative to DES is to use an asymmetric public key encryption system such as RSA (Rivest Shamir Adleman); a Lucas algorithm; PGP (Pretty Good Privacy); IDEA (International Data Encryption Algorithm), which is similar to DES but is a symmetrical crypto system with a 128-bit key; Seneca (used by the Australian government—128-bit key); or RC4 (40-bit key), used with commercial office automation products such as Lotus Notes. Each party uses a public and widely published key for encrypting the message but a private and secure key for decrypting it. Implementation of these algorithms is commonly achieved through the use of proprietary systems.

Encryption using DES keys is about 1,000 times faster than encryption using public keys in conjunction with the proprietary algorithms. DES employs an interchange scheme, whereas other algorithms use complex exponent processing. With DES, a new key is created for every "envelope" (or transmission) and often distributed using one-time pads (which can be stored on disks or CD-ROMs), whereas public keys can be kept in use for up to one to two years. However, the use of DES is strictly controlled, and the use of many encryption algorithms (particularly RSA) is protected by patent or copyright.

Encryption Technology.   Encryption scrambles *plaintext* requiring a *key* to decrypt or unscramble the data. In a typical system message, **m** (plaintext) is fed into an encryption algorithm, which is seeded by an enciphering key, **k(E)**, to produce a cryptogram or ciphertext, **c.** The idea is that the cryptogram should not resemble the message and should be such that an eavesdropper who obtains **c** should not be able to deduce **m**. For the message to be recovered, the cryptogram must be fed into a deciphering algorithm, which is seeded by a deciphering key, **k(D)** (see Figure 11–15).

Encryption offers the most comprehensive protection when combined with other kinds of protection, such as user authentication—for example, digital envelopes and digital signatures, to be discussed shortly. Encryption systems include both data encryption hardware devices and software packages. Many hardware-based encryptors are simple microprocessor-based "black boxes" that electronically encode data at the sending end and decode data at the receiving end. Several effective software packages are also available and run as applications programs on the user's system.

Hardware encryption devices provide certain advantages over software resident on a user's applications processor. For example, the installation of encryption hardware has a minimal effect on the user's existing computer system. Also, an encryption process employing hardware is virtually immune to unauthorized, undetected alteration. Software, on the other hand, is susceptible to programmer modification.

FIGURE 11–15

Encryption and decryption of plaintext by use of keys

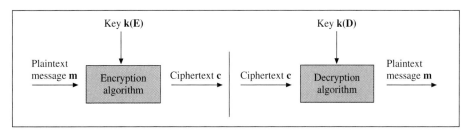

Key Management.   The success of an encryption system depends on its key management. Key management comprises the generation, distribution, entry, and destruction of key settings. Electronic and physical measures are used to safeguard the settings. Key settings are referred to as the *secret code*, the *key variable*, the *crypto key*, or the *key fill*. While in cryptography the encryption algorithm is usually common knowledge, transmission security is achieved through the safeguarding of the keys. For example, the DES algorithm is a published formula within the public domain. Distribution and handling of the keys are controlled and remain secret, ensuring that the encryption system operates properly.

Public keys are shared by all users in the network and are used to encrypt electronic communications. Decryption is accomplished by a *private* key that is different for each user.

Hybrid Cryptography and Authentication.   It is essential not only to protect a message in transit but also to be able to verify the authenticity of the sender. Two techniques are used for this purpose: digital signatures and digital envelopes.

Digital signatures. A digital signature is a unique code or bit pattern used to authenticate the sender of a message in a manner similar to using the frame check sequence (FCS) or cyclic redundancy check (CRC) for error checking a frame in a packet-switching network. The digital signature is calculated by applying the public domain MD4 or MD5 (message digest) hashing algorithm (designed at MIT, 1990–91) to produce a digest, which is then encrypted and appended to the message. The body of the message may be in plaintext or ciphertext. Encryption in this case can be carried out using either the DES symmetric private key method or one of the asymmetric public key systems discussed earlier. The receiver decrypts this message, decrypts the digital signature, and compares this with the digital signature calculated by reapplying the MD4/5 hashing function to the received message, as shown in Figure 11–16.

Digital envelopes. Sealing a **digital envelope** involves encrypting the message with a secret key and then encrypting the secret key with the receiver's public key. Upon receipt, the receiver decrypts the encrypted key with his or her private key and then decrypts the ciphertext with the secret key, as shown in Figure 11–17.

Router Filtering, Firewalls, and Bastion Hosts.   Interconnection to the Internet has generated much concern about security issues. As a result, topics such as router filtering, firewalls, bastion hosts, and application layer security are receiving a

FIGURE 11–16

Digest + public key = digital signature (sign and verify)

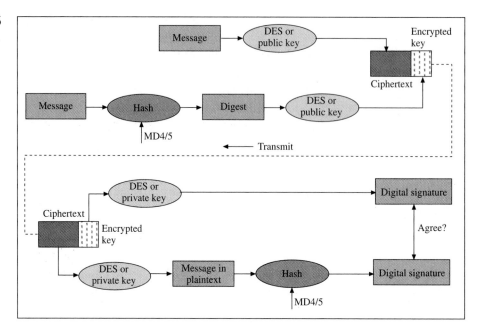

FIGURE 11–17

Secret key + public key = digital envelope (seal and open)

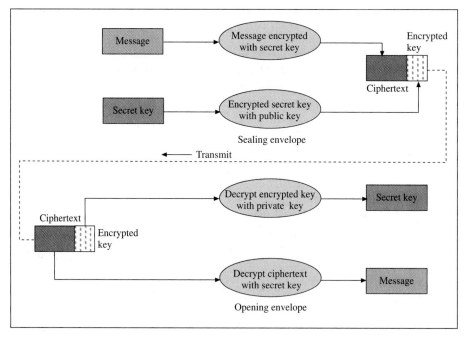

great deal of attention. Although strictly security issues, these topics were already discussed in Chapter 3 under "Performance and Security Issues" since they are so important.

Verification and Audit Techniques

Trojan Horses, Viruses, and Worm/Bacteria.   Instead of personally penetrating other computer systems, some irresponsible intruders specialize in writing programs that will do the job for them. Some of these programs merely commit minor pranks designed to show off their authors' cleverness; others commit far more serious infractions, such as destroying data, tying up networks, and violating security restrictions.

A common method used to introduce malicious software into a network is through the resources on the network, such as shared applications software. The intruder places malicious software in an enticing or new application, game, or other shared software. Common examples include shared software libraries, applications, utilities, or games; bulletin boards; public domain software; electronic mail; and file servers with public directories. Such software has various names depending on how it carries out its corruption process. The common ones are Trojan horses, viruses, and worms/bacteria.

Trojan Horses.   A *Trojan horse* is a malicious program that performs some useful task, such as sorting a disk directory, while at the same time carrying out some secret activity, such as introducing errors into data files, erasing files, or erasing the entire hard disk itself. The task the program is designed to perform is made as useful as possible to increase the number of people who use the program and hence fall prey to its hidden activities. Further, it can be timed to initiate in all copies of the program on a specific date. If users have made backup copies of their files, there may be no permanent damage. The lost data can be restored from the backup copies and the Trojan horse eliminated from the system.

Much more corrupting is a Trojan horse that performs its useful function but at the same time introduces hard-to-trace errors in the users' data files. The errors cause continuing problems, and the users will have great difficulty finding out what is wrong. On multiuser systems, Trojan horses can carry out other harmful activities. The program might pass secret data from a user authorized to access the data to an unauthorized user, or could install a so-called *trap door* that allows unauthorized users to gain access to the system.

Viruses.   A *virus* is a segment of code that, when inserted in an otherwise harmless program, converts the program into a Trojan horse. A program containing virus code can infect other programs by inserting the virus code into them. Worse yet, virus construction kits are available in journals and on the Internet—for example, VCL (Virus Construction Laboratory), 40HEX (Virus developer's journal), and others. Viruses are commonly spread by the exchange of infected disks between machines or individuals.

Whenever the virus is executed, it searches the disk for uninfected programs and infects them. Eventually, all the programs on the disk will become infected. If any one of those programs is transferred to another system, it will carry the infection with it and ultimately commit some malicious act, such as erasing a disk.

Over 3,500 known viruses exist. To aid in combating viruses, a number of *antiviral* or *vaccine programs* have appeared on the market, for example, Disinfectant and Gatekeeper (commonly used with Apple Macs) and F-Prot (File Protect) and Scan and Clean (commonly used with PCs). These programs work in several ways:

- They examine a suspected program for signs of infection.
- They detect the change in a program when it becomes infected. The antiviral program computes a "signature" for each file. After a program is infected, its signature will probably change, enabling the antiviral program to detect the infection.
- They monitor all disk activity and try to catch the virus in the act of infecting other programs.

Each antiviral program has to make some assumptions about where a virus is stored and how it does its work. Thus, no antiviral program can detect all viruses. Authors of viruses will attempt to use techniques that cannot be detected by any of the popular antiviral programs. This seems likely to lead to a technological "war" in which every advance in antiviral programs is offset by a corresponding advance in viruses.

Worms and Bacteria.   *Worms* and *bacteria* refer to programs that infect computer networks. Although not as destructive as Trojan horses and viruses, they can force a network to shut down until all copies of the hostile program have been removed. A worm program takes over and disables idle workstations on a computer network. Like the tapeworm after which it is named, a worm program is made up of many segments, each of which occupies a workstation. The segments propagate by finding uninfected workstations and starting new segments running on them. If a workstation is disinfected by deleting its segment, it will soon be reinfected by another segment. To get rid of the worm, the entire network has to be shut down while all segments are deleted. Bacteria programs, on the other hand, simply multiply themselves until they clog the network.

Intrusion Detection Techniques.   Figure 11–18 summarizes the main approaches used by intrusion detection systems. Each approach has advantages and disadvantages, and because no one approach by itself is sufficient for comprehensive intrusion detection, most packages now combine several of these techniques.

Audit Trail Analysis.   Early intrusion detection systems were often based on examination of the contents of system audit trails (manual review). As more research was carried out in audit trail analysis, two methodologies showed the most promise: statistical systems and expert systems.

Manual review.   Manual review of audit records is the most basic form of detecting intruders. It involves manually reviewing audit logs, looking for possible attacks or breaches of policy. Two major problems exist with this approach: a large volume of data and slowness of detection. Data reduction tools can be used to sift

FIGURE 11–18

Summary of intrusion detection methods

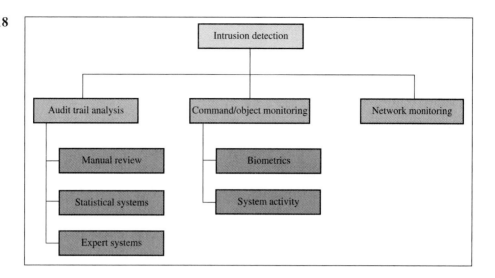

through audit data looking for "interesting" information. Frequently these tools format audit records to provide summaries of important data that can be rapidly investigated and acted on.

Statistical systems.   A more sophisticated approach to intrusion detection is derived from the application of well-known statistical methods. The use of statistics stems from the observation that most users follow readily discernible patterns of use. For example, during software development, a programmer is likely to be involved in an "edit, link, compile" cycle, with occasional breaks to perform housekeeping tasks such as checking files in and out of a source control system, backing up program files, or checking online documentation. By observing these basic working patterns, it is possible to build a profile of how a certain type of user is expected to behave under normal conditions. Currently most major intrusion detection systems incorporate some form of statistical detection.

An important part of this statistical analysis process is making sure that the appropriate raw data are collected. The three most common measures to which intrusion detection statistics are applied are event counters, interval timers, and resource measures.

Expert systems.   An *expert system* is a mechanism that attempts to encapsulate the knowledge of the various activities. Using this information, represented by *rules*, and information about the state of the monitored system, called *facts*, the expert system tries to arrive at the same conclusion a human expert would. For example, the expert system might contain the following rule:

If NUM_FAILED_LOGINS exceeds THRESHOLD then set
EXTERNAL_ATTACK_FLAG

This rule allows the system to determine the meaning of a high number of failed login attempts. If *EXTERNAL_ATTACK_FLAG* becomes set, this fact can be used by other parts of the intrusion detection system. For example, the following rule builds on the preceding one to increase the level of monitoring of a suspicious event:

If EXTERNAL_ATTACK_FLAG is set then INCREASE_MONITORING (AttackPoint)

The rules and facts of an expert system constitute the *knowledge base* of the system. It is this knowledge base that requires the most effort when designing an intrusion detection expert system. The relationship between rules and facts must be determined, and appropriate rules and behavior must be in place. It should be stressed that an expert system is only as effective as the knowledge base upon which it bases its findings. If the knowledge base is incomplete or has incorrect information, the expert system is likely to make mistakes.

Command/Object Monitoring.   This class of intrusion detection techniques is based on directly observing user or system behavior. These techniques can be useful for additional authentication methods (biometrics) or for immediate monitoring of user and system activities.

Biometrics.   Biometrics were discussed in the section on innovative security measures.

System activity.   Another approach to intrusion detection that often complements other techniques presented here is object and system activity monitoring. For instance, a steady increase in CPU load could indicate a worm attack, while a number of changes written to normally read-only executable files or system areas could indicate a virus attack.

Network Monitoring.   The final class of intrusion detection is network monitoring. This is particularly important in situations involving a large number of networked machines that are accessible to external users. For example, unusual connections between machines could indicate a "doorknob" attack, on which a user with a foothold in the local system is attempting to log into other local machines. Also, an unusual increase in overall network traffic might indicate worm activity.

A variety of products are available to implement the intrusion detection methods discussed here. These include

- Intrusion Detection Expert System (IDES).
- Information Security Officer's Assistant.
- Network Security Monitor (NSM).
- Distributed Intrusion Detection System (DIDS).
- Wisdom and Sense.
- Network Anomaly Detection and Intrusion Reporter (NADIR).

- Security Administrator Tool for Analyzing Networks (SATAN)—can also be used for auditing remote network servers.

Risk Analysis.   Given the high vulnerability of networks to security breaches, some measure for quantifying the risk associated with a network is needed. Some networks have thorough countermeasures in place, thus lowering the risk, while others operate with a higher risk of attack. *Risk analysis* is a method of quantifying that risk. The ultimate goal of risk analysis is to determine, through practical examples, how an intruder or a malicious insider could cause unauthorized disclosure of information, unauthorized modification of information, denial of service, or disruption in the continuity of operations. The issues that need to be addressed when assessing risk to LAN security therefore include

- Assets—what should be protected?
- Threats—from what do the assets need protection?
- Impacts—what are the immediate damages if the threat materializes?
- Consequences—what are the long-term effects if the threat materializes?
- Controls—what are the effective security measures?
- Risk—after implementation of the security controls, is the remaining risk acceptable?

In many countries, a separate organization such as the National Computer Security Agency is set up to assist in risk and other security issues. However, while an independent assessment is the best option, an internal assessment can do much to analyze and manage risk.

Performing Risk Analysis.   Frequently, software packages are used to assist in risk analysis, and the government security agency in each country makes recommendations on what software to use. One system that has been used for many years and recommended by the OSI bodies is CRAMM (**C**entral Computer and Telecommunications Agency Risk Analysis and Management Methodology). Others include LAVA (Los Alamos Vulnerability and Risk Assessment Methodology), RiskPAC (Profile Analysis Corporation for US Banks), and Catalyst (New Zealand Government Communications Security Bureau). More recent software packages offer graphical user interfaces and artificial intelligence–driven software to aid the risk analysis process.

A simple example of risk analysis follows.

1. *Defining and logically separating the network into elements.*   These elements include hardware, software, and communications, as well as supporting systems and components.

2. *Identification of threats.*   Next, potential threats against each network element are defined. This can be a long and laborious task, and the resulting list may not be complete. It is important, however, that the threat definition process have a specific focus and direction. For example, the threats identified should specifically target

elements or information that might compromise the integrity of the network. The number of initial threat models is usually large; however, many can be subsequently discarded.

3. *Determining vulnerability to threats.*   A given element's vulnerability to a specific threat is determined by combining the probability of threat occurrence and the element's susceptibility to the threat. Figure 11–19 gives an example.

The ability to select the appropriate category or level (3—high, 2—moderate, and 1—low) is a function of historical/empirical data, existing documentation, practical experience, and a comprehensive analysis. For instance, if the element's weakness to a particular threat is high and the probability of the threat occurring is moderate, the element's vulnerability rating is 3 (high probability of occurrence).

Consider a modem attached to a LAN via the telephone network. The *probability* of the threat that the LAN will be accessed illegally might relate to factors such as whether full login scripts are sent to users so that they learn about the operating system or whether auto-dialback software is in place. The *weakness* of a threat might depend on the level of sensitivity of the data, whether error correction software is installed on the modem, and so on. Typically the ratings assume the worst case to reveal security problems and concerns.

4. *Determining level of risk.*   To determine any given risk level, the severity of the threat and the element's level of vulnerability to that threat are combined. Figure 11–20 provides the information needed to make this determination.

5. *Implementing countermeasures.*   Implementing of countermeasures reduces or eliminates a risk. The value or *benefit* must be quantified against the *cost* of introducing the countermeasure and the residual risk determined (see Figure 11–21). Sometimes a single countermeasure can eliminate or reduce risk in more than one area. For example, encryption of data reduces the risk that data will be stolen or modified. Countermeasures fall into three main areas:

- *Access control.* Doors, locks, physical barriers, passwords, token access systems, authentication servers, encryption, and firewalls.

FIGURE 11–19   *Vulnerability Determination*

Element's Weakness to Threat	Probability of Threat Occurrence		
	High	*Moderate*	*Low*
High	3	3	2
Moderate	3	2	2
Low	2	2	1

Key:
3   High probability of occurrence
2   Moderate probability of occurrence
1   Low probability of occurrence

FIGURE 11–20 *Determining the level of risk*

Severity of Threat	Level of Vulnerability		
	High	*Moderate*	*Low*
High	3	3	2
Moderate	3	2	2
Low	2	2	1

Key:
3 High level of vulnerability
2 Moderate level of vulnerability
1 Low level of vulnerability

- *Accountability—audit trails.* Audit trails provide information on user logins, repeated incorrect password attempts, and so on.
- *Continuity of service.* Mechanisms that prevent loss of power, damage from flood or fire, and loss of service caused by malicious acts. Common methods include alternate routing, multiple processors, robust protocols, and fault-tolerant architectures.

6. *Determining residual risk.*   Residual risk is the remaining risk value after a countermeasure(s) has been applied. As Figure 11–21 shows, it may become necessary to repeat the two previous steps until the residual risk is less than some acceptable level. In some instances, such a rating is mandatory due to the sensitive and/or critical nature of a particular application or the damage that could be caused by information compromise, modification, or destruction. In these instances, residual risk can be lowered by applying additional countermeasures. Ultimately, however, a point of diminishing returns occurs at which the use of additional countermeasures may not increase the security of a system and may even degrade performance and operations and significantly increase system acquisition and maintenance costs.

In summary, risk reduction is a function of many interwoven functions, facets, and parameters, all of which must be examined. The ultimate decision to apply countermeasures must be determined by the network manager in conjunction with the organization and users. The identification of vulnerability alerts decision makers and creates additional security awareness. Nevertheless, the risk analysis process is not an end in itself but a catalyst for increased attention and reduction of vulnerability.

Rating Security

To provide a common basis for evaluating operating system security, two rating systems are in use. The national security agency's NCSC (National Computer Security Center) in the United States publishes the Department of Defense Trusted Computer Systems Evaluation Criteria, originally established for mainframe

FIGURE 11–21

Risk analysis process

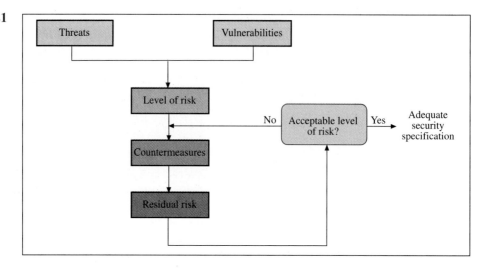

security classification. Systems are rated in four classes, D through A. D-level systems are unsecured. DOS is an example of an operating system in this class. C1-level systems must implement some kind of identification and authentication procedure as well as discretionary access controls. Well-administered NetWare or UNIX systems probably fall into this class. C2-level systems add control of object reuse (i.e., programs cannot steal one another's data), as well as the ability to audit user activities. Windows NT and NetWare 4.1 are examples of systems at this level. B-level systems are generally not used commercially because of their extensive restrictions. The most stringent level of certification is A, and apparently only one system in the United States is certified at this level. The most common choice is between systems at approximately the C1 or C2 level. While providing consistent evaluation criteria is an admirable goal, the NCSC's ratings do not encompass all aspects of security.

In Europe, the ITSEC (Information Technical Security Evaluation Criteria) separates the "security level" (discussed above) from "quality assurance" and uses ratings between E1 and E6. Thus, it is possible to have a host system that is rated A, B, C1, C2, or D (U.S. criteria) according to its features and rated E1 through E6 according to the level of testing to which the system has been subjected. The ITSEC further subdivides PCs (PC1 through PC4), hosts (E1 through E6), and networks (DX and DC). For example, an IBM AS400 might be rated as C1/E3.

Summary of Security Measures

Figure 11–22 summarizes security measures for PCs and LANs, which are the key gateway points required to prevent access to other LANs via the WANs. The figure rates the measures (ranging from medium to strong) against the cost (ranging from low to high). When combined, all of the measures provide multilayer or "onion skin" security that only the most determined and resourceful intruder could break.

FIGURE 11–22

Summary of security measures for PCs and LANs

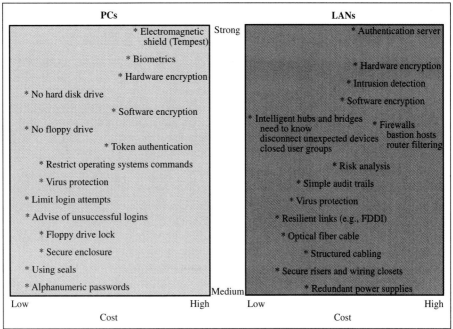

In conclusion, this section has outlined a range of security issues and related countermeasures. It is most unlikely that an individual network would encounter all of these exposures or required countermeasures. Each network must be analyzed to determine its risks as well as the appropriate levels of countermeasures. Furthermore, this analysis should be ongoing, not simply a one-time process when the system is purchased and installed.

A number of factors will increase the necessity for a stringent focus on security. These include

- Increased size, scope, and complexity of networks.
- More rapid access to the information resources these networks provide.
- A larger and smarter user population determined to test security perimeters.

Backup and Disaster Recovery

Stored data can be lost through fire, theft, malicious destruction, or, most commonly, failure of storage media such as disks and tapes. Most large computer installations periodically copy all of their stored data to tapes, or standard or compact disks and then store these in a remote location to prevent their loss in a fire or other disaster. Some organizations maintain (at a different location than the main system) a standby computer system to which they can turn if the primary system is destroyed. Organizations that do not maintain their own standby systems often have contracts with firms that specialize in supplying computer facilities on short notice.

Wise microcomputer users make backup copies of all disks containing important programs or data. The backup copies protect not only against disk failure but also against accidental erasure of files due to operator errors, as well as a variety of security breaches. Copy protection techniques that do not allow backup copies of programs to be made present serious risks to users.

Backup can be *incremental* (i.e., those files added or changed since the previous backup) or *full* (all files). The backup procedure can be initiated by an operator or run automatically under some form of timer control.

Although hard disks are reasonably reliable, they do fail occasionally; thus, data need to be backed up regularly. Backing up all the data on a hard disk is cumbersome and time consuming, but modern installations allow files that have been created or modified to be automatically backed up through the network to safe storage during off-peak times, such as nighttime hours.

A power failure can interrupt processing, cause loss of data, and damage equipment. These problems can be avoided by installing *uninterruptible power supplies (UPSs)*. When the power goes off, the UPS automatically switches the system to battery power. While the system is running on batteries, it can be shut down without damage to the hardware or loss of data, or local generators can be started up to permit continued operation.

A backup procedure that is becoming increasingly popular as a result of the requirement for virtual total reliability is RAID (redundant array of inexpensive disks). The idea is to group together several disk drives and use some type of drive redundancy to ensure that the array as a whole can survive and continue to operate satisfactorily if any one drive in the array fails. There are a number of RAID levels, which refer not to speed or performance but to *how* data are stored on the subsystem. RAID is defined over seven levels (RAID 0 to RAID 7), although most commercially available RAID systems fall into one of three levels (RAID 1, 3, or 5).

RAID 1 requires that data be read from and written to a pair of identical mirrored or duplexed drives. If one of the RAID 1 mirrored drives fails, the other takes over. RAID 1 is often the fastest RAID level because it requires little management overhead and associated CPU processing compared to other RAID solutions. However, RAID 1 is the most expensive RAID, essentially doubling the cost of all components, including drive controllers in the case of duplexing. Only half of the overall storage capacity of the media is available for use.

RAID 3, or simple bit parity RAID, stores bits across three disks, with error-checking information. If any one drive fails, its information can be inferred from the others. About two-thirds of the overall storage capacity of the media is available for use.

RAID 5, or block-striped RAID, stripes data over several drives (a minimum of three and often five to seven drives), with additional error-checking information. Any one of the three to seven drives can fail without crashing the subsystem. Two-thirds to six-sevenths of the total storage capacity of the media is available for use, depending on the number of drives.

If a drive fails in a RAID system, the network manager typically needs to remove the failed drive, replace it with a new drive, and start the drive-rebuilding operation. Most RAID systems allow for hot-swapping of drives, meaning a drive can be plugged in or unplugged without turning off power to the subsystem. Hot-swap capability is crucial for organizations running 24-hour operations.

Summary

No business network can be considered functional and reliable unless it comes under the control of a management system. Today management means more than alerting an operator that a network device has failed. Modern management involves monitoring, decision making, and implementation of these decisions. That is, the management system must be able to collect all the relevant information about the status and operation of the network. It must have the mechanism to decide on a suitable way to act, and it must be able to implement those actions. This means network equipment and the various applications they support must be equipped with the necessary hardware and software, something frequently lacking in many networks today.

Network management requires the implementation of a variety of tasks, including fault reporting, configuration, and change management, as well as performance, accounting, and security management. A network management system should have a software model of the physical network and should be updated by the monitoring information. This model keeps track of the network status (which components are operational, which are overloaded, and which are underutilized). In addition, the software model needs to be able to be used as a simulation tool to test improvement strategies.

The process of securing a network is vital. The time, effort, and money spent should reflect the value of the information assets residing on the systems attached to the network. Security needs to be considered very early in the system development process. After-the-fact retrofitting of security on a network will never provide as good a solution as a designed-in approach. Security can be pictured as an onion made up of many layers. Having defeated one layer of security measures, the intruder faces yet another.

Computers have given rise to new forms of crime and to new variations on old forms. Traditional crimes such as embezzlement may even be carried out more easily with computers, since computer systems will accept any transactions that obey certain formal rules even though the same transactions would look suspicious to a human auditor.

Unauthorized access to computer systems has become much more common since the PCs and modems needed to achieve it have become widely available. Most incidents of unauthorized access result not from the cleverness of the intruders but from poor or nonexistent security. Although persons found guilty of unauthorized access are being arrested and prosecuted, improved security techniques are likely to be a far more effective deterrent.

Malicious programs are one of the most recent threats to computer security. A Trojan horse performs a desirable service for its user while carrying out secret actions on behalf of its author. Viruses infect otherwise harmless programs, turning them into Trojan horses. Worms and bacteria can shut down a computer network. Users have demonstrated that they will make unauthorized copies of software if not somehow prevented from doing so.

Networks must be *managed* and they must be *secure,* since the core logistics for many companies is now the computer network (for example, networking is the business franchise for many vital industries such as banks and airlines). If the network is unavailable, the overall business activity comes to a halt and the company's competitive strategy becomes meaningless. Managing the network and guaranteeing the security of its data is an essential component of a company's plan and operation.

Key Terms

Application program interface (API)   392
Biometrics   411
Common Management Information Protocol (CMIP)   390
Data Encryption Standard (DES)   414
Digital envelope   415
Digital signature recognition   411
Kerberos authentication server   412
Management information base (MIB)   395
Remote monitoring MIB (RMON MIB)   398
Request for comment (RFC)   398

Simple Network Management Protocol (SNMP)   390
Simple Network Management Protocol-Version 2 (SNMP-2)   390
Smart card   411
Spoofing   411
Trojan horse   380
UNIX   393
Virus   380
Worm   380

Questions for Discussion

1. Why is user satisfaction an important network management objective? *PP 381-387*

2. What key issues are addressed in the management of a network? *PP 381-384*

3. Consider two LANs in different countries that are interconnected by a telecommunications company's network. Thus, there are three networks involved, and each has its own network management system. If you want to place a management center at one of the locations, what do you need to do? *PP 389-393*

4. What is the primary requirement of an integrated network management system? *PP 391-394*

5. A network management system that only monitors all hardware devices on the network, such as modems, NTUs, multiplexers, and

servers, suffers from significant inadequacies. Why is this so?

6. What key areas of functional management have been defined by the ISO and must be supported by any vendor implementing the CMIP management system?

7. Explain the difference between the physical and logical views of a network from the point of view of its management.

8. Explain the meaning of the paradox that there is a requirement to *restrict access* and at the same time to *share access* to data.

9. Suggest some measures you might implement in your organization to provide better security of data.

✗10. One of the most important issues in providing security in LAN networks is the requirement to enforce the *need to know* principle. Explain how this works in practice. *PP. 385-386*

11. Find out the names of some antiviral programs that run on computer systems that you use. How do these antiviral programs work?

12. For the organization where you study or work, first find out what stored and transmitted data are considered a security risk. (If loss of data poses no security risk, these issues are not a problem—but this would be most unusual.) Second, find out what data encryption method (if any) and software to protect against Trojan horses, viruses, and worms is in place. Now specify what encryption or software protection measures should be put in place and on what equipment they should be located to protect against unwanted intrusion as well as act as a filter for the introduction of new software in your organization.

13. The application of risk analysis to practical situations in which you work or study will be difficult without the use of risk analysis software packages. Consider such an environment and, by referring back to Figure 11–19, determine the *vulnerability* to a specific threat by combining the *probability* of threat occurrence with the element's *weakness* or susceptibility to that threat. (Hint: Consider the factors that affect the *probability* of a threat and the factors that affect the *weakness* of a threat in the example given under (3) on p. 422. Now, from the level of vulnerability you have determined for specific items or situations, determine the level of risk knowing the severity of the threat by using Figure 11–20.

In this way, you should be able to rate risk levels associated with various items or processes in your organization. However, a full determination of these levels can be carried out only with the use of risk analysis software packages.

12

FUTURE DEVELOPMENTS IN BUSINESS NETWORKING
Technology and Applications

Chapter Outline

Introduction   432

Change—A Driving Force for Future
    Telecommunications   433

Limitations on Networks and Future
    Developments   434

The Paperless Office and Its Effect on
    Business   436

Deregulation in the
    Telecommunications Industry   437

Important Technological Developments
    438

ATM (Asynchronous Transfer Mode)
    and Multimedia Applications   439

Other Developing Technologies   442

Seven Trends for an Electronic Future
    444

Learning Objectives

By the end of Chapter 12, you should
be able to

1. *Discuss* current limitations of
   networks and the future
   developments that may overcome
   those limitations.

2. *Evaluate* the concept of the
   paperless office and discuss
   potential business opportunities.

3. *Discuss* the effects of deregulation
   in the telecommunications industry
   and examine some of the new
   technologies that have evolved in
   conjunction with deregulation.

4. *Analyze* the new developments in
   asynchronous transfer mode (ATM)
   and multimedia systems as they
   apply to local and wide area
   business applications.

5. *Identify* a variety of new technologies
   that are likely to radically change the
   way we live and work.

6. *Describe* trends in electronic
   commerce that are likely to affect
   business and home entertainment
   systems.

Introduction

Now that we have crossed the threshold into the Information Age, we will need a new level of information access and communications dependent on telecommunications systems. What does the future hold for the ever-changing Information Age? This final chapter explores some of the possibilities and applications in this electronic future. Underlying these applications will be high-speed, transparent networks that give global access to a treasure house of information. Such wide-ranging access to electronic information has already brought new challenges. One key factor will be overcoming information overload. Filtering the plethora of messages and opportunities that are available will become an important factor in surviving and thriving in the Information Age. Key technologies that are now on the fringe of commercial technology will become mainstream on ramps to the information highway and virtual shopping mall of the future. The following scenario hints at some of the possibilities.

ISACSON MANUFACTURING, INC.

Jacob Isacson was the founder and CEO of Isacson Manufacturing, Inc., which produced molded plastic products and parts for a wide range of applications and markets. The company was in a very competitive market, but everyone planned well and worked hard. They used the best technology for their needs and found the best partners to work with. Such inter-firm cooperation had become increasingly common as communication technology made the transition to flexible organizations easier.

Jacob worked from his home three days a week. This meant that the two hours he would have spent commuting he could spend working from his virtual office at his home in the mountains. He found this arrangement far more productive and much more pleasant as he looked at the snow-capped peaks rising above the forested hillsides. Maybe he would go skiing with his wife and two sons after this afternoon's meeting, he thought.

Jacob sat on his back deck overlooking the valley and spoke to his portable computer. Instantly the screen came to life with a form requesting information. "Set up a meeting with Tom Jacks and Maria Jimenez for me at 2 PM today, please," Jacob requested. The **voice-activated intelligent scheduler** entered the names into the "meet with" field on the screen and "2 PM" into the "time" field and then read the setup back for confirmation. "Yes, that's right, thanks," Jacob replied and then asked if things were ready for the daily morning staff meeting. His scheduler announced that Judy Robb, his manufacturing supervisor, and George Odering, chief financial officer, were on the line. "OK," he said, and Judy's face came alive on his screen with George in the background. The meeting lasted 60 minutes, in which they covered the daily production, a few staffing problems, and George's need to get Jacob's electronic signature authorizing the weekly payroll and accepting the daily EFT/EDI payments list.

At 1:55 PM, Jacob's computer spoke up: "You have a virtual meeting with Tom Jacks and Maria Jimenez in five minutes. Is there anything that you need prepared for the meeting?" Jacob thought for a moment and then replied, "No, I think I'm OK." A few minutes later, his screen brightened up and said, "Meeting time, here come Tom and Maria. Tom is first in." A video image of Tom Jacks came into view, filling the screen. Tom was the CEO of Design Now, a CAD design firm that Jacob used for his new-product prototyping and

CAD to CAM setup work. "Hi, Tom, how's everything in Phoenix? Business good as usual?" They shared a bit of light news, until the computer interrupted to announce that Maria Jimenez was coming into the meeting. The screen automatically resized Tom's image to fill half the screen as Maria's face filled the other half. Maria was the owner/operator of the advertising and marketing firm that Jacob often used for new-product launches. "How are you, Jacob? You are looking well, it must be all that fresh air in Idaho—not much of it here in New York, I'm afraid!"

After a bit of small talk, Jacob steered the conversation to the latest product he had dreamed up. Tom wanted some drawings of what the product looked like. Jacob had done a sketch on his computer earlier, so he displayed the sketch on screen. As they carried on the meeting with voice only, they discussed the various aspects of the model—size, weight, color, moving parts, and other features—that were not evident from the drawing. Eventually Tom was satisfied that he understood enough to do a full CAD model of the product and said he would have it done by tomorrow. Maria asked about the market for this product and competing products. As they talked, Jacob summoned his **intelligent search agent** to find some information for him while they continued the meeting. Jacob filled in the search criteria with his pen so as to not disturb the meeting, and sent the agent on its way. The three of them continued to discuss the various pros and cons of the current design and the markets that might be open to it.

About 10 minutes later, the search agent flashed a light on the screen to let Jacob know that it had finished its first pass search. Jacob called up the initial hit list, scanned it, ticked off four items that looked particularly useful, and said, "Maria, I think I may have some answers to your marketing questions." He went on to quote the size of the market segment based on the U.S. Department of Statistics' latest figures and supporting information from a market research firm. Both sources maintained online database facilities for Internet searches. Then Jacob quoted from two reports, one from *The Wall Street Journal* and the other from a marketing trade journal, describing competing products. Finally, he showed them a video clip of a competing product launch that the market research firm had on file. This additional information gave them a new perspective on the project and some additional homework to do. Jacob confirmed that they were all free to meet again tomorrow at the same time, and everyone said goodbye.

Jacob asked his scheduler to set up a repeat meeting for tomorrow at the same time with the same people. He then said "go on standby" to his computer, got up from his chaise lounge, walked into the house, and announced, "Anyone interested in skiing?"

Change—A Driving Force for Future Telecommunications

Change is a key to the future. Few technologies are changing as rapidly as those found in computer communications. Today we are being offered microprocessors such as the Pentium and now the P6 (Pentium Pro), each of which is around five times faster than the previous technology. In storage systems, the cost per unit of storage is dropping every year. Today we are handling technologies that we hardly even heard of five years ago. The expected life cycle for equipment is frequently no more than three years. The idea of a two- to three-year capital cost recovery on investment is quite alarming. Frequently the old technology works perfectly well; however, the new technology is faster, can store more data, and offers the user access to applications software that allows the business to be more competitive.

It would be unrealistic to predict in a single chapter what technologies will be important five years from now. The business application drives the technology, not the reverse. ISDN is a classic example of this blunder. At the time ISDN was developed, it was a powerful technology, but nobody had any innovative ideas about how to use it. Multimedia-based applications with the potential to use ISDN networks were not mature at the time ISDN became available on the market.

There is, however, a clear vision for multimedia communication. Every indicator points toward the merger of voice, video, and conventional computer data. ATM is the enabling technology for multimedia systems and will be discussed briefly in this chapter. Fast and efficient location-independent communication is a driving force in business today. Further, rapid, global access to information at a realistic cost has become a reality as a result of the rapid developments in global networks such as CompuServe and the Internet.

The desktop workstation will be the interface that turns these visions into realities. Already multimedia workstations with 64 megabytes of RAM and 10-gigabyte (10,000 megabytes) hard disk drives are being piloted. These workstations will combine voice, data, and video business functions into a single multimedia communication and information system. It will matter little where data are stored, since an even greater variety of powerful search and retrieval tools will be available.

With every technological development comes an associated set of problems. These new advances in computer communication systems give rise to greater concerns about how to make these systems more reliable and secure and how to manage such complex integrated infrastructures. As businesses become more and more dependent on the information technology platform as a strategic and competitive way to do business, the failure of these systems becomes increasingly costly. Great care will be necessary, since selection of the wrong technology or the right technology at the wrong time can spell disaster that an organization may never survive. Furthermore, there will always be users who test security systems to the limit, creating new viruses and seeking ways to break encryption codes.

Limitations on Networks and Future Developments

The last five years have seen unprecedented growth and development in the telecommunications industry. It would seem that we could all have easy access to a wide range of applications operating on our networks and that interconnection to support the required applications and services would be a simple matter. Yet that is not the case. Although the world is now ringed with fiber optic cable and satellite systems and most businesses operate with some form of computer system, something is missing. Consider some of the limitations that we face today.

• Although electronic messaging is common in business networks throughout the world, interconnectability among many of these systems is still very limited. Some organizations, including many major companies, can still communicate only with text-based electronic mail systems and frequently are unable to include formatted documents, diagrams, and spreadsheets in their communications. To some degree, the Internet is helping to solve this problem; Internet mail is now widely accepted as the lowest common denominator for messaging. However, for the many organizations that do not have interfaces to the Internet, fax remains the only method for document communication, apart from mail and courier. The use of fax in these situations is cumbersome and expensive. Many of these problems relate more to the need for organizational and management change rather than to technological deficiencies.

• In most fax transmissions, data are taken from a database and entered onto a fax, which is then transmitted. At the receiving end, the data from the fax are then keyed into another database. This is an extremely wasteful, error-prone, and time-consuming practice when the systems at the sending and receiving ends are incompatible. Again, many of these problems are frequently more organizational and management related than technological.

• Although ISDN provides a single digital pipe into a business, most organizations still have separate connections for telephone, fax, data, and a variety of other telecommunications services. The problems this technology was designed to solve many years ago persist today.

• An office in Chicago has produced a document using Microsoft Word. It consists of text with several bold headings and fonts, a table, and a diagram. The manager wishes to transfer this document through a telecommunications network from his workstation to a colleague's workstation in Sydney. Because of so many incompatible protocols, he has to resort to faxing it (which means it will not be electronically stored at the destination) or mailing it on a disk (a five-day delay). Again, many of these problems are frequently more organizational and management related than technological. Therefore, both must be considered and resolved.

• A user has a file resident on her disk that runs under the Sun operating system and file structure. She wishes to transmit the file across a network (preserving the structure and layout) to a disk running under IBM's **Systems Network Architecture (SNA)** operating system. The solution would be to use the ISO product FTAM (File Transfer and Access Method), which has been available for some years but is seldom used.

• Many businesses still exchange invoices, purchase orders, delivery forms, and other documents via paper. This involves taking data in electronic form from one computer, printing it onto paper, and sending it the receiver, where it is then reentered into another computer and stored electronically once again. The problems here are very clearly not technical; they are related to organization and management.

These are just a few of many examples. The common problem in all these situations lies with the "islands of operation." Vendors' systems, particularly at the application level, are still largely incompatible despite the work of ISO and various de facto standards that now exist. Frequently customers become locked into one particular vendor's methods and systems, thus creating barriers to communicating with other vendor's systems. Although the global telecommunications companies now offer a widespread network of interconnecting links to almost every business imaginable, the applications at the upper levels have great difficulty in communicating.

The solution to many of these incompatibility problems is coming slowly, partly through the use of OSI standards and partly through the use of industry de facto standards. It is the user community that is demanding interconnectivity from the vendors, not the reverse. This has resulted in part from the widespread restructuring and reorganization going on in businesses and industries. Further, global networking has become available through the various telecommunications companies, which makes compatible interconnectivity so important to the users.

Fiber optics are becoming more widely used as high-bandwidth highways become available for multimedia applications such as color graphics, high-speed fax, and voice and video services. In turn, vendors are paying much greater attention to these compatibility issues. Thus, we can expect to see applications products coming onto the market that have the "stamp of compatibility," a key marketing success factor for these products.

The Paperless Office and Its Effect on Business

In the 1980s, computers were able to perform 10 million operations per second at a cost of a few cents. In the 1990s, as speeds accelerate further, cost/performance ratios are expected to improve by a factor of 100, with manufacturing costs becoming 20 percent to 30 percent lower. These powerful statistics go a long way toward explaining why the computer industry has experienced success with new products and new markets in recent years. Indeed, with technological advances of this magnitude, it would have been hard not to develop products that the market wanted.

The decrease in costs, together with the enormous growth in computational capacity, has significant implications for the office. It means that what was once considered a powerful company computer can now become the workstation on every manager's desk. This arrangement provides access to a vast range of company data, as well as the ability to process these data using conventional tools such as word processors, spreadsheets, and various file and database processing programs. Further, the paperless office can communicate this processed information rapidly to other managers, offices, and organizations on a worldwide basis.

The **paperless office**, which was widely predicted to arrive in the 1980s, never materialized. The prospects are better in the 1990s, particularly when multimedia applications are considered. This will bring a whole cluster of new problems that technology and society will need to address. The challenge for the users lies in finding out what is going on and applying this technology efficiently within their organizations. Users will also need to learn to think freely about the technology and its potential rather than in terms of a bygone market dominated by mainframes and central processors in which the only role for the PC was word processing, spreadsheets, and computer games. Such perceptions would be foolish considering today's massive expenditures on office automation products. Meanwhile, the faithful typewriter, the mainstay of the traditional workplace for a century, is virtually extinct.

In the previous section we discussed how electronic mail, while improving communication time and reducing the amount of paper transferred, has actually had only limited success because of the incompatibility among different vendors' systems. The incompatibility is one of the main reasons facsimile transmission has become so popular. In fact, fax has replaced telex as the common document transfer standard, even though a fax commonly starts out as a document in electronic form in a computer and ultimately becomes another electronic document in another computer once the data are rekeyed in at the receiver's end. The net result has been a huge increase in the use of faxes and thus an increase in the amount of paper in the office. It has been generally accepted for some years now that processing of paper documents by electronic means will go a long way toward reducing the amount of paper that is processed as well as increasing the speed with which business transactions can be carried out. The potential benefits are enormous. In Singapore, for example, the time needed for document processing has gone from three days to 10 minutes following the introduction of EDI at a national level. A trader who cannot process these types of documents within 10 minutes is out of the business. Other examples of the use of EDI as a critical business resource include Wal-Mart, Kmart, and General Motors, together with their small- and medium-sized suppliers.

One difficulty with EDI, as with electronic mail, is that a critical mass of users must agree that this is the desired method of operation from some point on. Achieving this agreement among competing companies has proven to be difficult. In spite of these major political obstacles, however, EDI is very likely to be a major player in the paperless office of the future.

Another potential benefit of the paperless office of the future lies in the increased complexity of the information that can be transferred in the form of multimedia communications. After all, when business partners meet, they frequently exchange much complex information in the form of verbal discussion, text, and graphical information. Electronic mail in its basic form is too limited for many types of communication. Thus, the introduction of high bandwidth to support multimedia communication among businesses that require a comprehensive interconnection of voice, video, formatted document transfer, and other office-related activities has the potential to reduce the amount of paper transferred, decrease the number of face-to-face meetings, and offer substantial cost savings and efficiencies.

Deregulation in the Telecommunications Industry

In recent years, **deregulation** has been a significant catalyst in moving telecommunications into a more competitive and efficient industry. The spin-offs have been cheaper products, global networks, and greatly improved services, particularly from the large telecommunications service providers. New Zealand was the first country in the world to deregulate its telecommunications industry in 1988; other countries, such as France and Germany, are not planning for full deregulation until around 1998.

Deregulation has undoubtedly been good for customers, as each network operator offers new and competitive services to gain a competitive edge. Further, deregulation has speeded up the modernization of the various telecommunications services. For example, in most deregulated countries, over 90 percent of the network and switching equipment is now fully digital. As a result, a whole new range of services and facilities have become available to the customer, thus improving the competitiveness of business operations.

Deregulation and the resulting competitive market are opening up a variety of new facilities and services that can offer more competitive ways of doing business. These include

- ATM services—high-bandwidth systems to support multimedia applications (see p. 439).
- Frame relay—an elastic bandwidth service for local area network interconnection.
- ISDN services—a moderate-speed and short holding time interconnection system offered as a dial-up or leased system.
- FDDI—high-speed fiber optic interconnection services (but likely to be superseded by ATM in the near future).
- VPN—virtual private networking, which allows users to derive their own private network from the public service.
- Switched multimegabit data service (SMDS)—a class of high-speed interconnection services supporting integrated multimedia such as voice, data, and video.
- Centrex—a private PBX derived from the overall telecommunications company switching equipment and supported at their switching exchange.

Important Technological Developments

The bandwidth requirements for emerging business applications such as client/server transaction processing, and image/graphics transmission, as well as for distributed database systems, are very different from those used in earlier applications. All of these modern applications process large volumes of data, transmit intermittent high-speed bursts, and are intolerant of long delays. To satisfy the requirements of these applications, the capacity management systems that allocate network bandwidth must offer access to high bandwidth on demand, direct connectivity to all other points in the network, and only consume the bandwidth actually needed.

Telecommunications companies offer a variety of services that can be used to fill these roles in different situations. It is essential that organizations carefully examine the variety of technological options available, evaluating the costs and benefits, performance features, and operational characteristics of these various interconnection services necessary to support modern business applications.

Wide area networks have been subject to great changes. Not too long ago, 9,600 bps links were considered to be moderately high-speed and 64 Kbps an expensive upper limit. Today 64 Kbps is only a very basic speed; 2 Mbps frame relay and ISDN, 100 Mbps FDDI, and now 155 to 2,488 Mbps ATM systems are all in use or planned as a basis for multimedia application communication. Bandwidth needs are expanding, and within the next few years a standard desktop workstation is likely to offer 100 Mbps multimedia communication for distributed business applications. Thus, flexible bandwidth allocations at realistic costs have become imperative to meet today's competitive requirements.

Thus, any considerations in the interconnection of local and wide area networks must include these changing technologies and application requirements. With today's distributed server and modern client/server architectures, it is acceptable for the interconnecting network to have to support online real-time color graphics, multimedia, and voice applications. This places high demand on the speed and reliability of the interconnecting network.

The positioning of existing and developing technologies was shown in Figure 4–15. Although new technologies such as ATM are likely to play a vital part in the support of future distributed business applications, the existing services will continue to provide the communications infrastructure for a long time to come. In fact, these services will become progressively enhanced over time. The only technology shown in Figure 4–15 and not discussed so far is ATM. This will become a key intercommunication technology to support multimedia communications over the next five years and is discussed more fully next.

ATM (Asynchronous Transfer Mode) and Multimedia Applications

Probably no other technology has drawn as much attention recently as have ATM and multimedia systems. Significant developments are now occurring in the fast packet-switching and broadband-ISDN areas. These various technologies all come under the general umbrella of what is called ATM technology. ATM has received substantial media attention and looks set to make a major impact on high-speed networking and as a transport system for multimedia business applications. The ATM protocol has the potential to remove the boundary between the local and wide area networking environments, thus obviating much of the protocol conversion commonly found in existing equipment interfaces between local and wide area networks.

One of the fundamental principles of ATM is to offer the end user a large variety of communication services through a single access point to the network, with each service potentially requiring a different bit-rate. Thus, a technique was needed to switch delay-sensitive information such as video or voice as well as information flows that are more intermittent and have widely variable bit-rates, such as those commonly found with LAN-to-LAN communication. ATM meets these requirements. It is a hybrid technique that combines the simplicity and very high bit-rates possible with circuit switching (currently used largely for voice or video transmission) with the flexibility of X.25 packet-switching systems, which are commonly used for many current business system applications.

In ATM, the basic unit of data transfer is called the *cell*. This appears as a packet having a fixed length with a header (including routing information used by the network) as well as an information field. The fixed format of the two fields ensures that the processing can be carried out by simple high-speed switching hardware, thus enabling faster processing speeds than are possible with traditional variable-length packet-based networks such as X.25 packet-switching and frame relay systems.

ATM is certainly the buzzword of this decade, appearing to be all things to all people. It is ideal for local, national, international, private, and public networks; scalable speeds; isochronous (real-time) and intermittent traffic; constant and variable bit-rate devices; and voice, video, imaging, and data. It is also capable of integrating these elements into one international broadband-switched network of the future.

Frame relay, in contrast, is positioned at the lower end of the ATM spectrum (up to 2 Mbps), but it uses variable-length frames and supports only conventional computer data transfer and not multimedia applications, which undoubtedly will be increasingly required in the future. FDDI is widely available and in common use now, in spite of its high costs, although it is unlikely to survive in the longer term as ATM systems become widely used. Further, ATM is an architecture that supports multimedia communication over a very wide range of scalable speeds. At the lower end of the bandwidth spectrum, 25 Mbps ATM hubs are starting to appear on the market, while at the upper end, ATM can be expected to offer speeds up to 2,500 Mbps.

Figure 12–1 shows how an ATM network will operate for future *wide* area multimedia application requirements. The center of the diagram shows the existing SDH (synchronous digital hierarchy) and SONET (synchronous optical network) systems, which form the lower layer infrastructure of modern telecommunications companies' networks. Above this, ATM provides a cell relay service that is totally independent of the network services or multimedia applications it is designed to support. Again, a bandwidth management system will provide capacity to existing network services such as frame relay, X.25, leased lines, ISDN, and other legacy services that will continue to be offered but will be transported over an ATM infrastructure. In the future, ATM networks will provide local area network interconnection services, bandwidth on an as-required basis, and possibly future ATM services that will have access to the raw ATM cell system.

For future *local* area business networking system requirements, ATM switches will interconnect to hubs and other switches that will form the distribution point for existing and future local area networks. Figure 12–2 shows a hub that has an interface for existing Ethernet and token ring legacy networks, but also has an ATM interface for ATM-capable workstations that will support the multimedia business applications of the future. Switched networks will therefore build on the local area networks and backbone routers now in place. ATM hubs and routers will link local area networks and established connections to enterprisewide networks, while ATM switches will connect departmental hubs and routers to form the basis of these new enterprise networks. Since ATM will be used in both the local and wide area environments, the distinction between *local* and *wide* will become rather arbitrary.

FIGURE 12–1

The ATM network comprising switching, bandwidth management, and networking services

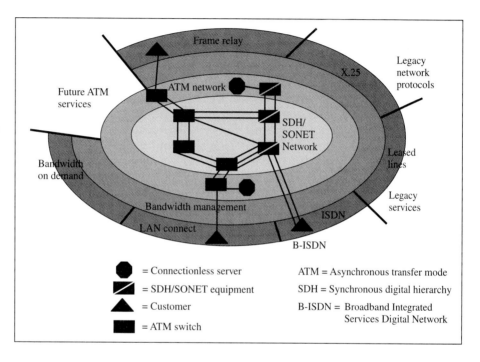

FIGURE 12–2

Departmental ATM hub and connection to the ATM network

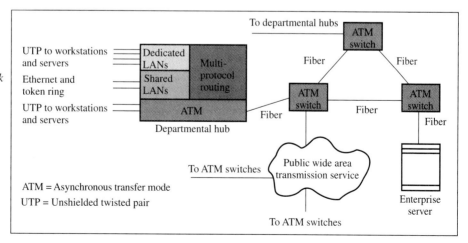

Other Developing Technologies

The first computers filled entire rooms, and it took about 30 years to create computers that would fit on a desk. The leap from desktop to laptop computers took less than 10 years. For much of this century, the mail and the telephone were the primary means of communication. Today faxes, voice mail, and electronic mail have all come into widespread use in less than a decade. What the next decade will bring is hard to predict, since change is occurring so rapidly that important technologies of the 21st century may still be sketches on a drawing board.

We can observe some significant and rapid developments. For example, few 15-year-olds are not "computer literate" today, and the wide penetration of PCs into the home has made the PC the appliance of the decade. In July 1994 there were 500,000 users of America Online; eight months later, there were 2.5 million users. Every 10 seconds a new home page is being created on the World Wide Web, and the number of Internet users is expected to reach 1 billion by the year 2000. One thing is certainly clear: The future will be digital—digital media, digital applications, and digital broadband information highways. The following sections suggest some likely options to consider for the next decade.

Building the Information Highways

Most of the developed countries have already started to embark on the information highway. They realize that to gain a share of the future lucrative multimedia market, they will need to have a broadband network in place. Probably no country is as advanced as Singapore, which aims to offer broadband superhighway access to every business and home by the year 2000. Broadband networks are coaxial and fiber optic systems that have enough capacity to carry full digital video, sound, and text between computers and, later, to TVs. In fact, fiber optic networks have almost unlimited transmission capacity. The objective is to give everyone everywhere an ultra-high-speed connection to any kind of information, including books, movies, news, business, and shopping. Already islands of such multimedia activity are developing, but it will be a few years before a universal integrated system is available.

The Internet is a good example of a system that is demanding the availability of these information superhighways. Already the Internet consists of more than 5 million interconnected computers in over 40 countries, with a current growth rate of 10 to 15 percent per month (see Figures 3–9 through 3–12 in Chapter 3). A variety of home-grown online services that offer access via the Internet are starting to appear. Bertelsmann, a large German publisher, has joined with American Online to offer services in many parts of Europe.

Personal Telephones

A telephone that can fit on a wrist like a watch (or, more likely, combined with a watch) and can be used from anywhere in the world has been a science fiction idea, but within a few years, it could become a reality. Cellular telephones are now small enough to fit into a shirt pocket at a reasonable price. The jump from the pocket to the wrist may not be all that far away. The problems for worldwide access have more to do with jurisdiction of the airwaves than with technology. At the present time, at least six international consortiums are negotiating with individual countries for the rights to offer worldwide telephone access. These consortiums are ready to invest billions of dollars into a mass of satellites so that at least one satellite will be accessible from virtually any point in the world. Telephone and fax services are already commonplace on many of the world's major airlines, although at present the charges are relatively high. Wrist telephones are expected to initially become standard equipment for international businesses, but the consumer market will soon follow.

Voice-Activated Computers

Voice as a method of computer input is already under development by IBM, Apple, and Microsoft. Such systems will not be like the slow, crude, error-prone devices that exist today. In the next four to five years, it is highly likely that these devices will be able to follow ordinary conversational speech, allowing for variation in inflection and rhythm, and therefore dominate the human–computer interface. Further, these computers will understand semantics. Thus, for example, when someone wants to search the Internet for all articles on new business developments in Asia, it will be possible to say, "Find me all articles on new business ventures in Singapore, Kuala Lumpur, and Hong Kong from 1994 on," and the computer will be able to intelligently interpret this instruction. Recently IBM released its VoiceType Dictation system, which runs on OS/2 and Windows platforms and includes special voice dictionaries for specific industry groups such as radiologists (19,000 words), medical practitioners (16,000 words), and journalists (30,000 words). In three to five years, voice-input systems are expected to become an integral part of conventional word processing systems such as Microsoft Word, WordPerfect, and Lotus Notes or even part of the underlying operating system.

This technology will not only apply to conventional desktop and laptop computers but will be available on other forms of electronic information-processing devices. So for example, a telephone will operate without a numeric keypad and respond instead to spoken commands. A conventional TV or video recorder will respond to spoken commands, thus getting around the problem of the lost remote controller. Automatic teller machines at banks will respond to spoken instructions and voice-based numerical data input and provide voice print security. It is highly likely that within the next 8 to 10 years, speech will become the primary channel for communication between people and machines. However, whole new security issues will also need to be resolved as voice-based systems develop.

Optical Computers

Huge advances in chip design have now taken the microprocessor close to the limits of the laws of physics. The electric currents that move around the circuits and switches in today's microprocessor-based telecommunications systems operate at the speed of light, but no faster. This results in the generation of heat, which is starting to limit much further reduction in chip size. Some computer researchers are moving away from using electricity to using light much as it is currently used in fiber optic cables. Further, scientists have found ways to use light to operate switching circuits and to store data. Already a primitive optical computer has been built, and further work on optical microprocessor-based transmission and switching systems is under way at IBM, AT&T Bell Labs, and NEC in Japan. It may be 10 years, however, before commercially available optical computers appear on the market.

Virtual Reality and Telecommunications

Virtual reality refers to the creation of an artificial environment that appears so realistic that it cannot be distinguished from the real thing. This term has been used very widely in recent years. The most successful example is the flight simulator used for pilot training. These systems have become so successful that trainees sometimes fly with a planeload of passengers on the rated aircraft the first time out of the simulator. New developments under way permit CAT scanners to create three-dimensional images of various parts of a patient's internal organs, making it easier to find tumors, for example, than with the use of conventional X-rays. Once these techniques are combined with high-speed ATM networks, it will become possible to instantaneously consult specialists located in other cities or even other countries. Other virtual reality developments allow an architect to show clients through a building before it has been constructed or to recreate historical buildings that have long since gone. Further into the future, virtual reality will permit people to learn to operate complex equipment from remote locations without ever touching the real thing.

Seven Trends for an Electronic Future

It is not easy to forecast the future, but in this section we will look at seven key trends that point to a future in which communication and information access are ubiquitous and to speak of electronic commerce will seem as archaic as talking about the telephone as a high-tech communication device. These key trends include

- Increasing miniaturization of communication and computing products.
- Increasingly powerful computing and communications systems.
- Increasing digitization of information.
- Increasing digitization of services (money, education, medical and other professional services).
- Increasingly intelligent systems (knowbots and intelligent agents).
- Increasing integration of business organizations (intraorganizational and interorganizational).
- Migration to common network technology for LANs and WANs (ATM and related technologies).

Let us look more closely at each of these trends.

Increasing Miniaturization

A major driving force toward the electronic future is the increasing miniaturization of communication and computing devices. In the era of room-size computers costing millions of dollars, the cost and inconvenience of electronic media were too high. However, in the coming era of intelligent wrist communicators and interactive computer/TV units, linked to a high-speed National Information Infrastructure (NII) at prices we pay for telephones today, electronic media and mass market acceptance will be a foregone conclusion. The semiconductor industry is pushing miniaturization into new domains. Soon digital phone/fax/modem facilities will become a built-in feature of the central processor. Whether it comes on a future P7, the PowerPC 608, or some later version, it is only a matter of time before communication capabilities are integrated at the chip level and included in a wide range of product types. Handheld **personal digital assistants (PDAs)** and pocket- and wrist-watch-based units will all ultimately be available with varying levels of capability based on the needs of the consumer. Ads such as "Buy this latest microwave and we will include absolutely free a preinstalled personal communicator with high-quality digital sound and omnidirectional microphone" may become commonplace in a decade as communication and computing devices become ever smaller and are incorporated into other products. No more chasing after a ringing phone or trying to locate the portable! A voice-activated unit will be built into the computer/TV, the bathroom mirror, the automobile, and the office desk. All of these communicators will offer direct links to the NII (or whatever the Internet grows up to be) at speeds suitable for their function.

Increasingly Powerful Systems

Computing and communication devices are becoming not only increasingly miniaturized but much more powerful as well. The past shows us a trend to the future. The original IBM-PC (circa 1982) was an 8-bit processor running at 4.77 MHz. Today's Pentium, P6 (Pentium Pro), Alpha, and PowerPC chips are 64-bit architectures running at 100 to 300 MHz. In less than 15 years, they have become hundreds of times more powerful and at prices as low as 20 percent of the cost (inflation adjusted). With nearly a 1,000 times price performance improvement in the last 15 years and similar improvements forecast for the next 15 years, it does not require a lot of imagination to see where things are headed. The same has been happening with communication devices such as the modem. Only 10 years ago, a standard modem ran at 1,200 bps and was the size of a shoebox. Now we have standard consumer modems at considerably lower prices running at 28,800 bps and higher with throughputs of well over 100,000 bps due to compression features. These units may also include a full Ethernet adaptor integrated with the modem and still fit onto a credit card–size device! The increasing power of these computer and communication devices makes them faster and more capable and bring to the user multimedia information opportunities that were unheard of a few years ago. Real-time videoconferencing and multimedia Internet with no wait at the desktop, the notebook, the telephone, or virtual vision glasses will become a certainty in due course under such growth scenarios.

Increasing Digitization of Information

The dramatic decrease in size and cost, coupled with the increased power of computing and communication devices, sets the stage for a market-driven push to digital information. The increasing digitization of information will culminate in ubiquitous electronic media with books, newspapers, magazines, and technical journals all being available and ultimately replacing paper versions of the same media. Many forms of media that are now one-way broadcast media, such as TV, will gain an interactive capability for many program types such as news, game shows, and talk programs. No more trips to the video store; digital video on demand will be one of the many services available through the NII.

The reason for this drive toward digitization will be economic, environmental, and market driven. The economies of electronic publishing are already flexing their muscles. It will be cheaper to produce and distribute electronic books, newspapers, and magazines than the paper versions. You can have them delivered via the NII to your computer or TV for reading, or have them read to you by your computer in your favorite synthetic voice, whether Garth Brooks, Marilyn Monroe, Eddie Vedder, or Tom Hanks. Electronic media are environmentally friendly. They use no raw materials, require very little energy to produce, emit no physical pollutants, require little physical storage space, and reduce transportation demands. They are a natural resource advantage, a marketing opportunity, and a cost savings. Electronic media will ultimately be market driven as well. An electronic book is far more amenable to creating an interactive story in which the user can participate directly, interacting with the characters and taking on a personal role. Digitization of rare books will make hard-to-find resources readily available to historians and history students alike. Digitized textbooks will put the latest versions at the fingertips of every student. Medical students, for instance, will have facilities to browse and search related resources such as online dictionaries of medical terms and detailed video clips of medical operations, allowing them to interact with the media to gain practice and confidence totally unavailable to them before.

Increasing Digitization of Services

Miniaturization, powerful systems, and digitization of information will bring about a major revolution that will affect business and the professions as much as the factory. The use of credit cards has already surpassed the use of checks and cash for many consumers. It is only a small step to full electronic money systems that may incorporate more integrated services with existing credit card systems as well as newer forms of payments, such as E-cash or cybercash for direct payment over the Internet/NII. Direct delivery of high-quality education is already starting to take place through many in-house business training and distance learning programs. As the first three trends proceed, the availability of delivery systems and powerful user communication and computing devices will make some areas of education and a much wider range of electronic education resources available. The availability of electronic services such as legal, accounting, and medical services is likely to come into wide use for competitive and cost effectiveness reasons.

Increasingly Intelligent Systems

Much research is going on in various institutions dealing with some of the challenges that are coming with this electronic future. One key problem is information overload. Having masses of digital information at your fingertips is a mixed blessing! How do you find what you really want without being overwhelmed by the sheer volume of it all? However, artificial intelligence and related research fields are yielding applications designed to help you cope. Intelligent voice recognition systems to provide a friendly, voice-activated interface together with intelligent agents offer one major avenue for automated assistance in finding the needle in the haystack. An *intelligent agent*, or *knowbot*, is a computer program that is capable of learning your preferences for information and then applying them intelligently to searches you request for particular types of information. For example, if you are in the automotive industry and have been using an intelligent agent for a number of weeks, you may have done Internet searches on automotive electronics and searched for articles about competitors' new product releases. When the intelligent agent delivers the results of the search, you read through the results, keep some articles, and throw others away. In this process, the intelligent agent begins to learn about the types of information related to your industry and your particular job based on the information you request. With each search, it better understands your profile and becomes increasingly successful at finding what you need.

Voice-activated knowbots are only one example of increasingly intelligent systems. Similar concepts can be applied to factory robot configuration for new-product assembly, computer system configuration, and communication network maintenance.

Increasing Integration of Business Organizations

Emerging telecommunications and computing capabilities described earlier have opened the way for better-integrated organizations, industries, and economies. Organizations that are well-integrated internally build a cohesive vision and corporate culture and tend to be more resilient and responsive to the demands of the marketplace. When such organizations partner with other high-quality organizations for their common good, they will be a market force to reckon with. Based on this presupposition, Figure 12–3 illustrates four regions of integration along the two axes of intraorganizational integration and interorganizational integration. The model proposes that higher levels of integration will yield higher levels of strategic impact on the organization's competitive position. The four regions include

FIGURE 12–3

Strategic impact of organizational integration

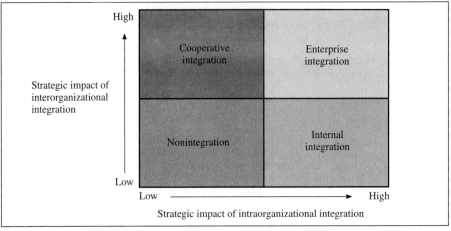

F. W. McFarlan, J. L. McKenney, and P. Pyburn "The Information Archipelago: Plotting a Course," *Harvard Business Review*, January–February 1983, pp. 145–56.

J. J. Vargo, N. Croke, and R. Hunt, "Information Technology and Organizational Integration in New Zealand Manufacturing," Working Paper No. 2/94, University of Canterbury, Department of Accountancy, Finance and Information Systems, Christchurch, New Zealand.

- *Nonintegration.* This region is characterized by organizational systems that are operated largely as stand-alone applications. The lack of shared data increases drag on information flows and reduces responsiveness to the environment. This combination yields low levels of strategic benefits.

- *Internal integration.* This region would be typified by increasing levels of internal integration, often beginning with administrative systems and increasing integration in manufacturing systems and ending with full CIM implementations that are integrated with administrative systems.

- *Cooperative integration.* Systems that support interorganizational activities typify this region, often beginning with E-mail, E-fax (faxing from a computer), and remote access to inventory levels; then progressing through electronic data interchange (EDI) of business documents such as purchase orders and invoices; and culminating in fully functional interorganizational systems (IOSs).

- *Enterprise integration.* This region is characterized by highly integrated systems, combining the best of internal integration and cooperative integration. The result is maximum responsiveness to the market environment due to an ability to effectively cooperate with trading partners as well as compete on cost and quality bases.

Migration to Common Network Technology for LANs and WANs

The extended discussion on ATM earlier in the chapter covered this important technology and the support it will provide for a common local and wide area network protocol. This move will both streamline network operation and interconnection and provide the building blocks for a highly scalable international information infrastructure (I^3).

Summary

This chapter has examined the direction that computer networking in business is likely to take over the next five years. It looks at key topics such as global communication networks and multimedia communication (the coming together of voice, data, and video), and it notes some of the limitations and risks likely to be incurred. A number of important developing technologies are discussed, including information highways, personal telephones, voice-activated computers, and the use of virtual reality in telecommunications. This chapter concludes with a view of the significant trends for our electronic future.

The number of new and developing networking services with the potential to support modern business applications is growing constantly. In this book, we have discussed a number of these services. Five years from now, we will likely have gone through still another technical revolution. Perhaps many of what we call "future" services now will be commonplace, and totally new technologies will be on the threshold. One thing is certain: The future of networking applications in business will be challenging, exciting, and highly profitable.

Key Terms

Deregulation   437

Intelligent search agent   433

Paperless office   436

Personal digital assistant (PDA)   445

Systems Network Architecture (SNA)   435

Virtual reality   444

Voice-activated intelligent scheduler   432

Questions for Discussion

1. Identify four limitations on networks and future developments. Discuss the political problems underlying these limitations. *pp. 434-436*

2. What benefits will accrue to businesses from the emergence of the paperless office?

3. How has deregulation in the telecommunications industry aided the advance of user services?

4. Why will high-bandwidth networks be increasingly important to businesses in the coming years? What bandwidth changes have developed in the last 10 years? *pp. 438-439*

5. Describe briefly how ATM networks will fulfill the demand for high-bandwidth in the future, and list some of the applications that will depend on this technology. *pp. 439-441*

6. Review Figures 3–9 through 3–12 in Chapter 3; then extrapolate the numbers shown in these figures to the year 2005.

7. What benefits would you see in having a wristwatch integrated with a full-function computer and communicator? What problems would you see with this, if any?

8. Describe an application of virtual reality using telecommunications that could influence your future career.

9. Discuss the seven trends for an electronic future covered at the end of the chapter. Put the trends in order of priority and justify your order.

Case Discussion and Analysis

1. Using a WWW browser, search for a business that markets its products or services using the Internet. Write a short description of the business, including the interesting technologies they are using and the home page address of the business.

2. Using a WWW browser, search for information on electronic commerce, intelligent agents, and other topics covered in this chapter. Write up your findings, including the home page address of the information source.

For both of the above items, good starting points could be the following WWW home pages:

http://galaxy.einet.net/galaxy.html

http://www.commerce.net

GLOSSARY OF TERMS

Acceptable Use Policy (AUP) Rules applied by many transit networks that restrict the uses for the Internet. Enforcement of AUPs varies with the network, but in almost every case outright "advertising" is unacceptable.

Analog signal A communication signal made up of a continuous wave pattern that varies in pitch or volume. When used to transmit computer data, a modem is used to convert from digital to analog and back again.

ANSI X12 and EDIFACT Two standards used for document transfer in EDI. It is likely that EDIFACT will become the world standard within a few years.

API See Application Program Interface.

Application Program Interface (API) Allows applications on PCs and mainframes to communicate with each other directly. APIs assist in the area of application program development because they allow PCs to connect at the application software level. A good example is IBM's Advanced Program-to-Program Communication (APPC/PC), although many vendors support their own proprietary versions of API.

Archie An Internet application program that will search Internet servers for a file of which existence is known but the location is unknown. A useful program for managing the tens of thousands of servers and millions of retrievable files on the Internet. Once the location of the file is discovered, FTP can be used to retrieve the file. See also Gopher, Telnet, WWW, and FTP.

Asynchronous The mode typically used for low-speed serial data transmission (usually 9600bps and less), in which each character (or byte) is transmitted separately with a start bit and a stop bit to delineate each character. The equipment to support asynchronous transmission is less expensive than that required for synchronous transmission, and it is used on dumb terminals and other less expensive equipment.

Asynchronous Transfer Mode (ATM) A new high-speed cell-based switching technology designed to act as a transport network for multimedia communications. It is designed to be transparent to both local and wide area networks and to support communication for many business applications, including text, business documents, voice, video, and other future application services.

ATM See Asynchronous Transfer Mode.

Attribute A data element that is a characteristic of an entity in logical data modeling. Often equivalent to a field of data in a physical implementation. For example, attributes of the entity "inventory" might include: ID number, description, quantity on hand, cost, and retail price.

AUP See Acceptable Use Policy.

Bandwidth The capacity of a communications channel. This is measured in bits per second for a digital channel and hertz for an analog channel.

Bastion host   See firewall.

Biometrics   Technique used to observe the characteristics of a person and his or her behavior in order to provide a much higher degree of security than that found with conventional user IDs and passwords. Examples include fingerprint scanners and observations of typing characteristics.

Bits per second (bps)   A measure of data transmission speed used in rating the transmission speed of modems, NTUs, etc. Bits per second may roughly be translated into bytes per second by dividing the bps rating by eight.

Brainstorming   A procedure for creative thinking and generation of ideas. All individuals present should participate and give any ideas they have, with no discussion of the items as they are recorded, as this could inhibit idea creation. After all ideas have come forth, then they may be discussed for their merits.

Bridge   A device which forwards traffic between network segments based on datalink layer information. Such segments have a common network layer address.

Bulletin boards   A form of electronic communication used over networks which allows all users to read and copy the posted messages.

Business process reengineering   A total rethinking of how specific functions of a business are accomplished, not simply to automate the existing functionality but to redesign the process to gain optimal results.

CAD/CAM   See Computer-aided design/computer-aided manufacturing.

CASE   See Computer-Aided Systems Engineering.

CCITT   Commitee Consultatif International de Telegraphique et Telephonique. (Consultative Committee of the Institute of Telegraph and Telephone). CCITT changed its name to ITU-T (International Telecommunications Union—Telecommunications Standards Sector) on March 1, 1993.

Centrex   A system whereby a business leases capacity from the Telecom authority on the switching exchange rather than lease or purchase their own PBX.

CEO   See Chief Executive Officer.

Channel noise   The environmental disturbances that may disrupt the flow of communication, cause a message to arrive in a garbled fashion, or prevent delivery of a message altogether. Examples of channel noise include audio, visual, psychological, and electronic.

Channel Service Unit/Data Service Unit (CSU/DSU)   See Network Terminating Unit (NTU).

Check float   The lag time between depositing a check in a bank account and the time the bank clears the check so that use can be made of the funds.

Chief executive officer (CEO)   The president, managing director, or operating head of an organization.

CIM   See Computer-integrated manufacturing.

Client/server   A software partitioning paradigm in which a distributed system is split between one or more server tasks that accept requests, according to some protocol, from (distributed) client tasks, asking for information or action. There may be either one centralized server or several distributed ones. This model allows clients and servers to be placed independently on nodes in a network. Examples are the use of various searching tools used on Internet, such as Archie, Gopher, WAIS, and WWW browsers, the file-server/file-client relationship in NFS, and the screen server/client application split in the X Window System.

CMIP   See Common Management Information Protocol.

Coaxial cable   A type of cable with a solid central conductor surrounded by an insulator, in turn surrounded by a cylindrical shield woven from fine wires. It is used to carry high-frequency signals, such as video or radio. The shield is usually connected to electrical ground to reduce electrical interference.

Collapsed backbone   A topology used in buildings where a router provides the focal point for network security, management, and configuration. UTP cable usually provides the connections between this router and the various floors or departmental workgroups. In this way, better control and management is possible, especially when multiple vendors' architectures are involved.

Common Management Information Protocol (CMIP)   Part of the OSI body of standards specifying protocol elements that may be used to provide network management. A highly complex protocol suite which has been slow to find its way onto the market, and to some degree its best features have been built into SNMP-2.

Communication channel   The means by which a message is passed between a sender and a receiver. Typical channels are mail, courier, fax, phone, e-mail, video conferencing, and face-to-face.

Communication model   A model that shows the process of interpersonal communication, which includes a sender, a receiver, a communication channel, channel noise, and the feedback process.

Competitive advantage   Where the use of a particular information technology application has given the organization an advantage in the marketplace over competitors in the same or related industries.

Computer-aided design/computer-aided manufacturing (CAD/CAM)   A system of software and hardware providing automated support for designing and engineering new products and product modifications, which is integrated with computer-controlled manufacturing equipment, such as numerical controlled machines and industrial robots.

Computer-aided systems engineering (CASE)   The process of using computer software to assist in systems analysis, design, and construction. The set of software applications used are variously referred to as CASE tools (where the individual applications are stand-alone), or CASE workbench (where multiple tools are integrated with one another). Examples of CASE tools include process decomposition diagrammers, entity-relationship diagrammers, association matrix diagrammers, screen designers, and automatic code generators.

Computer-integrated manufacturing (CIM)   A system that integrates CAD/CAM systems with automated logistics systems operating under JIT concepts. Typically included is rapid feedback from marketing to product design, engineering, and manufacturing to shorten time to market, quickening of product modifications, and implementation of quality improvements, all while reducing costs and increasing production flexibility.

Concentrator   A device that permits the sharing of a communications link with a number of attached links or workstations. See also multiplexer.

Concurrent access   Where two or more users can access the same application software and the same shared files simultaneously, with the system updating changes made by one user to the version being used by other users.

Connection-oriented   A type of transport layer data communication service that allows a host to send data in a continuous stream to another host. The transport service will guarantee that all data will be delivered to the other end in the same order as it was sent and without duplication. Communication proceeds through three well-defined phases: connection estab-

lishment, data transfer, and connection release. The most common examples are Transmission Control Protocol (TCP) and X.25.

Connectionless   A data communication system in which communication occurs between hosts with no previous setup. Packets sent between two hosts may take different routes. IP (Internet Protocol) is an example of a connectionless protocol.

Contact management   The process of following up with the many new contacts that all businesspeople make through both formal and informal channels.

Core competencies   The key areas of business (product lines and services) where a particular organization is internationally competitive and able to leverage their existing competitive advantage with further successful innovation.

Core logistics   A fundamental function of a company or industry, especially as regarding the procurement, manufacture, and delivery of goods and services. For example, salespersons making calls on customers; ordering, receiving and stocking inventory; and delivery of goods and services to customers are all core logistics.

Critical Success Factors (CSF)   The small number of factors which are critical to the success of a particular enterprise. For example, car style is a CSF for automobile companies, whereas variety of items is a CSF for supermarkets.

CSF   See Critical Success Factors.

CSU/DSU   See Channel Service Unit/Data Service Unit.

Data dictionary   A listing of the major data entities of an organization together with the attributes and other characteristics of the data.

Data Encryption Standard (DES)   A highly secure encryption standard pioneered by the U.S. government some years ago as a competition. It has remained a highly secure standard, and it is over 1,000 times faster than many of its competitors.

DCF   See Discounted Cash Flow.

DDN   See Digital Data Network.

Degrees of freedom   The freedom to take a variety of actions and make a range of decisions unconstrained by weaknesses in organization or technological infrastructure.

Digital Data Network (DDN) A wide area network designed for the transmission of high-speed digital data, often implemented using fiber optic cable. Current DDNs are capable of delivering multimegabit-per-second speeds, therefore allowing the transparent extension of a local area network to multiple sites in different parts of a city, different cities, or even different countries.

Digital envelope The encryption of a message with a secret key known only to the sender and receiver such that the receiver can verify that the message has not been tampered with during transit.

Digital signal A communication signal made up of a stream of binary digits (1 or 0) that represent data.

Digital signature A unique code or bit pattern used to authenticate the sender of a message—not a digital pattern of a person's normal signature.

Discounted cash flow (DCF) A concept used to compare incoming and outgoing cash flows from different periods of time caused by a capital investment, such as a new manufacturing facility or new information system. The process is very similar to compound interest methods and is most often represented by the Net Present Value method and the Internal Rate of Return method. In these methods, the further in the future a cash flow is, the less value it has today (present value).

Distributed processing (1) The use of multiple communicating computers to process application programs. (2) The distribution of a computing workload amongst multiple communicating computers that would otherwise be handled by one computer.

Downsizing (1) The process of reducing an organization's size to better match existing market demand and competition. This often includes major reductions in levels of management and other information-manipulation and information-passing people. In many cases such people are replaced by sophisticated information and telecommunications systems. (2) The process of replacing larger, more centralized computer facilities, such as a mainframe computer, with smaller computers, such as a LAN of microcomputers.

Dual-homed gateway A type of firewall where two network interface cards are installed in a computer. One of these is connected to the Internet and the other to the private network.

Dumb terminal A computer terminal (monitor, keyboard, and communications electronics) that simply sends and receives character data by means of a central computer. Although previously a primary technology, this type of terminal is rapidly being replaced by highly intelligent workstations and sophisticated terminals.

E-fax See Electronic fax.

E-mail enabled applications Traditional application software that has been enhanced to receive and generate E-mail messages so as to assist managers and other nontechnical workers to better access company information systems. Especially effective in organizations where E-mail has been enthusiastically received by knowledge workers and where the organization has many older-style mainframe applications, query languages, and batch file programs in place that normally allow limited access by knowledge workers due to the command line interface or esoteric language and syntax involved.

E-R diagram A data modeling diagram used to describe major data **entities** and **relationships** between them.

Economies of scale The value gained by an increase in production quantity or organizational size. This value may come as a result of increase in bargaining power, less wastage of time and materials, more ready access to capital markets or improved technology, or improved management expertise.

Economies of scope The value gained by being more able to market a wider range of goods and services to a wider range of geographically and culturally diverse customers. This value may arise as a result of better contacts in the community, enhanced manufacturing, or other technology that allows a greater responsiveness to customer demand or other factors.

EDI See Electronic Data Interchange.

EFT See Electronic Funds Transfer.

EFT-POS See Electronic Funds Transfer and Point of Sale.

Effectiveness The ability to make timely and appropriate decisions that produce persistent action toward specific quantity and quality outputs through the characteristics of adaptability and flexibility.

Efficiency The characteristic of an organization that permits it to produce the maximum quantity of outputs of a specified quality from a minimum of materials and human and organizational effort.

Electronic calendaring A diary system that allows users to book meeting rooms, equipment, and a variety of other services and facilities.

Electronic data interchange (EDI) The use of telecommunications to transfer business documents between organizations, and it may also be used for EFT. For example, a company using EDI may send an electronic purchase order (PO) instead of a paper one. The paper PO may take 1 to 14 days to arrive at the supplier, whereas an EDI PO will only take a matter of seconds.

Electronic fax (E-fax) The use of the fax transmission system to transfer E-mail and other documents directly into a computer for further processing, direct image capture, or printing out on a computer printer. This technology is implemented using a fax board in a personal computer or workstation.

Electronic funds transfer (EFT) Use of electronic payment methods, such as credit or debit cards, at the point of sale, for immediate credit to the seller's account. See also point of sale.

Encryption The process of converting a stream of data into a code that is very difficult to read by anything but a machine or user with a "key" to the code.

Entity Any group of persons or objects about which the organization wishes to keep data. A fundamental building block in a logical data model. Often equivalent to a record type in a physical implementation. Examples include customers, inventory, equipment, invoice, and checks.

Ethernet A network standard pioneered by Digital, (a major minicomputer manufacturer), Intel (major chip manufacturer), and Xerox, which is now used by over 80 percent of the LANs on the market. The standard uses a baseband bus network topology, together with twisted pair, coaxial cable, or other high-speed media, such as fiber optic cable. This system is capable of providing high-speed (10 Mbps) data communications for LANs. It is also commonly referred to as IEEE 802.3.

External factors Those characteristics over which the individual organization has little or no influence or control.

FDDI See Fiber Distributed Data Interface.

Features matrix A technique for comparing vendor proposals for the purpose of selecting the most suitable system proposal. The matrix typically consists of columns headed up for each of the vendor proposals under consideration, while the rows are labeled with the desired categories for comparing the proposals. Points are assigned for each of the categories and subcategories to allow ease of comparison.

Feedback The process of testing the received message with the sender to see if it was received accurately, or to provide additional information about the subject of the message. It gives an opportunity to verify accuracy and improve the overall quality of the communication. Feedback may consist of a variety of methods, including paraphrasing, asking questions, and making comments.

Fiber optic cable A form of telecommunication transmission media consisting of thin glass fibers bundled together inside an insulated cable. Capable of carrying voice, video, or data at speeds of up to 10 Gbps over 100 kilometers, and up to 10,000 Gbps over a few meters.

Fiber Distributed Data Interface (FDDI) A standard used in conjunction with fiber optic cable for transmission speeds of 100 Mbps. It has been defined as ISO9314 and incorporates the physical media dependant layer ISO9314/3, the physical layer ISO9314/1, the medium access control layer ISO9314/2, and the logical link control layer ISO8802/2.

File server A shared database on a local area network which provides access by multiple users to the files on the database. It is a shared resource primarily acting as a source of files but it can also carry out processing, although such a function should strictly be referred to as a *host server*.

File Transfer Protocol (FTP) An application program used to permit the sending or receiving of files (ASCII or binary). This is only possible if the user has an account on the remote computer that files are being transferred to or from. However, this limitation is addressed at many remote sites by setting up an anonymous FTP facility, which allows anyone to access certain files and retrieve them.

Firewall A dedicated gateway machine with special security precautions used to provide security from outside network connections and dial-in lines. The idea is to protect a cluster of more loosely administered machines hidden behind it from intruders.

Frame relay   A service for high-speed LAN interconnection in which bursts of data are accommodated with a variable allocation of bandwidth. Typically the speeds for this service lie between 64 Kbps and 2 Mbps.

FTP   See File Transfer Protocol.

Full-duplex   The ability of a telecommunication system to send and receive messages at the same time. Traffic is accommodated in both directions simultaneously. The telephone is an example of a full duplex device.

Gateway   The term *router* is now used in place of the original definition of gateway. Currently, a gateway is a communications device or program that passes data between networks having similar functions but dissimilar implementations. This should not be confused with a protocol converter. By this definition, a router is a layer 3 (network layer) gateway, and a mail gateway is a layer 7 (application layer) gateway.

Goal   The broad aims that an organization determines are necessary to achieve a mission statement.

Gopher   An application program used on the Internet to automatically find and browse various Internet resources (e.g., remote library card catalogues, online newspapers). This program incorporates some of the features of Telnet and Archie with other features, including a menu-driven environment. See also Telnet, Archie, WWW, and FTP.

Gopher client   A program which runs on a machine and provides a user interface to the Gopher protocol. Gopher clients are available for most workstations.

Gopher server   A program that runs off a server providing links to the Gopher client and finding various requested resources on the Internet.

Groupware   A class of information systems designed to support person-to-person processes in sharing documents and data, such as many database products. Other examples include messaging systems, scheduling and conferencing software, workflow software, and communicating word processors that allow multiple users to access the same document and data simultaneously while providing update and version control facilities to prevent the loss of data.

Half-duplex   The ability of a telecommunication system to send and receive messages in alternation. Traffic is accommodated in both directions, but in only one direction at a time. The typical walkie-talkie or short wave radio is an example of a half-duplex device.

Hertz (Hz)   One cycle per second. A Megahertz is a million cycles per second. Abbreviated MHz. A measure of computer speed or power. A processor running at 33 MHz is nearly seven times faster than one running at 4.77 MHz, if it is the same processor. The broadest approximate measure of relative computer power may be derived by multiplying the MHz rating by the word size.

Home page   A hypertext page that is the first point of contact with the WWW. A home page presents information about the organization or individual to whom it belongs and it provides hypertext links to other information that the creator has made available to the WWW.

Hub   A device connected to several other devices. In a message-handling service, a number of local computers might exchange messages solely with a hub computer. The hub would be responsible for exchanging messages with other hubs and nonlocal computers. Sometimes this is also referred to as a *star topology*.

Hybrid gateway   A type of firewall which uses a combination of protocols to limit Internet access to a private network. Access to the hybrid gateway can be made through the use of IP tunneling.

Hybrid manager   A manager capable of running a functional area of a business, while at the same time capable of recognizing IT opportunities and their application to various business needs.

IEEE802   The Institution of Electrical and Electronic Engineers which has been the standards-setting body for many of the local area network standards such as IEEE 802.3 (Ethernet) and IEEE 802.5 (Token Ring).

Information technology (IT)   The concept of IT encompasses the widest possible inclusion of technology that has a direct connection with information processing, storage, or transfer. IT includes telecommunications, software development, microprocessor design, and production and strategic information planning.

Integrated Services Digital Network   (ISDN) A wide area network designed to carry a mixture of data from many applications including voice, computer data, and fax.

Intelligent building   When local area network wiring is installed as part of a building's backbone services, such as electricity reticulation, air conditioning, or water. This term sometimes implies the use of associated computer equipment to control the various building services.

Intelligent hub   A hub with security and management hardware and/or software incorporated.

Intelligent search agent   A computer program capable of assisting a user in finding information on a single computer, local area network, or a wide area network such as the Internet. This type of application program (currently under development) has the ability to learn the user's information needs by assessing the various searches that are done for success, thus exercising some growing intelligence in the search process over time.

Interactive   Networked applications that communicate with one another in real time, with an online conversation thereby being made possible to users. Video teleconferencing, "chat" mode E-mail, and ordinary telephone are examples.

Interface   The shared boundary between two systems or subsystems that provides for interaction between the two systems. For example, a user interface is the shared boundary between a computer and a human that allows the human and computer to interact with one another.

Internal factors   Those characteristics over which the organization has some direct influence and control.

Internal Rate of Return (IRR)   A DCF method for calculating the estimated rate of return on an investment, given the projected positive and negative cash flows from the investment over its useful life. The IRR is computed based on the concept that a NPV of zero must use a discount rate equal to the projected actual rate of return. The IRR calculation iterates through the NPV calculation seeking a NPV equal to zero, substituting various discount rates into the calculation, and interpolating between them until the NPV equals zero.

International Standards Organization (ISO)   A voluntary, nontreaty organization responsible for creating international standards in many areas, including computers and communications. ISO produced the seven-layer model for network architecture (Open Systems Interconnection). Its members are the national standards organizations of 89 countries, including the American National Standards Institute (ANSI).

International Telecommunications Union   ITU-T (International Telecommunications Union—Telecom-

munications Standards Sector) is responsible for making technical recommendations about telephone and data (including fax) communications systems for PTTs and suppliers. Plenary sessions are held every four years at which time they adopt new standards. ITU works closely with all standards organizations to form an international uniform standards system for communication. Study Group XVII is responsible for the V, X, and I series standards. Previously known as the CCITT.

Internet   A set of some 50,000 interconnected networks supporting over five million computers in over 80 countries. Currently the number of users is around 20 million, yet the growth rate continues at 10–15 percent per month.

IP (Internet Protocol)   See Transmission Control Protocol/Internet Protocol (TCP/IP).

IP tunneling   A system where IP packets are conveyed transparently across networks using underlying protocols such as Ethernet or X.25 but without the user being aware of the requirements of this underlying architecture.

IRR   See Internal Rate of Return.

ISDN   See Integrated Services Digital Network.

ISO   See International Standards Organization.

IT   See Information Technology.

IT platform   The hardware and software platform that an organization has in place to assist in carrying out its business activities.

JAD   See Joint Application Design.

JIT   See Just-in-time.

Joint Application Design (JAD)   A method of structured group interviewing used to shorten the process of requirements discovery and system design while improving the quality of the information gathered. It consists of a trained facilitator, one or two additional systems analysts capturing requirements using CASE tools, and four to eight knowledgeable users with authority to establish requirements and make decisions for their functional area.

Just-in-time (JIT)   A system of inventory and manufacturing management that emphasizes the ordering and receipt of materials and other stock just in time to be manufactured or delivered to customers, thereby minimizing stock holdings and potential obsolete stock. This type of system is very often heavily dependent on computerized information and control systems with telecommunication access.

Kerberos authentication server   Kerberos is a security system developed as part of the Massachusetts Institute of Technology's Project Athena. Kerberos authenticates every user for every application. It is commonly used on the Internet and has been adopted by OSF (Open Software Foundation) as part of its DCE (Distributed Computing Environment). Kerberos relies on three components to watch over network security: a database, authentication server, and a ticket-granting server. All three components sit on a single, physically secured server that is connected to the network.

LAN   See Local Area Network.

Leverage   To gain advantage, allowing individuals to accomplish more than they would without it.

LLC   See Logical Link Control.

Local Area Network (LAN)   A telecommunication network allowing connection of computers, peripherals, and other devices that are in close proximity to one another (usually less than 10km) and are generally owned by the user organization. The major functions of a local area network are message processing and sharing of peripherals, data, and programs.

Logical Link Control (LLC)   The layer in the LAN architecture which is designed to provide end-to-end services independent of the underlying MAC and physical layers. Today this is often provided by the IP protocol.

MAC   See Medium Access Control.

Mail float   The time lag between posting a letter, check, or other item in the mail and the time it arrives at its destination.

Management Information Base (MIB)   Stores network resources, which are represented by managed objects.

Manchester encoding   A system used with Ethernet and token ring LANs to encode the transmitted bit stream in order to provide for accurate clocking and timing. This scheme is necessary with networks that operate at speeds of megabits per second.

MAU   See Medium Access Unit.

Medium Access Control (MAC)   The layer in a LAN architecture which defines the access mechanism to the physical layer. The two most common MAC standards in the industry are Ethernet and token ring.

Medium Access Unit (MAU)   The unit to which user devices are commonly connected. It originates from the IBM token ring networks and usually implies a star topology, with each peripheral device being attached by a 10BASE-T cable.

Megalink or T1/E1   A simple point-to-point unmanaged 2 Mbps interconnection service.

MIB   See Management Information Base.

Min/max analysis   A technique for comparing vendor proposals to reduce the number to a short list. Proposals are eliminated if they do not meet the organization's minimum system requirements or if they exceed the maximum budgeted cost for the system.

Mission critical applications   Business applications that are so critical to the daily functioning of the organization that if they are out of operation, the firm will be unable to conduct some portion of its business. For example, if an EFT-POS system goes down, the store using the system may be unable to complete customer sales.

Mission statement   The overriding statement of purpose held by an organization. See also goal and objective.

Modem   An electronic device for converting between serial data (typically V.24/RS-232) from a computer and an audio signal suitable for transmission over telephone lines, distinguished primarily by the maximum speed that it can support. Most modems support a number of different protocols, and they may either be internal, connected to the computer's bus, or external (stand-alone), connected to one of the computer's serial ports.

Mosaic   A GUI browser for accessing the WWW. Mosaic is the first major graphical interface to the Internet and is available in Windows, Macintosh, and X-Windows versions. This WWW browser has been tremendously successful and has encouraged many Internet users to create their own hypertext home pages, making a wide range of Internet resources readily available.

Multimedia   The presentation of multiple forms of sensory data to the user under computer control. For example, a multimedia encyclopedia stored on CD-ROM might integrate text, voice description, video segments, animation, and related sounds for a particular topic.

Multiplexer A device that combines several signals for transmission on some shared medium. A communications channel may be shared between the independent signals in one of several different ways: time division multiplexing, frequency division multiplexing, and statistical time division multiplexing.

Multipoint (multidrop) Terminals in a local area are terminated in a central switching station or concentrator, rather than being connected to the main computer directly as is the case with the star network. A number of these concentrators can be connected to the main computer by the same high-speed links. This type of network can considerably reduce line costs where large geographical areas are involved.

National Information Infrastructure (NII) The U.S. government-funded program to establish an integrated information highway to allow businesses to conduct electronic commerce more effectively, including EDI and other company-to-company commerce, as well as direct-to-the-customer commerce by using concepts such as at-home shopping via interactive TV. Often referred to as the *information superhighway.*

Net Present Value (NPV) A DCF method involving computation of today's value of cash flows that are projected to occur in the future using a discount rate (interest rate) to reduce the value of the future cash flows. The more periods (years or months) the cash flow is in the future, the more it is discounted and therefore the less value it has in today's dollars. After computation of the NPV, if the value is positive, this indicates that the investment is projected to repay itself along with interest, at a rate higher than the discount rate. An NPV of zero would indicate a rate of return equal to the discount rate and a negative NPV would indicate a rate of return lower than the discount rate. The projected rate of return from the estimated cash flows may be calculated by using the IRR concept.

Netscape A commercial development of Mosaic, including functional and security enhancements, which has become the most widely used browser on the WWW.

Network Terminating Unit (NTU) An interface between a data communications channel and a user's equipment in a similar way to which a modem is an interface between the PSTN and a user's equipment. The NTU takes one or more digital data streams and codes them for data transmission through the digital network. The coding technique commonly used is called Pulse Code Modulation (PCM).

Niche marketing The process of discovering and marketing an organization's products or services into specific market segments rather than to the whole market. To effectively do this, the organization must tailor their goods and services to better meet the need of that segment at competitive costs and quality.

NII See National Information Infrastructure.

Noninteractive Referring to networked applications that communicate with one another in a store-and-forward mode, so that messages arrive quickly at their destination but not immediately. This is typical of E-mail, where the messages are sent but may be held for a few moments by various computers along the delivery path until the computer has a free moment to forward the mail to the next location along the path.

NPV See Net Present Value.

NTU See Network Terminating Unit.

Object-oriented programming (OOP) This is different from conventional programming in that a set of built-in procedures define the behavior of objects, which provides a level of artificial intelligence not present in conventional programming. A good example is the desktop concept, with icons used to represent various objects on a desk such as folders, documents, and trash cans.

Objective The specific, realistic, and measurable targets that will allow an organization to achieve its goals.

OOP See Object-Oriented Programming.

Operating system (1) The group of system programs that provides access to system resources for application programs. Functions such as disk access, print access, and screen access are provided. (2) A user interface for manipulating files, running programs, and other basic tasks.

Operational efficiency The use of a particular information technology application has given the organization an increase in the cost-effective operation of its business.

Order entry An order entry (or order processing system) is one in which the customers' orders are fed to a database that initiates the shipping of orders. The primary objectives of the system are to initiate the shipping of orders, maintain a record of back-ordered items, and to produce sales analysis reports.

Overtrading   The process of growth within a business characterized by rapidly increasing sales that result in such demands on inventory and receivables that the organization moves into financial difficulties, especially in the form of a cash-flow crisis. The fundamental cause of this condition is insufficient capital investment to sustain the high level of growth.

Packet Assembler/Disassembler (PAD)   Hardware or software device for splitting a data stream into discrete packets for transmission over some medium, and then reforming the stream(s) at the receiver. Often used for conversion between asynchronous to synchronous data. The term is most often used for interfaces to X.25 networks.

Packet Switching Network (PSN)   A medium-speed wide area network designed for transfer of data packets among many users simultaneously.

PAD   See Packet Assembler/Disassembler.

Paperless office   The concept, widely predicted to arrive in the 1980s but still to happen, of a completely automated workplace using computer and communicatons technology in place of "paper."

Passenger name record (PNR)   A record representing a passenger's flight itinerary which is stored in the airline's flight reservations application.

Payback period   The length of time necessary to repay an investment, apart from any interest payments or return on the investment.

PBX   See Private Branch Exchange.

PDA   See Personal digital assistant.

Permanent Virtual Circuit (PVC)   A communications system in which physical or logical circuits are set up between the end stations such that no addressing is necessary following call establishment, similar to the way in which a telephone call is set up. The path through the network is defined by the virtual circuit numbers.

Personal digital assistant (PDA)   A hand-held computing device typically incorporating a digital pen pointing device instead of a keyboard for user input. The surface of the PDA is normally a touch-sensitive screen with icons representing the various applications, which might include an electronic diary, phone/address book, calculator, handwriting recognition, or sketchpad, as well as communication facilities, including fax, cellphone, and pager.

Personal productivity   Getting the most output from the limited time available. Efficient use of time leveraged by telecommunications-based information technology can help in producing more with less.

PNR   See Passenger name record.

Point of sale (POS)   A computer terminal or work-station functioning as a cash register check-out point at a retail store. The computer terminal is typically connected with an automated data capture facility, such as a barcode reader, and online data storage for recording sales, inventory maintenance, and credit verification. Also used with the term electronic funds transfer (EFT) as in EFT/POS.

Polling   A networking procedure in which each terminal on the network is polled (electronically asked) regarding its need to send a message over the network. If the response is affirmative, the terminal is given the opportunity to send its message, then control passes on to the next affirmative responding terminal.

POS   See Point of sale.

Primary key   A unique attribute of an entity that will allow a particular instance of that entity to be located. For example, the primary key for a customer would probably be the customer number.

Private Branch Exchange (PBX)   A communication switchboard. In more recent years, this familiar phone equipment has taken on a new character, incorporating private telephone and data communication and network control, allowing an organization to distribute an integrated data and voice system.

Protocol   The rules or standards governing communication over a network.

Prototype   A working model of an actual product or item that is used for testing and refinement purposes. This term is often used in information systems design to designate a rapidly developed working model of the system used to gain active feedback from the potential users of the system.

Proxy gateways   Firewall or bastion hosts that receive extra attention in order to provide for security between the Internet and a private network.

PSN   See Packet Switching Network.

PSTN   See Public Switched Telephone Network.

Public/corporate database   Database used to provide information via a wide area network. Information may be made available freely or charged for depending upon the service being provided.

Public Switched Telephone Network (PSTN)   The most extensively used network in the world designed for voice communication via the use of telephones, but it is still used in conjunction with modems and computers for low-volume data communication.

PVC   See Permanent Virtual Circuit.

RAID   See Redundant Array of Inexpensive Disks.

Recoverability   The ability of an organization to recover from a system failure regardless of the cause. Recoverability typically starts with data backup and may proceed to the extreme of replication of the full data center as a backup facility.

Redundant Array of Inexpensive Disks (RAID)   The essential concept behind RAID is to group together several disk drives and to use some type of drive redundancy to ensure that the array as a whole can survive and continue to operate satisfactorily if any one drive in the array should fail. RAID is available in various levels (RAID 0 to RAID 5), which refer to how data is stored on the system. Most commercially available RAID systems fall into one of three levels (RAID 1, 3 or 5).

Relationships   The logical associations or events that link entities in a data model.

Reliability   The extent to which users can rely on a system to be functional when they need it.

Remote Monitoring MIB (RMON MIB)   A MIB set up in a remote part of a network which gathers information about objects on that part of the network and reports this data back to a central management station in a timely manner.

Repeater   A device that propagates electrical signals from one cable to another. More recently, these devices have become more sophisticated and are now referred to as *hubs*.

Request for comment (RFC)   An invitation for comment issued on the Internet as part of the standards setting and updating process. Many industry standards have been created on the Internet using this process, as it provides a method for fast and widely distributed comment.

Request for proposal (RFP)   A document that an organization sends to suppliers asking them to propose a system solution to a need the organization has. The document will spell out what is required of the vendors and boundaries which the system should encompass.

Requirements analysis   The process of discovery used to yield a description of the new system requirements, including user, technical, budgetary, compatibility, internal, and external requirements.

Response time   Response time refers to the time a user has to wait between the time at which a request is made, a character is typed, or a command is sent to the system and the time at which the system responds. Response times over LANs may vary from sub-one-second times under normal conditions to tens of minutes on an overloaded system. Response times over WANs will also vary depending on the nature of the communication, distance to the host, host loadings, and transaction levels.

RFC   See Request for comment.

RFP   See Request for proposal.

Risk analysis   A method of quantifying risk associated with unauthorized disclosure of information, unauthorized modification of information, denial of service, and disruption in the continuity of operations.

RMON MIB   See Remote Monitoring MIB.

Router   A device that forwards traffic between networks. The forwarding decision is based on network layer information and routing tables, often constructed by routing protocols.

Screening router   This device is used to connect the Internet to private networks and can be configured to implement screening, which implies some form of packet filtering based upon source and/or destination addresses. Closely related terms include firewall, bastion host, dual homed gateway, and hybrid gateway.

SDLC   See Systems development life cycle.

Simple Network Management Protocol (SNMP)   The Internet standard protocol, developed to manage nodes on an IP network. As a result of its widespread use on the Internet, it has become a de facto industry network management standard.

Simple Network Management Protocol version 2 (SNMP-2)   A new version of SNMP which incorporates many new features resulting from five years of experience with SNMP. It also incorporates some of the ideas from the ISO management protocol suite (CMIP).

Simplex   A telecommunication system that is able to send or receive messages in one direction at a time. Radios and televisions are both simplex systems.

Smart card   A card resembling a credit card containing a microprocessor chip. Frequently used to generate short lifetime encrypted random numbers and act as a challenge/response system in order to authorize access to a workstation.

SNA   See Systems Network Architecture.

SNMP   See Simple Network Management Protocol.

SNMP-2   See Simple Network Management Protocol version 2.

Spoofing   This refers to the unauthorized modification of a message such that either the contents have been modified or that the message does not come from the apparent sender's address. IP spoofing is commonly associated with use of the Internet.

SQL   See Structured Query Language.

Star Topology   See hub.

Strategic leverage   The use of IT or other methods to gain more advantage from an organization's strengths, capturing opportunities that may have been beyond their grasp without the IT application or method.

Strategic partnership   A relationship built with another organization for the purpose of gaining a strategic advantage. This strategic partnership could consist of a range of relationships, including (1) a relationship with existing suppliers to leverage cooperative effort against a bigger foreign competitor, (2) a short-term consortium with a domestic competitor to allow penetration of an overseas market, (3) licensing agreements, (4) joint R&D arrangements, and (5) value chain partnerships.

Strategic planning   The process of establishing broad long-range direction, goals, and objectives for an organization's fundamental products and services, functions and processes, and resources and time frames.

Structured Query Language (SQL)   A standard language pioneered by IBM for retrieving information from a relational database.

SVC   See Switched Virtual Circuit.

Switched Virtual Circuit (SVC)   A communications system in which all intelligence lies in the end stations. Information is passed in frames or packets with a specific address for each in the same way that letters are sent in a postal system.

Switching costs   The cost for a customer to switch from one vendor to another.

SWOT analysis   A method of strategic planning that looks at an organization's internal Strengths and Weaknesses, as well as its external Opportunities and Threats.

Synchronous   The mode typically used for high-speed serial data transmission (usually greater than 9600 bps) in which a group of characters is sent in a synchronized fashion, without start or stop bits, but rather using timing circuits in the modem or transmission equipment to delineate one character from another.

Systems development life cycle (SDLC)   The cyclical process of developing an information system through analysis, design, implementation, evaluation, and maintenance.

Systems Network Architecture (SNA)   IBM's widely used seven-layer ISO model.

Tactical planning   The process of medium-term detailed planning needed to achieve strategic goals and objectives.

TBIT   See Telecommunications-based information technology.

TCP/IP   See Transmission Control Protocol/Internet Protocol (TCP/IP).

Telecommunications-based information technology (TBIT)   Any application of information technology that involves the use of telecommunications in the delivery of the application or technology.

Telecommuting   The use of computers and telecommunications to allow one to work at home, replacing physical commuting.

Teleconferencing   The use of electronic networks, sometimes in conjunction with video communications, to allow organizations to conduct a conference without all participants being present in the same place, which includes video teleconferencing, computer conferencing, and audio (telephone) teleconferencing.

Telemarketing   The use of computers and the telephone network to reach clients in their homes or offices.

Teleshopping   A system of at-home shopping in which customers consult a catalog or view TV advertising and order products over the telephone.

Telnet   An application program used on the Internet to log in to a remote computer. See also Gopher, Archie, WWW, and FTP.

Terminal emulation   Use of hardware or software to cause a terminal to behave or take on the characteristics of a different type of terminal.

Time to market   The time duration between conception of a new product or service through the design, engineering, and construction phases until final delivery of the product or service to the end customer.

Token ring   A computer local area network arbitration scheme in which conflicts in the transmission of messages are avoided by the granting of tokens, which give permission to send. A station keeps the token while transmitting a message if it has a message to transmit, and then passes it on to the next station. *Token ring* is also commonly referred to as IEEE802.5.

Toll-free 800 number   A system often used free of charge by customers to access companies who provide service or marketing information. The company providing the 800 number usually pays a fixed monthly rental for a specific number of freefone hours.

Topology   The layout or configuration of a network. Some topologies are designed for redundancy and reliability while others are designed for economy of interconnecting circuits.

tps   See Transactions per second.

Transactions per second (tps)   A measure of processing speed for transaction processing systems which indicates to maximum level of processing capacity of a system or group of systems.

Transmission Control Protocol/Internet Protocol (TCP/IP)   A communications protocol suite used for interworking, routing, and reliable message delivery. Originally a U.S. Department of Defense protocol suite developed for the Internet, it is now widely used for the interconnection of different vendor's equipment on both local and wide area networks.

Trojan horse   A malicious security-breaking program that is disguised as something benign, such as a directory lister, archiver, game, or a program to find and destroy viruses. A Trojan horse is also referred to as a *trap door.*

Unshielded twisted pair (UTP) Category 2, 3, & 5   Copper cable with the pairs specifically twisted so as to avoid electrical interference from outside sources. The number of twists per unit distance dictates the characteristics of the cable.

UNIX   This is a very widely used general purpose, interactive, time-sharing operating system developed by Bell Laboratories and implemented on most vendors' equipment. UNIX is also used and closely associated with the TCP/IP protocol suite.

UTP   See Unshielded twisted pair.

V.24 (RS-232)   A CCITT standard for serial port configuration that is widely used with microcomputers. Sometimes used synonymously with serial port, also called the RS-232 standard.

Virtual corporation   A temporary organization involving a number of unrelated organizations who cooperate together on a single project to design, produce, and/or market a product or service. See also *strategic partnership.*

Virtual private network   A telecommunication network derived from one of the standard wide area networks but made available only to a private group of users such as a particular company or set of clients.

Virtual reality   The creation of an artificial environment that appears realistic that it is difficult to distinguish it from the real thing.

Virus   A cracker program that searches out other programs and "infects" them by embedding a copy of itself in them, so that they become Trojan horses. When these programs are executed, the embedded virus is executed too, thus propagating the infection. This normally happens invisibly to the user.

Voice-activated intelligent scheduler   A program capable of responding to a user's spoken commands and comments in the process of scheduling appointments, meetings, and other tasks. The scheduler demonstrates intelligence by learning and remembering user preferences.

WAIS   See Wide Area Information Server.

WAN   See Wide Area Network.

Wide Area Information Server (WAIS)   An application program used on the Internet to search indexed database archives using keyword searches to find articles or information of interest.

Wide Area Network (WAN)   A telecommunication network allowing connection of computers, peripherals, and other devices, such as telephone and fax, that are at a distance from one another. This type of network is usually provided by a communication utility such as a telecommunications provider and is hired out to users.

Wideband DDN or Fractional T1/E1   64 Kbps up to 2 Mbps. A point-to-point interconnection service.

Windows NT   (Windows New Technology) Microsoft's 32-bit operating system developed from what was originally intended to be OS/2 3.0 before Microsoft and IBM ceased joint development of OS/2. NT is targeted at the workstation and corporate network market. It was released in September 1993. Unlike Windows 3.1, which was a graphical environment that ran on top of DOS, Windows NT is a complete operating system. It appears the same as Windows 3.1, but it provides true multithreading, built-in networking, security, and memory protection, and it is largely hardware independent.

Windows 95   Microsoft's successor to Microsoft Windows 3.1. It was released in late 1995 and resembles the graphical user interface of the Macintosh environment. The architecture and its successors is likely to have a significant impact over the next few years.

Workflow software   Software that routes electronic documents to the right people at the right time and keeps track of the document movement so that management can monitor task completion and project completion.

World Wide Web (WWW)   A highly flexible information service available on the Internet that provides ready access to a full range of Internet resources from various locations in an easy to use hypertext format. The WWW uses a "browser," an application program to "browse" through and coordinate Internet resources. See also Mosaic, Telnet, Archie, Gopher, and FTP.

Worm   A program that propagates itself over a network, reproducing itself as it goes and crippling devices around the network. Perhaps the best-known example was Robert Morris's "Internet Worm" of November 1988, a "benign" worm that got out of control and hogged over 6,000 SUNs and VAXs across the United States.

WWW   See World Wide Web.

WWW browser   A client program (known as a browser), such as Mosaic or Netscape, that runs on the user's computer and provides two basic navigation operations: to follow a link or to send a query to a server. Most clients and servers now also support "forms" which allow the user to enter arbitrary text as well as selecting options from customisable menus.

X.25   A CCITT standard for interconnecting to a packet switching network. This standard incorporates the bottom three layers of the ISO model and is used interchangeably with the term *packet switching*.

INDEX

100BASE-T, 154, 203, 204, 207
100VG-AnyLAN, 180, 197, 203, 205-207
10BASE-F, 174-175, 189, 191, 202
10BASE-T, 154, 174-175, 189-191, 194, 197
10BASE2, 174-175, 189
10BASE36, 174-175
10BASE5, 174-175
800 phone system, 16, 53, 142

Acceptable use policy (AUP), 92, 111
Access server, 410, 412-413
Accounting management, 384, 389, 390, 402
Active badge readers, 411
Address filtering, 116
Advertising, receiving leads from, 309
Airline computerized reservation systems (CRSs), 14
Alphanumeric pager; *see* Case study, Kangaroo Courier Company
Alternative selection, 354-363
Alternatives selection; *see also* Case study, Wilton Manufacturing Company
America Online, 95
American Bar Association, 72, 74
American National Standards Institute (ANSI), 155
Analog signals, 130-131

Analysis, organisational, 240-260; *see also* Case study, Rapid Delivery Couriers Corporation illustration of organizational analysis
Anonymous FTP, 98, 100, 102
ANSI X12, 80
ARPANET, 211
AppleTalk, 190, 191
Application gateway, 116-117
Application layer, 95, 152
security, 118
Application program interface, 392
Archie, 92, 99-103
Association matrix, 250-253
Asynchronous, 95, 136, 138-139, 157
Asynchronous transfer mode (ATM), 162, 197, 207-208, 439-441
in comparison with other technologies, 147, 150, 151, 173
AT&T Mail, 97, 117
ATM; *see* Asynchronous transfer mode
Attached unit interface (AUI), 189
Attributes, 253; *see also* E-R diagram
Audio; *see* Channel noise
Audit techniques, 417-423
Audit trail analysis, of intrusion detection, 418
Authentication server, 412-413
Automatic teller machine (ATM), 53, 54, 55

Automobile industry, competitive advantage illustrated, 13

Backup of data, 425-427
full, 426
incremental, 426
recoverability factor, 341
Bacteria programs, 418
Bandwidth, 125, 133, 148
Banyan VINES, 214
Baseband, 174
Bastion host, 117-118
Benefits cycle model,
Benefits cycle model, 231-234
illustrated, 233-234
Billboard, 111-112
Biometrics, 411
Bookmark, 103
Bps (bits per second), 125
Brainstorming, 251
Bridge, 188-190
example of use, 60, 62-63
Broadband, 174
Brouter, 192
Budgetary requirements, 330-331
Bulletin boards 77-78, 86
Bus, 175, 194, 195-6
Business process reengineering (BPR), 15; *see also* Workflow software
Byte Information Exchange (BIX), 79, 93

Cabling, 174-175
Caching, 105
CAD/CAM; *see* Computer-aided design and computer-aided manufacturing
Carrier, 131, 181
Carrier sense multiple access/collision detection (CSMA/CD), 174, 178-180, 204
Case study,
   ACD Manufacturing Group illustration of competitive advantage, 228-229
   American Hospital Supply Corporation, 8-9
   bank security, 385-386
   Best Manufacturing Company illustration of E-R diagram, 267-269
   brokerage company, 58-61
   Cole & Sons Manufacturing Company illustration of ineffectiveness, 227-228
   domestic appliance manufacturer, 66-68
   electronic white pages, 69-70
   Fast Clothes Company illustration of responsiveness 24-25
   fast-food distributor, 39-40
   hospital complex, 61-64
   IKEA, distributed network management, 381-383
   Isacson Manufacturing, 432-433
   JELFAB Ltd., SWOT strengths and weaknesses illustrated, 18-19
   Kangaroo Courier Company 10-11
   laptops, a potential security risk, 384-385
   LawNet system, 71-74
   Nicholls Fine Furniture, Inc. Illustration of threats 27
   Quality Toys Company, illustration of feedback, 304-305
   Rapid Delivery Couriers Corporation illustration of organisational analysis, 242-260, 263
   RHKJC, distributed network management, 383-384
   Richey Manufacturing Company, Inc., illustration of internal and external factors, 328-329

Case study—*cont.*
   Sing Lee Manufacturing Group illustration of SWOT, 30-31, 232-234
   Small Town Hospital illustration of opportunities 25-26
   Smith & Jones Company 2-4
   stalking the wily hacker, 386-387
   Superior Toy Manufacturing Company, illustration of feedback, 304
   Thompson Refrigeration Company, 93-95
   Venture Manufacturing illustrating environment of creativity, 279
   W.B. Bentley company, Inc. Illustration of JIT and EDI used to reduce risk, 282-283
   Wilton Manufacturing Company, illustration of network alternatives, 354-355
   World Wide Airlines, illustrations of system reliability, 339
Category (of twisted pair wires), 126, 174, 204, 205, 206
Cathay Pacific Airways, computerized reservation system failure, 20
CATWOE; *see* Rich picture diagram
Centralized network, 160
Centrex, 142, 438
CEO; *see* Chief executive officer
CERN, European Laboratory for Particle Physics, 102, 104
Change management, 384, 389, 390
Channel, 124-125
Channel noise, reducing, 302-303
Channel service unit (CSU), 132
Check float, 283
Chief executive officer (CEO), 13
CIM; *see* Computer-integrated manufacturing
Circuit switching, 127, 146, 147
Client/server, 208-209
Clipper-chips, 413
Closed user group (CUG), 409-410
Coaxial cable, 127-130, 174, 175
Collaborative research, support for, 306-307
Collapsed backbone network, example in practice, 66-67
Command/object monitoring, of intrusion detection, 418-419
CommerceNet, 114-115, 118

Committed information rate (CIR), 147, 148
Commodities and stockbrokers, 16
Common management information protocol (CMIP), 390, 395, 399-400
Communication, business types and TBIT, 311-313
   channels, 300
   effectiveness with networks, 299-302
   increasing message clarity, 300-302
   key points, 322
   model, 298-299
Communication channel; *see* Channel
Compatibility, compared to connectivity, 335-337
   technical requirement, 332
Competitive advantage, achieving through business networking, 11-17; *see also* Automobile industry, competitive advantage illustrated; Case study, ACD Manufacturing Group illustration of competitive advantage
   defined, 226
   example in manufacturing industry, 65
Competitive forces model, 237-238
Competitor, illustration of risk, 284
CompuServe, 77, 93, 97, 105
Computer-aided design and computer-aided manufacturing (CAD/CAM), 31
Computer-integrated manufacturing (CIM), bandwidth demanding application, 175, 198, 220
   as manufacturing system example, 64, 66
   as sample strength, 21
Concentrator, 135-138
   intelligent or wiring, 189
Concurrent access, 286
Configuration management, 384, 389, 390, 402
Connection and communication, 388
Connection-oriented, 95, 178-180
Connectionless, 95, 178-180
Connectivity, compared to compatibility, 335-337
   as a technical requirement, 332

Consultative Committee for International Telegraphy and Telephony (CCITT) 74, 131, 152, 154-5, 177
Contact management, 308-310
Cooperation, environment of 278
Copper distributed data interface (CDDI), 201, 207, 208
Core competencies, 12
Core logistics, 20
Cost-effectiveness ratio, 364-367
Cost feasibility, 355
Cost-benefit analysis, 86, 354-363
Cost-saving measures, 275-277
Creativity, environment of, 278
Critical success factors (CSFs), 238-242
  for internal and external requirements, 328-329
  implications for TBIT applications, 241-242
Cross-functional systems, 15
CSF; *see* Critical success factors
CSLIP (compressed serial line interface protocol), 95-96
Cybercash, 113, 446

Data compression, example of use, 60
Data dictionary, 253; *see also* E-R diagram
Data encryption, 414-416
Data encryption standard (DES), 414-416
Data modeling techniques, with interviewing, 324
Data models; *see* E-R diagram
Data service unit (DSU), 132
Databases, public and corporate, 77-79, 85, 86
Datagram; *see* Connectionless
Datapak (Hong Kong), 79
DCF; *see* Discounted cash flow
De facto standards, 156
Decentralized network, 160
Decisions, analyzing situations and making, 315
DECnet, 190
Decomposition diagram, introduced and illustrated, 248-250
  illustrated, 284
  with interviewing, 324
Degrees of freedom, 17
Demand priority protocol, 205

Deregulation, in telecommunications, 163, 437-438
Desktop Management Task Force (DMTF), 110, 400
Deterministic, 180
Dial-up (datel), 95, 96, 127, 150
Differential phase shift keying (DPSK), 174
Digital data network (DDN), 60, 132, 141, 143-145, 150
Digital envelope, 415
Digital signals, 130-131
Digital signature, 113, 411, 415
Disaster recovery, 425-427
Discount rate, 359-363
Discounted cash flow (DCF), techniques, 357
Disk drives, as a system reliability factor, 340
Disk operating system, 210
Distributed management environment (DME), 400
Distributed processing, 236
Distributed systems, 171
Document retrieval 312-314
Downsizing, 12
Dual-homed gateway, 116-117
Dumb terminal, 183-184

E-cash, 446
E-mail, benefits and drawbacks, 73-74
  in comparison with EDI, 82
  in conjunction with Internet, 97, 98, 99, 111-112, 116-117
  enabled applications, 286
  standards, 74-75
E-R diagram, illustration of, 267-269; *see also* Case study, Best Manufacturing Company introduced, 253-256
E1, 125, 145, 150, 151
Economies of scale, 232
Economies of scope, 232
EDI; *see* Electronic data interchange
EDIFACT, 80
Effectiveness, defined, 226; *see also* Case study, Cole & Sons Manufacturing Company illustration of ineffectiveness enhancing personal, 298-310
Efficiency and effectivenss, compared, 230

Efficiency, defined, 226; *see also* Case study, Kangaroo Courier Company measuring resource usage, 269-274
  organizational analysis to increase, 266-269
EINet Galaxy, 114-115, 118
Electronic calendaring, 75, 76, 84
Electronic commerce, 92, 111, 114-115
Electronic data interchange (EDI), illustrated 94, 282-283, 437; *see also* Wal-Mart Stores, example of EDI
  as Internet application, 111
  introduced 14
  a key to trading partner effectiveness, 289-292
  as networked application 79-83, 86
  in order processing, 37
Electronic diaries, 75, 76, 84
Electronic directories, 68-69
Electronic fax (E-fax), 19
Electronic filing, 312-314
Electronic funds transfer (EFT), 14, 54-55
Electronic funds transfer at the point of sale (EFT/POS), 14
Electronic future, 444
Electronic messaging, electronic mail (E-mail), 68, 70-71
Electronic publishing, 114
Electronic signature; *see* Digital signature
Encryption, 116, 118, 380, 406
Entities, 253; *see also* E-R diagram
Entity-relationship diagram; *see* E-R diagram
Environment of creativity, introduced and illustrated, 278-282; *see also* Case study, Venture Manufacturing
Environment, in Rich picture diagram, 257
Ethernet, 173, 176, 180, 189, 204
  fast, 203
  full-duplex, 207
Excess capacity, illustration of risk, 284
Expandability, as a technical requirement, 332-333

Expansion or proliferation; *see* Stages of growth model

Expert systems, of intrusion detection, 418-419

External considerations, 9

External factors, 236-237
  risks related to alternative selection, 369

Facilitator, for JAD, 325-326

Fault management, 384, 389, 390, 401-402

FDDI, in comparison with other technologies, 150, 151, 173

FDDI-II, 199

Feasibility, to assist in alternative selection, 355-356

Features matrix, 363-364

Feedback, improving, 303-304; *see also* Case study, Superior Toy

Fiber channel, 207, 208

Fiber optic cable; *see* Optical fiber cable

Fiber optic inter-repeater link (FOIRL), 174

Fiber distributed data interface (FDDI), 190-191, 195, 197-203, 207-208

File server, 171-172, 186-187
  example of use, 40, 59, 63

File server, software, 210

File transfer and access method (FTAM), 435

File transfer protocol (FTP), 92, 97-100, 103-104, 213

Financing methods, alternatives, 370-373

Finger, 111

Firewall, 117-118

Five component model, 243-245; *see also* Case study, Rapid Delivery Couriers Corporation

Ford Motor Company, encouraging the move to EDI 292

Foreign exchange, 55-58

Foreign exchange line, 142

Formalization or control; *see* Stages of growth model

Fractional T1/E1, 144, 150

Frame relay, 141, 147-149, 150-151, 173

Frito Lay, example of groupware ,15

Front-end processor, 136

Full-duplex, 127, 131, 157

Function and process diagram; *see* Decomposition diagram

Future value, 359

Gateway, 188, 192

Gateway server, 187, 192

Gbps (Gigabits per second), 125

Goals, 1; *see also* Strategic planning

Gopher, 100-104, 106, 117, 209
  client/server, 100

Group dynamics, in JAD, 325-326

Groupware, 15, 172
  supporting organizational groups, 285-288

Half-duplex, 131, 157

Hierarchical network, 158

High-level data link control (HDLC), 154, 177, 180

Home page, 104, 110, 112, 113

Host server, 187

Hot-swapping, of disk drives, 427

Hub, 158, 188-189
  "disconnecting unknown devices", 408-409
  example of use, 61, 63, 175
  "need to know", 408
  intelligent, 408
  switching, 207

Hybrid, as a network implementation strategy, 345

Hybrid gateway, 116-117

Hybrid manager, 6

Hypermedia, 104

Hypertext markup language (HTML), 103, 106

Hypertext transport protocol (HTTP), 102, 103

IEEE802, 177, 180

IEEE802.12, 205

IEEE802.3, 154, 194, 203

IEEE802.5, 154, 198

Implementation plan, for a network, 343-347
  justification of, 345-346

Information highway, 442; *see also* National Information Infrastructure

Information resources, ready access to; *see* Research and development

Information technology, 1

Initial costs and benefits, 357-363

Initiation; *see* Stages of growth model

Input-process-output model; *see* System model

Intangible costs and benefits, 357-358

Integrated services digital network (ISDN), 68, 145-147, 162, 197
  basic rate access, 146
  in comparison with other technologies, 150-151, 173
  primary rate access, 146

Integration of strategic planning with IT planning; *see* Strategic alignment

Integration, internal, cooperative, or enterprise, 448-449

Intelligent building, 175, 177

Intelligent distributed processing, 209

Intelligent scheduler 432

Intelligent search agent, 433, 447

Intelligent terminal, 183-184

Interface, 124, 143, 153

Internal and external factors, impact on competitiveness, 234-237; *see also* Case study, Richey Manufacturing Company, Inc.

Internal and external requirements, 326

Internal considerations, 9

Internal factors, 235-236

Internal rate of return (IRR), 359-363

International Airline Transport Association (IATA), 110

International economic change, motivator for use of TBIT, 6-7

International information infrastructure (I3), 448; *see also* National Information Infrastructure

International Standards Organization (ISO), 110, 152-156, 177, 200-201

International Telecommunications Union (ITU), 155

Internet, 68, 77, 91-120, 159
  architecture and protocols, 95-96
  business applications, 111-112
  as a business tool, 106-115
  client/server system, 98, 100-101, 102-3, 106

Internet—*cont.*
  gaining access, 96-97
  operation and performance,
      113-115
  overview, 92-93
  security, 113-118
  services and facilities, 97-98
Internet control message protocol
    (ICMP), 95
Internet Engineering Steering Group
    (IESG), 398
Internet Engineering Task Force
    (IETF), 98, 99, 110
Interorganizational transaction
    processing systems, overview
    14; *see also* Electronic data
    interchange
Interviewing, model of process, 324
    steps and process, 322-325
Intrusion detection, 418-421
Inventory, excess, illustration of risk,
    284
Inventory, obsolete, illustration of
    risk, 284
Inventory replenishment cycle, 14
Inventory system, 64, 65
Investment services, 55-58
IP address, 96
IP tunneling, 117
IPX (NetWare), 154, 190-192, 210
IRR; *see* Internal rate of return
ISDN; *see* Integrated services digital
    network
ISO 8802/3; *see* IEEE802.3
ISO 8802/5; *see* IEEE802.5
ISO model, 211
IT capabilites and organization
    impact, model, 11
IT platform, 236
ITU-TSS, 156

JAD; *see* Joint application design
Jam time, 175, 181
JIT; *see* Just in time
Joint application design (JAD),
    325-326
Just in time (JIT), 22, 64-65, 83
    illustrated, 282-283

Kbps (Kilobits per second, 125
Kerberos, 412-413
Key management, 415

Kmart, encouraging the move to EDI,
    292
Knowbot, 447

Leads, analyzing and qualifying,
    309
Leads, following up qualified,
    309-310
Leased circuits (leased line), 96, 127,
    142
Leasing, alternative financing
    methods, 371-373
Leverage, 20
Lexis, 72
Link access protocol, balanced
    (LAP-B), 154
Link access protocol, modem
    (LAP-M), 154
Link layer, 95, 154
Local area network (LAN), 34-35, 39
    benefits of using, 84-86
    costs of acquisition and use,
        215-218
    cost of failure, 217-218
    factors in selection, 218-220
    hardware and connectivity,
        183-186
    high-speed, 202-208
    major functions, 169-172
    operating systems, 210-215
    security management, 404-406
    servers, 186-187
    software components, 209-210
    standards, 177-180
Local loop, 141
Location independent work processes,
    16; *see also* USAA Insurance
    Company, example of location
    independent work processes
Logical link control (LLC), 177-179,
    190, 200
Lynx, 104

Macweb, 104
Mail float, 284
Managed objects, 395
Management, of change and
    organizational growth, 387-389
Management, mixed vendor, 389-390,
    391-395
Management and security, in business
    networks, 381

Management information base (MIB),
    395, 397
Manager-agent interface, 395
Manchester coding, 174-175, 180
Manual review, of intrusion detection,
    418-419
Manufacturing applications, 64-68
Marketing applications, 36-53
Marketing staff; *see* Contact
    management
Markets shrinking, illustration of risk,
    284
Maturity; *see* Stages of growth model
Mbps (Megabits per second), 125
MCI Mail, 97
Medium access control (MAC), 174,
    177-180, 190, 194
Medium access unit (MAU), 174
Megalink, 144
Mesh, 159-161
Message authentication, 410-411
Metropolitan area network (MAN),
    179, 180
Microcomputer, 183-184
Microsoft, LAN Manager, Windows
    95, Windows NT, 214
    Windows for Workgroups, 75, 76,
        190
Microwave, 128-130
Min/max analysis, 363-366
Miniaturization, as a system
    reliability factor, 340
Minitel, 53
Mission critical applications and
    systems, 21, 341
Mission statement, 2; *see also*
    Strategic planning
Models, to enhance analysis, 243
Modem, 130-132
Monomode fiber, 128, 199
Mosaic, 104-106, 112
Multidrop, 144, 158-160
Multimedia, 69, 114, 134, 202-204
    applications, 439-440
    workstation, 126
Multimode fiber, 128, 199
Multiplexer (mux), 133-135
    example of use, 60
Multiplexing, frequency division
    (FDM), 133
    in comparison with concentration,
        137-138
    statistical time division (STDM),
        133-135, 137, 145

Multiplexing—*cont.*
   time division (TDM), 133-135, 137
Multipoint; *see* Multidrop

National Center for Supercomputing Applications (NCSA), 102, 104
National Information Infrastructure (NII), 92, 112, 114-116, 446
National Science Foundation (NSF), 114
Net present value (NPV), 359-363
NetBIOS, 153, 211
Netscape, 104, 112
Netview (IBM), 394
Network, limitations, 434-436
Network components, 129-140
   determining sources of, 347-348
Network diagrams, annotated for interviews, 324
Network file system (NFS), 213
Network interface card (NIC), 204, 205, 211
Network layer, 154
Network management, 143
Network Management Forum (NMF), 110, 394, 400
Network performance standards, for user requirements, 337-343
Network terminating unit (NTU), 132, 143
News, 77, 94, 97-99, 101-104
Niche marketing, 227
Nonpaying creditors, illustration of risk, 284
Novell NetWare, 66, 76, 214
NPV; *see* Net present value

Objectives, 3; *see also* Strategic planning
Office automation (desktop automation), 68, 70-71, 75-76, 84
Official airline guide (OAG), 45
Open system interconnection (OSI); *see* International Standards Organization (ISO)
OpenView (Hewlett-Packard), 394, 400
Operating system, 168, 186
Operating systems, smarter, as a system reliability factor, 340

Operational efficiency; *see* Efficiency
Opportunities, taking advantage of, 25; *see also* Case study, Small Town Hospital illustration of opportunities
Opportunities and threats, 9; *see also* Case study, Kangaroo Courier Company
Optical computers, 443-444
Optical fiber cable, 127-130, 174-175, 197-202
Order entry , 36-37
Organizational groups, network applications to support, 285-292
Organizational feasibility, 355

P6 (Intel), 433
PABX; *see* Private automated branch exchange
Packet assembler-disassembler (PAD), 138-139, 145
Packet switching network (PSN), 42, 145, 150-151, 173
Paperless office, 436-437
Parallel, as a network implementation strategy, 345
Passenger name record (PNR), 41
Password, 410
Payback period, 357
PC LAN, 185-186
PDA; *see* Personal digital assistant
Peer-to-peer, 153, 154, 398, 399
Pentium, 433
Performance management, 384, 389, 390, 402-403
Performance, analyzing and measuring organizational, 266-276
Personal computer (PC), 183-184
Personal digital assistant (PDA), 13, 445
Phased, as a network implementation strategy, 345
Physical layer, 154
Pilot, as a network implementation strategy, 345
Plan, 111-112
Planning, organizing and controlling, 307-308
Platform; *see* IT platform
Plex network; *see* Mesh
Plunge, as a network implementation strategy, 345

Point of sale (POS),terminal system, 14, 37-38; *see also* Electronic funds transfer
Point-to-point, 144, 157, 175
Point-to-point protocol (PPP), 95-97
Polling, 158
PPP; *see* Point-to-point protocol
Present value; *see* Net present value
Presentation layer, 152
Pretty good privacy (PGP), 414
Primary key, 253; *see also* E-R diagram
Print server, 187
Private automated branch exchange (PABX), 10
Private branch exchange (PBX), 142, 158, 176, 194
Private line, 141, 142
Probabilistic, 180
Process diagram; *see* Function and process diagram
Prodigy, 95
Productivity, enhancing personal, 311-315
Project control, using budgets, 332
Propagation delay, 181, 182, 183
Protocol, 124, 154, 173
Prototype, defined, 278
Prototyping, attitude toward everything, 278
Proxy agent, 398
Proxy gateway, 116-117
Proxy server, 105
Psychological; *see* Channel noise
Public switched telephone network (PSTN), 35, 130-131, 141-142
Purchasing, alternative financing methods, 371-373
Purchasing system; *see* Case study, American Hospital Supply Corporation

Quality processes, support for iterative; *see* Research and development
Questionnaires, for interviews, 323-324
Questions, open-end and closed-end, 323

R.J. Reynolds, encouraging the move to EDI 292

RAID; *see* Redundant array of inexpensive disks

Rank Xerox, example of business process reengineering, 16

Reacting versus responding, 23

Recoverability, costs and benefits of, 341
  of network, 341-343

Recurring costs and benefits, 357-363

Redirector, 211

Redundant array of inexpensive disks (RAID), 426-427

Relational database management system (RDBMS), 209

Relationships, 253; *see also* E-R diagram

Reliability, of network as a user requirement, 338-339; *see also* Case study, World Wide Airlines

Remote monitoring MIB (RMON MIB), 398

Rental, alternative financing methods, 371-373

Repeater; *see* Hub

Request for proposal (RFP), 347

Request for quotation (RFQ), 347

Requirements analysis, 320-337

Research and development, personal efficiency and effectiveness, 305-307

Reservation system, 41-51

Resource usage, measuring improvements in; *see* Efficiency

Response time, as a user requirement, 337-338

Responsibility, environment of 278

Responsiveness, increasing, 23; *see also* Case study, Fast Clothes Company

Reuters, 58, 176

RFP; *see* Request for proposal

RFQ; *see* Request for quotation

Rich picture diagram, introduced and illustrated, 256-260

Ring; *see* Token ring

Risk, related to alternative selection, 369-371; *see also* Time and risk

Risk analysis, 421-423

Risk taking, a reward structure for, 280

Rivest Shamir Adleman (RSA), 414

Rlogin, 97

Router, 96, 88, 190-193
  boundary , 67, 116

Router—*cont.*
  example of use, 60
  filtering, 116
  screening, 116-117

Routing protocols, 192

RS-232, 132, 154

RS-422/423, 154

RS-449, 154

SABRE (American Airlines), 41

Satellite, 128-130

Scalability, as a technical requirement, 332-333

Schedule feasibility, 355

Screened host gateway, 116-117

SDLC; *see* Systems development life cycle

Security, in hospital environment, 62-63
  in LAN hardware, 406-410
  measures, 410-416
  in networks, 403-427
  rating, 423-424

Security management, 384, 389, 390, 403

Self-managing teams, used to gain short-term opportunities 280

Serial line interface protocol (SLIP), 95-97

Service access point (SAP), 178

Session layer, 152

Shielded twisted pair (STP), 126, 201, 204, 205

Shielding, cable, as a system reliability factor, 340

Signature block, 111

Simple management protocol (SMP), 398

Simple message transfer protocol (SMTP), 213

Simple network management protocol (SNMP), 390, 393, 396-397

Simplex, 131, 157

Skipjack algorithm, 413

SLIP; *see* Serial line interface protocol

Slot time, 175, 182

Smart card, 411

SNMP agent, 396

SNMP-2, 390, 397-398

Society for International Aeronautical Telecommunications (SITA), 57

Society for Worldwide Interbank Financial Telecommunications (SWIFT), 57, 110, 156

Spoofing, 410-411

Sprint, 93

Staff, managers and other; *see* Contact management

Stages of growth model, 246-247

Standardized general markup language (SGML), 106

Star, 157-159, 175, 194

Statistical systems, of intrusion detection, 418-419

Stock control system, 64-65

Stock management, 37-38

STP; *see* Shielded twisted pair

Strategic advantage, cycle of creation, erosion and reconstruction 9

Strategic alignment, described 6
  synergism illustrated, 7

Strategic direction; *see* Strategic planning

Strategic feasibility, 355-356

Strategic leverage, 2

Strategic model, combined, 237-239

Strategic partnerships, introduced, 12
  method of gaining competitive advantage, 227

Strategic planning, 2; *see also* Case study, Smith & Jones Company
  a foundation for analysis, 231
  goals 3, 5
  mission statement 2, 5
  objectives 3, 5
  process 4

Strengths, enhancing, 17-18
  leveraging, 20-21

Strengths and weaknesses, 7; *see also* Case study, American Hospital Supply Corporation and Case study, JELFAB Ltd.

Structured cabling, 406

Structured query language (SQL), 101, 172, 208

Switched circuits, 127

Switched multimegabit data service (SMDS), 438

Switching costs, 238

SWOT (strengths, weakness, opportunities, threats) method of strategic analysis, 7-11; *see also* Case study, Sing Lee Manufacturing Group
  illustrated, 233

SWOT—*cont.*
  illustrative model, 18
Synchronous, 95, 136, 138-139, 157
Synchronous data link control
  (SDLC), 138, 154, 180
Synchronous digital hierarchy (SDH),
  440
Synchronous optical network
  (SONET), 440
Synergism, IT strategy and corporate
  strategy, 7; *see also* Strategic
  alignment
System failure; *see* Cathay Pacific
  Airways, computerized
  reservation system failure
System model, used for efficiency
  measurement, 270-274
System requirements, model of, 321
System storage, as a technical
  requirement, 332-333
Systems development life cycle
  (SDLC), 321
Systems Network Architecture (SNA),
  140, 435

T1 circuit, example of use, 59-60
T1, 125, 145, 150, 151
Tactical planning, 5
Tandem exchange, 141
TBIT; *see* Telecommunications-based
  information technology
Tbps (Terabits per second), 125
TCP/IP, 153-154, 178-180, 190-192,
  211-213
  use with Internet, 95-98, 117
Teamwork, 15; *see also* Groupware
Technical feasibility, 355
Technical requirements, 332-333
Technological developments, 438-448
Technology risks, related to
  alternative selection, 369
Telecommunications-based information
  technology (TBIT), 5
  five key developments, 12
Telecommuting, introduced, 16
Teleconferencing, 83-84, 86, 150,
  202-203
Telemarketing, 51-51, 85, 142
  software, 52
Telephone tag, 14
Teleshopping, 52-53
Telnet, 99-104 , 213, 117
Terminal server, 187

Terminal, 183-184
Threats, defending against 26-28; *see
  also* Case study, Nicholls Fine
  Furniture, Inc.
  sample defended by TBIT, 28
Thriving on Chaos; see Time and risk
Tie line, 142
Time and risk, used to gain a
  competitive advantage, 276
Time-related situations, TBIT
  opportunities, 277
Token authentication, 411
Token ring, 173, 178-180, 182-183,
  194-196
Topology, local area network,
  193-197
  wide area network, 157-161
Total quality management, 285
Trading partner risks, related to
  alternative selection, 369
Traffic loading, as a technical
  requirement, 332-333
Transactions per second (tps), 7
Transmission Control Protocol/
  Internet Protocol; *see* TCP/IP
Transmission media, example of use,
  58, 59
Transmission speed, 125-6
Transport layer, 95-96, 153
Trap door, 417
Tree, 195-196
Trivial file transfer protocol (TFTP),
  116
Trojan horse, 380, 417
Twisted pair, 126-127, 174
Twisted pair distributed data interface
  (TPDDI), 201, 207, 208
Tymnet (USA), 79

Uncertainty, network opportunities in
  times of, 282-285; *see also* Risk
  and Case study, W.B. Bentley
  Company, Inc.
Underground cabling, as a system
  reliability factor, 340
Uninterruptable power supply (UPS),
  426
UNIX, 393, 395
Unshielded twisted pair (UTP), 126,
  175, 201, 204-207
USAA Insurance Company, example
  of location independent work
  processes 17

Usenet news, 77
User datagram protocol (UDP), 96,
  213
User requirements, 334-335
UTP; *see* Unshielded twisted pair

V.24, 132, 136, 154
V.35, 154
Vaccine programs, 418
Value added services, 163
Value chain model, 247-248
Vendor related characteristics,
  affecting alternative selection,
  368-369
Vendor risks, related to alternative
  selection, 369
Videoconferencing; *see*
  Teleconferencing
Virtual circuits, 178
  permanent (PVC), switched
  (SVC), 148
Virtual corporation, 13
Virtual private network, 34, 145, 163,
  390, 438
Virtual reality, 444
Virtual store front, 111-113
Viruses, 380, 417-418
Visual; *see* Channel noise, 303
Voice activated network, illustrated
  in Rapid Delivery Courier case
  251
Voice activation, 432, 443
Voice encryption, 413
Voice mail, 75

Wal-Mart Stores Inc, 82
  example of EDI 14, 292
Weakness, conquering, 20-22, 17-18
Weltanschauung; *see* Rich picture
  diagram
Wide area information server (WAIS),
  100, 101-104
Wide area network (WAN), 34-35,
  140-151
  benefits of using, 84-86
  cost of acquiring, 162-164
  integration, 161-162
  standards used in, 151-152
Wideband DDN, 144, 173, 163
WinSock, 97
Winweb, 194
Wireless LANS, 180

Workflow applications, introduced, 15
   supporting organizational groups, 288-290
Workstation, 183-184
   hardware and software costs, 215-216

World Wide Web (WWW), 92, 97, 102-4, 209, 442
   example of use, 94, 112-113
World Wide Web browsers, 103-106, 110, 112, 114
Worms, 380, 418
WWW; *see* World Wide Web

X.21, 147, 154
X.25, 145-147, 177, 192
   in comparison with other technologies, 150-151, 173
X.400, 68, 74-75, 213

Yellow pages, 111-112